MAWSON

PETER FITZSIMONS

MAWSON

and the Ice Men of the Heroic Age: Scott, Shackleton and Amundsen

WILLIAM HEINEMANN: AUSTRALIA

A William Heinemann book
Published by Random House Australia Pty Ltd
Level 3, 100 Pacific Highway, North Sydney NSW 2060
www.randomhouse.com.au

First published by William Heinemann in 2011

National Library of Australia
Cataloguing-in-Publication Entry

FitzSimons, Peter.
Mawson/Peter FitzSimons.

ISBN 978 1 74166 660 1 (hbk.)

Mawson, Douglas, Sir, 1882–1958 – Travel – Antarctica.
Explorers – Australia – Biography.
Antarctica – Discovery and exploration – Australian.

998.9

Jacket design by Adam Yazxhi/MAXCO
Jacket images courtesy of the Australian Antarctic Division. Front cover: Douglas Mawson in his 20s, by Swaine Studios; Sir Douglas Mawson, by Frank Hurley. Back cover: Mawson's men celebrate completion of their Winter Quarters, Cape Denison, end of January 1912, by Frank Hurley
Image on endpapers courtesy of the Mitchell Library, State Library of New South Wales, d1_18751
Internal and external maps and illustrations by Jane Macaulay
Relief drawing of Ross Island, the Great Ice Barrier and surrounds on p. xvii by Laurie Whiddon, Map Illustrations
Internal design by Xou, Australia
Typeset in Garamond by Xou, Australia
Printed and bound by Griffin Press, South Australia

10 9 8 7 6 5 4 3 2 1

To my eldest brother, David Booth FitzSimons, who first entranced me with the wonder of the story of Douglas Mawson many years ago and inspired me to write this story.

As has long been noted, just before the turn of the last century mankind knew more about the surface of the moon than it did about the seventh continent at the bottom of the world, the frozen lost land called Antarctica. In the famed Heroic Age of Antarctic Exploration that followed, the icy veils that had so long covered the face and form of this mysterious place were courageously lifted, one by one, to reveal that frozen face in all its terrible splendour. Though many men died in the process, four in particular became legends.

They were Ernest Shackleton and Robert Falcon Scott of Great Britain, Roald Amundsen of Norway, and Douglas Mawson of Australia. The climactic moments of their separate explorations occurred within a remarkably short period, 1907–14, and always at a time when others of the explorers were uncannily close to them on the continent.

This, then, is the story of that amazing time, and of those extraordinarily courageous men.

Sir Douglas Mawson's Expedition, judged by the magnitude both of its scale and of its achievements, was the greatest and most consummate expedition that ever sailed for Antarctica. The expeditions of Scott and Shackleton were great, and Amundsen's venture was the finest Polar reconnaissance ever made; but each of these must yield the premier position, when fairly compared with Mawson's magnificently conceived and executed scheme of exploration.

J. Gordon Hayes's assessment in 1928

Contents

PART FOUR: STRUGGLES

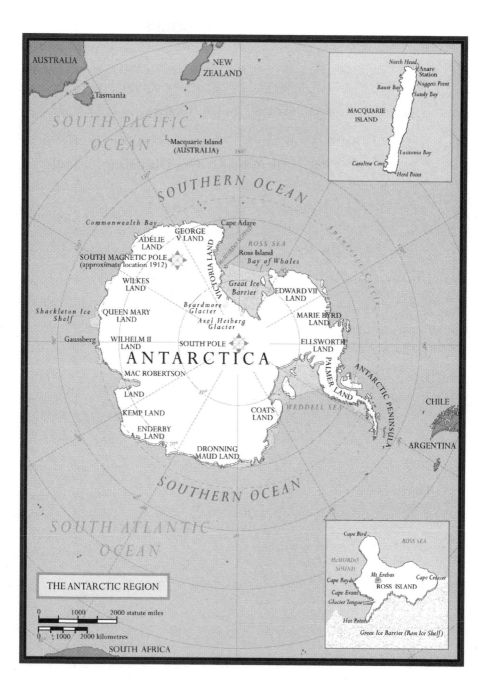

THE ANTARCTIC REGION

0   1000   2000 statute miles
0   1000   2000 kilometres

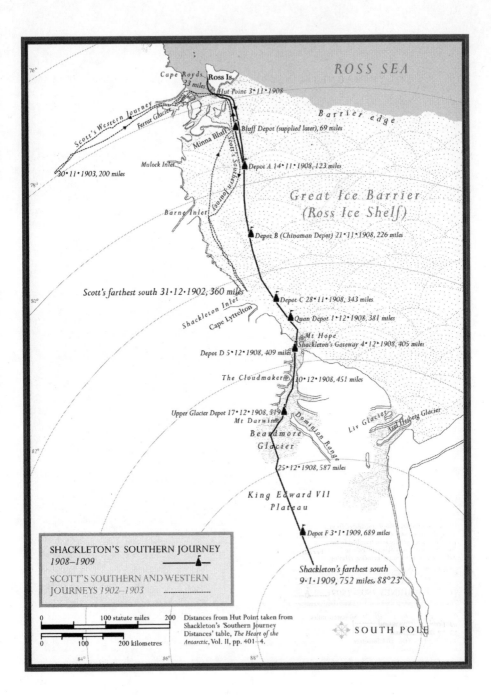

ROSS SEA

Cape Royds
23 miles
Ross Is.
Hut Point 3•11•1908

Scott's Western Journey

Ferrar Glacier

Barrier edge

Minna Bluff

Bluff Depot (supplied later), 69 miles

Mulock Inlet

Depot A 14•11•1908, 123 miles

30•11•1903, 200 miles

Barne Inlet

Great Ice Barrier
(Ross Ice Shelf)

Depot B (Chinaman Depot) 21•11•1908, 226 miles

Scott's farthest south 31•12•1902, 360 miles

Shackleton Inlet

Cape Lyttelton

Depot C 28•11•1908, 343 miles

Quan Depot 1•12•1908, 381 miles

Mt Hope
Shackleton's Gateway 4•12•1908, 405 miles

Depot D 5•12•1908, 409 miles

The Cloudmaker

10•12•1908, 451 miles

Upper Glacier Depot 17•12•1908, 519

Mt Darwin

Dominion Range

Liv Glacier

Axel Heiberg Glacier

Beardmore
Glacier

King Edward VII
Plateau

25•12•1908, 587 miles

Depot F 3•1•1909, 689 miles

Shackleton's farthest south
9•1•1909, 752 miles, 88°23'

SHACKLETON'S SOUTHERN JOURNEY
1908–1909

SCOTT'S SOUTHERN AND WESTERN
JOURNEYS 1902–1903

0   100 statute miles   200

0   100   200 kilometres

Distances from Hut Point taken from
Shackleton's 'Southern Journey
Distances' table, The Heart of the
Antarctic, Vol. II, pp. 401–4.

SOUTH POLE

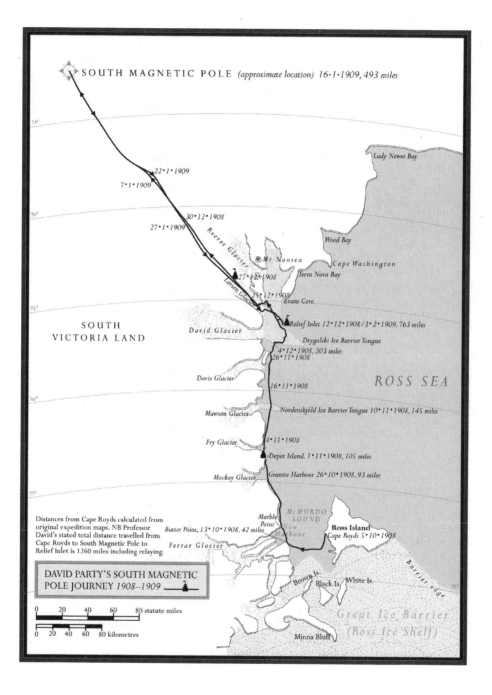

SOUTH MAGNETIC POLE *(approximate location) 16·1·1909, 493 miles*

22·1·1909

7·1·1909

30·12·1908

27·1·1909

Reeves Glacier

Lady Newes Bay

Wood Bay

⊙*Mt Nansen*

Cape Washington

27·12·1908

Larsen Glacier

Terra Nova Bay

25·12·1908

Evans Cove

▲Relief Inlet *12·12·1908 / 3·2·1909, 763 miles*

SOUTH
VICTORIA LAND

David Glacier

Drygalski Ice Barrier Tongue
4·12·1908, 203 miles
26·11·1908

Davis Glacier

16·11·1908

ROSS SEA

Mawson Glacier

Nordenskjöld Ice Barrier Tongue 10·11·1908, 145 miles

Fry Glacier

4·11·1908

▲Depot Island, *1·11·1908, 105 miles*

Mackay Glacier

Granite Harbour *26·10·1908, 93 miles*

Marble
Point

*McMURDO
SOUND*

Distances from Cape Royds calculated from
original expedition maps. NB Professor
David's stated total distance travelled from
Cape Royds to South Magnetic Pole to
Relief Inlet is 1260 miles including relaying.

Butter Point, *13·10·1908, 42 miles*

New
Harbour

Ross Island
Cape Royds *5·10·1908*

Ferrar Glacier

DAVID PARTY'S SOUTH MAGNETIC
POLE JOURNEY *1908–1909* ▲

Brown Is.
Black Is. White Is.

Barrier edge

0   20   40   60   80 statute miles

0   20   40   60   80 kilometres

Great Ice Barrier
(Ross Ice Shelf)

Minna Bluff

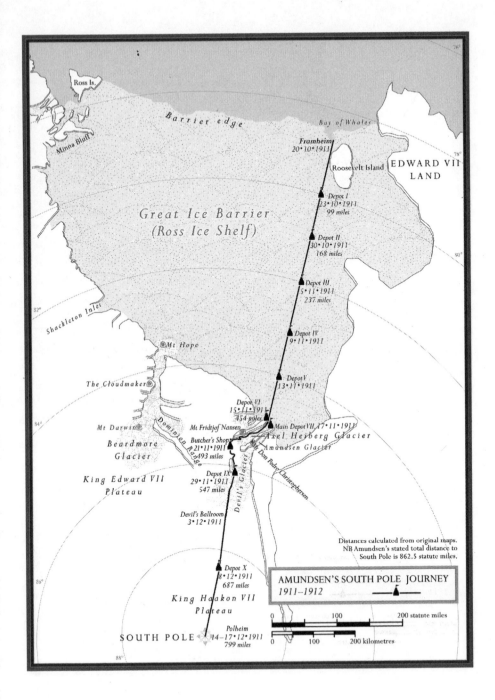

Ross Is.

Barrier edge

Bay of Whales

Minna Bluff

Framheim
20·10·1911

Roosevelt Island

EDWARD VII
LAND

Great Ice Barrier
(Ross Ice Shelf)

Depot I
23·10·1911
99 miles

Depot II
30·10·1911
168 miles

Depot III
5·11·1911
237 miles

Shackleton Inlet

Mt Hope

Depot IV
9·11·1911

The Cloudmaker

Depot V
13·11·1911

Depot VI
15·11·1911
454 miles

Main Depot VII *17·11·1911*
Axel Heiberg Glacier

Mt Darwin
Mt Fridtjof Nansen

Butcher's Shop
21·11·1911
493 miles

Amundsen Glacier

Don Pedro Christophersen

Beardmore
Glacier

Dominion Range

Depot IX
29·11·1911
547 miles

King Edward VII
Plateau

Devil's Glacier

Devil's Ballroom
3·12·1911

Distances calculated from original maps.
NB Amundsen's stated total distance to
South Pole is 862.5 statute miles.

Depot X
8·12·1911
687 miles

King Haakon VII
Plateau

AMUNDSEN'S SOUTH POLE JOURNEY
1911–1912

SOUTH POLE

Polheim
14–17·12·1911
799 miles

0   100   200 statute miles

0   100   200 kilometres

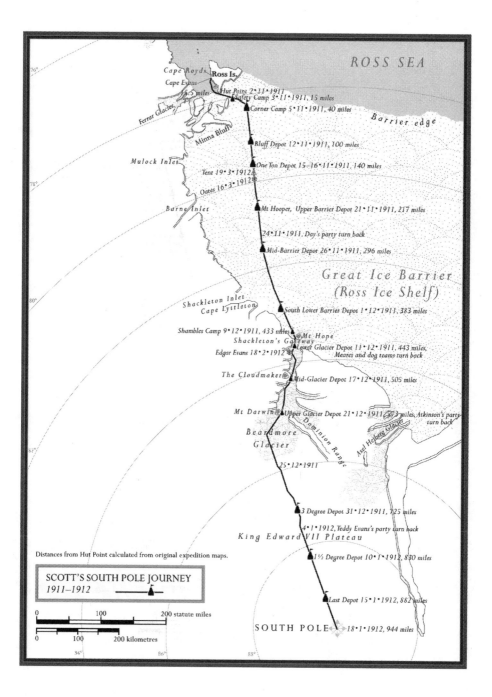

ROSS SEA

Cape Royds
Ross Is.
Cape Evans
Hut Point 2•11•1911
Safety Camp 3•11•1911, 15 miles
Corner Camp 5•11•1911, 40 miles

Ferrar Glacier

Barrier edge

Minna Bluff

Bluff Depot 12•11•1911, 100 miles

Mulock Inlet

One Ton Depot 15–16•11•1911, 140 miles

Tent 19•3•1912
Oates 16•3•1912

Barne Inlet

Mt Hooper, Upper Barrier Depot 21•11•1911, 217 miles

24•11•1911, Day's party turn back

Mid-Barrier Depot 26•11•1911, 296 miles

Great Ice Barrier
(Ross Ice Shelf)

Shackleton Inlet
Cape Lyttleton

South Lower Barrier Depot 1•12•1911, 383 miles

Shambles Camp 9•12•1911, 433 miles
Mt Hope
Shackleton's Gateway
Edgar Evans 18•2•1912
Lower Glacier Depot 11•12•1911, 443 miles,
Meares and dog teams turn back

The Cloudmaker
Mid-Glacier Depot 17•12•1911, 505 miles

Mt Darwin
Upper Glacier Depot 21•12•1911, 573 miles, Atkinson's party
turn back

Beardmore
Glacier

Dominion Range

Axel Heiberg Glacier

25•12•1911

King Edward VII Plateau

3 Degree Depot 31•12•1911, 725 miles

4•1•1912, Teddy Evans's party turn back

Distances from Hut Point calculated from original expedition maps.

1½ Degree Depot 10•1•1912, 830 miles

SCOTT'S SOUTH POLE JOURNEY
1911–1912

Last Depot 15•1•1912, 882 miles

| 0 | 100 | 200 statute miles |

| 0 | 100 | 200 kilometres |

SOUTH POLE 18•1•1912, 944 miles

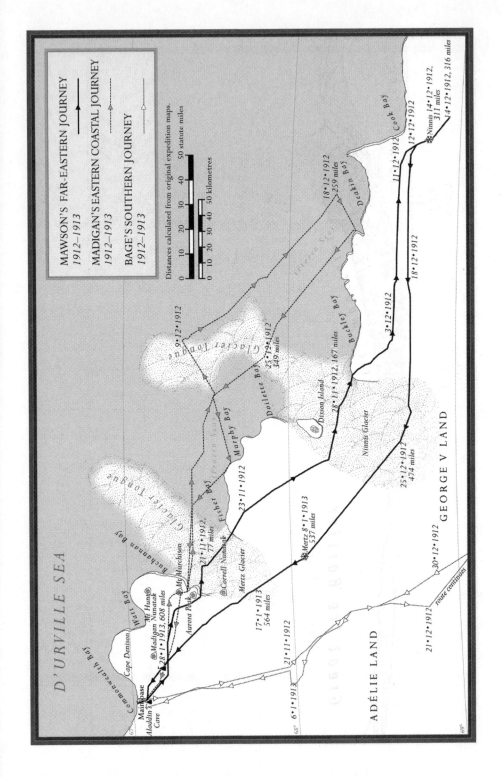

MAWSON'S FAR-EASTERN JOURNEY
1912–1913

MADIGAN'S EASTERN COASTAL JOURNEY
1912–1913

BAGE'S SOUTHERN JOURNEY
1912–1913

Distances calculated from original expedition maps.

0   10   20   30   40   50 statute miles

0   10   20   30   40   50 kilometres

D'URVILLE SEA

Cape Denison   Watt Bay

Commonwealth Bay

Mt Hunt
Madigan Nunatak
28·1·1913, 608 miles
Mt Murchison
Aurora Peak
21·11·1912,
77 miles
Correll Nunatak
Mertz Glacier

Buchanan Bay

Glacier Tongue

Fisher Bay

Murphy Bay

Doillette Bay

9·12·1912

25·7·2·1912
349 miles

Dixson Island
28·11·1912, 167 miles

Mertz 8·1·1913
537 miles

23·11·1912

17·1·1913
564 miles

21·11·1912

6·1·1913

Main
Base
Aladdin's
Cave

ADÉLIE LAND

21·12·1912
route continues

30·12·1912

GEORGE V LAND

Ninnis Glacier

25·12·1912
474 miles

3·12·1912

18·12·1912

11·12·1912

12·12·1912

Ninnis 14·12·1912,
311 miles

14·12·1912, 316 miles

Cook Bay

Deakin Bay

Buckley Bay

18·12·1912
259 miles

67°

68°

69°

xvi

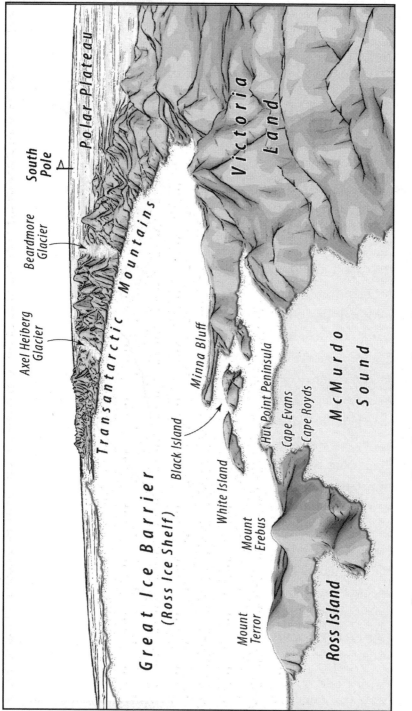

Polar Plateau

South Pole

Beardmore Glacier

Axel Heiberg Glacier

Transantarctic Mountains

Victoria Land

Great Ice Barrier
(Ross Ice Shelf)

Black Island

Minna Bluff

White Island

Hut Point Peninsula

Cape Evans

Cape Royds

Mount Erebus

Mount Terror

Ross Island

McMurdo Sound

Relief drawing of Ross Island, the Great Ice Barrier and surrounds

Background and Acknowledgements

'I bet I know what you're doing,' my wife said to me many years ago, when she saw me gazing intently at an Australian one-hundred-dollar note in my study.

'What?' I said.

'You're looking for your next biographical subject.'

Got me! Over the years, through writing stories and books about such Australian legends as Nancy Wake, Keith Miller, Phar Lap, Murray Rose, Les Darcy and Sir Charles Kingsford Smith, the battles of Kokoda and Tobruk, and the shipwreck of *Batavia*, I have made a practice of looking at beloved but long-gone Australian stories and trying to make them live and breathe again.

And Sir Douglas Mawson, whose image was on that note in my hand, really was a definite possibility. True, apart from his name and apparently well-deserved iconic status, I knew just about nothing about Sir Douglas, but in some ways that was the point. My generation had all but forgotten about him, and maybe it was time to look at him again, get to the bottom of why his story had been so beloved. But then, as ever I was wont to do, I forgot about it and went to other books, until . . .

Until in mid-2009, when my eldest brother, David, happened to tell me over a cup of tea something of the grandeur of the Mawson story and my publishers then took me out to lunch and suggested him again. But . . . when I soon established that three books had come out on him in just that year alone, I turned away from it once more.

Just a few months later, however, I received an email from out of the blue, from David Jensen, the Chair of the Mawson's Huts Foundation, wondering if I had considered:

> a biography on this great man, the most famous of Australia's Antarctic explorers and equal to Scott and Shackleton? No one has done it before in the 'make-it-live-and-breathe' manner you do your books, and he seems to fit into that very criteria you outlined last night on TV. Such a book would also help our cause. We have a team of volunteer conservation specialists departing Hobart early December to spend eight weeks on the ice working to conserve the historic site and we're planning a major documentary for screening next year. If you're interested in considering a book on him I'd be happy to help with family contacts etc . . .

And so it began.

For me, kindly helped by David Jensen all the way, the next two years were a fascinating journey – physically, intellectually and spiritually – to Antarctica, a place that I had never particularly contemplated before but now became, as my wife and family will attest, pretty much obsessed with. Beyond journeying to Antarctica itself, where I was thrilled to actually get inside Mawson's Huts, I also travelled, as a part of further research of the whole Antarctic story, to Hobart, Adelaide, Melbourne, Macquarie Island, Christchurch, Dunedin, London, Cambridge and Oslo, among other cities.

For, as it turned out, the more I got into writing this book, the more I found not only the story of Mawson to be absorbing but also the whole history of exploration in those parts. I was staggered that only a little over a hundred years ago, the continent had barely been set foot on, let alone explored. I adored the story of Shackleton's exploration there, and the fact that – even as Mawson and his men were setting off to the south – the famed Scott of the Antarctic and Norway's Roald Amundsen were in a race to the South Pole. I loved those latter stories so much that in short order, just as my previous book on Sir Charles Kingsford Smith had widened into a book on Smithy 'and those magnificent men', in this case I widened it from just Mawson to include 'the ice men of the Heroic Age'. It was fascinating to me that these titans of their time should have been so active, so close together in such a tight timeframe, and I decided to construct this book to encompass that frame.

And yet, in another way, this book is quite different from my more recent works, where, in an effort to make the story live and breathe, I have occasionally used just enough poetic licence so that – when all that remains of the historical record is in sober black and white – I can add the right hint of likely colour to give a true picture. With the shipwreck of *Batavia*, for example, there were only two primary documents left from 400 years ago, and I put an enormous amount of energy into cross-referring between those two documents to work out just what that colour should be.

With this book, however, there has been no need. So captivating were the stories of these titans at the time, and since, that research institutions were established, in part as shrines to these heroes. The Scott Polar Research Institute (SPRI) at the University of Cambridge is the repository for many of the letters, diaries, notes and papers from Scott's and Shackleton's expeditions, while most of Amundsen's papers are with the Fram Museum in Oslo, and Mawson's are spread between the Mawson Centre at the South Australian Museum in Adelaide and the Mitchell Library in Sydney, the latter holding the majority of the Australasian Antarctic Expedition (AAE) archive. It all meant that instead of just two primary documents to choose from, there were literally thousands of primary documents on which to invest literally thousands of research hours.

I am particularly indebted to the internationally renowned authority on polar history, Bob Headland, Senior Associate of the

SPRI and author of *A Chronology of Antarctic Exploration*, for his advice on the history of Antarctic exploration, including calculation of journey distances.

I would like to thank the staff of those aforementioned fine institutions for the expert help they gave and cite particularly Mark Pharaoh, the Senior Collection Manager of the Mawson Centre at the South Australian Museum; Naomi Boneham, Archives Manager, the Thomas H. Manning Polar Archives, SPRI; Georgina Cronin and Shirley Sawtell, Librarians, the Shackleton Memorial Library, SPRI; Stephen Martin, Historian and Curator, State Library of New South Wales; Tracy Bradford (and staff), Head, Manuscripts Section, State Library of New South Wales/Mitchell Library; Rowan Carroll, Director of the North Otago Museum; Julia Mant, Reference Archivist of the University of Sydney Archives; Gillian Simpson of the Australian National Maritime Museum; and the broad staff of the British Library.

Without exception, the families that I was able to contact of the explorers mentioned herein were good to me, and none more so than the Mawson family. I am indebted to Paquita Boston, one of Sir Douglas's granddaughters, and most particularly Emma McEwin, a great-granddaughter, who has written her own book, *An Antarctic Affair*, about the relationship between Sir Douglas and his wife, Paquita. With her impeccable pedigree, Emma was helpful throughout the writing of the entire book, and I warmly thank her for it. I am equally grateful for the help of other authors, including David Day, who is writing his own book on the history of polar exploration and with whom it was valuable to compare notes, and most particularly Alasdair McGregor, the winner of the 2011 National Biography Award, for his book on Frank Hurley.

All of Day, McEwin and McGregor – the last of whom I travelled to Antarctica with – were invaluable not only for their intimate knowledge of my subjects and overall Antarctica lore, but also for being able to guide me to where other treasures could be found. As far as possible, I went to original documents, drawing heavily on the aforementioned diaries, letters and contemporary newspaper accounts, but there are also the expedition books written by the explorers themselves, which were priceless, most notably *Home of the Blizzard* (AAE, 1911–14) by Mawson himself, Shackleton's *The Heart of the Antarctic* (British Antarctic Expedition, 1907–09/the *Nimrod* expedition), Scott's *Voyage of the Discovery* (British National Antarctic Expedition, 1901–04/the *Discovery* expedition) and *Scott's Last Expedition* (British Antarctic Expedition, 1910–13/the *Terra Nova* expedition) and Amundsen's *The South Pole* (the *Fram* expedition, 1910–13).

Beyond the principals, though, I loved the books by Captain John King Davis, *With the Aurora* (AAE) and *High Latitude* (covering several expeditions, including the AAE), Charles Laseron's *South with Mawson* (AAE), Apsley Cherry-Garrard's *The Worst Journey in the World* (the *Terra Nova* expedition) and, of course, Paquita Mawson's biography of her husband, *Mawson of the Antarctic*. The Royal Geographical Society's *Geographical Journal*, the 'go-to' source for expedition papers, maps and discussions, was invaluable.

Of the more modern books, there are many pearls, but Michael Smith's outstanding book on Lawrence Oates, *I Am Just Going Outside*, was a fount of information, as was Isobel Williams's book on Edward Wilson, *With Scott in the Antarctic*, Tom Griffiths' *Slicing the Silence*, Edward Larson's *Empire of Ice*, David Burke's *Body at the Melbourne Club*, Beau Riffenburgh's *Nimrod* and *Racing with Death*, Philip Ayres's *Mawson: A Life* , and 'Antarctica: Great Stories from the Frozen Continent', published by Reader's Digest. Jacka and Jacka's *Mawson's Antarctic Diaries* was constantly by my side.

Roland Huntford has of course done enormous amounts of work about Scott, Shackleton and Amundsen and their polar expeditions, and though I do not agree with all of his conclusions – most particularly his devastatingly low opinion of the virtues of Scott and the lack of virtue of his wife, Kathleen – I also found his scholarship extremely valuable.

In most of my historical books, I have called on my friend Dr Michael Cooper's twin passions for medicine and history to help inform me on the medical aspects of the story, and in this book I thank him warmly for his input, as ever. I am indebted also to Max Quinn and David Harrowfield of New Zealand, for their help in detailing the Oamaru aspect of the Scott story, and geologist Dr Stephen Gale from the School of Geosciences at the University of Sydney for his expertise on matters geological.

I thank Laurie Whiddon for the illustration of the Barrier, Transantarctic Mountains and Polar Plateau you see herein and Jane Macaulay, who designed the superb maps. For her help in all things to do with the form and texture of the book, I offer my deep appreciation to my treasured colleague at *The Sydney Morning Herald* Harriet Veitch, just as I do to my long-time researcher Sonja Goernitz, who was a great help across the board.

Let me, most importantly, acknowledge the work of my dear friend, principal researcher and all-round help on the writing of this book, Henry Barrkman. In my last book, *Batavia*, I wrote, 'I have never worked as closely with anyone in the writing of a book, and, by its end, he was more familiar with the primary documents than I was.' On this book, his input was more than double that, and it needed to be. Most of my books have 400–500 endnotes. This one, as I presented it to the publisher, had well over 2000 – a measure of the amount of highly detailed research that was done, and he ended up spending months in the archives at Sydney, Adelaide and Cambridge endeavouring to get to the very bottom of the story. So deeply were we immersed in the whole Antarctic saga that now and then I would fancy we were like trekkers ourselves. Time and again, when I fell into a crevasse of exhaustion or egregious error, he was the one who hauled me out, and this book owes his professionalism and intellectual rigour a great debt.

I thank all at Random House, particularly Margie Seale, Nikki Christer and Alison Urquhart for backing the project from the first, and my editor, Kevin O'Brien, for the thoroughness of his approach, his professionalism and for making his deadlines commendably malleable. True, we did have the odd disagreement over proper use of the past perfect – whatever that is – but he was kind enough to indulge my insistence. It was a measure of his skill that he could go through a manuscript that ten sets of experts had already cast their eyes over and *still* spot inconsistencies that needed to be put right.

In short, thank you, thank you all! My primary hope is that this book will do its subjects justice, and I hope you enjoy reading it, nearly as much as I enjoyed writing it.

Peter FitzSimons
Neutral Bay

Author's Note

There is little consistency among authors in this field, original or later, when it comes to the expression of expedition and journey distances. Distances may be expressed in statute (standard) miles, geographical (or nautical) miles, kilometres or a mixture of all three within the same book.

A geographical mile, synonymous with a nautical mile, only on land rather than at sea, is equivalent to one minute of latitude, and therefore one degree of latitude is equal to 60 geographical miles. Geographical miles are preferred for navigation because it is very simple to convert coordinates of latitude to distance.

In Mawson's Australasian Antarctic Expedition diaries, distances are typically expressed in statute miles, while Scott wrote in geographical miles throughout his *Terra Nova* diaries. Shackleton wrote *The Heart of the Antarctic* in statute miles (though he recorded both statute and geographical miles) until at his farthest south, when he changed to geographical miles to calculate the distance between his farthest south and the Pole.

In this book, I have chosen to consistently express all distances in statute miles, because to my ear it sounds more authentic to the period than the kilometre and because many readers will still be familiar with it. A statute mile is our regular land mile and is around 0.87 of a geographical mile. To assist the reader, where a quote includes geographical miles, I have endnoted the equivalent distance in statute miles (simply times by 1.15). For example, if you are located at 88 degrees 57 minutes south, you are one degree and three minutes and therefore 63 geographical miles from the Pole (90 degrees south), and 63 × 1.15 = 72.5 statute miles. There are minor variations in the lengths of geographical miles because the earth is not a perfect sphere and different organisations adopted different standards. For the purposes of this book, these may be ignored, as the differences are minuscule.

Also because it is what they employed at the time, I have used the Fahrenheit system to measure the temperatures, as opposed to Celsius.

Prologue

*What shall we say of our Douglas as an acknowledged leader
and organizer? This I will say – that if there be a corner of this
planet of ours still unexplored, Douglas Mawson will be the
organizer and leader of an expedition to unveil its secrets.*

Speech given by the Fort Street Model School's headmaster,
'Boss' Turner, to a school assembly in the late 1890s

It was in the time before the Dreamtime, nigh on 800 million years before people walked the earth.

A great and devastating cold, the coldest cold the world has known, fell upon the land we now know as Australia.

The snow tumbled down, the winds howled, the blizzards blew, the rivers froze, and such primitive organisms as had then evolved perished hard. In some parts, the land was simply submerged beneath an enormous cap of ice over four miles thick. As the snow continued to fall, decade after decade, century after century, for millennia, and became part of that ice cap, gravity caused the vast rivers of ice to flow, slowly, slowly – oh so slowly – out and down to the sea.

For tens of millions of years, the ice held the land in its terrible frozen grip until slowly, inexorably, sufficient warmth returned and it melted away. Where once there had been only snow and ice and howling blizzards, the earth gradually reappeared, and only a few million years later creeping plant life began to appear, followed by slightly more evolved organisms.

Over the next 500 million years, the earth's glaciers twice

reappeared, though it was never quite so cold again. Around 50 million years ago, the outline of the island continent finally became recognisable. Australia began to drift northwards, with its evolving cargo of flora and fauna. The centre of the continent began to desiccate, to lose even the barest hint of moisture, for where once there had been glaciers and snow there was instead sheer, white, blinding heat. The freezing wind had so ceased to shriek that the searing sun above not only shone, it *pulsed* . . . and the land became desert.

Yet that massive pressure of ice for all those millions of years in that time before the Dreamtime had made its mark. The moving ice had scoured and gouged the land beneath, plucking up rocks and boulder clay from far away and polishing them smooth before dropping them hundreds of miles from their source. Elsewhere, the signature parallel scratches of moving glaciers remained on the rocks to tell expert eyes something of what once was there.

Such an expert is the 25-year-old Douglas Mawson on this hot day in late September 1907. Yes, severe the landscape might be in these Flinders Ranges in the north of South Australia, just to the west of Broken Hill, with not a fleck of green to leaven the sheer burnt redness of it all, but – entirely ignoring the madness of being out in the midday sun in this manner – Mawson is a man in his element. A large fellow, of strong build and athletic movement, and yet with the intelligent expression of one who is lost in a world of intense reverie, he is picking his way among the limestone, shale, sandstone and quartzite rocks as he gnaws at myriad intellectual problems. His whole life to this point has been littered with signposts that have led him to be at this place, at this time.

In 1884, the two-year-old Douglas first came from England to Australia aboard the clipper ship *Ellora* with his older brother, William, and their parents, Robert and Margaret. The Mawsons were fleeing the economic depression that had gripped their native

Yorkshire. As the favourite family story goes, Douglas had shown his wherewithal and derring-do from the first.[1]

For on board that ship, somewhere out upon the seven seas on their way to their new home, the little one slipped unnoticed from the comfort of his mother's side in the galley and decided to go exploring . . . soon enough making his way out into the glorious sunshine and the refreshing sea breeze.

But if it was wonderful down here on the deck, where still no one had spotted him, how much better and brighter might it be up there . . .?

Up in the rigging.

And off he went. Hand over hand up the rat-lines, getting higher now, his feet gamely gripping to the spot where his hands had just been. His aim was to get to the very place, high above, where he had seen men walk sideways, and maybe he would have got there, too, but . . .

But suddenly there is a whole lot of shouting coming from below, and a little bit of familiar wailing – it does sound rather like Mother – before he is gripped by the strong hands of a sailor.

That worthy maritime man thinks he is 'rescuing' the wayward child but the said child has an entirely different impression. The little one thinks he is being unfairly thwarted from achieving his appointed goal. Screaming all the while, he is taken back to the deck by the grinning sailor, who deposits him at his parents' feet, saying only, 'Plucky little cuss! What will he do next?'[2]

And that propensity of young Douglas to push himself, to go further than others, to take calculated risks in his stride, and discover new worlds along the way is one that stays with him ever afterwards.

First up, this new rough-and-tumble world of Australia, where the family settled, offered many opportunities for his restless spirit to find an outlet. For, though they arrived there as a relatively well-to-do family, the Mawsons' money did not last long in the new land.

After first putting some of his capital into a citrus orchard out to the west of Sydney at Rooty Hill, where he settled his young family – a place where the boys could ramble – Robert Mawson then invested in pigs, followed by a new fruit-canning plant, only each time to achieve the same poor economic result. The family was closer to penury than prosperity, but the boys were flourishing regardless in a very outdoor, rustic life.

As Robert's finances were not quite so robust, however, the family retreated to the inner-city suburb of Glebe in 1893, allowing Robert to take a more secure job as an accountant. The family moved from house to house over the next few years, and the enterprising Margaret Mawson sometimes took in boarders to make ends meet. None of this affected the intellectual pursuits of the boys; to the contrary, they had both been outstanding academically.

Some 14 years later, as Douglas was about to graduate from his famous Sydney secondary school, Fort Street Model School, his headmaster, 'Boss' Turner, remarked to a school assembly, 'What shall we say of our Douglas as an acknowledged leader and organizer? This I will say – that if there be a corner of this planet of ours still unexplored, Douglas Mawson will be the organizer and leader of an expedition to unveil its secrets.'[3]

And when subsequently shining in the high academic realms among the even higher sandstone spires of the University of Sydney, which he attended from the age of 16 – gaining first an engineering degree and then a science degree majoring in geology, while Will studied medicine – Mawson was also remarkable for his physical prowess. In April of 1903, at the suggestion of his university mentor, Professor Edgeworth 'Tweedy' David, he travelled on a steamer to the New Hebrides, to conduct an extensive geological survey of the whole island chain. Though he fell ill to fever and nearly lost a leg to a dangerous infection, he managed to push his body to some of the most remote and dangerous parts of the chain – and returned four months later credited with having conducted the first systematic survey of the archipelago.

Great intellect, physical strength and courage stood beside another ingredient essential to Mawson's make-up . . .

One day, while sitting in the gloriously dappled light of the university refectory, Douglas Mawson happened to come across the poems of Robert Service, a favourite of explorers and a man sometimes known as Canada's Rudyard Kipling.

The lines of one particular poem, 'The Call of the Wild', which Service had penned after journeying to the Yukon River, where he had studied the soul-thoughts of the Klondyke gold seekers, played a symphony on Mawson's heart strings:

> Have you known the Great White Silence, not a snow-gemmed twig aquiver?
> (Eternal truths that shame our soothing lies).
> Have you broken trail on snowshoes? mushed your huskies up the river,
> Dared the unknown, led the way, and clutched the prize?
> Have you marked the map's void spaces, mingled with the mongrel races,
> Felt the savage strength of brute in every thew?
> And though grim as hell the worst is, can you round it off with curses?
> Then hearken to the Wild – it's wanting you.[4]

Yes, a symphony for a while, but by the time of its crescendo his soul became restless. After all, *theirs* was a life worth living. And it was these lines that moved him the most:

> Have you seen God in his splendours – heard the text that nature renders,
> (You'll never hear it in the family pew).

The simple things, the true things, the silent men who do things –
Then listen to the wild – it's calling you.

He listened. Oh, how he had listened.

After gaining a position as lecturer in mineralogy and petrology at the University of Adelaide in 1905, Mawson quickly became fascinated by South Australia's geology. Alone, and on occasion accompanied by his students, he often ventured forth on trips to even the most remote and roughest parts of the state.

On this day, however, his focus is purely on the signs of the ice cap that once was. As he walks along – his lean frame picking its way easily among the tangle of metamorphic, igneous and sedimentary rocks – he frequently pauses to draw small sketches and to take notes and photographs. Right there, for example, is the flat, smoothly polished rock surface bearing the telltale deep parallel scratches that he particularly revels in finding.

Exactly what caused that massive shield of ice to melt away and the climate to change so profoundly that there is now no natural ice within several thousand miles is not yet clear to Mawson, but the whole nature of what once was here remains profoundly fascinating to him. Completely absorbed by what he is seeing and learning, a strong desire begins to take hold. As Mawson would later explain it:

My idea was to see a continental ice-cap in being and become acquainted with glaciation and its geological repercussions. This especially interested me for in glaciological studies in South Australia I was face to face with a great accumulation of glacial sediments of Pre-Cambrian age, the greatest thing of the kind recorded anywhere in the world. So I desired to see an ice age in being.[5]

Yes, that's it. For him to truly understand how ice caps and glaciers form, and what they do to change a landscape, he needs to journey to lands where they still rule in a frozen kingdom. The same idea has occurred to other Australian geologists before him in times past, but this is different.

Douglas Mawson's own interest has come at a time when, though neither the North Pole nor the South Pole – the capitals of the very kingdoms where glaciers most prosper – has yet been conquered, both ends of the earth have been recently under siege from explorers. What's more, the siege has just reached a new stage of intensity, with the Anglo-Irishman Ernest Shackleton then and there mounting an expedition back to Antarctica. The rub is that the academic at the University of Sydney to whom he has been closest, and who wrote a strong reference for him to get his lecturing job at the University of Adelaide – Professor David – is so esteemed in the world of geology that he is going with Shackleton as nothing less than the head of his scientific team.

In his brief paper to the Royal Geographical Society in early 1907, Shackleton wrote, 'I do not intend to sacrifice the scientific utility of the expedition to a mere record-breaking journey, but say frankly, all the same, that one of my great efforts will be to reach the southern geographical pole.'[6]

And yet, scientifically, there is so much to find out. For they do not even know whether or not Antarctica is a continent. Perhaps it is a number of islands supporting a massive ice shelf. Or two large islands. All remains to be found. Of particular interest to Professor David is whether any evidence exists to suggest that Antarctica and Australia might once even have been joined.

Mawson is close friends with another geology-department member at the University of Adelaide, Walter Howchin, with whom he shares a common interest in glaciology. An ordained Methodist minister, Howchin is a geologising evangelist with a biblical view of geology, built on that one foundation stone of faith to beat them all: that God created the earth in six days . . .

Contemplating it all now, Mawson feels a great pang of regret that he is not going with Shackleton and David. He decides at least to write to the Professor to see if there might be any chance he can go too. There, in the middle of the desert, with the heat from the sun blasting from above and below, reflecting from the rocks, he wants nothing more than to go south, to see for himself the frozen land that lies there.

And therein lies another story. For that urge, to go south, young man, go *south*, is an urge that has been within mankind for many centuries, always beginning with a reverie as to just what the land that lies there might be like . . .

Introduction

Discovering Antarctica

In the years around 530 BC, the Greek philosopher and mathematician Pythagoras put aside his triangles and formed an equally fascinating theory: the world was *not* flat but spherical, like the moon and sun, and also symmetrical, with balance in all things.

It was an idea that slowly took hold, and a little less than 400 years later the philosopher Selukos of Chaldea postulated the existence of a southern land to counterbalance the known northern lands they were living on. But who lived there? That too was speculated upon as the centuries passed, and by AD 43 the Roman geographer Pomponius Mela went so far as to give its population a name: 'Antichthones' – a people separated from the northern hemisphere by the impassable Torrid Zone along the equator.

A century later, the hypothesis had, through constant repetition, crystallised enough that the greatest map-maker of his age, Ptolemy of Alexandria, drew 'Terra Australis Incognita', unknown southern land, on his world map. There it brooded, silently, lost, far down in the southern hemisphere opposite the Arctic Circle and boasting the South Pole as its centre.

Could it have a name beyond the 'unknown land'? Eventually, yes. It was Marinus of Tyre who in the second century AD coined the term 'Antarktos', Antarctic, meaning opposite to the Arctic. The Arctic itself had been named from the Greek *Arktikos*, 'Near the

Bear', in reference to the northern constellation Ursa Minor ('The Smaller Bear' or 'Little Bear' in Latin), which contains the North Pole Star, Polaris.

It had taken 700 years of human thought to theorise the existence of this place, draw it on a map and give it a real name. It would take nigh on another millennium and a half before navigation became sophisticated enough and ships were made hardy enough to open up the possibility of investigation.

For, back in 1492, while he was sailing the ocean blue in what is now the Bahamas, in the Spanish-constructed *Santa Maria*, the great mariner and navigator Christopher Columbus began to notice a very odd and troubling thing. The northern point of his compass was not pointing towards the unwavering North Star above the North Pole but tending half a degree to the north-west! And the further he continued, the more it varied. On 17 September 1492, he recorded in his log:

> Last night the pilots took a reading on the North Star and found that the compasses declined to the NW a full point. This caused some apprehension at the moment, but I ordered the north to be fixed again just before sunrise, and the needles were found to be true. This is because the North Star moves, not the compasses.[1]

Columbus's conclusion – that there was a slight difference between true north and the direction in which the needle was pointing – had no doubt been reached by other mariners previously. But the fact that a man of Columbus's capacity and renown documented it meant that it was taken seriously by the world at large, and over coming centuries the study of the phenomenon continued.

Bit by bit, mariners came to understand two things. The first was that the magnetic poles moved around from year to year, while usually remaining around 11 degrees offset from the geographic pole. The second was that the magnetic force that turned compass needles moved not only in a horizontal plane but also at an angle of vertical inclination with the earth's surface that brought the tip of the needle ever closer to vertical as they got closer to the pole, dipping towards the magnetic material at the earth's centre, which is likened to a bar magnet situated between the North and South Magnetic Poles.

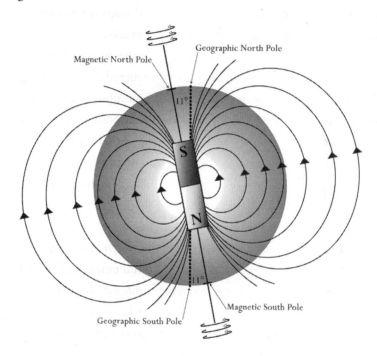

Dip compasses were therefore made to operate on two planes: the horizontal (the declination), which gives you the bearing of the magnetic poles, and the vertical (the inclination), which is the progressive increase in the dip of the needle as you move from the equator to the poles.

Compass needle in standard position.

Compass needle dipping towards
centre of earth at Magnetic Pole.

In 1576, Robert Norman was the first to describe the earth's magnetic dip (or inclination). His experiments also demonstrated that the earth's magnetic field was variable. It was not until 1700, however, that Edmund Halley (of the comet fame) prepared a worldwide map of the earth's magnetic field, enabling a far greater degree of accuracy when taking compass readings.

The first true breakthrough in actually finding out what lay at the bottom of the earth came on 17 January 1773. It was on this day when Captain James Cook – the celebrated navigator, don't you know, who had three years earlier guided his ship into Botany Bay on Australia's east coast – approached the first crossing of the Antarctic Circle in his ship HMS *Resolution*.

He was on something of a mission. In his words:

Whether the unexplored part of the Southern Hemisphere be only an immense mass of water, or contain another continent, as speculative geography seemed to suggest, was a question which had long engaged the attention, not only of learned men, but of most of the maritime powers of Europe.[2]

And now the British Admiralty had sent him to answer that question once and for all, steering first by way of the French navigator Jean-Baptiste Charles Bouvet de Lozier's discovery in the

South Atlantic of Cape Circumcision – no, really – to see if that place was part of the great southern continent and, if not, to proceed south from there. Cook's original secret instructions stated that, if the continent did indeed exist, wherever he located it he was 'with the consent of the natives to take possession of convenient situations in the country in the name of the King of Great Britain'. If he couldn't find it, he was to keep going south till he could go no more, 'prosecuting your discoveries as near to the South Pole as possible'.[3]

And so there he was on this auspicious day, in freezing conditions, continuing south and dodging ever-larger icebergs until his tiny ship at last crossed that long-coveted line on the map. And yet, though one might have expected Cook to feel exultant in his achievement, the truth was he was not.

What he mostly felt was sick.

Three weeks earlier, suffering from lack of fresh food, Cook had been 'taken ill of the bilious colic', accompanied by severe constipation and loss of appetite, and he had not really recovered since.[4]

Nevertheless, now that the line had been crossed he kept going, until HMS *Resolution*, accompanied by HMS *Adventure*, reached as far as 67 degrees 15 minutes south, at which position they could get no further as the ice became so thick in the ocean ahead of them that there was simply no way through.

In what would become a pattern for generations of men to follow, after having gone as far south as he could, Cook reluctantly turned north . . . and shortly thereafter fell even more ill. Relatively suddenly, in the extreme conditions, the now gaunt, pale Cook collapsed.

What was apparent to *Resolution*'s extremely capable surgeon, Patten, was that the good captain was in urgent need of fresh meat – not easy in such climes, and yet . . .

Up on the foredeck, the favourite dog of Mr Forster, one of Cook's senior officers, is heard barking . . .

. . . maybe there is a solution after all.

So it was that this dog was slaughtered and its meat presented by the cook to Captain Cook as a restorative. As to Mr Forster, although he felt a little grim about losing his favourite animal, he could at least take comfort that – perhaps in exchange for this dog's life – an entire species of animal, the emperor penguin, was named after him, *Aptenodytes forsteri*.

And the other consolation, of course, was that, in part thanks to the fresh meat, Captain Cook was able to recover. As Cook himself described it, 'Thus I received nourishment and strength, from food which would have made most people in Europe sick: so true it is that necessity is governed by no law.'[5]

Again, a significant pattern was set for generations of intrepid explorers to come . . .

But surely that record of farthest south could be bettered? With his every move carving the grooves of behaviour that generations of explorers in these parts would follow for many, many decades, Cook decided to have another go himself. On returning to New Zealand, he rested his men and revictualled his ship, and, late in 1773, he headed south once more. On 31 January 1774, he reached latitude 71 degrees 10 minutes south, crossing the Antarctic Circle for the second time, along a different course than before. With the sails and rigging of his ship now frozen stiff and heavy with ice, he then made the decision to turn back. He wrote:

> I will not say it was impossible anywhere to get farther to the south, but the attempting it would have been a dangerous and rash enterprise, and what, I believe, no man in my situation would have thought of. I, who had ambition not only to go farther than any one had been before, but as far as it was possible for man to go, was not sorry at meeting with this interruption; as it, in some measure, relieved us; at least, shortened the dangers and hardships inseparable from the navigation of the southern polar regions.

It was, indeed, *my* opinion, as well as the opinion of most on board, that this ice extended quite to the pole, or, perhaps joined to some land, to which it had been fixed from the earliest time.[6]

All up, Cook's circumnavigation of the globe in high southern latitudes between 1772 and 1775 at least gave some clue as to what the southern land consisted of. They knew now, for example, that it was *not* connected to any continents that lay north of it, and that whatever land there might be there, beyond and beneath all the ice, lay within the Antarctic Circle. 'If anyone goes further south than I have been,' said Cook, with perhaps a perceptible shudder of cold or horror or both, 'I shall not envy him the honour of discovery, but I will be bold to say the world will not be benefitted by it.'[7]

More significant than that information, however, in terms of what happened over the next century is that in the course of his travels – covering 60,000 miles – Cook had discovered islands, such as South Georgia, and affirmed they abounded with seals and penguins, with whales in the waters around them.

And so it began . . .

From the last decades of the 1700s, at first with a trickle, and then with a flood, man began heading ever further south, eager to reap not only the highly coveted and commercially precious fur-seal pelts, so prized for their warmth, but also the vast quantities of valuable elephant-seal oil and even some penguin oil, which would go on to light the lanterns of Europe and North America for most of the 1800s, bringing enormous profits to the sealing ventures. At first, there seemed no end to the riches available, and the industry took on the character of a gold rush, with each new arrival eager to plunder whatever they could, as quickly as they could, with no regard for the consequences.

In 1825, the British sealer Captain James Weddell – who, two years earlier, with his tiny ships, the 160-ton *Jane* and 65-ton *Beaufoy*, had managed to sail 214 miles further south than Cook for a new record of 74 degrees 15 minutes (pass the port) – made a horrifying estimation: 'I have been credibly informed that, since the year in which they were known to be so abundant, not less than 20,000 tons of sea-elephant oil have been procured for the London market . . . The number of skins brought from off South Georgia by ourselves and foreigners cannot be estimated as fewer than 1,200,000.'[8]

The slaughterers clubbed the seals to death before stripping the pelts and leaving the carcasses where they fell, often right beside their tiny pups, which, having lost their mothers, all died. No matter. You could kill and skin a fur seal in just under a minute, and though the extraction of the oil from an elephant seal took much longer – boiling it all down in big pots – just a single fur-seal pelt or 200 ounces of elephant oil was worth two pounds on the British market, the broad equivalent of two *months'* wages for an average farm worker in England. Similarly, elephant sealers used only the blubber, leaving the carcasses where they fell.

Just how far south those sealers voyaged was never properly documented because the locations of their profitable slaughter grounds remained top secret.[9] If a sealer found an unexploited island, one of his prime concerns was to forestall any competition.

Enter . . . Commander Jules Sébastien César Dumont d'Urville of France. In September 1837, having been farewelled from Toulon by King Louis Philippe himself, with two corvettes under his overall command, the *Astrolabe* and the *Zélée*, he headed off on a government-supported scientific voyage in search of the South Magnetic Pole and the mysterious land mass that might surround it. Two years and four months later, d'Urville's expedition took him to a location about 66 degrees 36 minutes south, 140 degrees 4 minutes east, and 1700 miles south of the southern tip of Tasmania.

On the remarkably calm evening of 19 January 1840, they found themselves in the very midst of a thick and troubling frozen forest of no fewer than 59 icebergs, but still they inched their way south, ever south, to the point that they at last crossed the Antarctic Circle.

And then, slowly, it happened . . .

'At 10.50 pm the sun disappeared,' the French commander recounted, 'and allowed us to see its high contours with the utmost clarity. Everyone had rushed on deck to enjoy the superb spectacle.'[10]

Land!

Too high and wide to be anything else. Land; they had seen it.

And slowly, slowly, despite the lack of wind, they were able to approach it. These men from the ever warmer climes of France now made their way through vast walls of ice towards the land so long imagined but never before certainly seen. For once, the icebergs fell back, just enough to allow them passage.

'Their sheer walls were much higher than our masts; they loomed over our ships, the size of which seemed dramatically reduced in comparison with the enormous masses. The spectacle they presented was both magnificent and terrifying. One could have believed oneself in the narrow streets of a city of giants.'[11]

At noon, they were finally within four miles of its rocky skirt at the base of a snow- and ice-covered coast, lying in a south-east to north-west direction, its precipitous cliffs leaving no accessible landing points. But there was no doubt that they were looking at the 'unknown land'.

Dumont d'Urville named it Terre Adélie, Adélie Land, after his wife (which surely pleased her), while he also named the comic, rotund little waddling creatures that abounded there the Adélie penguin (which likely pleased her a little less). D'Urville cruised north-west along the flat-topped ice cliffs up to 130-feet high to a position roughly south of Adelaide. No, in the face of those ramparts, there was no easy landing point, but he and his crew felt these ice cliffs were probably connected to land, though there was no way of telling.

On 28 January 1840, as d'Urville's exploration of the area was coming to an end, he encountered two vessels of the six-ship fleet of another explorer, Lieutenant Charles Wilkes, of the United States Exploring Expedition.

The 41-year-old Lieutenant Wilkes was in his flagship, *Vincennes*, and had entered the Antarctic Circle two weeks previously as part of a comprehensive exploration of the Pacific and the Southern Ocean, at the behest of his government, to chart these dangerous southern waters. On 19 January 1840, the water had turned a telltale muddy green, even as upturned icebergs encrusted with rocks began to appear . . . in the company of seabirds . . . and soon land was sighted from *Vincennes*.

Three days later, one of her sister ships, *Peacock*, hove to and soundings were taken. The measuring unit was 'fathoms', with each fathom equalling six feet, and when only 500 fathoms of a 1400-fathom sounding line returned covered in blue and slate-coloured mud, and a second sounding confirmed an even shallower depth of 320 fathoms, there was 'a burst of joy'.[12] With a rising shallow seabed established, that kind of sediment had surely been washed from nearby *land* over the ages, providing further proof of what they were witnessing. When an enormous king penguin was captured a short time later, and was found to have 32 pebbles in his craw, from 'the size of a pea to that of a hazelnut', Wilkes was duly satisfied and on 30 January 1840 named the new land 'The Antarctic Continent', though others would take a lot of convincing that it was indeed a continent.[13]

Unable to approach the land because of an imposing ice buffer, Wilkes turned west, erratically tracking the 'interminable' ice along the coast that lay directly below Australia for the best part of a month. In the process, he travelled along more than 2000 miles of coast before being halted by the formation he named 'Termination Land', which lay at right angles across their path.[14]

A year later, enter the dashing 38-year-old Scotsman Captain James Clark Ross, regarded as the most handsome man in the navy as well as an authority on terrestrial magnetism. In recent times, the burgeoning desire of the scientific community to both chart and understand the world's magnetic field had become so focused and passionate that it was referred to as the Magnetic Crusade, and it was Ross who was the lead Crusader.

Ross was appointed in 1838 by the British Admiralty to be leader of a four-year, two-ship expedition that had as its main goal the location of the South Magnetic Pole – just as, a decade earlier, he had located the North Magnetic Pole in far-northern Canada. His orders were 'even to attain it if possible, which it is hoped will be one of the remarkable and creditable results of the expedition.'[15]

In August 1840, Captain Ross arrived in Hobart and read accounts of the expeditions of Dumont d'Urville in the local newspaper. In November, Ross left Hobart in command of the naval vessels HMS *Erebus* and HMS *Terror*, so chosen because their mortar-bomb-resistant hulls were ideal should they encounter severe ice. This proved most prescient, for soon after crossing the Antarctic Circle and reaching 71 degrees south on 5 January 1841, he and his men encountered a sea infested with massive icebergs and heavy pack ice – flat sea ice not attached to the shoreline – extending right up to the southern horizon.

Of stoic blood, for six days the determined Ross headed south-west in search of the Magnetic Pole, fighting his way through the pack ice and into gale-force winds until he and the crew on his ships were amazed to break through into an open sea – a vast aquatic bulge on the other side of the continent to the Weddell Sea, far larger than a mere bay – which would later be named the Ross Sea.

Six days later, on 11 January, at approximately 71 degrees south – far further south than any man had ever been – Ross discovered (and named) the 12,200-foot peak Mt Sabine and shortly afterwards Cape Adare, a stubby finger of land in the north-western corner of the Ross Sea. The following day, making his way through 'inconceivable myriads of penguins . . . pecking at us with their sharp beaks',[16] he went ashore on Possession Island – the first land claimed for Britain's new sovereign, Queen Victoria.

Thwarted by unscaleable mountains in his attempt to reach the South Magnetic Pole,[17] for some days Ross proceeded southwards down the west coast of the Ross Sea, naming the land on his right Victoria Land in his queen's honour and its towering, ceaseless chain of mountains after Lords of the Admiralty. They proceeded, all the while making regular and highly delicate observations of the direction and intensity of the magnetic forces in this part of the world, and carefully recording them.

On 27 January, in the vicinity of 77 degrees south, *Erebus*'s lookout sighted a vast smoking mountain, so tall it rose higher than the otherwise all-encompassing ice could swallow. They named this almost 12,500-foot-high volcano – 'emitting flame and smoke in splendid profusion'[18] – Mt Erebus, and its smaller, inactive companion Mt Terror after their two ships. The land on which the volcanoes resided they called High Island (later to be named Ross Island). Ross named the large ice-enveloped bay separating Ross Island in the east from Victoria Land in the west McMurdo Bay (which became McMurdo Sound) after the highly regarded senior lieutenant of *Terror*, Archibald McMurdo.

Approaching the eastern limit of the north coast of High Island, Ross's confidence in reaching 80 degrees south waned as he caught sight of a 'low white line extending from its eastern extreme point as far as the eye could see to the eastward'.[19] It was a solid wall of ice stretching to the far horizons, so imposing and high, at up to 300 feet, that Ross recorded it was 'an obstruction of such a character as to leave no doubt upon my mind as to our future proceedings, for we might with equal chance of success try to sail through the Cliffs of Dover, as penetrate such a mass'.[20] After following the sheer cliffs of that ice barrier for some 250 miles, charting its contours all the way, he decided to name it – now there's an idea – after his queen, Victoria Barrier (also known at this time as the Great Ice Barrier and later renamed the Ross Ice Shelf).

In the course of this epic journey, Ross achieved an impressive 78 degrees 11 minutes south and had come within 160 miles of the ever-wandering South Magnetic Pole as it was situated in 1841.

Unknown to Ross at the time, subsequent exploration would reveal that barrier to be the largest ice shelf in Antarctica, at 188,800 square miles (nudging towards the size of France), around 500 miles across at its widest part and in places up to almost half a mile thick. It represented an enormous chunk of Antarctica's 5.4 million square miles.

And it was this discovery of the Ross Sea and the Great Ice Barrier – for 'barrier' would indeed become the operative word – that allowed access to a hitherto unexplored, vast area of Antarctica's coast, featuring scientifically valuable and accessible exposed rock in addition to suitable sites for future landings and the establishment of base huts for expeditions towards the icy heart of the vast continent.

The rub was this: all three of these major explorers – Commander Jules Sébastien César Dumont d'Urville, Captain Charles Wilkes and Captain James Clark Ross – returned to their homelands and reported what they had seen, in the case of Dumont d'Urville publishing a narrative of the expedition in ten parts in 1844. Nevertheless, over the next half-century or so, the world's interest in Antarctica slowed somewhat.

There were several reasons, not least that seals had been largely exterminated, penguins weren't worth killing and the rorqual whales couldn't be caught by existing methods and were less valued. Also, while much northern national energy was expended on such things as the Crimean War, the American Civil War and the Franco–Prussian War, the spirit of exploration found more certain satisfaction in the multitude of rich goldfields that sprang up overnight only to – all too frequently – fall back down during the day . . . before another one was inevitably discovered elsewhere.

The most celebrated exception to this general lassitude in exploring the southern higher latitudes was one expedition by the

British, led by James Buchanan, with Sir Charles Wyville Thompson as his chief scientist, on HMS *Challenger*, a steam-assisted corvette that had once patrolled Australian waters before conversion into a floating laboratory. The ship left Portsmouth in England in late December 1872 on a global oceanographic expedition that included 'sailing south towards the ice barrier as far as it is safe for an unprotected vessel to venture'.[21] The significance of this voyage was that for the first time biologists, chemists and physicists put their energies and skills together with navigators and maritime men to expand the frontiers of scientific knowledge alone. The ship returned four years later laden with examples of many newly discovered species of life and having sounded the ocean bottom around the whole southern continent. The renowned Scottish geographer and meteorologist Hugh Robert Mill judged it to be the 'greatest scientific voyage ever undertaken' and the *Challenger* report in 50 volumes a 'contribution to science so magnificent that it is beyond praise'.[22] One thing established beyond all doubt, after comparing the magnetic observations of the *Challenger* expedition with those taken by the expedition of Captain James Clark Ross, was that they were entirely different. The only conclusion was that the Magnetic Poles must move around, it seemed by as much as ten minutes of arc per year.

In the last decades of the nineteenth century, however, interest sprang anew with the advent of steam power in ships, which, in combination with the continued use of sails, made exploring the higher latitudes, both north and south, a less risky affair. While sails could still provide most of the power over long distances, steam power, with its attendant manoeuvrability, came into its own when negotiating pack ice.

The first true breakthrough in taking ships closer to the ends of the earth stemmed from Norway, where an explorer, oceanographer and internationally regarded professor of zoology by the name of Fridtjof Nansen had a revolutionary idea, inspired by a newspaper report that debris from the wreck of the American vessel *Jeannette*, sunk off the north coast of Siberia in 1881, had been found three years later off the south-west coast of Greenland. Clearly, that debris had drifted across the polar ocean, and his idea was to purposefully have his ship freeze in the Siberian ice and then have it drift across the North Pole, estimating this would take up to three years.

With that in mind, his ship, *Fram*, was built strong, with a specially rounded hull so that when the freezing ice pressed in around it, instead of being crushed, the vessel would 'slip like an eel out of the embraces of the ice',[23] and then sit upon it, as the ship was carried towards the North Pole. And that idea worked! After Nansen set off from Oslo on 24 June 1893, the ice closed in, and the mighty *Fram* suddenly popped up, exactly as planned, just as the wintry polar night descended. Their ice floe began to slowly, oh so slowly drift north. On 2 February 1894, they reached the 80th parallel, just three weeks before the sun returned. Nevertheless, an exceedingly long year beckoned – on 28 May, Nansen wrote, 'Ugh, I am tired of these endless white plains!'[24] – and just before Christmas they reached 82 degrees 30 minutes north, which was a new record for a ship.

By this time, however, Nansen had already left the ship with a companion, Hjalmar Johansen, and embarked on a push to the North Pole with dog-drawn sledges that carried kayaks for crossing open waters. They proceeded for three weeks vainly trying to get there – they got as far as 86 degrees 13.6 minutes north – and took another 14 months to get back. This included spending eight months in a crude shelter on an island in Franz Josef Land in the far north of Russia, waiting for weather and ice conditions to improve. *Fram*, meanwhile, kept slowly drifting, with her supremely bored crew, getting as far as 86 degrees 14 minutes north before Nansen's second in command, who had taken over, used dynamite to blast her free in the northern summer, and they made their way back to civilisation, three years after leaving.

The art of travelling to the higher latitudes was developing.

An enormous leap forward in the exploration of Antarctic climes came in the mid-1890s, when a Norwegian businessman from Tønsberg by the name of Henryk Johan Bull launched an expedition in his whaler *Antarctic* to search for right whales in the Southern Ocean. Hoping to revive the old gold-rush days, the ship was equipped with 11 'harpoon guns', recently patented by the expedition's financial backer Svend Foyn, capable of sending harpoons with explosive power and, at close distance, lethal accuracy deep into the whale.

It did not go well. In late 1894, they were obliged to go progressively further south in their search for the elusive whales, right to the point that the day after Christmas, with the midnight sun high in the sky, they crossed the Antarctic Circle and kept going. By this time, they had shot their bolt – in fact bolts, as all of their tackle, including their harpoons, had been lost, with no whales to show for it – and thought they might at least make some profit with seals.

On 16 January 1895, they sighted Cape Adare, and on 18 January they became only the second men since Ross, 54 years before, to land on Possession Island. Venturing further south to 74 degrees, they then turned northwards, and on 24 January they prepared their longboat to make an actual landing at Cape Adare.

Aboard the landing boat were the captain of *Antarctic*, four New Zealanders who had been recruited from Stewart Island, Bull and an acerbic Norwegian settler from Australia, the 30-year-old hobby scientist Carsten Egeberg Borchgrevink. The longboat approached the commodious peninsula, which gently sloped down from the steep rocks to the pebbly shore, but no sooner had its bow touched the gravelly bottom than, as he would tell it ever afterwards, regular seaman Borchgrevink jumped out! Ostensibly, this was to relieve the weight on the boat, allow the bow to get onto the beach and let the captain get onto the shore with dry feet. Rightly or wrongly,

Borchgrevink proudly (and regularly) declared that his was the first foot to be planted on Antarctica.

Also proud of the historic nature of the occasion, if also miffed at Borchgrevink's colossal presumption, Bull organised for a box with Norwegian colours to be attached to a pole erected on the beach, recording their arrival.

Though the men had only one whale to show for their trouble by the time they returned to Melbourne on 12 March 1895, they had achieved something far more significant. As Bull wrote, their expedition had:

> proved that landing on Antarctica proper is not so difficult as it was hitherto considered, and that a wintering party have every chance of spending a safe and pleasant twelvemonth at Cape Adare with a fair chance of penetrating to, or nearly to, the magnetic pole by the aid of sledges and Norwegian *ski-es*.[25]

Interest surged forward again . . .

At the sixth International Geographical Congress, held at the Royal Geographical Society's headquarters in London from 26 July till 3 August 1895, the Congress had – after having been addressed by none other than Carsten Borchgrevink on the possibilities of mounting a full-scale Antarctic expedition – passed a unanimous resolution:

> That this congress record its opinion that the exploration of the Antarctic Regions is the greatest piece of geographical exploration still to be undertaken. That, in view of the additions to knowledge in almost every branch of science which would result from such a scientific exploration, the Congress recommends that the scientific societies throughout the world should urge, in whatever way seems to them most effective, that this work should be undertaken before the close of the century.[26]

As a result of this same Congress, Antarctica was now generally considered to have been established as a continent.

Why the Antarctic and not the Arctic? One reason was that whereas the Arctic was no more than a mostly frozen ocean, the Antarctic was a massive land mass – some estimates put it at nearly twice the size of Australia – which could be laid claim to, with bases established to conduct terra firma exploration and scientific experimentation. And whereas in pursuit of the North-West Passage, a fair amount of information was already known about what lay within the Arctic Circle, next to nothing had been established about its southern counterpart. The North Pole was almost entirely surrounded by Eurasian countries – Russia, Norway and Denmark's Greenland, as well as Canada and the United States – whereas Antarctica was a long way from any powerful country, though nearest to South America, followed by New Zealand and Australia.

By those late 1800s, the last remaining undiscovered and unmapped land masses of earth lay in the extreme zones of the Arctic and Antarctic, and represented not just the final frontier but also the third imperative for exploration: geopolitical dominance. And so, the stage was set for what would become known as the 'Heroic Age of Exploration', a 25-year period as intense as it was brief.

In fact, the first group to spend the winter in Antarctica was not long away. On 16 August 1897, a scientific expedition sponsored by the Geographical Society of Belgium set out on the 110-foot converted Norwegian whaler *Belgica*, under the command of a 29-year-old lieutenant of the Royal Belgian Navy, Adrien Victor Joseph de Gerlache. The *Belgica* boasted an international crew – go south, young man, go south! – that included one American, the New York surgeon Dr Frederick A. Cook.

On 15 February 1898, just as the summer was disappearing and winter was on its way, the refitted *Belgica* crossed the Antarctic

Circle and continued to chart the largely unexplored Antarctic Peninsula – an extended finger of land that reaches from Antarctica up towards the southern tip of South America – until . . . just a little over a fortnight later, on 2 March, it shuddered to a halt as the pack ice closed in around it. With every passing hour, the ice became progressively more solid as the sunlight diminished every day. They were going to be stuck for the winter.

'We are now doomed to remain, and become the football of an unpromising fate,' recorded Cook in his diary.[27]

Mid-May, the sun fell below the horizon and darkness descended with frightening speed, starting to fully envelope them in one long Antarctic night. They were entirely unprepared to be the first group of men to ever spend a winter south of the Antarctic Circle. As the days and then weeks and then *months* passed, and the temperatures dropped, and the 'dense throbbing blackness of the polar night' became ever more menacing, so too did a certain blackness show up in the morale of the men, matched only by a slowly enveloping blackness of mind.[28] For madness now stalked them close as they tried to survive in their icy, dark, damp tomb and keep their sanity. One sailor became hysterical, while another was so disturbed by the pressure of the surrounding ice that he lost his reason.

Lieutenant Danco collapsed and died with heart palpitations on 5 June 1898. Two days later, a hole was hacked through the ice and his body was committed to the depths in a roughly sewn sailcloth bag. The captain of the ship and second in command, George Lecointe, retreated to his bunk, and, convinced he had not long to live, made out his last instructions. Later, Gerlache himself became incapacitated with anaemia. As many of the men turned pale with an absurdly greenish, oily hue, a fog of total despondency and physical and mental sluggishness settled over this frozen ghost ship of the Southern Seas.

But, cometh the hour, cometh the man. That man was Frederick A. Cook himself, who effectively took control of matters medical and mental. 'Mentally, the outlook was that of a madhouse,' Cook later wrote, but instead of despairing he simply got to work.[29] Realising that due to lack of sun, inadequate diet and low temperatures, many of the men were suffering from polar anaemia, and that the usual medicaments were proving ineffective, he devised what the sailors referred to as the 'baking treatment'.

The course of remedy was simple. The sick man was stripped naked and sat by the fire for at least one hour a day as a substitute for the healing sun's rays; only milk, cranberry sauce and fresh penguin or seal meat were to be eaten; bedding was dried daily and a laxative prescribed. As importantly, Cook recognised the need to perk up the patient's spirits, and in this he was willingly assisted by those crewmen still unaffected. What's more, it worked. Within a week, Lecointe had risen from his deathbed, and within two weeks he had returned to his normal duties.

As the wind continued to howl outside and the long, dark night continued, the men, when not sleeping 12 hours a day, wiled away the time playing card games – including gambling games – to keep their minds active and bring them back from madness. With his energy, humour, spirit and care, Cook got them through, and when the sun at last started to emerge once more from the inky depths that it had fallen into – first reappearing for a few minutes on 22 July – he could have taken a bow on the bridge for his achievements. Instead, he remained too busy in the long months ahead – as they remained in their icy prison – nursing the men's physical and mental health back from the brink. This was no easy matter, as frustration grew at the fact that they remained trapped, month after wretched month, until at last, on 14 March 1899, after 12 months and 12 days of imprisonment, *Belgica* finally moved into open water.

The efforts of Cook were deeply appreciated by one and all on the ship, and they would formally write of him:

His behaviour won the respect, indeed the admiration, of us all

... He was the most popular man on the expedition ... Upright, honourable, capable and conscientious in the extreme – such is our recollection of Frederick Cook.[30]

Still, it is doubtful that any admired him more than the Norwegian first mate who had observed closely just how Cook had managed to lead the men, fight the conditions and win through all at once. The name of the Norwegian was Roald Amundsen.

Meanwhile, so beguiled was Borchgrevink by the experience of setting foot on Antarctica, he had no sooner returned to Australia than he set about raising funds to mount his own expedition – the first to ever *intend* 'wintering over' in Antarctica. With the aid of dogs, it would also be the first to undertake sledging journeys on the continent.

His adopted country reluctant to back a 'foreigner', he travelled on a ship to England, where he secured financial backing to the tune of £40,000 from the millionaire publisher George Newnes. Thus, the 1898–1900 *Southern Cross* expedition was born.

On 17 February 1899, at Robertson Bay, Cape Adare, the *Southern Cross*'s anchor 'fell at the last *terra incognita* on the globe'.[31] Holding their noses against the 'ammoniacal' stench of guano, courtesy of a profusion of penguins, and with their 75 dogs back from uncontrolled slaughter of this enormous penguin colony, the crew unloaded the ship under gale conditions.[32]

On 1 March, as *Southern Cross* was departing, her crew dipped her flags and cheered in response as those left behind hoisted high the 'cut sandwich' (otherwise known as the Union Jack). Wise to the winter, as the temperature began to drop well below freezing, the prescient penguins packed their tuxes into their bags and made good their escape to the waters of the Southern Ocean, leaving the men alone ... very alone. On that desolate Antarctic shore, facing an unknown winter, they were as isolated as any ten men might possibly be.

'The long Polar night is dismal, very dismal, and in the terrible loneliness in that uttermost part of the world, character may well grow crabbed and gnarled,' recorded the Australian scientist Louis Bernacchi as winter set in.[33] The sea froze, and the temperature spiralled down to below minus 40 degrees, so low that the mercury froze in the thermometer and along with it the men's spirits. 'The darkness and silences weighed heavily on one's minds,' wrote Borchgrevink. 'The silence roared in our ears, it was centuries of heaped up solitude.'[34]

As the first penguin returned around October, zoologist Nicolai Hansen was in fact dying of a chronic intestinal problem. On his deathbed, he had asked to see that penguin and examined it with rare delight. The legacy of his demise: he became the first man to be buried on the icy continent.

On 28 January 1900, though, at last came a joyous cry . . .

'Post!' called out a neighbourly Captain Jensen, of the freshly arrived *Southern Cross*,[35] her masts and yards draped with ice. Overcome with joy, the men sprang from their bunks, competing for the hut's door before rushing headlong outside to see their relief ship returning to Robertson Bay. Borchgrevink's men received her like a long-lost lover. Starved of information for almost a year, the men soon devoured the newspapers, stupefied by all they had missed: the war on Transvaal, discoveries in telegraphy, the latest in European politics . . .

Not content with being the first expedition to winter on the Antarctic mainland, Borchgrevink and his men decided to venture south towards McMurdo Sound, landing at several locations on the coast of Victoria Land, taking magnetic observations and investigating the geology, flora and fauna. They carefully noted future sites for Winter Quarters with an eye to accessing McMurdo Sound and the possibility of sledging between the west and east coasts of a frozen Ross Sea in eight days. A disappointed Bernacchi (for Borchgrevink did not enter the Sound) theorised that a close examination of the Sound may well have shown a suitable site for their Winter Quarters.

The southern extent of the Ross Sea was wonderfully free of ice. With Mt Erebus as a landmark, they continued south-east, soon tracking Ross Island's northern coast from Cape Bird at the north-western tip heading east to Cape Crozier 48 miles away.

When they reached Ross's Great Ice Barrier, rising up from the ocean in places to an estimated height of 200 feet and stretching continuously far, far away to the east, Bernacchi recorded with awe:

> It was the most marvellous sight I had ever seen in my life, no words can adequately describe it.
>
> Imagination's utmost stretch
> In wonder dies away.[36]

Pushing through the almost open sea, the *Southern Cross* tracked the Great Ice Barrier east before reaching a break in its mighty ramparts at 78 degrees 34 minutes south, 164 degrees 32 minutes west.

Here, Borchgrevink and two of his companions landed, along with sledges, dogs and supplies. While having just achieved the distinction of making the first sledge journey in the Antarctic while at Robertson Bay, it was here that Borchgrevink sledged his way into the history books. On 17 February 1900, in reaching 78 degrees 50 minutes south, he became the first man to ever ascend to and journey across the barrier surface. In the process, he broke Ross's 60-year-old record of 78 degrees 11 minutes south by 45 miles.

In 1901, three national expeditions set out from Britain, Germany and Sweden, all to explore and winter on different parts of Antarctica. Their scientific programs were the greatest research effort on the continent to that date.

On 11 August 1901, a German Antarctic expedition set out from Kiel in northern Germany, under the command of Erich von Drygalski, a 34-year-old professor of geophysics at the University of

Berlin. His aim was to sail his opulently furnished ship, *Gauss*, south of the Kerguelen Islands and land on the virgin coast of Antarctica between 60 and 100 degrees east – if indeed that land even existed.

Here, with the aid of dogs, he intended to winter over aboard his ship, docked in the pack ice near the shore, planning to sledge inland towards both the South Magnetic Pole and the geographical pole come the spring. On 22 February 1902, sailing between two icebergs during an intense snowstorm, they heard a fearful grinding sound. The ship had become trapped in an ice field within frustrating sight of the distant coastal cliffs of what Drygalski named Kaiser Wilhelm II Land, situated approximately 80 degrees east, 2200 miles west of Cape Adare.

Despite their best efforts to release themselves with explosives, after three days the men resigned themselves to spending the winter preserved in ice, like insects in amber. Regardless, it was to be business as usual.

Drygalski immediately set about establishing a substantial scientific station on the surrounding ice floes so that they might still contribute to the international observation program soon to take place between the Antarctic expeditions in the area.

During the year the *Gauss* was trapped in the ice, seven substantial dog-led sledging journeys were made, involving up to eight men and four sledges. They carried out scientific investigations on the newly discovered mainland some 80 miles away. Their most important discovery was a 1200-foot-high volcanic plug, which they named Gaussberg in honour of their ship.

It was not until February 1903 that they managed to free the ship from her icy grip. They returned to Germany by the end of the year with news of this freshly discovered part of Antarctica.

Meanwhile, the most famous of all the early-1900s expeditions was about to get under way. One of the prime movers in British Antarctic exploration was an old English gentleman geographer and president of the Royal Geographical Society, Sir Clements

Markham. All whiskers, fob watches and pass the port to the left, Markham was on the lookout for outstanding young Royal Navy officers who might be made of the right stuff to lead a British Antarctic expedition for the Royal Geographical Society. (He had been appalled that the *foreigner* Borchgrevink had received British support for that *Southern Cross* expedition, while political tensions had precluded the navy from supporting Sir Clements's own dreams for a British Antarctic expedition.)

Such an acquaintance was a young English naval commander by the name of Robert Falcon Scott, born of a middle-class family in Devon with a long naval tradition. Markham had first come across Scott as a mere youngster of a midshipman who had won a hard-fought sailing race in the British West Indies. 'He was then 18,' he later recounted, 'and I was much struck by his intelligence, information and the charm of his manner.'[37]

It was noted by the writer Francis Spufford that Markham 'liked boys, [though] if he acted on the homosexuality he kept buried beneath a respectable marriage and an array of academic honours, he did so far away from home. Certainly far away from the midshipmen of good family . . .'[38]

As to mounting a British National Antarctic Expedition, though it took some time to go from resolution to actually putting the funds together to mount an expedition, Markham and Scott had a propitious meeting one afternoon when Scott was home on leave in June 1899. 'Chancing one day to be walking down the Buckingham Palace Road,' Scott later recounted, 'I espied Sir Clements Markham . . . and accompanied him to his house. That afternoon I learned for the first time that there was such a thing as a prospective Antarctic expedition; two days later I wrote applying to command it.'[39]

Two years later, Scott found himself to be doing exactly that, leading a joint Royal Society and Royal Geographical Society Antarctic expedition from the ship *Discovery*, which Sir Clements had commissioned at a price of £51,000. Among other things, the ship's wooden hull would lessen interference with the many magnetic readings she would take while at sea and frozen into ice. With that ship, Scott journeyed to Antarctica in 1902 and cruised along the same Barrier that Ross had 60 years earlier, noting that, contrary to Ross's uniform cliffs, the Barrier significantly varied in height, and also that it had receded further south since Ross's time. Scott established Winter Quarters aboard *Discovery* at Hut Point, at the southern tip of Ross Island in McMurdo Sound, and became the first to over-winter on the island.[40]

From the base, he and his team were the first to explore the vicinity and, most importantly for Scott personally, launch a southern journey. In part by trial and error, they determined that the best way to undertake such a journey was to march directly south across the Great Ice Barrier adjacent to Hut Point. Scott adopted the system used by the American Arctic explorer Robert Peary, undertaking a series of sorties into this harsh and unforgiving environment and establishing depots of supplies progressively further south. The idea was to take enough supplies for, say, a 200-mile journey, go to the 50-mile mark and leave enough supplies to fuel a later journey of 100 miles, then use the remaining 50 miles' worth of supplies to get back again.

On each sortie, they learnt more about how to deal with that environment and which of the team members were the best equipped, mentally and physically, to cope with it. One man who came to the fore was a boyish Anglo-Irish merchant marine naval officer by the name of Ernest Shackleton, an ambitious dreamer given to frequently spouting poetry. A showman to his core, with charisma to burn, during the winter he was also given to hamming it up for the crowd, pretending he had already been to the Pole and describing with wonderful detail to his absorbed if captive crowd in the hut how he was accordingly received by the kings and queens of Europe and feted by high society.

Though he had been engaged at the relatively lowly rank of third lieutenant in charge of the stores, provisions and entertainment, the enthusiastic Shackleton had so shone that Scott selected him and another man, by the name of Dr Edward 'Bill' Wilson, to make the final push to the South Pole in the later months of 1902 and first months of 1903. Though they had been initially aided by a 12-man support team and 19 dogs to help with the five sledges, neither stayed with the three principals for long. The dogs, lacking expert handlers, and with poor food, performed badly and proved to be of little use. Most of the hauling, thus, was done by Scott, Wilson and Shackleton, with each man carefully doing his bit to record the contours of this new territory they were discovering, with Scott charting, Wilson sketching and Shackleton taking photographs.

In blizzard conditions, without ever moving off the Barrier, they reached as far as 82 degrees 17 minutes south, though without a dejected Shackleton, who had been left some two miles or so behind to care for the eight surviving dogs. Scott's effort had extended 240 miles further south than Borchgrevink's, which itself had slightly improved on Ross's impressive farthest south of 78 degrees 11 minutes in 1841. After travelling approximately 360 miles south across the Barrier, Scott had come within roughly 500 miles of the Pole, though a newly discovered mountain range of 10,000 to 13,000 feet clearly lay between them and their goal.

Scott would have dearly loved to be able to continue, to find a way to get to the other side of those mountains,[41] but . . .

But at that point, in the last hours of the year, on 31 December 1902, with Shackleton coughing blood, fainting and no longer being able to pull his weight on the sledges, among a myriad of other problems – their food supplies running drastically low, their dogs so ailing they were nothing but a hindrance, and scurvy all round – Scott finally gave the order to turn back.

According to the second in command of the expedition, Albert Armitage, Wilson later told him that:

Wilson and Shackleton were packing the sledges after breakfast one morning. Suddenly they heard Scott shout to them, 'Come here you B.F.s [bloody fools].' They went to him, and Wilson quietly said, 'Were you speaking to me?' 'No Billy,' said Scott. 'Then it must have been me,' said Shackleton. After still receiving no answer, he lost his temper, and said to his leader: 'Right you are the worst B.F. of the lot, and every time that you dare to speak to me like that you will get it back.'

Before Shackleton left Antarctica, he told Armitage that he 'meant to return a better man than Scott'.[42]

Shackleton, who lived by his family motto 'By endurance we conquer', had indeed mustered all his endurance to make it back home. So debilitated did he become that for the last part of the journey he was forced to walk beside, rather than haul, the sledge and – causing further loss of pride – even be borne upon it nearing the end of the journey.

His spirit, however, remained undaunted. At one stage, when Shackleton overheard Wilson quietly telling Scott in a private discussion that he didn't think Shackleton would last the journey back to *Discovery*, Shackleton stirred, raised himself just a little and told them grimly, 'I'm not going to die; I tell you this – I shall be alive when both you fellows are dead.'[43]

Just over a month after turning back, on 3 February 1903, they successfully returned to their base. On the penultimate day prior to arriving home, they were, as Scott described it, 'as near spent as three persons can well be', after an expedition that had lasted 93 days.[44]

Given Shackleton's poor health when they finally did make it back, Scott felt obliged to send the Irishman home on the relief ship SY *Morning*, which had just arrived to deliver fresh supplies and take home any men who needed to go, while Scott and the others remained there for another winter.

However, according to Armitage, 'All the party without doubt were suffering from scurvy.' A greatly distressed Shackleton asked Armitage to intervene on his behalf. Consulting expedition doctor Reginald Kettlitz about Shackleton's health, Armitage was informed that, in fact, Scott himself was in a worse condition than Shackleton. When pushed on the matter, after beating around the bush, Scott told Armitage that if Shackleton 'does not go back sick he will go in disgrace'.[45]

Armitage was of the opinion that now that Scott had found his 'snow legs', acting on Markham's wishes, he was attempting to turn the expedition into a Royal Naval affair of his own conception. Ridding himself of all the merchant navy men such as Shackleton and Armitage was merely a necessary part of this process. Shackleton, a far more free-wheeling personality, never particularly cared for Scott's rank, and the latter resented it.

Scott now intended to do some further exploration, while for many of his men the challenge would be to free *Discovery* from the ice that had now frozen her in. Lest anyone jump to the wrong conclusion as to why Shackleton was being sent home, Scott wrote a report giving his reasons: 'It is with great reluctance that I order his return and trust that it will be made evident that I do so solely on account of his health and that his future prospects may not suffer.'[46]

On that account, Scott need not have worried. Shackleton had left Antarctica in tears. However, upon reaching London in June 1903, as the only man available of the three who had come so close to the Pole, he was lionised.

All hail Shackleton, the toast of the capital of the British Empire!

Despite *Morning*'s officers' reluctance to disclose what they felt was rightfully Scott's story, Lieutenant Shackleton sold his own serialised narrative of what had happened during their attempt on the South Pole to the *Illustrated London News*. Shackleton was even invited to give a lecture and lantern show at the prestigious Royal Geographical Society Christmas gathering – an extraordinary honour for one who, only two years earlier, had been more anonymous than a lost dog.

And yet, while Shackleton had embarked on the cocktail and lecture circuit, Scott's fine work in the Antarctic had gone on. After recovering over the course of the 1903 winter – and while Bill Wilson, with five others, was off Cape Crozier on an emperor-penguin-catching mission – on 26 October Scott ventured forth again, this time with Chief Stoker William Lashly, Petty Officer Edgar 'Taffy' Evans and four others to explore the 'western region' of Victoria Land.

Engulfed by a raging blizzard, the party were trapped on the Ferrar Glacier,[47] which climbs high into the Transantarctic Mountains behind Butter Point. At Desolation Camp, they were confined to their sleeping bags for 22 hours of the day for one whole week, enduring temperatures down to minus 24 degrees, the gale raging unceasingly around their ears, before a lull in the weather saw them resume the ascent through the thick fog. After two days of climbing, on 13 November, they crested the summit of the Ferrar Glacier, and on 14 November the weather cleared before them.

And there it was!

'We found ourselves,' Scott recounted, 'on a great snow-plain, with a level horizon all about, but above this to the east rose the tops of mountains, many of which we could recognize.'[48]

Here was a vast plateau, *the* Polar Plateau, at an approximately uniform altitude of almost 9000 feet, stretching out for so far that it seemed it might go to the South Pole itself.

The wonder of the moment was far from lost on Scott, who exulted, 'This great ice-sheet is unique; it has no parallel in the world and its discovery must be looked upon as a notable geographical fact.'[49] (In point of fact, Scott and his men were not the true discoverers of the Plateau, as the year before another party led by Scott's second in command, Armitage, had also seen it, before turning back after just a day.)

Although it meant turning their backs on the last familiar landmark, they set out on this desolate plateau. '[B]efore us lay the unknown,' Scott recorded. 'What fascination lies in that word! Could anyone wonder that we determined to push on, be the outlook ever so comfortless.'[50]

Four men turned back; three ants crawled west across the cruel giant's bleached tablecloth, William Lashly on Scott's left, Taffy Evans to his right, for two weeks yoked in harness and hardship and a bond between them that would not be broken.

Contending with the temperatures now plummeting as low as minus 44 degrees by night was one thing, yet it was the constant falls courtesy of negotiating the barb-sharp sastrugi (only broken by the heavy jerk of one's harness) and the cutting winds that cruelled them on this journey. Ah, the sastrugi. These, as new chums in Antarctica always discovered up close, are frozen ridges caused by the wind continuously blowing over an expanse of snow and carving out furrows in it. These furrows grow deeper, and the ridges commensurately higher, as the wind increases in velocity. In some ways, sastrugi are like the frozen waves of a stormy sea, with some higher than others – from just a few inches low all the way up to four foot high – and the worst of them were hideously difficult to get a sledge up, over and down again. All they could do was to keep going.

Their nostrils and cheeks were cracked, their lips broken and raw, and one of the thumbs of the enormous Welshman, Taffy Evans, bore deep, implacable cuts on either side of the nail, possibly the result of a slipped knife. Frostbite was welcome in the early morning to numb the pain, while jokes were most unwelcome at night, so painful was the process of smiling.

Nevertheless, by the end of November, as planned, they were to retrace their sledge-tracks home across 200 miles of this 'terrible plateau'. Scott admitted he didn't quite know where they were. His best guess: somewhere a long way west. He wrote at the end of the month:

Here, then, tonight, we have reached the end of our tether, and all we have done is shown the immensity of this vast plain . . . a scene so wildly and awfully desolate that it cannot fail to impress one with gloomy thoughts . . . But, after all, it is not what we see that inspires awe, but the knowledge of what lies beyond our view . . . beyond that horizon are hundreds and even thousands of miles which can offer no change to the weary eye, while on the vast expanse that one's mind conceives one knows there is neither tree nor shrub, nor any living thing, nor even inanimate rock – nothing but this terrible limitless expanse of snow. It has been so for countless years, and it will be so for countless more . . .[51]

That night, the men wondered whether future explorers would push still further across this cruel and desolate landscape. If so, they 'would have to leg it', commented Taffy Evans. Indeed, Scott thought they would.[52]

For 25 days, the three grimly struggled home through persistently gloomy light (a result of unexpected high-altitude clouds), laboriously hauling their recalcitrant sledge up and over high sastrugi, only to then encounter loose, fresh-fallen ice-crystal snow – the most turgid surface of all.

As with the previous season's Southern Party, their supplies proved inadequate. Heating the oil for their cooker was also an issue, and the men soon suffered the severest of hunger pangs. The big man Evans felt he hadn't eaten unless he had shovelled in a good steaming hot hoosh – the food *du jour, chaque jour*, in Antarctica for explorers on sledging trips, consisting of dried biscuit, lard and dried beef, all boiled up – and was the worst affected. His severely frostbitten face had dropped at the announcement of *rationing*, and now, after two weeks, there was not even any tobacco with which to console himself.

By the time the men reached *Discovery* on Christmas Day – to find the ship still frozen in at Hut Point, the open sea still 20 miles to the north in the area of Cape Royds – Scott had calculated that over that sledging season, nearing the limits of human performance, Lashly, Evans and he had man-hauled some 1098 miles at an average of about 15.4 miles a day, and had climbed a total height of just under 20,000 feet.

Over the ensuing six weeks, Scott's men feverishly attempted first to saw, then crack open with vast amounts of explosives 20 miles of ice. Whether it was these explosions that finally appeared to have paid off or, more likely, fortunate sea conditions was a moot point as far as Scott was concerned, but at last, on 16 February, the sea had broken out as far south as Hut Point. After the final charge was lowered into a tide crack and detonated, *Discovery* was at last freed.

As two relief ships, *Morning* and *Terra Nova*, had been standing by to assist, all three ships triumphantly now sailed together north out of McMurdo Sound.

Scott returned to London to a welcome (somewhat tempered by criticism of his management of the expedition) almost equal to the triumphant welcome that Shackleton had received when he had returned a year earlier. Which was where it got interesting. By the time that Mawson was about to become attracted to going to the Antarctic himself, Scott and Shackleton were mounting separate expeditions to return.

In early 1907, Scott had been having a very bad time, as the ship he was commanding, HMS *Albemarle*, had collided with HMS *Commonwealth* during naval exercises off the coast of Portugal. But the times were about to get more difficult still, for on a morning in mid-February he read a report in *The Times* from the week before headlined 'New British Expedition to the South Pole'. Shackleton, it seemed, had presented to the Royal Geographical Society his own plan for a fresh British Antarctic Expedition. In addition to attempting to reach the South Magnetic Pole, *The Times* reported, 'the main objects of the explorers is to follow out on the discoveries made on the southern sledge journey of *Discovery* . . . to carry the Union Jack still further south . . . If possible, the new Party will reach the geographical South Pole.'[53] Not only that, but Shackleton intended to launch this assault from Scott's old base at Hut Point in McMurdo Sound.

What made it even harder to bear for Scott was the notion that Shackleton would be going to Antarctica to mount a venture that would avoid the mistakes made by Scott. *The Times* opined that Scott's *Discovery* journey might have reached a higher latitude 'had it been more adequately prepared for sledge work'. And Shackleton's expedition would also avoid another mistake of his predecessor, for his ship would return to Lyttelton, New Zealand, for the winter to avoid being frozen in as *Discovery* had been.

Scott was stupefied. Returning to Antarctica himself had been his consuming passion, and he was planning to launch his own attempt on the South Pole from his old base in McMurdo Sound, the same spot that Shackleton was now laying claim to. As to the importance of being the *first* to the South Pole, Scott was under no illusion and had even taken careful notes of his long ruminations:

> The authorities and the public are apathetic and slow to be moved but he must be dull indeed who does not appreciate that there will be great glory for this man and for the country of this man who first of human beings stands on the axis of this world . . .[54]

But just how best to get there? That, too, was something he had contemplated long and hard, at one point even pondering how 'small roller wheels under the sledges might perform on the glacier?'[55]

At this time, though, the main thing was to warn Shackleton off what Scott considered his territory, and he was not long in dispatching a letter:

I see by the *Times* of Feb. 12th that you are organizing an expedition to go on our old tracks and this is the first I have heard of it. The situation is awkward for me as I have already announced my intention to try again, in the old place . . .

You see therefore that your announcement cuts right across my plans and to an extent . . . I needn't tell you that I don't wish to hurt you and your plans but in one way feel I have a sort of right to my own field of work . . .

I am sure you will agree with me in this . . .

Yours very sincerely,
R. F. Scott

P.S. I feel sure with a little discussion we can work in accord rather than in opposition. I don't believe foreigners will do anything much, the whole area is ours to attack. R. F. S.[56]

Reading it, Shackleton now fully understood why his own recent announcement of an expedition had done little to enthuse the Royal Geographical Society or inspire experienced expedition men such as Armitage, Skelton and Hodgson to enlist with him. Why, even his close friend Bill Wilson had declined a second-in-command position with Shackleton, because he was involved in a very important investigation of the disease then affecting the grouse in the north.

Any plans for Scott's new expedition were successfully kept confidential by all concerned as he needed to remain employed by the Royal Navy for several years. He was in tough financial straits following the *Discovery* expedition and also needed to earn a living while he planned his latest adventure. Furthermore, as was the custom, he did not want to go public until he had secured the necessary funds – not that for one moment did this minor matter stand in the way of the speculative Shackleton.

In a series of follow-up letters to Shackleton, Scott then pressed his claim in no uncertain terms to the area around McMurdo Sound:

> Of course my intention was to go to McMurdo Sound and our old Winter Quarters again! I cannot but look upon this area as my area until I signify my intention to desert it. Everything concerning it was discovered by our expedition and it is a natural right of my leadership to continue along the line which I made. I don't want to be selfish at anyone's expense, but still think anyone who had to do with exploration will regard this region as primarily mine . . .
>
> It must be clear to you now that you have placed yourself directly in the line of my life's work . . . two expeditions cannot go to the same spot either together or within the compass of several years – If you go to McMurdo Sound you go to Winter Quarters that are clearly mine . . .
>
> Well goodbye for the present, the subject is very close to my heart so please write openly and freely.
>
> Yours ever,
> R. F. Scott[57]

Privately, in a letter to the Secretary of the Royal Geographical Society, Scott Keltie, Scott allowed himself to air his principal grievance a little more savagely:

> Shackleton owes everything to me . . . I got him into the Expedition – I had him sent home for his health but I spared no pains to explain and publish reasons which should destroy any idea that reflected on his character – First and last I did much for him.[58]

And so it had come to this: Shackleton had risen from a deferential position on the *Discovery* expedition to now being a rival to Scott. As for Shackleton – notwithstanding the fact that Wilson and Scott had nursed him home from the Farthest South journey – he had not appreciated the way that Scott had subsequently portrayed his collapse. Scott's lecture on the expedition given at the Albert Hall, and also within the pages of *The Voyage of the Discovery*, published in 1905, had hardly been sensitive to Shackleton's reputation as a hero of exploration:

> For a time Shackleton was carried on one of the sledges, but for the most part he walked along independently, taking things as easily as possible. Our sail did most of the pulling . . . Shackleton is improving, but takes his breakdown much to heart.[59]

Scott had even gone so far as to refer to Shackleton as 'our poor patient' and 'our invalid'.[60]

Desperate to resolve the dispute, Scott suggested to Shackleton that they turn to the third man on their expedition to the south, Bill Wilson, a man 'who commands our respect and who could not be otherwise than straight'.[61] It is a wise choice. Shackleton's own regard for Wilson was so high that from the beginning he had offered him the position as second in command on his new South Pole expedition. Wilson, a very kind and deeply religious man, was by now a Scott man to the marrow of his bones, although his friendship with Shackleton remained strong. 'There is nothing I wouldn't do for him,' he later said of his greatest friend Scott, 'he is just splendid.'[62] On Scott's behalf, he wrote to Shackleton at the end of February 1907:

> My dear Old Shackles,
> I think you ought to retire from McMurdo Sound as a base . . .

but I do wholly agree with the right lying to Scott to use the base before anyone else . . .

I think that if you go to the McMurdo Sound the gilt will be off the gingerbread because of the insinuation which will almost certainly appear in the minds of a good many, that you forestalled Scott who had a prior claim to the use of that base.

I think that the tarnished honour of getting the Pole ever as things have turned out will be worth infinitely less than the honour of dealing generously with Scott. One never loses by being quixotic . . .[63]

Finally, thus, Shackleton ceded and cabled his former expedition leader:

To Captain Scott, Albermarle . . . Gibraltar,
Will meet your wishes regarding base. Please keep absolutely private at present as certain supporters must be brought round to the new position. Writing again fully. Shackleton.[64]

That formal letter followed, some ten weeks later, with Shackleton committing himself to working in an area to the east of McMurdo Sound, thereby avoiding all of Scott's familiar *Discovery* ground:

To begin with, as you know, I was unaware that you had any plans for another Expedition, and announced mine on February 12th, which plans were that I was going to make McMurdo Sound my base for the forthcoming Expedition.

I am leaving the McMurdo Sound base to you, and will land either at the place known as Barrier Inlet or at King Edward VII Land, whichever is most suitable . . .

If I find it impracticable to land at King Edward VII Land, I may possibly steam north, and then to westward and try to land to the West of Kaiser Wilhelm II Land . . .

I think this outlines my plan, which I shall rigidly adhere to, and I hope this letter meets you on the points you desire . . .

Yours very sincerely,
E. H. Shackleton[65]

It was a clever note from Shackleton, avoiding all mention of a desire to go to the South Pole, which would only have heightened their rivalry. Such a crusade to the bottom of the earth, however, remained very much his intent . . .

PART ONE

WITH SHACKLETON

Chapter One

Go South, Young Man, Go South

*At times, during the long hours of steady tramping across the trackless
snow-fields, one's thoughts flow in a clear and limpid stream, the mind
is unruffled and composed and the passion of a great venture springing
suddenly before the imagination is sobered by the calmness of pure reason.
Perchance this is true of certain moments, but they are rare and fleeting. It
may have been in one such phase that I suddenly found myself eager for more
than a glimpse of the great span of Antarctic coast lying nearest to Australia.*

Douglas Mawson, *The Home of the Blizzard*

*I never saw anyone enjoy success with such gusto as Shackleton. His whole
life was to him a romantic poem, hardening with stoical endurance
in adversity, rising to rhapsody when he found his place in the sun.*

Royal Geographical Society Librarian Hugh Robert
Mill, 'Life Interests of a Geographer'

28 September 1907, Mawson writes a letter

For Douglas Mawson, the idea to go to Antarctica has occurred at
a very propitious time. And so strongly has it gripped him that he
has no sooner returned from his foray into the Flinders Ranges to
his dumpy, dusty hotel in Broken Hill than he takes up his pen and
writes a letter to Professor Edgeworth David.

In the last gasp of his 40s, the charismatic professor with the handsome, wizened features has inspired in many of his University of Sydney students a love for geology, and Mawson remains in their front rank, with eyes shining bright. Some professors of David's stature are aloof to their students, rarely descending from their ivory towers, but not this man. Gregarious by nature, David has always been approachable, and so enduring has been the warmth generated in Mawson that the younger man delights in approaching him now.

'I should dearly have loved to have gone myself,' Mawson dashes off in his missive.[1] For his part, the Professor – only recently returned from practising snowshoeing and igloo-building in Kiandra near Mt Kosciuszko – is equally delighted to receive young Mawson's letter and immediately writes to Shackleton, recommending that the young fellow be included. Perhaps it is not too late after all!

And it all starts to move from there . . .

Early December 1907, Port Adelaide, Mawson meets his match

Mawson's ship has come in. On the first day of December, Shackleton's ship, RMS *India*, which has brought the renowned explorer from England to Adelaide, is making its first stopover in Australia, en route to Sydney and then Christchurch's port of Lyttelton. In New Zealand, Shackleton will meet up with *Nimrod*, the sturdy yet diminutive 40-year-old wooden sealer purchased in England for £5000, which will deposit the 16 expedition members somewhere along the frightfully frozen shores of the Antarctic continent. Professor David's letter to Shackleton has worked wonders, and only a short time after Shackleton's arrival at Port Adelaide Mawson is ushered into his presence.

'An attractive and interesting personality,' Mawson would record of his first impressions of the man he hopes will soon be his leader.[2] Dapperly dressed, Shackleton proves to be an impressive, very open and forward kind of man – all of which is quite unlike Mawson, who is far more patrician and reflective by nature. Beyond the Briton's charm, however, there is a physicality about him, a sense of raw animal strength, that is imposing. The explorer's broad shoulders and powerful frame mark him as a man practically *made* for hauling sledges through the polar wilderness, and no nonsense about it.

But to tin tacks: Mawson and his passionate desire to accompany the expedition to Antarctica. Although Shackleton's entire day in port is to be filled with one meeting after another, he is not particularly hurried with Mawson and gives him a fair hearing.

Mawson's passion for this adventure is something that Shackleton himself respects. As a much younger man, when he was on his first voyage with the British merchant fleet, his ship had rounded Cape Horn in a furious blizzard in the middle of winter. In the midst of the tempest, Shackleton found his thoughts turning to the south in an almost mystical manner, as if his destiny lay there. And that feeling has never really left him. A few years later, when he was 22, while crossing the Atlantic on a voyage from Gibraltar to New York, he had a powerful dream, which he later credited with turning him into an explorer. In the dream, he was standing on the bridge of the ship and turning towards the end of the earth. 'I seemed to vow to myself,' he later told a journalist, 'that some day I would go to the region of ice and snow and go on and on till I came to one of the poles of the earth, the end of the axis upon which this great round ball turns.'[3]

During this meeting, as out on the waters of Port Adelaide the ship-whistles of passing vessels periodically sing, and their own ship rises and falls on the wake, the young lecturer explains to this bubbling bulldog of a man that he does not want to be a member of the expedition per se, staying on for the duration, but rather desires to work his passage as a crewman down and back. What he wants is to see and study closely an existing continental ice cap, to understand glaciers and their geological consequences. He desires no pay from Shackleton for whatever work he does while there and will simply be satisfied with a return journey on the ship for recompense. What do you say, sir?

Shackleton, as a man who has already spent some time in polar climes, is very particular about just who he takes with him. The expedition leader would later describe something of his selection process:

> The personnel of an expedition of the character I proposed is a factor on which success depends to a very large extent. The men selected must be qualified for the work, and they must also have the special qualifications required to meet polar conditions. They must be able to live together in harmony for a long period without outside communication, and it must be remembered that the men whose desires lead them to the untrodden paths of the world have generally marked individuality.[4]

Mawson, in Shackleton's preliminary estimation, fits that bill well. And the fact that he comes so highly recommended by Professor Edgeworth David – whom the intrepid explorer is relying on to help raise some badly needed funds from the Australian Government – doesn't hurt either.

The upshot is that only three days after the meeting, Shackleton telegraphs Mawson: 'You are appointed Physicist for the duration of the Expedition.'[5] Though this is greatly surprising – geology not physics is Mawson's particular area of expertise, and he had only planned to go for a quick look – the opportunity is simply too good to miss, and the young scientist eagerly accepts, on a salary subsequently agreed to of 200 pounds per annum. He quickly takes formal leave of both the University of Adelaide and all things comforting and familiar, and dashes off to get ready to join *Nimrod* in Lyttelton.

Shackleton, in the meantime, goes on a whirlwind public lecture tour of Australia, visiting most particularly Melbourne and Sydney as he seeks to raise funds. On the back of the immense popularity Shackleton garners during the tour, Professor David continues to strongly urge the federal government to back him and writes another long, strong letter of recommendation, outlining the many benefits of the *Nimrod* expedition to Australia in particular. 'The Antarctic is of prime interest to Australia,' he writes to his friend, Prime Minister Alfred Deakin. 'It has much bearing on our weather and is a possible source of valuable minerals. Weather and magnetic studies will be of practical value to Australia. We cannot afford to neglect our nearest neighbour, our white sister.'[6]

Investing in Antarctic exploration, he explains, would advance the course of science and also aid the establishment of an Australian national identity. In addition, Shackleton has promised to donate many of the fauna and mineral specimens his expedition finds to Australian museums. It is such a compelling argument, and the Professor carries such weight, that on 13 December 1907, the heavily whiskered Deakin rises in the Lower House of the Federal Parliament in Melbourne and speaks in favour of the motion: 'That this House authorises the Government to advance a sum not exceeding £5000 for the purpose of supplying the necessary equipment to [Ernest Shackleton's] Antarctic expedition about to proceed to the South Pole.'[7]

In support of it, Deakin notes, in those grand, ringing tones that he has built his political career on, 'The sum of £5,000, although considerable to us, is, after all, not a large gift from the revenue of Australia. No similar demand is likely to be made for many years.'[8]

The motion is passed resoundingly, with the full support of the leader of the opposition Andrew Fisher, who acknowledges 'we owe a duty to ourselves and to posterity to explore the Antarctic regions'. The motion is duly passed, and the Shackleton expedition now has the money it needs. Another £1000 coming from the New Zealand Government makes the total finances just comfortable enough for the first time that Shackleton directs that all the money from his lectures in Australia be given to local charities. This is typical Shackleton: generous to a fault, right to the point of financial insanity. But he is loved all the more by Australians for it.

They can go . . .

24 December 1907, Lyttelton, and so begins Mawson's great adventure

Having departed Sydney Harbour five days previously in the company of Edgeworth David and Leo Cotton, Mawson finds himself aboard the SS *Wimmera*, rising and falling on the ocean's swell as the ship makes her way to the small port of Lyttelton, New Zealand, nestled in rolling green hills about half an hour from Christchurch. As well as meeting up with *Nimrod*, of course, he will also be meeting the rest of the Shackleton group for the first time and . . .

And here is one of them now. On the night of their arrival, just as Mawson is heading into a Christchurch bar for a drink with some of the others, he can't help but notice that a rowdy and dead-drunk patron is being carried out feet first. One of the other expedition members recognises the drunk. Why, it is Frank Wild, one of only two of Shackleton's former comrades on Scott's *Discovery* expedition who has accepted the invitation to go on this one, the other being Ernest Joyce.

Bemused, Mawson looks closer. This Wild fellow is built like a thermometer – all tiny, thin torso atop bulbous, powerful hips – no taller than five foot four inches, nor more than seven stone wringing wet, and probably in his mid-30s. But he is clearly tough and wiry. And, as garbled as his speech is, it is apparent that he has a thick Yorkshire accent, reminiscent of Mawson's own parents, who hail from that very part of the world. Wild's weathered and battered visage marks him as one who spends most of his life on the high seas – entirely appropriate for a man who loudly, if almost certainly falsely, claims none other than Captain Cook as his great-great-grandfather.

Though neither Mawson nor Wild knows it, this meeting is to be the beginning of a long and strong friendship between the two. The young Australian lecturer also meets soon afterwards such key expedition members as the very forward and rather rough-nut meteorologist Jameson Adams; surgeon and cartographer Dr Eric Marshall, who, though he once intended to take Orders, has recently completed his medical degree at Emmanuel College, Cambridge; and assistant geologist Philip Brocklehurst, an English baronet of notably aristocratic disposition and staggering wealth, who doesn't much like – what *is* that smell? – Australians, just on principle.

Early January 1908, Southern Ocean, hell at sea

A busy week of loading supplies and ensuring all is shipshape ensues, and after leaving Lyttelton on New Year's Day 1908 *Nimrod* is soon headed south, with a Union Jack presented to Shackleton by no less than Queen Consort Alexandra fluttering gaily from the foremast, as guns of farewell fire from Lyttelton heights and a crowd estimated at 30,000 wave them goodbye. So heavily loaded now is the small ship, with just three and a half feet of freeboard, that one of the shore party has even suggested that the proper place for the Plimsoll line is on the funnel.

In order to save precious coal, for when they will have to burn a whole lot of it to get through the pack ice, *Nimrod* is in tow behind *Koonya* on the end of two 60-fathom chain cables acting as buffer springs, in turn shackled to 120 fathoms of four-and-a-half-inch-thick steel wire. *Koonya* will take *Nimrod* as far as the pack ice before turning back. Now, while it is one thing to be a small vessel powering through the mighty Southern Ocean, being hurled from side to side with the roll of the waves, it is quite another to be towed through the same, meaning that there is an additional forward-jerking motion every time *Koonya* takes up the slack. As a consequence, the decks are never free of rushing water, and in the midst of a heavy gale that hits within an hour of leaving the port and simply does not let up the ship is constantly rolling from 40 degrees to 50 degrees each way, with Dr Marshall commenting in his diary at one point that the 'ward room is swimming in water. Not a dry or warm corner in the ship.'[9]

It is nothing less than, if not hell on earth, then at least hell at sea. English geologist Raymond Priestley certainly feels that way, confiding to his diary:

> The so called 'Scientists' Quarters' is a place that under ordinary circumstances I wouldn't put ten dogs in, much less 15 of a shore-party. It can be compared with no place on earth and is more like my idea of Hell than anything I have ever imagined before . . .[10]

And, of course, the ongoing storm that continues to throw them around makes it all immeasurably worse. So concerned is Shackleton that he signals Captain Frederick Evans of the *Koonya* to pour oil over troubled waters, directly on the sea at their bows, in a bid to quell the waves breaking over *Nimrod*. It seems to work a little, though they would surely be lost without the superb seamanship of the skipper of *Nimrod*, Captain Rupert England. He is an experienced mariner in steam and sail who has previously been to the Antarctic aboard *Morning*, one of the relief ships for Scott's *Discovery* expedition, where he met Shackleton, who deeply admires his seamanship. Yet still the seas remain so mountainous that *Koonya* is regularly lost from view. While the many ponies, dogs and sheep packed on board are constantly groaning their extreme distress, it is doubtful that they are as crook as some of the humans.

Mawson himself succumbs to seasickness such as he never believed possible, a nausea so compelling, so *propelling* that he not only throws up the last few meals in his stomach but also vainly tries to throw up meals from years past. It is all Mawson can do to crawl into a lifeboat and pull the canvas over him, so that at least he may be able to suffer in some privacy.

And it is precisely at this, the lowest physical moment of his life to date, that the canvas is pulled back and Mawson opens his bloodshot and bleary eyes to see the visage of *Nimrod*'s young chief officer, John King Davis. The two men look at each other for a few instants, each a little stunned to see the other, before the one who *doesn't* feel like death opens up. 'What are you doing there, why don't you get below?' shouts Davis above the roar of the gale.

The stricken Mawson gurgles back something incomprehensible, and then manages to just get out, 'Can't you stop this b-boat rocking?'[11]

No, Davis can't, but he can get something that just might relieve this fellow's wretched state a little. Some time later, he returns with some tinned pears, which he manages to feed Mawson almost in the manner in which a mother would feed a baby, except this baby actually wolfs them down before managing to get out a strangled, 'Thanks.'

It is not a cure-all, by any means, but it at least gives Mawson something in his stomach, and a few hours later, when Davis is off his watch at 8 pm, the Englishman is back again with more pears, at which point Mawson feels a little better. *Nimrod*'s chief officer coaxes him below decks, where he gives him steaming cups of hot cocoa. Even through his sickness, Mawson is impressed, both with the kindness of Davis and with the maritime man's whole approach to life. For, though still very young at just 26, the tall, whippet-thin, red-haired-and-bearded Englishman with the notably deep-set, piercing eyes looks much older, has already been at sea for over a decade and is obviously on his way to being a captain.

To some extent, Davis is bemused at his own presence on such a momentous expedition. As he tells Mawson, it was only a few months earlier, while on leave from his ship *Port Jackson*, that he tagged along with a friend to have a look at a London exhibition of the equipment that Shackleton was taking with him to the South Pole and happened to hear that the great man was having trouble finding a chief officer. Though he had previously not had the slightest interest in visiting Antarctica, an idle thought suddenly bubbled to the surface and popped: why not him?

At even his mild expression of interest, he was taken to another room, where, as he later recalled:

[A] man dressed in a blue suit sat writing at a table. He had thick black hair carefully brushed down and parted in the middle, heavy eyebrows, a piercing glance and a clean-shaven jaw of the variety known as 'bulldog'. There was about him the unmistakable look of a deep-water sailor. This was Ernest Shackleton.[12]

The older man snapped off a few cursory questions, decided that he liked the cut of Davis's jib and, shaking his hand, gave him directions as to how he might formally apply for the job to the captain of *Nimrod*. And that was where it all began!

Upon leaving through an outer office, however, the still dazed Davis noticed a large map of Antarctica on the wall and took his first good look. To his amazement, it was practically devoid of features, with much of its hypothetical coastline drawn with dotted lines, because even then, in the early part of the twentieth century, no one had actually *seen* much of it. To Davis, Antarctica, with its roughly circular vagueness criss-crossed by lines of latitude and longitude, looked like nothing so much as 'some gigantic, empty spider's web'.[13] To this point, Davis had no idea that there was a part of the world that effectively remained unexplored, something that enthralled him even more, and 'the first stirrings of a strange excitement and an enthusiasm began in my heart'. Soon enough, the job was his . . .

An ambitious, energetic man himself, Mawson admires those qualities in others, and the two form a bond from the first, frequently meeting for nightly conclaves thereafter. No matter that, led by Brocklehurst, many of the others on the expedition regard the Australians as mere (*sniff*, still there) colonials. Davis, whose parents had lived in Australia before he was born – his father working as an assistant master at Sydney Grammar School for four years – has more of a natural affinity for Australians than all others on the expedition, which helps their friendship further.

And of course, together with making new friends, Mawson is consolidating old relationships, particularly with his great intellectual mentor, Professor Edgeworth David. But now, things are a little different. On this expedition, their relationship is not one of master and student but rather colleagues in a common crusade of science, and if Mawson would certainly never claim to be the older man's equal, still they are far closer to equality than they have ever been previously. And Professor David is also popular with the other men. Davis would much later write of him:

None of us will ever forget Professor T. W. E. David or 'the Prof', as we called him, and after all these years the memory of his strength and humility, his well-stored mind, his courage and his old world courtesy always remain with me. The most thoughtless among us felt a compelling urge to do their best when they were in his presence. He had that rare gift of ennobling all he touched

... His lean, deeply-lined face with its high forehead and bright, kindly eyes might have been that of a poet rather than a man of science and his physique, though he was not a large man, was still that of an athlete . . .[14]

However, Dr Eric Marshall is not quite in accord with the chief officer's admiration. There are, he writes in diary, 'at least two Jonahs we can do without'. Those two Jonahs? Step forward Professor Edgeworth David and his 26-year-old protégé Dr Douglas Mawson, the last of whom is 'useless and objectionable, lacking in guts and manners'.[15] As far as Marshall can see, all Mawson does is lie 'in a sleeping bag at one end of the bridge vomiting when he rolled to starboard whilst the cook handed up food from the galley beneath him. He did no watches.'[16] As a matter of fact, Mawson is so useless in Marshall's view that they 'could leave him behind without regret'.[17]

But that doesn't happen, at least leaving Marshall more scope to vent even more of his spleen in his diary at the two Jonahs: 'Had a short talk with [Shackleton], who means to keep Prof. David on ice and also useless swine Mawson . . . No doubt [Shackleton] under David thumb who will take all credit for scientific results.'[18]

Some part of this animosity is simply for the fact that Mawson and Professor David are colonials. Two other Australians on the ship, Leo Cotton and a rather dour if strait-laced Boer veteran in charge of the ponies by the name of Bertram Armytage – no relation to the Armitage who was Scott's second in command – are similarly assumed to be not up to the mark because of it. Still, there is no doubting that Armytage has been more than courageous in keeping his ponies on their feet even in the worst of the lashing storms, so perhaps he will be of some use after all. They will see.

After 13 days of such storms, at last the weather clears for a tepid sun to emerge, allowing the ship to suddenly resemble, as

Shackleton describes it, 'a drying green on a Monday morning, as blankets, coats, boots etc are all recovering from a thorough salt-water soaking'.[19] As the men climb into the rigging, they keep a sharp lookout for'ard as they know the first of the icebergs must be close. Though they had left an Australian summer, it is falling progressively more cold, and they now must frequently rug up.

15 January 1908, Southern Ocean, *Nimrod* is cut loose

Icebergs, ho. With the sighting of these first icebergs, some 1400 nautical miles[20] to the south of Christchurch, the *Koonya* casts the towline off. Now, the faithful little *Nimrod*, fully unleashed for the first time, closes to transfer its mail to *Koonya* and to take on ten carcasses of sheep from the same.

That completed, the men on *Nimrod* gaze after *Koonya* as she dips her ensign and steams north into the thickening mist before quickly disappearing. Suddenly, they feel all alone. But at least there is much to do to take their minds off that solitude, including laboriously hauling in the 120-fathom towline and cables that lie dangling in the ocean beneath them before they can set sail. (And sailing it will mostly be, until they get to the pack ice, at which point their auxiliary engine will hopefully help manoeuvre them through the worst of it.)

That evening, just before midnight, in this strange half-light of the south, they cross the Antarctic Circle, with the icy waters against the bows making a constant, curious scratching sound that reverberates throughout the ship. They are getting close!

23 January 1908 and a fortnight thereafter, first aboard *Nimrod* and then at Cape Royds, Shackleton and his men get to grips

And there it is. After eight days of hard steaming, dodging icebergs all the way, the sky tells the story. There, straight to their south, is the 'ice blink', the white reflection in the sky that indicates that their goal, the Great Ice Barrier, lies dead ahead. This is confirmed a short time later when they spy, as described by Davis, 'a hard white line, as if drawn with an enormous ruler, beginning to materialise out of the blink, becoming sharper and more clearly defined as we draw near, until at last it stood fully revealed as the Great Ice Barrier itself'.[21] The Barrier's almost 500-mile-long front is flanked by precipitous ice cliffs of varying height, and its massive, flat, icy terrain provides proven entrée to sledging southwards towards the Antarctic interior and ultimately on to the South Pole.

Mawson, like all of them, and like all the men who have seen it in recent decades, stares, stunned, at these massive blue and white cliffs, towering 15 to 50 yards high above the ship, as he feels for the first time the frigid breath of the most frozen continent on earth tumbling over the cliffs and down upon them, battering them, freezing them to the marrow. Amid the beauty, there is a portent of danger in the air, almost a warning. This is a place of hidden horrors, a place to be taken seriously, lest those horrors hurt you. But its beauty is mesmerising.

As they steam east along the sheer ice wall at the bottom of the Barrier's white skirt – here satin smooth, there fissure fluted – 'the sun [is] reflected in every colour of the spectrum from the countless facets of the ice and snow'.[22]

Shackleton briefly considers the possibility of landing directly in the indent in the coast discovered and named as Balloon Inlet by Scott's *Discovery* expedition six years earlier as it travelled across the front of the Great Ice Barrier. Back then, Scott wanted 'the honour of being the first aeronaut to make an ascent in the Antarctic Regions'.[23] He was followed by Shackleton, who, wouldn't you know it, had flown higher.

Alas, now that inlet seems to have fallen victim to a vast calving and been subsumed by a far larger bay situated some eight miles further south than when *Discovery* visited. In place of the safe harbour that once was, they see this vast bay covered with about seven square miles of sea ice only six feet or so deep. Though it is tempting to land there because it would mean their starting point to get to the South Pole would be, by Shackleton's calculations, 90 miles closer than McMurdo Sound, there is a real problem. Strenuously supported by the veteran Wild, Shackleton has little confidence that the sea ice is stable enough to make his base upon. (Yes, the biblical parable had nothing to say about building one's house on ice – focusing instead on the virtues of rock over sand – but the principle remains.) The obvious danger is that they might put their base on a piece of ice that further calves off into the sea, leaving them stranded on a free-floating iceberg in the Ross Sea.

To add to their concern, ice packs and great bergs are rapidly moving into the bay from the north, threatening to sandwich *Nimrod* against the barrier cliffs. So Shackleton merely names the new formation Bay of Whales, for the large number of those superb mammals that he sees there, and the ship moves on along the Barrier, the men on it gazing open-mouthed at the wonder of the enormous caves in the face of the ice cliff, big enough to swallow them whole. Davis describes them as 'echoing cathedrals hewn out of sapphire and emerald and floored with the purple carpet of the eroding sea'.[24]

They are steering towards Shackleton's second choice, which is King Edward VII Land, around 70 miles to their east. Alas, *alas*, the ice pack simply will not allow *Nimrod* through to this part of Antarctica, meaning . . .

Meaning Shackleton must make a very difficult decision, and he gathers his men into the wardroom to announce it. Shackleton tells them he feels he has no choice – with both time and the ice pack pressing – but to land at the spot he specifically promised Scott he wouldn't, at Hut Point in the south-eastern corner of McMurdo Sound. Though he admits it is a case of 'damned if I do, and damned if I don't', there is no other option. 'I know in my heart I am right,' he says. 'We have to secure a solid rock foundation for our winter home.'[25]

He is encouraged to head to McMurdo Sound anyway by Professor Edgeworth David, among others, who tells him that they can achieve more for the world of science in that spot. Though Shackleton surely cannot ignore the fact that the other upside of going to McMurdo Sound is that it gives him the best known chance to launch a southern journey and possibly 'bag the Pole', the expedition leader maintains he makes this decision with an extremely heavy heart.

He now takes up pen and paper and 'writes his heart out' in a letter to his beloved wife, Emily, as *Nimrod* makes her approaches to McMurdo Sound. 'My conscience is clear, but my heart is sore . . . I have one comfort that I did my best.'[26]

Some aboard the ship, however, feel that Shackleton has *not* done his best and that they should have tried harder, none more so than – him again! – Marshall. With the 'build and arrogance of the class rugger forward', Marshall was beguiled back in England when hearing Shackleton's Antarctic spiel, asked for a position on the spot and was accepted . . . but he is now starting to regret it all.[27] What most gets his goat is that Shackleton has not pushed *Nimrod* harder through the pack ice. He writes in his diary that Shackleton:

> has certainly not rubbed an ounce of paint off [*Nimrod*'s] sides . . . He hasn't got the guts of a louse, in spite of what he might say to the world on his return . . . he has made no attempt to reach K.E. Land.[28]

Ever a man who is only a couple of degrees shy of being in a boiling rage in the first place, so strongly does Marshall feel on this issue that his rage soon enough spills over into a heated confrontation with Shackleton, as he accuses him of not making the effort he should have. In reply, Shackleton hotly denies Marshall's charge, maintaining he had in fact tried very hard indeed. The argument goes nowhere, but *Nimrod* does, as 450 miles to the west they sail.

With the breeze from aft and the wind in her sails, the ship travels in fine weather towards McMurdo Sound. On the foredeck, Mawson stands in the freezing cold, stunned by the vision of so many picture-perfect Antarctic scenes of the most wondrous beauty. It is like a Switzerland with its Alps on the seashore, 'the cliffs of Dover turned to ice',[29] as, thrusting triumphantly from the freezing sea, grand peaks and mountain ranges rise towards the heavens to heights of over 13,000 feet. As the explorers make their way to the southern gateway of the Sound, the sun illuminates perfectly the black rocks standing as silent sentinels on the shore, their ancient blackness in stark contrast to the sheer, virginal white of the fresh snow that lies at their base.

As Weddell seals and whales surround the ship, Adélie penguins sit atop the ice floes squawking and waving their flippers in welcome, or maybe mild protest, at these strange interlopers who have arrived on their strangely shaped and very mobile iceberg. As to the whales, they ram and breach the ice from beneath at regular intervals to spout before resubmerging and appearing some yards ahead.

And there, now, of course, is the famed and magnificent 12,500-foot volcano Mt Erebus, blowing a long trail of steam and smoke from its expansive cone into the sky. With its lower slopes obscured by cloud, it appears a castle in the air, basking beneath brilliant sunshine. Some 50 miles to the south-west, they can see a chain of mountain peaks (later to be known as the Transantarctic Mountains), the highest of which is the conical peak of Mt

Discovery. Named for Scott's ship, the 9000-foot beauty standing about 100 miles away is gazed at particularly intently by Shackleton, as it stands right by the route to the South Pole he intends to take in the spring.

But Shackleton, of course, has been here before. For those fresh to its wonder, the whole scene is a rhapsody, wonderfully captured by the words of Chief Officer John King Davis, who is witnessing it for the first time:

> With its white mantle of snow that like a chameleon changed to shades of blue, mauve, flamingo pink and delicate green where light and shadow dwell upon it, under an arch of sky that was pale to the southward and deep blue to the north, set in a sea that was for the moment calm and the colour of almost royal purple, this was the country of a dream. And the air! I had never breathed such a cold, dry, exhilarating draught before. As I filled my lungs with it I felt eager to perform feats of strength, prodigies of endurance. It made your senses tingle. You were ready to jump out of your skin![30]

And yet, when they arrive at McMurdo Sound on 28 January – much the same date as *Discovery* had arrived six years earlier – this time 20 miles of impenetrable frozen sea lies between their ship and Scott's old base at Hut Point.

Shackleton optimistically waits for Mother Nature to break the ice with the arrival of a northerly swell or southerly blizzard. However, by 3 February, with time and coal running low and Captain Rupert England ever anxious, Shackleton is unwilling to wait any longer. He orders *Nimrod* to retreat northwards along McMurdo Sound, heading back along the west coast of Ross Island and taking them a frustrating bit further away from the Pole.

Once a potential landing site is spotted, Shackleton, Wild and meteorologist Jameson Adams are lowered away in the whaleboat to scout the rocky headland. Soon, they identify a place perfect for their Winter Quarters, a flat spot located in a small level valley next to a freshwater lake.

On their return to the ship in the whaleboat, a penguin suddenly jumps out of the water and lands among the legs of the crewmen, which delights them. Dead sailors are said to occupy the bodies of penguins and albatrosses, and they consider it a wonderful omen. (Not that it prevents the sailors from engaging shortly afterwards in what might be termed 'spiritual cannibalism' by dining on roast penguin breast.)

Cape Royds is some 23 miles north of Scott's old base of Hut Point, beneath the shadow of Mt Erebus, which, with magnificent magisterial presence, towers over them. True, this spot, situated at 77 degrees 30 minutes south, is not ideal. Unlike Hut Point, it does not provide direct access to the Barrier, the beginning of any march from Ross Island to the Pole. From Cape Royds, an easy way south by land is stymied by precipitous cliffs and, for much of the year, the icy waters of McMurdo Sound immediately to the west. Any inland route south is blocked by the steep volcanic terrain to the east. There is no alternative. After wintering here, Shackleton's hope is that the Sound will be sufficiently frozen and firm that they will be able to travel across it to get to Hut Point. They can then start their push to the Pole from there in the spring.

And so, after they secure the ship to the ice that abuts the shore with ice anchors, the arduous task of unloading begins. The first bulky thing put ashore is the motor car, followed by the beasts of burden, both large and small. Shackleton has favoured using Siberian and Manchurian ponies, purportedly capable of hauling 1200 to 1800 pounds of equipment as far as 20 to 30 miles per day, and those eight shivering, shuddering, unhappy animals are now unloaded, as well as the mere nine dogs that have been brought. Then comes a largely experimental motorised sledge, which the men are intent on trying out for the first time amid such conditions.

Once the three modes of transport are securely on the shore, Mawson sees for the first time the extraordinary amount of the rest of the supplies emerging from the ship's bowels, as no fewer than 90 tons of coal, equipment and stores are put into sledges before being hauled away to apparently safer ground.

The sledges – made in that seat of all polar expertise, Norway, after Shackleton travelled there to organise it – are suitable for hauling by ponies or by men. They were constructed strong enough to stand up to the harsh environment yet supple enough to undulate with the terrain. Every component of the sledges – from runners to ropes – has been carefully selected and engineered to be able to comfortably carry 650 pounds of equipment and in actuality far more, as Shackleton has weight-tested his 18 11-foot sledges to more than 1000 pounds.

There are also ten 12-foot sledges suitable for pony haulage, together with two seven-foot sledges for work in and around the Winter Quarters and for short journeys. All are constructed of seasoned ash and American hickory with straps riveted on at regular intervals to hold the load in place so that should the sledge capsize, and even roll several times, its payload will remain well and truly secured.

With Mawson's help, those sledges are quickly put into operation and harnessed to the ponies to help transport such things as the dog-and-wolf-skin mitts, together with over 150 pairs of finnesko boots. These boots are made from the hocks of reindeers, specially shaped for the human foot and large enough to allow a bedding of absorbent sennegras – cut grass from Norway – to be squeezed underfoot for cushioning and to absorb moisture for as long as possible. A variety of sleeping bags are also piled up – ten singles and three large ones that might accommodate up to three men – made from the thick winter pelts of the reindeers for extra warmth and strengthened with seams and zips. In the mix are a dozen pairs of skis, not for sledging but for short trips and other duties around the main camp. A large part of the bulk now being loaded on the sledges is the food.

Based on Shackleton's previous experience on the *Discovery* expedition, he has chosen food containing as far as practicable the least moisture, and therefore weight, while still containing maximum nutrition. He wants food that will leave men feeling full for as long as possible after eating. With all this in mind, he has chosen as the mainstay of their diet what was originally a native North American recipe: pemmican, a mixture in approximately equal portions of high-quality meat – dried, pounded then powdered – and rendered fat. The fat is particularly effective in generating body heat. There is also no less than one ton of specially baked biscuits containing 25 per cent Plasmon (dried milk), tea to be drunk during the day, soporific cocoa at night, bag after bag of sugar, chocolate, cheese and oatmeal.

To cook all the food and heat the drinks, Shackleton has chosen kerosene-fuelled Primus stoves. The cooker, sitting on top of the stove, comprises an outer aluminium shell in which sits a ring-shaped vessel around which the heat circulates, itself containing the central cooking pot. Together with the Primus, the complete unit weighs around 15 pounds and, with a heat loss of only eight per cent, allows meals to be prepared from start to finish in half an hour.

Of course, the most important thing they unload is the prefabricated hut, which must be assembled on the shore as quickly as possible as it is their shelter that will get them through the winter. So important is this hut that its construction begins even as the rest of the unloading takes place, and piece by piece a wooden structure takes shape measuring 33 feet by 19 feet, with rough internal partitions made of sail canvas forming up a kitchen, darkroom, storeroom and laboratory at one end and a series of two-person cubicles along the other walls.

The whole hut has just one entrance, with both an outer and an inner door separated by a small anteroom, designed so that when one enters, the hot air can no more escape than the freezing air can rush unfettered straight inside, both blocked by the inner door. Only when the outside door is securely closed, and one has knocked off all the snow and ice inevitably attached to one's clothes, is it permissible to go inside.

Just to the side of the porch, Shackleton has his own small room – the only man accorded the privilege – while just next to that is the darkroom, where photographs can be developed, and next to that again the small laboratory, between the two entrance doors. As the men work, they frequently look up to see large groups of Adélie penguins that have come over just to see how they are getting on. Weddell seals also waddle up on their strange flippers to gaze at them with their huge, warm eyes. In the bay, large whales abound, frequently blowing their tops with vast geysers of vapour.

All these creatures, of course, can make their own arrangements to get through the winter, but not so the ponies and dogs that the men have brought with them. These animals will need shelter, and stalls are built for the horses on the lee side of the hut, while individual kennels are built a short way away, also substantially sheltered from the wind.

But quickly now!

For all during this time of discharging the cargo, the implacable elements are threatening to wreak catastrophe on the exposed anchorage. The cruel onshore winds make waves that threaten to break up that same ice on which they are landing the cargo. Meanwhile, with the tide, massive icebergs are drawn into the Sound – one of them 150 feet in height – where they come to ground and, once engulfed by fast ice, remain throughout the winter. They threaten to crush *Nimrod* up against the ice foot (itself now breaking away) and lock her into the Sound.

The tide cracks soon increase in number, threatening to open a gaping maw right between the piled up stores. Those stores must be dragged across them onto solid ground immediately, while a still anxious Captain Rupert England feels forced to shift *Nimrod* further round from Front Door Bay, first to Derrick Point and then to a new depot named Back Door Bay, in a bid to outrun the collapse of the ice foot. Vastly experienced in polar navigation, Captain England well understands the dangers of handling a vessel in these circumstances.

Should anything happen to *Nimrod* to prevent her returning to the United Kingdom that season, no one would know that Shackleton's party had established their base in McMurdo Sound rather than towards King Edward VII Land as intended. Additional stores meant for the contingency of *Nimrod* wintering over in Antarctica had been left behind in New Zealand to make way for other cargo. Now with her hold partially unloaded, with upset 'trim', the small ship is even more at the mercy of difficult sea and weather conditions. Captain England bears the responsibility of ensuring the safety of his vessel – the lives of all the men are depending on it.

At Back Door Bay, the ponies are employed to haul the remaining stores and coal from the ship across a tide crack boarded over with packing cases from the motor car. Two ponies are tethered alongside *Nimrod* waiting their turn to haul their sledges when suddenly the bay ice detaches, perilously isolating beasts from land. Bertram Armytage, who is leading the first sledge, only just manages to get his pony to jump across the widening crack before it can appreciate the danger.

Alas, the expedition's Scottish assistant medico, Dr Alister Mackay, who has the second sledge, has no such luck. His animal, Chinaman, panics, retreats to the back end of the floe and promptly lands itself in the freezing water. Fortunately, Mackay holds firm to the pony's lead rope and, now assisted by Mawson and David, manages to drag and lift the pathetically whinnying beast back onto the ice. It is time to give it some 'medicine'. A bottle of brandy is tossed down from the ship and half its contents hurriedly emptied down the shivering victim's gullet. Chinaman, swaying only slightly – and not yet seen to start telling glorious stories from his youth about how, had things gone differently for him, he could have won at Ascot instead of freezing his bollocks off down here – seems to settle down a little.

And so back to work.

With the aid of the ship's bow and engine, the floe is pressed back against the fast ice, whereupon ponies and men quickly cross to safety. Under these circumstances, *Nimrod* is forced to anchor offshore, as there is now insufficient draught adjacent to the land ice.

Suddenly, in another race against time, there is a strong sense among the men that they must complete the hut before the harsh winter conditions will make it near impossible to do so. Fortunately, there remains plenty of daylight, around the clock, and many of them work through three full circuits of that clock before dropping for a few hours' rest, and then going again. *Hurry, hurry, hurry!*

Few work harder in the course of the unloading and hut-building than Mawson, and Shackleton is impressed one morning to come across the young man, completely exhausted, in the ship's engine room. All through the previous day, and into the night, Mawson was unloading like a navvy, and now here he is asleep on the engine-room floor, 'his long legs protruding through the doorway, resting on the cross head of the engine'.[31] As the ship moves position and the pistons on the engine start pounding up and down, his feet start to move up and down with them.

Whatever else, this young scientist from Adelaide is a hard-worker, and if on first acquaintance Shackleton liked the cut of his jib, he likes him even more now. The one thing the two do not agree on, though – and this comes up occasionally in conversation as the unloading goes on – is the virtue of ponies, as opposed to dogs, in these parts. Shackleton believes in the strength of the ponies, noting that just one of them can pull up to 1200 pounds at a rate of three to five miles an hour, no matter how reluctant they might be to do so.[32] They can do the work of ten dogs and yet not require the effort of feeding ten yapping dogs at the end of a day's exhausting sledging. In addition, if one breaks down, the amount of meat it can provide for the sledging party is enormous.

Moreover, based on his past experience here, Shackleton has formed the firm view that when low drift is blowing in their faces, the dogs simply will not travel, and that as 'such drift was to be expected fairly often on the Barrier surface, even in the summer', the dogs are not a serious option.[33] Shackleton has brought nine dogs to do a little sledging work to supply the depots – all in the charge of his old comrade from the *Discovery* expedition, Ernest Joyce – but that is it. (While recruiting for this expedition, Shackleton happened to look out his office to see the vastly experienced Joyce passing on a bus and sent his secretary to fetch him, so he could make him an offer. Joyce signed on the spot.)

Mawson is nevertheless in favour of the dogs. True, a single dog can pull only a little more than its own weight, around 78 pounds, but what most impresses him is that the dogs are so *eager.* They only have to see a harness and they run into place, their tails wagging, practically begging to be all strapped in so they can start pulling. For Mawson, that enthusiasm for the task at hand is everything. And there are two other advantages in using the dogs. First, they are much more capable than ponies of living off the land. While every ounce of the ponies' food – compressed fodder – must be brought to Antarctica, the relatively small amount of dog biscuits can be augmented with seal meat and, *in extremis*, even the men's worn wolf-skin mitts and rawhide straps. Second, in their dog-eat-dog world, a weak dog could eat a dead dog and become a strong dog again, whereas the ponies cannot eat each other.

Despite these differing points of view, what Mawson really likes about Shackleton – as do nearly all of them – is the way he leads men. Mawson regards Shackleton as 'a most cheerful person . . . a born optimist [who] overflowed with energy'.[34] At a later point, he writes, 'To sum up his strong points, I would say that [Shackleton's] greatest assets were a never failing fund of optimism, great determination, unknowing of fear, ambition and a fine physique.'[35]

Shackleton also has the key talent of being one of them, without ever losing his aura of authority. A man's man, he leads from the front and imparts confidence to *nearly* all his men that they are in good hands. The holdout in this circle of admiration is the rambunctious Marshall, who still cannot forgive Shackleton for not pushing harder to reach King Edward VII Land. He proclaims in his diary that these days Shackleton 'only does any work when the cinematograph is working',[36] and while he's on the subject there are a few more thoughts he has to offer on his expedition leader:

> By God he has not played the game and is not capable of doing so and a consummate liar and a hypocrite. When he took me on he thought he had got a fool. No doubt he was right. He had got a man who was fool enough to take him at his word . . . To have sacrificed an appointment and prospects in order to join hands with a coward, a cad, who was incapable of keeping his word . . . He is incapable of a decent action or thought.[37]

These prove to be only his opening remarks.

Late February 1908, Cape Royds, Shackleton: 'O Captain! My Captain!'

On 18 February, Shackleton is on the ship while some of *Nimrod's* crew are on the shore. So terrible do conditions suddenly become that there is no way that Shackleton can get ashore or that the crew can come back before Captain England has *Nimrod* under way. He needs to get her to a more secure anchorage, where she can last out the blizzard in more safety, for a blizzard it is.

Shackleton's distress is great, for he feels his proper place is with his men ashore, and while the wind starts to shriek like Macbeth's witches he has no way of knowing if those in the half-completed hut will be blown away. And of course he knows that there is no alternative, that Captain England is responsible for the safety of the ship above all else. Still, things get the better of him 49 hours later when *Nimrod* is again approaching Cape Royds. Shackleton, as ever, is keen to get as close as they possibly can to continue the unloading – this time by whaleboat, for the ice has gone out with the swell – while Captain England is as solicitous as ever for the safety of his ship. But, in Shackleton's view, the skipper is far *too* cautious. This sets the scene for a moment of tight drama between the men.

When they are at a position off Cape Royds that Captain England regards as safe, he sets the engine-room telegraph to 'Stop'. This far and no further.

'Please go further in,' asks a clearly frustrated Shackleton.

'It is impossible,' replies Captain England.

Shackleton cannot bear it and dares to put his hand on the engine-room telegraph, to move it from 'Stop' to 'Slow ahead'. This is a serious breach of protocol. While Shackleton is the leader of the whole expedition, Captain England is the man ultimately responsible for the ship. Shackleton has no authority to do what he has just done. It is for this reason that Captain England places his hand on the telegraph once more.

'I am the master of this ship,' he says with some force. 'It is not possible to take her nearer land with safety.'[38]

In a pure clash of wills, there would be no contest. Shackleton would crush him like a grape. But in this instance, on this well-worn expedition battlefield, awash with maritime victories, Captain

England has the thing that truly counts, *authority*, and they both know it. After seconds of frozen tension as they both glare each other down, Shackleton cedes. Seething, he leaves the bridge. *Nimrod* stays put, and from this point on the remainder of the supplies must be laboriously transported ashore with whaleboat shuttles.

The whole process of unloading is, as Shackleton describes it:

> the most uncomfortable [period], and the hardest work, full of checks and worries, that I or any other member of the party had ever experienced. If it had not been for the whole-hearted devotion of our party, and their untiring energy, we would never have got through the long toil of discharging. Day and night, if such terms of low latitudes can be used in a place where there was no night, late and early, they were always ready to turn to, in face of most trying conditions, and always with a cheerful readiness.[39]

It is in shuttling the heavy coal bags – the last things to be offloaded, from the bowels of *Nimrod*'s hold – that the 'Orrr-stralians' truly come to the fore, and no one more than Bertram Armytage. Yes, he is quite a sober older fellow, not easily given to laughter or lightness, but between graduating a quarter-century earlier from Geelong Grammar – where among other things he excelled at rowing – and going to the Boer War, Armytage attended Cambridge, where he was the stroke of a triumphant rowing VIII for Jesus College. And though now 39 years old, he remains physically powerful, and those skills have not left him.

In the whaleboat, at the oars, Bertram Armytage shines, and in the company of Davis and Mawson – while Chief Officer John King Davis steers from the stern – he keeps pulling hard as they make endless journeys back and forth, loading and unloading at the end of each trip and getting progressively blacker with the coal dust until the job is done.

However seasick Mawson was just a few weeks earlier, he too is impressive for the amount of work he gets through, but it is Armytage who truly catches the eye. Shackleton, in a letter to Emily, describes him as:

> a splendid man, obedient, reliable, ready for any work . . . gets on with all, extremely popular because he is a man of the world and knows the ways of younger men . . . [Armytage] was the first to make the English section reconsider their attitude to Australians.[40]

But at last it is done. The Antarctic summer is almost at a close, the days starting to shorten, the wind lifting, when the final filthy bag of coal is blessedly put ashore. Davis, who has the carriage of this last load, reports the fact to Shackleton, who is working hard on the still only half-finished hut.

Shackleton stands and puts his fists on his hips, his brow knitted in thought. 'Well done!' he responds. 'Now get away as soon as possible and tell the captain to sail at once. Good-bye.'[41]

And that is it. No ceremony. No words wasted. In short order, the exhausted men on the shore pause briefly as they see *Nimrod* sail away, feeling even more alone now than when *Koonya* cast them off, but at least mustering the spirit to answer the three cheers from the men of *Nimrod* that come floating to them o'er the freezing waters.

Aboard *Nimrod* in the fading light, men such as John King Davis feel some satisfaction and no little relief that their own end of the job has been successfully completed. For his part, Captain England is feeling entirely exhausted – he will shortly hand over command to Davis for the next 24 hours so he can rest, even though they are still in precarious waters – but he is also relieved to be away from the powder keg of a man that is Shackleton.

Entirely unknown to Captain England, however, below decks is a letter from Shackleton addressed to his agent in Christchurch,

Joseph Kinsey. Inside that letter is another letter, which Shackleton instructs Kinsey to deliver to Captain England only once returned to Lyttelton. It will inform the captain that, owing to his mental state and health, he is to hand over *Nimrod* to his agent within two weeks, when he is to 'sign off the register as master', and instructions have been issued to appoint his replacement.

Shackleton wants nothing further to do with him and explains as much in a letter to his wife: 'England must resign as he has not been very well and has delayed things greatly by loss of nerve. I am very sorry for him but must consider the safety of the Expedition.'[42]

Stepping into the breach, at least temporarily, will be Chief Officer Davis, who will further take the opportunity during the fallow winter months to sit the exam in New Zealand to gain his Extra Master's certificate, to become a fully fledged ship's captain.

For those who remain at Cape Royds – particularly men such as Mawson, who are here for the first time – there is an enormous and enduring sense of wonder at the sheer other-worldly feel of being in Antarctica.

The day after the ship's departure, the land party lays in a supply of fresh meat for the winter. To this end, they slaughter about 100 penguins at the nearby rookery. So trusting are these delightful, strange creatures, so entirely unafraid of man, that there is no need to shoot them. They can simply be slaughtered where they stand. Even after the first few dozen lie dead at their feet, still the others shuffle forward to see what is going on, and many suffer the same fate. From there, without being plucked or dressed, they are merely flung onto the roof of the hut, where they are soon frozen into place, to be retrieved by ladder as required.

From the door of the now completed hut, the men enjoy spectacular views of the Sound and the western mountains. Most delightful is the polar sun shining off those mountains, making, as Professor David describes it:

tints of greenish-purple, blue and amethyst on peaks rising above grand glacier-cut valleys, and golden light reflected on the surface of the great glacier. [It felt like] one was seeing something in the way of world beauty never seen anywhere else and one longed to be able to convey the glory of it to those who dwell equator-wards of the Antarctic Circle.[43]

Immediately in front of the hut is a small body of water, later named Pony Lake, and to the left is a sheet of ice that becomes known as Green Park, where the men will play hockey and soccer.

Despite the loss of their only crate of beer – fallen into the water during the unloading – the men are content with all their endeavours and look forward to exploring in the vicinity of Winter Quarters.

And even for the old hands, such as Frank Wild, there are fresh wonders. One day, shortly after arriving, he is on a short walk away from the hut when he hears an enormous booming sound, rather like thunder. Walking towards it, he comes to a beach on the northern side of Ross Island, where the Ross Sea has frozen over to a thickness of three to four feet. But it is under pressure now! For, to Wild's stunned amazement, a powerful north wind has set the whole frozen mass into a very slow motion. He later recounts:

The ice was being pressed on to the land as it was checked, [and] masses of it were forced into the air. Some of the sheets reached a height of sixty feet before they collapsed with a crash as loud as any heavy gunfire. This was going on along several miles of coastline, and was a most awe-inspiring sight and sound.[44]

There are other wonders in this strange, frozen world that are completely staggering. The softly spoken 41-year-old biologist James Murray – whom Shackleton has brought to be in charge of the base hut when they all depart on their sledging expeditions

– discovers one of them. He manages to build a small dredge that can be lowered on a rope through a fissure in the ice and then briefly dragged along the bottom, scooping up a wide variety of marine life, including small fish and crustaceans. Once they come to the surface, of course, they are effectively snap frozen before he can get them back to the hut for study.

And here is the weird part. Among his trawl of specimens harvested from the bottom of the ice lake, Murray discovers microscopic animals: rotifers, commonly called wheel animals, and tardigrades, referred to as water bears or moss piglets. But hang on a minute, what's this? Upon thawing out a chunk of fungus the rotifers have long called home – frozen as solid as a bottle of milk on a Bathurst porch in the middle of winter – Murray discovers that the rotifers come back to life, albeit ever so slowly. Shackleton, though hardly a man of science, describes this phenomenon as 'one of the most interesting biological discoveries that had been made in the Antarctic'.[45]

Compelled, Murray devotes enormous amounts of time to studying the rotifers' ability to exist under the most extreme conditions. It is not long before many of Shackleton's men are to be found standing in a semicircle around the biologist's table, keenly watching on as Murray does his damndest to kill the specimens off. He heats them up in water almost to boiling point, which they survive, then promptly takes them outside and exposes them to minus 50 degrees, repeating the process again and again to little effect. On the basis of this, the scientists speculate that the creatures may have been frozen for thousands of years.

There are other amusements and good-natured ribbing among the happy crew. While opening a box of provisions one day, Wild finds a small piece of brick and thinks the opportunity too good to miss to pull the Professor's leg. Taking it to Australia's finest geologist, he hands it over and says to him – truthfully – that he has found this geological specimen near the hut and is wondering if it might possibly be of some interest. With barely restrained excitement, Professor David gets out his magnifying glass and makes an instant determination: 'One of the best specimens of conglomerate I have ever seen, Wild.'[46]

Ah, the delight with which this celebrated answer is repeated to everyone in the hut, and the friendly laughter that ensues . . .

Amid the laughter and levity, however, the expedition has its worries. Within the first month, no fewer than four ponies – Billy, Sandy, Nimrod and Mac – have died, three of them from consumption of the pleasantly flavoured salty Antarctic sands, salt that has come courtesy of the blizzards, which spray the seawater onto the land. (When Sandy's gut was opened up, it was found to contain 12 to 14 pounds of sand.) The fourth pony died from eating shavings in which chemicals have been transported. This means that, of the original ten ponies, only four remain – Quan, Socks, Grisi and Chinaman – as Doctor had to be put down during the voyage and Zulu shortly before they landed.

The loss of these ponies hits the man whose job it is to care for them, Bertram Armytage, particularly hard. A little lugubrious at the best of times, he seems to become ever more withdrawn, to the point where Shackleton has to ask him to 'snap out of it'.[47] Armytage tries but is only partially successful.

Early March 1908, Cape Royds, Mawson scales the heights

But to work. Sledging. Though it is not possible to carry out any significant sledging expeditions – such as depot-laying – given their position beside the Sound, with the Professor's encouragement Shackleton decides to get at least one thing accomplished before the winter shuts them down, and that is to send a party to scale the summit of nearby Mt Erebus. The amazing clarity of the atmosphere and lack of any scale objects makes it very difficult to estimate distances. In actual fact, the summit of Mt Erebus is 34 miles from Cape Royds. It is close enough that, on occasion, when the wind is blowing in their direction, they even fancy they can smell a whiff of sulphur.

Back in 1904, in the last part of Scott's *Discovery* expedition, a party that included Frank Wild and Ernest Joyce managed to ascend just a little higher than 3000 feet of its full 12,500 before being forced to descend. Now, despite being far and away the oldest man in the party, the ambitious Professor David is particularly keen to make the ascent himself to have a close look at this active volcano, and Shackleton agrees. It will be an important achievement for their expedition to have Mt Erebus geologically assessed. Oddly, however, despite the past experience of Wild and Joyce in making the ascent, Shackleton does not select them to support Professor David but instead sends Mawson, in the company of Dr Alister Mackay. They are to be backed up by a support group of Jameson Adams, Dr Eric Marshall and Philip Brocklehurst, to help carry supplies to a spot where the primary group can launch on the summit.

Though they are of course still very early into their whole expedition, Mawson has already impressed Shackleton greatly as a willing worker whose whole academic background in geology makes him perfectly qualified to collect important data about the volcano, and the fact that he is on this expedition to Antarctica on David's request makes him the best man to support the Professor.

As to Dr Alister Forbes Mackay, the expedition's 29-year-old Scottish physician, he, too, is robust and a willing worker, and his medical expertise may prove useful should the Professor get into any trouble making such a strenuous assault. Most importantly, it will give these men, new to such climes, precious training and experience for the forthcoming sledging trips of the summer.

5 March 1908 and for four days thereafter, scaling Mt Erebus

It is no small thing to leave the warmth and relative security of the hut in these first days of the polar autumn to venture out into the frozen wilderness, but now the time has come. And, naturally enough, as they venture forth their eyes are drawn to the prize, the three craters of Erebus high above them – one lower, extinct crater and two higher ones, of which one is extinct and the other, the highest of them all, is not only still active but also positively billowing steam and huge volumes of ash before their very eyes. That steam is so strong it extends, as the Professor describes it, 'at least 2000 ft above the summit in about half a minute, and spread out to form a vast mushroom shaped cloud'.[48]

The initial part of the journey is not too onerous as the two parties, with the assistance of the other expedition members, drag a single sledge loaded with supplies and weighing 560 pounds up the first slopes. Having manhandled the sledge across a moraine (a pile of loose debris left on the ground by a glacier long-since gone), the snow begins to fall as they ascend a small yet steep glacier on hands and knees before confronting . . . the loathed sastrugi, which continually topples the sledgers and is the cause of much cursing all round.

Having camped for the night at an altitude of 2750 feet with temperatures falling to minus ten degrees, the men are soon faced with a steepening ascent as they begin to climb the mountain in the morning. Their journey has turned into a gut-busting slog as they truly get into it, heaving, straining, hauling with every ounce of their strength to continue upwards, ever upwards on the icy, freezing slopes, their steps taking them into increasingly thin and cold air. In such cold, at such height, each breath is difficult, paradoxically almost burning the throat and lungs as it freezes them from the inside. As gruelling and difficult as it is, though, it is also thrilling to know they are stepping out where no humans have ventured before.

On the frigid evening of 6 March 1908, they are a little under halfway to the top at a height of 5630 feet and make camp among fragments of volcanic lava. The following morning, it is decided by Adams that his support party – himself, Marshall and Brocklehurst – although ill-equipped, remain strong enough to continue to the summit with the main party. Having cached the sledge, equipment and supplies in a depot, they all set out, tightly roped together and carrying three days' worth of food to tackle the steep ascent, now a gradient of 1:5 (for every five yards forward they climb a yard), by way of cutting steps.

Far, far away down at the Winter Quarters of Cape Royds, Bertram Armytage feels a sudden surge of excitement as, through the deer-stalking telescope that he has trained on the volcano for the last couple of days, he can suddenly and distinctly see six tiny dots pushing higher, before the weather closes in and they disappear. Still, it is something to tell Shackleton, who is interested to hear that the six are going well and have stuck together.

That evening, the six men camp at 8750 feet above sea level, the temperature so cold at minus 20 degrees that the hairs in their nostrils freeze and crunch when they squeeze their noses and every breath forms a thick cloud, which crackles as it freezes. On this night, a blizzard as wildly furious as it is bitterly cold springs up, which almost sees Brocklehurst lost forever down the mountainside in pursuit of one of his wolf-skin mitts.

The conditions are so off-putting that the six men are confined to their tents for the whole of 8 March without any water because a flame cannot be kept alive to thaw some snow. Nevertheless, their mood remains one of exhausted exuberance. Despite the difficulties, they are getting there, and if the wind would just abate they are only perhaps a day's march from the summit.

And sure enough, the weather having cleared, at 4 am on

9 March the six resume the cripplingly steep ascent, the angle of which is now – literally – a breathtaking two steps up for every three steps forward. When they are just 800 feet below the summit of the main crater, the going gets extremely difficult, yet despite this Mackay most unwisely splits off from the main party and attempts to go it alone. He first passes out of sight and then, shortly afterwards, passes out entirely. When they find him again, he is just recovering from a dead faint, brought on by altitude sickness, and he is sternly admonished to stay with them thereafter. Chastened, he does.

By the late afternoon of this day, they manage to reach the summit of the second extinct crater, though it is hard going as the oxygen is so thin that they can only move slowly, meaning their bodies are generating little warmth. First their feet and then their hands start to feel like blocks of ice.

Brocklehurst, a hard man who represented Cambridge in lightweight boxing in 1905 and 1906, has been walking for nine hours with his feet in such a deplorable, frostbitten condition that when his ski boots (he chose not to change into his finneskos) are removed, both his big toes are *black*, with another four toes severely frostbitten.

The medical doctors, Marshall and Mackay, work frantically in a bid to restore circulation – furiously rubbing the flesh – and it is decided that Brocklehurst should remain in the camp while the men investigate the rim and interior of the extinct crater. Here, they discover lumps of lava, feldspar crystals and fragments of pumice beneath the snow before being captivated by ice-bound fumaroles – volcano vents – one of which almost consumes an over curious Mackay.

The five men return to camp at 6 pm to tend to a slightly improved Brocklehurst and have dinner while admiring the most wondrous of views from the bottom of the world.

10 March 1908 and the day thereafter, Mt Erebus, reaching the peak

Oh, wonder of wonders! For, early this morning the rarest of all sights greets the campers. As described by the Prof:

> All the land below the base of the main cone, and for 40 miles to the west of it, across McMurdo Sound, was a rolling sea of dense cumulus cloud. Projected obliquely on this was . . . the huge [shadow of the] bulk of the giant volcano. The sun had just risen, and flung the shadow of Erebus right across the sound, and against the foothills of the Western Mountains. Every detail of the profile of Erebus was outlined on the clouds, could be readily recognised. There to the right was the great black fang, the relic of the first crater; far above and beyond that was to be seen the rim of the main crater, near our camp; then further to the left, and still higher, rose the active crater with its canopy of steam faithfully portrayed on the cloud screen. Still further to the left the dark shadow dipped rapidly down into the shining fields of cloud below. All within the shadow of Erebus was a soft bluish grey; all without was warm, bright and golden. Words fail to describe a scene of such transcendent majesty and beauty.[49]

Once again leaving Brocklehurst to put up his feet, the party of five sets off at 6 am on the morning of 10 March, and, after a gruelling 2000 feet, by 10 am the geological nirvana for Professor Edgeworth David and Douglas Mawson is reached. Conquering a summit that has never known the tread of a human foot is no small thing, and they now look over the lip of the active volcano and down into the crater of hell. That crater is some half a mile wide and 900 feet deep, and far below they can see the source of the billowing stream of sulphury smelling smoke and ash that now towers, sways and swirls 1000 feet above them.

In a subsequent report, Professor David writes:

> We stood on the verge of a vast abyss, and at first we could see
> neither to the bottom nor across it on account of the huge mass
> of steam filling the crater and soaring aloft in a column 500 to
> 1000 ft high. After a continuous loud hissing sound, lasting for
> some minutes, there would come from below a big dull boom,
> and immediately great globular masses of steam would rush
> upwards to swell the volume of the snow-white cloud which ever
> sways over the crater. This phenomenon recurred at intervals
> during the whole of our stay at the crater. Meanwhile, the air
> around us was extremely redolent of burning sulphur.[50]

All up, it is a curious combination of heat from the mouth of the
fuming volcano meeting with the freezing winds that are whipping
around their ears, but there is little time for reflection. Mawson
takes photos (with some difficulty, as his camera has become
jammed with frost) and takes a hypsometer measurement to
determine their altitude, while Edgeworth David takes geological
samples of feldspar, pumice and sulphur.

There is, yet, just enough time to take in the view from the top
of the bottom of the world, and at one point Mawson again gazes
with some interest at the land lying far to their west, land which
he knows no one in the course of history has ever set foot on. It is
something to conjure with, and it is an image he knows instinctively
that he won't forget, but there is no time for a long reverie.

The men are exhausted. They have strenuously ascended from
their 7 March depot with only three days of supplies, they have
endured extremely low summit temperatures along the way with
little water and now there is the critical condition of Brocklehurst's
frostbitten feet to consider. Getting back to Winter Quarters as
quickly as possible is of paramount importance.

That means risks have to be taken, and the party decide they will complete the 8000-foot descent to the base of the main cone that day. Returning to their camp to eat a hurried meal, pack up and pick up the broken Brocklehurst (who insists on shouldering his usual heavy load, which contains the cooking utensils), they begin sliding down an initial section of rubbly rocks, before quickly coming to an abrupt halt overlooking a steep *névé* (glacial ice slope).

How to tackle this slope, precisely? By letting the force of gravity have its head, much the same way 'The Man from Snowy River', in Banjo Paterson's famous poem of two decades earlier, had done so. (The only two possible alternatives are to retrace their steps to the point above them where the rocky spur had deviated from the main glacier ridge or cut steps downwards into the *névé* slope, and they are really no alternatives at all, because they would both take too much time. They *have* to get down quickly.)

So be it. As one, they watch with great interest as their jettisoned loads somersault with gay abandon – and bounce . . . and *bounce* . . . and BOUNCE – down the mountainside before finally thumping up against a rocky ledge that lies some 600 feet below. They, of course, cannot bounce, but there is another way. For now, sitting on their bottoms, they launch themselves down the slope, managing to control their slide as they gather speed by driving their ice-axes into the steely *névé*, as ice sprays everywhere . . .

Slope one safely negotiated, the *glissade* is repeated again and again, until they have mercifully descended a total of 5000 feet in four hours and reach the gently inclined terrace where the depot lies. There has been some damage to their clothes and equipment, including the loss of an aneroid and a broken hypsometer, but the main thing is that their lives and limbs are still intact and they have escaped the cruellest temperatures of the high altitudes in these high latitudes.

After making camp for the night, they resume the return trek at 5.30 the next morning, with the going extremely hazardous as the sledges are pushed and pulled across the sastrugi whipped up by the blizzard of 8 March. Then, with a blizzard threatening while they are still several miles out from the hut, they abandon their sledge in a spot where they can easily find it later and make a final dash for home.

Happening to leave the hut at around 11 am is none other than Shackleton himself, who spies six slowly moving men making their way over the ridge towards him. 'Did you get to the top?' he shouts, running to meet them. Adams gradually gestures with one hand to the heavens. Insisting upon verbal confirmation, and receiving it, Shackleton now races towards the hut, and soon the others come pouring out to greet the conquerors.

Hail! Hail! All hail!

The six hardy explorers tumble into the hut, as Marshall records it, 'Bruised all over, [and] nearly dead.'[51]

Handshakes and champagne all round is the order of the day, which, according to Shackleton, 'tasted like nectar to the way-worn people. Marshall prescribed *a dose* to us stay-at-home ones, so that we might be able to listen quietly to the tale the party had to tell.'[52]

Mid-March 1908, Europe, Captain Scott gets news

By now, Scott is heavily engaged in his preparations for his next Antarctic expedition, which includes travelling to Lauteret in the French Alps via Paris to witness first-hand the trial of his motor sledge by fellow Antarctic explorer Dr Jean-Baptiste Charcot. It is for this reason he is in Paris when he learns from the *Continental Daily Mail* that Shackleton – contrary to their handshake agreement – has gone ahead and established a base at McMurdo Sound! Scott is deeply disappointed and feels betrayed.

In a letter to his soon-to-be wife Kathleen Bruce, Scott writes:

Did I show you his agreement with me – it was a perfectly plain distinct statement absolutely binding in an honourable sense – he definitely agreed not to approach our old quarters . . . it makes it definitely impossible to do anything till he is heard of again . . . you can guess something of my thoughts.[53]

And yes, Kathleen can. Ever since the two began courting, their bond has been almost mystic, despite the facts that at 38 he is ten years her senior, they are of entirely different backgrounds and he is as strait-laced as she is bohemian by nature.

Though Kathleen is far from elegantly turned out – refusing to wear jewellery, eschewing corsets, careless in her dress – and not classically beautiful, her striking Mediterranean looks, courtesy of a Greek grandfather, give her instant impact. A sculptress who lived for five years in Paris studying her art while also 'vagabonding' about Europe, she just has an *allure* about her that Scott, like many men, finds simply irresistible.

As to Kathleen, from first meeting Scott she has been convinced that he is destined for greatness far above and beyond the mere fame he enjoyed as a result of the *Discovery* expedition, and that is precisely the kind of man she has long harboured a desire to bear a son to. She cannot wait to marry him and bear that son.

Chapter Two

Into the Night and Out into the Wilderness

*I have served with Scott, Shackleton and Mawson and have met Nansen,
Peary, Cook and other explorers, and in my considered opinion for all
the best points of leadership, coolness in the face of danger, resource under
difficulties, quickness in decision, never failing optimism and the faculty
of instilling the same into others, remarkable genius for organization,
consideration for those under him and obliteration of self, the palm
must be given to Shackleton, a hero and a gentleman in very truth.*

Frank Wild

Alone, alone, all, all alone. Alone on a wide wide sea!

Samuel Taylor Coleridge's poem 'The Rime of the Ancient Mariner', quoted by
Ernest Shackleton in his diary on 20 November 1908 to describe the Barrier

Factus non Verbus (Deeds not words)

Omnia Desuper (All things are from above)

Viribus Unitis (With united strength)

These Latin mottos were jotted down by Mawson in his diary on
the Shackleton British Antarctic Expedition, 1907–09

Late March 1908, Cape Royds, as the darkness descends

The heady battle between the forces of light and darkness is ongoing throughout the Antarctic year and is always fought at a furious pace. Only twice a year, during the equinoxes, are these battles so evenly fought – with exactly 12 hours of both – that the two sides can call it a day.

Daylight duration changes slowly near midsummer and midwinter, but the rate of change of the hours of daylight is much faster near the equinoxes, as the dark comes earlier and lasts longer in autumn, while, conversely, in spring the daylight rapidly lengthens. At this time, however, at Cape Royds, darkness is surging forward at the startling rate of 14 minutes a day, with seven minutes of difference between the times of sunrise and sunset from one day to the next.

When the men of *Nimrod* arrived in Antarctica, the daylight accompanied them around the clock, never leaving their side. Only a few weeks afterwards, the sun was disappearing below the southern horizon for an hour each night. By the end of March, the darkness has strengthened its grip to last for just under 14 hours in the 24-hour cycle. With each passing day, as the minutes freeze and fall away like icicles on the face of time, so too does the night come falling from the sky with increasing rapidity.

At the Pole itself, the six-month night has already commenced, while here at Cape Royds, approximately 840 miles (as the crow flies, or 900 miles by foot) to the north, the sun can only manage to rise a short way above the horizon before the terrible gravity exerted by the forces of darkness quickly suck it back down again. With the limiting of the daylight hours equally limiting outdoor activities, there is a greater need than ever for indoor amusements, and sometimes it emerges in strange ways. One of the strangest, and most amusing, is when the expedition's artist George Marston dresses up as a woman – using costumes brought to Antarctica specifically for the purpose of mounting amateur theatrical productions – and begins to move around the hut, attempting to embrace member after member, and pressing his attentions upon them. Most take it in good fun, though there are two notable exceptions. One is the prickly Mackay, who threatens to spit at Marston unless he is left alone. The other is Mawson, who is not particularly amused at all and, once all has settled down again, merely remarks in a sad, tired tone, 'It was all very well but he was not the thing.'[1]

April to July, Cape Royds, the onset of winter

And so back to work. Always back to work. Survival in Antarctic times is not passive, it is active. Very active. If the work of the early weeks has been as intense as it has been narrowly focused on establishing themselves, the chores thereafter, as it gets darker and colder and autumn turns to winter, have to be even more intense, as survival gets more difficult. As to the scientific work, that, too, proceeds apace.

The geologists of the expedition, Professor David and Priestley, work overtime to collect rock samples from within a roughly four-mile radius of Winter Quarters, which they will study over the course of the coming winter. Biologist James Murray is kept occupied with his study of the local marine life, dredging the dozen or so small lakes just discovered in their immediate vicinity as well as dredging through the sea ice in the tidal cracks. The number of sea urchins, sponges, worms, starfish, coral, snails and bivalves that come up from the depths is staggering, leading Murray to conclude, 'The sea bottom here appears to be covered by a continuous carpet of living things.'[2]

Mawson, meanwhile, is engaged in the study of the structures of various forms of ice and snow in the lakes and surrounding countryside, as well as atmospheric electricity, and making preparations to record the effects that the imminent aurora australis will have on the earth's magnetic field, as it has been established that there is a definite link.

With all men returned to Winter Quarters, a work schedule is established for maintaining the scientific instruments and taking meteorological observations – air temperature and humidity, atmospheric pressure, wind force and cloud direction – every two hours around the clock. Each night, the appointed nightwatchman ensures the hut fire is kept burning and that there is enough hot water for breakfast, takes the observations, maintains the acetylene gas plant that works the lighting and settles the juddering, shuddering, shaking and miserable ponies, unused as they are to the confines of their stables.

At the height of winter, Joyce, Marston, Wild and the mechanic Bernard Day spend many a long night publishing, with the aid of a hand-press, *Aurora Australis* – a book comprising certain articles and poems by such expedition members as Mawson, David and Shackleton himself, who also acts as managing editor, and illustrated by Marston, who is a very talented artist.

Another key job in these long winter months is to begin to prepare the sledges for the coming journeys of the summer, and that includes getting the food ready. Down in this part of the world, the base of the breakfast of champions – not to mention the lunch and dinner of the same – is pemmican. Offering the key combination of the highest calorific value for the lowest weight – the spoiling of which is said to have contributed to the tragic fate of Burke and Wills on their Central Australian expedition of 50-odd years before – the pemmican could be boiled with melted snow on the sledging trips and mixed with almost anything, from oatmeal, dried biscuit and butter to diced pony and dog meat to make a 'stodgy porridge-like mixture served hot'[3] known as hoosh. This could be made to vary in taste and consistency by the amount of snow dug up from the floor of the tent or grabbed from outside and thrown into the pot. It's one of those foods that taste all the better the more privations one is suffering. In London or Sydney, inedible. In the wilderness of Antarctica, you wouldn't trade it for caviar. In the words of Mawson, 'Eating hoosh is a heightened form of bliss which no sledger can ever forget.'[4]

Early August 1908, Cape Royds, storms within and without

'It was the best of times, it was the worst of times, it was the age of wisdom, it was the age of foolishness, it was the epoch of belief, it was the epoch of incredulity, it was the season of Light, it was the season of Darkness, it was the spring of hope, it was the winter of despair . . .'

Professor David's magnificent stentorian tones roll through the hut. Throughout this winter, it has become one of the favourite activities at the end of the day to gather around him as he gives a reading of a chapter from Charles Dickens's *A Tale of Two Cities*, *The Pickwick Papers* and so forth, and sometimes continuing into the wee hours to such gales of laughter and incredulity at a new twist in the tale that Shackleton himself would call from his bunk that it was 'time . . . all "good" explorers were in bed'.[5]

For all those fun times, though, enduring the long, dark night of the polar winter can have a strange effect on a man's psyche. In early August, a 90-mph blizzard frustrates commencement of the spring sledging season. And it is not only the weather that rages on, as the long winter of their discontent continues. On one howling morning, the cook William Roberts, cooped up in the tiny cubicle he shares with Dr Mackay, is rather innocently tying up his boots with the support of the sea chest that contains Mackay's belongings when something snaps in the medico's head. A somewhat erratic man at the best of times, Mackay – he who had so unwisely attempted to go it alone on the ascent of Mt Erebus – decides that he so little likes Roberts's boot on his sea chest that he lunges at him, falls upon him and begins to wring his scrawny chicken neck.

Shouts! Gurgles! Come hither! There is a fight! Come *quickly*!

It is Mawson who gets there first and, far bigger and stronger than the feisty Scotsman, manages to quickly haul him off the gagging Roberts, allowing the two men to retreat to their respective corners. Shackleton, needless to say, is beyond furious and even wonders out loud if the best solution might be to shoot Mackay. Well, perhaps not. Still, an air of barely restrained tension settles over the hut for most of the shore party.

Another bubbling blue sees the ever rambunctious Marshall threaten to take Frank Wild outside to 'hammer' him.[6] As Priestley comments wryly in his diary, it is 'lucky evidently that the Winter [is] almost over instead of just beginning'.[7]

At least there are two men between whom there appears to be little tension, despite living cheek by jowl by towel, and they are Dr Douglas Mawson and Professor Edgeworth David. Both scientists appear to be too occupied with work to have any time for tension with each other. Shackleton's account of their quarters is evocative:

The last compartment was the dwelling-place of the Professor and Mawson. It would be difficult to do justice to the picturesque confusion of this compartment; one hardly likes to call it untidy, for the things that covered the bunks by daytime could be placed nowhere else conveniently. A miscellaneous assortment of cameras, spectroscopes, thermometers, microscopes, electrometers and the like lay in profusion on the blankets. Mawson's bed consisted of his two boxes, in which he had stowed his scientific apparatus on the way down, and the Professor's bed was made out of kerosene cases. Everything in the way of tin cans or plug-topped jars, with straw wrappers belonging to the fruit bottles, was collected by these two scientific men. Mawson, as a rule, put his possessions in his storeroom outside, but the Professor, not having any retreat like that, made a pile of glittering tins and coloured wrappers at one end of his bunk, and the heap looked like the nest of the Australian bower bird. The name given, though not by the owners, to this cubicle was the 'Pawn Shop', for not only was there always a heterogeneous mass of things on the bunks, but the wall of the darkroom and the wall of the hut at this spot could not be seen for the multitude of cases ranged as shelves and filled with a varied assortment of note-books and instruments.[8]

Mid-August 1908, Cape Royds, Shackleton ventures forth

Like animals awoken from hibernation, the coming of the light prematurely stirs Shackleton and his men, who come blinking forth from their cosy Winter Quarters into the white of day. With the weather still freezing and the sun still reluctant to return in full, it is of course far too soon to be heading out, yet Shackleton has little choice. Unable to lay depots back in March, he must do so over the ensuing months, while McMurdo Sound is still frozen, and he is keen to get started.

And so it is time to put their work of the winter to the test, to get out their sledges, pack their supplies and head off to their appointed destinations. In an effort to blood the newcomers and give them a 'baptism of frost',[9] Shackleton institutes a program of sledging journeys to supply Hut Point (which will serve as an advance base for the sledging expeditions to begin in October) and points further south en route to the Pole.

As to the major sledging journeys, Shackleton has decided that

Jameson Adams, Dr Eric Marshall and the energetic quartermaster cum jack of all trades Frank Wild will be the ones to accompany him on his push for the holy grail of the Geographic South Pole, using the four surviving ponies to cover the distance there and back of around 1800 miles.[10]

Meanwhile, the Northern Party of Edgeworth David, Douglas Mawson and Alister Mackay can trek using Shanks's pony alone – the power in their own legs – to cover the estimated 480 miles in the opposite direction, to where the South Magnetic Pole is thought to lie, up on the Polar Plateau, north-north-west of Cape Royds.[11]

Brocklehurst, missing what was his most severely frostbitten big toe, amputated by Marshall shortly after the descent of Mt Erebus, will form part of the Western Party, accompanying Priestley and their pony master, Bertram Armytage, to first lay a depot for the Northern Party before undertaking a geological expedition to the western mountains they could see on the far side of McMurdo Sound. This would include ascending the Ferrar Glacier, which Scott climbed six years earlier, to look for fossils.

The remaining men, organised into various tight groupings, will provide support for the major sledging expeditions and carry out minor expeditions closer to the base.

With the exception of a disappointed Brocklehurst – who had wanted to make an attempt on the South Pole himself – it is a division that suits the three parties of men. From the beginning, Shackleton has been all too aware that, whatever advances are made in scientific knowledge on this expedition, the wider public will judge his success or failure on how close they get to the point of the planet upon which its axis turns – the 'Great Nail', as the Americans would have it.

And there will also be great kudos to 'bagging' the South Magnetic Pole. Following form, Shackleton provides written instructions to Edgeworth David, Mawson and Mackay:

You will leave Winter Quarters on or about October 1, 1908. The main objects of your journey are to be as follows:

1 To take magnetic observations at every suitable point with a view of determining the dip and the position of the Magnetic Pole. If time permits, and your equipment and supplies are sufficient, you will try and reach the Magnetic Pole.
2 To make a general geological survey of the coast of Victoria Land . . .
3 I particularly wish you to be able to work at the geology of the Western Mountains, and for Mawson to spend at least one fortnight at Dry Valley to prospect for minerals of economic value . . . I consider that the thorough investigation of Dry Valley is of supreme importance.[12]

(Shackleton was particularly keen to exploit the economic potential of whatever valuable minerals might be discovered in Antarctica, as he would return to England with debts in the vicinity of £20,000.)

The main thing, though, at least from Professor David's point of view, is to get to the South Magnetic Pole. As Professor David well knows, to actually be the first to stand upon the point where the balance needle of the specially constructed dip compass points down at an angle of 90 degrees would give a man prestige for life within the scientific community and even the wider public.

Early October 1908, Cape Royds, Mawson sallies forth

And so comes the day: 5 October 1908. Shackleton is not there to see the Northern Party off, as he left a fortnight earlier on a depot-laying trek in preparation for his own journey, which will begin at the end of October, but at least everyone else left in their hut turns out to wave them fond farewell.

The Party might not have any natural horsepower to drive them forward on their journey, but they do have the horsepower provided by the motor car – 'a 12–15 horsepower New Arrol-Johnston, fitted with a specially designed air-cooled four cylinder engine and Simms Bosch magneto ignition' – which has been brought to these parts more on a trial basis than anything else.[13]

Alas, after travelling only a few miles, poor visibility due to the deteriorating weather conditions forces the mechanic and designated driver of their motor car, Bernard Day, to call it a day and turn back. It is time to abandon this current experiment – the earliest attempt to use motorised transport in Antarctica – as a near failure, and David's party must now put themselves in harness.

David, Mawson and Mackay press on into the polar wilderness as they first cross the frozen McMurdo Sound and then begin the hard slog up the wildly beautiful coast of Victoria Land.

But it is not easy, and Mawson can't help noticing very early in the piece that one of the problems is . . . well . . . it's the Prof. No matter that the Sydney University academic has been a great mentor to young Douglas over the years, and went out of his way to get him on this extraordinary adventure in the first place, his eccentric ways are getting on Mawson's nerves.

Every morning before breakfast, akin to a religious ritual, the Prof has to change his double layer of socks, which seems more than a little precious to the younger man. Every night as they bunk down, the Prof, after dilly-dallying around doing God knows what, is always last into their three-man sleeping bag and somehow manages to sit on both of them as he gets himself into position.

And it doesn't even stop there. When at last the Prof, always dressing in his bulkiest clothes, does get into the bag, he has no hesitation in taking the central and therefore warmest position, which pushes Mackay and Mawson to the far corners. Neither of the younger men is happy about it, but for the moment they keep their peace.

And, quietly, the Prof feels equally frustrated, confiding to his journal:

A three-man sleeping-bag, where you are wedged in more or less tightly against your mates, where all snore and shin one another and each feels on waking that he is more shinned against than shinning, is not conducive to real rest.[14]

Early October 1908, Great Ice Barrier, Shackleton and his men lay the last of the depots

It has been a long and arduous man-haul, but at last, on 6 October, Shackleton's six-man depot party, consisting of Adams, Marshall, Wild, Joyce, Marston and himself, have arrived at their intended destination.

For now, after this two-week journey, during which they were beset by blizzards of such freezing ferocity that temperatures plummeted to minus 59 degrees, Shackleton feels that they have come as far south as they dare across the Barrier to lay this depot. Any further and they would risk not being able to return safely, to begin the journey proper in under a month's time.

They have still done well for all that and have established their 'Depot A' – including one gallon of kerosene oil for cooking and, as importantly, 167 pounds of pony maize – at 79 degrees 36 minutes south, some 130 miles from Hut Point towards the Pole. The location is marked with an upright sledge and a bamboo rod supporting a black flag that, once let fly, furiously flaps fare thee well. And now they turn back to Winter Quarters, ready to launch again in a few weeks' time.

Late October 1908, north of Marble Point, Victoria Land, Professor David cedes the lead

Yes, Professor David is the designated leader of this party of three, but just under a fortnight since the men left Cape Royds things are beginning to change. On the day of 18 October, the Prof starts to see things double; then he starts to feel as if a hundred grains of sand are rolling around on his inner eyeballs; then his eyes begin to water in a futile attempt to wash those imagined grains away; and by the night he cannot see at all, as his terrible case of snow-blindness takes hold.

All he can do is climb into his sleeping bag and hope that his eyes will be better on the morrow, but it is all to no avail. For when he wakes, the dim light of the polar dawn appears to be frozen that way. Mawson and Mackay may be able to see clearly in the burgeoning daylight but he cannot, as all remains dim.

Under such circumstances, it is clearly untenable for the Prof to take his position as the foremost man on the long rope attached to the sledge, responsible for picking out the way ahead, and so he does the obvious thing. That is, he cedes the position to the younger, stronger and better sighted Mawson.

And even when the Prof's eyesight improves over subsequent days, Mawson has proved himself so good in that lead position, showing a great ability to pick out the best track, that the Prof insists he keep it for the remainder of the journey. At least for the moment, though, the Prof remains overall party leader.

After a few more days' hard hauling, Mawson comes to the conclusion that getting to the South Magnetic Pole is simply going to be too hard and they would be better off sticking closer to the coast to chart it, as well as undertaking the planned geographical and geological surveys at chosen sites. Personally, it is this geological exploration that most interests Mawson – examining, among other things, the similarity between this coast of Antarctica and the southern coast of Australia – and he has some quiet resentment at the Prof's seeming obsession with the glory of being the first to reach the South Magnetic Pole.

The Professor, strongly backed by Mackay, overrules him. It is the principal target they have been set by Shackleton, the one with the most kudos bar the Geographic South Pole itself, and that is where they will head.

28 October 1908 and the day thereafter, Cape Royds, Shackleton receives a sign

The last few days have been spent overhauling the sledges and ensuring the ponies are in good condition. All of the food for the journey is prepared, weighed and apportioned to the last ounce, along with all the equipment being carefully stowed and balanced on the sledges. The sledge-meters, the bicycle-like wheels that are towed behind each sledge, have been oiled. Each revolution of the wheel clicks on a register to determine just what distance has been travelled, thereby establishing their position on the map. The harnesses have been checked and checked, and then, just to be safe, checked again.

Shackleton writes instructions for work to be concluded in his absence in addition to the steps to be taken in the event of the Southern Party's failing to return. And they have all written their last letters to loved ones, 'to be delivered in the event of our not returning from the unknown regions into which we hoped to penetrate'.[15]

Finally, all is in readiness. Tomorrow, they will depart Winter Quarters and begin their attempt on the South Pole!

Shackleton is feeling very positive about it all, eager to get started, and then . . . something occurs that gives him further heart. As they are all sitting down for what is essentially their farewell dinner, a shaft of evening sun enters the hut through the ventilator, shining a perfect circle of light on the picture on the wall of His Majesty the King that hangs there. 'Slowly it moved across and lit up the photograph of His Majesty the King,' writes Shackleton the following day. 'This seemed an omen of good luck, for only on that day and at that particular time could this have happened.'[16]

All bodes well. Tomorrow, Shackleton and his three men will start 'to strive to plant the Queen's flag on the last spot of the world'.[17]

The next day blooms gloriously. It is a cloudless morning, with such brilliant sunshine that all things, including their prospects, are sparkling. At 10 am, each man of the Southern Party – Shackleton, Adams, Marshall and Wild, who are to lead the ponies Socks, Grisi, Chinaman and Quan in turn – gird themselves to head south, and ever south, hopefully unto the turning point of the world itself.

Now, the two men who are to remain at the hut, the biologist James Murray and the cook William Roberts, gather to warmly farewell them. Shackleton is moved:

> A clasp of the hands means more than many words, and as we turned to acknowledge their cheer and saw them standing on the ice by the familiar cliffs, I felt that we must try to do well for the sake of every one concerned in the expedition.[18]

Shackleton, as is his right, leads off, taking his party down from the hut to the firm sea ice, which will give them a relatively easy start to the journey. Shackleton's heart is singing, as he is wonderfully aware that, after four years of planning and passion, fund-raising and tying off thousands of loose ends, the journey of his dreams has at last begun.

And yet, they have barely been going for an hour when Socks falls lame, likely having injured himself on some sharp ice. It comes as a bad shock, as Quan had the same affliction for a full week, and now they find that their troubles in this field are not over.

All they can do is go on and trust that he will slowly come good . . .

29 October 1908, north of Granite Harbour, as the Northern Party change plans

By the end of October, negotiating the deteriorating ice is so difficult that they must relay the two sledges, with all three of them hauling one forward before going back to get the other one – meaning they have to trudge a total of three exhausting miles for every pathetic mile they manage to advance. It is so laborious and time-consuming, yielding an average of just four and a half miles a day, that it now becomes obvious they will never be able to reach the Magnetic Pole *and* sledge back to Butter Point, located almost opposite Cape Royds on the coast of Victoria Land, because of what will have become an open sea.

Shackleton's instructions had stated that, on their return, the Northern Party would join up with the Western Party at Butter Point, where they would find 600 pounds of supplies put in a depot for them. Such was Shackleton's already high regard for Mawson that he instructed him that, at that point, he would take charge of a three-man party – Priestley, Brocklehurst and himself – that would explore the Dry Valley and surrounding area. Professor David would then lead the other two men, his fellow Australian Bertram Armytage and the Scotsman Dr Alister Mackay, back to Cape Royds.[19]

But, with the slow-going, the situation has changed, and they must adapt to it. So the young Mawson presents a fresh proposal to his mentor and Mackay, based on his reluctant realisation that engaging his passion for geology will no longer do, under the circumstances. Now, he says, they must give up all else *bar* the attempt to reach the South Magnetic Pole. In order to preserve a full ration of sledging food for the 480-mile inland journey, he proposes that, as they travel north along the frozen edge of McMurdo Sound and until they head inland, they must live as much as possible on seal flesh and 'local food' such as penguins.[20]

On this outward journey, Mawson explains, they must establish a depot on the 'low sloping shore' of the Drygalski Ice Tongue, in full view of the coast, to which they will return and survive, again on seals and the like, until rescued by *Nimrod* at the beginning of February, as per Shackleton's contingency plan.[21]

This Drygalski Ice Tongue, jutting into the Ross Sea from the coast of Victoria Land, is the result of the confluence of a large glacier and several tributary glaciers descending from the western mountains. As those glaciers feed into a central ice sheet, the Drygalski Ice Tongue is forced out at the opposite – sea – end, just like toothpaste forced from a tube, in this case frozen toothpaste.[22]

This time, in a further sign that the dynamic of leadership has shifted, Mawson's proposal is unanimously adopted, and the resourceful Mackay soon sets about constructing a biscuit-tin stove capable of running on seal blubber alone, allowing them to preserve all their kerosene for the inland leg of the journey.

Still, Mawson – first and foremost a geologist – takes time to identify geological specimens in the area. The gneiss specimens are of particular interest, as they do indeed closely resemble the types he has identified in the Broken Hill area, and they potentially contain minerals that are of promising commercial value, which will please Shackleton. And he is also busy throughout the journey, of course, taking magnetic and geographical observations, all of which are faithfully recorded and marked down in notebook after notebook, which he fills and carefully stores.

1 November 1908, 12 miles north of Granite Harbour, with Professor David's Northern Party

On this day, the Northern Party find the time to write precious letters to their loved ones. Once finished, the letters are bundled together and secured in a tall cairn that the Party have built by the shore, so that it can easily be spotted by *Nimrod* when she comes looking for them. It is perhaps a non-personal letter, however, addressed to 'The Commander of the *Nimrod*', which is the most important one of all:

> Dear Sir,
>
> I beg to inform you that we intend leaving here to-morrow in continuation of our journey towards the Magnetic Pole. We have to work our two sledges by relays, which, of course, means slow progress only about four miles[23] per day. At this rate we hope to reach the north side of the Drygalski Ice Barrier here at the point where a slow sloping shore is marked on the Admiralty Chart of the Antarctic Sheet III. We propose to make a depot there marked by a black flag similar to the one we are leaving here at the island at south side of entrance to Granite Harbour.[24] We propose to travel inland from the 'low sloping shore', and if possible reach the Magnetic Pole and return to depot. We estimate that this may take six weeks, so that we may not return to the coast at the low sloping shore depot until about January 25. We propose to wait there until the *Nimrod* calls for us at the beginning of February.
>
> Trusting that we shall not be putting you to any great inconvenience.
>
> I am dear Sir, yours very truly,
> T. W. Edgeworth David.[25]

1 November 1908, Lyttelton, New Zealand, *Nimrod* makes ready to depart

In the meantime, the 'dear Sir' in question proves to be Lieutenant Frederick Evans RNR of the Union SS Company of New Zealand, the former captain of *Nimrod*'s tow-ship *Koonya*. After the sacking of Captain England, it is Evans who has taken command for this important trip – the judgement has been made that John King Davis is likely too inexperienced – and it is he who now oversees the loading of her stores, with Davis by his side. It is Captain Evans's expectation that they will be able to leave in about a month.

3 November 1908 and four days thereafter, south of Hut Point, Shackleton's Southern Party have many a breakthrough

Despite the blizzard of yesterday, today the party leaves Hut Point (which they first reached on 30 October) under a brilliant sky, excited to begin the approximately 900-mile trek to the South Pole. The pony Socks is much better.

And though they soon encounter snow so deep that the freezing beasts sink up to their bellies in it, by day's end a respectable 12 miles has been reeled in, and while the men puff away on that 'most ideal smoke a man could wish for after a day's sledging', the shattered ponies chomp on their reward of after-dinner biscuits.[26]

The following day, an initially overcast sky and further soft snow does not prevent them completing an even more promising 16 miles. 'Everyone is fit and well,' enthuses Shackleton as the cloud clears away to the north, revealing Mt Erebus in all its majesty.[27] Yet to the south there lies only growing darkness. While they sleep, the sky turns overcast and a light snow begins to fall.

The dull landscape bleeds into the dull sky. There are no points of reference, no shadows, and all is entirely featureless. Now, the only way they know they have struck sastrugi is when the sledges begin to stand upright before them. It is like they are walking upon a white floor, surrounded by four distant white walls, walls that, nevertheless, provide no impediment to the wind.

But what treachery lies beneath this floor! Apparently solid ice covered with snow is often no more than a snow bridge across a crevasse – the latter formed as massive sheets of ice move slowly over the undulating land below and . . . crack. After the crack first appears, the snowdrift blowing across it forms a cornice – an overhanging edge of snow – which continues to grow until it meets the far side of the crevasse and more snow is dumped upon it. While at the edges, this snow bridge can be relatively strong, in the middle it is weak, and as Shackleton's party proceed it is a relatively frequent occurrence for either man or pony, or both, to break through at the weakest, middle part.

Sometimes, only their legs go through and they can pull themselves out. Other times, man and pony break through entirely and have to be pulled out by the harnesses and ropes they are attached to. The obvious danger is that if a crevasse is wide and deep enough – so deep you could never hope to plumb its depths – it will swallow them whole and not even need to burp.

Confined to their tents on 6 November by a blizzard, Shackleton comprehends the effect any further delays will have on their supplies, given they are already well behind his initial hope of averaging 18 miles per day:

It is very trying to be held up like this, for each day means the consumption of 40 lb of pony feed alone. We only had a couple of biscuits each for lunch, for I can see that we must retrench at every set-back if we are going to have enough food to carry us through. We started with ninety-one days' food, but with careful management we can make it spin out to 110 days.[28]

This 'careful management' means the rations are cut by just under a quarter, while their daily tobacco rations are also quickly smoked away in the anxiety of it all.

What to consume, then, if not food, while confined to their tent in a blizzard? Books. Shackleton has *The Taming of the Shrew*, Marshall devours George Borrow's masterpiece *The Bible in Spain*, Adams has Arthur Young's *Travels in France*, while Frank Wild enjoys Charles Dickens's *Sketches by Boz*.

All up, the challenges of being in this land at least come as no surprise to the vastly experienced Shackleton. When *Nimrod* left New Zealand nearly a year earlier, the *West Coast* editorial opined:

> A constant fight with the most severe of elements will have to be sustained, fierce storms of sleet, hail and snow, may and in all probability will be encountered, and King Frost will exact his toll in every form if not successfully met and baffled.[29]

And they were right!

As the party sets out once again at 8 am, on 7 November, weather conspires with the terrain to hold horrendous sway. At lunch, men and ponies drop as one, having progressed but one terrible mile in five appalling hours as now a blizzard halts their day. Of the many problems confronting them, one is that when the temperature drops, the sweat on the lee side of the ponies quickly freezes, meaning they require extra care once they stop.

And the problems do not end there, because many of them, including the leader, Shackleton, starts to suffer from snow-blindness. In the four days since leaving Hut Point, averaging less than 12.5 miles each day, they have not even covered 40 miles of the estimated 1800-mile return journey to the Pole. If that journey is the length of the alphabet, they are only a little over halfway to the letter 'B'.

9 November 1908, on sea ice, approaching the Nordenskjöld Ice Barrier tongue, the Northern Party all take the strain

Things are becoming more strained by the day, and nothing more so than the dynamic between Edgeworth David and Mackay, though Mawson's own relationship with the Prof is also becoming tense. Over the last month, the authority of the Prof has weakened while the open irritation of Mackay with him has strengthened, and the consequent efforts of the Prof to mollify the Scot have increased. But the worst of it is the manner in which the Prof tries to do the mollifying.

'We don't seem,' Mawson notes ruefully in his diary, 'to be able to save what we should in the way of provisions accruing by unforeseen circumstances as the Professor gives any such away to Mac whenever he thinks to please him.'[30]

And it is a very serious issue.

In such an environment, doing such heavy physical work, each of them has the hunger at mealtimes of two men – alas with food for only one. It is therefore doubly important that such food as they have be shared absolutely equally, in a manner where there can be no resentment. So it is that they observe the customary method of division that has been tried, tested and proved by other polar explorers over the years and become standard practice.

If the ration for breakfast, say, is a Plasmon biscuit, then the man doling them out would place them on the cover of the cooker in a row, and then, after one of his two companions turns his back, say to him, 'Whose?' That person with his back turned would nominate the person to have it, before the next biscuit goes in the same fashion.

Another sign of how important food has become to them is their devotion to gathering in crumbs. At the beginning of their journey, biscuits would be broken and the crumbs would fall wherever. By now, however, the biscuits are broken over pannikins, so that every precious skerrick can be retrieved and consumed. And, beyond conversation concerning the business of their expedition, there is only one subject guaranteed to gain their complete attention. 'We could discuss nothing,' Professor David records, 'but the different dishes with which we had been regaled in our former lifetime at various famous restaurants and hotels.'[31]

But Mawson's point remains. They are going through their food provisions way too fast if they are going to do what needs to be done. Plus, they need to have enough in reserve so that they can withstand unforeseen circumstances, such as blizzards or accidents. As it is, they are already very close to the wire, and there are other problems apart from food. Mawson admits to himself:

> The Prof is certainly a fine example of a man for his age, but he is a great drag on our progress . . . it is difficult to judge but seeing that he travels with thumbs tucked in his braces, and general attitude, one concludes he lays his weight on the harness rather than pulling.[32]

In such an intense environment, where they are with each other for 24 hours a day, day after day, for weeks and then months – up to and including, of course, sleeping together at night in a three-man sleeping bag – it is natural enough that even the most minor foibles start to grate on the others' nerves.

16 November 1908 and three weeks thereafter, Great Ice Barrier, Shackleton feels 'alone, all alone'

After Shackleton locates the first depot he laid down in September, they leave behind a sledge and other provisions for the return journey before proceeding south across the barrier. As they go, they regularly raise six-foot-high snow cairns made from roughly cut blocks of snow and mark them with black flags to help guide them home.

While things have been at least a little better since those first difficult days, and they have increased their daily distances, still they are not without serious problems. For their poor, pathetic ponies – always shuddering, whinnying and looking at them rather accusingly with their large, sad eyes – are getting progressively more miserable as they struggle for purchase on the difficult surface of the Barrier, with each step usually breaking through the snow crust to a depth of up to ten inches. Their actions at night prove even more concerning. Quan regularly chews through his tether, while Socks prefers chewing lumps of the other ponies' tails – resulting in predictable equine outrage – while Chinaman is quite the worst for wear across the board, though the effect that the snow crust has had in chafing his fetlocks is particularly worrying.

As to the men themselves, they are caught between exhaustion and exhilaration, strangely bouncing between the two and sometimes settling on both at once. Shackleton writes on 20 November:

At one moment, one thinks of Coleridge's 'Ancient Mariner': 'Alone, alone, all, all alone. Alone on a wide wide sea!', and then when the mazy clouds spring silently from either hand and drift quickly across our zenith, not followed by any wind, it seems uncanny. There comes a puff of wind from the north, another from the south, and anon one from the east or west, seeming to obey no law, acting on erratic impulses. It is as though we were truly at the world's end, and were bursting in on the birthplace of the clouds and the nesting home of the four winds, and one has a feeling that we mortals are being watched with a jealous eye by the forces of nature. To add to these weird impressions that seem to grow on one in the apparently limitless waste, the sun to-night was surrounded by mock suns and in the zenith was a bow, turning away from the great vertical circle around the sun. These circles and bows were the colour of the rainbow.[33]

It is a strange, extraordinary world of terrible beauty, and the following day – just a little over three weeks after beginning their push – the weakest pony, Chinaman, is the first to pay the ultimate price for having been forced into it. Like Scott, Shackleton has no stomach for killing, and the grisly task of shooting the poor beast ultimately falls to Frank Wild. With a single revolver bullet to his brow, Chinaman's life is instantly no more. Still, his throat is immediately cut and his blood pours out to stain the whiteness. Thereafter, Wild and Marshall get to grips with the carcass and, in even more bloody fashion, carve 150 pounds of horsemeat away from the bones. The resultant large chunks become 'a welcome addition to our bill of fare'.[34] Some of those chunks are to be taken with them, while the rest of what was Chinaman is stacked up at the base of a snow cairn.

And it is not just Chinaman's carcass that is sacrificed for their assault on the South Pole. Now, his harness is used to fashion stays for the upturned sledge, and a black flag attached to a bamboo pole will signal this depot and its cache of meat to the returning explorers.

There are just three ponies remaining, hauling 500 pounds each, though as the conditions under-hoof of the Barrier suddenly improve they do start to make better time.

Just under a month after leaving base, on 26 November, they push beyond 82 degrees 16 minutes south and so break Scott's record, both in terms of 'farthest south' and the time taken to get there. The men celebrate by drinking to each other's health with two tablespoons each of Shackleton's orange liqueur, previously given to him by his wife, Emily. (A very typical, thoughtful gesture from Emily Shackleton. Five years his senior, she was a 28-year-old, tall, beautiful sophisticate when he first met her, in 1897. He was all but instantly smitten, and she returned his ardour in kind and raised him one, so that a happy and devoted marriage soon ensued.)

Getting to this spot so early in the season – at times spurred on by Marshall's 'Forced March' tablets, a cocaine preparation, which seems to aid their stamina – is a sign of how well they are going. For, as Shackleton knows all too well, it took 59 days to get to this point with Scott, while they have accomplished it in just 29 days. And here's cheers! Afterwards, they smoke and talk a while before turning in, Shackleton pausing only to write excitedly in his diary:

November 26. A day to remember, for we have passed the 'farthest South' previously reached by man . . .

To the south, south-east ever appear new mountains. I trust that no land will block our path . . . One wonders what the next month will bring forth. We ought by that time to be near our goal, all being well.[35]

They push on, unsure of what lies ahead but eager to keep going all the way to the Pole. What they do know is that it will not be easy, as the surface of the Barrier becomes rougher, more broken and more dangerous the further they move south. The range of mountains to their west, marching with them slowly, side by side, starts to outpace them and curves around to confront them, clearly lying between them and the Pole. Are they to be blocked outright?

Perhaps; perhaps not. All they can do is pull on, stripped down to their shirts, under a hot sun that glares off the snow with such intensity that they must wear their tinted-glass goggles at all times and chew on raw frozen horsemeat to cool their throats.

Soon, they are mesmerised by what appears to be, as Frank Wild records in his diary, a 'brilliant gleam of light' in the sky above the southern horizon.[36] And yet, so rough is the terrain they now find themselves in, it takes them nearly a week to find its magic source.

But it is worth it. For, on the afternoon of 3 December, they have no sooner climbed to the summit of one of the foothills of those mountains than they can see it.

Marvellous!

There, before them, lies what Shackleton subsequently describes as 'an open road to the south . . . a great glacier, running almost south and north between two huge mountain ranges'.[37] A glacier reflecting the sunlight and lighting the way forward to the promised land! They believe . . . they believe. And they are beyond thrilled.

'[I] shall never forget the first sight of this promised land,' records Marshall.[38]

Wild is almost equally exuberant:

> The view that was now opened up to us was worth double the labour. The glacier which we now see must be the largest in the world; it is 30 miles in width and we can see over 100 miles of its length.[39]

Though for the moment they reverentially refer to it as the Great Glacier, or The Glacier for short, at a later point Shackleton will christen it the Beardmore Glacier, in honour of his friend and principal sponsor for this expedition, the Anglo-Scottish industrialist William Beardmore. But a great glacier it indeed is, stretching in fact 170 miles, ascending up to the Polar Plateau to a height of 10,000 feet.

Gazing with wonder, the men can see where the glacier tumbles into the Barrier – a frozen river pouring into a frozen pond – violently breaking up its surface in the immediate vicinity into enormous pressure ridges and crevasses, and causing those long undulations they have been negotiating for so many miles.

In short order, the men move through a pass situated in the last curve of the glacier flanked by granite pillars 2000 feet high – 'a magnificent entrance to the "Highway to the South"', which will become known as Shackleton's Gateway – and they are soon upon this fast-rising 'open road'.[40] Alas, Grisi and Quan having by now taken bullets, like Chinaman before them, the one surviving pony, Socks, is now hauling one sledge, while the men, straining with every fibre of their being, haul the other sledges upwards, ever upwards, onwards, ever onwards.

First week of December 1908, south side of the Drygalski Ice Tongue, the Northern Party treks through a maze

Having travelled only 50 miles north from the Nordenskjöld Ice Barrier Tongue in a miserable 20 days, David's party now has to confront the behemoth that is the Drygalski Ice Tongue. Although only 25 miles or so wide, this labyrinthine ice formation proves to be heavily crevassed and criss-crossed with many deep valleys, with the way through these valleys being regularly blocked by perpendicular walls of snow, sometimes making it feel like one big white maze without end.

The Party skirt east for three days, and any early optimism in negotiating a smooth crossing soon turns to increasing frustration – with the ice and each other – as they now confront wave after wave of perilously crevassed, jagged ice formations up to 100 feet high.

It is for all the world as if a massive, storm-tossed sea has suddenly snap frozen, and instead of negotiating it with a boat, the men must laboriously climb each wave with their fully laden sledges – always in danger of capsizing – and crunch their way down the other side, careening this way and that, perpetually teetering on the precipice of complete disaster.

7 December 1908 and several days thereafter, Beardmore Glacier, the Southern Party eat like a horse

Not long after Shackleton and his men have set off again after lunch on this cold day, there is a sudden cracking sound, a wild whinny of panic, and they look up to see poor ol' Socks disappearing down a crevasse, while just about taking Wild with him for his trouble.

For Wild was walking beside Socks when the snow bridge collapsed, and in the next instant his feet go into space and he feels a violent blow on his shoulder, which proves to be the pony. Wild is extremely fortunate to throw out his left hand and grip on to something, which proves to be the ledge of the chasm, while Socks keeps tumbling down the seemingly bottomless chasm beneath him. A great piece of luck – at least for them, if not the pony – is that the harness connecting Socks to the sledge has snapped, leaving all of their supplies and equipment still at the top, while the pony continues to plummet to oblivion.

Gasping, heaving, the other three men quickly haul Wild back to the top and secure the sledge. Then, all four lie on their bellies and creep once more to the edge. 'Socks must have been killed instantly as we could hear no sound from below, and could see nothing but an intense black depth,' a shaken Wild records in his diary.[41]

Without that unfortunate animal's horsepower, there is nothing left to haul the 1000 pounds on the sledge bar their own manpower, and they spend some time fashioning the sledge harnesses to fit themselves instead. Initially, they have some doubt as to whether it is even going to be possible, but, though it does prove to be something of a trial to get the heavier sledge started, to their surprise the four men are able to get both sledges moving.

In supremely difficult terrain, they also have to resort to relay work. Sometimes, it is so difficult that the only way they can proceed is to use their ice-axes to cut steps into the sastrugi, to get up and over it, and then use a rope and tackle to haul the sledges up to them – with the knife-sharp crest of each one often taking shavings off the sledge runners. Time and again, the men fall painfully on the icy surface, and they finish each day completely exhausted, but one way or another they manage to keep moving.

And if they are pulling like a horse, at least they would soon also be eating like a horse – less in terms of eating a great deal, as the expression runs, than in eating the fodder that was intended for poor old Socks. It tastes shocking, but they have no choice if they are to keep going. And even then, Shackleton decides that if they are to achieve the South Pole, rations will have to be cut further.

11 December 1908 and the day thereafter, northern side of the Drygalski Ice Tongue, Professor David finds himself in a spot of bother

Nearly there now. After 11 days' hard slog, they have nearly covered the 25 miles across to the northern side of the Drygalski Ice Tongue. By this point, the conditions underfoot have mercifully improved a little: the sastrugi have at last diminished to the point where the ice waves have levelled off somewhat, and crevasses are no longer a constant threat to life and limb. They are able to make camp about a mile from the edge of the Ice Tongue, with fine views over Terra Nova Bay.

Satisfied with this rare moment of relative repose, Mackay decides to go off with his field-glasses to search for a path down the other side of the Ice Tongue to what will later be named Relief Inlet, while Mawson stays in his tent carefully changing photographic plates under the darkness of his sleeping bag and Professor David takes the opportunity to go a little way off and sketch the Bellingshausen Ranges.

Around 30 minutes after they have all separated, Mawson is

fully engaged with his work, deep inside his sleeping bag, changing the photographic plates on his camera, when he hears a slightly odd thing. It is the voice of the Professor, Edgeworth David, ol' Tweedy, coming from somewhere behind him . . .

'Mawson, Mawson.'

'Hallo!' replies Mawson.

'Oh, you're still in the bag changing plates, are you?' asks the Professor.

'Yes, Professor.'

Silence for some time . . .

'Mawson!'

'Hallo?' replies Mawson.

'Oh, still changing plates are you?' asks the Professor.

'Yes.'

More silence . . .

'Mawson!'

'Hallo. What is it? What *can I do*?' asks Mawson.

'Well, Mawson, I am in a dangerous position. I am really hanging on by my fingers to the edge of a crevasse and I don't think I can hold on any longer. I shall have to trouble you to come out and assist me.'[42]

Mawson rushes out to see, and it's true! The Professor has fallen into a crevasse barely ten yards from the tent and with outstretched arms has just managed to cling on to the edges and not be swallowed up holus-bolus by the bottomless crevasse. He really doesn't want to be a bother, but he does feel he has to be rescued, and Mawson quickly obliges.

The following day, 12 December, they reach Relief Inlet, where they intend to establish their depot before pushing on to the Magnetic South Pole; however, the low, sloping shore so clearly marked on their Admiralty map fails to materialise. With little alternative, they construct a prominent ice cairn a little further inland from the shore than preferable, yet still – please God

– within fair sight of the passing *Nimrod* when it comes. Here, they depot one of their sledges, geological specimens and spare clothing, together with another letter detailing their plans, and head inland to the spot where, paradoxically, nigh on every compass on earth is keenly pointing bar their own – for it becomes progressively more sluggish the closer they approach.

19 December 1908, on the central ice sheet approaching the Transantarctic Mountains, Mawson suspends . . . judgement

It is the measure of the man. No matter the already huge weight they are hauling on their sledges and the difficulties of getting them over the hostile surface, Mawson is totally absorbed in growing his collection of geological samples, constantly taking his pick of whatever terrain they are covering and adding small amounts of weight to the sledge he is hauling. (No greater passion for geology hath any man than this.)

But for his next trick . . .

Mawson disappears, like a magician through a trapdoor. Having only time to utter a cry of alarm, he drops through a snow bridge and comes to a rest of sorts, albeit dangling at the limit of his eight-foot toggle-ended rope.

He is entirely swallowed up by the underlying ten-foot-wide crevasse. Mackay and David immediately rush over and grab onto their comrade's rope. Now upside down in the crevasse, his life hanging literally by a collection of threads, Mawson does what for him is the obvious. He first wanted to come to Antarctica to study glaciers after all, and he now uses the opportunity to gather some of the fine crystals at this depth that have piqued his interest.

Finally, Mackay lowers an alpine rope with a bowline to help bring him up, and soon Mawson's head comes crashing through the snow ledge, as he is mercifully delivered back from the brink of the bowels of the earth. They push on.

Christmas Day 1908, 2000 feet above sea level, on the ascent of Larsen tributary glacier, Professor David and Mawson tell Mackay to 'stick this in your pipe and smoke it'

What do you give a man on Christmas Day who has just about nothing when you have even less to give? It takes Mawson and Professor David some time, but they finally work out the appropriate gift. In recent days, Mackay has been suffering from snow-blindness, meaning that not only is his vision impaired by having what amounts to sunburnt eyeballs but also he is in great pain. Understandably, therefore, Mackay is feeling low, a mood made worse by the fact that he has run out of pipe tobacco and can no longer smoke. And so the perfect gift . . .

All of them have been using sennegras as a liner for their boots to soak up moisture, provide insulation against the cold and make their feet more comfortable. Why not offer some of that grass to the inveterate smoker Mackay, so he can stick it in his pipe and smoke it?

Eureka! In no time at all on this howling Christmas morning, Mackay is again happily puffing away, seemingly untroubled by just where this grass has been.

Alas, by this time the rest of their problems are not so easily solved. Both Mawson and Professor David have mild cases of frostbite, with the tip of the Professor's nose turning black, just as a part of Mawson's right cheek is, and all three of them have lost skin from their lips for the same reason, with Mawson awaking each morning to find that the frozen blood around his mouth has sealed it shut.

Boxing Day 1908 to New Year's Day 1909, Beardmore Glacier, Shackleton proceeds with some 'grub scoffing useless beggars'

It has been a long haul, but finally their open road to the south, the glacier they have been oh so laboriously climbing for the last three weeks, starts to flatten out. They are delighted to find themselves atop what proves to be the Polar Plateau – at a height of some 10,000 feet above sea level – with a seemingly flat vista between them and the South Pole. This is, of course, the same Polar Plateau that Scott had stepped out on five years earlier, after Shackleton had been sent home, albeit a different part of it.

Not that the going is easy for all that.

After nearly eight weeks of solid trekking, of which the past three weeks have been pure man-hauling, their bodies are exhausted and starting to break down. Tumbles over ridges remain frequent, as do falls down crevasses. Compounding their problems is the fact that the weather has turned foul. An icy headwind cuts through their woefully inadequate jackets and headgear, further delaying their progress. They still have over 300 miles to get to the Pole, yet only three weeks of rations remain. Under such trying conditions, relations between the men are strained. 'Following Shackleton to the Pole is like following an old woman,' the ever-acerbic Marshall, always in a mood like a toothache, records in his diary.[43]

As it happens, Frank Wild feels much the same about Marshall, while remaining an unabashed admirer of Shackleton. 'I sincerely wish he would fall down a crevasse about a 1000 ft deep,' the Yorkshireman writes of Marshall in his diary. 'He certainly does not pull the weight of the extra tent and his kit, and that leaves the weight of his food for us to pull.'[44]

A few days later, he adds:

I can now quite sympathise with Scott when he says, 'Wherever my destiny may in future lead me I hope it will not again be to the interior of the Antarctic Continent.' For the future I am not going to remark on M.'s not pulling but will make special mention of it when he does. I am afraid S. is working too hard today, he has a bad headache today.[45]

And still he is not done:

Neither A. nor M. have been pulling worth a d—, and consequently S and I have to suffer, I am quite certain we are pulling two thirds or more of our load.

If we had only had Joyce and Marston here instead of these two grub scoffing useless beggars we could have done it easily.[46]

Food being a problem from almost the outset, they cut rations back still further and also rationalise their gear to lighten their load. When planning the journey, Shackleton did not realise that fuel and food are far less efficient at this altitude. At 10,000 feet, his hard-working party is sucking in air containing only 70 per cent of the oxygen available at sea level. The result is that they frequently feel giddy, have headaches – with Shackleton suffering particularly badly – and are more short of breath than usual. They push on, and by New Year's Day Shackleton's calculations place them at 87 degrees 6.5 minutes south, which is a new record for both northern and southern latitudes, and according to him they are now within 200 miles of the South Pole.

9 January 1909 and the day thereafter, Polar Plateau, Shackleton reaches the point of no return

So near and yet so far. Over the last few days, their progress has been slowed by the howling blizzards, the rigours of the terrain, the altitude of 11,200 feet and the facts that their boots are worn out and the sennegras depleted. They have only one set of clothes, frostbitten feet and hands, and cut faces. The slow realisation dawns on Shackleton that, while they are capable of getting to the South Pole, they will not have sufficient food to get back. Still, he wants to get at least within 100 miles of it, shattering previous records and demonstrating that it is possible. At that point, they will turn back.

All are aware that they are nearing the point of either return . . . or no return.

'You'll stick by me if I go on,' a heaving Shackleton says hopefully to a straining Adams beside him, as they haul forward, with their every step into the eternal whiteness increasing the chances that they will finish in the eternal blackness.[47]

Adams is far from sure. Looking at his leader, he can see that Shackleton is just about played out, far more than any of the rest of them.

For his part, Marshall has made it absolutely clear that he has had enough of this madness and begs Shackleton to turn back. And Marshall, too, is concerned at Shackleton's physical deterioration and exhaustion, saying to Adams as he nods towards the madly stomping leader, 'He will go bust if he goes on another hour like this.'[48] Something has to give.

Finally, just after 9 am on 9 January 1909, after no fewer than 73 days' travelling south, south, south, ever and always *south*, Shackleton, too, comes to the conclusion that enough is enough. Though not quite at the end of the world, they can just about see it from here, and though his most ardent desire is to continue to the turning point of the world . . . there is no escaping the fact that they have now reached their own turning point.

Shackleton calculates that they are within 97 geographical miles of the Pole, and he calls for everyone to stop.[49] (Using statute miles, they are 111 miles away, but by using geographical miles they are under the golden 100, and it just sounds a lot better.)

'We have shot our bolt,' Shackleton writes in his journal, 'and the tale is 88° 23' south.'[50] At this point, Shackleton asks Frank Wild for the Union Jack flag that Queen Alexandra gave the expedition leader 18 months before, along with the Bible. Wild has been using the flag as a veritable blanket, its heavy silk keeping him not quite warm but at least warmer than he otherwise would have been. Wild retrieves the flag from his kit and reluctantly hands it over, and they plant it right beside a small brass cylinder containing stamps and documents.

Standing there as the flag flaps frantically, Shackleton turns his field-glasses to the south, gazing longingly in the direction in which the South Pole lies. All he can see is a flat, white, frozen plain, surely extending to the Pole itself. It looks cruel and unforgiving, and yet maddeningly attainable if only they had more supplies with them and more ponies to help haul during the Barrier stage.

Looking at him, Wild feels admiration and sympathy for Shackleton in equal measure. The admiration is for how hard Shackleton has pulled to help get them there. 'All through this journey,' Wild would later recall, 'Shackleton strained every muscle and nerve to the limit, as he always did, during the twenty years I knew him, when strenuous action was called for. I am convinced this was the reason for his breakdown when with Scott and Wilson.'[51]

The sympathy is for the fact that Shackleton has not quite achieved his life's dream but is turning back for the ultimate safety of them all. It might have been just possible to keep going, but, as leader, he had wider responsibilities. 'I am perfectly certain,' Wild asserts, 'that had Shackleton only himself to consider he would have gone on and planted the flag at the Pole itself.'[52]

Still, they have gained the record for travelling the farthest south, and that is really something. They celebrate that evening by having an extra lump of pemmican with their dinner, a taste of sloe gin and, for Wild at least, a cigar from H. Upman's, which he has been keeping for this very day. And then, the following morning, they turn their sledges around, set their makeshift sails to catch as much of the bitter wind as possible and head north, to get to Hut Point, where – with the waters clear for passage – it has been arranged that *Nimrod* will 'occasionally look' for them in the event they have not returned to Cape Royds by 10 February. If *Nimrod* cannot reach Hut Point yet due to ice, the men at Cape Royds Winter Quarters have been instructed to watch for Shackleton's flash signal from the Glacier Tongue between Cape Royds and Hut Point from noon to 1 pm each day.

Going just as fast as their frostbitten feet can carry them, their urgency now is twofold. In the first place, they have to move fast to prevent their rations from running out well before they can reach succour. Second, if they don't get to Hut Point by 1 March, the returning *Nimrod* will, as per Shackleton's specific instructions, have left for New Zealand without them, obliging them to spend another winter in Antarctica. So, push they must, and push they do – though in fact their only way forward is to *pull*, hauling forward their wretched sledges over all terrains. The only saving grace is that the wind is now blowing from behind them, and, by putting up sails, their sledges are at least helped along a bit.

Chapter Three

Getting Home

Antarctica is a world of colour, brilliant and intensely pure. The chaste whiteness of the snow and the velvet blackness of the rocks belong to days of snowy nimbus enshrouding the horizon. When the sky has broken into cloudlets of fleece, their edges are painted pale orange, fading or richly glowing if the sun is low. In the high sun they are rainbow-rimmed.

Douglas Mawson, *The Home of the Blizzard*

15 January 1909 and the day thereafter, nearing the South Magnetic Pole atop the Polar Plateau, Edgeworth David, Douglas Mawson and Alister Mackay chase an unseen force to the ends of the earth

It has been a brutal journey, which has seen them ascending 5000 feet in 20 days on little more than half-rations. A potentially catastrophic concoction of strong blizzards, bad surfaces, freezing temperatures, exhaustion, starvation and anxiety about getting back to the Drygalski Depot has cruelled them all the way.

Part of the problem is the ever-changing position of the South Magnetic Pole over the years, which wanders the terrain like a drunken nomad. Before 1902, it was shifting eastward. Since then, it appeared to be moving north-west, and now it seems to be 40 miles north-west of where it was estimated to be by fellow Australian scientist Louis Bernacchi, on Scott's *Discovery* expedition. The men are not so much going to a particular spot on the map as working out just where it might be on the map on the day they will hopefully manage to intercept it.

Frustratingly, much of it amounts to approximations, guesswork and gut-feel. On one occasion, after a hard day's hauling, Mawson takes a reading only to discover that it is maddeningly further off than when they started the day.

Mawson is relying on his dip compass, which has been progressively, and now rapidly, standing more vertically (towards the centre of the earth) the closer they come to their goal. After marching seven miles in the afternoon, he sees that the compass needle is just 12 minutes off being straight up and down, and he calculates they are within 13 miles of their journey's end.

The next day, after two miles, the Party leave everything non-essential they can in a prominent position to return to later, enabling them to travel light for the six or so hours they estimate it will take them to reach the region that Mawson has made an educated guess at. As Mawson explains to David and Mackay, calculation of the *precise* location of the South Magnetic Pole would take a month of observations – all he can do in a day is make his best estimate that they are as close to its location as his observations allow.

After 13 miles of marching, they arrive in the desired position – 72 degrees 25 minutes south, 155 degrees 16 minutes east, at an elevation of 7260 feet. As Mackay notes in his diary, their compass still points sluggishly towards the north-west, suggesting while they are in the Magnetic Pole's suburb, they are not exactly in its home.[1] But they are very close! True, this location does not have the same mythical glamour that the Geographic South Pole does – a spot that does not move from year to year and is the southern point of the axis on which the planet rotates – but it is something, all right. No one has been on this spot before them; many have tried and some have died.

'It was an intense satisfaction,' the Prof recorded, 'to fulfil the wish of Sir James Clarke [*sic*] Ross that the South Magnetic Pole should be actually reached, as he had already in 1831 reached the North Magnetic Pole.'[2]

Planting the light flagpole they have carried all this way in the snow, they soon have the Union Jack gaily and proudly flying before a slight southerly wind.

And now for the ceremony, with Professor Edgeworth David, as their leader, making a brief speech. Precisely following the script Shackleton has given them to read out on this occasion, he declares, 'I hereby take possession of this area now containing the Magnetic Pole for the British Empire. Three cheers for the King. Hip hip . . .'

'Hurrah!'

'Hip hip . . .'

'Hurrah!'

'Hip-hip . . .'

'HURRAH!'[3]

A quick pause as they take a photo to mark the occasion, using a piece of string connected to the camera trigger. All of the men observe protocol and remove their hats, notwithstanding the temperature being minus 16 degrees, while they give the best chattering, frozen smile they can and Edgeworth David pulls the string. And then it is time to quickly head back to where they have left all of their supplies, to make this last dash. 'With a fervent "Thank God" we all did a right-about turn,' writes David, 'and as quick a march as tired limbs would allow back in the direction of our little green tent in the wilderness of snow.'[4]

They, too, are now on an unforgiving timetable.

Four months earlier, Shackleton had written his instructions in ink, meaning they are now set in stone, and they state clearly to the captain of *Nimrod* that if there is no sign of Edgeworth David's Northern Party at Cape Royds by the end of January, then, on 1 February, the ship should proceed north along the coast to search for them, not travelling any further north than 'the low beach on the north side of the Drygalski Barrier, keeping as close as practicable to the shore and making a thorough search for the party'.[5] Now, it is obvious to Professor David's party that they have no hope of meeting *Nimrod* at Cape Royds, meaning that, from here, they will need to trek the 270 miles to the northern side of the Drygalski Barrier right by the coast in 16 days – a challenging average of a tad more than 16 miles a day.

They are in a very difficult position, complicated by the fact that Mackay has turned nastier than ever on Professor David, frequently ripping into him verbally as the older man ambles, rambles and shambles along. The Prof keeps trying to get back in Mackay's favour by offering him more chocolate and biscuits, but Mackay will have none of it.

'Why shouldn't *Mawson* have it?' Mackay demands.[6]

20 January 1909, Upper Glacier Depot, Shackleton's Southern Party take the path less travelled back to Hut Point

After 11 days' hard-hauling, getting thinner by the day, at long last Shackleton and his men are back on the 'highway to the south' that they first spotted two months earlier, but, mercifully, this time it is taking them to the north, back to safety. As they begin their descent, the frigid air of the Polar Plateau falls behind, and oxygen becomes more plentiful. Upon making camp, exhausted but relieved, Shackleton takes up his pen and writes:

We arrived at our depot at 12.30 pm with sore and aching bodies. The afternoon was rather better, as, after the first hour, we got off the blue ice on to snow. However bad as the day has been, we have said farewell to that awful plateau, and are well on our way down the glacier.[7]

24 January 1909 and two days thereafter, Butter Point, 42 miles' march from Cape Royds, the Western Party break the ice

In the meantime, the third of Shackleton's sledging groups, the Western Party of Raymond Priestley, Philip Brocklehurst and Bertram Armytage, have been having a tough time of it themselves. Led by Bertram Armytage, they managed to ascend the Ferrar Glacier, but their search for fossils was fruitless, with heavy snowfall, blizzard conditions and poor maps all conspiring to hamper them.

Complicating things is that the relationship between the tightly wound Armytage and the loosely insolent English baronet Philip Brocklehurst has turned as icy as the terrain they are covering. From the beginning, the aristocratic Englishman has not been content to follow the orders of a colonial – it seems against nature. When, early on, Armytage denied his request to have an extra pannikin of water every day so he could brush his teeth, things began to deteriorate.

Indeed, it fell to Priestley to communicate between the two as they made their way back to the coast – finally, on 14 January, pitching camp on the sea ice at the foot of Butter Point, where it was intended they rendezvous with the returned Northern Party. Alas, of the Professor, Mawson and Mackay there was no sign, so Armytage took an important decision. Shackleton's written instruction was that if they hadn't appeared by 20 January, he was to take his party to the Glacier Tongue, 'if the ice permits', in order that they might be easily spotted by *Nimrod* and picked up. Bertram did precisely that, leaving most of their supplies at Butter Point for the use of the Northern Party, should they turn up.

But would the ice permit? Armytage thought so. After having a close look, he took the view that it was stable, so they put up the tent.

When Priestley awakes on this morning of 24 January, however, and walks out of the tent, he cannot help but notice that something is different . . .

They are afloat in McMurdo Sound! Surrounded by water!

Armytage and Brocklehurst are awoken seconds later to his panicked shout: 'We've broken out – we're on a floe drifting!'[8] It is close to their worst nightmare, with only falling into the endless blackness of a deep crevasse beating it. Quickly, they strike camp and head north along the floe to search for any way back across, trying to ignore the fact they are in danger of being swept out of McMurdo Sound and into the Southern Ocean, along with ignoring the snouts of the killer whales that now abound all around. The Western Party might have missed breakfast, but the whales – assuming them to be some kind of strange penguin – are hoping *they* haven't.

Alas, there proves to be no way back, and their only recourse is to wait and see if the ice floe might tend back towards the fast ice. The three pass a desperate day, with the only positive point being that Armytage and Brocklehurst shake hands, on the reckoning that in these desperate straits to beat *all* desperate straits they must put aside their unstated quarrel and be united.

And, in the end, Shakespeare's notion that 'there are tides in the affairs of men' is proved right, for at midnight that tide changes direction, to bring them a change in fortune. In the direction they are now heading, they can suddenly see that one edge of their floe might possibly nudge a fringe of fast ice on the western shore, just 200 yards ahead!

More shouts. More mad scrambling. The tent is collapsed in record time, the sledge thrown together, and when, just minutes later, the ice floe does indeed momentarily give a frozen kiss to the shore, they jump for their lives, pulling the sledge with them, and then watch in horror as the floe they had been on heads north to the open sea.

Barely able to believe their good fortune, the three extremely relieved explorers make it back to Butter Point, where, the following morning – praise the Lord! – they soon see *Nimrod* coming their way. When she finally manages to manoeuvre alongside the fast ice at 3 pm on 26 January, they are able to scamper aboard.

By this time, all safe, Brocklehurst and Armytage have tacitly agreed to resume their silent hostilities, and Captain Evans notes in his log that 'a chill more than the ice' exists between the two.[9]

No doubt about it, Antarctica could do strange things to men, even among, as Captain Evans later notes, well-bred university men like these:

> Unmannerliness so primitive was the symptom in their cases of that nervous ill-health which afflicts in varying degrees all the members of a little community condemned to a most irksome intimacy by confinement within one small room through the long months of a Polar night.[10]

26 January 1909, 70 miles south-east of Hut Point, Scott's man, Ernest Joyce, resupplies Bluff Depot

On this day, the first of two dog-hauled sledge journeys led by Joyce arrives to supply Bluff Depot, directly due east of Minna Bluff, leaving the food and fuel that Shackleton's Southern Party will heavily rely on for the last 70 miles of their return journey. Having negotiated heavily crevassed country and numerous falls through the ice, Joyce and his three companions erect two bamboo poles flying three black flags atop a ten-foot snow mound, giving a total height of 22 feet (clearly seen from a distance of eight miles). Beneath them, they have laid down 500 pounds of provisions.

Late January 1909, Beardmore Glacier, Shackleton's Southern Party push on

Trudging, falling, trudging, trudging, trudging, falling. Shackleton's Party are suffering from a devastatingly cruel mixture of starvation, dysentery, intermittent blizzard conditions and a nightmare of one-foot-deep snow and sastrugi – the last like whipped up meringues.

Compounding it all for Shackleton is terrible snow-blindness, which so reduces his capacity to operate that, as they come to crevasses, Wild has to tell him which direction to take and where to jump, so he can stay clear of disaster. Inevitably, he falls far more often than the others, but he never complains.

Most days, their rations are reduced to just a few miserable biscuits and some even more miserable horse meat, no longer augmented by the pony maize, as this was exhausted some three weeks back. Things are deteriorating rapidly, and it is a close-run thing as to which is the worst: the physical condition of the men themselves, their spirits or their dilapidated sledge. Probably, it is a tie between the men and their low spirits, as at one stage the already deeply unhappy Adams collapses from hunger. (Like so many men, Adams was beguiled by both Shackleton and his description of the White Continent during a chance meeting two years earlier. He surrendered a Royal Navy promotion to enthusiastically enlist on the *Nimrod* expedition – only to now find himself more dead than alive.) For his part, Wild is suffering worst from the dysentery – almost certainly brought on by consuming some decayed flesh of the pony Grisi – and this, together with an uneven surface and bad light, means that on at least one day they are lucky to drag him five miles.

One of the strange things about descending the glacier is that they can see so far ahead. At the foot of the glacier is a large, perpendicular rock where they have left a major depot, and they can see that rock from 60 miles away. Alas, they are still 20 miles away when their all but last skerrick of food is consumed, and they must march on with little in their stomachs but the growing sound of gnawing. Many is the time that the man most weakened, Frank Wild, falls into a crevasse in his soiled pants and is in such a pitiful state that, while hanging in his harness above the black abyss, he prays that the rope will break so that his pain can be over. Yet despite their physical difficulties, Shackleton insists they retain the burdensome geological samples they have collected along the way.

Just before leaving the glacier for the last time, Shackleton crashes through the soft snow, plunging into a crevasse, only the jerk of his harness beneath his heart stunning and saving him. 'There is the last touch for you, don't you come up here again,' Shackleton imagines the glacier to be warning.[11]

Finally, however, there is relief of sorts. 'Thank God we are on the barrier again at last . . .' Shackleton writes on 28 January, having spent just over a week on the descent that has included 'some of the worst surfaces and most dangerous crevasses' they have ever encountered.[12]

Even once upon the Barrier, however, the perilous difficulties remain. Both Shackleton's leadership and his generosity of spirit are more than tested – and both pass muster like the prize thoroughbreds they are. In a gesture that Wild would remember all his life, the expedition leader sacrifices the one biscuit he has been allotted for the day's rations and gives it to the ailing Wild. Wild records in his diary that night, 'I do not suppose that anyone else in the world can thoroughly realize how much generosity and sympathy was shown by this. I do and by God shall never forget it. Thousands of pounds would not have bought that one biscuit.'[13]

Shackleton barely manages to record in his own diary, with quivering hand, 'Please God we will get through all right. Great anxiety.'[14]

31 January 1909, Drygalski Ice Tongue, Mawson and Mackay rally while the Prof teeters on the brink

Having now successfully descended the Larsen tributary glacier onto the central ice sheet that feeds into the Drygalski Ice Tongue, the three exhausted explorers are now well aware that they must negotiate 'a chaos of crevassed and serac ice'[15] – serac ice being a field of icy pinnacles – between them and their point of potential rendezvous with *Nimrod* at the Drygalski Ice Tongue.

They may be just 16 miles from their Drygalski Depot, yet now it is 16 miles of intervening fast-melting ice they must cross. *Quickly.* The Party are suffering their respective afflictions: Mawson an injured leg, David a badly frostbitten and potentially gangrenous foot, Mackay a bout of snow-blindness. Between the three of them, they are lucky to make up one fit man. On one occasion on this day, both Edgeworth David and Alister Mackay narrowly escape disappearing down the same crevasse by clumsily throwing their arms out either side of the snow bridge.

It is, as Mawson describes it in his diary, 'an awful day of despair, disappointment, hard travelling, agonising walking – forever falling down crevasses'.[16] They cut themselves a way across to the shore, skirting alongside one of several semi-frozen lakes, Mawson himself falling after a snow bridge collapses. Their tempers grow shorter than an Antarctic winter's day.

The Professor is quite a sight. The trousers of his windproof oversuit, known as Burberrys, are so badly ripped it is a close-run thing as to whether they are deemed actually on or off – but there is little doubt that he would have been arrested in Pitt Street for wearing the same.

'You are a bloody fool,' snarls Mackay one more time, after a hobbling David yet again disappears down a crevasse.[17] And Mackay does not let up. At a point when Mawson is far enough away that he cannot hear him, Mackay plays the strongest card he has in his deck. As the designated doctor on this expedition, he is ultimately responsible for the health of them all, with the authority to determine what ails them. With that in mind, he now tells the Prof that he will declare him insane unless he soon, formally and in writing, relinquishes the leadership to Mawson, as per Shackleton's original instruction should calamity arise.

It is Mackay's view that so debilitated is the Prof, such a shambling and incompetent wreck has he become, that calamity has now arisen. And he intends to act upon it. The Prof has been told.

Late January to early February 1909, Cape Barnes, McMurdo Sound, *Nimrod* takes shelter, on her mission to pick up the explorers

At this advanced stage of the season, the pack ice in McMurdo Sound is beginning to break up and move north. Reluctant to move any further south of Cape Royds, *Nimrod* impatiently takes shelter in the lee of an iceberg against the frequent blizzards in order to preserve her precious coal.

Her men wait by for that blessed brief moment when the Ross Sea might sufficiently clear to allow the ship to approach Hut Point and quickly get out again before it freezes them in. With Professor David's Northern Party three weeks overdue and Shackleton's party also still out, Captain Evans grows anxious. As each day passes with no sign of them, and the thermometer continues to fall, it becomes ever more likely that *Nimrod* will be forced by the freezing over of the Ross Sea to leave for the north before either party is picked up.

Complying with Shackleton's instructions, on 1 February Evans crosses the Sound and heads north – dangerously hugging the coast of Victoria Land – in search of Professor David's party.

2 February 1909, northern side of the Drygalski Ice Tongue, with Edgeworth David's Northern Party

Onwards, onwards, onwards they plough with great haste and determination through fresh snow, racing with time lest they miss *Nimrod* – which, if all is well, should have been travelling north up the coast looking for them since the day before. They barely stop to eat, and sleep is a luxury they can no longer afford. The Prof's feet are so useless that he has taken to walking on his heels, doing the best he can this way.

In any case, Alister Mackay really has had enough of David's performance as leader, his constant stumbling into crevasses, his general incompetence and decrepitude, his trousers so torn he can barely keep them up. Mackay's rage is so great, Mawson notes, that when they are both in harness and the Prof's posterior presents itself, the Scotsman appears – with barely deniable intent – to kick him in the backside.[18] Again and again, Mackay demands in his thick brogue that the Prof stand down as leader and hand over to Mawson. Finally, on this day, exhausted as he is, the old man – for that is what he now is, and no mistake, so worn down does he appear – can resist no more. He formally suggests to Mawson that he take over. In response, the young lion tells his old mentor, the one responsible for bringing him on this expedition in the first place, that he does not like the idea of it and will have to think it over.

After a few miles, they strike that same *barranca* (broad valley) in the central ice sheet they had met on their way out and must now cross. Now so close to the coast, a proliferation of seals and penguins can be seen all along the canyon floor . . .

But wait! There, in the distance! Mawson spots the flapping depot flag from the other side of what he refers to as a 'steaming crack' – an enormous ravine in the ice – that they must cross to reach their depot.[19]

It is with some difficulty that they crash the sledge to the floor of the *barranca*, only to find there is no suitable slope on the other side to haul it up again – meaning they are forced to trace their way back to where they started. Nevertheless, it is something to have spotted the depot, and in celebration the sizeable excised liver of one of the two emperor penguins Mackay has slaughtered on the ravine floor bubbles away in the camp stove that night. That taste! That softness! That wonderful feeling of a full belly and returning strength and purpose . . . It proves to be as deeply appreciated and savoured a repast as they have ever known.

The fact that they now have fresh meat available in the form of seals and penguins at least means they are unlikely to starve in the short term. But still they need to get to the Drygalski Depot, not just for its food but because it is situated at the point where the passing *Nimrod* will spot them and retrieve them. What is passing now is time, and it becomes ever more urgent to find a way to navigate across the ravine, before it is too late. It may be that *Nimrod* is just hours away. Such worries continue to plague the totally exhausted – and now teetering on deranged – expedition leader, Edgeworth David, who also has escalating physical problems. One of his feet has gone numb, and both his boots appear to be frozen. They *need* to get to the depot, find *Nimrod* and get away.

The worry of it all is debilitating, and something about the Prof is definitely not all right. While Mack is off hunting seals, the exhausted and befuddled 51-year-old has started to commit to paper, in duplicate, his letter of resignation as party leader. The mantle is to be transferred to his protégé, Mawson – who now feels he has no choice but to reluctantly concur with Mackay that their leader is, for the moment, 'partially demented'.[20]

And yet, Mawson, concerned at this needless humiliation of his mentor before it is *absolutely* necessary, tells David he 'does not like the business' and states that David should leave matters 'as they are until the ship fails to turn up'.[21]

But that is not good enough for Mackay, who gets wind of it

when he returns and writes in his diary that night:

> I have deposed the Professor. I simply told him that he was no longer fit to lead the party, that the situation was now critical, and that he must officially appoint Mawson leader, or I would declare him, the Professor, physically and mentally unfit. He acted on my proposal at once.[22]

Unknown to the three men, just 15 minutes after they turn in that night, *Nimrod* passes by from between two cables and three-quarters of a mile offshore. In part because of a large iceberg off the coast and because a light wind is carrying a snowdrift that obscures visibility, neither the depot flag or tent are spotted.

3 February 1909, Relief Bay, the Northern Party keep their eyes peeled

After snatching five hours' sleep, stomachs satisfied with more than a soupçon of boiled penguin meat, the Party head off, this time along the north bank of the steep-walled ravine, passing by a multitude of seals at rest on the canyon floor beneath them. So pressed for time are they, so urgent their mission, that there is simply no time to slaughter the seals to stock up their provisions. After travelling one and a half miles inland in search of a crossing, they come to the narrow snow bridge across the main canyon and at 10 pm that night, the spent Party at last arrive at Relief Bay.

However, having come in on the wrong bearing, they must camp a little beneath their depot, yet still within good view of the coast. Following Mawson's sumptuous meal of seal blubber, blood and oil, with a side order of fried meat and liver, he and David turn in, while Mackay commences the first four-hour watch, his eyes glued to the coast for any glimmer of *Nimrod*.

4 February 1909, Relief Bay, the Northern Party make tracks

Still no sign of the ship. It is a brutal, desperate decision they must make. They must either prepare to dig themselves in at their nearby depot – building a snow cave to keep them from the wind – which would enable them to winter in that very conspicuous spot (now that they are on the coast again, they should be able to kill enough penguins and seals to get them through), or immediately attempt the 230-mile trek back to their base at Cape Royds.

Mackay, not believing that *Nimrod* will search for them, is all for starting straight away for Cape Royds. He proposes they take with them a cooker and adequate seal meat for sustenance, leave a note for *Nimrod* telling them of their plans and get going! David and Mawson are quite opposed, however, and opt for waiting it out until the end of February, allowing ample time for *Nimrod* to rendezvous with them there.

The discussion is right at its most intense – this is, after all, a matter of life and death – when suddenly, at about half-past three in the afternoon, two shots ring out. They are quite distant, but they are shots all right! There is a sudden pause in the conversation as the three men try to work out what it can *possibly* mean, when it is Mawson who realises there can be only one explanation: *Nimrod!*

In an instant, the young scientist is up and out of the tent, yelling back to the others, 'It's a gun from the ship!'[23] By the time Mackay and David get out of the tent themselves, Mawson is already 100 yards in front of them, impatiently calling for them to follow him at speed, just as soon as they have found and brought the thing he has forgotten. 'Bring something to wave!' he calls back over his shoulder.[24]

Professor David heads back inside to grab a red rucksack and is quickly on his way out to see his dream of all dreams coming true. After his long, exhausting and debilitating trek, suffering fatigue to the point of incapacity, snow-blindness, severe frostbite to his feet to the very edge of gangrene and fearing many times that death was right upon him, not to mention the constant humiliation at the hands of Mackay, finally, finally . . . salvation has arrived. For there, coming up the inlet, is the mighty *Nimrod*, no more than 400 yards from him, her men on the deck, her smokestack breezily billowing, her three sail masts cutting the mist like beacons of salvation.

Upon *Nimrod*, Chief Officer John King Davis, who is peering out from the lookout on the main topmast, bellows, 'There they are!' A mighty cheer is raised as others rush up from the decks below, to see first one, then two, and then a third man rush out of the tent on yonder hill. Hurrah! Three out of three accounted for.

And only half a minute later, while all the crew cheer to the echo, they can make out who is who, as they crowd on the shore. There is Mackay, waving at them furiously from the shore, and there is the Professor. But where . . . where is Mawson? The answer comes when Mackay shouts to them in his thick Scottish brogue, 'Mawson has fallen down a crevasse! Bring a rope!' Almost in the same breath, though, Mackay shouts other news: 'We got to the magnetic pole!'[25]

While that rope is being retrieved and a shore party is assembled, Mackay and David rush over to the fissure to find the crestfallen Mawson still peering up at them from 18 feet below. They are too physically weak to extract him, but, of course, the cavalry has just arrived from the ship. It is Davis who quickly responds, leading a rescue party over the ice to where Mawson has been swallowed up.

When they first met, over a year earlier, when Mawson was seasick in the lifeboat, Davis's first words to him of course were, 'What are you doing there, why don't you get below?' Now, the question is rather why doesn't he come on up, and Davis is just the man to make it happen. In short order, the grizzled mariner bridges the opening with a piece of timber and, with a rope around his waist, is lowered away. Deftly tying the rope around Mawson's waist, Davis gives the signal for the Australian to be hauled into the daylight, and the process is repeated for Davis's extraction. All three of the intrepid explorers are soon bundled back onto *Nimrod*, together with their gear and their oh-so-precious records, and they are safely back on board the ship amid warmth, food, hot tea and other people – in other words, civilisation! Mackay, who believes the Prof's condition to be so poor that they would never have made it back to Cape Royds, declares their salvation 'enough to make a man turn religious'.[26]

But gee, they smell. Captain Evans insists they have baths before doing anything else, and then a splendid hot meal follows. Gathering around as they eat and talk, the crew of *Nimrod* are thrilled to hear of the success of the expedition and that, in the course of a staggering man-hauled sledge journey of 1260 miles in 122 days (this figure includes the considerable relaying of sledges), they actually made it to the South Magnetic Pole – a real coup for the entire expedition, although David feels that, had they had dogs, they could have completed the journey in half the time.[27] Courtesy of Mawson's efforts, they have also succeeded in charting with approximate accuracy the outline of the coast in this part of Antarctica plus the position of several newly discovered mountains.[28]

And Mawson, Mackay and the Prof listen in turn to the adventures of the Western Party, including their narrow brush with being lost forever on an ice floe. All up, it is a wonderful evening of bonhomie and feasting, telling stories and catching up. Still, it seems Mackay, for one, has overdone it, for afterwards Brocklehurst, hearing a 'noise like a seal calling',[29] investigates. It proves to be Mackay, holding his belly as he writhes in agony on his bunk. After being on starvation rations for so long, his stomach is not used to so much rich food and drink all at once.

Mawson, at least, is able to keep going, and there is even a little time for him to hear something of the story, from his friend Davis, of how they came to find them, and how lucky it was that they didn't miss them entirely. As Davis tells him, if the ship had missed them, it would have been all Davis's fault. For Davis was the man on watch the night before, as they steamed north towards Cape Washington, cautiously hugging the coast, eagerly looking for some sign that they were alive, when they passed by a group of icebergs just off the Drygalski Ice Tongue. Four hours later, when Captain Evans came on deck, he first remarked that there seemed no chance of finding anyone now and that they would have to turn back shortly as their coal supplies were getting perilously low. He then asked whether Davis's examination of the coast had been thorough.

Davis initially replied, 'Yes,' but then he hesitated momentarily before saying that there had been a group of bergs he'd seen four hours earlier at 4 am that had obscured a close examination of the coast behind them. The good captain immediately took him up on it and crisply had him fetch and then read out the orders that Davis had just put his initials to. Wretchedly, realising where this was going and the mistake he had made, Davis read aloud, 'The Officer of the Watch is to examine every feature of the coastline and ensure that the ship does not pass any inlet or bay without searching it.'

'Now,' Captain Evans bored in, 'did you or did you not pass any inlet or bay during your watch this morning?'[30]

Davis felt that they very likely had not, but he was now beset by doubt and ultimately had to reply that he simply could not be sure.

And so they returned on their previous course and carefully threaded their way *behind* the icebergs, whereupon they first came upon what seemed like a perfect dock in the Drygalski Ice Tongue. Then, as the sun swept low above the mountain peaks to the westward, shining upon the snow-covered, gently undulating slopes, they spied a black flag flapping from the top of what would prove to be a green conical tent!

And Mawson, of course, knows the rest. Yes, it has been a close-run thing, and yes, it was Davis's mistake that would have seen them still left there, but he is nothing if not honest, and the bond between the men grows.

But for now, to bed. A *real* bed!

As Professor David writes in his diary that night, 'None but those whose bed for months has been on snow and ice can realise the luxury of a real bunk, blankets and pillow in a snug little cabin.'[31]

Pass the pillows. Inevitably, though, now that the three men are out of danger themselves, they have the luxury of wondering – not for the first time, but certainly for the first time at any length – how the Shackleton Southern Party are getting on. Did they get to the Pole? Are they safe? Will they be able to get back to Hut Point in time, by 1 March, for *Nimrod* to pick them up and pluck them to safety? Just how are they going?

And, of course, they are not the only ones wondering.

5 February 1909 and five days thereafter, 70 miles south of Hut Point, Scott's old companion Ernest Joyce arrives at Bluff Depot

A difficult man, Ernest Joyce. It is the opinion of Eric Marshall, always willing to record his full and frank views of others, that he is 'of limited intelligence, resentful and incompatible'.[32] And yet no one doubts his overall ability when sledging. It was for that reason that Shackleton recruited him for this expedition, to look after the dogs and do precisely what he is doing now: resupplying the depots that he and his men will be relying on upon their return from their assault on the South Pole.

For Joyce and his companions, this has been a long, hard haul, fraught with danger and difficulty, but on this day his second supply journey reaches Bluff Depot. This time, they carry with them luxury items such as apples and mutton brought from *Nimrod*, which met them at Cape Royds back on 15 January.

Joyce has been hoping all this way to find Shackleton's Southern Party camped there, and to be able to surprise them with their wondrous food supplies, but to their disappointment Bluff Depot is just as lost and lonely, freezing and windswept as when they left it, and of Shackleton and his men there is no sign. All they can do for the moment is wait, day after weary day.

Concerned that the Party has not arrived at the depot by 10 February, Joyce decides, contrary to Shackleton's orders to return, to venture further south towards the Pole in search of the overdue party. After finding nothing but the outward tracks of the Southern Party, they turn back towards Bluff Depot and are just approaching it when . . .

When they see them!

For, suddenly in the far distance, they can just manage to make out an erected tent and men walking about!

Alas, alas, as they move closer, the men and the tent slowly dissolve before their very eyes.

'It is curious what things one can see in circumstances like these,' writes a disconsolate Joyce, of how they have been expecting Shackleton's party to appear 'out of the loneliness'.[33]

The Southern Party are now 18 days overdue. Where oh where can they be?

Mid-February 1909, upon the Barrier, 225 miles south of Hut Point, the Southern Party run over a Chinaman

They are struggling. Their hunger has been 'too awful to describe', at times all four suffering from diarrhoea and too ill to march. 'We cannot keep our thoughts, waking or sleeping, from food and our conversation continually turns to it,' Frank Wild records.[34]

Just when it appears that they will all perish, though, they are extremely fortunate to run over a Chinaman . . . specifically, *their* Chinaman, the first pony they shot, some three months earlier. After thawing and cooking the good-sized liver – always the softest part – they devour it with relish. Then, when Shackleton catches sight of red-stained snow, further investigation uncovers a frozen core of Chinaman's blood – and they soon have a most welcome beef-tea-like addition to their scant supplies.

Under renewed horsepower, with abatement of the sastrugi, for a time the going proves relatively easy; however, in between picking up cairns they are often down to half a pannikin of horsemeat and a few biscuits a day, so their energy abates in equal measure and the men again grow exhausted.

Shackleton's spirits are lifted at least a little when, on his 35th birthday, 15 February 1909, the normally taciturn Marshall somehow spirits up a cigarette as a present for him, which he smokes with delight, sucking it deeply into his lungs and blowing it to the winds with all the *savoir faire* of a lord of the realm.

So exhausted are the men that to get into the tent each night they must raise their legs into the sleeping bags by hand, as though their lower limbs are separate from their bodies. At night, the cold is like a living thing, constantly striking at them. The only things remotely warm in their world are the primus stove when they are cooking on it – just how close can you get your frostbitten fingers to the flame without actually burning them? – and their own hot breath in their sleeping bags at night, where they leave just enough space at the top for oxygen to get in without letting the hot air out.

Still, they battle on, day after day, the sledge harnesses biting their stomachs from without and devastating hunger attacking them from within. Lively, almost childlike, debate ensues at mealtimes and nearly always centres on their favourite subject – food. Should one eat one's biscuits in one sitting or, like Shackleton, save a little something to aid sleep at bedtime? Well, *I* think . . .

The week of determined walking finally pays off on 20 February when they reach Depot A at 79 degrees 36 minutes south. There, they fill their bellies with hoosh and a blackcurrant pudding that they make with a tin of Hartley's jam and biscuits, followed by fat Tabard cigarettes, the smoke of which bites their lungs with exquisite beauty. 'Never was a meal more enjoyed and I am sure there were never four more grateful than us,' records Wild in his diary.[35]

Spurred on by the anticipation of more sumptuous and plentiful supplies at Bluff Depot, Shackleton and his men are up and about at just after 4.30 the next morning, raring to go. Despite the winds picking up and the temperature plummeting, death so closely stalks them if they tarry that, tapping into what feels to be their last reserves of physical and spiritual strength, they manage to reel off another 20 miles, and then with desperate dynamism another 20 miles the following day.

Tracks! On 22 February, the Party come across the tracks of four men and their dogs, which they assume to be made by Joyce's party, heading towards the depot that Shackleton ordered them to establish from 15 January. They follow the tracks closely. Inspecting one of the strangers' camps, Shackleton feels sure that *Nimrod* has arrived, as he recognises new brands of goods among their refuse. Shackleton's men are so desperate that they scrounge like monkeys among the remnants of the camp, growing irrational when they find but a few blocks of chocolate and a biscuit.

22 February 1909, in the lee of the Glacier Tongue, *Nimrod* waits for the Shackleton party to turn up

What to do? It is the question that both Captain Evans and biologist James Murray – who has become nominal expedition leader in Shackleton's absence, though that means little when they are on *Nimrod*, where the skipper commands – have been wrestling with over for the past two weeks since picking up Edgeworth David, Mawson and Mackay. For, while that was indeed a great breakthrough, the fact remains that Shackleton and his men remain missing well after their expected return date of 10 February.

Compounding the problem is that Shackleton's written instructions issued to Murray are ambiguous as to whether he wants a rescue party located at Cape Royds or, as he later has it, Hut Point. In his initial instructions prior to heading for the Pole in late October, Shackleton stated that if the Southern Party have not arrived by 25 February then Murray is to appoint a three-man rescue party to be stationed at Cape Royds and sufficiently supplied for seven men for an additional winter. However, Shackleton's later instructions appear to countermand this, saying the rescue party should be at Hut Point, which would seem to make more sense in terms of proximity to the Southern Party's return journey.

At least it is clear who he wants to lead the relief party: Douglas Mawson, whom Shackleton regards as strong, capable and potentially a good leader. An extraordinary step, perhaps, to give such responsibility to such a young man who joined the expedition only at the last minute and has minimal rank compared with others – but perhaps Shackleton recognised the similarity with his own position vis-á-vis Scott on the *Discovery* expedition seven years earlier. For Shackleton, too, had joined Scott as a relatively anonymous third lieutenant and had risen to the point of accompanying Scott on his attempt on the Pole through ability alone. Mawson was like that. Most importantly, however, before they had headed off on their separate expeditions, Mawson had told Shackleton he was available – no small thing when he was being asked to spend another year in this place. Mawson had come a long way from the man who, 18 months earlier, had only wanted to go on a quick trip to Antarctica. Now, he was contemplating spending two years straight there.

If the Southern Party still have not arrived by 1 March, Mawson will lead the rescue party that must set out to look for them.

Late February 1909, Great Ice Barrier, the Southern Party reach Bluff Depot and then the haven of Hut Point

And then they see it. Far, far on the farthest horizon of the frozen white waste all around, they spy as if in a vision an ethereal light, a flash of something wonderful beckoning them forth. For it can only be one thing: Bluff Depot! And sure enough, as they proceed, they begin to see the huge white shape of the depot emerging, and from atop its ten-foot brow a cleverly positioned biscuit tin is reflecting the sun at them.

At last arrived, on this day of 23 February they tear upon the food supplies and give thanks to their old comrade Ernest Joyce. Joyce's trip means that instead of just the pemmican, pemmican and a little more pemmican that they had been expecting, they suddenly find nothing less than eggs, cakes, gingerbread, crystallised fruit, even a fresh saddle of roast boiled mutton from the ship, Carlsbad plums and, most welcome of all, a full plum pudding! Like ravenous wolves on baby chickens, the four men take enormous bites of these prized foods and gulp it all down in massive chunks, trying to ease the hunger pains that have been with them now for months.

'Good old Joyce,' the exhausted but elated Wild writes in his diary.[36]

But careful . . .

Warned by Scott and Wilson's experience on the *Discovery* expedition of what happens when one overeats after a period of starvation, Shackleton advises the others not to overdo it. In the end, however, they all ignore the warnings and gorge themselves, meaning that all four of them are reduced to lying, gasping, in their sleeping bags for many an hour thereafter, four anacondas that have swallowed a pig each and must try vainly to digest it all.

Though their immediate danger of starving to death has passed, what has not is the enormous distance they have to cover in the very limited time that remains before *Nimrod* will have to leave to avoid being frozen into the ice for another year. Even now that things are looking up, a blizzard of such ferocity has hit that they must stay in their tents – Marshall with Wild, Shackleton with Adams – for another day before getting moving. Marshall, at least, is glad of it. Of them all, he is the one who has suffered most from the overeating the day before, and his diarrhoea is severe. Beyond that, he has been feeling so poorly over the previous weeks, so thoroughly run down and exhausted, that for the next 24 hours he barely moves from his sleeping bag, until the blizzard abates and they are on their way once more.

On 25 February, though they get away all right, after lunch Marshall grunts that he simply cannot walk a foot further. No matter that the worst of the journey is now well behind them, that they have moved to within two days' march of Hut Point and safety. The truth of it is that Marshall is physically finished. On this afternoon, he sinks to the snow, and no amount of coaxing or cajoling can get him to move again. All they can do is get him into a tent and try to keep him warm. Collapsing in these climes is problematic at the best of times, and Shackleton – who is not without sympathy, given that Marshall's experience is similar to his own on the *Discovery* expedition – is left with a hard decision. Whatever he is going to do, it will have to be done quickly, and so Shackleton decides.

They will leave Adams here to care for Marshall, with most of the food and supplies, while he and Wild make a mad dash for Hut Point both to get *Nimrod* to stay long enough that they won't have to spend another wretched winter there – an unthinkable option – and to get help, so that Marshall and Adams can be rescued. Carrying a prismatic compass, sleeping bags and food for but one meal, they set off in the late afternoon of 28 February.

And yes, Shackleton and Wild are both exhausted, both debilitated after four solid, gut-busting months of sledging, much of it on starvation rations, but the two 35-year-olds are not without some advantages. It is Wild's strong view, based on his long experience, that while a young man would likely best a man of 30 to 40 years in a short and strenuous contest such as a soccer game or boxing bout, when it comes to an exercise lasting days, weeks and months of solid toil, then 'the older man invariably beats the youngster'.[37] And sure enough, after a hard slog that includes finally discarding the sledge to make faster progress across the ice, and trying to compensate for Wild's fast-failing feet, at ten o'clock that night they finally make it to Hut Point to find . . . no *Nimrod* in the harbour and nary a soul in the hut!

Not in all of their struggles to this point, in all of their yearnings to arrive, had they *ever* imagined arriving 'in such a cheerless fashion'.[38]

However, inside the hut they find a letter, telling them that *Nimrod* was there over a week earlier and that they have on board the Edgeworth David Party, who successfully reached the South Magnetic Pole. Though it is too dangerous to have *Nimrod* moored close by due to the difficult ice and sea conditions, they would anchor in the lee of the Glacier Tongue until 26 February in the hope that Shackleton and his party would soon turn up.[39]

This is a problem. For it is now 28 February. Are they really, *now*, forsaken here? Shackleton is perplexed; his premature abandonment, if that's what it is, appears to directly contravene what he believes were his orders: 'If we had not returned by 25 February, a party was to be landed at Hut Point, with a team of dogs, and on March 1 a search-party was to go south.'[40] Ice conditions permitting, *Nimrod* was meant to remain in the vicinity until 10 March, in the event they were quickly found. Based on this, Shackleton's expectations were threefold: there would be men and food in the hut, a lookout stationed at Observation Hill, behind Hut Point, and *Nimrod* on hand until 10 March to fetch them off.

And yet it appears that, with the Southern Party having been out for 120 days, with food for only 91 days, come 25 February Captain

Evans has for the moment overruled Shackleton's instructions for Murray to supply Hut Point and drop off a relief party.

Meanwhile, aboard *Nimrod*, the protests of the Shackleton faithful, including Mackay and particularly Brocklehurst, grow louder with each passing hour. Brocklehurst writes in his diary, 'We are beginning to dislike [Captain Evans's] attitude. He considers himself too important and it looks as if he is going to make himself head of the Expedition.'[41]

In addition to their frustration with Evans is the fact that the proposed relief party to be headed by Mawson is only composed of colonials – nary a Brit in sight. Outrage. Meanwhile, this international conflict disguises the fact that no southern search party has been launched, no lookout established on Observation Hill, no supply of the *Discovery* hut accomplished. Rather, *Nimrod*, under Evans's command, has languished, inert, near the Glacier Tongue. Though at Hut Point there has been a little food left for the missing men – onions, plum pudding, biscuits, together with a Primus lamp and a little oil – there has certainly been no search party. And nor has anyone thought to leave them sleeping bags.

Yet Shackleton, a British bulldog on two legs, is simply not the type to resign. Just as it goes dark, a short time after they arrive, Wild and Shackleton try in vain to ignite the Magnetic Hut, an outbuilding of the main hut. It is their hope that the resulting blaze, together with the Union Jack they have put on the hill, will serve as beacons of hope – as signs that they are ruddy well alive and expect to be picked up by *Nimrod*, if indeed she has stayed beyond the 26 February deadline and is still in the area. Surely they would have given them another few days' leeway?

And even when the hut refuses to burn in the first instance, there is no capitulation from Shackleton. He and Wild simply pass an extremely cold, uncomfortable night sitting up with a piece of roofing felt tied tightly around them in a futile attempt to get warm, and then in the morning they try again.

This time, mercifully, the hut, she blazes.

And sure enough, almost as if it is the phantom of a ship long-ago lost coming to them through the mists of time, just as their desperation is nearing its blackest ebb, *Nimrod*'s crow's nest suddenly appears atop the fog that lies low above the water.

'No happier sight ever met the eyes of man,' Frank Wild records of his vision of the ship.[42] And perhaps they are inordinately lucky the ship is still there? But, on the other hand, Frank Wild always believes in helping luck along the way, and before their extraordinary trek began he secretly sewed a bean into Shackleton's trouser bottoms, in the Irish tradition that it would bring him good fortune.

And good fortune it is, for the ship is in fact returning to Hut Point to drop off Mawson and the wintering party that will begin the search for what would likely be the Southern Party's miserably frozen cadavers somewhere out there. Perhaps it is prudent not to tell Shackleton this right now . . .

Yet now *Nimrod* approaches Hut Point to see two wild men on top of the hill frantically waving the Union Jack. As recorded by Mackay:

[W]e heard a cheerful yell and a clatter of feet on the deck above. We all tumbled out and rushed for'ard to the fo'c'sle head . . . There was a crowd there some saying that they had seen a flash signal, and some a figure besides Vince's Cross.[43] Soon we could make out two figures plainly and the excitement was tremendous. We all danced about and cheered and waved our arms, and then fell to punching each other.[44]

A boat manned by Armytage, Mackay and Mawson is quickly lowered away and, after picking up the two men, is now back within shouting distance of *Nimrod*. It is Chief Officer Davis who asks the question on behalf of the ship, shouting out, 'Are you all well? Where are the other two?'

'We left Marshall and Adams twenty miles back,' comes the reply. 'They're all right!'[45]

All within earshot recognise Shackleton's voice, meaning the other wild man – all dirt and beard and hair – must be Frank Wild. And then one of the crew, forgetting himself a little but unable to resist asking the other question they have all been wondering, shouts out, 'Did you get to the Pole, sir?'

'No,' says Shackleton, in words he has surely been aching to say for weeks, and intends to say for *years* more, 'but we got within ninety-seven miles of it!'[46]

The mightily relieved Captain Evans soon welcomes both men on board. A hot bath is run in the engine room for them, and they are offered a special box of delicacies from Fortnum & Mason that has been kept for this specific occasion. Neither man, however, wants anything so fancy. What their bodies crave is warm fat and lots of it, and while they sit there in the smoke-filled wardroom and tell some of their story, a small and smoking mountain of piping-hot bacon and fried bread is brought to them from the galley. They consume it at a great rate before – like a couple of frozen Oliver Twists – they call for still 'more!'. All of the ship's company is of course delighted at their survival, but, as Davis would later recount, 'To Shackleton these welcome diversions seemed only an interlude, for he was merely waiting for a sledge to be equipped before setting out again to bring in the two men he had left behind.'[47]

And no matter how much Captain Evans implores Shackleton to let any of a dozen of his own men from the ship lead the relief party, the exhausted leader will have none of it. Out of the question, Captain. For the instant the freshly provisioned sledge is ready, the expedition leader so newly and miraculously saved from the polar wilderness girds his loins, fixes his harness and heads out into it once more. In the company of Mawson, Mackay and one other, he is to retrieve the men he was obliged to leave behind.

Watching them go, just three hours after the initial rescue, Frank

Wild is standing on the bridge beside Captain Evans. A short time earlier, Shackleton asked Wild if he would go back for the men. Wild had told Shackleton straight, 'Yes, if you stay aboard as there is no need for the two of us.'[48]

A fair point, by any measure, but Shackleton – who just like Wild had not slept for the previous 52 hours – replied with an irrefutable point of his own: 'I *must* go.' And so he now does, with the mood on the ship one of deepest admiration for their leader, best expressed by Captain Evans, who remarks to Wild, 'Shackleton is a good goer, eh?'[49]

3 March 1909, Hut Point, Marshall is surely surprised

And in the end it is a close-run thing, but Shackleton, Mawson, Mackay and the fourth man, New Zealand crew member Michael Thomas McGillion, do indeed get to Adams and Marshall while they're both, mercifully, still alive, though both very hungry. (One can't help but wonder, under the circumstances, if, upon seeing Shackleton and Mawson as two of his rescuers, Marshall alters his assessment of the former as not having 'the guts of a louse'[50] and the latter as 'useless and objectionable, lacking in guts and manners'.[51]) As a matter of fact, after his long enforced rest followed by eating the precious food, Marshall is improved enough that he is even able to take his place pulling the sledge, and they all set off back to Hut Point in an exhausted state.

It is an extremely difficult journey, but after jettisoning most of their equipment – including one of the two sledges, the tent and the cooker – so as to be able to better negotiate the climb over to Hut Point, they arrive just before midnight. This time, they raise a signal by bursting open a tin of carbide, 'pump-shipping [urinating on it] and setting a light to it', and their aim is achieved.[52] The flare is spotted nine miles away at the Glacier Tongue by the lookout on *Nimrod*, and within a few hours the total expedition is at last reunited on board. Having marched over 100 miles in five days, and not having slept for the last 55 hours, the heroic Shackleton, promptly and deservedly, collapses in a wet heap.

March 1909, Southern Ocean, *Nimrod* sails home

And so, at 8 am on 4 March, now with all of their merry crew back on board and the winds abated, it is time to leave this frozen continent. Already, the icy hand of hand of winter is starting to tighten its grip, as the waters surrounding McMurdo Sound begin to freeze over. There is no time to spare. As *Nimrod* continues north up the coast of Ross Island, the bow and sides of the tiny ship are constantly buffeted by small chunks of ice three or four inches thick, some of which are just on the point of joining together solidly as the temperature falls, before the determined *Nimrod* once again splits them asunder. This time, Marshall need have no worry that Shackleton has 'not rubbed an ounce of paint off [*Nimrod*'s] sides',[53] for the ship loses far more than that as she ploughs forward, lurching only a little as she breaks through some of the thicker ice. In just a few hours, those on board can see the familiar landscape of the hills around Cape Royds, and they know they are within mere miles of their hut, which is soon within sight.

As they pass it, all of the men crowd onto the windy deck, and when they see the hut, standing a little forlorn and windswept in the far distance, they pause for a last look and then give a spontaneous, rousing three cheers. In the words of Shackleton:

> The hut was not exactly a palatial residence . . . but, on the other
> hand, it had been our home for a year that would always live in
> our memories . . . We watched the little hut fade away in the

distance with feelings almost of sadness, and there were few men aboard who did not cherish a hope that some day they would once more live strenuous days under the shadow of mighty Erebus.[54]

Shackleton, as a matter of fact, is already planning it. On the way back from their Pole attempt, while sharing a tent with Wild, the expedition leader asked him if he would be interested in making another attempt. If only he'd known, he might not have asked . . . For in fact, only a short time before, Wild had penned in his journal, 'This trip has completely cured me of any desire for further polar exploration, nothing will ever tempt me to face that awful glacier and terrible plateau again.'[55] And yet, so highly does he regard Shackleton, sitting there facing him, his jaw jutting forward as he awaits his answer, Wild replies without hesitation, 'Yes!'

Which is to the good. The problem they have now is that they have no sooner boarded *Nimrod* than they receive news from Captain Evans that Scott is preparing for his own next Antarctic expedition, which means . . . they must hold off for a couple of years. It might be possible for Great Britain to muster the resources to send one expedition to the South Pole but not two. 'That knocks us out, Frank,' Shackleton breathes to Wild, 'we *must* give Scott his chance first.'[56]

Ah, but there is another on board with them who is already making his own plans and is untroubled by news of Scott, for he intends to explore the possibilities of mounting an expedition on behalf of another nation: Australia. As they sail away, the original idea of Douglas Mawson to explore and chart 2000 miles of Antarctic coast west of Cape Adare – that region that lies directly below the southern shores of Australia – is beginning to crystallise.

The 26-year-old Mawson bears little resemblance to the ingénu who just over a year ago spent the majority of the outward journey seasick and supine in a lifeboat and was one of the most junior members of the shore party. This Mawson really has risen in the ranks to the point where he was the one selected to lead Shackleton's relief party, and to then accompany the great man to rescue his stricken comrades – and he stands astride *Nimrod*'s foredeck sniffing the Antarctic sea breeze with relish.

The three-week journey back to New Zealand barely provides the young scientist enough time to contemplate the magnitude of the accomplishments now attached to his name – first to scale Mt Erebus, first to get to the South Magnetic Pole and involved in the longest recorded unassisted sledge journey – not that this man of science is particularly interested in such accolades.

He has further learnt about the art of leading men from Shackleton, and how energy, selflessness and generosity of spirit are the keys to it. He has tasted leadership himself on the return leg of the South Magnetic Pole expedition, and the responsibility sat comfortably across his broad and capable shoulders. Above everything else, he has proved to himself that he has what it takes to prosper amid all the madness of Antarctic exploration – physically and, most importantly, mentally.

Mawson knows all too well that he is still not satisfied and won't be satisfied until he has achieved more in these parts. Since that day he sat atop Mt Erebus, observing along with his party that phenomenal sight of the shadow of the volcano cast long across 'the screen of low lying cloud like a Goliath's magic lantern show',[57] the feeling he has left something major undone has only grown.

Scientific endeavour aside – for it is now so much more than that – this strange and fascinating land is more than in his blood. The desire to return to this rarest of all lands, to explore the 2000 miles of coastline that lie ever untrodden and still unclaimed now resides deep in his marrow. It is odd, but, somehow, the further to the north they go, the more Mawson's mind returns to the south and the things he wishes to accomplish there.

Early March 1909, Oslo, Amundsen plans an expedition

At this same time, already in the far, *far* north, a handsome if weather-beaten 36-year-old Norwegian man by the name of Roald Amundsen is focusing his own thoughts on the even further north – in fact, on the North Pole itself. In many ways, his background is similar to that of Mawson, in that he is a curious combination of ambition, intelligence and physical prowess – while also possessed of an overwhelming belief that there is little the world can throw at him to which he is not equal.

Born and raised in Borge on the eastern coast of Norway, Amundsen comes from many generations of dashing seafarers on his father's side, giving him such a sense of adventure that, while growing up, he would frequently leave his bedroom window open during winter to toughen himself up for the terrible trials that he hoped awaited him. This was balanced a little by having a mother who was insistent that her notably accomplished fourth son would become a doctor instead. Amundsen bowed to her wishes while she was alive and began medical studies at Norway's University of Oslo, but as soon as his mother died when he was 21 the strapping young man – he is well over six foot tall, with a lean and powerful frame – headed off to sea.

Inspired by Fridtjof Nansen's feat of crossing Greenland in 1888, Amundsen visited Antarctica in 1897–99 on Belgium's *Belgica* expedition, where, after the ship had been frozen in, he was very impressed by how the American surgeon Frederick A. Cook worked so hard to keep them alive and sane through that terrible winter. And while so many of the others of that expedition had suffered during that time, and hated every moment of it, with Amundsen it had been the reverse. There was something about extreme conditions that he liked, nay, *loved*, and he had used the experience to focus on his long-held ambition to be the first man to get to the North Pole.

First, however, he needed to prove himself as an explorer and leader in his own right. From 1903 to 1906, in his tiny 70-foot square-sterned sloop *Gjøa*, he had succeeded in being the first to find and force the famed and fabled North-West Passage, managing to sail the boat, with his crew of six, right across the top of the world, from Oslo through the Atlantic and Arctic Oceans – pausing only to live for a time with a Netsilik Eskimo tribe, so he could study how they survived and even prospered in such extreme cold – into the Pacific Ocean and down to San Francisco, California, where the men were met with a hero's welcome.

On the basis of this success – after all, others had been trying to do it for no fewer than 300 years – the now legendary Amundsen was able to gather sponsors for the very project he is now focused on. On 9 February 1909, the Norwegian legislature passed a resolution that allowed the ship that had helped make Nansen famous, *Fram*, to be loaned to Amundsen for his expedition, while a sum of 75,000 Norwegian kroner (just over £4000) was granted for repairs and necessary alterations. The ship had the perfect pedigree for what Amundsen wanted to do now.

Late March 1909, New Zealand, Shackleton and his men have their homecoming

First, on 23 March 1909, *Nimrod* arrives in Stewart Island, just below the South Island of New Zealand, and two days later, amid great fanfare, she sails into the place where it all began: Lyttelton, New Zealand.

On arrival, thousands upon thousands of cheering people turn out to greet them, and the press pronounces them international heroes:

FARTHEST SOUTH
SHACKLETON'S MAGNIFICENT JOURNEY
WITHIN NINETY-SEVEN MILES OF POLE
TERRIBLE HARDSHIPS ENCOUNTERED
PROFESSOR DAVID AT MAGNETIC POLE[58]

Accolades for their remarkable achievements stream in from scientists and others from all over the world. Her Majesty Queen Alexandra relays her congratulations, as does King Edward VII, who cables Shackleton, 'I congratulate you and your comrades . . . on having succeeded in hoisting the Union Jack . . . within 100 miles of the South Pole and the Union Jack at the South Magnetic Pole.'[59]

The men are instructed not to talk to the press about the expedition as Shackleton has an exclusive agreement with the *Daily Mail*. Yet, after a year and a half away from civilisation, the adventurers do have one urgent question for the Fourth Estate. 'I say, who won the Burns–Johnson fight, eh?' is the first question posed by one of them to a journalist.[60] (The journalist tells him with wonder that the black American Jack Johnson absolutely thrashed the Canadian white man Tommy Burns so badly in front of 20,000 screaming fans in Sydney that, in the 14th round, the police themselves had to step into the ring to stop the fight.)

Within an hour of docking and after hurried farewells, a notably dishevelled Professor Edgeworth David (he is initially refused embarkation because customs staff think him an undesirable) is bound for Australia aboard the SS *Maheno*.

Meanwhile, the excitement over the collective achievements of the Shackleton expedition continues to grow. Shackleton's success is regarded as a reflection of the worth of the whole British race, with a writer for *The Sphere* newspaper opining that, 'So long as Englishmen are prepared to do this kind of thing, I do not think we need lie awake all night dreading the hostile advance of the "boys of the dachshund breed."'[61]

Spontaneous warm tributes to Shackleton immediately stream in to the *Daily Mail* from around the globe, most particularly from the English-speaking world, following syndicated news of his Antarctic adventure. 'The fascinating thing about Mr Shackleton's report is the story of the struggle rather than the results of the struggle,' waxes *The Globe* of New York. 'All of us feel loftier in our inner stature as we read how men like ourselves pushed on until the last biscuit was gone.'[62] Not forgetting the great strides forward that have been made for science, the *Daily Mail* declares that Shackleton's discovery of coal and limestone brings fresh evidence that not only was Antarctica once joined to South America and New Zealand, it also 'corroborates a theory that the moon represents a part of the Earth, torn off what is now the Pacific Ocean'. As to his exploration of the enormous polar tableland stretching all the way to the South Pole, this 'supports the view that Antarctica is a continent and not a mere collection of islands'.[63]

All of which acclaim leaves Captain Scott in a dashed ticklish position. Mustering public enthusiasm as needs must, that good man says:

I have not had time to look at Mr Shackleton's expedition in all its bearings, but there can be no doubt that most magnificent journeys have been made and that the work altogether has been conducted in a splendid manner. It appears that the Manchurian ponies, like the dogs in our own southern sledge trip, only helped in a portion of the journey. The really brilliant part appears to have been accomplished by the men themselves dragging their loads . . . In whatever measure that remaining distance [to the South Pole] is computed, it is for England to cover it![64]

There is great rejoicing at Shackleton's alma mater, Alleyn's College, Dulwich, where it so happens that Professor David's brother is the chaplain. A half-day holiday is declared, and every boy – rally, school! – subscribes a halfpenny towards a congratulatory telegram.

One of Shackleton's former masters, Mr William Escott, who is still at the school, fondly remembers the lad for the press:

> He never rose high in the school, or applied himself seriously to his books, but his merits were always recognized as being out of all proportion to his place in the form. He was considered rather delicate. He was always full of energy but could never put his nose to the grindstone – a rolling stone gathering no moss, but a lively and pleasant fellow.[65]

And, of course, Mrs Emily Shackleton at their residence in Edinburgh – where the Shackletons moved for his work with the Royal Scottish Geographical Society – is herself both thrilled and overwhelmed with hearty telegrams of congratulations. 'I am supremely happy to know of my husband's safety, for I have had no word of him for about a year,' she says.[66]

Not that the acclaim is universal, however, with Scott's man, Sir Clements Markham, weighing in with a casual cross-court backhand worthy of the tennis tournament that is all the rage these days, Wimbledon. 'A very wonderful performance,' he notes acerbically to the *Daily Mail*. 'That Lieutenant Shackleton could do so much in such a short time seems almost inexplicable.'[67]

If Sir Clements has anything to say about it – and he most certainly will – his man Scott will have the last word on the whole affair . . .

PART TWO

THREE
MEN GET
ORGANISED

Chapter Four

Australian Heroes

One of the oft-repeated questions for which I usually had a ready answer, at the conclusion of the [Nimrod] expedition was, 'Would you like to go to the Antarctic again?' In the first flush of the welcome home and for many months, during which the keen edge of pleasure under civilized conditions had not entirely worn away, I was inclined to reply with a somewhat emphatic negative. But, once more a man in the world of men, lulled in the easy repose of routine, and performing the ordinary duties of a workaday world, old emotions awakened, the grand sweet days returned in irresistible glamour, faraway 'voices' called . . .

Douglas Mawson, *The Home of the Blizzard*

30 March 1909 and three days thereafter, Sydney, home is the sailor

And there he is!

Despite squally weather, a large crowd, of whom a fair bulk are students from the University of Sydney, has been gathered at Circular Quay since the wee hours of the morning to welcome back their chosen hero of the British Antarctic Expedition. A wave of excitement rolls through them as they first recognise the familiar figure. Yes, there is no mistaking the distinctively tall man standing on deck, wearing his celebrated accoutrement, even if he does look a little thinner.

'I see you've got your old brown hat on!' one of the students calls out.

'How are you feeling?'

'Tip-top. Jolly well, thanks.'

'Find it cold here?'

'I find it jolly hot.'

'By gad he's energetic. David's fame is now magnetic!'[1]

Only a few hours later, Professor David – whom most, led by the press, have exuberantly mistaken for the expedition leader – is being traditionally welcomed to a special luncheon in his honour at the University of Sydney's magnificent Great Hall, the most venerable setting in an academic environment in all of Australia. No fewer than 600 enthusiastic students join together with their professors in the unbounded song of praise written in his honour, 'The Book of Exodus', sung to the tune of 'Waiting at the Church':

David has gone with little sling and stone;

Looking for Goliath at the Pole;

Living on candles and penguin marrow-bone,

Not to mention pyroxene and amphibole . . .[2]

In his own remarks to the throng, however, the Prof is not only gracious but also eager to deflect the glory away from himself towards a more worthy recipient. 'Just as Shackleton was the general leader, so,' he says, 'in all sincerity and without the pride that apes humility, I say that Mawson was the real leader and was the soul of our expedition to the magnetic pole. We really have in him an Australian Nansen, of infinite resource, splendid physique, astonishing indifference to frost.'[3]

The desire to honour the Prof goes far wider than the University of Sydney. For the sign outside the Town Hall a few days later, where the official reception is about to be held to welcome 'Tweedy' home, reads 'House full'. So pressing are the 3000-strong throng that Professor David's wife, Cara, not to mention Attorney General Billy Hughes, struggle to gain entry. (Hughes only manages to get in, *The Sydney Morning Herald* reports, 'by getting on the back of an alderman, who spoke through a keyhole to an attendant'.)[4]

'It was almost as difficult to get into this gathering as it was to work up to the magnetic pole,' jokes David, in reference to the fact that he himself stood outside the barred entrance for half an hour before someone recognised him.

Having welcomed him, Lord Mayor Allen Arthur Taylor and a jocular Billy Hughes join the crowd in a hearty round of 'For He's a Jolly Good Fellow'. And that he is, that he most certainly is! For now, Professor David again warms to the theme that most possesses him since returning.

'I would like to point out,' says the Prof, 'and I say it with great emphasis, that the magnetic pole was not discovered by myself, that it was not located by myself, but that it was fixed by that great scientific man Douglas Mawson.' *(Applause.)* 'He is a man Australia can be proud of, he was educated in New South Wales, was a pupil of old Fort Street School, and a shining light of Sydney University . . .'[5]

Not that the academic is being entirely honest, for all that. The Professor is also pleased to report that never once on their journey to the South Magnetic Pole did they have 'the slightest disagreement', bar that one minor moment when Dr Mackay expressed some slight disenchantment with Mawson, a good camp cook, having put sugar in their hoosh. Warm applause all round, and a vote of thanks given by the Lord Mayor saying he only wished he had booked the reception for the Domain, where they could have accommodated 30,000 and not the 3000 they have here.

April 1909, Sydney and Adelaide, all hail Mawson

Two weeks later, it is Mawson's turn to return to new-found fame (though little fortune, as Shackleton has not yet paid him). Once again, it begins with a special luncheon at the University of Sydney, this one in the company of the Prof. Another celebratory dinner is held at Mawson's alma mater, Fort Street, where the rather bemused geologist again finds himself lionised. Yet both these glorious occasions pale into insignificance against the welcome he receives in his adopted city of Adelaide.

Eyes right, and all hail the conquering hero!

Along with a bevy of University of Adelaide dignitaries, no fewer than 100 of Mawson's students amass on the central platform at Adelaide Railway Station to welcome home South Australia's newly adopted favourite son. Alighting from his carriage, Mawson is stunned to see the students rushing towards him, and before he can protest they have placed him on their shoulders and are chairing him towards a waiting truck.

Crowds of cheering students follow in the wake of the vehicle as it makes its way up North Terrace to the university union room, where another 200 or so undergraduates are waiting to give him 'the tiger' – their slang for a resounding cheer – before greeting him in song:

Raw feet, raw feet, down a hole,
Rough meat, rough meat, on the Pole;
Seal fat, seal fat, come and see,
Douglas Mawson, DSc![6]

Quite overcome and dumbfounded, Mawson thanks not only the crowd for their 'novel' welcome but also Providence for allowing him to return again to his old friends in Adelaide. 'After spending some time in the polar regions the heartiness of this welcome has made me feel quite warm and I should like some of the ice from the South to cool me,' he jokes, the crowd instantly breaking into yet further applause.[7] A tip-top fellow this Dr Mawson clearly is.

14 June 1909, London's Charing Cross Station, Shackleton and Scott have an odd meeting

There he is! When the great – oh yes, he is – Ernest Shackleton, his wife, Emily (who had travelled to Dover to greet him) and members of his expedition arrive at Charing Cross at precisely ten minutes past five on this delightfully balmy Monday afternoon, they are met by a large gathering of the press and 600 cheering supporters on the platform.

The first to shake Shackleton's hand and pat him on the back is his father, followed by his five sisters and two children, Raymond and Cicely, who all embrace him. Also among the throng are the president and other office bearers of the Royal Geographical Society, Captain Robert Henry Muirhead Collins, representative of the Australian Government, numerous dignitaries from the exploring community and one other person of great significance . . .

For there, a little to the edges and patiently waiting his turn to offer Shackleton a welcome home upon his triumphant return from the farthest reaches of the planet, is none other than Captain Robert Falcon Scott.

True, it was not that long ago, on learning of Shackleton's landing at McMurdo Sound, that Scott wrote a letter to the Royal Geographical Society secretary Keltie, saying that he would never associate with Shackleton again and even branding Shackleton 'a professed liar', but now, like so many others, Scott is irresistibly drawn to Shackleton's limelight.[8]

But his is a scientific, not personal, excitement, mind. As he wrote to his friend Major Darwin, president of the Royal Geographical Society, three months earlier, 'the private feeling incurred by past incidents cannot affect my judgement of his work. That excites my interest and admiration and to an extent that can scarcely be felt by those who have no experience of Polar difficulties.'[9]

One can but wonder at the emotions felt by Shackleton as he

graciously takes Scott's proffered hand, but he could be excused for feeling vindication for having been once referred to by Scott, in public, as 'our invalid'. Now, it is Scott who seeks an audience with *him*.

June and July 1909, London, Shackleton and Scott correspond

The following day, when an elaborate lunch is hosted by the Royal Societies Club in honour of Shackleton and his men, Scott is there again! Responding to president Lord Halsbury's rousing tribute, Shackleton rises to the occasion, doffs his cap to Scott and says, to murmurings of great approval, 'Every expedition that went out was a pioneer for another expedition.'[10]

All up, London's latest hero goes on, it was owing to the knowledge he gained under Captain Scott that he was able to push the British flag a little further south.

The relationship between the men is thus, if not quite repaired, at least a little patched up for public display. Still, it cannot have escaped Shackleton's attention that despite Scott's previous proprietorial air towards McMurdo Sound, he still has no compunction in thanking Shackleton for revealing there exists an accessible route to the South Pole in the form of the Beardmore Glacier, at the foot of which lies 'Shackleton's Gateway'.

Nor is Scott coy about it. In fact, at the legendarily exclusive Savage Club, in his speech after dinner in honour of Shackleton on 19 June, he concludes, 'All I have to do now is thank Mr Shackleton for so nobly showing the way.'[11] Scott also chooses to make reference to the fact that Shackleton's team was laid low by exhaustion, snow-blindness and dysentery, and 'their struggle onward must, it seemed to him, appear to every Englishman as grand'.

In his stride now, he goes on, 'Polar travel is not founded upon the desire for gain, but upon the desire for knowledge, and polar travellers above all things must be sportsmen. A true sportsman is not jealous of his record, or slow to praise those who surpassed it.' But to his main point. It is important, he notes, that the Pole must be conquered by an Englishman, and Scott has just the man in mind, an unsurprising selection. 'Personally,' he says, 'I am prepared and have been for the past two years, to go forth in search of that object.'[12]

Two weeks later, Scott even confides to Shackleton some of his own plans for making a second assault on the South Pole, writing to him in his tight, spare style, while adopting a tone that appears to acknowledge him for the first time as a genuine equal, one who has achieved a glory of his own:

> If as I understand it does not cut across any plans of your own, I propose to organise the expedition to the Ross Sea which as you know I have had so long in preparation so as to start next year . . .
>
> I am sure you will wish me success; but of course I should be glad to have your assurance that I am not disconcerting any plans of your own.[13]

Shackleton replies shortly thereafter, crisply but politely, that Scott's plans:

> will not interfere with any plans of mine. If I do any further exploration it will not be until I have heard news of your expedition, presuming that you start next year. I wish you every success in your endeavour to penetrate the ice and to land on King Edward VII's Land and to attain a high latitude from that base.[14]

If Scott and Shackleton have patched things up to the point where they can at least communicate, the man they both respect so much, Bill Wilson – the third member of their 1902–03 trek towards the South Pole – has no hesitation in writing a strong letter to Shackleton, as part of a process where he formally breaks off the friendship:

> I allow that you were in a very difficult position there you know. But I wished to God you had done anything in the whole world other than break the promise you had made, the very making of which showed that you allowed a right to Scott . . .
>
> But why in the name of fortune did you promise to do the second best thing and then do the very worst!
>
> You took Scott's job practically out of his hands against his wish and knowing that he has been hoping to finish it . . . Not one man in a thousand would have treated you [so well] as he has.[15]

Another man who cannot forgive is the redoubtable Sir Clements Markham, who regards Shackleton as something of a fraud, lionised now because 'the exaggerated praise of cleverly engineered newspaper articles raised him to the crest of a wave . . . above his chief'.[16]

Shackleton does not see it like that at all and hugely enjoys his fame – now at a level far beyond what it was when he returned from the *Discovery* expedition, and certainly now far beyond that of Scott himself.

Early August 1909, Broken Hill, Mawson returns to the heart of the red continent

It is an exceedingly odd thing to have left the all-white heart of a frozen continent and then just a few months later find yourself not far from the scorched red heart of another, but such are the times, and such is the life of Douglas Mawson.

For the young and now widely celebrated lecturer has no sooner resumed work at the University of Adelaide than he travels to Broken Hill to conduct geological research in the Barrier Ranges for his Doctorate of Science and to deliver a couple of lectures on the Shackleton expedition to the good citizens of that dusty town.

At the time of Mawson's visit, Francisca 'Paquita' Delprat and her sister Leintie are summer-holidaying in Broken Hill with their father, the BHP silver-mine general manager Guillaume Daniel Delprat. The two young women and Mawson are separately invited to dinner at the Boyds' residence, Mr Boyd being the underground manager of the BHP silver and lead mine in Broken Hill.

Well . . . hello!

Though not a man given to exclamation marks in either expression or emotions, Mawson is nevertheless extremely impressed with the gorgeous young Paquita from the first. Attractive, self-confident and cultured, she is Dutch-born and lived in Spain before arriving in Australia at the age of seven. At six feet tall, the 17-year-old with long, dark hair and alabaster skin is nothing if not arresting in appearance. What's more, educated in the sciences of chemistry, biology and particularly geology – which she has studied closely at her school of Tormore House in North Adelaide, in part because of her father's line of work – she is not only able to speak Mawson's language, which to the young geologist is no small thing, but also able to speak it in a delightfully alluring and exotic accent, with a lilt here, a tilt there and a *rrr*eally *rrr*iveting way of *rrr*olling her rrrrs.

Rrrravishing!

For her part, this is not the first time that Paquita has seen the tall, slim Mawson. On a misty day in Adelaide only a few weeks prior, his smile towards a friend down by the sporting fields of Adelaide University, where she is studying, caught the ingénue's attention.

Mawson, a man not known among his friends for great flights of passion, leaves that evening completely taken with the gorgeous young woman. And Paquita is all but equally smitten. He is clearly a man of pleasing aspect, who has a fine intellect, not to mention a certain fame to rival and even surpass that of her distinguished father. In this evening they have spent together, she has also more than confirmed the attractiveness of his most notable feature. As she would later describe it, 'He had the most wonderful smile . . . And he had a very, very fine big mouth and a smiling mouth – what do you call it? – *generous* mouth, you know? And he could really . . . he could twinkle, you know?'[17]

Early September 1909, Shetland Islands, news from the top of the world

It is only a single, brief telegram, with small, spare type, but it generates huge headlines in millions of copies of newspapers around the world:

EXPLORER COOK PLANTS THE STARS AND STRIPES
AT THE NORTH POLE
COOK REACHES THE TOP OF THE WORLD
AMERICAN FIRST TO TOUCH THE NORTH POLE
HUNTED BY ALL NATIONS FOR 400 YEARS[18]

Filed at Lerwick in the Shetland Islands on 2 September 1909, the telegram carries the staggering news that American explorer Dr Frederick A. Cook – he who first made his fame by virtually taking over the leadership of the *Belgica* a decade earlier – had, after a 'prolonged fight with frost and famine', reached the 'Great Nail' of the North on 21 April 1908. So difficult was the return journey, he says, that it took him a year to get back to his base in Annoatok,

Greenland, and a further five months to reach north Scotland!

The world at large is thrilled at the news that its top has been claimed, and yet, only a week after it breaks, *another* American explorer, Robert E. Peary, announces that *he* reached the pole on 6 April 1909.

COMMANDER PEARY ALSO REACHES NORTH POLE: DID NOT MEET COOK[19]

With the two explorers both having claimed the North Pole, the press is not long in inveigling that famed explorer Amundsen into the controversy. In response, the intrepid Norwegian maintains that the world is needlessly obsessed with such things, most particularly given that the North Pole is not to be found on terra firma in the first place. No, far more important, Amundsen says, is the contribution the explorers have made to *scientific* knowledge of the Arctic's geographical conditions. 'What work is left will be sufficient for all of us.'[20]

All of which said, Amundsen still enthusiastically supports the claim of his old friend, Cook. After what happened on the ice-bound *Belgica* over that terrible winter, Amundsen still feels he owes the doctor his life, and the two have established a friendship born of mutual respect that has lasted and grown through the years.

'No one doubts Peary,' comments Amundsen in a newspaper interview. 'Why doubt Cook? I know both Cook and Peary have been at the Pole. I am not anxious that anyone has been there because I am going there myself next year.'[21] He says elsewhere, 'The possible results for Dr Cook's achievements will have no influence on my projected expedition. I am not planning to reach the point of the pole. My trip will be for oceanographic investigation.'[22]

Against that, no sooner has Amundsen learnt of Cook's claim than he is, quietly, on the next train to Copenhagen, where he knows Cook is being feted by royalty. Amundsen wants to investigate whether or not his own dream is still alive. After the two have spoken, the Norwegian is more firmly convinced than ever that his dream of being the first man to the North Pole is now definitively dead, and he begins to conceive a new plan . . .

In the meantime, of particular interest to the polar exploring community is that only shortly after Peary makes his claim, rumours circulate that he is preparing afresh for an assault on the South Pole as well! *The New York Times* goes so far as to print a short article on page one – headlined 'PEARY TO SEEK SOUTH POLE?'[23] – claiming the explorer has ample furs, sledges and other equipment necessary for the expedition.

Bit by bit, the eyes of the polar exploring community have not only turned south, they have also begun to focus.

13 September 1909, London, the British Empire moves on the only bit of land on earth where the sun sets but once a year

On the day that Robert and Kathleen Scott's first child, Peter, is born – fulfilling Kathleen's long-held ambition to have a son to a great man – that man himself, Robert Falcon Scott, publicly announces his plans. He is going to try to finish what he started. He is going to mount another expedition to the bottom of the earth: 'The main object of the expedition is to reach the South Pole and secure for the British Empire the honour of that achievement.'[24]

Bravo. Bravo. *Bravo!*

Scott, says the president of the Royal Geographical Society, Leonard Darwin, will 'prove once again that the manhood of the nation is not dead, and that the characteristics of our ancestors, who won this great empire, still flourish amongst us'.[25]

It is clear that immortality and enduring honour will rest with the man and the country that gets there first, and the only remaining question is who will it be and which country will have the honour? In fact, there are many contenders from many nations, and Scott surveys them all with a slightly wounded air. After all, though the Antarctic continent is too blessed big to really claim in the name of the British Crown by simply planting a Union Jack upon one small part of it, his own and Shackleton's expeditions have covered an enormous amount of ground across it and it *feels* as if it is part of the British Empire, even if it is too cold, with too few obvious treasures, to formally colonise.

At the Shackleton dinner at which he spoke, Scott had stressed that point. The South Pole must be claimed by an Englishman, and Scott presented himself as just the man to 'go forth in search of that object'.[26]

And who are these others, apart from the possibility of Peary? From Germany, Lieutenant Wilhelm Filchner, an experienced campaigner, announces that not only will he make an attempt on getting to the South Pole but also he and his team will be the first to march right across the entire Antarctic continent, finishing in McMurdo Sound, while the Frenchman Jean-Baptiste Charcot and the Japanese explorer Lieutenant Nobu Shirase have their own plans. One who announces no plans at all is the famed Roald Amundsen – but he is known to be going to the North Pole, which is to the good.

Late September 1909, Australia, Mawson feels obliged to hide his true feelings

By this time, Mawson's attraction to Antarctica is slowly burgeoning into a full-blown love affair. Lying at the very heart of this love affair are the 2000 miles of largely unexplored Antarctica shoreline, 'the great span' of coast stretching east to west directly south of Australia, between Cape Adare, south of New Zealand, and

Gaussberg, to the south of the Indian Ocean. Like any other lover, Mawson longs to again catch a glimpse of his 'Land of Hope and Glory', to examine it and discern its exact nature. For in his mind, this whole region really might be like the great British patriotic song of that time:

> Land of Hope and Glory, Mother of the Free
> How shall we extol thee, who are born of thee?
> Wider still and wider shall thy bounds be set;
> God, who made thee mighty, make thee mightier yet,
> God, who made thee mighty, make thee mightier yet.

However, like many a love affair that is to stand the test of time, near its beginnings he still feels obliged to hide its true contours from passing observers. When frequently asked in the first weeks of being back home whether he might return to the Antarctic, Mawson replies with an *almost* emphatic 'No'.

The thing is, he is not yet quite ready to acknowledge to himself, let alone the world, the power of those feelings he experienced while down south. Now that he is returned to the world of mere mortal men and workaday life, though, now that he again has ample time to contemplate things, freed from the daily burden of merely surviving, again and again his feelings – like a whale regularly breaching the water's surface to blast out and suck in air – naturally return to those 'grand sweet days'.[27]

At first a whisper, soon a cry, the voices call:

> ... from the wilderness, the vast and Godlike spaces,
> The stark and sullen solitudes that sentinel the Pole.[28]

Mawson strongly believes that the natural focus of any Australian or Australasian – for he is thinking that New Zealand could also contribute – Antarctic expedition is the part of Antarctica that lies directly beneath the south coast of Australia. It is land that has remained unexplored since Dumont d'Urville named a small part of it some 70 years ago; it is land on which Australia, on behalf of the British Empire, should make good her rightful claim.

7 December 1909 and a week thereafter, from Adelaide to the seven seas, Mawson is on the move

It is a pleasant thing for Mawson to be on SS *Mongolia* leaving Port Adelaide for England. And it is not just the pleasant sea breeze, the bright sunshine or the lovely vista of the Adelaide Hills falling back behind. It is that, after long consideration, he is taking firm action to fulfil what has become a cherished dream.

With letters of introduction from Professor David, Mawson is ostensibly setting out for the Old Dart to meet prominent Antarctic explorers, including Scott, and their financial backers to assess the lie of the land. Whether he is to mount a purely Australian expedition or, more financially practical, join an already established explorer on his expedition remains to be seen. All Mawson is sure of is that he does want to get back to Antarctica, to that unexplored shore, as soon as possible – and that the best way to get south is to first go north, to England.

Strapped for money as he is – for Shackleton has still not paid him his wages from the *Nimrod* expedition – Mawson must travel second class, and yet he is fortunate to meet a couple of professors in first class, Warren and Berry, who inform him that Scott has asked Professor David to suggest a geologist for his forthcoming expedition. This sounds perfect. When the *Mongolia* breaks her journey in Fremantle, Mawson immediately cables Scott to arrange a meeting.

14 December 1909, Buckingham Palace ballroom, Shackleton kneels

It is the climactic moment in the life of the *Nimrod* expedition, even though the ship herself and members of that expedition have been back in Britain for nearly six months. For it is the day that many of the key members of the expedition are to be honoured with awards in an investiture in Buckingham Palace's grand ballroom.

Many of them find it odd to see Shackleton himself, whom they will always remember as a commanding figure covered in the polar regalia of Burberry trousers, balaclava and finnesko boots, completely covered in snow and ice to the point that not even his nose is showing, now attired in the full court dress of a single-breasted, black, silk and velvet coat with a stand collar, gauntlet cuffs, the right number of cut steel buttons in all the right places and black jacket with white-lined tails. With it go black britches, black silk stockings, black patent-leather shoes, a dark hat, a steel sword and a black scabbard. His white gloves and white bow tie complete the garb. He looks self-conscious and ill at ease, and for good reason. Within minutes, he will be knighted by none less than the British king.

The other members of the expedition, too, had been asked to turn up in court dress, but mercifully this strict requirement had been eased somewhat after it had been delicately explained to the Lord Chamberlain that many of the recipients simply would not have the wherewithal to muster court dress and it had been agreed they could turn up in 'blue suits'.[29]

There is little time to reflect on such things, for at just a few minutes before eleven o'clock an admiral of the fleet, under full sail, with all regalia billowing, strides into the room staring straight ahead, just a few seconds before the room is filled with the sound of blaring trumpets. And then there is His Majesty King Edward VII himself in the full uniform of a field marshal, at the head of members of his court, now walking forward to take his place upon the throne dais, beneath a velvet dome.

At the prompting of aides, members of the *Nimrod* expedition line up to receive from the king their Polar Medal, to recognise their sterling efforts. Their numbers do not include Douglas Mawson, as he is on the high seas, nor Edgeworth David, as he has been denied leave by the University of Sydney, meaning the only Australian team member there is Bertram Armytage. Oh so proudly, the fastidiously tidy 41-year-old from Victoria, educated at Geelong Grammar and Oxford, stands to attention as King Edward VII pins the coveted Polar Medal to his chest, right beside his other medals from the Boer War. It is undoubtedly the proudest moment of his life.

And now it is Shackleton's turn.

On knees still hurting a little from his trials in Antarctica, Shackleton kneels before His Majesty, who takes his silver sword and lightly touches him first on the right shoulder and then on the left, at which point the polar explorer lightly kisses the sovereign on the back of the hand. And then . . .

Arise, Sir Ernest.

Sir Ernest Shackleton does so, before, as previously instructed, backing away from the king so as not to turn his back on the sovereign. It is, to this point, the crowning achievement of Sir Ernest's life – bestowed an honour by His Majesty not even accorded to Captain Robert Falcon Scott.

Early January 1910, Scott's offices in London, some key recruits are accepted

Have you heard? Scott is off to the South Pole again, and he is looking for recruits! When word circulates within and without the international polar fraternity that Scott is up for a new expedition, over 8000[30] applicants are keen for a 'start' in the southern 'show'.[31]

The hub for all the recruiting activity is Scott's expedition headquarters at 38 Victoria Street, London, halfway between Westminster Abbey and Victoria Station, where Scott himself is meant to occupy the largest room – but that is only nominally. For if not in the secretary's office wading through what practically amounts to a snow cairn of applications, as often as not he is to be found elsewhere, in deep conversation with the providores of one patent foodstuff or another.

Meanwhile, in another room nearby, scientists sit cross-legged hearing out inventors of newfangled appliances – see how this stove runs on virtually no fuel? – while in yet another room stands an extremely sturdy, rough sort of Welsh cove sorting out all the sledge gear. Oh, do be careful on your way out that you don't tread on that there *Discovery* sledge with your great big clod-hoppers! Through it all, there is a constant scattered flotilla of naval officers coming in and out of the offices, gathering stores and depositing them in colour-coded three-ply Venesta cases.

Scott's first and most crucial appointment is the chief scientist, his best friend, Edward 'Bill' Wilson, who almost eight years earlier had been with Scott and Shackleton when they made their first major push towards the South Pole. The 38-year-old Wilson is a man for all seasons, and most particularly winter: an artist, a doctor, a zoologist, a proved performer in polar climes who has Scott's complete confidence. Together, they know precisely the kind of man to sign up, as well as who to avoid. They want men who will prosper in such ferociously testing terrain, rather than wither. And they need a lot of them for this major expedition. No fewer than 65 will have to be recruited, of whom 31 are to be left behind after their ship, *Terra Nova* – one of the two rescue ships of *Discovery* back in 1904 – returns to lower latitudes of sunnier disposition.

While Wilson appoints the scientists, Scott sets about recruiting the rest of the crew. Together, they decide to accept the applications of five trusted members of Scott's previous expedition on *Discovery*.

Scott knows well the virtues of petty officers Thomas Williamson, William Heald and Thomas Crean and is happy to have them, together with, most particularly, Chief Stoker William Lashly and Petty Officer 'Taffy' Evans.

Six years before, both Lashly and Taffy Evans were with Scott when he sledged up the Ferrar Glacier and onto the Polar Plateau, hauling west across Victoria Land into the unknown for 17 days, and, almost like wartime comrades, there remains a great bond between them. Scott recorded shortly afterwards:

> Evans was a man of Herculean strength, very long in the arm with splendidly developed muscles . . . Lashly had been a teetotaller and a non-smoker all his life, and was never in anything but the hardest condition . . . With these two men behind me our sledge seemed to become a living thing, and the days of slow progress were numbered.[32]

Meanwhile, another Evans, Lieutenant Edward Ratcliffe Garth Russell 'Teddy' Evans – who first went south on SY *Morning*, which left to resupply *Discovery* in December 1902, and again a year later on a relief voyage to evacuate Scott's party if *Discovery* could not be freed from the ice – has been in the process of planning his own Antarctic expedition. With support from Sir Clements Markham, he approaches and is accepted by Scott as his second in command.[33] For Evans, a qualified navigating officer and of excellent physical fitness – with a 'wildly beautiful' wife, Hilda, who is full of ambition for him – it has not been an easy decision to fold his own plans into Scott's, but the lure of being on such an expedition, on such a patriotic venture, is finally impossible to resist.

In terms of the scientific make-up of the expedition, Wilson decides on three geologists, of whom two are Australians: Griffith Taylor[34] and Frank Debenham, the latter being another student of

Professor Edgeworth David's, who had in fact been recommended to Scott by Mawson. The third is the redoubtable Englishman Raymond Priestley, who, along with Edgeworth David and Murray, made many geological, animal and plant discoveries in the land and lakes around Cape Royds while on the *Nimrod* expedition and went to Australia thereafter to work with the Prof some more. Canadian Charles 'Silas' Wright is selected as the physicist along with George Simpson from the Indian Meteorological Service and 28-year-old naval surgeon turned parasitologist Edward Atkinson, who will be one of the expedition's doctors.

Two non-scientific officers are selected: Bernard Day, the mechanic who worked on the motor vehicle on the *Nimrod* expedition, and Apsley Cherry-Garrard, graduate of Christ Church, Oxford, where he read Classics and Modern History. Initially, the short-sighted Cherry-Garrard is rejected, despite stumping up £1000. However, when he suggests to an impressed Scott that the expedition team can keep the money regardless, the 24-year-old is re-interviewed at expedition headquarters and included as zoological assistant to Wilson. The balance of officers is made up of Royal Naval personnel.

Another significant signing is the enigmatic Cecil Meares, a man who had become fluent in many languages when employed as a British spy, has travelled all over Russia and is familiar with its ways and people. A man's man, an adventurer with tousled hair, Meares is soon despatched to deepest, darkest eastern Russia to make the critical purchases of the expedition sledge dogs and – more problematically – the ponies.

Without any expertise at all in ponies, Meares must at the outset rely on the one specific instruction Scott has given him as to what kind he wants – as on this point, 'the Owner', as Scott is referred to by his men, is most insistent. He wants ponies with *white* coats. Shackleton clearly stated in his account of the *Nimrod* expedition, *The Heart of the Antarctic*, that while his white ponies were the least tractable, they did prove the most hardy.[35] And so that is exactly the kind that Scott wants.

From the beginning, Scott is also most particular about the fact that, though he is planning a multi-pronged attack on the Pole involving motor sledges, dogs, ponies and man-hauling, there will be a hierarchy in operation. Scott, like Shackleton, plans to test the motor sledges in Antarctica by transporting cargo from ship to shore, and then in the late summer, all being well and ice conditions permitting, they will greatly assist in the establishment of depots as far south as possible. The following spring, Scott hopes to use them to transport the Pole Party and supplies all the way across the Great Ice Barrier surface to the foot of the Beardmore Glacier.

Now, should the motors break down at some point crossing the Barrier – and, judging by their past performances, that seems more than likely – the ponies, assisted by the dogs, would completely take over hauling the sledges to the bottom of the glacier. At this point, Scott is sure, based on Shackleton's experience, they would be useless in trying to get *up* the glacier. So, there at the foot of the glacier, the ponies would be slaughtered and a proportion of their meat cached in a depot to be consumed on the return journey. The important thing, though, is to have *enough* ponies. Shackleton made do with four, and on his return to New Zealand had been quoted in the press saying that getting to the Pole was simply a matter of having more ponies and more provisions – and Scott had taken note.[36]

As for the dogs, Scott has no stomach for doing the same to them. Based on his previous experience during the *Discovery* expedition, he regards them as unreliable and does not think they can negotiate uneven surfaces over any great distance and go all the way to the Pole – certainly not without being driven to death.

As a navy man, Scott possesses limited experience in handling and driving a pack of dogs. Yes, with encouragement from Nansen he will reluctantly include 33 of the canines in his plans, but he does not plan to slaughter them like the ponies or use the weakening ones to feed the stronger ones, as that would be way too cruel. Much better to preserve the lives of the dogs and have them return home safely than use them as 'pawns in the game, from which the best value is to be got regardless of their lives'.[37] No, the dogs will stop at the foot of the glacier and head back to Winter Quarters, ready to bring fresh supplies out to the depots in a few weeks' time and afterwards come out again to help the South Pole Party get back.

Beyond all other considerations, the truth of it is that Scott is a sledging purist who simply does not believe the use of ponies or dogs on the Polar Plateau quite . . . *proper*. He really does believe in man-hauling, pure and simple. For him, it is almost a philosophical thing, and he makes no apology for it. He later writes:

> One cannot contemplate the murder of animals which possess such intelligence and individuality, which frequently having such endearing qualities, and which very possibly one has learnt to regard as friends and companions . . .
>
> In my mind no journey ever made with dogs can approach the height of that fine conception which is realised when a party of men go forth to face hardships, dangers, and difficulties with their own unaided efforts, and by days and weeks of hard physical labour succeed in solving some problem of the great unknown. Surely in this case the conquest is more nobly and splendidly won . . .[38]

This view is very much in keeping with that of his mentor Sir Clements Markham, who is a great believer in the virtues of propulsion by the pure, magnificent power of their bodies alone. According to Sir Clements, an estimated three-month march between McMurdo Sound and the South Magnetic Pole, for example, could easily be covered 'without the cruelty of killing a team of dogs by overwork and starvation'.[39] No, Sir Clements has always been firm: 'Nothing has been done with them to be compared with what men have achieved without dogs.'[40]

For now, Scott will have to prepare a complex set of contingency plans should one of the modes of transport fail on the South Pole journey, particularly the motors, as they will be hauling such a large proportion of their supplies.

Scott also hires one Victor Lindsay Arbuthnot Campbell, a straight-backed 35-year-old naval officer from Brighton with a long, lean face and an air of quiet authority, whose job it will be to command a small party making a separate landing on an unexplored part of King Edward VII Land to map it.

Mid-January 1910, London, Douglas Mawson arrives, anxious to meet Scott

For a man such as Mawson, who left English shores at the age of two, over a quarter-century earlier, it is wonderful to return, a scientist on the ascent, to the land of his birth, to experience first-hand the splendour, grandeur and sheer excitement of London, the largest city in the world, the capital of the British Empire.

Though he does very little sightseeing, he does allow his old friend from *Nimrod*, John King Davis, to show him around the likes of the Tower of London and, particularly, Madame Tussauds, where they delight in viewing the tableau of *Sir* Ernest Shackleton accompanied by Adams, Marshall and Wild at his farthest south, admiring the detail of Shackleton's face and the all-too-familiar grey and blizzarding background landscape.

While Mawson also takes time to look up relatives outside London and visit academics in Cambridge and Oxford, he is here on business Antarctic and does not tarry long before arranging his meeting with Scott.

When the two meet at Scott's offices just north of the Thames, confusion competes for airspace with the smoke plume issuing from Scott's pipe. After receiving Professor David's cable recommending Dr Mawson, and then the cable from Mawson himself requesting a meeting, Scott immediately assumed that the Australian wanted what all of the other thousands of men who have contacted him in recent weeks want: to join him on his *Terra Nova* expedition to the South Pole. The difference in this case, as Scott makes clear to Dr Mawson from the first – his words cutting through the hustle and bustle of activity outside his office door – is that he would be delighted to have him. As a matter of fact, he very nearly *insists* upon it.

As a keen student of the *Nimrod* expedition, Scott, like the rest of the polar community, is well aware of the Australian's extraordinary all-round capabilities. Professor David has heaped garlands of praise upon Mawson's broad shoulders, his high opinion confirmed by the writings of Ernest Shackleton, who has documented the young Australian geologist's leading role on the record-breaking man-haul to conquer the South Magnetic Pole, among other things.

As Scott is a man who believes in the purity of man-hauling, Mawson's ability in this department – together with his scientific acumen and obviously good character – is highly desirable. In fact, so keen is Scott to have Mawson commit to him that on the spot he not only guarantees he will be a member of the final party that marches to the South Pole but also offers to pay him handsomely for the privilege – £800 for the two years Mawson will be away is not an inconsiderable sum, when the average wage at the time is just £3 per week. The one thing that Scott cannot offer him is the chief scientist's position, as that has already been taken by Bill Wilson.

In response, Mawson stuns Scott by making it clear that he has no interest in any 'boy's own adventure' attempt on the South Pole; it holds little vocational interest for him at all. No, Captain Scott, he has something else in mind, entirely. 'Have you thought of exploring the uncharted coast west of Cape Adare?' Mawson asks. No, Scott has not.[41]

Mawson follows up with a rather impassioned exposition of so doing, pointing out that since the days when Dumont d'Urville and Charles Wilkes spotted and charted odd wisps of that coast, *no one* has even seen it, and to this day no one has set foot on it. And it is high time! And so to the point of the exercise for the Australian. 'I'll join you,' Mawson tells him, 'if you'll land me and a party of three on that coast.'[42]

If Mawson and his small party could be left there, they would independently undertake valuable scientific research and geographical reconnaissance along the largely unexplored coast – an area that is 'crying out' for investigation. Back in 1899, Borchgrevink and his men established that Cape Adare, with its relatively accessible landing sites and huge penguin rookeries, was a good place to make a base for the winter, despite its difficult situation for access to the interior. And right next to such a base, you have one of the greatest ranges of rocky coast on the Antarctic continent. Geological studies already undertaken at its eastern and western limits indicate that a connection once must have existed with Australia between Cape Adare on the one side and Gaussberg on the other. The magnetic pole is close to the coast inland of Cape Adare,[43] allowing further magnetic observations, and the area's meteorology and biology essentially remain unexamined. Mawson goes on, his words tumbling forth in his passion for the project and the need to make Scott see its virtues.

In addition to adding to the body of Antarctic knowledge, the region may well open up economic opportunities for the Empire – through the potential discovery of viable deposits of coal and minerals as well as exploitation of its ocean's resources.

Scott acknowledges it to be an interesting idea . . . but at the conclusion of the three-hour meeting he has made no commitment to take Mawson and a small party to Cape Adare. Nevertheless, he has pressed Mawson to allow his name to be put down as a member of the expedition, to be confirmed by the Australian within three weeks.

In a second meeting, however, which includes Scott's right-hand-man Bill Wilson, it is not long before an impasse is reached. Scott is very keen for Mawson to come, but the Australian is equally insistent that he will not do so unless his plan for a Coastal Party is agreed upon. Scott, who has pledged to establish bases at both McMurdo Sound and King Edward VII Land, feels fully committed and simply will not agree to Mawson's request. For one thing, he is most intent on getting to the South Pole, and, as he explains with some firmness, bordering on irritation, dropping a secondary group at Cape Adare will be a dashed distraction, don't you see?

There seems to be only one way to proceed, and yet when Mawson floats the possibility of mounting his own expedition, Scott bridles. Why, don't you know, it has always been Scott's intention to explore the coast west of Cape Adare, and he has now more or less set his mind to 'picking the plums' out of that area when *Terra Nova* returns to pick up his expedition.

Well then, Mawson tells Scott, if he cannot be landed where he wants, the only capacity in which he would have considered enlisting was as chief scientist, but as Bill Wilson already fills that position, he will not 'henceforth accept a post on the expedition'.[44]

Despite the fact that Wilson appears to be the very roadblock that keeps Mawson from joining the expedition, the English scientist comes out of the meeting feeling positive, recording in a subsequent letter to Professor Edgeworth David, 'We both of us really liked what we saw of Mawson – he is obviously capable and keen on his work.'[45] Yet Mawson does not return the compliment and is likely the only man ever to have recorded a negative thought about the all-but-universally popular Wilson, when he writes unambiguously in his diary, 'I did not like Dr Wilson.'[46]

But, in the meantime, surely, old bean, they can keep talking? With this in mind, on Wednesday 26 January Scott invites Mawson for dinner at his fashionable, albeit small, Georgian terrace at

174 Buckingham Palace Road so they can continue to discuss it, and . . .

And so this, then, is Kathleen Scott. An alluring and artistic woman, as charismatic as she is independent, Kathleen is attracted to men of power and intellect. Her close friends include George Bernard Shaw, James Barrie, Max Beerbohm and Henry James, while the great French sculptor Auguste Rodin (her one-time teacher, and admirer of her sculptures) attended her wedding to Scott. These famous men are, in turn, attracted to her candour, generosity, loyalty and optimism, as well as, most likely, her flirtatiousness.

Mawson immediately joins the ranks of Mrs Scott's ardent admirers, but still he refuses to commit to the *Terra Nova* expedition unless her husband agrees to take him to Cape Adare. And still Scott does not agree. Mawson expresses his frustration in a letter to famed British geologist Sir Archibald Geikie:

> This area is crying out for investigation. It offers the greatest range of rocky coastline anywhere obtainable on the Antarctic Continent, the cliff exposures cross the strike of the older rocky complex; it is here a connection must one-time have been effected with Australia . . . and it is an almost unknown coast for meteorology and biology. In my opinion it is the pick of the Antarctic for scientific investigation and I deplore Capt Scott's inability to include part of it in his programme.[47]

Bit by bit, Mawson comes to the conclusion that the only way he can achieve what he wants is to undertake his own Australian expedition – a Herculean task in terms of preparation, but he has done the work of Hercules before in the Antarctic, and there now appears to be no other choice.

Who, in England, could most help him to mount such a venture if not Scott? Of course, there could only be one man. None other than *Sir*, if you please, Ernest Shackleton . . .

At this point, Shackleton is on a speaking tour of Europe, still trying to pay the outstanding bills from the *Nimrod* venture. (He had hoped that the sales of *The Heart of the Antarctic* would wipe out a lot of that debt, but, sadly for him, all of the excitement over Scott's announcement that he was heading for the South Pole made his own account rather like old news. Yes, he got close, but Scott, well, he was going to finish the job.)

As it happens, Shackleton and Mawson have already been in touch.

'ON NO ACCOUNT SEE SCOTT TILL I RETURN,' Shackleton had rather presumptuously cabled him from Europe.[48] Mawson had no qualms about ignoring that directive because, firstly, Shackleton is no longer quite 'the Boss' he was, at least not to Mawson, plus the Australian has no interest in getting personally involved in the Shackleton versus Scott rivalry.

Still, when Shackleton returns to England at the conclusion of the Continental leg of his lecture tour, Mawson is earnestly there waiting for him on the docks at Plymouth. Three years earlier, of course, when Shackleton's ship pulled into Adelaide, it was Mawson who requested to go on board to have an audience with him. Now, it is Shackleton, all hustle and bustle and hail-fellow-well-met, who is quick to come off the ship so he and Mawson can travel back to London together on the train and have time to talk.

It is odd for Mawson to compare the Shackleton of Antarctica that he knew with the figure that sits before him now, as outside the train window the English countryside flies backwards through the night. Shackleton of the Antarctic had been all Burberry, boots and ice forming on his whiskers. But this one, *Sir* Ernest Shackleton, is besuited, polished and groomed, as befitting a gentleman who has been appearing before large audiences.

He remains the same old Shackles underneath, however, with the same charisma and gregarious nature, the same restlessness to be off on other adventures. The Anglo-Irishman's head is awhirl with get-rich-quick schemes, as a consequence of one too many coffee-house conversations in Budapest. According to Shackleton, Hungary's version of Lasseter's Reef lies just around the next pass, old chum, if only he can organise to get the mining rights to it.[49] It could be the answer to Shackleton's ongoing financial woes, for, despite his great fame now, and the fact that the British Parliament has granted him £20,000 to settle his many debts, he is still a long way from satisfying his creditors.

But to the business at hand, the thing that Mawson's head is awhirl with: a journey to Antarctica, with a main base established at Cape Adare. Mawson is delighted with Shackleton's response. 'You ought to go yourself! I could get you support.'[50]

Typical Shackleton. If Scott is blocking you on a matter Antarctic, well, dear boy, just do it anyway. And Shackleton knows just the person who can help Mawson to do it. Why . . . Shackleton himself! 'Australia helped me on my south polar expedition in 1907,' says he, '[so] let me be the first to assist you in England . . .'[51]

In equally typical generous fashion, Shackleton offers Mawson space in his own offices at 9 Lower Regent Street in downtown London to get the English end of the expedition organised – an offer that Mawson is quick to accept. And, true to his word, it doesn't take long for Shackleton to get his eye back in – working all the old angles and contacts to raise funds for a fresh expedition.

The most important breakthrough comes after Shackleton arranges for Mawson to travel south to Plymouth to visit his good friend and noted steel industrialist Gerald Lysaght, a keen yachtsman who, out of friendship for Shackleton and eagerness to have some part of such a great venture, generously supported the *Nimrod* expedition. Mawson spends five hours alone with the potential benefactor explaining details of the expedition, and Lysaght soaks it all up. So well does it all go, in fact, that when Shackleton places a follow-up call the next day, the result is the promise of £10,000 towards their expedition. This could really happen!

Not surprisingly, seeing just how much money could be collected, Shackleton's enthusiasm grows from there, and not long afterwards he comes into the offices early one morning to make a peremptory announcement, as casually as he might say he was just ducking down to the shops to get some tobacco: 'I have decided to go to the coast west of Cape Adare and you are to be chief scientist.'[52] Just like that!

Although feeling somewhat done over, the ever-practical Mawson realises the charming Shackleton's worth as a proven fund-raiser – as a matter of fact, on the spot he claims he can lay his hands on a further £70,000 – and reluctantly takes the suggested demotion. After all, this is not about the pursuit of personal glory, it is about expanding the frontiers of science, and it matters little who commands the expedition so long as those frontiers are pushed back.

15 February 1910, London, Mawson's plans begin to crystallise

It is all starting to come together, and Mawson is fairly certain now of his course. Hitching his wagon to Shackleton's steam train – *he's a good goer, eh?* – makes a lot of sense. In an elegantly penned letter to his old friend from Sydney University, the geologist Griffith Taylor, Mawson sets out his thoughts:

> I am almost getting up an expedition of my own – Scott will not do certain work that ought to be done – I quite agree that to do much would be to detract from his chances of the pole and because of that I am not pressing the matter any further. Certainly I think he is missing the main possibilities of scientific work in the Antarctic by travelling over Shackleton's old route. However he must beat the Yankees . . .[53]

21 February 1910, London, Shackleton is careful

With the chance of returning once more to the scene of his greatest triumph, and the money starting to flow, Shackleton remains passionate about the whole expedition. Careful this time not to have any repeat of the ill will between him and Scott, though, Shackleton divulges all of his plans by writing Scott a letter:

> I am preparing a purely Scientific Expedition to operate along the coast of Antarctica commencing in 1911. The Easterly base is Cape Adare and the farthest west, Gaussberg . . . I am particularly anxious not to clash with your Expedition, nor in any way to hinder your pecuniary efforts.
>
> With this object in mind I have decided not to appeal for public funds, either Government help or for donations from Societies, as I am being strongly supported by individuals.[54]

12 March 1910, Melbourne, one of Shackleton's expedition members decides to say goodbye at the Melbourne Club

While the likes of Shackleton returned from the *Nimrod* expedition to find fame and at least half a fortune, and men such as Mawson had been so inspired that they want nothing more than to return to Antarctica as soon as possible, the aftermath of the polar experience had not been a happy one for them all. Such a man is Bertram Armytage, who had, of course, been the only other Australian on that expedition apart from Mawson and Edgeworth David.

He had been well enough regarded to have successfully led the Western Party of Raymond Priestley and Philip Brocklehurst to the top of Ferrar Glacier. A taciturn and moody man at the best of times, things have not panned out for him at all since returning, however. A highly coveted position at the Imperial War Office in London had been denied him, for one thing.

On the evening of 12 March, he quietly checks into Room 24 at the exclusive Melbourne Club on Collins Street and then gets busy. First, he dresses himself in his impeccable dinner suit, then he dons all of his Boer War and Polar Medals – the Queen's Medal, the King's Medal, the silver Polar Medal that he'd personally received from King Edward VII – before putting a towel down on the floor. Lying upon it, and carefully ensuring his head is fully upon the towel, he takes out his colt pistol and puts the muzzle to his temple.

Then he pulls the trigger.

It is 6.20 pm.

A shot rings out, and around the Melbourne Club the startled members suddenly pause. What *on earth* was that? It sounded very like a shot. When Armytage's door is opened with the master key, he is found on the floor, a grievous wound on his temple and the towel saturated with his blood. He is dead.

Astonishingly, he has written no note nor left any clue as to why he has done this. As they would find out in days to come, he has left behind a grieving wife, Blanch, who would shortly receive a cheery letter from him that he penned just three days earlier.

In the endless speculation that follows, the least that can be agreed is that the experience of having gone through the long, dark night of a polar winter had *not* been good for his mental equilibrium.

Mid-March to late April 1910, Hungary's Carpathian Mountains, Mawson and Davis pursue wild geese

Strange, where the winds of adventure blow you . . .

In early March, Mawson and Davis find themselves in the Carpathian Mountains at Borpatak near Nagybanya, on the border of Hungary and Bukovina. Following up on Shackleton's insistence that not only is there gold in them thar hills of Hungary but that the goldmine might be purchased at bargain-basement prices, they have gone to investigate. Their former expedition leader has been informed that the mine in question is so rich that the local peasant who owns it has already made a fortune using the most primitive mining techniques.

As it pans out, however, the only yield from this enterprise is two months' squandering of their valuable time. A peasant the mine owner might be, but he is shrewd and proves to have about as much interest in selling his gold mine at the preposterous sums that Shackleton offers as sailing to Antarctica. It is a pity. The fortune they need to get to Antarctica will not be coming from here.

17 March 1910, London, Scott gathers his men

In Scott's offices, the recruiting process goes on. In these last months of preparation, a 27-year-old God-fearing Scotsman, Henry Robertson Bowers, is appointed to the expedition as storekeeper on the strong recommendation of Sir Clements Markham.

As Bowers – who comes to them from the Indian Marine Service, where he had been assigned to catch pirates in the Persian Gulf and survey the Irrawaddy River – is a squat man with a barrel chest, flaming-red bristly hair and an enormous beak nose, animated by great energy and organisational ability, he is of course known as 'Birdie' Bowers. And he is tough, too. When he falls through the main hatch while loading *Terra Nova*'s hold, landing 19 feet down on a pile of pig iron, he simply picks himself up, dusts himself off and continues on his merry way. This is *precisely* the kind of man they are looking for.

While home on leave from military service in India, another man has become interested in joining Scott's expedition. Lawrence Edward Grace Oates, known to most as 'Titus' Oates after the seventeenth-century English conspirator, is a man in the mood for adventure.

Of the landed gentry, the dyslexic Oates was educated at Eton, after which his application to Oxford was rejected due to a below-par academic record, which the outspoken and independent lad quickly blamed on the incompetence of his teachers. Such were the times that the obvious career for such a well-born man was the army, and accordingly, with the influence of his doting mother, Caroline, he received a commission in the 6th Iniskilling Dragoons. Although this was his second choice after the Greys, it was nevertheless one of the most highly regarded cavalry regiments in the British Army and provided the ideal opportunity to indulge his passion for horses.

Though he did extremely well in the army, it left him far from unmarked. His left leg is shorter than his right as a result of a bullet through the left thigh, courtesy of a battle against the Boers in March 1901. It was in this same action that he earned the nickname 'No Surrender Oates' from his admiring regiment, and for which some felt he deserved nothing less than the Victoria Cross. Just six months after being invalided home, Oates rejoined his regiment in South Africa.[55]

Though the limping Oates's spirits slumped during those inactive military years since the Second Boer War, an increasing passion for horses served as some substitute for the excitement of real action. An outstanding horseman, he won several Military Cups, helping to add to an already impressive résumé.

Now, though? Now, his outward demeanour of comfortable English gentleman turned army man belies a tense, somewhat world-weary, 30-year-old man. In India, he had been long resentful of his superiors and, as a consequence, military life in general. In one of his many letters to his mother, he had commented with disdain on the army's latest drive to recruit men with brains, 'A man with brains knows too much to join the Service.'[56]

While Oates was on furlough in England in the middle of 1909 – fired up by the huge public fanfare surrounding Shackleton's return in June – Scott publicly announced plans for the *Terra Nova* expedition. Oates was presented not only with an exciting alternative to his current life prospects but also with the ideal opportunity, felt by so many children of the age, to serve his King and Country.

Returning to India, Oates sends Scott a straightforward note in application, which soon sits towards the top of the mountainous pile in Scott's offices. A terse, independent man, Oates is an unlikely candidate for Scott. Nevertheless, aspects of the man do commend him. One thing is that having an old Etonian British Army officer – a war-hero cavalry officer no less – would surely boost not only the expedition's profile in all the right quarters but also the men's morale.

But it is Oates's proven expertise with horses that is the major point in his favour, as while Scott prefers the purity of man-hauling, he is nevertheless a firm believer that it is horses – specifically Manchurian ponies with white coats – that will do most of the back-breaking work of getting to the South Pole. Among Scott's present troupe of mostly scientists and mariners, knowing one end of a pony from the other may well be crucial.

Equally attractive to Scott is Oates's offer to contribute the not insubstantial amount of £1000 of his own money towards the cost of the expedition *and* forego his salary for its duration. This is a significant amount of money to Scott, given the constant burden of attempting to reach the £40,000 initially estimated as necessary to undertake the enterprise. (The concept of expedition members paying to claim a place on an Antarctic expedition is by no means a new one. The *Nimrod* expedition's assistant geologist, Philip Brocklehurst, the second Baronet of Swythamley Park,

Staffordshire, paid a staggering £2000 to secure a place on that expedition.)

Just on the basis of Oates's written application, then, Scott decides to offer him a position. On this 17th day of March – which turns out to be Oates's 30th birthday – the War Office cables the commander in chief, India, granting Oates his freedom.

In general, so high is the quality of applicants that inevitably there are many very good men who do not make the cut. One such army man not able to convince Scott of his worth is a young lieutenant in the Royal Fusiliers, Belgrave Edward Sutton Ninnis, even though he has a strong pedigree in the field. Ninnis's father had gone on the famed British Arctic Expedition of 1875 to 1876 as a surgeon, and the 23-year-old Belgrave is keen to duplicate the feat on a major polar expedition of his own. Alas, he does not make the selection.

Another man comes to the expedition in an interesting way. While on a trip to Norway in early March to see tests of the motor sledge as well as to purchase furs and the finest traditional ash and hickory sledges, Scott takes the opportunity to meet Fridtjof Nansen to apprise the famous Arctic explorer of his plans and ambitions for his Antarctic expedition. In response, Nansen is somewhat underwhelmed to hear that Scott intends to favour motor sledges and ponies instead of what the Norwegian believes is the correct way, which is dogs and skis. Nansen believes it is imperative that Scott's men be good skiers, and with that in mind he recommends a keen 20-year-old Norwegian Antarctic explorer in waiting, Tryggve Gran.

An interesting fellow, Gran, whose own interest in Antarctic exploration was piqued a year earlier when he posed as a journalist so he could meet Scott's great rival, Shackleton, in Oslo, while the latter was on his never-ending world lecture tour. 'Shackleton,' he later recounted, 'was a master of the art of involving his audience in the inner meaning of his topic. One could almost say that the splendid slides were superfluous. I drank in his every word. I fastened especially on his remarks about skis.'[57]

A small parenthesis here.

In fact, another person of particular interest sat spellbound in the audience that day. As later recounted by Shackleton's wife, Emily, as her husband spoke, Roald Amundsen sat with 'keen eyes . . . fixed on him, and when Ernest quoted Robert Service's lines, "The trails of the world be countless", a mystic look softened his eyes, the look of a man who saw a vision'.[58]

Close parenthesis.

So enamoured had Gran become with the whole idea of the South Pole that he, too, was mounting an expedition, with Shackleton's active encouragement. 'Go ahead with your plan, my boy, and do it right away,' Shackleton told him, adding an unusually frank and public expression of support for a potential competitor of Scott's.[59] Nansen, concerned over Gran's lack of experience and Scott's reluctance to use skis, arranges a meeting between the young greenhorn and Scott. As a result, Gran starts to consider throwing in his lot with the Englishman, if Scott would ever agree to it . . .

The clincher comes a few days after their first meeting, when Gran accompanies Scott to the Norwegian village of Fefor to witness further trials of the motor sledge and . . . all too inevitably . . . its axle snaps clean in two.

What to do? For, as it happens, time is of the essence. Scott is due back in London the following day, and the nearest workshop is well down in the valley, ten miles away. Gran's hand is up in an instant – he could do it! Soon, snow powder flying back in Scott's face, Gran is swooshing off down the deep valley on his skis, the broken 25-pound axle strapped to his back like a samurai's sword. Within five hours, he is back to lay the expertly repaired part at Scott's feet.

An instant convert to both the virtues of skiing and the abilities of this young man, Scott offers Gran a position on his staff as expert ski instructor, at the same time offering to buy out the equipment Gran has already purchased in preparation for his own expedition. And so it is that two aspiring expedition leaders in their own right, first Teddy Evans and now Tryggve Gran, are subsumed by the *Terra Nova* expedition under the leadership of the Owner, the irrepressible Captain Robert Falcon Scott.

One more thing, however. Now that Gran is a fully fledged member of the Scott expedition, he takes steps to arrange for Captain Scott to visit Roald Amundsen, whom he knows. Given that Amundsen has announced that he will soon be heading to the North Pole, Scott is interested to see if they might be able to do something together in the field of science, whereby, using the same instruments, their two parties could make magnetic-field measurements simultaneously in the north and south for later comparison.

Alas, though the meeting is all arranged through the good graces of Gran and Amundsen's brother Gustav, when Scott turns up at Amundsen's home, the Norwegian explorer is not there, leaving Gran severely embarrassed.[60]

Scott heads home to continue his preparations . . .

Chapter Five

Departures

I think Shackleton was the most wonderful organiser who came into the world, bar none. And the king of leaders and adventurers . . . He was quite irresponsible about money . . . we rather had a dispute about that . . . Of course money meant nothing to him, you see; he didn't know the meaning of the word except spending it.

Sir Jameson Adams, member of the *Nimrod* expedition

It is only given to us cold slowly wrought natures to feel this dreary deadly tightening at the heart, this slow sickness that holds one for weeks. How can I bear it. I write of the future, of the hopes of being more worthy; but shall I ever be – can I alone, poor weak wretch that I am, bear up against it all. The daily round, the petty annoyance, the ill health, the sickness of heart – how can one fight against it all. No one will ever see these words, therefore I may freely write. What does it all mean?

A scrap of Robert Falcon Scott's diary when he was 21

18 May 1910, London, Mawson loses patience with Shackleton

Finally, Mawson has had enough. Despite all of Shackleton's promises about the huge amounts of money that would flow in from his many sponsors, and the Hungarian gold mines once they have done the deal, the sobering truth is that four months after Shackleton's committing to lead the expedition, Mawson finds himself all alone in London – Shackles has gone on a lecture tour to America – with just about no money raised, apart from that pledged by the wealthy industrialist Lysaght. Worse still, Mawson notes that he *still* hasn't been paid his wages from the *Nimrod* expedition and he hasn't even received expenses from his time spent wildly chasing Hungarian geese.

This is a problem for Mawson on many fronts at once – not least his personal finances. It is not that he is financially moribund, and as a matter of fact he is a man who always has an eye out for financial opportunities in his own field of endeavour, with a track record of investing in interesting finds of minerals that he comes across in his professional capacity. The big returns on all such investments, however, are likely far in the future, and he really does need his pay from the *Nimrod* expedition now.

But at least equally important is the fact that Mawson has had no contact with Shackleton for weeks, and he has no idea whether Shackleton is still committed to the expedition or not. Mawson decides that the only way to resolve it is to confront Shackleton personally, and with that in mind he decides to return to Australia via the United States, where he soon tracks the explorer–entrepreneur down to Omaha, Nebraska, resolutely standing amid the debris of his failed speaking tour.

For three days, the two men go at it, thrashing out issues extending from the coming Antarctic expedition to monies outstanding from both the *Nimrod* expedition and the Hungarian venture that has still come to nothing. It takes some doing, but in a smoky Omaha hotel lounge Mawson finally makes Shackleton agree to put his signature to a binding contract, engaging him to pay Mawson the outstanding £400 for the *Nimrod* expedition and appointing him chief scientist of the next expedition, or leader if Shackleton reneges, in which case Shackleton will still be committed to helping to raise funds.[1] Satisfied, sort of, and with Shackleton promising to keep in touch, Mawson continues on his journey home. And yet, despite Shackleton's stated intent to continue with their plans to go to Antarctica if he can free himself from other projects and commitments, Mawson, quietly, is not fully counting on it. 'By this time he had many get rich quick schemes in view,' Mawson records in his diary, 'and I felt that the chances of his getting to Antarctica were lessening.'[2]

Mid- to late May 1910, Scott's London offices, a stranger arrives

Even Sherlock Holmes – the fictional creation of that keen Scott supporter Arthur Conan Doyle – would surely have been confused. For the bowler hat perched jauntily on the back of the head of this man who has just entered Scott's Victoria Street offices bespeaks a confident gentility. But his shabby raincoat, buttoned up to the neck to hide his collar, suggests he has known roughness, too, an effect heightened by the fact that he clearly has a slight limp.

For Scott and his men, it is all the more confusing, for they have been expecting a spick and span cavalry officer, with hair pomaded and a waxed moustache in the classic fashion. This fellow standing before them, however, appears at first glance to be a more than somewhat dishevelled farmer with kind brown eyes.

'I'm Oates,' the man drily announces.

And so he is. Following an hour-long discussion with Scott, Lawrence Oates is taken over to *Terra Nova*, where he puts himself to work with great zeal and enthusiasm. Soon realising that 'the Soldier', as they affectionately call him, possesses more than a little seamanship – it turns out he has also been a keen yachtsman in his time – the ship's officers engage him to assist with the fit-out.

It is not long before Lieutenant Campbell makes application to Scott that Oates be immediately taken on as a midshipman rather than – and this is briefly considered – travel to Siberia to catch up with Meares and assist in the procurement of the ponies and dogs. With Scott's blessing, on 31 May, Oates is signed on as a midshipman in the yacht RYS *Terra Nova*, at the peppercorn salary of one shilling per month. He is not a man in it for the money – for he does not need money. He wants adventure and a change from army life.

1 June 1910, the Thames, London, Scott's expedition begins

Time for a few words, chaps. In the aft of *Terra Nova*, Captain Scott gathers his crew and a small group of distinguished visitors to him so he can speak to them of what a great privilege and honour it is to sail under the White Ensign of the Royal Navy, this 'white emblem of British naval achievement', which, quite appropriately, soon breaks out of its folds to greet the sunshine and the pleasant, cooling breeze.[3]

At 1700 hours *precisely* (the British do it so well), *Terra Nova* is warped out of the South-West India Dock and slowly towed out into the River Thames.

Surveying the massive crowd lining the quay, who are enthusiastically cheering them off, and waving back at them, one of the men, the heavily moustachioed English photographer Herbert Ponting, who is standing beside Captain Scott, whimsically asks him, 'If this is [our] farewell, just what [our] homecoming will be like?'

'I don't much care for this sort of thing,' Captain Scott replies simply. 'All I want is to finish the work we began in the *Discovery*. Then I'll get back to my job in the Navy . . .'[4]

Shortly thereafter, Scott and his wife leave the ship in the Kent port of Greenhithe. While *Terra Nova* sails on to Cardiff to do some final preparation work and fill her coal bunkers, they stay behind so the expedition leader can engage in more fund-raising. They intend to briefly catch up with the crew in Cardiff, return to their fund-raising and then catch a fast ship that will allow them to join *Terra Nova* in Cape Town. In Scott's absence, *Terra Nova* is under the leadership of the expedition's second in command, Lieutenant Teddy Evans.

3 June 1910, Oslo, Roald Amundsen is aboard *Fram*

In the forenoon, the famed little ship leaves her mooring beside Akershus Fortress, the mediaeval castle that protects the ancient port. Slowly at first, and then with more confidence, she moves down the harbour and towards the open sea.

Though Roald Amundsen still has quite a few weeks of travelling along the Norwegian coast to pick up further supplies for their voyage – as well as a quick oceanographic survey to do in the North Irish Sea, serving to demonstrate to his king, Nansen and sponsors that he is on the right track – he feels a great weight being lifted from his shoulders. Mostly, he is pleased to have made a successful getaway from Oslo, unhampered by the growing number of creditors who have been pressing him lately. It has been no cheap exercise to make ready to get to where he wants to go, and after incurring bills that he simply cannot pay it is doubly good to be getting away.

13 June 1910 and two days thereafter, Cardiff, Taffy's going to speak!

The officers and crew of *Terra Nova* have had a tough time of it since arriving in Cardiff. The ship no sooner took on an additional

300 tons of fuel and nearly 100 tons of Insole's best Welsh steaming coal, together with the lubricating oils, than a rather disturbing problem showed up. As she settled more deeply in the water, alas, some of the seams that were previously above the water began to leak, auguring 'a gloomy future for the crew in the nature of pumping'.[5]

But most of those problems are forgotten now, as, two days before their departure to the south, the Lord Mayor of Cardiff and the Cardiff Chamber of Commerce are hosting a farewell banquet in the finest room of the Royal Hotel. Captain Scott has again joined his men for the occasion, to ensure that all is now shipshape with *Terra Nova* and to be personally presented by the Lord Mayor with a much appreciated cheque of £1000 for the expedition fund. Scott makes a gracious speech in reply, promising that *Terra Nova*'s first port of call on her return to Britain will be Cardiff, and he sits down to thunderous applause, when . . . when . . . *Taffy's going to speak!*

A roar goes up from the men of *Terra Nova* as they see the giant sway to his feet and call for silence. He is the biggest man in the room, a veteran of the *Discovery* expedition and a native South Welshman, and it is a sign of Petty Officer 'Taffy' Evans's high standing in the room that he has been placed on the high table between the Lord Mayor and Captain Scott.

But now he has something to say. He has no notes but – as has ever been the case through the ages, as ever it will be – in much the same manner as the drink has flowed down his throat on this evening, so too do his true feelings now flow out of him. Itsh about Captain Shcott and what a fine man he ish. 'No one else would have induced me to go there again,' he shays, 'but if there is a man in the world who will bring this to a successful issue, Captain [Shcott] is the man.'[6]

Thunderous applause all round. And more celebration. Much more. So much celebration for Taffy, in fact, that in the wee hours of the following morning it takes no fewer than six men to get him back aboard *Terra Nova* and safely to bed. Scott forgives him. For if Taffy adores Scott, that great affection is returned from Scott to Taffy. The two go back a long way, having served on HMS *Majestic* before the turn of the century, where Scott was a torpedo lieutenant, which was in turn before the two had man-hauled together over vast distances on the *Discovery* expedition. In terms of social class, the two are a long way apart, but there is just something about Taffy, his working-class, no-nonsense approach, his extraordinary physique, general good humour and animal masculinity, that Scott deeply admires.

And he needs such good men. For even if all goes perfectly, they will be away for a long time and engaged in terribly hard work. The plan is for them to arrive in Antarctica in late December/early January, to build their hut and do some early sledging expeditions to establish depots, before getting through the winter to make their assault on the South Pole in the spring.

Finally, all is in readiness, and on 15 June, with the recently presented Welsh Red Dragon gaily fluttering from the masthead, *Terra Nova* sets sail for the south, to the strains of a full-throated rendition of 'Auld Lang Syne' coming from the choir set up on Penarth Head:

> For auld lang syne, my jo,
> for auld lang syne,
> we'll tak a cup o'kindness yet,
> for auld lang syne.

Those on the Head stay watching until finally the hardy little ship disappears into the thick maze of coal ships waiting in the Bristol Channel to load. Time to go home.

Mid-June 1910 and several months thereafter, Adelaide, Mawson spends precious time with Paquita

Ah, Paquita . . .

Adelaide's hero returns from England via America in mid-1910 to immediately return to work, delivering 'extension lectures' on his Antarctic discoveries. But there is a key difference to the way things used to be. Now, Paquita sits in the front row of each and every one of his lectures, gazing at him adoringly, much as he gazes back, her face the natural resting point for his eyes after every quick flicker around the hall to ensure he has everyone's attention.

After returning from Europe, Mawson did not tarry in contriving a way to see Paquita again – at first on the pretext of visiting her naively flattered brother, William – and their attraction to each other has been as instantaneous as it has been intense. She even manages to bring out in him a hitherto hidden playful side, and for one of his lectures he turns up in full polar outfit, complete with balaclava, windproof jacket, thick pants and so on, only to take off one garment after another as the lecture proceeds until . . . until . . . he says, 'Perhaps I'll stop now . . .?'[7] At this, he removes the last layer of clothing . . . revealing to the relief and then amusement of all that he is wearing a dinner suit underneath. Ah, how they laugh, and none harder or with more warmth than the sparkling Paquita. *Rrrrravishing!*

Late June 1910, mid-Atlantic, Oates gets the attention of *Terra Nova*'s men

Gentlemen! A toast to Napoleon Bonaparte!

In the galley of *Terra Nova*, the assembled officers, crew and scientists are just finishing their dinner when they are surprised to hear Oates propose this curious toast. Bemused, they toast the former French emperor. Oates, as it turns out, is devoted to the memory of Napoleon, whom he regards as not only the finest soldier who ever lived but also no less than the 'high priest of his religion' – the religion of duty.[8]

As to *Terra Nova* – referred to by the men as 'the old bus'[9] and said by Oates to have 'two speeds, slow and slower'[10] – she continues to plug away.

They are a happy bunch, all of the crew getting on well together, helped by the fact that in the absence of their expedition leader, Scott, the shackles of formal discipline are not so tight. 'It was a grand scrap, a free-for-all, though no-one quite knew what it was all about and no-one cared.' So the Australian geologist Frank Debenham – another of Professor Edgeworth David's protégés – describes the all-in wrestling matches that 'raged up and down between the solid wardroom table and the cabins for a long time and great was the damage to shins and elbows'.[11]

When the games are on, the captain of the ship, Lieutenant Teddy Evans, is right in the thick of things, but for the most part he is devoting himself to the far more serious task of whipping this loose outfit of men into a solid whole. Aside from compulsory 'watches', he ensures that the ship's entire complement assiduously applies itself to such myriad steamship duties as painting the bulwarks, working the pumps, shifting cargo, stoking the coal and, most arduous of all, wielding 'the devil', a heavy, rake-like tool used to break up the mass of incombustible matter known as 'clinkers' and reshape the furnace fire.

One in, all in, me hearties. They're off on a grand and thrilling adventure to help one of Great Britain's most celebrated men go after a great and worthy goal. As the men work hard for the common good, an atmosphere of bonhomie and strong camaraderie is soon established.

And very soon the men's personalities are borne out. The warm and generous Bill Wilson is something of a father figure to them all: omniscient, a tireless, selfless worker always there to lend a sympathetic ear. Birdie Bowers is the cheerful, superbly organised commissariat, with a shopkeeper's knowledge of the whereabouts of every item stored in every case as if he has known it all his life. Lawrence Oates is the enormously popular hard-working Soldier, already thick as thieves with the twinkling doctor 'Atch' Atkinson, with these two ever ready to crack a joke or pull a prank on the others.

With the men sleeping on deck in hot weather, rushing to the railings to admire the passing by of a Portuguese man-of-war – a jelly-like marine invertebrate – leaping over the side to take an early-morning wash, joining in evening sing-song: though the days are long, they somehow pass quickly. Somehow, even as the tireless heartbeat of the steam engine pulses away – *chonk-chonk-chonk (pause) chonk-chonk-chonk (pause)* – and the sail stands taut before the breeze, the laughter never seems to stop.

'This is the rowdiest mess I have ever been in,' Oates would write to his mother a few weeks later. 'We shout and yell at mealtimes just as we like and have a game called Furl topgallant sails which consists of tearing each other's clothes off . . . the whole place a regular pandemonium.'[12]

16 July 1910, London, Scott's departure cheers Shackleton

And now it is time for Scott, accompanied by Kathleen, to board a train to take them to a fast ship, the RMS *Saxon*, to Cape Town to catch up with *Terra Nova* there.

An intimate group of friends and well-wishers assembles at Waterloo Station to farewell the Scotts, including Sir Edgar Speyer, who is the treasurer for the expedition, Dr Scott Keltie, secretary of the Royal Geographical Society, and Lieutenant Wilhelm Filchner, leader of the German Antarctic Expedition, which is set to head south the following May.

Also present – in an exact reversal of how it was just 13 months earlier, when he arrived back from Antarctica – is Sir Ernest Shackleton, who, along with Sir Edgar Speyer, engages in earnest conversation with Scott on the platform, just before the expedition leader is due to board the train, which will take him to Southampton, where his ship awaits.

'Goodbye and good luck,' says Shackleton, shaking Scott's hand.[13]

And then . . . 'Three cheers for Captain Scott!' Shackleton enthusiastically shouts as the train begins to pull out. 'Cheers for Mrs Scott!'[14]

'See you at the South Pole!' Scott calls out of the carriage window; not, however, to Shackleton but to Lieutenant Wilhelm Filchner.[15]

And with that, the train pulls out. In Scott's luggage, carefully folded, he has two Union Jacks graciously presented to him by Her Majesty Queen Alexandra a fortnight earlier. Her Majesty asked that the first flag be planted at the farthest point south that they reach – hopefully the South Pole – while the second is to be first planted there and then brought back.

Scott intends to do exactly that.

Late July 1910, Adelaide, Mawson courts

By now, Mawson is a regular attendee at the Delprat family dining table in Tynte Street, North Adelaide, as, bit by bit, William fades into the background of Mawson's discernible attention and Paquita moves well forward. The real breakthrough comes when, out of the blue, Douglas calls her and asks if she would care to go to the theatre with him, bringing one of her sisters. 'That did rather put ideas into my head,' Paquita later recalled of the occasion. 'It was a musical comedy but I don't think I remembered a word of it next morning.'[16]

Upon his next invitation to dinner, he and Paquita are 'left alone' afterwards, to pore over Mawson's photographic albums of Antarctica and the New Hebrides. And here are the natives in their grass skirts, here are the mountains, and here is one of the most extraordinary geological formations I have ever seen . . .

As the weeks go by, Mawson's visits to the Delprats become ever more frequent, expanding to include long, languid afternoons at the family's holiday home in Brighton, El Rincon, as all tacitly come to understand the two are 'courting'. As the temperature warms pleasantly, so too does Mawson's love affair with the 'little one' start to blossom, alongside the scarlet bottlebrush native to that state.

Surrounded by a loving and gregarious family, Mawson realises he has lived too long the spartan life of the intellectual. It is not that his own family is not close, particularly, but . . . well . . . they certainly have not been as close to each other as are the Delprat family. While Paquita is the second youngest of seven children who see each other all the time, together with their loving parents, that has not been Douglas's experience. In the first place, there was just him and his older brother, William, as children of the family, and while the Delprat family have certainly travelled around the world as Mr Delprat has pursued his sterling career in mining, the Mawson family have been rather simply blown around by the prevailing economic winds.

The bottom line is that there is warmth to the Delprat family life that Mawson knows he has been missing out on, and he wants more of it. With Paquita. Maybe even having a family of their own one day . . .

25 July 1910, Vladivostok, Cecil Meares gathers dogs and ponies as it rains cats and dogs

Here they all stand by the Vladivostok quayside in the mounting rain, two-feet deep in mud and manure: Scott's four men, 19 ill-behaved ponies and 30 yapping dogs awaiting shipment.[17]

The leader of the troupe is the exhausted Cecil Meares. Since leaving London in January, his peripatetic journey has seen him travel over 5000 miles across Russia on the Trans-Siberian Railway to Khabarovsk, before taking a horse-drawn sleigh 660 miles north along the frozen river Amur to what surely must be the most remote, most appallingly bleak town in all of Russia, Nikolayevsk-on-Amur.[18] This flyspeck of a port on the coast of the North Pacific Ocean is well known to Meares for the quality of its dogs and dog-drivers, and it was there, with the assistance of the young Russian 'dog-boy' he hired, Demetri Gerof, that Meares assiduously tested then purchased 30 dogs. From there, he got them back to Vladivostok by steamer and then train.[19]

So far, so good, and Meares is confident that he has good dogs. When it came to the procurement of the ponies, however – the central driving force of Scott's expedition – Meares handed the job over to an acquaintance, who in turn enlisted the assistance of an experienced, diminutive Vladivostok jockey by the name of Anton Omelchenko.

The ponies were found 315 miles north-west of Vladivostok in a market in Harbin, Manchuria, and, following Scott's strict instructions, they were purchased less for their pedigree or form or strength than for the fact that their coats are the requisite white.[20] The names given to each pony are to correlate strictly with a list coming from London, generated by the schools, clubs and individuals who have donated the cash necessary and so have secured naming rights.

After a long and gruelling journey to Vladivostok, these ponies are to be sent on an arduous 52-day sea marathon to Lyttelton in New Zealand, where they will await the arrival of *Terra Nova*.

Clearly, it is to be an extremely difficult task, and to assist him Meares has engaged Anton as the expedition's groom for the ponies and Demetri Gerof as his assistant dog-driver. Meanwhile, Captain Scott's brother-in-law, Lieutenant Wilfrid Bruce (Kathleen's older brother, who gave her away at their wedding), has also arrived to lend a hand – though, to be sure, the no-nonsense Meares regards this rather effete gentleman as 'a little too kid glovey' to be of any real use to him.[21]

10 August 1910, Norway, *Fram* weighs anchor off Fredriksholm

It has been an exceptionally busy two months. Since being farewelled from Oslo by King Haakon many weeks before, Amundsen and his men have conducted their brief survey in the North Irish Sea before returning to the Norwegian coast, gathering the things they need and doing essential maintenance for the expedition ahead. A large prefabricated hut and essential stores, including half a ton of gun-cotton and rifle ammunition, are loaded aboard, together with no fewer than 97 yipping-yapping dogs – some of Greenland's finest, courtesy of the Royal Greenland Trading Company – which are quickly quartered in a specially constructed false deck. Meantime, the motor is overhauled and the hull coated with a hardy waterproof substance. It has all been so exhausting. But now, with the wonderful clarion call 'The anchor's up!', they are full speed ahead, finally, truly, on their way.

Their reported route will take them right down to the South Atlantic, round Cape Horn into the Pacific Ocean and up to San Francisco for a brief stopover, before they will again head north to the Bering Strait – which separates Russia and Alaska and is the gateway to the Arctic Ocean – till they get to within the Arctic itself.

Yes, the American Robert Peary claimed to have got to the North Pole last year – while Frederick A. Cook's own claims have been bitterly disputed – but Amundsen has told one and all that his is a *scientific* expedition, and therefore the fact that someone else has got to the North Pole first is neither here nor there to him.[22] For all that, some keen observers are surprised at this enduring enthusiasm, as it is so often the way of these things that once someone has planted their flag in a previously unclaimed spot, the net level of interest and passion for the pursuit from other would-be claimants drops away to near-nothing, but for whatever reason Amundsen professes to be as keen as ever.

Against that, a few things are striking some of his 18 fellow expedition members as a little odd. The dogs, for example . . .

Jeg forstår ikke. I don't understand. Why are we transporting dogs all the way around the world – including around the murderous Cape Horn – when we could just as easily pick up dogs in Alaska, a place where they abound and are easily available to buy? And what use will a prefabricated hut be out on the ice pack, and which of us would be fool enough to live in it? *Ikke mig.* Not me.

It is all very confusing. For the way of exploration in the Arctic is to stay with the ship. And, speaking of the ship, why is the after-deck completely weighed down with coal sacks? Surely that, too, could have been bought in San Francisco?

15 August to early September 1910, Cape Town, Captain Scott is troubled

So fast is *Saxon*, and so slow is *Terra Nova* – caught without any wind in the doldrums – that even though Scott left Great Britain nearly six weeks after his comrades, he nevertheless arrived in South

Africa on 2 August, almost two weeks before them, and has had to wait, hoping they will soon appear.

At last, on 15 August, *Terra Nova* arrives at the Simon's Town naval base just east of Cape Town, where she will undergo some minor repairs while the men are granted leave.

Some two and a half weeks later, on 2 September, *Terra Nova* is once again steaming south, but now there has been a significant change in her command structure, as Scott has taken over. As expedition leader and a naval commander to boot, this makes a certain amount of sense, but there is more to it than that.

Scott's thoughts are already beginning to focus on the push to the South Pole, and – trying to work out which of the men are the best mentally equipped to accompany him – he decides he wants to get to know them better. Obviously, someone must give up his quarters, and that proves to be a disappointed Bill Wilson. Drat! He has been thoroughly enjoying *Terra Nova*'s atmosphere of bonhomie but is now obliged to change places with Scott and catch the faster RMS *Corinthic* to Melbourne, in the company of his own wife, Oriana, plus Kathleen Scott and Hilda Evans. For his part, Lieutenant Teddy Evans is equally unhappy with Captain Scott's decision, as it simply doesn't sit right with him to effectively be relieved of his command of the ship from Cape Town onwards, no matter the leader's reasons.

Something else troubling the expedition is news received from London that fund-raising efforts back in Britain have not been going well. Yes, they have raised the originally budgeted £40,000, but as costs have now blown out to £50,000 there is a £10,000 shortfall. With efforts to raise the funds in South Africa producing only a meagre £500, it now falls upon Wilson to attempt to raise this extra money in Australia, which is unlikely to prove much more promising.

Wilson puts his finger on what appears to be the core of the problem in a letter home to a friend:

I fear it is no easy job there as the government has already published its intention of giving no money at all to Scott's expedition. This is the result of the proposal to start an Australian expedition and Mawson, an Australian, having failed to get appointed to our expedition on his own terms, will no doubt have Shackleton to back him.[23]

Well, they will just have to make the best of it. As Scott sails east from Cape Town, with the mighty Roaring Forties at his back, another small ship is approaching its destination . . .

6 September 1910, Madeira, Amundsen unveils a secret

On 3 September, after nigh on four weeks at sea, *Fram* eventually pulled into the small island of Madeira off the coast of Africa, on her way to the North Pole. It was a great opportunity to replenish their supplies and, as a consequence of the mechanics needing two days to inspect the propeller, give the crew some much needed time ashore.

After three days, all seems ready. The propeller is fixed, and the *Fram* is gagging to the gunwales with precious and soon to be rare freshwater (including 1000 gallons stowed in the longboat), together with a plentiful supply of fresh fruit and vegetables. All up, the *Fram* holds sufficient supplies for seven *years* at sea, or even frozen upon it, without the need to put into port.

The men have written letters to their families, and they are just three hours away from their scheduled time of departure.

But it is now that Roald Amundsen – 'the Chief', as his men refer to him – calls a meeting for the entire crew. He has something he needs to tell them. He needs them up on deck right away.

But what is this? As the men gather, grumbling at this

unexpected interruption to their final preparations, they find Amundsen has a curious look on his face . . . and something else besides. He is standing before a large map that he has pinned on the mainmast. A map of . . . of . . . they look closer . . . Antarctica. *Antarctica?*

Yes, Antarctica.

Amundsen speaks to them clearly, in his always authoritative if slightly high-pitched voice. He is sorry, and he hasn't been comfortable leaving his true intentions hidden for so long, but there was no choice. Had he told them in Norway, the secret would likely have got out, and they would almost certainly have been prevented from going by the sponsors whose money was contingent on a push north, not south. Only now does he feel he can tell them their true destination, which is not the North Pole at all. Rather . . .

Rather, he makes clear to them, gesturing to the map of Antarctica and uttering the magic words '*Sør Pol*', that he intends heading to the other end of the world entirely.

As later described by first mate Lieutenant Fredrick Gjertsen — one of only two ship's officers who had, under written agreement, been privy to Amundsen's plans from the start — 'most stood there with mouths agape staring at the Chief like so many question marks'.[24]

An exception is Olav Bjaaland, an accomplished Norwegian skiing champion and highly skilled carpenter whom Amundsen has personally selected for his unique combination of talents. No sooner has he heard the news from Amundsen than he shouts, 'Hurrah, that means we'll get there first!'[25]

Not necessarily. For this to happen, the others of the expedition must also agree, and there is reasonable hesitation in the air. After all, they have been *had*. Though it remains unspoken, there is no way around it. Amundsen, their leader, has *lied* to them, and he has been lying for some time. If he is capable of such subterfuge in the mostly sunny latitude they have been part of for the last few weeks, then just how would things be in the polar extremities? In such an environment, with their lives likely hanging by a thread, or more likely a rope, they surely need a leader they can trust implicitly, and Amundsen has just unequivocally demonstrated that a large portion of their trust to this point has been misplaced.

On the other hand, it *would* be exciting to make a push to the South Pole, to try to get there first, and they can see how, under the circumstances, Amundsen has kept their true destination from them to this point. And so the emotions course through Amundsen's men.

The silence after Bjaaland's initial enthusiastic response is a fair indication that the men are working their way through both sides of the equation.

Though for his own part Amundsen remains confident he has done the right thing – to have made his plans public earlier would have risked having the whole expedition 'stifled at its birth'[26] – the project consequently now hangs in the balance.

Amundsen deems it only fair to now ask each and every member individually whether he is ready to travel to the South Pole rather than the North. 'So then, who is coming?' Amundsen asks matter-of-factly, almost as if he is inviting them to go for a small jaunt to yonder bay.

A stony silence ensues, the men caught as flat as the map behind Amundsen. How far does faith in his leadership carry them – a one-year detour all the way to the bottom of the world? It is one thing to commit to the exploration of the well-known and celebrated North Pole, but what about to the South? Those who go ashore here will have paid passage home, so maybe now is the time to opt out of this subterfuge? But how would they feel then, if they are seen to have run away just as Amundsen is planning to plant the Norwegian flag in what is one of the most coveted last unclaimed spots on earth?

And there *is* the extra pay to consider.

Like ice breaking, their resistance begins to crack.

Hjalmar Johansen nods that he will come. Bjaaland says he will come, as does Helmer Hanssen, the renowned dog-driver and navigator born and raised inside the Arctic Circle, who had accompanied his old friend Amundsen on their journey through the North-West Passage – learning from the Inuit the fine art of driving dogs. He is happy to follow Amundsen not just to the end of the earth, as he thought he was doing, but to *either* end, as it turns out now.

Amundsen's spirits soar with four parts jubilation and one part sheer relief that the whole thing hasn't suddenly come unstuck, as Lieutenant Kristian Prestrud, ice pilot Andreas Beck and the whaler Oscar Wisting also nod, as does Sverre Hassel, though he has been forewarned and has already given his agreement. Though Adolf Henrik Lindstrøm, who also accompanied Amundsen on the North-West Passage expedition, is cooking, the Chief doesn't even have to ask – of course Adolf is in. As to the rest, one by one the men step up and say *ja*, yes, they are indeed coming on the greatest adventure of their lives.

With their goal now clearly defined and history beckoning, enthusiasm soon replaces doubt, and acclaim for their leader replaces angst at his subterfuge. 'There was so much life and good spirits on board that evening,' Amundsen later recalls, 'that one would have thought the work was successfully accomplished instead of being hardly begun.'[27]

Two hours later, just before they cast off to head south, one man is let off the *Fram*. This is not a disloyal crew member but in fact the man most loyal of all to Roald Amundsen. That is, his older brother by almost two years, Leon, is not to go with them, for he has no interest in exploring. In three weeks or so, though, once they are well on their way and have a good head start in their race to the Pole, Leon is to do several things. First, he must observe the key protocol that the King of Norway be informed of the change of plan, then he must post the letters that the men have written to their families back in Norway and send the Englishman Robert Falcon Scott a cable, and finally he must inform Fridtjof Nansen and the press what his brother is doing . . .

Meanwhile, as the *Fram* leaves the hot port of Madeira, Amundsen settles down in his cabin to do more of what he has already done a lot of: reading every account he can get his hands on about how earlier explorers to Antarctica fared in order to work out the best way to proceed.

12 October 1910, Port Phillip Bay, Melbourne, Scott's *Terra Nova* arrives

For Dr Bill Wilson, it has been a very long trip from Cape Town to Melbourne on RMS *Corinthic*. Yes, it has been lovely to spend time with his beloved wife, Oriana, but against that he has also had to spend time with the extremely strong-willed wives of Scott and his second in command Evans. There have been . . . tensions among the women, most particularly between the latter two. (Quietly, Kathleen has taken a very dim view of his Oriana as well, describing her in a letter to a friend as 'an absurd prig'.[28])

And now, no matter that *Terra Nova* has arrived in the dead of night and in squally weather. At Kathleen Scott's fierce insistence – for she feels that her husband would expect her to come – a highly agitated Wilson soon puts the three wives and a mailbag aboard a small motor launch and they head out into Port Melbourne to welcome their beloveds. It is no easy matter in such darkness and with a running sea to find the right looming shape that is *Terra Nova* – though at least Oriana proves to be an absolute brick as they plough through uncomfortably large waves.

'I hope it will never fall to my lot to have more than one wife at a time to look after,' comments Wilson in his diary.[29]

Presently, Kathleen Scott hears her husband's voice, and she calls out to him repeatedly. There is no reply, but still Kathleen insists to Wilson that they continue. This results, as she confides in her diary, in her 'getting more and more unpopular . . . but at last we got close to the beautiful *Terra Nova* with our beautiful husbands on board. They came and looked down into our faces with lanterns.'[30]

In short order, the women are on board, being warmly welcomed by their husbands as news is excitedly exchanged of what has been happening to them all over the weeks since they last saw each other in Cape Town. But this is all only brief, for with the motor launch still awaiting them the three men take the opportunity to return to land and the far more comfortable accommodation in the hotel where their wives are staying.

And it is here, back in the hotel, that Kathleen gives 'Con', as she calls her beloved husband, the post that has been awaiting him. Among it all is a cable, in an envelope on crisp, yellow paper. Scott opens it and reads:

```
Beg  leave  to  inform  you  Fram  proceeding
Antarctic Amundsen.[31]
```

Cry treason!

Well, perhaps not treason, as Amundsen is not an Englishman – and clearly not a gentleman – but it certainly feels like a betrayal. In Scott's view, the Ross Sea region, stretching from King Edward VII Land in the east to Victoria Land in the west is his domain first and foremost by virtue of his expedition there, and after that at least Britain's domain because of what Shackleton had done on his own recent expedition. And while he, Scott, has been totally public about his plans from the beginning, here is this Norwegian skulking around under the cover of darkness and only telling them of his plans very late in the piece.

Perplexed, Scott returns to *Terra Nova* the next morning, immediately summoning to his cabin the one Norwegian on his expedition, Tryggve Gran, to uncharacteristically seek his opinion. Maybe Amundsen's countryman can shed some light on this most perplexing of cables. 'What can you make of this?' Scott asks a soon to be equally baffled Gran.[32]

For the moment, there is little to be done but greet the news with starchy stoicism and get on with it. That Scott does, but he is nevertheless careful to keep the cable secret from the rest of the crew, for fear that it might badly affect morale. The one thing he does do, in the hope of getting just a little more information about what he is up against, is to cable Nansen in Norway asking if he can shed some light on Amundsen's destination.

Nansen's reply is to the point: 'Unknown.'[33]

Mid-October 1910, Adelaide, Mawson writes a letter

Knowing that Captain Scott is now in Australia – the papers have been full of it – Mawson writes to him:

Dear Captain Scott,

. . . I am extremely glad to see your expedition so well set out and regret to think that so grand a chance is lost to me. No further steps have been taken by me towards raising funds for my projected expedition. I am doing this on purpose so that you may never regard me as a usurper of funds which might otherwise have gone towards your enterprise. After you have got away, I shall endeavour to raise the money necessary to equip an expedition. Do not ever place to my door the blame of having in any way influenced the Commonwealth Government in their decision not to give your Expedition money. This was done whilst I was in Europe and without their knowledge of my ever intending an expedition.

If I can be of assistance to yourself or any member of your staff please let me know. Unless you come this way, I think it unlikely that we shall meet before you leave. You would get a full house were you to lecture here.

With all sincerity,
Douglas Mawson[34]

In fact, however, by the time that Scott receives the letter, the Australian Government has come good, at least a little, with acting prime minister Billy Hughes publicly announcing the federal government would be giving his expedition £2500, half of the amount he was asking for.[35]

28 October 1910, Lyttelton, New Zealand, Oates is off his ponies

Terra Nova steams into Lyttelton, near Christchurch, and shortly thereafter Lawrence Oates gazes for the first time on the 30 Siberian dogs and, most importantly, the 19 cold-weather breed of Manchurian ponies that Cecil Meares and Kathleen Scott's brother, Lieutenant Wilfrid Bruce, RN of HMS *Arrogant,* have managed to transport to the quarantine station on Quail Island, five miles into Lyttelton Bay.

After a circuitous voyage around the Pacific, the animals arrived six weeks earlier. To Meares's credit – far more than Wilfrid Bruce's, as Meares's fears had been right and he had not proved himself to be much 'hands-on' help at all – not a single dog has died in that time nor one pale pony perished, but . . .

But with just one look, Oates is nothing less than appalled, most particularly with the ponies, later describing them to his mother as 'without exception, the greatest lot of crocks I have ever seen'.[36]

The Owner, needless to say, doesn't see it like that at all, or, if he does, he refuses to acknowledge that there might be a problem. As a man who has been at sea since the age of 13, Scott's experience with horses and ponies is rudimentary at best and totally ignorant at worst. Despite that, he has no hesitation in saying he is 'greatly pleased' with the beasts.[37] For starters, just as he has demanded of Meares, all the ponies have the required white coats, and this gives him confidence that they will prosper in the Antarctic conditions.

Needless to say, Scott is little impressed by the presumptuous Oates's unbidden opinion and his all too obvious attempt to absolve himself of any responsibility should the ponies break down in Antarctica. Oates, however, has not even broken into stride when it comes to expressing his unhappiness over the ponies. For he and Scott disagree not only over the condition of the animals but also over the requisite quantity of feed for the expedition. Scott wants to take just 30 tons of forage, whereas Oates *insists* on 45 tons.[38]

He what? He *insists*.

Scott bristles. How *dare* Oates question his judgement?

Oates is hampered in replying in the manner he would like to by the fact that Scott is his superior officer, but he is deeply aggrieved.

This clash between the two Englishmen from different branches of the armed services is not merely one of a difference of opinion but also of a difference of personalities, as would later be noted by their colleague Frank Debenham:

Between Oates, dry and caustic, humorous and solid, shrewd and quietly genial, objective in his outlook – and Scott, shy and moody, and temperamental and sensitive, quick in mind as in action, with the soul of a poet – a 'sentimentalist' Cherry called him – there can have been little in common. Their natures jarred on one another . . .[39]

The heated conversation goes for all of an hour, with Oates refusing to give up. He is neither a volatile man nor particularly quick of mind (Wilson once said to him, 'The way thoughts flash through your mind, Titus, reminds me of snails climbing up a cabbage stalk'[40]), but he is as dogged a man as ever lived and wins through persistence what he cannot by persuasion pure.

And so it is that Oates finally triumphs, after a fashion, and Scott agrees to take the extra tonnage of fodder in place of steaming coal.[41] (And even then, Oates manages to up the ante and smuggles a further two tons aboard.)

Despite the heat of the argument, the army man is not particularly one to bear a grudge and is inclined to a benevolent view once an argument is finished. Oates writes a short time later:

Dear Mother,

I have had a great struggle with Scott about the horse forage. When I tackled him he said not one oz over 30 [tons] so it's no use arguing however we argued for one hour. He told me I was a 'something' nuisance but has given way which shows he is open to reason.[42]

For now, Oates busies himself supervising the construction of 15 stalls under the forecastle of *Terra Nova*, with another four to be built on the outside deck, so that the beasts will hopefully arrive in Antarctica still able to pull sledges. It is too late to get other ponies bred for Antarctic conditions, so they will just have to make the best of it. From this point on, Oates's key focus is getting the inadequate beasts he has been given the charge of to be as adequate as possible for the crucial task assigned them. In the coming summer, they will haul the fully laden sledges across the Barrier to the foot of the Beardmore Glacier, at which point man-hauling will take over.

As to Scott, Evans, Wilson and their wives, a good deal of their time in Christchurch is spent with social engagements, during which Captain Scott is frequently asked to make a speech outlining the expedition's goals and answering whatever questions anyone might have.

One question that pops up regularly is very simple. *Why?* As in, why on earth are you trying to get to the very ends of the earth? What will it actually prove? What is the blessed *point?*

Scott's answer rarely changes: 'How can we expect to know anything of the mighty universe of which the world is but an atom, if we don't explore to its uttermost recesses our own little globe?'[43]

Early November 1910, Adelaide, Mawson writes

After Scott has replied to Mawson on 22 October, wondering what the Australian's own plans are, Mawson writes:

Dear Captain Scott,

. . . It is with great sadness that I write, for it seems to me that one great chance of a lifetime has slipped away. It is not the notoriety of reaching the Pole that I refer to: it is lost companionship of great spirits – that alone which makes life a harvest of joy, raised upon a battlefield of suffering.

. . . With regard to the expedition on which I expect to embark at the end of next year the following are the outlines:

The arrangement with Shackleton is that he may or may not be in charge – when last I saw him he fairly definitely stated that he could not get away – I understand how unfortunately he is placed.

If I am in charge it will be Australian and headquarters at Hobart.

We hope to have a good ship with the *Nimrod* as tender; the *Nimrod* will deposit coal at Cape Adare probably. We think of leaving four men at Cape Adare, another batch as near the Magnetic Pole as possible, to take a year's reading, and sledge inland to it. We hope to have two more land parties between Gaussberg and Adélie Land. These latter parties can knit up the coast line but will do very little in the hinterland. Every branch of scientific work will be attended to so far as equipment permits. Regard will also be had for economic resources; Australia will be the gainer should anything eventuate . . .

My best wishes go with you for the safety of your expedition, for the alleviation of your hardships and for your final success.

Sincerely yours, now and always,
Douglas Mawson[44]

23 November 1910, Lyttelton, dockside with *Terra Nova*, Captain Scott gets unwelcome news from Great Britain

Public excitement about the impending departure of *Terra Nova* has built to the point that Scott has been obliged to have a 'NO ADMITTANCE EXCEPT ON BUSINESS' sign erected on the gangway – a rare unfriendly note in an otherwise warm relationship between the expedition and the Christchurch community.

Still, Scott has many other worries. Now, just a few days before he leaves for Antarctica, the news has reached New Zealand that Amundsen is also on his way to the South Pole, and the press ask Scott for a public statement. While normally Scott would not have deigned to even acknowledge the existence of a rival, the fact is that his own crew are now also aware of Amundsen's change of plans. Just the day before, his Norwegian expedition member Lieutenant Tryggve Gran received a whole folder of Norwegian newspaper cuttings detailing Captain Amundsen's intentions. So, for the sake of expedition morale, and to relieve the pressure of the press, Scott feels obliged to speak.[45]

Striking what he feels is just the right tone – British equanimity itself, atop a very stiff upper lip – he calmly explains to the press reporters pushing in around him at the docks, like baby chicks around a mother hen, that he is well aware of Amundsen's change in plans. And yes, he has also heard rumours that the Norwegian intends to proceed to McMurdo Sound – he in fact received a telegram from London several weeks earlier informing him that Amundsen had ordered from the British Admiralty special charts of the McMurdo Sound/Ross Sea area, which was a real worry. However, let Captain Scott be very clear on this point. The English expedition leader thinks that Amundsen choosing this particular approach 'is highly improbable'.[46]

Far more likely is that Amundsen will make for the Weddell Sea on the far side of Antarctica from McMurdo Sound and the Ross Sea, establishing camp on Graham's Land. The ascent to the pole from there is far smoother and more gradual, if also a longer distance compared with the shorter, rougher approach from McMurdo Sound. Scott adds:

> It has been suggested that Amundsen's action is a breach of etiquette in view of our known plans, but that is not at all the proper view. There is no reason whatever he should not attempt to reach the Pole from any quarter except that for which we are known to be bound. Personally, I should welcome friendly competition, which could only lead to a better knowledge of the Antarctic Continent and its physical condition, but it is, I think, a matter for regret that Amundsen should have kept the details of his plan secret.[47]

Nevertheless, may the better man win, what?

'If the rumour is true that Amundsen hopes to reach the South

Pole from a spot on the coast of West Antarctica,' Scott says to a particularly persistent journalist, 'then I wish him good luck.'[48]

Scott's public point is that Amundsen can do as he jolly well pleases. Scott's expedition, with all its attendant scientific programs, will proceed as planned.

Truly, however, Scott remains more than a little worried about Amundsen, as are his backers in London.

Late November 1910, Adelaide, Mawson makes news in a different field

It is all very, very odd. Most people, since forever, had thought that the value of the country around the Flinders Ranges was just about nothing. Nothing could grow on it, no animal could graze on it, it is too far from anywhere for anyone to really want to live there, so how could it be worth anything?

But now the papers run with an interesting bit of news. Douglas Mawson, the chappie who had gone to Antarctica with Shackleton – you know the one – has announced that he has discovered a huge mineral-bearing lode of great scientific and, potentially, economic interest to Australia. Apparently after travelling on camel – no, really – to that unforgiving country of the Northern Flinders Ranges around Mt Paynter, he was led by some old-timers to some finds that they found interesting, and he agreed. According to Mawson, he has discovered quite a few unusual minerals including high-grade radioactive materials within a radium bearing formation.[49]

Still, a canny man, Mawson. Before this announcement had been made public – he had actually gone up there a month earlier – he has made his own investment in the small company that has been established to investigate the find. They say that radium may be very valuable one day.

28 November 1910, Port Chalmers, Dunedin, a battle royal breaks out

The Oates and Scott contretemps is not the only conflict brewing among the men, as the Evanses – Teddy and Taffy – are also having more than a wee spot of bother. Second in command Evans has been less than impressed with Taffy ever since the petty officer's unseemly behaviour in Cardiff. Part of Teddy's frustration is that Taffy is clearly a favourite of Scott's, whereas the relationship between Teddy and Scott is strained, owing somewhat to the growing strain between their wives.

Matters came to a head in Lyttelton two days earlier when, after the Bishop of Christchurch blessed *Terra Nova*, an extremely drunk Taffy careered off the gangplank (some say actually pushed by Teddy), and 200 pounds of drunken humanity plunged headlong into the harbour. Scott dismissed the hulking Welshman on the spot, only to all too predictably soften and reinstate him the next day, much to the chagrin of Teddy. To keep Taffy out of Teddy's eyesight, and harm's way, once the gigantic drunk sobered up – and it took a while – he was put on a train from Christchurch to Dunedin. *Terra Nova* is docking there on a brief stopover to take on coal, and Taffy has now rejoined them.

And it is here that heightened tension among the wives, particularly between the domineering Kathleen Scott and Teddy's wife, Hilda, breaks into the open. The men have grown to dislike Mrs Scott's intrusion into the expedition preparations and are given to wondering just who is running this show: the Owner or his good wife. A frosty silence tends to descend over the crew whenever she is around . . . and heads down, lads, for here she comes now.

On this, *Terra Nova*'s last full day at Port Chalmers before she heads south on the morrow, the underlying tension suddenly bursts into the open. First, Teddy – likely encouraged by his wife – has a set-to with Captain Scott over what he sees as his shortcomings, including his too lenient treatment of Taffy, and then the tensions between the wives spill into the open. Kathleen Scott's and Hilda Evans's fond farewells to their respective husbands end in a fierce shouting match between the two ladies. Halfway through the fight, Wilson's wife, Oriana, enters the fray, adding her tuppence worth. In a letter to his mother describing the scene, the highly amused Oates writes:

> *Mrs Scott and Mrs Evans have had a magnificent battle; they tell me it was a draw after fifteen rounds. Mrs Wilson flinging herself into the fight after the 10th round and there was more blood and hair flying about the hotel than you would see in a Chicago slaughter house in a month. The husbands got a bit of the backwash and there is a certain amount of coolness which I hope they won't bring into the hut with them.*[50]

Mercifully, they are saved, if not by the bell then at least by the shrill tones of the steam whistle of a ship about to leave.

29 November 1910, Port Chalmers, Dunedin, and so . . . goodbye

Kathleen Scott chooses not to farewell her husband with a traditional kiss, because she does not want the crew to see him sad. Oriana Wilson has no such concerns. After *Terra Nova* sets off at 2.30 pm in bright sunshine from Dunedin Harbour, Oriana stays on board right until they get to the heads, at which point a tug takes her off. As *Terra*

Nova pulls away, Bill Wilson stays at the bow waving happily at his beloved wife, as does she from the bow of the tug, and they continue to do so until they can see each other no more. He describes this emotional farewell in his diary that night as 'a goodbye that will be with me till the day I see her again in this world or the next – I think it will be in this world and some time in 1912'.[51]

And so *Terra Nova* struggles south, so heavily overladen that what was her Plimsoll line – before being personally painted over by Lieutenant Teddy Evans – is now a good two yards below the surface. On board are 32 men running the ship and another 33 men who, if conditions are right, are to be landed at Cape Crozier at the eastern end of Ross Island. A handful of them are hoping to get to the last word in South, the Pole itself.

Meanwhile, every square inch of deck above and below water has either cargo or a claimant. While 405 tons of coal has been stowed in bunkers in the main hold, another 30 tons lies in sacks on the upper deck. The main deck allows little room to move for the disassembled material to build the huts, the sledges, travelling equipment, larger scientific instruments and machines, not to mention the motor sledges, the ice-house filled with three tons of ice, 162 carcasses of mutton and three carcasses of beef. A finishing touch to this scene of controlled chaos: the 33 snarling dogs on the deck, chained just far enough apart that they can't savage each other.

Below, the crew and the men of the landing parties – all 65 of them – are living and working tightly together, with many a 'hot hammock' that is claimed by as many as three men in eight-hour shifts on the day, and . . .

And what is that smell? That would be the urine and excreta of the ponies above seeping through the leaky decks onto everything below. And all of this is before they have hit any storms. On the day before leaving, Lawrence Oates wrote to his mother, 'I only pray to heaven we don't get very heavy weather going south, or there is bound to be trouble.'[52]

Chapter Six

Journey to the Bottom of the Earth

[Captain Scott] cried more easily than any man I have ever known.
What pulled Scott through was character, sheer good grain, which ran
over and under and through his weaker self and clamped it together.

Apsley Cherry-Garrard, *The Worst Journey in the World*

Long have I waited lonely,
Shunned as a thing accursed
Monstrous, moody, pathetic,
The last of the lands and the first.

Douglas Mawson quoted these lines from Canadian poet Robert Service
in his address to the Australasian Association for the Advancement of
Science, as he sought funding to mount an expedition to Antarctica

1 December 1910, Adelaide, Mawson receives news

After no contact with Shackleton since August – when Shackleton
had at least reassured him that the promise of Lysaght's £10,000 was
still secure – Mawson is a man confused.

After all, this has been going on for nearly a year! Shackleton's
enthusiasm for leading the expedition has waxed and waned and
then waxed and waned some more and even gone off on an entirely
different tangent.

At one time, Mawson even read in the English newspaper *The Sphere* that Shackleton was planning an expedition identical to the one that Mawson had presented the plans for in January – with no mention of Mawson himself taking part in it – and that he had already presented those plans to the Royal Geographical Society. The next time, he heard that Shackleton had abandoned all ideas about leading an Antarctic expedition.

One way or another, it cannot go on, and after Mawson writes to Shackleton in desperation, insisting that Shackleton either commit or resign, at last on this day a cable from Sir Ernest arrives at Mawson's Adelaide residence, withdrawing from the expedition.

Mawson is not surprised, and if anything he is very pleased. It gives him the certainty he needs. If this is going to happen, it will be because he and he alone has made it happen, and he sets out to do exactly that. Mawson is now the man. And not having Shackleton on board will remove a large part of the British flavour of the expedition, which also pleases him. He later writes:

For many reasons, besides the fact that it was the country of my home and alma mater, I was desirous that the Expedition should be maintained by Australia. It seemed to me that here was an opportunity to prove that the young men of a young country could rise to those traditions, which have made the history of British Polar exploration one of triumphant endeavour as well as of tragic sacrifice. And so I was privileged to rally the 'sons of the younger son'.[1]

And one of the roles of those younger sons, he is sure from the beginning, will be to:

afford the world an opportunity of seeing what Australians can do. It is a big project, which has the effect of bringing Australia prominently before European countries . . . Australia gains the prestige of being strong enough to investigate and claim new territory.[2]

2 December 1910 and the day thereafter, Southern Ocean, when the weather starts getting rough, the tiny ship is tossed

So overladen is *Terra Nova* that when the shifting wind blows force nine from the south on this day, as described by Wilson:

> the waist of the ship was a surging, swimming bath, and one went there at the risk of being drowned alive in one's clothes before getting out again, or else being broken up amongst the ruck of petrol cases, or else mistaking the outside of the ship's rail for the inside in a green sea and not finding one's way back again by the end of whatever rope one happened to seize as the deluge engulfed one. It was really terrific.[3]

Scott himself is in the thick of it, waist-deep at the poop-deck weather rail, the maelstrom boiling and bubbling all around him. Birdie Bowers and four others attempt to clew in the last remaining jib. Trying to reduce the sail area catching the wind, they are in an extremely precarious position out on the bowsprit, 'being buried deep in the enormous seas every time the ship plunged her nose into them with great force'.[4]

Down below, the scene is equally terrifying, as coal dust carried in the water that is flooding into the engine room sees Lashly spending hours deep in water unsuccessfully trying to keep the pump valves clear to remain operational. Furious attempts are made to clear the room and keep the heart of *Terra Nova* beating. The smaller auxiliary pump is commissioned, and manned by the stokers, who battle against the roaring wave of water within the room, which slams from side to side at the vicious whim of the raging ocean.

Under dim lamplight, the engine room resembles a scene from Dante's *Inferno*. The occasional glare from one of the momentarily sprung furnaces affords a view of clattering, steaming pumps, against which the waters rise inch by inch. This is not 'hell or high water', this is both.

'The seas through which we had to pass to reach the pack-ice must be the most stormy in the world,' Apsley Cherry-Garrard would write. 'Dante tells us that those who have committed carnal sin are tossed about ceaselessly by the most furious winds in the second circle of Hell. The corresponding hell on earth is found in the southern oceans.'[5]

Terra Nova finds herself among the highest waves and heaviest winds that the men – even some of the old salts, gnarled by decades on the seven seas – have ever seen. The port whaleboat swings from its davits and is wedged under the bridge deck even as part of the bulwark is carried away, along with 60 cases of petrol and 20 cases of lubricating oil. A dog is lost overboard, its broken chain snaking away into the spume, while the ponies are in a trouble all their own.

And look there! Right into the green maelstrom fearlessly stride Titus Oates and Atch Atkinson, doing everything they can, at the risk of their lives, to keep the ponies on their feet and resistant to the tons of water washing over them.[6] Despite this magnificently courageous effort, still one of the ponies expires in its stall.

'I am afraid it's a bad business,' Scott suggests to Cherry-Garrard, just as Oates, once more risking life and limb, ventures aft to report another pony has gone down. Meanwhile, Meares has his hands full, hauling on the chains of other dogs washed overboard, lest they die by hanging rather than drowning.

In the rolling seas, the situation is becoming ever more desperate. With *Terra Nova* leaking like a wooden sieve, the wind screaming like an evil witch and the pitching of the ship worse than ever, the engines are cut for fear of a steam explosion as a result of the rising water. But now smoke is spotted coming up through the seams in the afterhold, which is full of coal, liquid fuel and gas built up because of the battened-down hatchways. The threat of fire is patent, and the only likely solution is to flood the ship – an action that would surely result in her foundering.

In a stolen moment, Wilson confides to his diary, 'The ship all the time rolling like a sodden, lifeless log, her lee gunwale under water every time . . . the sky was like ink and water was everywhere.'[7]

When both steam pumps give up the ghost, the situation becomes more than merely critical. And yet, Teddy Evans does not panic. A good man in a crisis, he organises all available officers and staff to be brought in to clear water from the stoke hold by hand, for that is the only place that can be reached with buckets. Two hours on, two hours off, the waterlogged men, some nude in the heat 'like Chinese coolies',[8] work solidly throughout Friday and into the early hours of Saturday relaying buckets with great difficulty to and from the stoke hold up the steep steel ladders to the upper deck. All the while, however – in the manner of maritime men since the dawn of time – they sing at the top of their lungs every song they know. All sing:

> My Betty is a bonny lass,
> my Betty wears a thumb,
> and often looks into a glass,
> but 'tis a glass of rum.
> Bess, Bess, Bess, Betty, Bett,
> hasten to my arms,
> and then a fig for Kate.[9]

It is only just under 24 hours later, after nearly five tons of water have been bailed, that the boilers are able to be refired and the pump restarted. The most dangerous work of all was done by Teddy Evans and Birdie Bowers – crawling below and cutting through to the pump shaft to free it of a 'coal ball', a potentially devastating bolus of coal dust and oil, which had been clogging the pump.

And yet . . . is it a sign? As described by Wilson:

> There came out a most perfect and brilliant rainbow for about half a minute or less, and then suddenly and completely went out. If ever there was a moment at which such a message was a comfort it was just then – it seemed to remove every shadow of doubt, not only as to the present issue, but as to the final issue of the whole expedition – and from that moment matters mended and everything came all right.[10]

Not that they have escaped the storm fully unscathed for all that. Apart from the damage to the bulwarks of the ship, they have lost two ponies, one dog, ten tons of coal, 65 gallons of petrol and a case of the biologists' spirits. Their own spirits, however, have been restored with the realisation that by pulling together they have managed to thwart complete catastrophe, surviving seas with waves estimated at up to 35 feet high.

The nautical equivalent of a baptism of fire, there is great satisfaction that they have been severely tested and survived. Now shaking herself down like a dog after a deluge, *Terra Nova* proudly pins back her ears and sallies – all sing – 'all way on down south, way on down south of London town'.

Early December 1910, Adelaide, Mawson indulges his love and engages his passion

Although thoughts of marriage flutter like butterflies, Mawson remains faithful to his other love: the 'Australasian Antarctic Expedition', as he has decided to call it.

In between university lectures and outback field trips, Mawson makes frequent journeys to various parts of Australia, trying to raise funds. As well as spruiking to potential donors the scientific rewards of the expedition, he also emphasises the considerable contribution it will make to Australia's growing sense of nationality.

On those few evenings he isn't occupied, Mawson meets Paquita, a good stick, who helps him to compose and carefully check the specific make-up of the materials, equipment and supplies that will be required. And while Paquita is stunned at the endless lists that Mawson keeps making of the things they will need – right down to how many bars of soap they will need for 26 men across four bases, men who will not be bathing often – once she realises that he is going whether she likes it or not she is determined to do everything she can to support him, and sits with him throughout the day and into the night, helping him.

And now let's see. For the main base, we will be needing no less than 16 tons of food, to keep 12 men alive for a year, not forgetting a couple of dozen dogs, coal for heating, fuel for the primus stoves, equipment for six sledging teams, needles and threads for myriad tasks, and perhaps two dozen thimbles, no, make that three . . . while for the second base, we'll need food for seven men and . . .

And so on.

Such intimate and important work brings the couple even closer, and late one Sunday afternoon, while the two are at the Delprat's Brighton holiday home, El Rincon, Mawson stays on far later than is usual. While the rest of the family gather around the piano inside, singing along to the old-time standards, Paquita and Mawson are snuggling up and gazing out to sea from their favourite spot on the veranda. After the hot day, before that sparkling ocean, it is hard to believe that on the other side of the water lies a frozen land from which Mawson has only recently returned and to which he is now more certain than ever he will soon be heading back.

But on this, day, for once, Antarctica is not foremost in Douglas's mind. Somewhere in this dream-like moment, as the waves rise and fall on the beach in rough rhythm to the gay music and robust singing emanating from within, both Douglas and Paquita realise their feelings are in perfect harmony. In the stillness of that late afternoon, there remains no question: Douglas and Paquita are deeply in love, meaning there remains only one thing to be asked. And Douglas has no sooner asked that question than Paquita has agreed to marry him.

For Paquita, 'it all seems like a dream'. 'Adelaide's hero', 'so tall, so good-looking and so much in demand', has asked her to marry him!¹¹ For his part, Douglas is equally smitten and wastes no time in formalising their commitment.

My Dear Mr Delprat,

and I hope with your consent

*My Dear Father*¹²

So begins Mawson's letter to Paquita's father, Guillaume Delprat, observing the protocol of the day as he asks for the formidable businessman's 19-year-old daughter's hand in marriage . . . at a future date. Mawson continues:

Love has run out to meet love with open arms — it is the ideal story. Naturally you will be interested in my position and prospects for the future which, I must confess are not as good as I should desire when considering its reflection upon one so good as Paquita. There is, however, dogged grit in our family (though I am sorry to say it) which has dragged us over many obstacles and will never forsake me while I have my being . . .

At the present moment I am looking forward only to your consent to my union sometime in the future with your treasured daughter Paquita. In all probability I shall go to the Antarctic for 15 months from the end of next year, then I shall return with your consent to my dear love . . .

Be merciful —

Yours very truly

Douglas Mawson

P.S. Mrs Delprat will be interested to read this.[13]

Ol' man Delprat immediately responds by return post. He is more than happy to welcome Douglas into the family but quickly comes to the point concerning the wisdom of proposing to his daughter only to have her anxiously left dangling for 15 months while he travels to Antarctica. 'Do you think it a fair thing to make a woman go through?' he asks his prospective son-in-law, pointedly. 'Do you think it helps you to build up the home you want to provide her with?'[14]

In short, Douglas should think seriously about cancelling his proposed expedition. Somehow, however, Mawson manages to bring the old man round – there is never a worry with Paquita – and the engagement is formally announced. The preparations for the expedition remain on the basis of full steam ahead and let the devil take the hindmost.

Reporters, unsure which of Delprat's four daughters is Mawson's fiancée, have him engaged to each one in turn, and Paquita carefully installs the articles and photographs in her album.

'Douglas Mawson, the brilliant young scientist who covered himself with glory in the Shackleton expedition . . . has undertaken to lead one expedition to the South Pole and another to the church,' reports *The Bulletin*.[15]

Mawson's hard-working mother, recovering from a recent stroke, writes to Paquita, 'I am very glad to know that Douglas has found a girl he can love, as I know he is difficult to please.'[16]

30 December 1910 to New Year's Day 1911, Southern Ocean, *Terra Nova* is on the very shores of the frozen continent

And always it is like this. Though Antarctica can be formidable in her defences against all those who would choose to land on her by brute force alone, she is inclined to cede to seduction. So, with Birdie Bowers up in the crow's nest for much of the time, spotting the ice obstacles before them and calling warnings to the bridge, *Terra Nova* keeps moving through the heavy pack ice. And when she has to get to grips with the ice, she performs wonderfully well, Scott recording with great satisfaction that, 'as she bumped the floes with mighty shocks, crushing and grinding a way through some, twisting and turning to avoid others, she seemed like a living thing fighting a great fight'.[17]

Finally, the ship is in clear water and the frozen continent lies before them. By the following day, the first of the New Year, they can even see the familiar sight of Mt Erebus, and Scott practically feels as if he has come home. Not that Lady Antarctica is *quite* as accommodating as he had hoped, however. The seas around being too rough to make a landing at his intended destination of Cape Crozier, they are obliged to move to the next best option, which is the very familiar McMurdo Sound, where the *Discovery* expedition was based.

4 January 1911, Cape Evans, Scott's party make their base

So it has always been; so it will always be. And yes, so it is on this occasion. Nearing the end of a long and difficult journey, on 4 January 1911 there is a rising excitement among the men of the ship as their journey's end approaches. Their collective gaze roves along the shoreline, looking for the spot where they will land.

With ice blocking the way to his old base of Hut Point, Scott settles on establishing his Winter Quarters at Cape Evans – formerly called 'the Skuary' and now renamed for his second in command – some seven miles south of Cape Royds and 16 miles north of Hut Point. It is Scott's hope that this will be 'a place that would not be easily cut off from the barrier'.[18] And so it is that on this picture-perfect day, the skipper, Lieutenant Pennell, carefully nudges *Terra Nova* forward until they are able to neatly anchor right up against an area of fast ice that is about a mile and a half away from the solid land where the hut will be constructed.

With the ship secured, the unloading can begin, led by the 17 surviving ponies. One by one, they are put in a 'horse box' and carefully unloaded from the ship to the ice by derrick, to be led delicately across the ice to the land, where they delight in rolling in the snow, snorting, rolling, snorting some more, whinnying at the sheer pleasure of it all! Yes, the snow upon the ice is relatively soft 'neath their hooves on this amazingly warm day, and not quite as comfortable as solid land would have been, but for the ponies anything is better than being cramped in tiny stalls upon that wretched, rolling ship, so constantly awash in green seawater.

5 January 1911, Ceylon, Kathleen Scott heads back to England

Kathleen Scott is missing her husband terribly but at least busying herself at every stop along the way, sightseeing. On this day, she has risen early to see Ceylon's magnificent Buddhist shrine, the Temple of the Tooth, before the ship's departure that afternoon. And yet at dinner on the ship that evening on the high seas, an odd thing occurs. A naval man, also returning to England, one Captain Blair, muses mildly, 'It seems rather absurd for me to drink this soup, because I'm going to drown myself directly.' Which he then does. Man overboard. He is not found. The ship sails on.

5 January 1911 and five days thereafter, Cape Evans, Scott and his men get to grips

The rested ponies are put to work and are soon seen to be pulling their weight, and then some, relaying anything from 12 to 18 hundredweight across the ice from *Terra Nova* to the hut site that Scott has selected. Despite remaining under the close and watchful eye of Oates, though, the ponies are anything but consistent. Relatively weak ones such as Blossom, Blücher and Jehu seem exhausted after hauling for only a very short way, while others such as Weary Willie, Snippets and Hackenschmidt are forever fractious, bordering on impossible to deal with. As a matter of fact, Hackenschmidt, of possible Arabian extraction, possesses the unfortunate habit of kicking out with both fore and hind legs at whoever draws near to him, and he is so athletically dangerous that he is named for the Estonian professional wrestling champion, famous for the same quality.

And then there is the most vexatious of all: Christopher, who is sweet as a mother's kiss until within sight of a sledge, at which point he turns as suddenly violent as Mr Hyde, kicking out and biting anyone displaying the unforgivable presumption of trying to approach him with the traces, even including the experienced Oates.

One notable exception to these oh so problematic ponies is Punch, who has a constantly calm nature allied with a willingness to work, and Oates takes a particular shine to him because of it.

Part of the problem with all the shivering creatures is their total unfamiliarity with the work they're being asked to do. Unsure of their footing on the smooth ice, spooked by the trailing sledges, annoyed by their traces and swingle trees (the wooden bar immediately behind the pony used to balance its pull), they strain to escape, and the ensuing tumbles and falls cause minor injuries to man and beast alike. 'There is no doubt that the bumping of the sledges close at the heels of the animals is the root of the evil,' Scott records in his journal.[19]

Two or three ponies get away from their handlers, careering off in all directions, although the guilty usually return soon after like sorry lost dogs. The real dogs, meantime, are also being used to haul supplies and equipment – usually with more effect – though even they have their problems, and it's not long before one of the dog teams joins the act, dragging its driverless sledge and fallen dogs in any direction until recaptured.

And then there are the other conveyances . . .

'The motor-sledges are working well,' Scott writes, after their engines mercifully start on the afternoon of landing, 'but not very well; the small difficulties will be got over, but I rather fear they will never draw the loads we expect of them.'[20]

Four days into the unloading process, a massive crack rends the air, as the ice beneath their feet breaks and splinters. In an instant, the heaviest motor sledge has broken through the floe and is heading to the freezing seabed 60 fathoms below, nearly taking a man with it.

There are other close calls . . . For, look there! There, right beside the ice astern of the bow of *Terra Nova*, eight agitated killer whales suddenly appear, lifting their massive snouts out of the water. Something is exciting them, but what?

Scott calls to photographer Herbert Ponting to try to get a picture of them. That worthy begins to do just that and is standing on the ice floe next to two tethered dogs when everything goes crazy. From beneath, the whales start ramming the ice so fiercely that it begins to crack and rock wildly! The dogs bark, the ice booms, there are shouts aplenty, and it is all the terrified Ponting can do to jump back before it all splits asunder. The badly shaken photographer would later report that the breath of whale was 'like a blast from an air-compressor'.[21] Fortunately for the dogs, the ice on which they are standing remains intact despite the constant ramming, and so the killer whales are denied hot dogs for breakfast. Scott records in his journal:

> It was clear that the whales shared our astonishment, for one after another their huge hideous heads shot vertically into the air through the cracks which they had made. As they reared them to a height of six or eight feet it was possible to see their tawny head markings, their small glistening eyes, and their terrible array of teeth – by far the largest and most terrifying in the world. There cannot be a doubt that they looked up to see what had happened to Ponting and the dogs.[22]

A far more benign presence are the local penguins, which are particularly attracted to the sound of the men roaring out songs and nursery rhymes. 'She has rings on her fingers and bells on her toes, and she shall have music wherever she goes', the men bellow out to the besuited birds, who excitedly huddle together on the floe to hear the full gala performance. Alas, when soloist Meares, for an encore, proceeds to launch into 'God Save the King', the penguins' response is less positive. As one, the previously fascinated group waddles off and dives 'headlong into the water'.[23] Sigh. Everyone's a critic . . .

All up, the work goes on, and Scott is satisfied that by 10 January *Terra Nova* is all but unloaded and the hut coming along apace. The whole process, however, and the responsibility of it has so consumed Scott that to some of his men he has appeared remote. As Wilfrid Bruce reports back by letter to his sister, Kathleen Scott:

He talked very little to anybody and sometimes days passed without my saying more than a few words to him, but I think Wilson and Evans probably saw a little more of him, and by the time things were landed and got a bit settled, he bucked up a lot and said many pretty things to us.[24]

11 January 1911, Sydney, Mawson sees a dream projected

It is a gathering of the good and the great of Australia's scientific community, at Australia's oldest and grandest university – a meeting of horn-rimmed glasses, high foreheads and starched collars, surrounded by towering sandstone edifices upon which ivy grows. For, on this auspicious day, Mawson places his plans before a gathering of the Australasian Association for the Advancement of Science at their meeting at the University of Sydney.

Using a machine and lantern slides that allow him to project enormous images up on the wall, Mawson speaks with a curious mixture of passion and academic restraint as he sets out his plans. What he wishes to do, he announces to these great men of science, is to head to the huge unexplored scientific frontier that lies right beneath Australia and establish no fewer than three bases upon the 2000-mile sweep of Antarctic coastline, west from Cape Adare to

Gaussberg – a coast that has never known the tread of man.

As the scientists listen with rapt attention, he explains how each base would have equipment to record temperature, humidity, wind speed and direction, barometric pressure, cloud cover, hours of sunshine and fluctuations in magnetic declination – all of which can be collated upon their return to give an entire picture of the meteorological and magnetic conditions in that part of the world. And that is not all. From those bases, he and his men would venture forth on their sledges to explore the terrain for major features, for mineral deposits, for fossils that might indicate Antarctica's history from many millions of years ago. They would map a coast that has previously gone all but unsighted, let alone mapped. And beyond all this, that which would be good for the sciences would be good for Australia, showing the rest of the world just what Australians were capable of.

He is here to seek their backing for him to approach other sponsors with their imprimatur, and also to get some of their own money as a good start.

He finishes with a patriotic flourish, in passionate tones:

Can our scientific societies remain content to allow distant countries to poach on their inherited preserves? Can Australians remain heedless of this land of great potentialities lying at our doors? Can our national conscience remain unstirred in the face of achievements to be accomplished, achievements such as have ever formed girders in the constitution of nations.[25]

Blessedly, at his conclusion he is not only met with loud applause but also, far more importantly, the Association gives him its unanimous endorsement and grants him £1000 of its funds, albeit with some hefty strings attached. In return for its money, the Association seeks assurance that Mawson is and will remain the leader of an *Australian* expedition, the results of which will be published in *Australia*; the expedition will remain in the control of *Australia*; the committee will choose the personnel (with Mawson's final approval); the committee will decide the scientific program; and its £1000 will only be used to purchase scientific instruments.[26]

Agreed. Agreed. Agreed. Agreed. Agreed.

Mawson is delighted to go along with it all, for in his eyes these demands are nothing less than reasonable.

The Association also appoints a committee composed of the president of the Australasian Association for the Advancement of Science (AAAS), Professor Orme Masson of Melbourne University, together with Professor David of the University of Sydney and Professor George Cockburn Henderson of the University of Adelaide – who are charged with drawing up a suggested scientific work program for the expedition, appointing staff in conjunction with Mawson, promoting the expedition and carrying out the raising of funds in their respective states.

Together, this committee will also approach the Commonwealth Government with the purpose of enlisting its support. Yes, when the then prime minister Alfred Deakin moved the motion three years earlier to give £5000 to the Shackleton expedition, he expressly said, 'No similar demand is likely to be made for many years,' but things have changed.[27] This really is an Australian expedition, and it is only appropriate that it is supported by the Australian Government.

14 January 1911, Bay of Whales, Amundsen makes his base[28]

Perfect. After their long journey from Norwegian shores, lasting now 22 weeks and four days, *Fram* at last pulls into Amundsen's intended destination. He will establish his Winter Quarters – *Framheim*, as in 'home of the *Fram*' – here in the Bay of Whales, located not on land but on the Great Ice Barrier, some 450 miles to the east of Scott's position on McMurdo Sound.

It is a deeply considered decision by Amundsen. After long study of every map of this area he has been able to get his hands on from previous expeditions, he has come to the key conclusion that this small bight is the very one that James Clark Ross observed and charted in 1842. Yes, the shape is slightly different, as bits have broken off and reformed, but the basic form is constant enough that he is prepared to bet his life – literally – that the thing that has arrested the fearful force of the Barrier at this very point is 'something that was firmer than the hard ice – namely, the solid land. Here then the barrier piled itself up and formed the bay we now call the Bay of Whales.'[29]

Yes, there have been changes at the western edge even since Shackleton's *Nimrod* expedition was here (it was Shackleton who gave the Bay its name, due to the abundance of whales that were found here), but nothing has substantially changed at the face of the Barrier. And, unlike Shackleton, the lucky Norwegian has found the bay clear of pack ice and totally accessible. The point is that this carefully calculated risk – two miles in from the shore as added protection against the ice they are on calving off into the sea – puts them 70 miles closer to the South Pole than Scott and his party at McMurdo Sound, with initially easy access to the path south.

Notwithstanding that Amundsen is far removed at this starting point from the Beardmore Glacier discovered by Shackleton – as yet, the only proven route to the Pole – Amundsen is confident in the power of his dogs and that if there is a way up to the Polar Plateau from here, they will be able to cross it.

An added advantage for Amundsen is that the weather by the Bay of Whales is far more benign than at McMurdo Sound. Many of Antarctica's blizzards originate from the Transantarctic Mountains, which are much closer to the Sound than they are to the Bay.

20 January 1911, McMurdo Sound, Scott and his men make a home

Within two weeks, the wooden hut, measuring 50 feet by 25 feet, is finished. It is replete with double boarding on both sides of the frame and a seaweed 'quilted' lining, with a boarded and similarly insulated floor that also boasts a top layer of felt.

A porch entrance houses the acetylene gas generator fitted by the mechanic Bernard Day to light the hut, and he has also professionally installed the ventilator, cooking range and stove, taking particular care to route the chimney pipes first through the living quarters in the manner of rough central heating. Whatever else, it is unlikely that the cold will prove too severe a problem so long as the stove stays alight.

In the middle of the hut is a wall made of crates of supplies, and this also serves as something of a class border, with – in the British maritime fashion – the officers' quarters, the Wardroom, positioned on one side and the enlisted men's quarters, the Mess deck, on the other.

The place is not without some comforts from home, and if the penguins and seals are seen to cock their heads quizzically at about this time, it is likely because for the first time the strains of Enrico Caruso and Nellie Melba are soaring across their frozen world, as the gramophone is one of the company's favourite forms of entertainment.

And Oates? He has little free time at all, as he continues to concentrate on the health of the ponies. It seems to the others that he is tending to them all through the night and day, feeding them, calming them, ensuring that enough ice has been melted so they have water to drink, taking them out for exercise, doing what he can to keep them comfortable and warm, trying to ensure they can sleep properly despite the freezing conditions and allowing them to recover from the dreadfully hard labour they have endured in dragging the heavy loads over the treacherously slippery ice.

Scott is an admirer of his devotion: 'Oates is splendid with them – I do not know what we should do without him.'[30] For his part, Cherry-Garrard is an equal admirer of all of Oates's work with the ponies, and the troublesome pony Christopher in particular, noting approvingly that Oates's 'management of this animal might have proved a model to any governor of a lunatic asylum'.[31]

Of course, Oates has Anton Omelchenko to assist him, but the horse-groom can barely utter a word of English and is frequently in moods of deepest melancholia caused by general homesickness and specific worries as to how his one-legged girlfriend is getting along without him back home in Russia. Despite that, he is a hard-worker, who returns Oates's admiration for him in spades. As the Norwegian expedition member, Gran, will later recall, the one bit of English that Anton has mastered is the one he uses in reply to most questions put to him: 'Captain Oates good to horses, good to Anton.'[32] But even with Anton's help, it is an uphill, frozen struggle, and Oates continues to worry about the ponies' suitability for the crucial task that has been set for them.

On this, the night before they leave for their first excursion to the south – to lay the depots in preparation for their summer assault on the Pole – Oates has been frank in his letter to his mother:

I can see myself being kept pretty busy as none of the people here know anything about the ponies and they are a fairly rough and obstreperous lot . . . The transport is of course the great question and between you and me things are not as rosy as they might be . . . Scott and Evans boss the show pretty well and their ignorance about marching with animals is colossal. On several points Scott is going contrary to what I have suggested . . . That is the growl I have got . . . the ponies have improved out of recognition since coming ashore they are fat but of course soft . . . they have no exercise no-one being available for the job. This is a point Scott cannot see the [sense] of but if he wishes to march with soft animals I am content. We shall I am sure be handicapped by the lack of experience in trekking which the party possess . . .

I wonder what has happened to Amundsen? Scott thinks he has gone to the Weddell Sea to try for the Pole from there. If it comes to a race he will have a great chance of getting there as he is a man who has been at this kind of game all his life and he has a hard crowd behind him . . .

Don't think from what I say Scott is likely to endanger anyone, it will be quite the reverse and I may be maligning the man altogether as I admit I am annoyed at him not taking my advice more freely about the marches . . .[33]

And speaking of being annoyed, Scott was actually a lot more than that when, a week or so before heading south on the depot-laying journey, he and Meares made the brief journey 16 miles down the coast to *Discovery*'s former base at Hut Point. The expedition leader is furious at what he finds.

Shackleton, the last man to have used it, when he was there in 1909, has left the bloody door open! The result is that the hut is all but unusable. What was once a sheltered space has had snow blowing into it over two years, and this has now turned into a solid block of ice, as in the perpetual modern struggle between Antarctica and the human imprint, Antarctica is forging forward. 'It is difficult to conceive the absolutely selfish frame of mind that can perpetrate a deed like this,' Scott writes of his feelings. 'Finding that such a simple duty had been neglected by one's immediate predecessors disgusted me horribly.'[34]

Late January 1911, Adelaide, Mawson leaves on an important mission

January has been a rather profitable month for Mawson. In addition to the £1000 pledged by the AAAS, he has raised a further £5000 from private backers. Together with the £10,000 pledged by Lysaght, he has now amassed – dot three, carry one, subtract two – £16,000 in the kitty, a fair start, what with the newly established committee dedicated to raising more.

So, with fund-raising matters well in hand in his own country (however, still well short of the – *small cough* – £40,000 required to mount an expedition), Mawson decides to head to the old country. It is a trip he must make to raise fresh funds from the expatriate well-heeled Australians living there, make good on the promises of the British supporters he has won on the previous trip, secure a suitable vessel, purchase specialist supplies and recruit whatever Britons he might need for his crew. And of course he is particularly anxious to secure the promised Lysaght money.

Thankfully, the council of the University of Adelaide – his principal employer, after all – grants its outstanding and celebrated young lecturer the time off that he needs.

27 January 1911 and two weeks thereafter, leaving Glacier Tongue, McMurdo Sound, the Wicked Mate makes an amazing discovery

And now it is time. Taking their leave of Captain Scott and his men, Chief Officer Victor Campbell, accompanied by, among others, surgeon Murray Levick and geologist Raymond Priestley, orders his men to weigh anchor.

An archetypal Royal Naval officer, albeit of very shy disposition, Campbell has gained the ironic sobriquet the Wicked Mate for his highly controlled manner. After a few words of quiet command from him, *Terra Nova* slowly heads off towards the eastern limit of the Ross Ice Shelf, 450 miles from McMurdo Sound, where Campbell intends to establish Scott's Eastern Party and they will be the first to explore that part of the mainland known as King Edward VII Land.

Once in the vicinity, it is not long, however, before Campbell encounters precisely the same severe ice and sea conditions that stymied exploration of the area by both Scott in 1902 and Shackleton in 1908. 'Of all the desolate places in the world none can compare with this place,' Wilfrid Bruce writes in a letter to his sister Kathleen. 'Sheer 100 ft cliffs of ice, rolling smooth hills behind, all white. Not a dark speck or break of any kind could we see . . .'[35]

Try as they might, there is no way through, and Campbell must reluctantly turn the ship around and sail back along the front of the Ross Ice Shelf. They soon identify an indent, which presents another possible place to land. This is the Bay of Whales.

In 1902, Scott had discovered and named the smaller Balloon Inlet in the vicinity in honour of his first Antarctic balloon flight, aboard the *Eva*. However, since that time, a calving of ice had broken away to form the new and larger bay that Shackleton had named and that they are now slowly entering.

At around one o'clock that night, the ship is suddenly stirred into life as the amazing word spreads. Another ship! A ship has been sighted docked in the sea ice in the Bay of Whales! Among all the chaos – men grabbing for clothes and cameras and clambering onto the deck – the name on the side of this foreign ship is clearly discernible just a few hundred yards off under the summer night sky. It is the *Fram*! They are astonished, as they all somehow accepted Scott's reasoning that Amundsen would do the right thing by themselves and England and make his own assault on the Pole from the other side of Antarctica. But here he is! It is unfathomable.

Still, in the wee small hours of the morning – as bright as it is – Campbell, who has lived in Norway and can speak the language, is first to make his way across to the stubby, curiously funnel-less *Fram*, where he soon learns from the startled watchmen that Amundsen is at the Norwegians' hut, which has been built well back on the ice shelf, and that he is expected back at the ship in the early morning.

Campbell, imperturbable by nature, combines his 'great cool' with humour and warmth and . . .[36]

And here is Amundsen now, going like a steam train! Atop a rocketing sledge, his imposing figure suddenly appears, cracking a whip above his vanguard of immaculately responsive sledge dogs, who bound forward as if there is no greater joy known to them than doing precisely this. The Norwegian looks almost like a king in his element, perhaps a prince of the polar climes, master of all he surveys, as he glides across the ice at a great rate of knots but with perfect control of his animals, before he brings them to a sharp and expertly executed halt. In person, he proves to be a large and powerful man, with piercing, deep-set pale-blue eyes topping an aquiline nose and flourishing moustache that somehow manages to make him look every inch the conquering explorer. Either that or the last of the Vikings . . .

The worst thing, though? Amundsen is *so* friendly and welcoming. One might have thought that he would regard them as great rivals; he might have been stand-offish, to say the least. As it is, he could not be more hospitable, offering them breakfast up in the hut. Campbell and two of his men take him up on it. *Framheim* proves to be a very small construction of no more than 20 square yards, with a table in the middle that can be pulled up to the ceiling when not being used for mealtimes.

From the well-equipped kitchen, Amundsen's cook, Adolf Lindstrøm, presents a square meal from the *Fram*'s copious regulation stocks. Lindstrøm certainly knows what he is doing. He was with Amundsen seven years earlier on the *Gjøa*, when she became the first vessel to go through the North-West Passage, and though he is a mechanic by trade he has become a cook on this expedition to replace the one whom Amundsen sacked in Madeira.

Amundsen appears quite happy to show the British whatever they'd like to see. Looking around, they are amazed to find that not only do the Norwegians have a side annex that houses over 100 dogs but also they are well on the way to constructing a subterranean series of rooms connected by tunnels and it includes such things as a sauna and a library!

As charming and hospitable as Amundsen is, it is clear that he is first and foremost an explorer who is entirely focused on winning the race to the South Pole. On the other hand, there is nothing about him that appears to wish anything but the greatest success to the Scott expedition. As a matter of fact, generosity itself, Amundsen graciously invites Campbell and his party to make a base wherever they like, *right here* if they want to, as of course the Antarctic is free for everyone. Look, if Campbell would like to make use of Amundsen's dogs, then he is welcome to do that too! Personally, Campbell would have been prepared to accept, but he is quietly discouraged by other members of the party – not quite the done thing, don't you see – and, being unable to act without Scott's permission, declines with profuse thanks for the offer.

Still, Amundsen's apparent lack of worry about Scott's expedition is close to depressing. And it is to get worse. Having invited Amundsen over to *Terra Nova* for lunch, the Englishmen cannot help but notice, once again, that as the Norwegian arrives on a sledge pulled by five dogs, those dogs are perfectly behaved. A single whistle from Amundsen and the dogs smoothly pull up for all the world as if they are connected to a braking system.

And do you note how, after Amundsen alights from his laden sledge, he nonchalantly turns it upside down to prevent the dogs pulling away without him, but they show no inclination to do so? Their master has stopped and so must they. They don't howl, they don't fight with each other, they simply drop in their tracks and await his return.

It is all so thoroughly dispiriting that Priestley can barely concentrate on his lunch. It is such a far cry from the mangy mutts they have brought with them and the poor, pathetic ponies – two of which the Eastern Party have on board – Oates has been nurturing since they left New Zealand that it is hard to enjoy the meal.

For their part, Amundsen and his men are relieved to confirm that *Terra Nova* carries no antenna and therefore no wireless, as they know that, after the race to the Pole, there will be another race to get the news to the world. And they are also pleased to be treated to a banquet that, compared with their own well-regulated diets, is nothing short of sumptuous. That's the British for you, top heavy with all the trimmings. (Notwithstanding the very odd smell of – *can it really be? Yes, I am all but certain* – horse piss.)

Scott's dogs, Amundsen and his men note, are just one part of a multi-pronged attack on the Pole, and they have been transported south while exposed to all weathers on the roof of the ice deck. This is in stark contrast to how it was on the *Fram*, where their own 116 crack sledge dogs had a specially constructed deck all to themselves. For the Norwegians, the dogs are not a mere prong, they are the *driving force* of the southern journey. With the special attention they have received, the tightly calibrated diet fed to them at carefully worked out times of the day, they have arrived in Antarctica healthier than when they left home. (Scott's dogs, on the other hand, have arrived in Antarctica sick as . . . well, sick as dogs . . . in part because of the rigours of the journey itself, and also because they have been fed a diet of Norwegian dried fish, which is thought to have become tainted en route through the tropics.)

The more the conversation continues over lunch, the more the British men realise that these Norwegian fellows are *serious*. Serious about dogs, serious about preparation and serious about getting to the South Pole first, though they are not so impolite as to state the latter. The Englishmen realise as well that, so long as the Norwegian camp on the edge of the Great Ice Barrier doesn't calve off into the ocean – which they still see as a possibility – the Bay of Whales has one colossal advantage. As it is one degree higher in latitude than McMurdo Sound, it means that if this were a 100-yard dash to the Pole, Amundsen would effectively be starting from the seven-yard mark . . . and probably earlier in the season than Scott, because ponies are more sensitive than dogs to the cold.

Not that they can't give the Norwegian a couple of worries of his own. Towards the end of the meal, Amundsen wonders whether Scott's motor sledges are, perhaps, proving successful . . . *ja*? Ah, yes, the motor sledges. 'One of them,' explains a mischievous Campbell, referring to the one that now rests 60 fathoms down on the ocean floor, 'is already on *terra firma*.'[37]

Of course, the assumption that Amundsen makes is that Scott has succeeded in motoring across the Barrier to the foot of the Beardmore Glacier! Neither party says a word, Amundsen not wishing to appear desperate to seek further information, Campbell more than happy to leave the Norwegian wondering – a rare victorious moment in a day of defeat.

But that is all it is – a moment. At lunch's conclusion, Amundsen heartily shakes all of their hands, sincerely wishes them well, climbs back into his sledge and, as they all look on, utters a quick, incomprehensible word in Norwegian, at which point – can you *believe* it? – all of the dogs smoothly start off as one and are soon charging away, leaving the stunned Britons in their ice-sprayed wake.

Soon after, with tail between legs, *Terra Nova* slips her bonds, and Campbell bids farewell to that land he had so looked forward to exploring.

All up, the Norwegians have made a big impression on the British men, and they are under no illusions as to what they are facing. Raymond Priestley writes in his diary that night:

We have news which will make the Western Party as uneasy as ourselves and the World will watch with interest a race for the Pole next year, a race which may go any way, and may be decided by luck or by dogged energy and perseverance on either side . . .

If they get through the winter safely, they have unlimited dogs, the energy of a nation as Northern in type as we are ourselves, and experience of snow travelling that could be beaten by no collection of men in the world . . .

One thing I feel, and that is that our Southern Party will go far before they permit themselves to be beaten by anyone, and I think that two parties are very likely to reach the Pole next year, but God only knows which will get there first.[38]

Kathleen Scott's brother, Wilfrid Bruce, seems to have less doubt. For he has been stunned by the single-mindedness with which the Norwegians are pursuing the South Pole to the exclusion of all other things. While his brother-in-law's party is awash with scientists of all descriptions, pursuing everything from geological surveys, biological analysis, collection of meteorological data and magnetic variations, as well as charting the coast and trawling the seabed for specimens, Amundsen does not have a single scientific sideline and is doing no research at all. For only one thing interests him . . . 'They have 120 dogs and are going for the Pole!' Bruce writes in a letter to his sister. 'No science, no nothing, just the Pole!'[39]

Terra Nova continues her miserable retreat west, briefly calling in at Cape Evans to send a note from Campbell to Hut Point for Scott, reporting the staggering developments. They have to drag two miserable ponies through the freezing waters to shore. After what they have so recently seen of the discipline, efficiency and ease with which Amundsen's dogs move in exactly this kind of landscape, it is nothing short of pathetic. It is becoming ever more apparent that these shivering beasts will be more trouble than they are already not worth when they hit the steep terrain that is now their destination – north up the coast of Victoria Land towards Cape Adare.

Meanwhile, back at *Framheim*, not long after Campbell's visit, Amundsen makes what he calls 'a strange discovery'.

'Nearly all of us had caught cold. It did not last long – only a few hours – and then it was over. The form it took was sneezing and cold in the head.'[40]

17 February 1911 and the day thereafter, One Ton Depot, 140 miles south of Hut Point, Scott's dogs run rings

For the last fortnight, Scott's depot-laying party has been trudging through the snow – moving at around one-third of the rate of Amundsen's dogs – as their ponies and dog teams haul almost a ton of supplies to be left in their most southerly depot.

Along the trail from Hut Point, they have already laid other depots, upon which the Southern Party will rely for guidance and sustenance, particularly on the home leg of their journey from the South Pole in the coming summer. One of the most important of these, Safety Camp, lies just 15 miles south of Hut Point and is so named because it is built on old Barrier ice, beyond the tide cracks and crevasses, and therefore thought to be stable. Another is Corner Camp, some 25 miles further on and located right at the point where their route to the Pole dog-legs to get around a heavily crevassed area. From there, it is about 60 miles to Bluff Depot, where their route heads directly away from the land and due south along 169 degrees east, straight towards the Beardmore Glacier.

Now along that dead-straight route south they are in train to establish their major depot, ideally at 80 degrees south, some 80 miles south from Bluff Depot and 180 miles from Hut Point. It is important to get this major depot as far south as they can, as it is to be their last major outpost from which they will launch on the South Pole the next summer, and the first they will return to on their way back. The further south they get it, the safer they will be.

Alas, the ponies are not proving a great success. On days when Amundsen's team with their many dogs are making 20 miles in their own depot-laying exercise, Scott's team is laid up in tents, the summer blizzards too much for the ailing ponies. They are going nowhere fast. The only thing quick about them is their speed of deterioration.

Spooked by the uneven and ever softer terrain, the unfortunate nags soon grow exhausted from their endeavours. But, again, it gets worse. Scott's own dogs – which are barely suffering despite the freezing conditions and despite Scott's belief that they would be useless this far out on the Barrier – sense easy targets in the sick ponies. A few days previously, when poor pony Weary Willy fell first behind the main group and then to the ground, exhausted, the dogs instantly and instinctively turned into a veritable wolf pack and begin tearing into him, gouging his flesh with many bites before Gran and Meares could beat the brutes off with sticks.

With their problems mounting by the day, they can go little further – in Scott's mind at least. On the evening of 17 February, he announces to the others that on the morrow they will do just one half-day's march and establish their final depot there, even though that will be 38 miles short of their intended target of 80 degrees south.

For Scott, the deciding factor is the state of the ponies. He has already been forced to send three back to the base, concerned that otherwise they will die, and now it is obvious that Weary Willy is on his last legs. Scott's fear is that if they do keep going to 80 degrees south, the rest of the ponies will also be lost.

Not all in his party agree, and the strongest in his opposition is Oates. Almost from the beginning of their time together, Oates has had his doubts about the qualities of Scott's leadership, and just before heading off on this depot-laying expedition he wrote a frank letter to his mother to that effect, saying of his leader:

he would fifty times sooner stay in the hut seeing how a pair of Fox's spiral puttees suited him than come out and look at the ponies' legs or a dog's feet — however I suppose I think too much of this having come strate from a regiment where horses were the first and only real consideration.[41]

While for the most part Oates has kept his own counsel on the many matters on which he disagrees with the expedition leader, now he feels that he must speak out, as it is so important. His firm view is that they must push on and establish the depot at least another 30 miles closer to the Pole, as per their original plan. Establishing it just half a day's march away, he says, will still be too far away for the Pole Party to get back to on their return journey. All they need do now, he says, is to kill the ponies for meat as they collapse and push on. Scott, though, won't hear of it and dismisses Oates's urgings seemingly without truly listening to them.

Now, Oates is a soldier, trained to be obedient to his commander. But this is not a military outfit, after all, meaning that instant obedience and acquiescence is not legally enforceable. He decides to try one more time to convince Scott, choosing his words carefully but still exhorting him to establish the base further to the south, as their Norwegian colleague Tryggve Gran listens in closely and Weary Willie whinnies pathetically nearby with the other surviving ponies.

Scott is now becoming irritated at Oates's outrageous refusal to bow to his wishes. 'I have had more than enough of this cruelty to animals,' he replies to Oates, 'and I am not going to defy my feelings for the sake of a few days' march.'

'Sir,' Oates replies, unaccustomedly icily, but he means it, 'I'm afraid you'll come to regret not taking my advice.'

'Regret it or not, I have taken my decision as a Christian gentleman.'[42]

And that is that. The following day, with the wind 'cold and biting', Scott decides not to undertake any further half-day march south.[43] And so it is that, here at Camp 15, 79 degrees 28.5 minutes south, and still 40 miles away from the intended depot location, Scott and his men build what they call One Ton Depot. They have come some 140 miles from their starting point, which is around one-third of the distance of over 400 miles to the base of the Beardmore Glacier.

Now working quickly, they unload the fuel and the food from the sledges, systematically stacking the boxes atop each other in the now accustomed manner. They start with a snow base a little raised from its surrounds, put the flat boxes of food on top of that and then continue in a pyramidal shape from there, with the smaller things such as biscuit boxes and fuel containers being piled on in successively decreasing layers until a pile some six feet high, weighing over 2000 pounds, is formed. The sizeable tinplate Plasmon biscuit tins are placed near the summit to act as reflectors and the noticeable red fuel tins at the very apex. Around the whole pile, they stack snow and upright sledges adorned with tea tins, before finally affixing a black flag to a raised central bamboo pole, so that the cairn may be seen from a good distance.

Oates, a brooder by nature, continues to worry about this decision of Scott's regarding the horses and many other decisions besides. His thoughts form the foundation of later letters to his mother: 'Myself, I dislike Scott intensely and would chuck the whole thing if it were not that we are a British expedition and must beat those Norwegians.'[44] Several days later, he writes, 'The fact of the matter is that [Scott] is not straight, it is himself first, the rest nowhere.' Four days later, Oates feels he might have been a little too harsh on Scott, warning his mother, 'please remember that when a man is having a hard time, he says hard things about other people which he would regret afterwards . . .'[45]

For his part, Scott thinks that Oates is a 'cheery old pessimist' and writes, 'The Soldier takes a gloomy view of everything, but I've come to see that this is a characteristic of him.'[46]

Another whom Scott takes a relatively dim view of is Cecil Meares, who keeps banging on about the virtues of the dogs as opposed to the ponies. Scott confides to his diary, 'Meares, I think, rather imagined himself racing to the Pole and back on a dog sledge.'[47]

In fact, that describes precisely what Amundsen intends to do.

22 February 1911, Bay of Whales, Amundsen and his men head out

On this day, the Norwegian expedition leader and eight men set off on their seven sledges hauled by 42 dogs to undertake the second and farthest south depot-laying expedition.

Lindstrøm, left behind to keep the home fire burning, doesn't tarry too long in farewelling his compatriots. Under an overcast sky, Amundsen looks back to see his quartermaster broadly smiling . . . before scuttling back inside to the warmth of the stove almost before the last sledge has drawn away on the most arduous of sledging expeditions to date – deep into the frozen soul of this forbidding land. While Lindstrøm's next weeks are spent beside the warmth of the hearth, Amundsen and his men battle soft snow, hard headwinds and devastating blizzards, all as part of their program to make preparations for their coming attempt on the South Pole in the spring.

Over a period of eight weeks, Amundsen and his men are able to establish three depots, all in a direct line between *Framheim*, lying at 78 degrees 38 minutes south, and the South Pole, the *closest* depot of which is at 80 degrees south. The next is at 81 degrees south and – most crucially, because it is 237 miles along their journey – the last is at 82 degrees south. This last depot is 175 miles closer to the Pole than Scott's One Ton Depot, allowing the Norwegian to make a final push from roughly 550 miles away, whereas Scott must launch from his major source of supply approximately 725 miles from the Pole.

In total, Amundsen's depots contain three tons of provisions, including 22 hundredweight of fresh seal meat. The whole operation has been extremely successful, and Amundsen has every reason to be satisfied both with the amount of supplies laid so far out on the Barrier and with the fact that they have been able to gain experience in Antarctic conditions and refine the methods they will use to attack the Pole. These refinements include improving the speed with which they can make, and break, camp, working out the best method for dividing and packing supplies, and determining just which of their equipment is absolutely necessary and what can be safely left behind.

Most crucially, on a barrier surface ever prone to throwing up whirling clouds of powdered snow and thick mists that cut visibility,

Amundsen has devised a method for carefully indicating the location of each of his depots with a comprehensive series of markers (20 bamboo poles flying black flags for the 80-Degree Depot, and broken-up packing cases for the 81- and 82-Degree Depots). The markers extend six miles east and six miles west of each depot, and each one is numbered and marked with the distance to the depot. So sophisticated and efficient is this system that, at times, lines of Norwegian dried cod are used as markers on the way out and as dog food on the way back. Yes, there will be extraordinary risks awaiting them when they make their push on the Pole, but for now Amundsen spares no effort from himself or his men to reduce those risks as much as possible.

22 February 1911 and two and a half weeks thereafter, Great Ice Barrier, Scott's men head back

It has been a long haul. Leaving behind One Ton Depot, the British began to journey home in two groups, the dog teams heading out first, followed by Oates and Bowers's party with five ponies bringing up the rear, the men forever treading in the crisp rings made by the hoofs of the exhausted ponies just ahead of them.

For both parties, danger is all around. The day before, after Scott unwisely decided to take a shortcut by missing out on Corner Camp – thus putting them in the middle of the crevasse field that the route to Corner Camp had been designed to miss – the party's entire team of dogs was almost lost down a crevasse, hurtling one after the other like rabbits down a hole. Perhaps feeling guilty over having placed them in the field, Scott lowered himself on a rope 65 feet into the crevasse to rescue the last two dogs, muttering all the way back up, 'I wonder why this [crevasse] is running the way it is, you expect to find them at right angles.'[48]

And still it is not the most appalling thing that happens at this time. For it is on the next day that Scott finally picks up the note left for him by Campbell informing him of Amundsen's presence at the Bay of Whales. Scott's face reacts curiously: first going grey, then blanching, before turning angry red. How dare this Norwegian bounder stray into their territory and presume to mount his own expedition? Most of the others on the Scott expedition feel the same . . . only more so. They are in favour of a confrontation, physically throwing the blighter out if necessary. As Cherry-Garrard would later recall, 'We had just paid the first instalment of the heart-breaking labour of making a path to the Pole; and we felt, however unreasonably, that we had earned the first right of way.'[49]

It just isn't quite . . . quite . . . *right*.

Scott now sits waiting for three weeks at Hut Point for the sea to sufficiently freeze over to allow him to return to Cape Evans. It has been a brutal, demoralising experience.

'Our party is divided,' writes Gran of the pervading mood in the cramped quarters, 'and we are like an army that is defeated, disappointed and inconsolable.'[50] Of the eight ponies that Scott started out with, six have been lost on the return journey to Hut Point: three perished due to cold and exhaustion, one drowned and two had to be destroyed after becoming trapped on the unstable ice adjacent to Hut Point. One Ton Depot has not been laid as far south as he would have hoped, and now it appears that one Roald Amundsen is firmly moving into his territory. Always, the spectre of the Norwegian is there, looming ever closer.

Though Oates doesn't care to express his views out loud, he has written a letter to his mother expressing his concerns, which will await the return of *Terra Nova* to be delivered:

What do you think about Amundsen's expedition? If he gets to the Pole first we shall come home with our tail between our legs and no mistake . . . I must say we have made far too much noise about ourselves . . . photographed steaming through the fleet etc: it is rot and if we fail it will only make ourselves look more foolish. They say Amundsen has been underhand in the way he has gone about it but personally I don't see it as underhand to keep your mouth shut. I myself think these Norskies are a very tough lot.[51]

In the end, things calm and sanity prevails. In the tempest of all his feelings, Scott writes in his journal, 'One thing only fixes itself definitely in my mind. The proper, as well as the wiser, course for us is to proceed exactly as though this had not happened.'[52]

Chapter Seven

Trials and Errors

For a polar campaign the great desideratum is tempered youth. It is the vigour, the dash, the recuperative power of youth that is so necessary to cope with the extreme discomforts and trials of such exploration, which approximate to the limit of human endurance and often enough exceed it.

Douglas Mawson, *The Home of the Blizzard*

Late February 1911, London, Mawson receives bad news

And so it has come to this. After repeated enquiries by Douglas Mawson as to where the industrialist Lysaght's promised £10,000 is – none of which receive a straight answer from Shackleton – Mawson writes to Lysaght directly. Coming to understand that Shackleton and Lysaght have had a falling out of late, he tries to salvage what he can, using a favoured tactic of promising sponsors a percentage of any economic discoveries: 'Surely I can rely on you for £1,000 anyway – this would give you a good interest in the results.'

In response, Lysaght's wife is frank. Her husband is unwell and can't see him, but he has in any case already paid the money to another. 'All that he could afford,' she says, 'indeed more – he did for Sir Ernest Shackleton this time last year.'[1]

Shackleton!

Scarcely bringing himself to believe that the worst really has happened, Mawson discovers after more heated enquiries that

Shackleton has 'invested' Lysaght's money 'in other ways', the nature of which Mawson might guess as somehow being tied up with one scheme or another. The point remains: Lysaght's funds have fallen through, and Mawson is left with a gaping hole in the very finances he needs right now, particularly for the purchase of a suitable vessel.

Undaunted by such financial fragility, Mawson decides to go even deeper into debt, by moving on the canny suggestion by Kathleen Scott to include an aeroplane on the expedition – if for nothing else because of the amount of publicity it would generate, for who could forget the magnitude of the reception Louis Blériot received upon crossing the English Channel just two years previously? And it has only been a little over a year since none other than Harry Houdini flew the first plane in Australia, when he got off the ground just outside Melbourne, before taking it up to Sydney and flying it there at Rosehill Racecourse. The flight captured the public imagination in precisely the way Mawson hopes to do with his polar expedition, and he has come to the conclusion that by announcing to the public that they have bought a plane and are going to fly it in Antarctica – doing a demonstration flight in Australia on the way through – fund-raising would be made all the easier.

Enquiries are made to purchase a French plane, letters are written, commitments are made, and he moves on to the next and most crucial thing of all: recruiting the first of his most senior staff. While these will mostly be Australians, there are a few important foreign exceptions. Not only are men required with the right skills and expertise but also, like the most robust of Antarctic vessels, they must be made of the right and sternest stuff. There is little use being a well-skilled man if you are unable to endure the harshest conditions on earth, the privation, the isolation . . .

Early March 1911, Montreal, John Davis receives good news

It's not working. And nor is he. Like a reformed alcoholic trying to stay sober, start a new life and put his old life out of his head, John King Davis has journeyed to the east coast of North America, far removed from all things Antarctic, where he is hopeful of finding a job with the Canadian Northern Railway shipping service. Yes, he has loved his Antarctic experience, but in some ways he has loved it too much, for it is so all-consuming, so devouring, it leaves little room for much else. Maybe in Canada he'll find the 'else' part – and at least by going he won't be endlessly hanging around, waiting for Shackleton's next expedition to Antarctica to happen.

Yes, he feels, as his train pulls into Montreal station, he has made the right decision. But the problems prove to be many. Upon arrival, he is taken from the station to the hotel in nothing less than a sleigh. In temperatures of just ten degrees, it is hard not to think of his times in the frozen far south. And, as his bowler hat provides inadequate protection, he discovers in the sanctuary of his hotel room that the climate has achieved something that the Antarctic did not. After the journey in the sleigh, his ears are lightly frostbitten.

Now, while Canada has been described to him as a land of opportunity, a place where a young man can quickly make his fortune, it has to be said that those opportunities are not jumping out to grab him, wrestle him to the ground and fill his pockets full of cash. The job with the shipping service fails to materialise, and he is at a loose end, looking at the possibilities of finding work in Calgary instead, when there is a knock on the door. It is opportunity. But not the one he is expecting. For he now receives a cablegram from his old friend Dr Mawson. The cablegram informs him that Mawson is in London, mounting a polar expedition of his own. He wants Davis to be skipper of his ship, and second in command of the expedition. Is Davis interested?

Very, very interested indeed. And to hell with his previous reasoning that he needed to get away from Antarctica. All of that is instantly forgotten, and no matter that there are no other details of the expedition offered. 'Here,' he later recounted, 'was a definite offer and there could be only one answer. Seeing again in my mind's eye the frozen and mysterious ramparts of the last continent and counting the land of opportunity well lost for such a cause, I cabled an acceptance.'[2]

Mid-March 1911, London, Mawson is getting organised

Delighted to receive an affirmative answer from Davis, Mawson, in London, continues recruiting. Key appointments are the men he intends to put in charge of the Greenland sledge dogs he is about to purchase, dogs that he hopes will haul him on his proposed Far-Eastern Journey to explore and chart parts of the coast directly south of Australia. (Having seen the failure of Shackleton's ponies on the *Nimrod* expedition, Mawson is more convinced than ever that the answer to animal locomotion in polar climes lies in many light, fast dogs that, *in extremis*, can be eaten as you go, and not in a few heavy ponies, which need to be butchered and stored.)

To begin with, to look after these dogs Mawson likes the look of Lieutenant Belgrave Edward Sutton Ninnis of the Royal Fusiliers. When he turns up at Mawson's tiny offices at 9 Lower Regent Street, Ninnis proves to be a strapping, fine figure of a man, standing six foot four inches, with a splendid record as an athlete put in the shade only by his excellence at playing polo. Yes, there is the small matter that the 23-year-old has no experience with dogs, but that is countered by the fact that he comes across as a man who is capable of turning his hand to *anything*, and that is precisely the kind of man that Mawson wants. Though Ninnis previously applied to be a part of Scott's expedition and was rejected, Mawson now readily accepts him.

Another who makes the cut is a 27-year-old Swiss citizen and lawyer, Dr Xavier Mertz, who is an accomplished mountaineer and expert skier, good enough to have won the ski-jumping championship of Switzerland two years earlier before becoming the world champion in the discipline shortly afterwards. Of an affluent engineering family, the heavily moustachioed Mertz is an affable and adventurous young man of many skills, who was about to join the family business when he heard of Mawson's expedition and immediately journeyed to London to meet the Australian. In so doing, he displays a spirit that impresses Mawson.

True, Mertz has no more experience with dogs than Ninnis, but still Mawson decides to take a chance and puts the two foreigners in charge of the Greenland dogs that are to be purchased through the Danish Geographical Society. Instinctively, he feels they will work well together.

There are a handful of other non-Australasian recruits, including none other than Mawson's old friend from the *Nimrod* expedition, the Yorkshireman with the penchant for whisky, Frank Wild, who got to within 97 nautical miles of the Pole under Shackleton's leadership and, before that, was an able seaman on Scott's *Discovery* expedition. Mawson is honoured to have a man of such experience with him, even if, at the age of 37, Wild will also be the second oldest. He appoints him to command the expedition's central base, the one to be established next along the coast from the main base, where Mawson and the bulk of the men will be.

Mid-March 1911, Cape Evans, Scott and his men settle in, as Oates has a 'fit'

In the realm of the intellectuals, with all this scientific carry-on, all this collection of data and endless speculation about the whys and wherefores and whatnots of magnetic inclinations and declinations, whatever they are, geological formations and meteorological phenomena, it is not that Oates is *completely* uninterested, just that it is not quite his thing. He has come to this expedition as a man from the army, where entirely different things are valued – courage, marksmanship, horsemanship and so forth – and it takes some time to adjust.

The scientific fellows, whom he refers to mock-derisively as 'the faculty', have odd ways about them. Such as their absurd lack of desire to drink brandy. The thing is, the scientists actually *have* brandy here at the lower ends of the earth, but the faculty won't let any of them at it, for the brandy is reserved for 'medical comforts'.

On sledge journeys near and far, the bottles of brandy go out but always return unopened. Maybe the faculty are quietly quaffing the brandy on the side and simply not sharing? This, at least, is a theory he puts past the man who has become his great friend on this expedition, Atch Atkinson, who is greatly amused by it.

'Saw 'em again this morning,' Oates would growl to Atch, 'all full.'

'But say,' Oates asks of Atch one day, 'what do they give 'em for anyway?'

'Oh, fits,' Atch replies.

And just how does one throw a fit?

Well, Atkinson explains, generally by throwing oneself to the snow, crawling about on one's hands and knees and having a lot of uncontrolled spasms.

Doesn't sound too hard.

Later that same day, when the time is right, Bill Wilson – sometimes affectionately known to the men now as Uncle Bill – looks up to see Oates before him, on his hands and knees on the snow, trembling and twitching violently.

'Look at that man,' says Atch in Wilson's ear, with what he hopes is a suitable tone of alarm. 'He's got a fit.'

'Yes, he's got a fit all right,' Wilson replies dryly. 'Rub some snow down his back and he'll soon be all right.'[3]

28 March 1911, London, word of Scott's doings in the Antarctic breaks

News of Captain Scott's safe passage to McMurdo Sound in early January reaches London by cable the day after Scott's ship has safely returned to Stewart Island, New Zealand.

While the press coverage leads on the staggering news of *Terra Nova*'s 'discovery' of *Fram* in the Bay of Whales in early February, Mawson is far more focused on the report that Scott's second party have landed at Cape Adare, *precisely* where Mawson told Scott he intended to go. Mawson even gave him all his plans to that effect!

There is no way around it. Though Mawson does not want to think ill of Captain Scott, it really seems as if, after the Englishman refused to drop him and some companions at that very spot because he said it didn't fit in with his projected program, the blighter has then gone and plucked the plum from Mawson's plans and incorporated it into his own . . . all without Mawson!

In response, Mawson is full and frank in the views he gives on the subject to the *Daily Mail*:

It surprises me very much to hear that Captain Scott has landed a party at Cape Adare in face of the agreement between us and in view of the information I gave him. When I was in England last year it was practically arranged that I should accompany Captain Scott. I was only, however, prepared to join if Captain Scott would land me with a party at Cape Adare to carry out magnetic work along the northern coast of the Antarctic Continent. After maturely considering this, Captain Scott decided that it could not be done, at any rate the first year. Then it was that I arranged to organise an Australian expedition for scientific work along the coast between Cape Adare and Gaussberg.

My plans were put before Captain Scott and there was no secrecy in the matter. Australia has supported Captain Scott, but in the face of the information now to hand some dissatisfaction is inevitable in the Commonwealth. Captain Scott personally wrote to me the last thing before leaving Australia and asked me to furnish him with full details of my plans, and this I willingly did, giving him all particulars, including the statement that I intended to land at Cape Adare. Naturally I am sorry that circumstances have driven Captain Scott to take the course he has done.[4]

One interested reader of these remarks is Kathleen Scott, who quickly writes him a warm note in an attempt to mollify him. Mawson has a great regard for Scott's wife and is quick to respond himself, standing by his central point before softening somewhat:

Dear Mrs Scott,

. . . I do wish Captain Scott had been franker with me – instead of it all proceeding from my side. I think it is quite unnecessary for explorers to act in the way Amundsen has done.

Had Captain Scott truly desired to settle an Eastern party on K.E. VII Land this year it seems to me that the men he has had pluck enough to do it. The K.E. Land well wants doing and none but a strong expedition like Captain Scott has can do it. Any old ship from Australia can land at Cape Adare.

So you saw my complaint in the *Daily Mail* – it was rather rotten wasn't it. I was woken up after midnight by a telephone message on the phone and that is how they put it.

I am glad for your sake that Captain Scott has much the best chance of getting to the Pole, though he will have a hard race . . .[5]

Shortly thereafter, Kathleen Scott graciously invites the strapping Australian to a long lunch at her home, which goes some way towards placating him.

For his part, Sir Ernest Shackleton, also in London, has no intention of being left out on either issue, and he weighs in with typical self-assuredness, starting with the Scott/Amundsen 'Race for the Pole'. He tells the *Daily Mail*:

> Captain Scott will undoubtedly follow my route. Both men are experienced. Captain Scott has the advantage in my mind in equipment, being well supplied with motor-sledges and ponies. But against this must be set the hereditary knowledge of skiing and handling of the dogs that the Norwegians possess. The ice conditions will be much the same for both.

As to who has the *right* to operate where, he is equally forthright:

> One of Scott's parties is wintering in the area which Dr Mawson, who will shortly start, has included in his sphere of exploration. What concerns the public most is, who will get to the South Pole first; and I for one consider it a moot question. I personally want to see the British flag flying on the spot towards which we struggled in 1909 for so many weary months, frost-bitten, cold and hungry.[6]

And that's that, then.

Early April 1911, London, Davis arrives to meet with Mawson and finds the ends are loose

And there he is!

Mawson is standing at Euston Station when – after John Davis's long journey from Canada, across the Atlantic to the port of Liverpool and then by rail – his train pulls in.

Despite their jointly serious natures, the two are hail-fellow-well-met, gripping hands tightly in the same manner as they are about to get to grips with their great adventure, but it is not long before Davis is surprised. Mawson being Mawson, Davis has been expecting that when it came to the organisation, he would find all the 'i's dotted, all the 't's crossed and nary a loose end to be found anywhere.

To his amazement, however, he finds that the Australian has no funding in place, no ship, no supplies, no equipment, and every end he can see is loose! Davis realises he has been invited to be master of a ship that doesn't actually exist yet, or at least is not in the explorer's possession.

On their way back to Mawson's tiny office at 9 Lower Regent Street, which is of course where Davis's whole Antarctic adventures began with Shackleton nearly three years earlier, they begin to talk. It becomes clear from the first that this is to be a different kind of polar expedition, that it has nothing to do with trying to claim the South Pole and is all about advancing the cause of science, with a bonus of making a significant territorial claim for Australia on that part of Antarctica. He also learns of the significant problems Mawson has had with fund-raising, and the work that remains.

And so it begins. Over the next weeks, they pound the pavements, knock on doors and pursue every contact they have, trying to get to people who are not only wealthy enough to contribute but who will also care enough to help what is fundamentally an Australian venture at the very time that Scott – an *Englishman*, by God – is already getting ready to make his own push on the Pole.

For Mawson and Davis, it is not easy to keep going under such circumstances, to keep knocking, keep ringing, keep asking for a meeting on the off-chance it will actually lead to something solid, but they have no choice. Not for nothing would Mawson write of this time, 'The whole of my stay in London was about as distressing a time as could be imagined.'[7]

In his letters to Paquita, however, while acknowledging that there are difficulties, he is ever and always upbeat in his conclusions:

Everything here is very unsettled and I am looking forward to better times, possibly busier. No word as to funds has come from Australia and I am in the dark as to what has been done there. I am confident of success, however. Although I have asked for £40,000 for the Antarctic Expedition, I can if necessary conduct a very creditable one in a ship of Nimrod or Pourquoi Pas class for as little as £25,000. I tell you this so that you need not feel so anxious about the funds. If you know me aright, you will understand that once having said I am intending to go to the Antarctic I shall go, even if it is in a whaleboat (excuse the fact that it would not be possible to do this). Captain Davis is here now and we have been going into details regarding ships — I have a private agent in Norway enquiring also. Several suitable ships may be had, there is no anxiety on that account.[8]

No, no anxiety on account of ships being available, but huge anxiety when it comes to getting the money to pay for a ship and an entire expedition. Both men are nearly in despair – the more so when in the space of a fortnight negotiations to buy both Scott's old ship *Discovery* and the French ship *Pourquoi Pas* fall through – when at last comes a breakthrough.

10 April 1911 and the day thereafter, London, Mawson addresses the Royal Geographical Society and goes on with it

On this day, Mawson outlines his plans for his Australasian Antarctic Expedition to a meeting of the highly prestigious Royal Geographical Society. He tells this august gathering of the good and the great of the geographical world that, at year's end, a ship's complement of 50 men will head south from Australia, with almost every member of the land party a specialist scientist recently graduated from the universities of Australia and New Zealand. Now, although it *was* his hope to chart the whole of the coast stretching from Cape Adare to Gaussberg, given that Captain Scott has now landed his own party at Cape Adare – small furrowing of the brow – he has done the only thing he could do and has modified his plans, no longer intending to make his own central base there.

From Hobart, they will instead pass through the Roaring Forties and Furious Fifties to Macquarie Island, 930 miles south-south-east of the Tasmanian capital, where they will establish their first base, leaving a party of five men. They will be left there to conduct meteorological, biological and geological studies, while also setting up wireless antennae that, ideally, will allow their Antarctic base to reach them and allow them to communicate with the Australian mainland.

Then, broadly along the path forged 70 years earlier by Dumont d'Urville, Charles Wilkes and James Clark Ross, they will head ever further south along the meridian of 158 degrees east until they reach the ice pack. If possible, they will push through the ice to get to the continent itself and there establish the main Antarctic base, of 12 men – equipped and provisioned to survive a year – before proceeding to the west to drop two more parties of six and eight men respectively. All three bases will be at a sufficiently large distance apart for a full picture to be built up of the conditions of that part of the Antarctic continent. Once established in the midsummer, they will get through the winter and then, in the coming of the spring, all three parties will explore and chart the continent in their area, linking up with each other on sledging expeditions, so that a complete charting of the coast can be effected.

And even as the ship is doing all this, and then afterwards, she would take soundings and conduct marine sampling along the way to find out more about the contours and content of the ocean floor between Australia and Antarctica.

Mawson explains that, from the main base, a party will once more head towards the South Magnetic Pole, to determine exactly how far and in what direction it has moved since Mawson himself went there three years before, all as part of a process whereby members of the entire expedition will collect valuable magnetic, meteorological and biological data about Antarctica. Their ship, meantime, will have returned to Hobart, before heading back to Antarctica a year later to pick them all up.

In response to Mawson's paper, President Leonard Darwin – white-haired and pointy-eared, rather like his famous father, Charles – expresses regret over the fact that Scott's second party has landed at Cape Adare. And yet this regret is not owing to the consequences for the Mawson expedition but rather to any effect it may have on the overall objectives of the Scott expedition. Judging by Darwin's statements, it was not quite the done thing, not quite *sporting*, for Amundsen to have landed at the Bay of Whales, but still quite all right for a part of the Scott party to have taken up at Cape Adare.

Still and all, what, what, the society recognises the scientific value of the AAE and graciously donates the sum of £500 to the Australian's cause.

It is a small amount, yes, but far more valuable is the Royal Geographical Society's seal of approval, which will surely help further donations start to flow.

Thus buoyed, the following evening Mawson dines late into the night at the Travellers' Club with publishing magnate William Heinemann. As a man who has not only published Shackleton's *The Heart of the Antarctic* but also lays claim to introducing the literary works of H. G. Wells, Robert Louis Stevenson and Rudyard Kipling to the world, Heinemann is one whose stature equals his wealth, and it is enormously important for Mawson to gain his support. Happily, all goes well, and the deal is struck – Mawson will receive an advance of £1000. Bit by bit, in dribs and drabs, the money is starting to come together. And it is not just from his personal efforts . . .

22 April 1911 and several days thereafter, Australia, Mawson's finances are helped by well-connected friends and a 'Sydney girl'

The open letter to the editor of the Adelaide *Advertiser* that appears on this day – signed by Professor Orme Masson, Professor Edgeworth David and Professor G. C. Henderson – makes no bones about it. Their fellow Australians, from whom they are seeking donations, must understand that the Mawson expedition is set on a higher plane than merely claiming boasting rights for being first to the bottom of the world.

For all that, it is perhaps the lack of 'sporting excitement' in the whole venture – with no push to be first to the South Pole – that fails to grip the imagination of the public. Though Masson takes it upon himself to write to nearly 500 of the wealthiest graziers in Australia, the net result is just 'one promise of £20, two to consider the matter . . . and one promise of fresh meat',[9] though this is countered somewhat by small amounts that continue to drip in from some of the more humble members of the public.

After Professor David addresses a gathering at Sydney Town Hall, he shortly after opens a letter addressed to him in which he finds two £1 postal notes, signed simply, 'Sydney Girl'.[10] Equally impressive, from another field, that well-known Melbourne girl, the great Nellie Melba, contributes £100.

The truly big money, however, is always going to come less from the public at large than from the public purse – and on this front things are going better. In what is now Mawson's home state of South Australia, the premier commits £5000 for the expedition, while Victoria goes to £6000 and New South Wales to £7000. After a meeting in Melbourne Town Hall chaired by Governor General Lord Denman, attended by the prime minister, the Hon. Andrew Fisher, the leader of the opposition, the Hon. Alfred Deakin and many other dignitaries, the Commonwealth Government commits £5000, just as they did for the Shackleton expedition. And, after representations by Lord Denman, the British Government commits £2000.

25 April 1911, London, Mawson's ideas take flight

In the absence of her husband, Kathleen Scott has remained a deeply involved member of the polar community. On this day, she writes to her Australian friend Douglas Mawson, whom she has corresponded with since meeting him early the previous year.

Dear Dr Mawson,
I believe I can help you about aeroplanes. Think you can do far better than Blériot if you mean to take a monoplane. There is a

machine that the Vickers people have bought which is infinitely more stable, heavier and more solid and will carry more weight. Its cost is £1000 but I think it could be worked to get it for £700 or even less . . . being sincerely.

Kathleen Scott

Suggest yourself for lunch any day or dinner if you let me know before.[11]

Mawson immediately follows up, as the Vickers sounds like exactly the modern machine he needs to capture the public's imagination. It is with a similar passion – to be on the prow of modernity – that Mawson has decided to pioneer radio communications within, and from, Antarctica. It was only a little under a decade earlier – 1902 – that Marconi demonstrated it was possible to communicate via radio over long distances, and Mawson is determined that his expedition will have the state-of-the art equipment so that all three bases on Antarctica will be able to communicate with each other. The base will be at Macquarie Island, which will be a relay radio station to Hobart, and from there to all the world.

Late April 1911, London, Mawson and Davis find a vessel for their dreams

There is good news, and there is better news. Davis has found a whaler just *made* to go to the Antarctic with.

Yes, *Aurora* – a steam yacht – is over 30 years old, having been built in Glasgow in 1876 for whaling in the northern seas, but she is solid and superbly designed for the task set for her. Her oak hull gives her great elasticity should the ice press in upon her, while her greenheart hardwood sheathing will enable her to withstand whatever abrasion she will encounter from butting up against the jagged edges of ice floes. For the heavy work of breaking through the pack ice, the 'cutwaters' of the acutely sloped and overhanging bow are protected by iron plates, allowing the ship to rise above any ice impediment before crushing it down.

The ship's power is provided by a coal-fired steam engine – helped by sails to allow the coal to be burnt only frugally and to act as insurance should the coal run out – capable of driving her at up to ten knots. At 165 feet long, 30 feet wide and 18 feet deep, she is capable of carrying over 600 tons: 150 tons of cargo and three times as much in coal.

Not least important is the reasonable price – Davis advises she can be purchased for just £6000, less than half the original asking price.

1 May 1911, London, Mawson rattles the tin

The key problem that Mawson and Davis have after they sign the contract to buy *Aurora* is actually having the ready cash. Their fund-raising efforts to this point have simply not produced the money they need.

Enter Sir Ernest Shackleton, who, just when they need him most, at last comes good. It is courtesy of his intervention that Mawson succeeds in gaining an audience with the greatest media magnate of his day, Lord Northcliffe, of Amalgamated Press Company, the owner of the *Daily Mail, Daily Mirror* and *The Times*. Lord Northcliffe is made up in fairly even parts of acute business acumen, diverse passions, huge generosity of spirit and an enormous appetite for work. On the parquet floor of his home's lounge room lies the skin of a massive polar bear, shot and skinned on the Jackson–Harmsworth Polar Expedition to the Arctic that Northcliffe sponsored. However, more often than not he is to be found here in his spacious and elegantly appointed office in Fleet Street's Carmelite House. This is where Mawson has come to make his pitch.

Ahem. If the good lord could just front them for £12,000, they would have the bulk of the money they need to purchase a ship, fit it out and buy the first of the specialist supplies and equipment they require. And the *Daily Mail*, with a circulation of well over a million copies, could have the newspaper rights to the story once they have completed their journey.[12]

Northcliffe hears out Mawson's plans. It is his view that that sort of money could be raised from the readers of the *Daily Mail* in as little as two days, but he needs to be sure. It is out of the question for the paper to push it and then be associated with failure. After more discussion and more assurances, Lord Northcliffe agrees to publish an appeal within his pages for support of Mawson's venture.

2 May 1911, Cape Evans, Scott's men hunker down as winter approaches

There are strange soccer games and there are strange soccer games, but this, *this*, surely is one of the strangest of them all. For on this morning, on a 'pitch' marked out the previous day on the badly cracked sea ice not far from the hut, two teams, captained by Oates and Tryggve Gran – who is good enough to have played in Norway's first international match, against Sweden, even if they did lose 11–3 – go up against each other.

The players include the Canadian Silas Wright, who has only ever played ice hockey; Griffith Taylor, whose own sport is 'rugger' and is bemused to find the rules of soccer so different; Anton, the five foot nothing Russian groom who has likely never seen a soccer ball let alone kicked one; a laughing Captain Scott himself; and two of the biggest men in the navy, Tom Crean – an extremely capable Irishman, raised on a farm in County Kerry before joining the British Royal Navy – and Taffy Evans, a noted Welsh player. All of them find breathing difficult in the biting wind at a temperature of ten degrees below, but it is a great deal of fun, with much high hilarity interspersed with many solid falls on the terrifyingly slippery surface, one of which causes a serious knee injury to Frank Debenham.

Nevertheless, both teams play like German bands, with their enthusiasm matched only by the amount of noise they generate. The two stars of the show prove to be Atch Atkinson and Tryggve Gran, though it is widely agreed that the real winner on the day is the blizzard that springs up just after half-time.

With that howling wind behind you, even a small kick on the icy surface can go a very long way . . . including right into the goal, allowing one team to beat the other like a red-headed stepson and go to an unassailable 3–0 lead. The other side gives no quarter, but so freezing are the conditions, so powerful the wind, that it is decided that 20-minute halves are quite sufficient and the two teams finally leave the pitch shaking with cold but deeply satisfied, resolving to have a return bout.[13]

8 May 1911 and a month thereafter, London, Mawson and Davis receive good news

On this delightful spring morning, as London produces all too rarely, Mawson and Davis excitedly purchase the first edition of the *Daily Mail* to see on page nine, boldly emblazoned and running almost the entire length of the column, an open letter from Sir Ernest Shackleton addressed to the editor, beneath the headline:

AN APPEAL FROM SIR E. SHACKLETON
THE AUSTRALIAN ANTARCTIC EXPEDITION
A DEBT OF HONOUR

Sir – Will you allow me, through your columns, to make an

appeal on behalf of the Australian Antarctic expedition under the command of my old comrade Dr Douglas Mawson?[14]

Shackleton begins by reminding the reader how much Australia has done, 'financially and otherwise', for polar exploration, particularly his own expedition and that currently being undertaken by Scott. Australia is now set to send out her own expedition, 'to draw back further the veil that shrouds the greatest unknown area of our world'.

As there is a propitious gathering in London of many of the good and the great from all over the British Empire for the coronation of George V on the 22nd day of the following month, and they will be all plumped up on imperial pride and pageantry, Shackleton makes a well-aimed appeal to them. For how could men of the Empire forget that the fine man Mawson – with his bountiful academic credentials and extraordinary abilities as an explorer – was a member of that three-man party who raised Queen Alexandra's Union Jack at the South Magnetic Pole? It was the greatest unsupported sledge journey the world has known, north or south! Shackleton knows from experience that Britons can and will be counted upon:

> The Australian expedition has its sentimental side. We are as anxious today as we have ever been that Britons shall keep their place in the vanguard of Polar exploration. For these reasons I appeal with confidence to the British nation to come to the aid of Australasia in this great enterprise.
>
> ERNEST SHACKLETON
>
> Cheques should be addressed to the Editor, The Daily Mail, Carmelite House, E.C.[15]

And that is just the beginning. For the next two days, posters appear all over London proclaiming '£6,000 WANTED TODAY!', backed by favourable editorials imploring readers to do the right thing, all while the editor of the paper, Thomas Marlowe, is quietly contacting leading businessmen in England and Australia to ask them to contribute.

The response to Sir Ernest's appeal is 'instant and magnificent', an overwhelming overnight success. The following day, the *Daily Mail* reports that by 7 pm the previous evening a staggering £6000 has been pledged in donations large and small, half of the total sum called for. The largest single donation to date is £2500 (the same amount donated to Scott's *Terra Nova* expedition) by Sir Anthony Hordern of the well-known Sydney emporium.[16]

Yet not everyone gets misty-eyed at the thought of Mawson, an Australian, receiving British financial support. For no sooner has the appeal appeared than Edgar Speyer, treasurer of the British Antarctic Expedition, and Sir Clements Markham KCB write to all the newspapers in protest. They thunder that because the *Terra Nova* expedition – currently being undertaken by Captain Scott, whom they characterise as the 'founder of the Antarctic Land' – is still short by £8000 to £10,000 in its funding, that is *precisely* where British people's money should be invested.

This, Speyer and Sir Clements vociferously proclaim, is before:

> new schemes are taken up and funds are diverted from the patriotic objectives which are now in the course of our tried explorer. One important expedition ought to be provided for before any appeal from promoters of any other scheme is listened to, which is intended to divert support from a well-equipped expedition actually in being.[17]

In response, the editor writes that while they are happy to run this above letter in their pages, the intention of Scott's 'unmannerly sponsors' is clear: 'It appears to us extremely ungracious, in view of the generous support which Captain Scott as well as Sir Ernest

Shackleton had received from the Australian Government and people.'[18]

Fortunately, the churlishness of Edgar Speyer and Sir Clements Markham appears to have next to no effect, as the required money is raised within a week, together with many British firms promising a vast array of standard and specialised foodstuffs free.

As the *Daily Mail* notes: 'We imagine as to cigars, cigarettes, and tobacco, owing to the generosity of the British-American Tobacco Company and Messrs Sandorides, the expedition will be able to smoke to their hearts' content without coming to the end of their stock.'[19] No doubt a good part of this largesse is stimulated by the fact their product names will be freely advertised when Mawson's stores go on display at the Imperial Exhibition, Crystal Palace, the following week, but Mawson is no less grateful because of it.

Overcome by the tide of British generosity, he now writes to the *Daily Mail* editor on his own behalf:

Sir,
Please allow me to thank the readers of the *Daily Mail* and Sir Ernest Shackleton for the magnificent effort which has resulted, in less than a week, in the supply of so large a sum of money and so great an amount of stores for myself and my companions in our forthcoming Antarctic expedition.
With renewed thanks,

Yours faithfully,
DOUGLAS MAWSON[20]

Most importantly though, the Mawson expedition now has the money it needs to actually pay for the ship it has already bought. The next major task is to continue recruiting the rest of the crew, and to that end an advertisement is placed in Northcliffe's London papers by Captain Davis on 7 June 1911.

Happily, the applicants come from far and wide. Such is the glamour of polar exploration at this time – to go where Scott and Shackleton have been! – that Davis is soon besieged by young and adventurous seamen seeking a position. He holds the interviews aboard *Aurora* and is soon well on his way to filling his roster for the ship, while most of the shore party will come from interviews with young scientists and the like in Australia.

Early June 1911, Adelaide, Paquita awaits

Meanwhile, Paquita waits at home, meeting the postman daily in the street for the longed-for latest letter from her beloved fiancé. Although Mawson is a devoted correspondent, because of obvious delays in receiving seamail Paquita receives her most up-to-date information regarding Mawson's current activities through the press.

Her Douglas, she finds, is continuing apace in London making preparations for the expedition. He is recruiting new expedition members, tirelessly meeting a whole range of Antarctic experts, courting the rich and influential for further funds and seemingly working on a dozen fronts at once.

6 June 1911, Cape Evans, Scott celebrates

It has been another good 'day' and night, the two blending into each other almost seamlessly, as it is only the intensity of the darkness that varies. On this evening, Captain Scott is particularly content as he fills out his daily journal and reviews the productive day. A moment earlier, he stepped outside to see that 'the moon has emerged from behind the mountain and sails across the cloudless northern sky; the wind has fallen and the scene is glorious . . .'[21]

Today, he and his crew have celebrated his 43rd birthday with an immense decorated cake, which they devoured at lunch, followed not long afterwards by a special celebratory dinner, where they enjoyed excellent seal soup, roast mutton and redcurrant jelly, fruit salad, asparagus and chocolate. 'After this luxurious meal everyone was very festive and amiably argumentative,' Scott records in his diary.[22]

Ah, but soft now. For as he writes, he pauses for a moment to take it all in. In the nearby dark room, he can hear one group passionately discussing political matters, while a few others lingering at the dinner table are divided over the origin of matter, while and yet another group debate military matters. As Scott listens in, the individual snatches of conversation sometimes meld together in most ludicrous fashion. True, such debates rarely have any conclusive 'winners' but they give a great deal of pleasure to all involved, most particularly when one man or t'other imagines he has at least been triumphant in making a particular point, if not necessarily winning the whole debate. Scott sums up: 'They are boys, all of them, but such excellent good-natured ones; there has been no sign of sharpness or anger, no jarring note, in all these wordy contests! All end with a laugh.'[23]

Not that there is not plenty of work for them to do, for all that, in their preparations for their forthcoming sledging journeys. One of the most important of these is overseen by Oates – to try to get the ponies, most of which appear to be little more than skin and bones, in as good a shape as possible for the severe trial that awaits them. It is obvious that the bitter cold of the Antarctic winter and their depot-laying journey have entirely worn them out, and they seem to always be starving.

In an effort to put some meat on their bones, give them some strength, Oates tries giving the nags extra supplies of food to go with their compressed fodder – a mixture of oilcake and oats, which was intended to be saved for the polar journey itself but which Oates feels they now must get immediately.

The other factor is ensuring that the ponies get exercise, and at Oates's behest Scott orders all those who are going on the forthcoming trips to daily take one pony out on a small walk in the darkness, weather permitting. And yet, if the men meet this task with a certain level of reluctance, it is more than matched by the reluctance of the ponies themselves to venture out in the freezing conditions, and they all too frequently lash out with their hind hooves against any living target foolish enough to come within range.

Early June 1911, London, Mawson's ship is fitted out

From the moment *Aurora* arrives at South West India Docks on the Thames – where she is to undergo an extensive overhaul and refit in preparation for a new phase of her career – Douglas Mawson is impressed with her roominess, among other things. 'With the *Aurora*,' he exults, 'I believe Shackleton would have reached the pole. So cramped were the conditions [on *Nimrod*] that from that cause alone he lost several ponies.'[24]

Not that the ship doesn't need a lot of modifications before becoming the specialist exploring vessel Mawson needs, capable of travelling as far south as any. She must become a 'barquentine', powered by both sail and steam, capable of travelling vast distances to get to the frozen continent then quickly manoeuvring through the pack ice under her own power – and still capable of sailing away if she runs out of coal.

New accommodation quarters are constructed for the crew on the below deck, with a new foremast fitted. Sails – a *sine qua non* on Antarctic voyages – are stowed to take advantage of the region's westerly winds and economise on coal but perhaps more importantly included as an alternative means of propulsion should the propeller become inoperable as it punches away through the pack ice – a real possibility.

Now, as she is a ship devoted to pure scientific endeavour, two laboratories are conveniently located on the upper deck, and to assist the scientists in their endeavours steam is laid on to a forward steam-windlass to be used for manipulating the deep-sea dredging-cable. As she is to spend much of her time well sealed up against the cruel Antarctic weather, particular attention is given to ventilation throughout. For the purposes of having both a sure supply of fresh water and emergency ballast, six large water tanks are installed in the bottom of the hold.

After the refit is complete, the specialist equipment and supplies that Mawson and Davis obtained in England are loaded aboard, including no fewer than 3000 cases of stores and 48 Greenland sledge dogs of various shapes and sizes (arranged through the Danish Government). As to the motor launch and wireless station masts, they, along with other equipment, are being built in Sydney and will be loaded when *Aurora* reaches Hobart.

As they all work away together, the likes of Ninnis and Mertz and the other new recruits get to know Mawson, at least a little, for the first time, even as they come to understand a little of the excitement of what awaits them.

'I can hardly believe that I am off on a Polar Expedition,' Ninnis records in his diary with enormous enthusiasm. '[Mawson is] a splendid fellow. He is quiet and a scientist all over; also a gentleman, ditto. My respect for him increases daily.'[25]

Late June 1911, South West India Docks, *Aurora* receives a fragrant visitor

It is an immutable natural law, since time immemorial, that when a beautiful woman comes among sweaty, working men, every man is instantly aware of her attractiveness and his own unworthiness. So it is on the day when the great Anna Pavlova, the famously accomplished and beautiful Russian ballerina – who first came to major fame, by the by, when she was playing the title role in the famed ballet *Paquita* – sweeps aboard *Aurora*, shimmering success, fame and beauty all in one.

A friend of the all but equally internationally renowned Australian opera soprano Nellie Melba, Pavlova met Mawson during the London social season and accepted his invitation to visit the ship with the wonderful name. (As an eight-year-old growing up in St Petersburg, she was stunned when she first saw *Sleeping Beauty* performed and dreamt of one day growing up to dance just like Princess Aurora – a dream she has recently realised.)

She is gracious to one and all, charming them with her poise and beauty. To Mawson, she gives a small silk doll,[26] to the totally smitten Ninnis, a signed photograph, which he clasps to his chest like the Crown jewels. To all, a few words and a smile . . .

It is hard to tell, but perhaps the thing that pleases her most is a panting young husky bitch, all slobbering tongue and thick fur, which she picks up and fondles. Forevermore, this husky is known as Pavlova in her honour. Soon enough, the dancer is gone, but her memory lingers far longer than the delicious waft of perfume she trails behind her, and all feel deeply honoured to have received such a visit from such a lady.

One other episode that is particularly touching to Davis occurs at around this time . . .

As captain of a ship going to Antarctica, he receives an invitation from James Young Buchanan, who 39 years earlier went to Antarctica himself aboard the *first steam-powered vessel inside the Antarctic Circle*, HMS *Challenger*, as a physicist. This dear old gentleman respectfully requests Davis's company at a dinner at his home in Norfolk Street, where he would like him to meet two other men who were on the same voyage, Sir John Murray and Admiral

George Richard Bethell of the Royal Navy.

Davis accepts, and at the end of the 'delightful and memorable evening'[27] – dining in an exquisitely furnished room where the light from the roaring fire dances upon the gleaming silverware along with the light from the shaded candles upon the table – after discussing the events of the old days and the plans of Davis for the new days, Mr Buchanan calls for the butler.

Very good, sir, yes, sir, of course, sir.

Shortly thereafter, the butler returns with an old bottle of Madeira, at which point the host of the dinner, savouring the moment, warmly commands him, with no little ceremony, 'Open the *Challenger* Madeira!'[28]

This particular vintage, he explains to Davis, was first bought on a stopover at the island of Madeira on their way to the Antarctic in 1872, and it is only ever brought out for such special occasions as this. Joined by his two old shipmates, Mr Buchanan then raises his glass and the party drink a toast to the Australasian Antarctic Expedition of 1911 and to its leader, Dr Douglas Mawson.

It is a wonderfully kind gesture, deeply appreciated by Davis, the more so when, a few days later, two bottles of that same Madeira arrive at the *Aurora*, with a note suggesting they should be opened when Dr Mawson reaches Antarctica.

PART THREE

ANTARCTICA UNDER SIEGE

Chapter Eight

Under Way

In no department can a leader spend time more profitably than in the selection of the men who are to accomplish the work.
Douglas Mawson, *The Home of the Blizzard*

I am convinced that this exploration is going to be of permanent advantage to Australia. It will, moreover, afford the world an opportunity of seeing what Australians can do. It is a big project, which has had the effect of bringing Australia prominently before European countries. It presents Australia in a new light. Australia gains the prestige of being strong enough to investigate and claim new territory.
Douglas Mawson, *The Sydney Morning Herald*, 8 September 1911

27 July 1911 and a week thereafter, River Thames, *Aurora* slips away in the night

Just before midnight on 27 July, with the Commonwealth blue ensign and the white Royal Thames Yacht Club pennant fluttering astern from her masts, the refitted and partially loaded *Aurora* is pulled away from the South West India Docks by a small steamer. Once under her own steam, she creeps down the Thames at midnight, heading for Penarth Harbour, five miles south-west of Cardiff city, to take on a full load of coal.

The reason for such an unearthly hour of leaving is that Captain Davis is effectively fleeing the reams of red tape the British maritime authorities have been tying around his ship before allowing her to go to sea. A couple of days previously, a Board of Trade official came aboard to personally inspect the ship and told Davis that unless 'four additional eight-inch hold ventilators are installed',[1] *Aurora* simply could not leave.

Under pressure, and running out of time to meet Mawson in Hobart by early November as planned – for Mawson had departed several weeks earlier by passenger ship, to continue fund-raising and organising things in Australia – Davis decides his ship might as well be 'forfeited to the Crown, as indefinitely hung up in London'.[2]

Unfortunately, the Greenland sledge dogs secured on the deck of the tiny ship quickly dispel any hope for a silent exit. Celebrating their long-awaited departure, the 48 dogs positively outdo each other, setting to with 'such a deafening chorus of barking, yelping and howling that the pilot had considerable difficulty in making his orders heard'.[3] The worst of it is that it really only takes one dog to start howling when, through some canine code known only to them, all the others feel obliged to join in, and all of the dogs howl in concert, if not in harmony, making such a row it practically makes conversation impossible. Attempts by Ninnis and Mertz to quell the mutinous mutts prove futile, the dogs' tumult easily winning out over Captain Davis's bellowed orders to his crew. Far from being a silent exit, it is a moot point as to whether, on decibels alone, they might have outdone Big Ben.

Poor weather en route to Cardiff makes things grim. Mertz confides to his diary:

> *Aurora* was rolling all day long. Sometimes the ship was on the crest of a wave then it plunged into the waters as if it wanted to hit the sea-bottom, and once again try to reach the sky. Water swirled over the deck, even in cabins. That was uncomfortable. Fortunately I was not seasick and I was secretly proud of this fact.[4]

The worst of it is that the incoming water spoils some of the stores and, to the dismay and horror of the 21-strong crew, reveals significant leaks in the living quarters. Still, one would have thought this best discovered now rather than later, when the temperature of any uninvited Antarctic seawater would be south of freezing. Nevertheless, so shocking is the experience that some of the crew scarper from the ship in Cardiff, intent – call them crazy if you will – on doing their time on watertight vessels instead of a miraculously floating sieve.

Oddly enough, while their experience at sea has shown beyond doubt that *Aurora* has problems when it comes to seaworthiness, only a short time after the men arrive in Cardiff comes the welcome news from a Board of Trade official that London has relented and 'provided *Aurora* was measured for a load-line and a Plimsoll mark was cut on the vessel',[5] the ship would be free to go.

Once the departed crew members are replaced by others, they are all but ready to go, bar one thing. The Australasian Antarctic Expedition is in what Captain Davis – often referred to by his crew as 'Captain Gloomy' – is pleased to label as 'very low financial water',[6] with no cash to pay for the coal they need to get them to Australia. (The money raised by the *Daily Mail* campaign has been a Godsend but has only gone so far.) Fortunately, he manages to negotiate a whole consignment of coal on the promise that they would pay in three months, so on 4 August the journey proper begins.

8 September 1911 and a week thereafter, *Framheim*, Amundsen wishes he hadn't

Though the calendar says they are now over a week into spring, and therefore with the passing of winter they should be able to make their push for the Pole, Antarctica itself has no interest in such a calendar. Four days into their attempt, Amundsen, the seven men with him and about 90 dogs pulling four sledges between them are well out on the Barrier and risk freezing to death.

The temperature falls so low, to an unimaginable minus 61.6 degrees, that the fluid in their compasses congeals. At this temperature, it is possible for men's teeth to not only chatter but shatter, and – though unknown to the Norwegian – exactly that has recently happened to Apsley Cherry-Garrard of Scott's party, on a trip he has taken over the polar winter with Bill Wilson and Birdie Bowers.

In the face of his obvious mistake in having left too early in the season, Amundsen takes the even more obvious decision. That is, once they reach their first depot at 80 degrees south, the one they set up back in February, they add to its stores, leaving themselves just enough supplies to get back to *Framheim*, and on 14 September they head back at all possible speed.

Even then, it is a close shave. For the following night, with 46 miles still to go to safety, it is discovered that two of Amundsen's men, Helmer Hanssen and Jørgen Stubberud, have badly frostbitten heels. It is now more urgent than ever that they return to the warmth and safety of their hut as quickly as possible, and so keen is Amundsen to do so that he breaks the usual protocol in extreme conditions of sticking together come what may. His own sledge is soon careering so quickly across the Barrier that he leaves the other three sledges in his wake.

Amundsen and the two men with him arrive back at *Framheim* on the afternoon of 16 September, a good eight hours before the last sledge, which gets in well after midnight, after blundering around in life-threatening temperatures. 'Heaven knows what they had been doing on the way!' writes Amundsen.[7]

On that last sledge is the veteran to beat all veterans of polar travel, Hjalmar Johansen, who has been careful to bring up the rear and ensure that everyone is safe. He is a big-drinking 44-year-old, as tough and durable as the leather in the old boots he wears, who once saved Nansen's life in the Arctic. Though Amundsen never wanted him on this expedition – his drinking makes him unreliable, and his stature makes him an alternative leader to himself – Nansen insisted and Amundsen reluctantly agreed. But now Johansen turns on Amundsen, in front of all the others, publicly upbraiding him for having left them out there while looking after his own safety. 'I don't call it an expedition,' he thundered. 'It's panic.'[8]

Within the room, all is silent. What Johansen has said is broadly true and they all know it. Amundsen's actions the day before had not been his finest hour. And it is also true that Johansen is the only man with the authority to confront the leader in this manner. What will Amundsen do in reply?

They are not long in finding out. In the face of what could have become a mutiny, Amundsen responds quickly. First, he moves away from the public confrontation . . . and then back towards the men in question separately. He divides and conquers. Isolating Johansen and the one man who has supported him, Kristian Prestrud, he talks privately to each of the others in turn and gains a pledge of loyalty from them. And then he announces publicly that neither Prestrud nor Johansen will be going on the next attempt on the South Pole. Instead, they can explore King Edward VII Land and good luck to them. Johansen will not even be the leader of that and will have to follow Prestrud's orders. It is the final slap-down to Johansen. His authority restored, Amundsen now focuses on getting ready to go again, once the weather is a little bit warmer.

13 September 1911, Cape Evans, Winter Quarters, Scott has a plan

After hours, turning into days, into weeks, into months . . . calculating distances, weights and rations, on this morning Scott is at last ready and announces to the gathered men his final plans for conquering the South Pole. In six weeks' time, he tells them with typical resolution, they will begin to execute his multi-pronged plan, which will see 16 men setting out with sledges hauled by ponies, dogs and motors across the Barrier as far as the base of the Beardmore Glacier. Of those prongs, it is the ponies he is most relying on to break the back of the work, with the dogs and motor sledges acting as backup only.

From the beginning, he has had little confidence in the dogs – as witness the fact that he has brought so few of them – and it has been obvious from the first that the experimental motor sledges are so prone to breaking down in the freezing conditions they are unlikely to haul a serious weight of supplies too far into the interior.

As to detail, setting out in the vanguard of this assault on the Pole would be four men in the two surviving motor sledges: Teddy Evans, William Lashly, Bernard Day and former naval steward Frederick Hooper. The main party, with the ponies, would comprise ten men – Scott, Taffy Evans, Wilson, Bowers, Cherry-Garrard, Atkinson, Wright, Crean, Oates and Irish naval man Patrick Keohane – and they would leave a week later, as they would be moving faster than the first party. The last to set off would be the dog teams led by the Russian dog-handler, Demetri, and Cecil Meares, but once they have hauled their loads to the bottom of the Beardmore Glacier they would turn around and head back. The ponies, alas, would not be so lucky. Their reward, once they have got the bulk of the sledges to the foot of that glacier, would be a bullet to the brain, whereupon their flesh would be stored for provisions, After that, good old British man-hauling would take over.

Twelve men, three groups of four, would then man-haul the sledges to the top of the glacier and commence the journey across the plateau. As they progress, first one support group – whose job it will have been to bring to that point more supplies than they need, leaving behind the excess for the other groups to consume on the return leg – would peel off, then the other support group would follow suit and return home, leaving behind the final group to make the last daring thrust. The composition of the final group to make the assault on the South Pole – hauling the sledge themselves an estimated 275 miles to the Pole from the top of the Beardmore Glacier,[9] and then another 900 miles back to Hut Point – would be named en route.

It is Scott's carefully calculated estimate, based on the differing speeds of the ponies, the dogs and man-hauling, that they will be away for 148 days, of which just 47 man-hauling days will be on the Polar Plateau, about two miles above sea level, where the temperature will be sub-freezing and the oxygen nearly one-third depleted. While Scott has allowed himself 31 days from the top of the Beardmore Glacier to the Pole, marching an average of 8½ miles per day, he expects to double the rate on his return and complete the same distance in just 16 days. Their sledges, of course, will be getting progressively lighter as they eat their way through much of the weight. Even with this increased rate of return, however, Scott has noted:

Hence only by a miracle can the Pole party get back in time to catch the ship. Latest date possible for ship March 15th if party gets away November 1 they can only get back by March 21st. Based on 148 days total.[10]

But is it even realistic to think that men could survive so long in such conditions, while hauling sledges? Not even Scott is sure of the answer to that most crucial of all questions. 'I don't know whether it is possible for men to last out that time, I almost doubt it,' he confides to Frank Debenham in a moment of great self-doubt.[11] But he is equally determined that they will find out, come what may.

One who is not impressed with Scott's complicated thrust to the South Pole is Lawrence Oates, who writes to his mother, 'It is trying to work three kinds of transport that knocks me. They can't do it in the army, so I am jolly sure Scott is not going to.'[12] (Again, even Scott has his doubts on this, writing of the differing speed of his ponies, 'It reminded me of a regatta or a somewhat disorganized fleet with ships of very unequal speed.'[13] And yet the same problem is all the more true of the other means of transport.)

For all that, Oates's chief concern is that his ponies do the best they possibly can under the circumstances. His ambition is for the ponies to actually make it across the Barrier to the Beardmore Glacier, at which point he would like to help to get the sledges the 170 miles to the top – far and away the most difficult part of the exercise – and then turn back. Let the others have the glory of bagging the Pole. Personally, he is fast losing enthusiasm for the project.

20 September 1911, London, Kathleen Scott awakes with a start

It is all so very unsettling. After having a very bad nightmare about the fate of her husband, Kathleen awakes to see her two-year-old son, Peter, who has only just learnt to talk, come very close to her and say very emphatically, 'Daddy won't come back.'[14]

Late September 1911, off the coast of Cape Town bound for Hobart, a test of courage aboard *Aurora*

It is a time for 'mad dogs and Englishmen', some two decades before the Noel Coward song of the same name made the phrase famous. On this occasion, one of the Greenland dogs has been severely affected by the hardships of the voyage thus far and drops to the deck after a severe fit. Is it dead . . .? No! For in an instant it suddenly rises and starts charging loose, barking furiously and snapping its massive jaws at all in its path. The cry of 'mad dog!' goes up, and the response is immediate.

Quick as a flash, all the deck hands tear up the rigging like monkeys up a tree, to escape those snapping jaws. Aroused by the commotion, other crew members emerge from the fo'c'sle companionway below to appraise the situation and immediately jeer at their faint-hearted shipmates above, until . . .

Until suddenly, the charging, snarling dog bolts at them, and with discretion being the better part of valour they decide to join their cowardly comrades after all, as the whole ship falls to chaos bar the officers, who, safe on the bridge, find the whole thing comical in the extreme. With the dog now disappeared beneath the fo'c'sle head, it is the job of Mertz and Ninnis to go and shoot it. This they appear to do, for it is with great satisfaction that the men in the rigging hear a shot and then a report that the job has been done. Perhaps a little sheepish, the crew members descend, until they hear the uncertain voice of Ninnis coming from below . . .

He calls to Mertz that he thought he shot the right dog but now sees one with similar markings between some barrels, so there might have been a mistake, and . . .

And quickly lads, up the rigging! Up the rigging they all go once more until, 'after the confirmation of the first execution . . . they could be prevailed upon to descend'.[15]

Ah, the laughter afterwards, once it is all safe once more.

It has been a good trip so far, as the little ship, propelled by steam and sail and the ministrations of her cheerful crew, has made relatively good time, covering an average of around 185 nautical miles a day, all the way to Cape Town and thereafter. The weeks have passed and storms have blown, all with no ill effect on the ship, and they have continued to get to know each other better.

Xavier Mertz has proved particularly popular for his willingness to turn out in all weathers, often with Ninnis in tow, to do whatever needs to be done to help the ship's officers and crew. Mertz has proved to be a quick learner in all matters nautical and after only a few weeks has turned into a very capable seaman, able to 'hand, reef and steer' with the best of them.

As to Ninnis, the young giant of 23 has at least pleased Captain Davis by studying the basics of navigation, as he feels it may well be a useful skill to have in the polar wilderness, where the compass is frequently groggy, there are all too frequently no landmarks and all you have is the angles of the stars (when you can see them) and sun to calculate your position. Against that, however, Davis does quietly have misgivings about the lack of application of Ninnis to other, more mundane, tasks and quietly records in his diary his view that the well-heeled Englishman is 'lazy and ignorant and appears to think that to boast of being hopelessly incompetent is extremely smart . . . He is one of those people who go through life always depending on some one to pull him out of difficulties.'[16]

Perhaps harsh, but certainly one of the foremost of those people helping him out is Mertz, as from the first days on the voyage the two are inseparable.

A part of Mertz's popularity is owing to the fun the others of the crew have been able to have with him through his attempts to learn the English language. When, for example, the ship was taking coal aboard at Cardiff, the Swiss man went ashore with the others and had a brief night out on the town. Upon being introduced to some lovely Welsh girls, Mertz, who proves to be something of a ladies' man, removed his hat, bowed low with Continental courtliness and reached for the very word that the English speakers seemed to use whenever they wanted to emphasise anything: 'How do, bloody fine day isn't it?'

Ah, but it had got better still.

By the time *Aurora* was approaching Cape Town, Mertz's grasp of English had vastly improved – in part through a penchant for reading the Sherlock Holmes books of Arthur Conan Doyle – and yet he was not above taking tips on how to improve it still, and the crew had been keen to tell him. On this occasion, for example, when he asked *Aurora*'s chief engineer, 'Oh, Gillies, is it perhaps possible you can tell me what time the pilot will come on board?' that gentleman was quick with his reply.

'I don't know,' the ancient mariner told him. 'You had better ask the captain but for goodness' sake don't say "the pilot", that is only a vulgar sailor's term, the proper name is "'harlot".'

So it was that only a short time later, Captain Davis arrived on deck to be asked by Mertz, 'Oh, Captain, is it possible you can tell me what time ze harlot comes on board?'[17]

Ah, how they laugh.

And Ninnis, notwithstanding Captain Davis's sometimes gloomy countenance when contemplating him, loves it all. 'I cannot realise my luck,' he records as his impression of the whole of their experience in his diary. 'At times I lie awake, simply hugging myself for joy. Here I am practically in my second childhood, so simple and infantile are our pastimes.'[18]

Captain Davis is perhaps the only man on board not easily amused by the antics always going on around Mertz, which is perhaps what Mertz is referring to when he writes in his own diary a short time later, 'Davis says very little, this man thinks too much about how to keep to the route, and about all his duties.'[19]

Still, not even Davis could help but be charmed by Mertz's joyous nature. Among other things, the Swiss is known to do such things as climb up the mainmast in rare moments of leisure and sing his entire repertory of university songs.

He fits in. He is a good egg. He is adored by the others, not least Ninnis, who is himself at least popular with the rest of the crew, despite the chest of fancy clothes the Englishman keeps beneath his hammock and his rather dandy-ish ways.

2 October 1911 and the month thereafter, Sydney's Central Station, a journey is joined

At last, at last, Frank Hurley has his chance. The accomplished young photographer from Sydney's inner-west is desperate to impress this fellow Dr Douglas Mawson with his talents, all with a view to being installed as the official photographer for the expedition, but it has been hell's own job to track the doctor down.

Notwithstanding the fact that the two have grown up just a stone's throw from each other in Glebe, they have for most of their lives lived in entirely different worlds. Mawson has pursued a life of intellectual endeavour, has always been studious and serious, and comes from a solid family, whereas Hurley dropped out of Glebe Public School and has lived more by the seat of his pants than anything else. And yet, like Mawson, Hurley has developed a capacity to be single-minded and passionate, in the younger man's case by pursuing one thing, pure and simple: photography.

But now, at last, it may be that their worlds are about to collide. Huffing and puffing just like the steam train beside him, which is getting ready to head south from this platform, Hurley at last has his target in his sights. After chasing him unsuccessfully all over town, now, here is Dr Douglas Mawson, readying to board a train to Melbourne.

Armed with a recommendation to Mawson from Kodak salesman Henri Mallard – urging the expedition leader to take on the young photographer – Hurley does not waste a minute and soon presents both himself and his claims to the position, his hopes all . . .

All aboard!

After all that, Hurley has run out of time. Or has he?

It takes a little doing, and Hurley has to be quick, but in the time between Mawson boarding the train and it starting to chug out of the station, the photographer is able to finagle a ticket as far as Mittagong, which will give him the crucial two hours he needs to impress upon Dr Mawson just what an asset he would be to the expedition, and this includes showing him something of his portfolio.[20] He also makes it clear that he is so desperate to go on this expedition that he will do it 'absolutely free'[21] – exactly what Mawson himself offered Shackleton three years earlier when he was in the same position.

The two part company at Mittagong, with Hurley jumping off to head back north on the next train, and the wonderful thing is he has only been home a couple of days when a telegram arrives from the good doctor saying, 'You are accepted.'[22]

As Hurley later characterises that telegram: 'Three simple words, but they threw open the golden door of adventure for me.'[23] And Mawson would insist on paying him a fair wage: £300 on return of the expedition.[24] Typical of Mawson, however, he not only wants Hurley for the skills he has – which will be useful for fulfilling their press contracts and chronicling their time in Antarctica – but also requires him to develop new skills that they might need and quickly arranges for him to receive instruction in cinematography with the Sydney film production house Gaumont and Co. Ltd.

From the beginning, Mawson has a very clear idea as to what collection of skills he will need from his men in Antarctica – skills far more numerous than the number of people he can take – and he is assiduous in ensuring that new recruits gain them before departure.

Young Hurley is, of course, beside himself with joy at such news and tells all and sundry, including his mother, who still lives in Glebe. Now, as it turns out, this rather anxious woman is not quite so enthusiastic about her son sailing off into the great unknown. In fact, she is appalled. On hearing the news from her excited lad, the recently widowed woman resolves that she must do something to stop this folly, and a few days later she takes up pen and paper to write directly to Mawson:

Dear Dr Mawson,

I hear that my son Mr J. F. Hurley has applied for the position of Cinematographer and Photographer to your expedition. Now I tell you this is not in fairness to himself as he has an internal complaint. I am certain that he is not strong enough for the position. He has never roughed it in any way during his life. He has lung trouble so bad that if he started I do not think he would come back and in justice to myself I think you should put him right out of your mind. In conclusion I want to ask you a favour, and that is, do not mention to my son that I have written to you, and you will greatly oblige.

Yours truly,
(Mrs) M. A. Hurley[25]

It is a communication that takes Mawson aback more than somewhat, as 'internal complaint' could mean anything from tuberculosis to a weak heart. The young chap looked healthy enough and had certainly been eager, but so dire would be the consequences of having an invalid with them in Antarctica for 12 months – far removed from proper medical care – that it is unthinkable to take him unless he is absolutely sure.

Against that, Mawson knows from experience with his own mother what a needlessly protective species they can be. Without breaking faith with Hurley's mother's request for confidentiality, Mawson assays to ascertain Hurley's true state of health and question whether he is 'sufficiently strong for the arduous work of the Antarctic'.[26]

The confused Hurley, not knowing where such a damaging assertion could have popped up from, replies that of course he is strong enough. 'I think there are some fabulous reports in circulation which I am pleased to say are absolutely untrue,' he replies with some feeling.[27]

To break the impasse, Mawson arranges for an independent medical examination to be conducted on Hurley, who passes with flying colours. He proves to be as healthy as *two* trouts and sends on to Mawson his clean bill of health. Mawson honours his original offer and goes on to contract Hurley to a salary of £300, which will, nevertheless, be only payable after they return to Australia, hopefully in April 1913. In return, Hurley hands over the copyright to all of the work he'll do on the expedition, so it can be used 'to raise necessary funds to meet liabilities'.[28]

Agreed. Agreed. Agreed.

Hurley is not particular over contractual niceties. He just wants to go on this extraordinary venture, and in the time remaining he throws himself into learning cinematography and assembling the film and equipment he will need to record 12 months of activities in the strange land where he is bound.

Another expedition member recruited at this late time is geologist Charles Laseron. A warm man with a wonderful sense of humour, Laseron is somewhat taken aback by Mawson's abrupt manner and the fact that the great man's first question to him is whether he can cook. Laseron confesses he has made a damper or two in his time, but that his early creations probably remain somewhere in the bush in a state of 'semi-petrification'.[29]

He ends up making a strong impression on Mawson. However, rather than issue a formal letter of acceptance, Mawson sends Laseron a letter advising him to undertake a crash course in taxidermy at the Australian Museum and . . . by corollary . . . Laseron is on the team.[30]

Though he makes a few exceptions, Mawson steers by the star that the great desideratum is tempered youth: 'It is the vigour, the dash and the recuperative power of youth that is so necessary to cope with the extreme discomforts and trials of such exploration, which approximate to the limit of human endurance and often enough exceed it.'[31]

It has been far from easy for Mawson back in Australia as, apart from recruiting – even managing to take on the odd Australian who has seen ice and snow before – he tirelessly continues to raise much-needed funds and attend to myriad details. Based on his past experience, he knows that it is the simplest of decisions he makes now that may mean the difference between success and failure in a year's time.

5 October 1911, Cheltenham Park Racecourse, Adelaide, Mawson's men have a mishap

It is just six o'clock on this amazingly still morning when Lieutenant Hugh Watkins, with none other than Frank Wild as passenger, and with the hard-working English ground engineer Frank Bickerton watching nervously from beside the hangar, takes off on a demonstration flight at the racecourse, in front of a fascinated crowd of many thousands of South Australians. For this is the monoplane that Adelaide's favourite adopted son, Dr Douglas Mawson, is going to take to Antarctica in a couple of months, don't you know? A Vickers, they say it is – whatever that means – imported from France. It's worth something like £700.

Noisy, fragile-looking little thing, isn't it? But, notwithstanding they say it can cover a staggering 300 miles in the five hours it can stay aloft, no sooner has the 34-foot-long bird taken to the skies than . . . gravity triumphs after all. Before their very eyes, the plane comes crashing to earth with a terrifying screech of metal, clearly damaged beyond repair. Both wings are shattered, one cylinder in the engine is broken, the tail is broken in half and the nose of the plane is broken beyond recognition, looking like nothing so much as a 'dismembered caterpillar'.[32]

Mercifully, and amazingly, once extricated from beneath the wreckage, both the pilot and the passenger manage to stagger, if not quite walk normally, away from it. Though injured – with such varied afflictions as cracked ribs, bruises and cuts – they are not too badly hurt. They recount that though they got to an altitude of about 200 feet, they first hit a fierce air tremor and then got straight into an air pocket that dropped them to 100 feet. They were then finished up when they hit another air tremor that meant the very ground whose surly bonds they had so recently escaped was now rushing up towards them.

As Frank Wild subsequently explained it to a friend, 'We were then on the centre of the racecourse and as the earth rushed at us, all my past life did not panorama before me. I felt no fear, just had time to think "Frank old boy your days of exploration are done . . ."'[33]

But no, he would live to trek another day.

As the expedition is already in difficult, if not desperate, financial straits – representation to various state governments through-out October proving fruitless – Mawson, once he hears news of the crash, takes the only sensible course available to him. A deeply disappointed Lieutenant Watkins is sent back to England on the next ship, his expedition over before it has properly begun. Realising, however, there is still some mileage to be gained with the public, Mawson decides to retain what is left of the dismembered plane for use as an air-tractor – a wingless aeroplane, where the propeller's thrust is used to move a laden sledge forward.

20 October 1911, *Framheim*, the Norwegians get busy

Yes, the attempt to launch on the Pole five weeks earlier was aborted because of the extreme cold, but as the weather has warmed that has all been forgotten. Some nine months after arriving in these climes, all is now in readiness for the Norwegians to launch for real, a launch from which there will be no turning back, come what may.

On this misty morning, a light breeze from the east soon clears the air. Amundsen and his four companions, Olav Bjaaland, Oscar Wisting, Sverre Hassel and Helmer Hanssen – each one of them hardy, robust men with vast experience in travelling through harsh terrains, for they have been simply born to it – ready themselves to set off. As they do so, the rest of the Norwegians crowd around to say their personal farewells, including a notably surly Johansen, who is shortly to depart on his own far less glorious trek with Prestrud.

As distinct from Scott's multi-pronged attack on the Pole, Amundsen's plan is simplicity on skis and sledges. The five men on skis are taking four sledges packed with supplies, and each sledge is pulled by 13 dogs. That is far more dogs than they need to pull a sledge, but Amundsen intends to slaughter many of their number during the journey to provide food for both the men and the remaining dogs. 'Slaughter', however, is far too emotional a word for the cool-headed way that the Norwegian looks at it. He later recounts:

> Every dog we took south with us meant fifty less pounds of food to be carried and cached. In my calculations before the start for the final dash to the Pole, I figured out exactly the precise day on which I planned to kill each dog as its usefulness should end for drawing the diminishing supplies on the sleds and its usefulness should begin as food for the men.[34]

This, of course, is far removed from Scott's notion that he does not want to use the dogs as 'pawns in the game'. But now, it really is time.

Doffing an imaginary cap to cook Adolf Lindstrøm – as if to say 'Until we meet again, my friend' – Amundsen climbs onto Wisting's sledge and, with his trademark lack of formality, sets out.

The unburdened sledges – after having already established over a ton of supplies in the depots at 80 degrees, 81 degrees and

82 degrees south, the men need only a small amount of supplies to get to the first depot – are a joy for the dogs to pull, and with one sharp command from Amundsen they enthusiastically apply their shoulders to the harness.

Soon, the party is passing cinematographer Prestrud, positioned down on the sea ice, cranking his handle for all its worth. Amundsen's seeming light-heartedness is all a play for posterity, all done in the knowledge that if they do win the race to the Pole – and for the Chief it most certainly is a race – then this footage will be particularly significant. For the folks back home, and perhaps around the world, Amundsen makes like landed gentry, wielding the whip over the lead dogs with a light flick of the wrist as the sledge passes into the distance. The show over, the explorer glances over his shoulder to take a look – would that it not be his last – at what is for him the most beautiful place in the world. Soon, to those that they leave behind, they are devoured by the landscape, black blobs disappearing into overwhelming whiteness.

Such is the way of the Antarctic.

Mid-October 1911, Indian Ocean, on the high seas with *Aurora*

In bringing *Aurora* across from Cape Town to Hobart, Davis has been enduring some of the worst gale conditions that he has ever encountered – a shrieking tempest all but unceasing – which means they have no choice but to batten down the hatches and battle on the best they can. With the exception of 16 October, the gales and squalls are relentless until, mercifully, around 20 October conditions vastly improve. Still, the morale of the crew remains high, and the little ship proves she can take heavy weather, which will be vitally important for the journey to Antarctica.

Mid- to late October 1911, Cape Evans, things come to a head for Scott

Lawrence Oates has finally had enough. He is sick of being in Antarctica, sick of the unending boredom of it all, sick with worry about the inadequacies of the ponies in his care, which are being asked to do the impossible, and, most particularly, sick of Robert Falcon Scott. All these months later, he still blames Scott for the first of the ponies having drowned, including his own favourite, Punch, and remains bitter over his clash with the expedition leader during the depot-laying journey in February.

He has little confidence that, despite his efforts, the crocks of ponies that Scott has given him to work with are up to the task of getting to the bottom of the Beardmore Glacier. Once more, he writes to his mother at around this time and gives his summation of the animals he has to work with:

Victor: Narrow chest, knock knees . . .

Snippets: Bad wind sucker. Doubtful back tendons off fore legs. Pigeon toes. Aged.

Jehu: Suffering from debility and worn out . . .

Chinaman: . . . has ringbone just above the coronet on near fore. He is different to the other ponies perhaps pure Manchurian. I think [he is] the oldest pony of the lot which is saying a good deal, both nostrils slit up.

A more unpromising lot of ponies to start a journey such as ours it would be almost impossible to conceive.[35]

All put together, is it all worth it? He thinks not.

The only way out he can see is to formally resign, refuse to head south with the expedition when it leaves in a few days' time, write a cheque to Scott for the expenses he has incurred and then wait throughout the summer for *Terra Nova* to return, at which point he would simply go back to England.

It is now that the 'Father Confessor' of them all, the man beloved by the whole expedition party, Bill Wilson, gets involved. A special man is Bill Wilson. Birdie Bowers, for example, regards him as 'the most manly and the finest character in my own sex that I have ever had the privilege to meet'.[36] (And Wilson himself, by the by, has a similar high regard for Bowers, thinking him 'the most unselfish character I think I have ever seen in a man anywhere'.[37])

In this instance, the key is that Wilson is a man whom Oates also regards very highly, notwithstanding the fact that while Oates is a hero of the Boer War, Wilson was an outspoken opponent of it. In the face of Oates's intended drastic action, Wilson, with the aid of Meares and Teddy Evans, manages to bring him back from the brink. But only just.

One thing that helps to bring Oates around is the possible honour of being among the first men to reach the South Pole. He writes to his mother on 28 October:

I have half a mind to see Scott and tell him I must go home in the ship but it would be a pity to spoil my chances of being in the final party especially as the regiment and perhaps the whole army would be pleased if I was at the Pole.[38]

(True, just like the loved ones of everyone in the hut, his mother won't see this letter until the *Terra Nova* returns for them in

February, but it helps him feel close to her to write directly.)

Hanging over them all is the spectre of Amundsen and his wretched dogs, though there remains a strong feeling that the Norwegian may be in for a few cruel surprises if dogs are indeed the only transport he is relying on. As Birdie Bowers writes to Kathleen Scott:

> Certainly to trust the final dash to such an uncertain element as dogs would be a risky thing whereas manhaulage though slow is sure and I for one am delighted at the decision. After all it will be a fine thing to do that plateau with manhaulage in these days of supposed decadence of the British race. Anyhow whether we succeed or not we all have confidence in our leader and I am sure that he will pull it through if any man will.[39]

The Owner himself is not quite so sanguine, and thoughts of Amundsen frequently gnaw at him. Just where is the Norwegian? How far are his preparations along? At what point will he depart? What route will he take? Of course, Scott has no answers to any such questions, but they won't go away. As he writes himself in a letter to Kathleen:

> I don't know what to think of Amundsen's chances. If he gets to the Pole, it must be before we do, as he is bound to travel fast with dogs and pretty certain to start early. On this account I decided at a very early date to act exactly as I should have done had he not existed. Any attempt to race must have wrecked my plan, besides which it doesn't appear the sort of thing one is out for . . .

You can rely on my not saying or doing anything foolish — only I'm afraid you must be prepared for . . . finding our venture much belittled. After all, it is the work that counts, not the applause that follows.[40]

Late October 1911, Adelaide, Mawson makes ready to depart

Her Douglas is just about to go, just about to leave her again, this time to go to Hobart to join up with *Aurora*, and then on to Antarctica. Before he departs, though, Paquita and her mother are frantically trying to finish one last task to help him. The younger woman has decided that as he is going to a land where everything is white, it might be useful, darling, and cheery if her fiancé has some things that are brightly coloured. With that in mind, she and her mother are now sewing together a dozen or so bright-red, orange and yellow linen 'Paquita' bags 'for small food packages or personal items'.[41]

Beyond just their bright colours, she hopes they might prove helpful in one way or another. She is worried about him. Under the strain of everything, he has become thinner in the last months. So much responsibility devolves upon him and him alone.

Not for nothing does he say to her, just before setting off, 'Personally I feel I would never have the energy to get up another expedition. I am prepared to go on exploring for the rest of time, but it is the organization from which one shrinks.'[42]

And not long afterwards, after their final tender embrace, he is gone, upon a ship that will take him to Hobart.

Though upset, at least Paquita has many activities to keep her busy, the foremost of which is preparing for her own trip. Given that

Douglas is to be away for well over a year, and on his return they will be married, her mother has decided to take her to Europe for much of the following year, to show her something of the land of her birth and to visit relatives, and so she may gather things for her trousseau.

1 November 1911, Cape Evans, Scott and his men get started on their great adventure

Captain Scott does not really like Teddy Evans, and he has been disappointed with his efforts on this expedition to date, for many more reasons than he has been too hard on Taffy. Three days earlier, he had written to expedition secretary Joseph Kinsey:

> Teddy Evans is a thoroughly well meaning little man, but proves on close acquaintance to be rather a duffer in anything but his own particular work. All this strictly 'entre nous', but he is not at all fitted to be 'Second-in-Command', as I was foolish enough to name him. I am going to take some steps concerning this, as it would not do to leave him in charge here in case I am late returning.[43]

This low opinion of Evans's capacity has perhaps been instrumental in sending him off a little over a week earlier – well removed from Scott's own departure – with Day, Lashly and Hooper aboard the two sputtering motor sledges. Each motor sledge was groaning under the weight of a ton and a half of kit at an average speed of around one mile per hour, which is to say much slower than a couple of very sick ponies. The day before, Wright and Keohane also departed, driving the two slowest ponies: Jehu and Jimmy the Pig.

And today, Scott himself will leave with the main body of men and ponies in three staggered and sometimes staggering detachments ranging from slowest to fastest. As he makes his last-minute preparations, Scott is keenly aware that he is about to depart on the journey of his lifetime . . . or indeed the journey of his death.

Meares, Demetri and the dogs will bring up the rear in a couple of days' time. Travelling faster than the heavily laden ponies, the dog party is expected to meet up with the main party some 140 miles away at One Ton Depot, or even a little further beyond.

Before heading out into the wilderness, Scott makes his last entry into the diary that he leaves behind: 'So here end the entries in this diary with the first chapter of our History. The future is in the lap of the gods; I can think of nothing left undone to deserve success.'[44]

Scott takes some comfort from the fact that he will be travelling with his best friend, Bill Wilson, who is in fact close enough to Kathleen Scott that he writes to her himself before departing: 'On the whole our prospects are very good and I would much rather have them than Amundsen's for all his dogs. However you will know what he has done probably before we shall.'[45]

To the South Pole and back from their starting point is approximately 900 miles each way, but of course whereas the crow could fly straight, they would be plodding every step of the way, the first part of the journey behind their ponies, up, over and around obstacles.

Meanwhile, unknown to them, both motor sledges have already given up the ghost, with seized engines in the freezing conditions. Incapable of pulling heavy loads over difficult surfaces, the motor sledges have blown up before reaching Corner Camp, only 40 miles south of Hut Point.

The four men who started out with those infernal machines now put themselves in harness, and, all pulling together, stagger along as they bear the weight of 740 pounds of supplies, sufficient for one four-man unit for six weeks. They are expecting to meet Scott at One Ton Depot or further south still.

4 November 1911, Hobart, the end of the beginning

Hobart ahoy! After a journey lasting exactly 100 days from the South West India Docks on the Thames, the tough little whaler heads up the Derwent River into the Tasmanian capital, pausing only to drop the dogs off at the Nubeena Quarantine Station. Though the usual way of things after a long voyage is for the crew to be given a fair measure of shore leave, on this occasion there is no time. Rather than seeing a diminution of activity as sea duties are left behind, Davis is soon pushing the crew as never before to get *Aurora* cleaned out, scrubbed down and all shipshape, engines tuned and the hull cleared of the marine growth that has attached itself since the ship left Cardiff.

Though the expeditioners have brought much equipment and food with them from London, still the amount to be added from Hobart is nothing short of extraordinary. And now, meticulously overseen by both Douglas Mawson, who is there to meet them, and Captain Davis, the 'beef' – the sailor's term for manpower – are soon heaving and straining as they wheel to the ship everything from Antarctic-specific clothing, including windproof oversuits, fur mitts of wolf skin and finnesko ski boots, to items such as fur-lined sleeping bags as well as stocks of alcohol, diverse scientific equipment, dredges and sieves, Norwegian sledges, collecting jars and boxes, mountaineering equipment, medical supplies, skinning knives and forceps, harnesses for the sledge dogs, water and, of course, endless bags of coal.

5 November 1911, Depot III, 237 miles south of *Framheim*, Amundsen is very, very pleased

Seventeen days into Amundsen's southern journey, progress has been excellent. Yes, they have had some dangerous mishaps, which have included a few occasions of dogs, sledges and men tumbling higgledy-piggledy down crevasses, but all the men at least (for they do lose a few dogs to misadventure) have been hauled safely back to the surface, and they are on track, on time.

Early on in the trek, the men came across a cairn they built the previous April – a six-foot-high construction of blocks of snow cut out with large snow-knives, heaped upon each other, together with a black flag on a bamboo pole – still standing all these months on, and clearly visible for miles on a good day. It gave Amundsen an idea, and he immediately put it into action. From that point on, every few hours on their journey, they build another cairn, and within each cairn they leave a written record of the day, the time that it was constructed and, most crucially, the exact bearing towards the previous cairn they have built to the north. While they are heading out into a trackless wilderness, they are ensuring that on their way back there will be a heavily signposted highway to get them home. A bonus for the dogs is that the building of each cairn gives them some precious rest – and for the male dogs it provides particular relief.

As to their first food depot, 99 miles from *Framheim* – the one they laid in mid-February, nine months earlier – it took them just four marches to reach it. Oddly enough, even though they are averaging over 20 miles a day, their days do not feel too strenuous and they generally do not finish them feeling too fatigued. Amundsen can take great satisfaction that his careful planning has been vindicated, and of his many triumphs to this point a key one has been the modification of the sledges. When he purchased them in Oslo, they weighed 150 pounds off the shelf, but over the winter Olav Bjaaland, the skiing champion and carpenter, skilfully managed to reduce them to just a third of that weight, somehow without losing strength, flexibility or even durability.

It is the dogs, of course, who are doing the hard work, hauling the men and supplies, and it is those dogs who most need rest, so after just five hours in harness, with that mileage accomplished, Amundsen insists they stop where they are and rest, before they go again. He is rewarded by the fact that, for the most part, both dogs and men keep healthy, and just a fortnight after beginning their journey they arrive at the farthest south base, at 82 degrees south, on time and with growing confidence.

All is on track, even if that track is getting higher and colder as they proceed.

7 November 1911 and a week thereafter, south of Corner Camp, Oates's growing concern about the ponies' lack of oats

No one likes to actually say anything. But in the midst of this blizzard, where the ponies can no longer move and must be sheltered behind urgently built snow walls, and Scott and his men are effectively trapped in their tents, no one can help but notice that when Cecil Meares and Demetri and the dogs arrive with a flurry of snow, they appear to be entirely untroubled by the atrocious conditions that have stopped the rest of them. An irritable Scott, however, insists he is little impressed that the dog party have caught up with them 100 miles and a week before schedule – undoubtedly embarrassed at having sternly instructed Meares before departure that they would not be able to afford to wait for them at One Ton Depot.

'Meares has played too much for safety in catching us so soon,' he writes in his journal, 'but it is satisfactory to find the dogs will pull the loads and be driven to face such a wind as we have had.'[46] Somewhere deep within Scott, beyond even his embarrassment and irritation, there must be the stunned and sorry realisation that his reckoning that the dogs would not perform with such drift in their face on the Barrier is completely wrong.

Worse even than that, a week later at One Ton Depot, the bitter truth is now apparent – at least to some. It is not just that the dogs are fast but also that the ponies are slow. Notwithstanding that, from the second day of the journey, Scott has switched them to night marching, so that the surface will be colder and firmer underfoot for the nags. In the recent blizzard conditions, their hooves are constantly plunging deep beneath the surface, and it is all they can do to keep going. The dogs, of course, just scamper along the top. Can Captain Scott admit out loud that a terrible mistake has been made? Of course, he cannot.

The others, however, have no need to be so dismissive of the obvious, as they are not the ones who insisted from the first that this expedition would be relying on ponies and not dogs. (And white-coated ones, at that, as if that makes any difference. If true, one would hate to see what condition these pathetic brutes would be in if they had dark coats.) For the question stands: if Meares and his relatively untrained dogs are able to move so quickly, just how must Amundsen and his dogs be faring? It does not bear thinking about.

Oates and Meares, at least, are able to quietly talk about the situation, and both agree: Scott really has made a serious error. Beyond just the reliance on ponies rather than dogs, there has been the ongoing problem of coordinating the separate teams to arrive at the same depot at roughly the same time. It is all so thoroughly depressing.

Oates's overall grim mood has been compounded – first there was the discovery of the two abandoned motor sledges, and now there is the discovery that the ponies have lost condition far more rapidly than he expected. While Scott remains blithely optimistic about his ponies – 'I think that a good many of the beasts are actually in better form than when they started,' he enthuses – it is telling that a plan is made to soon sacrifice two of the ponies, Jehu and Christopher, to keep the dogs going much further than originally anticipated.[47]

Oates writes in his diary, 'We both damned the motors. 3 motors at £1000 each, 19 ponies at £5 each, 32 dogs at 30/- each. If Scott fails to get to the Pole he jolly well deserves it.'[48]

And then Oates falls asleep, completely exhausted. Tomorrow will bring yet more of the back-breaking work he has been doing to this point. Part of the problem is the pony Christopher that he is responsible for. In these conditions, the wretch has proved to be virtually uncontrollable, even by so experienced a horseman as him. In fact, so much so that the only way they can get the animal into the harness in the morning is to have four men throw him to the ground and hold him down, even as the brute tries to have his revenge by biting and kicking. Under such circumstances, Oates and his party must simply keep him going all day long rather than stop for lunch, because it is just more trouble than it's worth to get him started again once they stop. This means that they have spent the last week feeling extremely hungry for the last half of the day – with their bodies burning energy that food is not providing – but there is no other way.

No doubt about it: Christopher is, as Bowers later terms it in his diary, 'A thoroughly bad egg.'[49]

Mid-November 1911, Queen's Wharf, Hobart, the preparations for the Mawson expedition continue – bend your backs and stow, m'lads

While most of the things being loaded on board *Aurora* are essential for keeping the men sheltered, warm and fed for a long period of time in an unforgiving climate, several things are included to nurture only their minds.

The AAE library, which is a mix of Mawson's own collection and books donated by their London patron C. D. Mackellar, boasts a large number of polar-expedition books and scientific reports as well as various fiction titles, such as the *Trail of '98* by Mawson's favourite, the 'Yukon Poet' Robert Service. Mawson is also careful to include another dog-eared and much-loved book from his library: the Roman emperor and philosopher Marcus Aurelius's self-dedicated *Meditations*. It is a book with a philosophy – contained in a series of Aurelius's disconnected thoughts to self – that resonates strongly with Mawson's own. Aurelius is a great believer that inner freedom and peace is to be attained firstly through submission to Providence, and secondly through rigorous detachment from everything not within your own power to alter. Man is but a small part of Nature, and while he may fight hard to alter those things that can be changed, he must accept those that cannot . . .

For Mawson, such a philosophy is made for Antarctic exploration, and Aurelius's teachings strike a chord that rings true from the beginning. He is keen that others might also read it on the voyage and draw strength from it.

But, back to work with the loading, as hundreds of four-gallon containers of kerosene, to be used as fuel for the sledging stoves, and high-quality benzine to power the air-tractor, motor launch and generators are all brought on board – while *Aurora* herself has 386 tons of coal. For support, Mawson charters a Bass Strait packet, *Toroa*, to take some of the stores, as well as 17 expedition members, 50 live sheep, another load of precious coal, and most of the equipment and supplies for those staying on at Macquarie Island. *Toroa* will take them as far as that island before unloading some of her supplies there, transferring the rest to *Aurora* and then turning back.

Toroa's vastly experienced Captain Holliman is well known by the sobriquet 'Roaring Tom', as there is little he says beyond 'pass the salt' that is not a roar.

18 November 1911 and the rest of that month thereafter, foothills of the Transantarctic Mountains, Amundsen affirms speed is of the essence

Having laboured mightily to ascend 2000 feet over the course of 15 miles, and then scale an even steeper ascent of another 2000 feet, on this afternoon they come to a small, very flat terrace, a tiny pass between the mountain peaks that surround it on nearly all sides. Which way now?

The only possibility is to return the way they have come, in the hope of finding an easier passage through these mountains, or try to get to the spot they can see far to their south, where there appears to be a series of stepped terraces, between mountains that Amundsen dubs Mt Fridtjof Nansen and the 12,000-foot Don Pedro Christophersen.[50]

Alas, to get to those terraces they have to give away their hard-won altitude and drop sharply into the valley that lies before them – not what they were expecting – and those terraces may lead to a dead end, making a retreat even more difficult.

Amundsen, alone, briefly turns back to the northern end of the pass to take one long last look at the Barrier and the way they have come. They cannot go back. There can be only one decision. They must go on.

To successfully (though not exactly safely) negotiate the first 800-foot descent, Amundsen's men wrap thin ropes around the runners of their still heavily laden sledges to act as brakes and proceed to drive the dog teams headlong down the mountainside. Applying the same crude method, they then manage a second, steeper descent, slipping and sliding their way to the bottom and at times cannoning their sledges into each other in the downhill argy-bargy, though fortunately with no significant damage.[51] Now on the valley floor, the men cross two small, steep glaciers, climbing another very difficult 1250 feet as they relay their two sledges – foot by foot, rope jerk by rope jerk – up and onto another plateau, standing at 4550 feet, one of the steps they have seen from afar.

And then it happens. Long have they laboured, far have they come, now, now is their reward. Turning westward towards Don Pedro Christophersen, they are stopped in their tracks by the most wonderful sight. For there, before them, they see a vast glacier, running across them from the north-east to the south-west and stretching right up from the Barrier between the lofty mountains and on to the Polar Plateau.

Just as Shackleton found the Beardmore Glacier years earlier, now another 'highway to the south' has opened up before Amundsen and his men, an undiscovered glacier that Amundsen names Folgefonni (though he will later rename it the Axel Heiberg in honour of his patron on the *Gjøa* and *Fram*).

True, this is a far shorter and far more brutal glacier than the Beardmore, as it rises viciously 8000 feet from the Barrier up to the Polar Plateau in just 20 miles. But Amundsen immediately realises, as he later recounts, 'It was by this glacier that we should have to gain the great plateau; we could see that.'[52]

Speed is of course of the essence in stealing the prize from Scott, and they waste no time in beginning. By 20 November, travelling predominantly by line of sight, the Norwegians are in position to begin their climb, and with dogged persistence they reach the Polar Plateau just one day later, with both men and the dogs completely exhausted. Yet there is cause for great satisfaction. 'This day's work – nineteen and a quarter miles,[53] with an ascent of 5750 ft – gives us some idea of what can be performed by dogs in good training.'[54]

Only a month after leaving *Framheim*, Amundsen and his four companions have managed to keep moving at breakneck speed, pioneer an alternative route and get one ton of supplies to the top of the plateau, enabling them to put the final part of their plan into place, which is to get their dogs ready for the dash to the South Pole. Yes, the Norwegian men have been courageous, but Amundsen is under no illusions as to where most of the credit lies – with their dogs. 'They lay flat down and hauled, dug their claws in and dragged themselves forwards,' writes Amundsen.[55]

And yet, despite their sterling service, half these dogs must now be killed. After all, the party's supplies are at the top, the worst of the hard hauling is done and the hard reality is that the dogs are now more useful as an internal rather than external power source. With little ceremony, therefore, he commands that the 24 weakest dogs be shot by the individual sledge drivers they have so admirably served up till now.

As the first shots ring out, the Norwegian leader does feel emotional after all, and he finds himself pumping the Primus up to full in a futile effort to stifle the shattering crack of each brutal betrayal – as shot on shot echoes eerily across the white, ever more lifeless plain.

'A trusty servant lost his life each time,' Amundsen sorrowfully records in his journal, as each man now takes a knife and disembowels his many victims lest the meat be spoiled.[56] It is as brutal as it is bloody, and no sooner have the steaming entrails fallen upon the snow than they are ravenously devoured by the surviving dogs. Indeed, so much of their one-time companions do they eat that Suggen, Wisting's dog, subsequently staggers about the camp with his stomach somewhat misshapen.

The Norwegians do not quite have the stomach for that themselves, and, in an odd case of humanity meeting caninity, out of respect the men do not partake of the dogs that night and wait until the next morning. Now, the carcasses of the dogs are flayed, with their meat an enticing vision – albeit foul smelling – rich red and soon laid out against the pure white of the snow. With the skills of a master chef, Wisting prepares the meat into a dog soup. Over the next two days, a few of those 24 dogs are devoured with no small satisfaction – much of the feasting observed by the dogs that remain – while the rest are either put in a depot to be eaten on their return journey or put on the sledge to be taken with them.

For Amundsen, the appearance of the dog cutlets recalls 'memories of old days, when no doubt a dog cutlet would have been less tempting than now – memories of dishes on which the cutlets were elegantly arranged side by side, with paper frills on the bones, and a neat pile of petits pois in the middle'.[57]

The camp becomes known to them as the Butcher's Shop on the strength of it. Then, after frustratingly pausing for four days because of a blizzard, the five men and 18 surviving dogs, hauling three sleds, push into the howling headwinds. The South Pole is now just over 300 miles away. Not that it is going to be easy for all that . . .

Only a few days later, the men find themselves in very dangerous territory, which they call the Devil's Ballroom – essentially a glacier criss-crossed by deep crevasses covered by thin snow bridges. To the untutored eye, it looks like much of the glacier they have so recently ascended, but in fact they have to go slowly for fear of falling to their grisly deaths into the frozen bowels of the ice world below, from which there would be no escape.

21 November 1911, Sydney Harbour, off on the great adventure

Some days are diamonds, and this is one of them. On this glorious day of late spring, Sydney Harbour seems to sparkle like never before, as an excited Frank Hurley makes his way to the Union Steam Ship Company's wharves in Darling Harbour . . . And there she is! She is the SS *Paloona*, the very vessel that will take him and several other young men who are to join the expedition down to Hobart. There, they will meet up with Dr Mawson himself on *Aurora*.

The band of excited well-wishers that is there to see them off includes many professors from the University of Sydney as well as leaders in the scientific community who have a stake in this expedition. The atmosphere is one of barely contained excitement. This be adventure! This be the start of pushing on to new frontiers. This be, for many of them, including Hurley, their first major trip to anywhere, let alone the mysterious shore of a frozen continent still to know the tread of human feet.

And so to business. The gangplank is hauled up, the lines untied, and slowly, surely, SS *Paloona* pulls away towards Sydney Heads. Still waving the well-wishers goodbye until they are out of sight, Frank Hurley stands beside the other expedition members, most of whom he has never met before.

Bit by bit on their way to Hobart, the men will come to know each other better. There is, among others, Charles Laseron, who is now bemused to find himself to be a half-trained taxidermist, and John 'Jack' Hunter, a young biologist from Mawson's alma mater of Fort Street Model School, who also like Mawson went on to graduate with two sterling degrees from the University of Sydney, in his case science and medicine. The man who will be in charge of the wireless on the main base, the gentle giant Walter Hannam, is also on the deck and beside himself with excitement. He would soon write in his diary:

Today marks the start in life that I have longed for since I was a child and read Nansen's *Furthest North* . . . We have first started on the [*Paloona*] for Hobart where we sail on our voyage of discovery and as it is a lovely day with no sea we are sure to have a good time and of course are full of curiosity as to what our future home will be like.[58]

New Zealander Arthur Sawyer is to be in charge of the crucial wireless at Macquarie Island. There are two medical doctors in

Archie McLean and Evan Jones, the latter being a newly graduated young medico from Sydney University.

Of them all, though, it is the 26-year-old Dr McLean who makes the strongest impression on the others from the first. A joint arts and medical graduate from the University of Sydney, blessed with great physical strength, he has a fondness for greeting all and sundry with the phrase 'Hallo, Dad'. He does this so frequently that he is oft referred to as Dad – a moniker that he doesn't particularly chafe under.

21 November 1911, Mt Hooper (Upper Barrier) Depot, 220 miles south of Cape Evans, Scott has a face like a tired old sea boat

There they are.

For the last six days, Teddy Evans's motor-sledge cum man-hauling party have been anxiously awaiting the arrival of Scott and his party, and now at last, just before 5 am, the first of Scott's crocks, Jehu, Chinaman and Jimmy the Pig, together with their drivers, pull into the spot Teddy Evans has named Mt Hooper Depot. Soon thereafter, the entire troupe is joyfully reunited once more, and a unit of provisions, two boxes of biscuits and three tins of paraffin are deposited at the base of a cairn with a large black flag atop it.

And yet, if Evans's men are a little shocked at how poorly the ponies look, Scott and his men can't help but notice how exhausted and downright skinny Evans and his men are, particularly Day, who is positively gaunt. The abandonment of the motor sledges on 2 November just beyond Corner Camp has meant that Evans and his men have had to man-haul 740 pounds of supplies on their ten-foot non-motorised backup sledge around 175 miles here to the Mt Hooper Depot, and in such conditions, doing such labour, their strength has clearly ebbed as their bodies have deteriorated.

As exhausted as they are, however, Evans's party has still managed to cover the 77 miles between One Ton Depot and Mt Hooper Depot in approximately the same time it has taken Scott and the ponies. This only provides further evidence that the leader has made a terrible mistake in the choice of ponies. Oates records in his diary that, as a consequence, Scott carries 'a face like a tired old sea boat'.[59]

The numbers are grim. Only three weeks and roughly 220 miles into what Scott has estimated would be a 21-week and 1800-mile round journey (a week behind schedule), men and beasts are suffering markedly. True, the ponies are intended to get them only to the base of the Beardmore Glacier, but when it comes to men, if this decline is what occurs after only a fortnight of man-hauling, what would any of them be like after three or four months of it?

The one bit of good news? 'We haven't seen anything of Amundsen,' Day jokes with the newly arrived.[60]

23 November 1911, Tasmania, SS *Paloona* sails up the Derwent River – Hobart ahoy!

And there, boys, is the freshly painted *Aurora*. For as *Paloona* sails into Hobart only a couple of days after leaving Sydney, she immediately makes her way to the Queen's Wharf, where the hardy ship of their dreams awaits. She is a tough-looking little vessel, over which dozens of people are swarming, carrying cargo, while aloft singing sailors are hauling on lines, checking the sails and halyards and all the rest, all watched by the myriad sightseers on the wharf.

There she is, boys! It is a vision to behold, and it is with a great sense of privilege that the excited young men from Sydney make their way through those sightseers and – by virtue of the fact that they are actually a part of this expedition – head up the gangplank to meet their new companions for the first time.

Here is Xavier Mertz – 'How you are, bloody fine day, isn't it?' – and this is Belgrave Ninnis, together with the redoubtable Captain Davis, who seems a bit . . . gloomy. (Don't worry about it, lads, he's just a bit like that, even at the best of times.)

But here, too, is a cheery New Zealander, chief magnetician Eric Webb of the Carnegie Institute, who will be in charge of the magnetic observations, side by side with the 23-year-old scientist Cecil Madigan from Adelaide. He has recently been awarded a Rhodes scholarship, but Mawson has persuaded the tough and capable young man – one of his students – to defer it in favour of enlisting on the AAE. His role will be to take charge of all the meteorological measurements while the expedition is down south, and at first acquaintance he seems well suited to the task. Physically tough and intellectually rigorous, Madigan is possessed of a vivacious personality quite in contrast . . . well, it has to be said . . . quite in contrast to Dr Mawson himself.

A formidable figure, weighed down somewhat by the many responsibilities now lying upon his coatless shoulders – and with his sleeves rolled up, so he can better exert his own elbow grease – Mawson has little time or inclination for bonhomie in these frantic days, and if the new chums do question him on any matter, they usually find his answers to be 'short shrift, earnest and hurried'.[61] He has endless lists to mark off, and dozens upon dozens of decisions to make, so he simply has no time for light chit-chat of any description. In the words of Charles Laseron, their leader is, at this point, 'rather austere and reserved'.[62]

Not that there is much time to get to know him anyway, or have idle chit-chat with the others, as everyone, new or old, must immediately pitch in to the task at hand, which is getting *Aurora* shipshape, fully loaded, fuelled and ready to go. It is devastatingly hard work, most of it, and yet if it is not quite the time of their lives, it is at least the time of their lives to this point. By day and into the early evening, all the men of the Mawson expedition continue to work like mad things on and about *Aurora*.

All of the 5200 separate items that have been assembled by the Hobart dock – weighing mostly 50 to 70 pounds each – have to be numbered, daubed with different colours according to whether they are destined for Macquarie Island, Main Antarctic Base or Western Base, brought on board and carried down into the bowels of the ship. They are so packed that they are accessible as required, with the packages for the first base at the top and so on. All too frequently, they need to be repacked. And then there is all the timber for the huts that must be built when the expedition gets to the bases, and the air-tractor, and the enormous poles of Douglas fir that will become the wireless masts, together with the wireless equipment itself. And heave, and heave, and . . . heaaave!

Perfect. Mawson notes that, whatever else, the hard physical work is 'just what was wanted to make us fit'.[63] At the other end of the scale are the smaller, more delicate things, such as fresh eggs, which are carried and stored on board with nearly as much care as is devoted to the many delicate scientific instruments that also must be stowed.

The work starts at dawn and goes until well after dark. And then, the men quickly scrub up and head out onto the town to enjoy themselves in the traditional manner of seafarers, warriors and adventurers before they head off for a long period, since time immemorial. Ah, but these are not just any men. To the lovely lassies of this great Tassie town, they are nothing less than, as Archie McLean puts it, 'young gods of explorers striding among the hospitable townsfolk . . .'[64]

'Hobart girls, what ho!' Laseron writes in his diary. 'The name *Aurora* is acting like magic, and most of the chaps are doing well with the fair sex. Strawberries and cream is the chief item of diet, and the shops are rarely empty.'[65] Life has never been better.

24 November 1911 and four days thereafter, 63 miles south of Mt Hooper, life gets progressively worse for Scott's Southern Party

With their leader constantly measuring their progress against where that interloper Shackleton was up to at the same time on his push, the spectre of the hard-striding bulldog is always with Scott's party, and always just up ahead.

Into the driving snow and bitterly cold wind, with Christopher still requiring Oates and several others to throw him to the ground and wrestle the harness on him every time, and several of the ponies deteriorating by the day, the men have fallen further behind the schedule that Scott originally set. The agitated Scott insists they must continue to maintain their recent average of 15 miles per day.

This measuring of themselves against Shackleton goes right to the point where Scott, encouraged by Atkinson and Oates, refuses to shoot a pony for food for the dogs until they are all beyond the point on the Barrier that Shackleton reached when his own first pony was slaughtered.

Shortly thereafter, it is established that the pony who will soon go to the dogs is Jehu. At Scott's reluctant command – he has long hated the idea of killing animals but now realises there is simply no choice – Oates takes Jehu back up the track and kills the pony with a single shot to the temple. And Oates himself is affected, recording in his diary that night that 'it's a brutal thing killing these poor ponies. The sad part is Jehu has plenty of march left in him but the dogs have to have food and forage is becoming short.'[66] The 23 dogs are not the only ones glad for the feed, as Jehu provides the delicacy, seldom savoured before now, of fresh meat for the 14 men. It is the particularly grim fate of the ponies that after having suffered for so long – first to get to Antarctica, then to drag such a heavy weight so far through such appalling conditions – their final resting place is in the bellies of the men who have done this to them.

Nevertheless, the slaughter of individual ponies at regular intervals is a pattern that Scott hopes to continue from now on, as their food supplies are gradually consumed and the total load lightens.

As to the dogs, their own role in taking supplies forward had originally been planned by Scott to be minimal compared with that of the motor sledges and ponies. They were to provide a supporting role and assist in carrying forward supplies as far as the middle of the Barrier (around 81 degrees 15 minutes south) and then return to Winter Quarters, so they could ready themselves to head out on the Barrier once more in the late summer, first to resupply the depots, and then on a second trip to help Scott's party return home from the South Pole. However, with the abject failure of the motor sledges, things have changed. Rather than Cecil Meares, Demetri Gerof and the dog teams, it is now Day and Hooper and the two dogs in the worst condition who are duly the first to be turned back that night, bearing a message from Scott to be delivered to Cape Evans:

We are making fair progress and the ponies doing fairly well. I hope we shall get through to the glacier without difficulty but to make sure I am carrying the dog teams farther than I intended at first – the teams may be late returning, unfit for further work or non-existent.[67]

By this time, focus is starting to narrow on just who the final four to push for the Pole will be. Typical is the pronouncement of Wilson to his wife in one of the many letters that Day and Hooper are taking back with them, saying he hopes to be picked by Scott 'just for your sake'.[68] All are keenly aware that great honours and fame await whoever bags the Pole first, though a large measure of the delight is due to the pleasure this will bring their wives, parents and families.

And yet, if Wilson has his moments of trepidation, wondering if it is even possible to get to the Pole and back alive, he is still able to draw deeply on his religious faith to give him strength. Before he left, Oriana had given him a pocket testament and prayer book to take with him, and he frequently reads it at night in his tent, always feeling strengthened by its holy words. 'What a perfect piece of faith and hope!' he writes in his diary, referring to the prayer book. 'Makes me feel that if the end comes to me here or hereabouts there will be no great time for O. to sorrow. All will be as it was meant to be.'[69]

The Scott party struggles on, and a few days after Jehu it is the worthy Chinaman who pays the ultimate price. The Canadian Charles 'Silas' Wright describes it with a curious mix of delicacy and bluntness. 'Chinaman died tonight of senile decay complicated by the presence of a bullet in the brain,' he writes in his diary. 'Poor old devil, he never shirked and was capable of reaching the Beardmore. Dogs had to be fed . . . The smallest and the oldest of the lot and the first to cross every degree of latitude. Would eat some of him – only Atch refuses.'[70]

1 December 1911, Hobart, Belgrave Ninnis contemplates the worst

In a brief break in their preparations, Belgrave Ninnis takes a little time out – as do most of them – to write some last letters before they leave civilisation behind for at least a year. In an elegant yet masculine hand, he writes to his dearest friend in London, a fellow by the name of H. E. Meade, or, as Ninnis calls him, Zip:

Dear Zip,
We sail tomorrow afternoon on the voyage to Antarctica, and prior to this interesting event, I am writing to ask a favour. In the

event of my being snatched to the skies (or the reverse) during our trip, will you, when the news of this event reaches you, please write to, or see, Cox's people, and find out if they have forwarded to my father the letter I sent them weeks ago. I told them when I wrote that they were to send on this letter when they heard of my death but not before . . .

My 'dec' notice is sure to catch your eye somewhere . . .

B. E. S. Ninnis[71]

1 December 1911, South Barrier (Lower) Depot, things get bloody . . . for Scott's party

It is a very beastly business. On this day, it is the turn of Oates's pony Christopher to take a bullet, but it is not easy. This time, just as Oates fires his pistol at the pony's head, in character the pony bucks a little, and the bullet only wounds him. Terrified, and spraying blood from his forehead onto the pristine whiteness, the bucking brute of a thing charges to the end of his pony lines until, at last, Oates is able to let off another, more successful shot that drops him and kills him. He dies as he has lived, and as far as Bowers is concerned they are well rid of him.

But Birdie does not feel the same way about his own pony, the brave and worthy Victor, who is still strong enough to have been able to easily haul 450 pounds of supplies into the camp. Such is Birdie's empathy for this lovely animal that he gives him one of his own precious ration biscuits to chew on, just as he, too, is shot.

A beastly, bloody business indeed . . .

With the meat of the ponies safely cached, they push on, with a previously penned poem by Bill Wilson for the expedition paper, the *South Polar Times*, surely capturing something of their experience:[72]

The Silence was deep with a breath like sleep
As our sledge runners slid on the snow,
And the fate-full fall of our fur-clad feet
Struck mute like a silent blow
On a questioning 'hush', as the settling crust
Shrank shivering over the floe;
And the sledge in its track sent a whisper back
Which was lost in a white-fog bow.
And this was the thought that the Silence wrought
As it scorched and froze us through,
Though secrets hidden are all forbidden
Till God means man to know.
We might be the men God meant should know
The heart of the Barrier snow,
In the heat of the sun, and the glow
And the glare from the glistening floe;
As it scorched and froze us through and through
With the bite of the drifting snow.[73]

Chapter Nine

To the South!

*I may say that this is the greatest factor – the way in which the expedition
is equipped – the way in which every difficulty is foreseen, and precautions
taken for meeting or avoiding it. Victory awaits him who has everything
in order – luck, people call it. Defeat is certain for him who has neglected
to take the necessary precautions in time; this is called bad luck.*

Roald Amundsen, *The South Pole*

*It was with beating hearts, and a strange feeling of exaltation that we
started on what will probably be the greatest adventure of our lives.*

Charles Laseron, Diary

2 December 1911, Hobart, aboard *Aurora*, Mawson has a dream departure

What a time they have had getting away! It has not just been the
loading of supplies adequate for 32 men spending over a year in
Antarctica aboard *Aurora* and *Toroa*, the last-minute lectures to
raise further funds, the endless checking that they have everything
they will need, but also the receptions, the farewells, the celebratory
church services. Two days earlier, the premier of Tasmania hosted
a reception for them, and the previous Sunday a special service had
been held for them at St David's Cathedral.

Speaking of matters religious, why, who might this be tottering
up the gangplank? Mind your manners and watch your language,

lads, lady on board! And indeed she really is. Pleased to meet you, Lady Baron, and thank you very much to the Hobart Ladies Auxiliary of the British and Foreign Bible Society for the very useful bibles. Without a chaplain aboard, this is just what we need.

Occupying a prominent position on *Aurora*'s rigging is the Tasmanian Tourist Association's gift of a signboard bearing the words 'To the Antarctic, and Success!' with a finger pointing ahead. While *Aurora* is flying the blue ensign and the Royal Thames Yacht Club burgee, all over the wharf and on the surrounding boats and warships hovering close, Union Jacks and Australian flags are gaily flying.

And the telegrams pour in. No less than Her Majesty Queen Alexandra, consort and now widow of King Edward VII, forwards a message of farewell to the expedition, in which she warmly wishes Mawson and his crew 'every success and a safe return'.[1] The governor general, Lord Denman, writes wishing Mawson's expedition good luck and success in bringing honour to the Commonwealth.

Dockside, Mawson gives his final statement to the press, leaving no doubt as to the primary purpose of the expedition: 'On leaving Australia to hoist the Australian flag in a land that geographically belongs to Australia, I wish to express my deep thanks for the assistance the federal and some state governments have given to me in forwarding this enterprise.'[2]

Now, together with the ship's company of 24, plus Ninnis and Mertz, Dr Mawson comes on board with another 11 men – half his team, as the other half will follow in the support ship the *Toroa* – making it 38 who wave fond farewell to the crowd.

At 3.55 pm, Captain Davis gives the order to cast off all ropes. Precisely as the Town Clock tolls 4 pm, the hardy little whaler pulls away from the wharf. In response, cheering breaks out from the gathered crowd and the band strikes up the hymn 'God Be With You Till We Meet Again' – as they all wish Godspeed to the first Antarctic expedition under Australian leadership.

Frank Hurley, a man with a keen eye for the vision splendid, is stunned at the mixed magic colours and beauty of it all. In their wake, launches gay with fluttering bunting follow them tightly and exuberantly. Far behind, over Hobart town, a purple mist merges 'into a marvellous blue where the deep green slopes of Mt Wellington sweep gradually up to a precipitous basalt dome'.[3]

Near the summit of that marvellous mount, a wispy trail of smoke from a fire unknown arches high to the heavens 'neath a windless sky. And, as the ship heads down the Derwent, 'the silvery limbs of the eucalyptus trees which clothe the slopes on either side with rich green forests, stood out in crisp detail and were reflected in the unruffled turquoise waters'.[4]

It is a perfect, dreamy departure that could not have been more different to the way *Aurora* left their dock on the Thames five months earlier.

A brief pause to load the 38 surviving yip-yapping dogs from the Nubeena Quarantine Station – with Ninnis and Mertz once more to the fore as in days of yore, tethering each dog to a spot on the bulwarks of the upper deck – and then they are truly on their way. That night, at 8.45 pm, the signal station at Mt Nelson, south of Hobart, sends a warm message of farewell, safe journey. Out of the darkness to the south comes the flashed message in Morse code in reply, as the ship bobs up and down on the heavy swell: *Everything snug on board; ready for anything. Goodbye.*[5]

Godspeed. On they press, into the night, towards the land of the midnight sun.

Down below, many men, such as Frank Hurley, do it tough on this first night as the wind and sea rise in sympathy with each other, to the point where the small vessel is soon being tossed around in a full-blown gale. Up one wave, down another, and broadsided by the next, much of the deck cargo soon begins to shift around, some of it crashing into the bulwarks at the side of the ship, as the crew works frantically to apply extra ropes to secure it. There are some terrifying moments in that long, dark night, but the boat lives to see the troubled dawn. Less a baptism of fire than a terrible drenching, it is the first warning to the new chums of Mawson's party that what they are embarked upon is not just a romantic adventure but also a perilous pursuit with real, life-threatening risks. And, like those risks, the gale does not lessen as the days go by.

8 December 1911 and three days thereafter, Depot X atop the Polar Plateau, Amundsen's party pass a worthy milestone

On this auspicious day, Amundsen and his team pass an important milestone. Three years before, on Shackleton's journey towards the South Pole, the Briton made it to 88 degrees 23 minutes south, just 111 miles from the bottom of the world, and on this day the Norwegians have gone past that. Yes, their bodies are breaking out in sores and some of them have frostbite, but they are still making good time, and very nearly *having* a good time.

Personally, Amundsen has only one real worry: where is Scott? Is it to be their fate that they will get to the South Pole only to find the Englishman there waiting for them, or might he have even left a long time previously, leaving only a flapping Union Jack? It would be an unimaginable disappointment, but it has to be a possibility. After all, he knows that Scott's people have been using a combination of motor sledges and ponies, and though Amundsen is of the firm view that his dogs are better equipped for the tough terrain than Scott's ponies, it may be that the motor sledges have worked. Back in late January, that fellow Campbell said that one of the motor sledges was 'already on terra firma'. What if they all worked that well and Scott has been able to quickly transport vast amounts of supplies across the Barrier? It really would be a terrible horror to find himself beaten. Amundsen resolves to push harder still.

Kjør, hunder, kjør! Mush, you dawgies, mush!

As the men proceed south over the next few days, of course this fear that they will see signs of the English ahead of them rises. They continue to nervously scan the horizon for any sign, and . . .

And, *there!*

In all of the endless whiteness, something black has shown up.

It is dog-driver Sverre Hassel who cries out. 'Do you see that black thing over there?'

God. Yes, they can.

'Can it be Scott?' someone shouts, voicing the thoughts of them all.

Bjaaland skis over to investigate. His relief is overwhelming. 'Mirage,' he pronounces, lightly. 'Dog turds.'[6]

8 December 1911, Pacific Ocean, Mawson and his men find that Providence asserts herself

And still the gale blows. The waves grow progressively higher and more ugly as the ship makes her way through the Roaring Forties and then the Furious Fifties.

'Hell, grim Hell, sodden watery Hell,' Belgrave Ninnis describes the three kinds of westerly winds to a friend in a letter.

> Perchance you have heard of the 'Roaring Forties'. Well, for eleven days they've been roaring. This is famed as the roughest place on God's earth, and, by Jove, it has lived up to its reputation. Things are coming to a pass when one comes to a meal in oilskins and sea boots.[7]

It is so bad below decks in the middle of the night that the water streaming through the cracks in the planking and onto Belgrave Ninnis's head is heavy enough to make him reverse his position on the bunk and have it pour onto his feet instead. By the time he rises at 6 am to feed the whimpering dogs, he has slept little. And then, he is just in the act of getting the dogs their first bucket of fresh water from the pump amidships when a massive wall of green water bursts over the starboard bulwark and in an instant knocks him from his feet, sweeps him down the deck and pins him under the winch with a few tons of green sea on top of him.

The biologist and artist Charles Harrisson, who has been helping Ninnis, loses his feet to that same wave and, after having the wind knocked out of him by being hurled against the timber stack on the deck, finds himself being washed along in the company of half-drowned dogs. As the water at last releases him, he finds Ninnis crawling out from under the steam winch. In a unanimous vote, they decide it will be better 'to leave watering the dogs until later'.[8]

On the bridge, Mawson watches the waves breaking over the ship with mounting horror, unsure if the next one would carry away the 'indispensable huts amidships, or would a sea break on the benzine aft and flood us with inflammable liquid and gas?'[9]

Perhaps the only man happy in such weather is the intrepid Hurley, who, realising the superb film and photo opportunities to be had, is regularly seen climbing high into the rigging with his camera or cinematograph to try to capture it. Nothing seems to scare him.

How did they survive such seas in their small and severely overloaded vessel? According to Mawson, in a letter to Paquita, it is because:

Providence has asserted itself right from the beginning . . . Aurora rolls day and night without ceasing. I have been trying to sleep on a couch and almost nightly find

myself on the floor a few times during my watch below.
The seas breaking over the ship have deluged everything
– it is a horribly repulsive feeling to be dropped from the
couch into two or three inches of water flowing backwards
and forwards on the floor. We have managed to keep the
dogs alive so far.[10]

9 December 1911, Shambles Camp, at the bottom of the Beardmore Glacier, Scott's ponies are all done in

There is wet, very wet, wet through, wet to the bone . . . and last of all the wet you get when your entire world is filled with wet above, wet below, wet coming at you in a howling wind and wet right through your clothes, your kit and everything you come in contact with. It is this wet that now completely and wretchedly soaks the Scott party, as the howling blizzard that has been besieging them for a week drives moisture into everything: tents, bags, gear, clothing, men and ponies. All are wet right through, with tobacco juice flowing from Oates's bag and time itself miserably dripping, as the temperature is just far enough above freezing to keep them bitterly cold *and* sodden all at once.

Slowly, they keep on hobbling forward regardless, with the summer blizzard so strong at times that the landscape is totally obscured. They are the worst conditions, with 'the most excessive snowfall', that Wilson has ever seen, and – as a veteran of Antarctica – he has seen a lot.[11] Knee-deep in snow, the men drive into cruel southerly winds, the starving ponies sinking up to their bellies. It is looking like they are not to be lucky with the season, and instead of the relatively calm polar summer they have been hoping for they are destined for a devastating one.

The reward for the stricken ponies' efforts by day is to be buried deep in drift by night, though Wilson for one keeps aside his biscuits for his stricken pony Nobby to nibble upon. Despite the terrible deterioration of the surviving ponies, still, through the careful ministrations of Oates, the poor suffering beasts just manage to keep going, dragging their wretched sledges behind them – their agonised neighing blending with the drone of their drivers chiding them onwards, ever onwards – and at last, at last, on this day at around eight in the evening, the Scott party finally approaches the foot of the Beardmore Glacier. They camp within sight of the magnificent granite pass known as Shackleton's Gateway, now about ten miles away, and not far from the point where the frozen river collides with the frozen sea at a 90-degree angle to create an entire confusion of huge shattered shards of ice.

The fact that the ponies have struggled on this far is an enormous achievement for Oates, and one acknowledged by the others. Wilson, always the most generous of companions, is, as ever, the first to offer his congratulations. Striding up to Oates, he takes him by the hand and says, 'I congratulate you, Titus.'[12] As to Scott, his hope of passing through Shackleton's Gateway well ahead of Shackleton's time and then travelling some ten miles or so up the glacier with the ponies still in hand has been blighted by the highly unusual summer blizzard that fate has sent – *this season of all seasons, when they are making their attempt!* – which he feels somewhat bitter about. Despite his earnest hopes, Providence has not been kind to them. Nevertheless, he rises to the occasion, immediately adding, 'And I thank you.'[13]

While Oates is pleased with the efforts of his charges, he now has a rather important duty. He must kill all five of them. They have completed their appointed task and will obviously be no good on the deeply crevassed surface of the glacier that awaits them. And the other factor is food. Two days earlier, Scott had been forced to break into his glacier rations (oil and biscuits) to keep them all going, so the horsemeat will help to redress this shortfall. With one bullet to the brow, clinically administered by Oates, each beast of burden instantly dies for the cause. In the now dreadfully familiar fashion, the meat is soon hacked from their bones and built up into a sizeable cairn that will act as a depot for the returning parties. The ponies' only tombstone is a tall flagpole to mark where their frozen flesh lies.

It is, of course, a very messy process, making the whole place look like an abattoir, which provides the inspiration for a name for this spot. 'Shambles Camp' – yes, that will do nicely, as 'shambles' is an old word for abattoir.

While there is sorrow at the bloody dispatch of such loyal servants of the expedition, there is also, extraordinarily, some relish at the prospect of taking over the job of the ponies themselves. With no more horse-handling, a nice spot of man-hauling soon awaits, and Wilson for one looks forward to it. 'Thank God,' he writes in his diary, 'the horses are now all done with and we begin the heavier work ourselves.'[14] For all that, he, too, has enough affection for his own pony, Nobby, to give it one of his supper biscuits before it is shot.

A good night's sleep and then they will go on.

11 December 1911 and two days thereafter, Macquarie Island, Mawson and his men receive a surprise

Around noon on this blustery day, Captain Davis uses the knowledge gleaned on his previous trip to Macquarie Island, aboard *Nimrod* in 1909, and a favourable wind to guide *Aurora* through the rocky entry into Caroline Cove. This small and slightly sheltered indent – well known to the old-time sealers – lies on the south-western tip of the island.

Mawson orders the whaleboat to be lowered away, and it is soon passing through the 80-yard channel, carefully taking soundings all the way to ascertain whether it is deep enough for the mother ship to follow. A profusion of pesky penguins leap all around, and the men crowd the deck to get a look at this welcome respite from the sea. For it is land all right, and lots of it, as they all gaze in wonder upon this craggy, high island – about halfway between Hobart and Antarctica – running north and south and measuring some 21 miles long by three miles wide at its widest point.

High above and far away, a lone waterfall cascades into a single silver stream of pure water that runs down into a distant valley. Right before the men lies a summer-holiday scene, a veritable mediaeval bestiary come alive. This particular inlet is backed by a thick tussock-grassed hillside upon which thousands of squawking penguins fuss about in their black-tie outfits, attending their egg-full rookeries and sounding, to Davis's ear, like an 'animated cocktail party'.[15] When the men land on the rocky shore, however, the penguins instantly crowd around them and turn into 'a band of schoolboys out on a long vacation'.[16]

A little further along the beach, what at first appear to be huge rocks on the shore and then massive slugs are in fact enormous elephant seals, lazily disporting themselves at regular intervals in mud-wallows. Kings of their realm, they barely deign to acknowledge the visitors beyond, bellowing the odd half-interested roar, which is in contrast to the many anxious seabirds of all varieties that circle all around, screeching a warning at these invaders to keep well clear of their nests. For their part, an army of squawking and squeaking royal penguins, with distinctive golden feathers on their heads, collectively arch yellow eyebrows at the invaders, as a nonplussed leopard seal, unimpressed at having his midday nap interrupted, reluctantly slithers slowly seaward. For all of the awed mariners, there is some sense of having entered a natural wonderland, lost in time, practically untouched by man.

Despite such scenes of original harmony, though, the exceedingly shallow approach almost leads to *Aurora*'s demise when she runs aground on submerged rocks just outside the bay's entrance, causing what is considered at the time to be only minimal damage. The decision is taken to set a course for the north end of the island. Specifically, Captain Davis wants to head to North East Bay, on the eastern side of the low spit at the northernmost tip.

A stiff south-east breeze greets the ship at the new destination, and Davis anchors *Aurora* as near to the shore as possible to await more favourable winds. But what's this? As they move closer to the coast, two apparently uninhabited huts a little way up the beach are espied and, more curiously, what appears to be the battered bones of a recently shipwrecked schooner lying on its sad little side among the cruel and unforgiving rocks.

Amid concerned discussion on *Aurora* about the dangers to shipping of plying their trade in uncharted waters, most particularly after their own scrape along the submerged rock, a strange little man is seen to emerge from one of the huts, catch one glimpse of the ship and then rush back inside. He almost immediately re-emerges with a coterie of cohorts, who now – rather like ants tearing out of a suddenly disturbed nest – excitedly rush hither and thither along the shore in an unnecessary attempt to attract *Aurora*'s attention.

Soon, upon the shore, a platform of sorts has been constructed from planks and barrels, upon which a flag is raised, and a semaphorist now excitedly communicates that they are the surviving crew of the shipwrecked New Zealand sealer *Clyde*, now living among the small community of blubber collectors that is stationed there. After several attempts to reach *Aurora* in their small boat end in capsizing, *Aurora* follows the signaller's advice and finds safe anchorage on the western side of the spit, which Davis suggests be named Hasselborough Bay, after the island's discoverer, Frederick Hasselborough. The sealers are now able to successfully row out to them.

On her maiden voyage, it appears *Clyde* was fully laden with seal and penguin oil collected from this permanent base. She was preparing to depart when, in a large easterly gale on 14 November, just a month ago, her anchor cables were snapped, she broadsided onto the beach and soon broke up. Her men are greatly relieved to learn that *Aurora*'s support vessel *Toroa*, expected in a few days, would be able to transport them back to Australia – provided, of course, they can bend their backs with the crews of the two ships to help unload all they need to on Macquarie Island. Done!

Further, with an ever-watchful eye on the budget, Mawson informs them that *Toroa* will take out the seal and penguin oil already collected on *Clyde*, and he expects to fetch a reasonable profit on the open market.[17]

Together with George Ainsworth, who is to command the Macquarie Island group, Mawson settles on the northern end of the beach as the site for the permanent hut, in the lee of the large hill found there. The wireless communication station itself is to be built atop that hill, the 350-foot-high knob at the northern end of the spit creatively named on the spot as – wait for it – Wireless Hill. The engineers Bickerton and Gillies commission the motor launch, and *Aurora*'s onerous weight is slightly lessened by the transfer of goods and equipment to shore.

On the afternoon of 13 December, under the loud ministrations of her captain, Roaring Tom, the *Toroa* arrives, and, as she carries the majority of the supplies for Macquarie Island, the motor launch is again used to bring into shore her supplies, including 55 live sheep, as well as to shuttle other supplies, such as a precious 90 tons of coal, to *Aurora*.

In the course of unloading and exploring their new surroundings, the men are not long in discovering the signs of human activity on this island. For there, about 300 yards south of where they have set up their hut, are the industrial works built in 1890 by a former New Zealand politician from Invercargill by the name of Joseph Hatch.

These works include steam digester tanks, to rapidly render the penguins, and open iron pots used to initially render the elephant seal blubber. The further-refined elephant seal and penguin oil can be used for a wide range of purposes, everything from lamp oil to industrial lubricants to leather-harness oil.

The first of the sealers got to the island in July 1810 and simply went berserk, as they waded into the massed animals with their clubs and guns and knives. They killed no fewer than 30,000 fur and elephant seals in just one bloody year – soon enough wiping out the fur seals and severely denting the population of elephant seals.

Nevertheless, by killing penguins and a few elephant seals and boiling them down for oil in his industrial works, Hatch and his men are still able to make enough money these days to make it profitable, and the results of their most recent efforts are all around for the new arrivals to see, and *smell*. In the landscape around the huge steel boiler and down by the beach, there are many rotting carcasses of seals and elephant seals – for once the sealers have taken the blubber, they have no interest in the rest and simply leave the remains there to rot and reek in the sun, to be consumed by those carrion-eating birds, skuas and petrels.

Both Mawson and Hurley, particularly, are appalled at such environmental carnage and resolve to do whatever they can in the future to stop the slaughter.

11 December 1911, Lower Glacier Depot, Scott's dogs are turned back and the pure man-hauling begins

There has been a small change of plan. Although originally Scott intended Meares, Demetri and the dogs to accompany the Southern Party only as far as the Mid-Barrier Depot – lying at 81 degrees 15 minutes south – a combination of the abominable weather and the terrible condition of the ponies means they have been kept on over two weeks longer than anticipated.

With the killing of the ponies, however, the dogs have efficiently stepped *once more unto the breach, dear friends, once more*, and hauled 800 pounds of supplies forward to Lower Glacier Depot. As before, no one likes to comment on just how extraordinarily efficient the dogs appear to be, as that would only heighten their concerns as to just where Amundsen might be right now.

Nevertheless, because the dogs have other crucial tasks to perform, in terms of later resupplying the depots for those who will be returning from the Pole, Scott cannot keep the dogs going south. They have already come much further than they have been provisioned for and now, in these lower reaches of Beardmore Glacier, he deems it time to bid farewell to Meares and Demetri. With a wave, a whoop and a flick of the whip, the dog teams are turned for home, bearing the message from Scott: 'Things are not as rosy as they might be, but we keep our spirits up and say the luck must turn.'[18]

This lack of rosiness most certainly extends to Meares and Demetri, who now have a long struggle ahead to drive the dogs some 450 miles back over the inhospitable Barrier to Hut Point. Despite Bowers's comment in his diary that the dogs will 'rush Demetri and Meares back like the wind', the fact that they have turned back so late in the season and so far away means that, even if the conditions turn perfect for them, they will not be able to satisfy Scott's original brief from two months earlier. That brief had it that, once returned north to Hut Point, they were to have a short rest and then set out in late December/early January to resupply One Ton Depot no later than 19 January with adequate rations and 'as much dog food as you can conveniently carry'.[19] These rations are to sustain, firstly, the returning parties and, secondly, another rendezvous party that will head further south from One Ton Depot a few weeks later, to speed home Scott's party when they are making their own way back from the Pole. (Yes, it *is* complicated.)

As it is, though, Meares and Demetri will only likely be back at Cape Evans by mid-January, and it would be unthinkable to immediately turn around to resupply One Ton Depot, even if they and their dogs were to prove physically capable of doing so.

As to those remaining with Scott, now that the ponies are shot, the dogs are gone and the ascent of the glacier proper begins, the physically most gruelling part of the journey awaits. From where they have established Lower Glacier Depot – some ten miles along and up from Shambles Camp – they must haul their sledges towards the South Pole up the Beardmore Glacier, the summit of which is 160 miles away and some 10,000 feet above sea level.

They begin . . .

11 December 1911, Adelaide, home of the Delprats, Paquita receives a letter

Such a pleasure! Even though her Douglas is now well on his way to Antarctica, before leaving Hobart just over a week earlier he penned his fiancée a letter, and on this day she receives it. Eagerly, she tears the letter open, and she lingers over every word, loving the affirmation of his love, before he soon enough gets to more temporal matters:

You may be sure that I am going away this time far happier than last time when you were not awaiting my return. You may be sure I will look after myself compatible with a dutiful endeavour to accomplish . . . I had to cease writing this afternoon when the Premier came and now at 12.45 am. Saturday send a few more lines. I am very sleepy and you must excuse. We have had a farewell tonight by the Premier, a great crowd of people attended. I gave two lectures here to raise cash this week and got £60 clear. We have a fearful quantity of deck cargo and are leaving behind some of our stores. With good weather we shall reach the Antarctic without fail, very heavy weather may wash some of our cargo overboard. The men are all good. Au revoir till you get a billet-doux from Macquarie Island.[20]

The relief she feels at receiving it is nearly as great as the relief she felt a few days earlier when she discovered that she was not pregnant after all. Truly, she has been extremely worried. Shortly before he left, she and Douglas had kissed ever so passionately and, as far as she is aware, this might have been enough to cause her to be with child. But it had been all right![21]

13 December 1911, Beardmore Glacier, Scott's party ascend as the weather closes in

The wind she howls, the thermometer she drops, the blizzard she never ceases. In the last nine hours, Scott and his men have made less than five miles.

Following directly in the wretchedly lengthy strides of Shackleton, Scott has grown even more obsessed with comparing his progress against his erstwhile pioneering companion's and becomes increasingly agitated the further they slip behind – now five and a half days.

'Skis are the thing, and here are my tiresome fellow-countrymen too prejudiced to have prepared themselves for the event,' Scott writes in his diary.[22]

While Wilson sits on a packing case sketching each of their camps, Oates broods as only Oates can. There are now 12 men left, each soul expected to haul 200 pounds upwards, ever upwards to the summit. What is almost worse is that the snow is deep and loose. As Bowers records in his diary at the end of another day of shattering effort, where it has taken all their energy just to keep the sledge moving for a few hundred yards, before the whole thing sank so deeply into the soft snow it became a snowplough:

> The starting was worse than pulling as it required from ten to fifteen jerks on the harness to move the sledge at all. I have never pulled so hard, or so nearly crushed my inside into my backbone by the everlasting jerking with all my strength on the canvas band round my unfortunate tummy . . .[23]

Morale is lower than the barometer and keeps falling with it. That evening, Scott writes in his diary, 'I had pinned my faith on getting better conditions as we rose, but it looks as though matters are getting worse instead of better.'[24] Of all his worries, it is the wretched weather that troubles Scott the most. It slows them, exhausts them, depletes their supplies for little gain and pushes ever closer to winter the time when – should they get all the way to the Pole – they will be making their return. It may well be touch and go . . .

14 December 1911, Polar Plateau, Amundsen's party are nearing the South Pole

'Halt!' Amundsen cries out to the other four men: Hanssen, Wisting, Hassel and Bjaaland. On the back of the three sledges, they check the meter attached to the small wheel that measures distance travelled. It says 862.5 miles, the exact distance from *Framheim*, Bay of Whales, to where the South Pole is to be found. They are really *here*. Or at least hereabouts . . .

And the best thing – in this entirely featureless white spot, on this entirely featureless white plain, with only their instruments and mathematical calculations to tell them it is any different from anywhere else – is that there is not the slightest sign of Scott or his men. No flag, no tents, no detritus of previous campsites, no tracks have they crossed in previous days and *no grinning Englishmen*, which perhaps would have been the worst of all. Amundsen is entirely confident they are the first here and have beaten the British expedition cold, make that freezing.

It means he can now actually do – a version of it, at least – what he has long dreamt of doing since the days of growing up as a little boy in Norway, keeping the window open at night to toughen him for the trials ahead. From the back of his sledge, Amundsen retrieves the flag they prepared the night before.

But the climax is not a solo act. They have journeyed here together, and, *av Gud*, by God, they will plant it together. At Amundsen's generous invitation, thus, all five Norwegian men grip the flagpole with their frostbitten hands, lift the point a couple of feet above the surface and then drive it hard into the snow, before stepping back.

Amundsen enunciates his words carefully, having thought long about what he would say: '*Dermed planter vi deg, elskede flagg, på Sørpolen, og gir dette platået som det står på navnet Kong Haakon VII Vidde.* Thus we plant thee, beloved flag, at the South Pole, and give to the plain on which it lies the name of King Haakon VII's Plateau.'[25]

In an instant, the fierce wind captures the fabric of the flag and whips it straight out with a sharp crack, making it perfect – and hold it, click – for the photographs that Bjaaland takes.

Left with time to reflect, the leader enters into a strange sort of sentimental reverie:

> The goal was reached, the journey ended. I cannot say – though I know it would sound much more effective – that the object of my life was attained. That would be romancing rather too bare-facedly. I had better be honest and admit straight out that I have never known any man to be placed in such a diametrically opposite position to the goal of his desires as I was at that moment. The regions around the North Pole – well, yes, the North Pole itself – had attracted me from childhood, and here I was at the South Pole. Can anything more topsy-turvy be imagined?[26]

That night, they celebrate their achievement. Sadly, there is no champagne, but they do allow themselves the South Pole equivalent: a little extra seal meat from their rations, which goes down well. The conversation in the tent is exuberant as they chew over the grandeur of their accomplishment and set about inscribing everything they possess with that name they now own: '*Sørpolen*', South Pole.

But now for the *pipe de résistance*. For the first time, inside the tent, the men take up their pipes, Wisting donating his whole supply of tobacco to the man who has made them all famous. Not only that, from that point forward he takes it upon himself to cut plugs of tobacco and put them in Amundsen's pipe regardless of the weather. If he could have smoked the pipe for his hero as well, he surely would have.

One of the advantages of navigation in the land of the midnight sun is that it is possible to make calculations at both midday *and* midnight, and on this evening, as midnight approaches, Amundsen makes ready with his sextant. The sun has been circling steadily around the horizon at almost exactly the same height for the last few days – at close to 23 degrees, which is equivalent to the tilt of the earth – but it is the midday and midnight measurements that count.

As the clock strikes 12, he measures the angle of the sun above the horizon and from that calculates their latitude at 89 degrees 56 minutes south. At just four minutes off the 90 degrees south they need to get to, they are just a little over four miles away.

15 December 1911, Beardmore Glacier, Tryggve Gran has a vision

Dreams are strange things. They come with the most exquisite detail, which, no matter how moving, how profound, how revealing . . . fades . . . fades . . . fades . . . with the waking hour. And so it is on this morning for Tryggve Gran. As he tells the others of Scott's party, he had a long and seemingly vivid dream, but upon waking all he can remember is reading a telegram that proclaimed: 'Amundsen reached Pole, 15–20 December'.[27]

15 December 1911, Macquarie Island, Mawson's Australasian Antarctic Expedition flies the fox

The work in unloading the *Toroa* has been so efficient that now, just two days after arriving, the little ship, with the shipwrecked sealers aboard and their salvaged oil, is ready to set sail for home.

The men already on the island have also loaned Mawson a flying fox to line-haul an engine and dynamos up to the top of Wireless Hill, where they intend to erect the two 100-foot-high antennae. The antennae themselves, however, are too heavy to allow the use of the flying fox's counterweight and have to be laboriously hauled up using manpower alone. (And heave . . . and rest . . . and heaaave . . . and rest . . . and *heaaaave* . . . and rest.) The men have been working tirelessly for 16 hours a day, none harder than Mawson himself, who increases the respect his men feel for him by leading from the front.

As he writes to Paquita in a letter that will be borne back by the *Toroa*, 'The last few days have been strenuous ones but I like it – I am in my element. Hard physical work agrees with me.'[28]

15 December 1911 and two days thereafter, South Pole, Amundsen makes sure

If they are not right upon the South Pole itself, they can certainly see it from here, and to ensure there can be no dispute Amundsen organises his men to cover the ground within a 12-and-a-half-mile radius from their current position. Unlike his friend Frederick A. Cook, and the unseemly squabble that occurred between him and Robert Peary as to who got to the North Pole first – and indeed whether either got there at all – Amundsen will leave no doubt that he really has been the first to reach the actual South Pole.

With that in mind, as Amundsen later describes it, at 2.30 on the morning of 15 December, three men – Wisting, Hassel and Bjaaland – 'went out in three different directions, two at right angles to the course we had been steering, and one in continuation of that course'.[29] Each man carries a marker, a sledge runner identified by a black flag, to which is tied a bag containing a note for Scott with the bearing and distance of their main camp. Throughout all of the next day, Amundsen and Hanssen take further observations and this time calculate they are five and three-quarter miles from the Pole itself.

By mid-morning of 16 December, once all three men have safely returned from their solo 25-mile journeys and rested, they start to move their camp to where these calculations indicate the true South Pole is.

With Bjaaland leading, they set out, Amundsen bringing up the rear. Once they have made camp in the new position – which looks *exactly* like the old position on this featureless white plain, but anyway – they take observations every hour for 24 hours to ensure they have in fact reached their mark. With the uncertainty of the instruments, they are taking no chances, having journeyed this far. Come noon on 17 December, Hanssen and Bjaaland do as they did at the old camp and venture out to mark a distance of five miles from their location, before returning.

At dinner that evening, Bjaaland takes it upon himself to make an excellent impromptu speech, congratulating them all and honouring their leader for their achievement. It is a great day for them and a truly great day for Norway. To top it off, Bjaaland then stuns and delights them all by offering them their pick from a silver cigar case filled with cigars that he has carried all this way!

Ah, how sweet it is.

'A cigar at the Pole!' exclaims Amundsen. 'What do you say to that?'[30]

The cigars distributed, like Wisting and his tobacco, Bjaaland now presents the esteemed leader the case containing four remaining cigars as a memento.

And the South Pole itself, of course, needs its own memento of their visit, the best monument they can construct under the circumstances. They have planned this moment for many months and from the sledge take the tent they have brought all this way for this specific purpose. As they unfurl it, they are greeted with a surprise message pinned inside by their comrades: *'Velkommen til 90'*, Welcome to 90. They call it *Poleheim*, as in 'Home of the Pole'.

On the top of the tent, a little Norwegian flag is lashed fast, and underneath it a pennant, on which 'Fram' is painted. The tent is well secured with guy ropes on all sides. Inside the tent, in a little bag, Amundsen leaves a letter addressed to HM the King of Norway, giving information of what they have accomplished, together with a covering letter for Scott. On the chance that they are lost upon their return trip, Amundsen hopes that Scott would be able to deliver the news of his accomplishment to the world. The royal letter, which Amundsen wrote two days earlier at the old camp, reads:

Fram Expedition

15 December 1911

Your Majesty,

Allow me to inform you that yesterday, on the 14th December, after a successful sledge journey from our Winter Quarters at Framheim, five men from the Fram expedition – myself included – arrived at the South Pole area. According to our observations, the position was 89°57'30"S. We left for the pole on 20th October with four sledges, 52 dogs and provisions for four months. We have ascertained the southernmost point of the Great Ross Ice Barrier, about 86°S, as well as the point where Victoria Land and King Edward Land meet. Victoria Land ends here, while King Edward VII Land continues southward to 87°S, where we found an impressive chain of mountains with peaks up to 22,000 feet. I have taken the liberty – with your permission, I hope – of naming them the Queen Maud Range.

We have found that the great inland plateau begins to slope gently downwards from 89°S, with an altitude of approximately 10,750 feet. Today we marked the geographical South Pole with a radius of 8 km and raised the Norwegian flag. We have called this gently sloping plain, on which we have succeeded in establishing the position of the geographic South Pole, King Haakon VII's Plateau, with, I hope, Your Majesty's permission. We will start the journey back home tomorrow with two sledges and 16 dogs. We are well provided with provisions.

Yours sincerely,
Roald Amundsen[31]

And, almost in the manner of a time capsule, they also leave in the tent a sextant with 'a glass horizon, a hypsometer case, three reindeer-skin foot-bags, some *kamiks*[32] and mits'.[33] And then they are on their way, retracing their path along their old tracks and frequently looking back at the little tent they have left there, until it soon enough sinks from view and their gaze now resolutely turns to the north, to their base at the Bay of Whales. They have done it, they have made it first to the South Pole. Now, they must get back safely and tell the world that they have done so.

20 December 1911 and the day thereafter, Beardmore Glacier, as Scott's party approach the top, Birdie has a screw loose

It is a real blow. On this brutal day of hauling, they have just stopped for the blessed respite of lunch – ah, how sweet to be able to remove the wretched harnesses that so chafe their skin – when Birdie glances at the dial of the sledge-meter to see how far they've come and makes the 'disastrous discovery'.[34]

Somehow or other, as they have been making their way up and over endless bumps in the ice that morning, a screw has come loose and the registering dial has fallen out! The significance of the loss of that dial is enormous, as, with the theodolite and compass, the sledge-meter is one of their key navigational tools. It is out of the question to head to the Pole without one. If they can't find the dial, the next party to turn back will have to do so without knowing how far they have travelled – making their navigation far more difficult. This is such a dim prospect that Birdie insists on walking back two miles with Bill Wilson to see if they can find it, but there is no sign.

That evening, the expedition leader decides it is time to split up. All this way, Captain Scott has been contemplating just who should make the final push for the South Pole and knows that the time is right to thin it down still further. From three units of four men, only two units will continue.

Scott has been dreading this moment, as all the men have pulled to the limits of their strength, but now four good men have to be deprived of their just reward: the chance to bag the Pole. Ahem. Those four men who will return from the Upper Glacier Depot to Cape Evans the day after tomorrow are: Atch Atkinson, Silas Wright, Apsley Cherry-Garrard and Patrick Keohane. Because they are to be led by Dr Atkinson, their group is to be referred to as the Doctor's Party.

Silas Wright – who has previously been singled out by Scott as a man of great potential – is undoubtedly the most furious at this instruction. Why, to begin with, he has no doubt that both he and Cherry-Garrard are in much finer fettle than their sledge leader to this point, Teddy Evans, who is to remain with Scott.

As far as Silas is concerned, Teddy has no business going on, and the previous evening he recorded in his diary his strong feelings: 'Teddy the damn hypocrite, as soon as he sees the Owner's sledge stopped and they are watching us come up puts his head down and digs in for all he's worth.'[35] On this night, he writes, 'Scott a fool . . . Too wild to write more tonight.'[36]

Wilson, who is going on, is nevertheless dashed upset about Cherry-Garrard, for whom he has a great affection. To try to soften the blow, he takes him aside and quietly explains to the young Oxford graduate that it was a toss-up between him and Titus as to who would have to return. In response, an emotional Cherry-Garrard asks Uncle Bill whether his performance has disappointed Scott. 'No, no, no,' Wilson insists firmly. Apsley has done splendidly, and he mustn't think that. As a matter of fact, Wilson confides, he himself half-expected not to go on from the foot of the glacier. It is just one of those things.[37]

Atch Atkinson, on the other hand, is more than happy to turn around, as he feels completely done in, though he is disappointed and concerned that his great friend Oates, whom he believes is beginning to suffer badly, won't be returning with him.

Just one thing though, Doctor, before you head off. In an informal conversation with Atkinson the following night, Captain Scott tells him that after he has safely returned to base he wants young Demetri and him – not Meares, as he is expected to return with *Terra Nova* for family reasons – to bring the rendezvous party with the dogs out to meet the Southern Party on their return from the Pole.

The following day, it is time. There is a great sadness between them all as they say goodbye with warm handshakes, pats on the back, best wishes for a safe return to the Doctor's Party, while they in turn wish a successful assault on the Pole to those who are going on. Scott says some nice words to those departing about the sterling service they have rendered them all, and then it really is time. As the two parties finally split, one heading north, the other heading south, the weather starts to close in, with thick snow from above and the snowdrift from the wind quickly helping to obscure the vision between the two parties.

'The last we saw of them as we swung the sledge north,' Cherry-Garrard records in his diary, 'was a black dot just disappearing over the next ridge and a big white pressure wave ahead of them . . .'[38]

Though still sad that he is not to be one of the chosen ones, Cherry-Garrard, trudging south, has little doubt that Scott will get there. 'Anyway he has only to average seven miles a day to get to the Pole on full rations – it's practically a cert for him.'[39]

Up close, that 'black dot', the two parties of four men, continue to trudge forwards doggedly – alas, without dogs – towards the bottom of the world. The two sledges are still heavily laden, as they carry food, tents and 12 weeks' supply of oil and fuel. Each man has 190 pounds to haul forward, as by this time they have eaten their way through much of what they have been carrying. One sledge is hauled by Scott, Oates, Wilson and that unstoppable workhorse to beat them all, Taffy Evans. The other is hauled by Bowers and Crean, together with two of the men who were with the motor sledges and have been in exhausted harness ever since, Teddy Evans and William Lashly. These two are still the worse for wear for having been man-hauling for so long, and Lashly, who used to have a barrel chest, now just has a chest.

24 December 1911 and the day thereafter, Macquarie Island, Mawson and his men head south

Farewelling Ainsworth's Macquarie Island Party, *Aurora* now makes for Caroline Cove at the base of that island, where she hopes to replenish her water supply before heading south for Antarctica. This task proves slow going, as the only water not rendered undrinkable by penguin excreta is to be found in a virtually dry gully 80 yards inland of the beach. Two large barrels are slowly filled and transported to *Aurora* by boat before the laborious process is repeated again and again. The men grow weary, and at 11 pm work is suspended until the morning. However, poor sea conditions during the middle of the night drive *Aurora* against the rocks of her narrow berth, and, having lost a kedge anchor,[40] the ever cautious Captain Davis, perpetually fearing the worst, decides to immediately put out to sea with *Aurora*'s water tanks less than full.

Conditions considerably improve towards dawn, and *Aurora*, with 50 men and their howling dogs aboard, is soon steaming south, always south, along the 157th meridian of longitude.

Christmas Day 1911, Polar Plateau, Scott's party's festive feast

As Christmas Days go, at least it is memorable. Alas, though they manage a very long march of 17 miles, not all of it is pleasurably memorable.

Though it had been a relief, three days earlier, to have reached the top of the Beardmore Glacier and start out upon the Polar Plateau, the men now find themselves in terrain criss-crossed by crevasses into which one or the other of them is inevitably and constantly falling. Mid-morning on this birthday of Jesus, Lashly – who has himself turned 44 on this day – has the worst drop, when he falls in so heavily and deeply that he jerks Crean and Bowers off their feet and hangs there, suspended, until they can regain both their feet and their composure and haul him out again. It has, of course, been a moment when Lashly has been left contemplating the gaping maw of his own mortality, and yet, to Scott's surprise, 'his fall has not even disturbed his equanimity'.[41]

That evening, there is at least some Christmas cheer for dinner when Birdie is able to produce something he has had hidden all this time, even from the official weigh-in before departure. It consists, as he records, of:

> a good fat hoosh with pony meat and ground biscuit. A chocolate hoosh made of water, cocoa, sugar, biscuits, raisins, and thickened with a spoonful of arrowroot. Then came 2 1/2 square inches of plum duff each, and a good mug of cocoa washed down the whole . . . I positively could not eat all mine.[42]

Simple, yes, but it gives them more pleasure in this terrible terrain than the best meal provided by the best chef in London might provide in normal times.

And yes, of course all of them are missing their families and loved ones on this day, as they contemplate how strangely the world turns that they should find themselves so very far away from them, in fact near the turning point of that world. But something else that gives them good cheer is that they have still seen no sign of the Norwegians! Though the Norskies have, of course, started from a different point on the Barrier, as far as the Scott party know there is only one way up to the Polar Plateau in this part of the world, which is via the Beardmore Glacier, and it is a very good sign that there has been no trace of the foreigners.

Following their Christmas dinner, the men are positively sated and exhausted. 'I should have liked somebody to put me to bed,' records Bowers before turning in.[43]

28 December 1911, Axel Heiberg Glacier, Amundsen spots a problem with the dogs

For the Norwegians, the return from the Pole to this point has been more than satisfactory, and they have been making even better time than Amundsen expected. The weather has been remarkably benign, with the sun mostly shining and the wind nearly always at their backs, allowing them to put up improvised sails on their sledges. The dogs, at least the surviving ones, have pulled extremely well, and never more so than after devouring good portions of the dogs that have been killed to keep them all – humans and dogs – in fresh meat. For *days* after such a feast, the dogs are noticeably stronger. The problem, however, is that maybe they are eating too much. For, as Amundsen notes, the dogs have now changed in condition from when they left the Pole and are 'putting on flesh day by day and getting quite fat'.[44] As a matter of fact, the same may be happening to Amundsen himself, as he has found that he absolutely adores eating dog cutlets, and there are plenty to go around.

29 December 1911 and five days thereafter, Southern Ocean, aboard *Aurora*, Mertz sings

Whales ahoy! As *Aurora* steams onwards, whales surround the ship, followed shortly thereafter by extraordinarily large albatrosses hovering above, while petrels dip and dive across the tops of the waves, all of it a sure sign that land lies nearby.

At 4.20 pm four days later, in foggy conditions, the cry of 'Ice on the starboard bow!' is heard for the first time, and soon *Aurora* is confronting her natural enemy: a terrifying iceberg as big as a three-storey building, slowly, silently and menacingly emerging from that fog. On the bridge, Davis's watchful eyes narrow as he appraises its dimensions: 80 feet high, three-quarters of a mile long, half a mile wide, with the typical flat top of a salt-free Antarctic iceberg that has calved off from a massive ice sheet. (As has long been noted, the Arctic ones tend towards having a narrow apex, typical of salty bergs that have come from the sea edge of land ice.) This'un is really only a tiddler compared with the bergs he has seen in his time – ah, the stories he could tell you – and yet, as the fog lifts, they are able to get a closer look at it, and all those new to polar regions are instantly awestruck.

They are revelling in what Charles Laseron describes as 'the most beautiful sight of our lives'.[45]

The berg is full of vertical cracks, which, owing to refracted light, make it look like a massive bright sapphire. Ice caves, and masses of ice nearly separated from the main mass, all reflect the same gorgeous blue. More and more bergs now appear, all of them carved into a thousand fantastic shapes and forms, and full of 'caverns of ethereal blue; gothic portals to a cathedral of resplendent purity',[46] which sheer take their frozen breath away as the men gaze in awe upon them.

In some spots, you can see, as clear as day, the giant vision of a man's face staring at you from just inside the berg wall; at others, a beautiful fresco of lace, and all of it experienced through a silence so profound it is as if you are in a frozen cathedral of nature. No one speaks, as it just wouldn't be right in such a holy moment.

The one man who is most certainly not taken in by the beauty is Davis, most particularly as the fog descends again and the bergs come thicker still. He redoubles his vigilance as more and more impossibly large chunks of ice suddenly appear from the murk, rushing at the ship from all forward angles. They are like scattered soldiers protecting the shores of Antarctica, and though there are not enough to repel *Aurora* yet, there are at least enough to make everyone aboard wary. Or almost everyone.

For then, a short time later, they hear it.

It is a strange, ululating, sing-songy chant . . . coming from parts unknown, instantly whipped away by the wind. They look at each other, stunned. Is this the mating call of an unseen sea lion? The dying cry of a whale they have just hit?

And then they realise. It is Mertz. Up in the rigging. As recorded by Hurley, 'Mertz, aloft in the crow's nest, was in high ecstasy, and entertained us and the denizens of the pack by warbling loud yodels.'[47] For Mertz, it really is thrilling, reminding him of all the snow and ice in Switzerland, so far, far, away. Australia had been interesting, to a point, but he much prefers this kind of environment to the Australian or tropical sun. The rest of the travellers are just thrilled to have a sign that they are at last nearing their destination.

Forward, ho! Forward along that same mysterious coast that Dumont d'Urville had sighted and named Adélie Land 71 years before, without ever setting foot on it. They are the first to have seen it since and will hopefully be the first to set foot upon it, if they can just get in close enough.

But soon, the ice-soldiers are thicker still, and larger, and more dangerous. The bow of *Aurora* pierces the light brash – small fragments of floating ice – before the thickening pack ice inevitably stymies her progress.

Davis is not taking any chances, and, as if he is a cavalryman riding a horse at a fiercely packed line of infantry holding pikes, time and again he sheers off to the side, trying to find another way through, before turning around entirely to get into open space . . . and then going in hard once more. Answering Davis's constant staccato orders – 'Starboard! Steady!', followed nearly instantly by 'Hard-a-port!' – the two helmsmen work feverishly, swinging their hardy vessel now to port, now to starboard, in an attempt to dodge the numerous bergs and floes in their way, all the while ignoring the rudder chains screeching in protest at being so frequently pulled and pushed this way and that.

Soon, the ice closes in, and *Aurora* shudders each time she strikes even the smallest fragments of the brash ice bow on, pushing them just enough to one side to scrape and groan past. The dense pack extends as far as the eye can see, with hardly daylight now between the gargantuan ice blocks, as the baby bergs obey Mother Nature's lightly cuffing hand and squeeze themselves tightly into whatever tiny space is available.

Despite the white, there is no sense of lingering Christmas in the air, no echo of 'Jingle Bells' on the wind; rather, the constant bass note of ice faces groaning and grating upon other ice faces fills the air with a screeching and maudlin warning. Sometimes, there is no avoiding a large floating chunk of ice, and *Aurora* strikes it full on, jolting everyone forward as the hardy little ship recoils for a moment . . . before she surges forward to strike again. Sometimes, the ice cracks upon this attention, its shattered remnants scraping along the side of the ship, and sometimes it doesn't.

Ultimately, though, *Aurora* is forced back out to sea, pushing further and further west in an attempt to track along the pack, probing here, probing there, probing everywhere until a way through is found. It is wall-to-wall continuous white towards the coast, with the sky above a pale glare, reflecting the sun from the large tracts of ice, an effect obvious even in overcast conditions and known as 'ice blink'. Only a 'water sky', indicated by a darker shadow on the horizon where open water would likely lie beyond, would encourage Davis to take *Aurora* into an ice pack. There is no choice but to probe in this manner, and yet it makes progress so slow that the engines continue to munch through coal as though it is cheap popcorn.

Still the ice pack shows no sign of giving way to their relentless sallies.

A pity, of course, that they can't land at Cape Adare, where Mawson wanted to from the start, but, regrettably – *more gnashing of teeth from Mawson* – that spot has been claimed by Scott's men after Mawson made the mistake of trusting Scott with his plans.

The problem is not just that Cape Adare presents a known place to establish Winter Quarters, but also that it is both relatively close to the South Magnetic Pole and within wireless distance of Macquarie Island, so it is highly desirable. The further to the west they go, the harder the sledging journey will be to get to the South Magnetic Pole, and the more difficult it will be to have easy wireless contact. But there is nothing for it. Scott's men have taken the spot, and that is that. It is a damn shame.

At last, however, on 3 January, there comes what might be a breakthrough. At five o'clock in the morning, the chief officer, Toucher, comes down from the bridge to report that the fog is clearing and he can see on the port side what might be land ice – that is, ice so high it surely must be attached to the land, rather than being a massive iceberg. Davis and Mawson immediately join him on the bridge and confirm Toucher's belief. Just a quarter of a mile away, a wall of ice disappears into the mists high above. If it is a berg, it is the biggest they have ever seen. There is a possibility that it is an ice-capped low island, but it is far more likely to be Antarctica itself.

Proceeding slowly, *Aurora* continues tracking westward along the sheer wall, until, just after seven o'clock in the morning, that wall gives way a little and turns to the south, beckoning them in.

This way, this way, you are so close . . .

3 January 1912 and the day thereafter, Polar Plateau, Scott and his men are getting closer to the South Pole

So close, but still so far! They are now at a latitude of 87 degrees 32 minutes south, with just 175 miles to go. While trudging stoically forth, Scott has been agonising, as ever, over who will make the final push for the Pole with him. The expectation of the others all along has been that the final group will be a simple matter of starting with the Owner and then selecting the next three strongest.

Now, he has made his decision, and on this morning of 3 January, with wind howling all around, Scott goes first to the tent of Teddy Evans, Bowers, Crean and Lashly and asks all but Teddy to leave so he can talk to him alone. With precious little preamble, Scott tells him the stark news – he, Scott, will only be taking his own team on to the pole; Evans's team would now have to turn back.

. . .

The wind roars mightily but is ignored, forgotten.

. . .

Evans is stunned, slapped across his gaunt face by every word. Two years earlier, Scott *promised* him that if he folded his own nascent expedition plans in with Scott – becoming Scott's second in command – he would be guaranteed a place in the Pole Party so long as he was fit enough, which, despite his thinness after so much man-hauling, he still feels he bloody well is. And yet now, Scott, without a word of explanation, let alone apology, has openly gone back on his word! This from a self-proclaimed 'Christian gentleman'?

Scott tries to mollify the obviously upset Teddy Evans by telling him that the reason he must return is because he is the only man with the navigational skills necessary to lead the party the 770 miles to Cape Evans without a sledge-meter . . . but it has little effect. Ideally, Scott would have liked to take all eight men on to the Pole. However, this is simply not logistically practicable, for they do not have enough food.

What makes matters worse, however, is that Scott now asks Teddy if he could 'spare' Bowers, to join up with Scott's existing team and go to the Pole? So there it is. Teddy Evans can't even make the final group when it is expanded to five! And he has to go back with just *three* men!

It really does seems like a crazy decision. The whole expedition to this point has been built on four-man units – with the tents designed to hold four, the sledges drawn by four, carrying supplies for four and all the depots on their way back being provisioned for four.

Yes, a five-man team can better deal with a man falling ill, but, against that, with five there is more chance that that will occur. And it also means that the three-man team will find it commensurately more difficult and be in real trouble if just one man goes down. The decision will clearly throw both teams out of kilter. Evans's three-man team will have to strain to haul a four-man sledge home, while with Scott it will not be obvious how to have five men in harness pulling a sledge piled precariously high with supplies. At night, Scott's party will have an extra man crowded into the tent; at mealtimes, they will need another half an hour to thaw, prepare and serve the men, requiring more fuel in turn.

The other three men are brought back into the tent, and Scott gives his orders. The four men to accompany him to the Pole are . . . Bill Wilson, Lawrence Oates and Taffy Evans from his own team, plus Birdie Bowers from Teddy Evans's team. The remaining three, William Lashly, Thomas Crean and Teddy Evans, are to head back to the base.

And that is that. Though in the naval culture that pervades in the Scott party, the decision is not one to be argued with, some bitter disappointment does show through. Crean, in fact, openly weeps, such is his turbulent emotion at not being selected to make the final push. Even the usually imperturbable Lashly – the man who saved Scott and Taffy Evans on the *Discovery* journey to Victoria Land – is seen to be affected. Still, Lashly at least has the wherewithal to wish Scott well and to assure him that the rest of them wouldn't mind too much so long as Scott thinks himself in a good position to reach the Pole, having benefited from all the help they have been able to give him. Beyond hurt and anger at their own omission, however, there is also some muffled dismay at what they see as Scott's lack of judgement in his selections.

For example, from the beginning of the ascent of the Beardmore Glacier, Oates has been clearly limping – likely through aggravating his old Boer War wound. A fortnight earlier, as Atkinson was preparing to turn around, Oates told him that he did not feel fit to go on. Yet Scott has selected him to go on? The huge Taffy Evans is another who seems to be suffering a great deal, visibly starting to weaken, and it seems obvious that Lashly would have been a better choice. But there can be no open revolt. This is Scott's show, and there is to be no going back on his decision.

One part of the decision that Scott does not share with them, however, is his desire to spread the glory of being in the Pole Party among the services, with Oates representing the army and Taffy Evans the lower decks of the navy. And, now that Scott has dropped Teddy Evans, Birdie Bowers is the only competent navigator available. As to Uncle Bill Wilson, well, Scott could never contemplate being without him for such a journey.

Still, the true Christian gentleman, Wilson once more does everything he can to comfort those who have missed out, most particularly the bitterly disappointed Teddy Evans. The one thing that makes Evans feel just a little better is that Bill promises to take to the Pole a small silk flag that his wife has given him to be flown there.

All those who are continuing south to the Pole pen hurried letters to their own loved ones for the returning party to take back with them. Lawrence Oates writes to his brother:

Dear Bryan,

We shall get to the Pole alright – I suppose by the time I get back you will be a big fat man with half a doz kids – If that filly of mine looks like racing will you think about sending her to Halich . . . Blowing cold here — Best chin chin — Remember me to Cissy.

L. E. O.[48]

Birdie pens a heartfelt missive to his mother:

I am now sending you a note from what is perhaps the most unthinkable spot on this round world . . . you will be pleased to hear that Captain Scott has selected your offspring to accompany him to the Pole . . . If God be for us who can be against us? . . . I feel proud of my parentage that has given me a constitution and physical strength to stand such a test . . . did you ever think your son would get to the Pole? I think the British flag will be the only one to fly there . . . This polar business must be cleared up once and for all.[49]

What Bowers does not say is that there is a small complication where he is concerned. For, three days earlier, along with the rest of Teddy Evans's team, he followed Scott's instructions and left his skis eight miles shy of Three Degree Depot. (Scott, it seems, thinks the surface they are on is better for walking than for skiing. The returning party will pick up their skis later, while those going to the Pole retain theirs on the likelihood they will soon come to easier surfaces.) It all means that while the rest of Scott's party have their skis with them now, Birdie Bowers alone will be forced to – exhaustingly – stomp all the way to the Pole and back to where he has left those skis, before things will be easier for him.

Wilson pens a note to his beloved Oriana, saying:

You know my love for you — it's just myself, and all I do and all I pray for is your good. Be strong in hope and in faith if you hear no more of me after this till next year . . . I believe firmly that we have a lot to do together when we meet again.[50]

The following day, before they split, the smaller party of Lashly, Crean and Teddy Evans decide to stay with the larger party going south for a short way, to ensure that it is feasible for the three-man and the five-man teams to operate before their final separation.

It seems to be.

At ten o'clock in the morning, at 87 degrees 34 minutes south, 46 miles south of Three Degree Depot, and 175 miles north of the Pole, it is time to say their goodbyes.

The emotion as they part is even higher than the last time the group split up, as this time one party really is going for the Pole itself, while the other is composed of three men who want nothing more than to be with them.

But now, there is nothing for it. In a howling wind, at a temperature of minus 17 degrees, the larger group of five get themselves back into harness. As they take the strain and begin to get the sledge moving once more, the bitterly disappointed Teddy Evans – it is happening, it is really happening right now, his dream coming asunder before his very eyes, and he cannot quite believe it – at least rallies enough to lead his men in three cheers for Scott and his party. Poor Crean is half in tears.

The formation adopted by Scott is to have himself, Bowers and Wilson in the front row, all taking the strain together on three separate tethers attached to their harness, with Oates and Taffy Evans behind on their own tethers, rather like the front five of a rugby scrum.

As they move off, Bowers looks positively dwarfed by the others around him. They are now five men with only four pairs of skis, Bowers on foot slightly behind Scott and Wilson. As Birdie is a much smaller man to begin with, he marches in finneskos alone and with each step sinks several exhausting inches into the snow, before pulling his foot out again to take his next. But no matter, he still has pluck, and as he steps out he waves the little White Ensign that Teddy Evans has given him.

Oates, too, feels Teddy Evans's bitter disappointment at the fact that the nominal second in command is not going with them and calls out, 'I'm afraid, Teddy, you won't have much of a "slope" going back, but old Christopher is waiting to be eaten on the barrier when you get there.'[51]

There is a little more banter of this nature, covering the sorrow and deep emotion they're all feeling, and then the three men who are turning back stand there mutely, watching them go, as the five men and their now solo sledge get progressively smaller. The last discernible figure the three can see before Scott's remaining party fade into the sheer white nothingness is Lawrence Oates, at the back on the left, who, several times, turns back and cheerily waves. Then the white Polar Plateau swallows the black specks whole . . .

Chapter Ten

Cape Denison

*We had found an accursed country. On the fringe of an unspanned
continent along whose gelid coast our comrades had made their
home – we knew not where – we dwelt where the chill breath
of a vast, Polar wilderness, quickening to the rushing might of
eternal blizzards, surged to the northern seas. Already, and for
long months we were beneath 'frost-fettered Winter's frown'.*

Douglas Mawson, *The Home of the Blizzard*

4 January 1912 and several days thereafter, Southern Ocean, Mawson's men enter a strange new world

Getting close now!

When *Aurora* encounters a glacier tongue, a sounding reveals
a mud bottom at a shallow 395 fathoms, which – just as Lieutenant
Charles Wilkes, of the United States Exploring Expedition, assumed
after doing similar soundings in 1840 – must mean they are on the
continental shelf, with Antarctica itself very close. Passing by this
massive ice behemoth, which extends 130 feet above the water, the
explorers are entranced by the grandeur of the deep blue and green
caverns and vast grottoes like giant mouse holes at irregular intervals
along its length. Over the next few days, they track shoreward along
the ice tongue and a now optimistic Mawson searches for a suitable
place to establish his Winter Quarters, if they can only find solid land.

All up, all of the men aboard *Aurora* who have not been to these parts before have a sense that they are entering a strange new world, unlike anything they have experienced before. The sun, for example . . .

It rises in the very early hours, practically in the south, sweeps low across the horizon until well after midnight, before sinking, again in the south, for but a brief rest of a few minutes before emerging again in practically the same spot!

As to Mawson, he is beyond thrilled to now be so close. And it all feels so different from his previous visit. 'You will be in Europe ere this letter gets to you,' he writes to his fiancée. 'The excitement will be very great but I hope Paquita *occasionally* thinks of Douglas. Perhaps it is your love warmth that already shades me from cold, for I doubt if I feel it so much as the last time.'[1]

6 January 1912, Polar Plateau, 1½ Degree Depot, Taffy reveals . . .

A week earlier, Taffy Evans and Tom Crean carefully and skilfully shortened the two 12-foot sledges, as their lightened loads no longer required them to be so long. Alas, in the process, one of the tools slipped and Taffy badly cut his hand, leaving a severe open wound.

What to do? Of course, what he has always done: tough Taff soldiered on, hiding the wound from Wilson and Scott . . . until now, when it can be hidden no more. At first view, as Taffy rather sheepishly removes his gloves and shows Wilson the terribly infected cut, the older man is shocked, noting that the wound is well filled with pus, while Scott, too, is anxious, hoping the hand won't give the Welshman any trouble. In these parts, as he well knows, a cut like that can be more than problematic – it can be a death sentence.

Adding to Taffy's discomfort, in the minus-20-degree temperatures the men's hairy faces have turned into ice masks and their hands on their ski poles feel like frozen blocks, for the simple reason that they're not far off being exactly that. Yet the indomitable Birdie Bowers marches on – nothing seems to slow the man down – while the Owner remains thankful that he and the others are still on skis.

6 January 1912 and four days thereafter, Southern Ocean, Mawson and his men skirt the shore

And now the coast they have been following – for they did indeed spy their first bit of land on the previous day – starts curving inwards, and the men become aware that they are steaming into what looks like a large bay, which is promising. Now, every telescope and field-glass they have on the ship is brought to bear on this piece of coast. To the east lies the wall of the glacier tongue they have been following; to the west they can see a 2000-foot-high snow-covered promontory, obviously too towering to be anything other than land, suggesting that this is all but definitely Antarctica itself.

By day's end, far, far to the west they can see a cape that could well be the cape that d'Urville reported seeing in 1840 and named Cape Découverte. Perhaps, then, what lies before them now is the very Adélie Land that the French mariner named for his wife.

Sure enough, just before a calm and sunny noon two days later, the men spot a promising rocky outcrop about 15 miles off the port side. Venturing closer, by 3.30 pm they are about one mile off the rocks, beyond which they can see white slopes that look like an easy passage to the interior. This is looking better and better, as Belgrave Ninnis is quick to note:

Discovered new land [yesterday] . . . It is a bleak, desolate coast, snow covered hills with here and there patches of bare rock, and cliffs of ice. The shore is dotted with small rocky islands.

All yesterday we were trying to push along it, but the weather was very foggy with a heavy snowfall and we had to go very cautiously indeed . . .

We have just discovered what looks like a good landing place for our hut, and any minute we may receive the order to land stores that will see us working day and night until the ship leaves . . .

This place has an extraordinary formation and I am already gripped thereby. Is so huge and white and quiet and . . . forbidding looking.

If Scott and Amundsen fail to reach the Pole I shall soon be down here with a British Expedition . . . but of this more anon, I have so many Expeditions promised that goodness knows where I shall be soon. But we shall, bar accidents, meet ere then.

I am enjoying myself more than I can possibly describe. You would love it . . .

Well now fare ye well. Welcome me with open arms if I return and weep over my distant and frozen corpse if I don't, and cast thoughts after me as I head my devious and crevasse ridden ways . . .

Yours sincerely,
B E S Ninnis[2]

Aurora drops anchor as close as possible to this promising shore. Now, following a satisfactory reconnoitre in the whaleboat, Mawson returns to his ship and directs the small motor launch to be lowered away. Negotiating their passage past a series of islets, the launch slowly chug-chugs towards a small inlet in the rocky coast, towing the whaleboat loaded with stores as it goes. There is not a breath of wind, and it is warm enough that Mawson and the seven men with him are wearing neither mitts nor overcoats. They soon find themselves in an idyllic, tiny, landlocked harbour – an aquatic indent into the coast, about the size of a football field – flanked on both sides by some rocky ridges heading down to the shore, all of it teeming with Adélie penguins in their thousands, and Weddell seals and their pups in their hundreds.

One thing is for certain: they will not starve here, at least not in the summer months, and nor will their dogs.

As the landing party step ashore at eight o'clock on this balmy evening, they fulfil Mawson's dream of the last four years and become the first men in history to lay foot in that 2000-mile continental expanse between Cape Adare and Gaussberg.

Arise, and step forward Douglas Mawson, Frank Wild, Cecil Madigan, Frank Bickerton, Alexander Kennedy, Eric Webb, Robert Bage and Frank Hurley, the last of whom with camera in hand as the expedition's official photographer records it all . . . with one minor setback. While Mawson is accorded the honour, by the others, of being the first man in the history of the world to step ashore on this particular piece of Antarctic coast, Hurley all but instantly has the unintended honour of being the first man to sit in these parts, after he slips over on the ice.

No matter. With the sun shining down on their heads, and adventure and achievement thrilling their souls, Mawson applies one of the privileges of being expedition leader to name this general area Commonwealth Bay, with Cape Denison at its head – the last named for leading expedition donor and Sydney newspaper proprietor Hugh Denison – and the little harbour they hope to call home for the next year Boat Harbour.

The glacial slope behind that harbour that they had seen from the ship looks to be smooth and crevasse-free, which will provide a clean start for the sledging parties' journeys of exploration, although to the left and right of the rocky shore are heavily crevassed sheer ice cliffs, with only two patches of rock showing through as far as the eye can see.

Even though the most crucial thing is that they have finally discovered solid land, with a suitable, sheltered boat harbour and a wide, flat site where their Winter Quarters can be constructed close by the shore, still the place is not perfect.

To begin with, the position is a lot further west than Mawson ever envisaged. In fact, having pushed so far west and used up valuable coal supplies, Mawson immediately takes the decision to consolidate his three intended landing parties into just two: Mawson's Main Party, to be based here at Cape Denison, and Wild's Western Party, to be transported with luck no further than 500 miles west of their present location, so that Mawson's Far-Eastern Party and Wild's Western Party may meet up during the spring and summer sledging journeys.[3] Yes, it is not perfect, but this is where they will make their base.

The shallowness of the water close to the shore prevents *Aurora* coming nearer than one mile, which means that the serious unloading will have to be done by boat. (Landing cargo on the Antarctic shore is typically accomplished by bringing the ship in close and unloading onto the fast ice adjacent to the shore. The goods are then sledged away to the nearby destination.) And though the harbour is relatively sheltered from the worst of the ocean's fury, and they have landed in comparatively calm conditions, they only manage to get two loads ashore before a vicious wind howls down at them south from the interior, a wind as bitter as it is unrelenting, and they are soon chilled to the marrow of their bones.

It is, in fact, so bad that one of their men, Arch Hoadley, soon has frostbitten fingers, and the motorboat gets swept away from *Aurora*, with the three men on board only narrowly escaping being hurled onto one of the rocky islets before its engine can be restarted. 'Nothing I had experienced in the Ross Sea or in any other part of the world,' Davis writes later, as one who has sailed the seven seas for decades on end, 'came up to the gales and blizzards of Commonwealth Bay for sudden violence and frequency.'[4]

Once all of the men are safely back on board *Aurora*, albeit feeling frozen, they retreat to the warmth of the mess room. Mawson gives the order that, once the gale abates, unloading is to begin again immediately, and yet it is not until the morning of 10 January, some 30 hours later, that the wind falls enough to make that remotely possible.

All hands on deck! With the aid of a derrick fashioned from two lengths of the wooden masts intended to hold up the antenna for the wireless, the men begin to fill the launch and two whaleboats with the supplies on board that were designated for the first two wintering sites, which have now become one, as they try in vain to ignore the whipping wind.

But it is a fearful business all right. Davis has *Aurora* as close to the shelter of the ice cliffs as he can manage, in 13 fathoms of water, but the wind remains strong enough to drag the anchor a little before it mercifully holds. Still, with the wind blowing upwards of 70 mph, the waves come thick and fast. And though these waves are not enough to trouble the ship, they are plenty big enough to trouble the whaleboats and motor launch, and the men are only able to continue to get those boats away in the lulls, which last no more than three hours at a time. The key is to make sure all the boats are loaded to the gills, and the motor launch then tows the two whaleboats – often together with an additional 'raft' made of hut timbers or wireless masts – into the small harbour.

9 January 1912 and the day thereafter, Polar Plateau, Scott and his men set a record

In all the extremity of their situation – exhausted, starving, freezing – there is at least one good thing that occurs on this ninth day of January. That is, they surpass the point farthest south that Shackleton attained precisely three years earlier, which was 88 degrees 23 minutes

south. It is certainly something. Another bit of good news is that there
is still no sign of Amundsen and his Norwegians.

In nearly exactly the same position, albeit with only four men
and supplies for substantially fewer days than his outward journey
took, Shackleton decided that, while he could get to the Pole, he
would be very unlikely to get back again with all his men alive.
Shackleton's logic was revealed in a conversation he had upon his
safe return to England, when he said to his wife, Emily, 'I thought,
dear, that you would rather have a live ass than a dead lion.' She had
replied, 'Yes, darling, as far as I am concerned.'[5]

Scott, however, carries with him to the Pole a communication
from his wife, Kathleen, of an entirely different nature. It is a letter,
written in pencil on a torn piece of paper, that includes the passage:

*Look you – when you are away South I want you to be
sure that if there be a risk to take or leave, you will take
it, or there is a danger for you or another man to face, it
will be you who face it, just as much as before you met
[Peter] and me. Because man dear we can do without
you please know for sure we can . . . If there's anything
you think worth doing at the cost of your life – Do it. Do
you understand me? How awful if you don't.[6]*

Scott understands. It is *not* that his wife has a death wish for him
– far from it – but in the equation of decision-making, he mustn't
think about her and their son, because they would be all right. She
believes in his greatness and must put honour and the possibility of
achievement before everything else.

So, whereas Shackleton of course turned back, Scott now goes on, exultantly noting in his diary 'RECORD' before getting into harness once more and pulling south, south, south, ever more south towards the axis of the world, and pausing only to lay down one week's provisions at 1½ Degree Depot, so they can lighten their load for this last dash to the pole.

By camp on the night of 10 January, they are only, according to their navigator Birdie's calculations – his enormous beak nose nodding ever so slightly up and down as he works it out – let's see, 85 miles from the Pole, carrying food supplies to get them through 18 days.

12 January 1912 and several days thereafter, Cape Denison, Mawson takes a dive

In such wind, the conditions ashore are more than merely grim, with no shelter yet constructed, though the unloading proceeds apace. The first real drama arrives in the full light of just before midnight on this howling day, when suddenly the wind increases to the point that all loading and unloading is immediately stopped and the major focus of those onshore at the time – Mawson, Wild and four others – is simply surviving. Quickly, as the wind punches into them, knocks them over, screams into their ears and tears at their mouths, noses and every loose part of their clothing, they grab the heavy cans of benzine and form them into a wall, which allows them to build three other walls a little more easily. Bizarrely, as they build, they can't help but notice that though the hurricane is howling, there is not a cloud in the sky above and the sun is shining brightly.

With the walls at last constructed, for a roof atop their makeshift 'Benzine Hut' they put planks weighed down by more cans of benzine, and at last they gain some respite to spend the night in a little more protected comfort. The following morning, once the wind has abated enough for the unloading to continue, the others come ashore and pick up where they left off. They work with urgency, eight hours on, eight hours off, eight hours on, and fill each 24-hour period in that manner as the work indeed goes on around the clock.

As busy as they are, however, there is still time to steal glances at the teeming life apparent all around in this strange place. For while the frozen land itself supports no native terrestrial fauna, the waters have life that 'vies in abundance with the warmer waters of lower latitudes'.[7]

Adélie penguins and Weddell seals swarm around them in stupendous numbers, while baleen whales and 20-foot killer whales muster round and bob up for a look-see at *Aurora*'s stern. Leopard seals and crab-eater seals are sighted on the ice, 100 one minute, none the next, showing total sangfroid unless their ice platform is accidentally disturbed by a discourteous passing vessel. Flocks of various petrels – silver-grey fulmars, the snow petrel, the Antarctic petrel, the Wilson's storm petrel and Cape petrels – may be seen skimming the water in search of food or congregating atop the enormous icebergs, chatting away without a care in the world.

Ah, but back to work and the endless unloading, together with getting together the rudiments of the permanent Winter Quarters they are building. A key installation is of course the large stove in the main hut's kitchen area, which, apart from allowing them to cook, will also warm the larger construction. And yet, just as they are nearing final assembly, they discover that several important parts have gone missing. Recalling that a box fell into the harbour in the first part of the unloading, Mawson says to Laseron, 'Come on, Joe, let us see if we can get it.'

Taking the whaleboat out into Boat Harbour, they manage to locate the box in freezing waters at a depth of about six feet. Alas, despite their best efforts, they are unable to pick up the elusive box with any sort of improvised hook, pike or any other such makeshift fishing device. The solution is obvious, if shattering. But Mawson does not hesitate. Saying simply, 'There is only one thing for it,' he strips off and jumps in to retrieve it. As his body hits the water, a jolt goes completely through him as the air explodes from his lungs, followed by a general feeling of numbness, which quickly gives way to an extraordinary sensation – like a ringing in his ears, except it is all over his entire body. He emerges blue with cold, but the box is secured.

Lo and behold, when the contents are explored it is discovered to contain . . . tins of marmalade. More than fortunately, the missing pieces of the stove are found elsewhere shortly afterwards and the stove is soon assembled, if not yet fired up. That chattering sound? Nothing. Just Mawson's teeth. He will warm up, once they get the stove sorted.

15 January 1912 and the day thereafter, Polar Plateau, Scott has never had such work in his life

Things are becoming ever more difficult. Bowers's wristwatch – crucial to determining their position, as by 'shooting' the angle of the sun at a precise time it is possible to work out their latitude – has been found to be unreliable. This is just one of many worries, with Scott having written in his diary at lunch four days earlier:

> I never had such pulling; all the time the sledge rasps and creaks. We have covered 6 miles,[8] but at fearful cost to ourselves . . . Another hard grind in the afternoon and five miles[9] added. About 74 miles[10] from the Pole – can we keep this up? It takes it out of us like anything. None of us ever had such hard work before . . . Our chance still holds good if we can put the work in, but it's a terribly trying time.[11]

Still, buoyed along by the reckoning that they are at most two days shy of their goal, on this night Scott records in his diary:

It is wonderful to think that two long marches would land us at the Pole. We left our depot to-day with nine days' provisions, so that it ought to be a certain thing now, and the only appalling possibility the sight of the Norwegian flag forestalling ours . . . Only 27 miles[12] from the Pole. We ought to do it now.[13]

Up early the next morning and in good spirits, they push on hard, pulling their sledges as they go, and have seven and a half miles under their belts by noon. A noon theodolite reading shows them they are but 24 miles from the prize – tomorrow will surely see them reach the Pole.

Their exhausted excitement is palpable. Long have they suffered, but soon, *soon* the object of their deepest desires will be at hand, and they will be able to plant the Union Jack upon *the* most coveted remaining spot on earth.

That afternoon, at about 5 pm, they are all marching along with rising expectation, exultation and exhaustion when the sharp-eyed Birdie Bowers suddenly stops. What do you think that thing is in the far distance, something oddly black in the pressing whiteness all around?

Nothing, Birdie, you are seeing things. It will prove to be no more than an odd formation of sastrugi throwing a strange shadow and is of no concern.

Still, as they march onwards, all of them focus on this far-off object, the fear in their hearts gripping them ever more tightly as the black thing gets progressively larger and less and less like a natural feature, and more and more like their worst nightmare come to life.

After 30 minutes, that nightmare really does become real. For now there is no denying it. What they clearly see just up ahead is . . . is . . . is a black flag tied to a sledge runner.

Dear God.

The Norwegians.

Blighters must have come up by another glacier – for there was certainly no trace of them on the Beardmore Glacier. The flag's flapping ends are badly frayed, indicating it has been there for some time. Not far away, they find the remains of a camp, mixed with the tracks of many skis and sledges and an enormous number of *dog* paws. It is difficult to gauge the age of the tracks with any certainty, but Wilson notes they are 'probably a couple of weeks, or three, or more . . .'[14]

It makes little difference now. They are tramping across old ground. Far from trumpeting success, they are trumped; far from being the headline act in the piece, they are little more than old news, their late arrival only serving as a backdrop to enhance the legend of what will be perceived as Amundsen's greatness.

It makes little difference now.

17 January 1912, Polar Plateau, Scott finds an awful place

After a sleepless night comes the bleak, bitter morning – somehow, never more bleak or bitter a morning have they seen – as Scott's party awakes to the dreadful marching conditions of a force four to five headwind with a staggering wind-chill factor of minus 22, which only serves to lower further their already wretched spirits.

Once started, they follow in Amundsen's sledge tracks, now appallingly apparent, and pass two of his cairns before, for some strange reason, the Norwegians' tracks seem to drift too far to the west. They adjust and go straight on to where they think the South Pole lies, hoping against hope (for that is all that is left to them) that Amundsen has lost his way. And still this provides little comfort, as Oates, Evans and Bowers are suffering severe frostbite of the nose, cheeks and feet, and Taffy's hands are painfully blistered, while the wound on his knuckle is giving him hell.

At their lunch camp, Birdie takes fresh bearings and calculates they are at 89 degrees 53 minutes 37 seconds south – roughly seven and a half miles from their destination. That night, after marching that distance through severe winds and a temperature of minus 21 degrees, they feel they are on the spot at last. Scott records his feelings in his journal:

> Great God! this is an awful place and terrible enough for us to have laboured to it without the reward of priority. Well, it is something to have got here, and the wind may be our friend to-morrow . . . Now for the run home and a desperate struggle. I wonder if we can do it.[15]

Birdie, meanwhile, consoles himself, as he writes in a letter to his mother from the Pole:

My Dearest Mother,

A line from the spot might not be out of place . . . I don't suppose you thought your son would be at the apex of the Earth. Well here I really am and very glad to be here too. It is a bleak spot . . .

Now the greatest journey home. It only remains for us to get back. Fortunately we are all fit and well and should be back to catch the ship in time for the news . . .

It is sad that we have been forestalled by the Norwegians, but I am glad that we have done it by good British manhaulage. That is the traditional British sledging

*method. This is the greatest journey done by man unaided
since we left our transport at the foot of the glacier...
I could not have better companions – we are a most
congenial party – five is a pleasant little crowd when we
are so far from home.*[16]

Oates embraces no such romantic notions and takes an entirely different tack in his diary:

> I must say [Amundsen] must have had his head screwed on right. The gear they left was in excellent order and they seem to have had a comfortable trip with their dog teams. Very different to our wretched manhauling.[17]

18 January 1912 and the day thereafter, South Pole, Scott is asked to deliver a letter

After Bowers and Scott calculate they are three and a half miles from the Pole, one mile *beyond* it and three to the right, they are off again early. Trudging, trudging, trudging along. By now, all of their expectation, all their excitement, all their exuberance at being about to conquer the South Pole has long gone, and all they are left with is exhaustion pure. Only an hour after beginning, they spy precisely what they have been fearing: Amundsen's small, compact tent still held aloft by a single bamboo pole. The wave of disappointment that has towered above them since the day before now comes crashing down all around and drowns them in sheer misery.

Inside the tent, they find a note pinned to the bamboo staff recording that the Norwegians reached this point on 16 December 1911, 32 days earlier, and listing the men who would have their names etched in history's finest front pages forever more, reducing the Englishmen, surely, to a mere footnote:

Roald Amundsen

Olav Olavson Bjaaland

Helmer Hanssen

Sverre H. Hassel

Oscar Wisting

16 December 1911

And Scott finds, too, left in a prominent position where he can't miss it, an envelope with his name on it. Opening it, he finds two pieces of paper. One of them is addressed to King Haakon of Norway, advising the Norwegian sovereign – it seems, though he cannot be sure, as he does not understand the language – of what Amundsen and his men have done. The other letter is to Scott himself, and the Englishman reads it with a heavy heart:

Dear Captain Scott, – As you probably are the first to reach this area after us, I will ask you kindly to forward this letter to King Haakon VII. If you can use any of the articles left in the tent please do not hesitate to do so. The sledge left outside may be of use to you. With kind regards I wish you a safe return.

Yours truly,

Roald Amundsen[18]

It is close to the moral equivalent of a dagger to the heart. In one fell swoop, Scott has gone from being a man hoping to write his own name in the history books as the conqueror of the South Pole to being a mere postal delivery boy for his rival. Nevertheless, he has no choice. He has been asked to deliver the letter, so, as the honourable English gentleman he is, deliver it he must.

Scott in turns leaves his own note at the tent, informing whosoever should arrive in the future that his party has also now been here. After this, pausing only for Bill Wilson to purloin some of the silk strips from the Norwegian tent seams, together with some other minor effects, they continue on towards where they estimate the precise pole lies, around one and three-quarter miles away. Continuing on after lunch, they discover one of Amundsen's upturned sledge runners half a mile distant, which they believe to be his mark for the Pole itself.[19]

Birdie's location sightings at lunch calculate they are now less than a mile from the Pole. At this point, which they name 'Pole Camp', they build a cairn and plant in the ice what Scott refers to as 'our poor slighted Union Jack', before Birdie Bowers uses a string connected to his camera to take some photographs of the five exhausted Britons: Captain Robert Falcon Scott CVO; Dr Edward Adrian Wilson; Lieutenant Henry Robertson 'Birdie' Bowers; Petty Officer Edgar 'Taffy' Evans; and Captain Lawrence Edward Grace 'Titus' Oates.

With a weariness that goes to the very core of their beings, they then turn their sledge to the north – back to Cape Evans.

Scott's written words drip with pathos: 'Well, we have turned our back now on the goal of our ambition and must face our 800 miles[20] of solid dragging – and goodbye to most of the daydreams!'[21]

Now retracing their tracks – and as if once is not enough – Scott's team suffer again the indignity of marching past the sneering black flag of Amundsen's party that they had first passed on 15 January.

Almost by way of exacting retribution, they strip the bamboo pole of its flag, which Scott squirrels away into his kitbag to rest alongside a small piece of the slighted Union Jack they have so recently and so sullenly raised. As to the flagpole, it is fashioned into a makeshift mast for their sledge sail. And so it is that the Britons' progress rests upon, and is constantly shadowed by, the Norwegians. The going is tough, made worse by the fact that they must drag their sledge up a slight slope, as the precipice of the Polar Plateau is some 2000 feet higher than the Pole. All they can do is to trudge on, as they begin to pick up the first of Amundsen's directional cairns, and then their own at regular intervals, until inevitably the paths of the cairns part company, even as the wind picks up and the temperature drops . . .

'I'm afraid the return journey is going to be dreadfully tiring and monotonous,' Scott opines in his diary on Friday 19 January. 'We are going to have a pretty hard time this next 100 miles[22] I expect.'[23] And likely longer. For with the pole achieved, albeit without the 'reward of priority', there remains only one thing left to do.

Survive.

And there is only one way to do so. After racing Amundsen all the way to the Pole, and losing, they must now race back to the hut ahead of the fearful winter that will soon spring up from behind them . . . and they dare not lose that race, for *everything* would be lost with it, including their lives, and they know it from the first.

If they are quick enough, and do survive, there is a chance, just a chance, that they can be the first to bring news to the world that the South Pole has been conquered, even though, regrettably, it was not by them.

19 January 1912 and three days thereafter, Cape Denison, Mawson and his men are left alone

With a flourish, Douglas Mawson finishes off a letter to Paquita, which he intends for Captain Davis to take back to Australia to be put in the post to her:

Know O'Darling that in this frozen South I can always wring happiness from my heart by thinking of your splendid self.

There is an ocean of love between us dear.

Your loving Douglas[24]

And now it is time to say their farewells to each other. With everything offloaded from *Aurora* and time pressing – beyond the oasis of clear water, they know, the ice-soldiers will soon be beginning to mass once more, to prevent the little ship from breaking free – it is important that the ship not tarry a moment longer. Davis still has to drop Frank Wild and his seven selected men – Andy Watson, George Dovers, Morton Henry Moyes, Doc Jones, Alexander Kennedy, Arch Hoadley and Charles Harrisson – some 400–500 miles along the coast to their west, so as to be able to take their own meteorological and scientific observations simultaneously with those being taken by Mawson's party and the men left at Macquarie Island.

Ideally, as they proceed along the coast, they will 'cache provisions at intervals . . . in places liable to be visited by sledging parties'.[25] For the sledging parties of Wild will also explore as much of the coast and immediate interior as possible, and if both parties can get their antennae up and their radios working it may be possible for them to liaise – and have a western sledging party from Mawson's group meet up with an eastern one from Wild's group. A word before you go, though, lads.

For now, to bid them proper farewell, Mawson and Davis gather all the members of the two parties together with the ship's officers in *Aurora*'s tiny wardroom. To mark the occasion – albeit for reasons best known to himself, and coming from a cache unknown – Frank Wild is dressed in the full garb of Sir Francis Drake, replete with Elizabethan hose, causing much merriment. Glasses are handed out, and the bottle of the finest Madeira given to Davis in London by the three old *Challenger* shipmates six months before is opened.

They first make a toast to their gallant British predecessors, who gave them this wine after coming to these parts in 1874, nearly 40 years earlier, as well as to previous Antarctic explorers such as the Englishman Ross, the Frenchman d'Urville, the American Wilkes, and all of their men who came here another quarter-century before that. As Davis drinks the fortified wine, gazing at the bearded, eager faces of his youthful companions – the 18 men in Mawson's party who are to be left here, and the seven others who will accompany Wild to the west – he remembers vividly and fondly that evening with the three old gentlemen in Mr Buchanan's house in Norfolk Street where they wished him, and them, the men of the new generation, Godspeed upon their rare adventure.[26]

Mawson then makes a brief, elegant speech, particularly wishing the Wild party well, while also expressing the thanks of them all for the work of Captain Davis to get them to this point and wishing him and *Aurora* a safe return to Hobart.

Good health, good luck, here's to the King, and if the good Lord smiles upon us we will all see each other in just under a year's time when mighty *Aurora* comes back to gather up both parties. Here's cheers, and fare thee well!

With that, there are handshakes all around, even as some last-minute letters are scribbled, to be added to the mailbag for loved ones at home – a bag already containing the four letters Mawson has written to Paquita over the last five weeks. And then, at 8.45 pm, Mawson and his men climb back into their whaleboat to return to their barren shore, all of it to the strains of 'Auld Lang Syne' being sung by those on *Aurora*, led by the rich baritone of Frank Wild.

'Goodbye and do your best!' Mawson calls out to them, as

his last words to those on the departing ship.[27] Whatever else, he is confident that, in men with the capacity and vast experience of Davis and Wild – whose two figures on the stern of the ship are now getting smaller as their own boat separates from the departing *Aurora* – he has put the work to be done in the best of hands.

Aboard *Aurora*, Davis soon has the boiler up to full steam, and the little ship is chugging her way around the headland, making for the north-western horizon. Wild, now calm and reflective, remains standing by the stern, the cold nipping at his ears, as he gazes back for his last glimpse of where they have left their comrades. Shortly thereafter, he shares his feelings with a friend in a letter:

> I for one could not help thinking that our goodbyes were to some of them forever. It is a fearful country where they are landed. Except for less than a mile around the Winter Quarters, the coast is a perpendicular ice wall from 100 to 300 ft high, and it rises back rapidly to about 2000 ft – we cannot see beyond that. From the base there is a fairly clear track leading up to the slope about 200 yards wide. Even that is not free from crevasses, and on either side of this track the ice is so horribly broken up that nothing but a bird could cross it; and, except Mawson himself, none of the party has had the least experience.[28]

That experience, however, is soon coming as fast and furious as the howling wind and its spitting darts of icy sleet. As a temporary measure, the Mawson party make their new home in four tents and the small shelter constructed from the benzine cases. Though Mawson and his men are now entirely isolated, there is relief that the intense preliminaries are at last over and their actual adventure proper can begin. 'I was glad it was over,' writes Ninnis that night in his diary. 'I could have wept with the greatest of ease.'[29]

But to work. While most of the exhausted troupe turn in for the night by 10 pm, Mawson and a tight coterie of men stay up to discuss the next steps in building the huts. They are able to consider the erection of two huts here, rather than the original one that has been planned, because the consolidation of the three Antarctic parties into two has left a surplus of huts at this base. It is decided to have one larger hut for the living quarters and one smaller hut in its lee, to serve as a workshop, with a single doorway between a common wall. Mercifully, construction is expected to be relatively quick, as the buildings have been previously assembled and each piece of timber numbered before being taken apart again. Most importantly, a master plan for both huts tells how all the king's horses and all the king's men can put it all back together again.

For a place to build them, Mawson has already selected a site about 50 yards from the water's edge on the sheltered side of a large pile of rocks for the sake of some respite from the vicious winds roaring down the slope at them from their south. There is just enough space on this fortuitously level expanse of rock for the two strong-beamed prefabricated huts to be constructed – and the first thing the following morning they all begin.

Dynamite has to be employed to blast holes in the rock for the foundation stumps. However, the freezing weather does not aid detonation. The men circumvent this by carrying the explosives close to their bodies, in pockets and even inside their undergarments, to keep them warm. (No greater commitment to a task hath any man than this.)

With the explosions organised, the next problem arises: what to use for tamping material around the stumps being put in for the foundations, when there is no earth or clay? Fortunately, it is not only in the fields of chemistry, physics and biology that genius strikes, and as soon as someone suggests using guano from the penguin rookery the problem is solved. By packing the guano tightly around the stumps and then pouring water upon it, which instantly freezes, it is as if the foundations have been set in stone. The other way is to urinate upon the guano. (How does one urinate in freezing conditions? The answer, as they all learn immediately, is very, very quickly. And, by the by, it is the uncircumcised men who are the best protected for the task.)

Next day, the first of the stumps are in place.

Day after endless day, the work is hard and long – they start at seven o'clock every morning and go right through until eleven o'clock at night – but it is deeply satisfying. Their home is taking shape before their eyes, and all are conscious that their survival, and at the least their comfort, depends on getting the job done right. As they work on these splendid days, the wind blows cold, the sun shines hot and the sapphire-like icebergs in the sparkling bay float pleasantly in the swell. There are regular visits from groups of interested Adélie penguins that want to see how the strange new creatures are getting along, while the only concern of the Weddell seals basking 'in torpid slumber on the shore' is that these strange visitors not make too much noise.[30] In brief breaks for quick meals that include the last of the fresh supplies of meat, fruit and vegetables, the men dine in the environment that Antarctica most specialises in – al fresco to beat all al frescos – upon tables made out of kerosene cases.

The mood among the men as they work is nothing short of joyous. They have arrived, they are at the beginning of a great adventure and they are delighted at the progress they are making. And the scenery around them, the newness of it all, is as exciting as it is invigorating. Belgrave Ninnis is loving it all: the wonder of their environment, the work, the camaraderie, the joy of crawling into their separate sleeping bags after a tough day, all 'snug and warm, with pipes and cigarettes, and a cheerful haze filling the tent . . .'[31]

First thing the following morning, they are into it once more, making progress on their hut, their sanctuary, as bemused penguins chatter between themselves about what all this hammering, sawing and talking between these strange creatures with the extraordinarily long flippers can possibly be all about.

The common feeling is well expressed in a letter from Mawson to Paquita:

What an exultation is ours – the feeling is magical – young men whom you would scarce expect would be affected stand half clad without feeling the cold of the keen blizzard wind and literally dance from sheer exultation – can you not feel it too as I write – the quickening of the pulse, the awakening of the mind, then the tension of every fibre – and this is joy.[32]

21 January 1912 and four days thereafter, Polar Plateau, Scott's Southern Party are hit by a blizzard

The calculus of catastrophe is always on their minds.

With a blizzard now halting their push towards 1½ Degree Depot, their constant calculations – of food on hand divided by days remaining to the next depot – always have the ghastly spectre of death hanging over them. From here, they know it is 51 miles to 1½ Degree Depot and they have six days' food in hand. At 1½ Degree Depot, they will pick up supplies for another seven days to feed and warm them for the next 103.5 miles . . . It should be just enough if they are not too much further delayed by unseasonal blizzards like this one, but they will be in real trouble if it does not lift.

Fortunately, on this occasion it does, though their problems are not over. The temperature spirals down to minus 30 degrees, which is unheard of for this time of year. The sun and constant freezing wind catches the minute spicules of falling snow, creating a blinding haze that obliterates Scott's party's former tracks and obscures their sighting of cairns. In such difficult conditions, the only way to keep up a reasonable day's average is to pull harder, for longer, making the men ever more exhausted and ever more hungry, as the deficit grows between the energy they are expending and that coming from the meagre amount of food they are eating.

'I don't like the look of it,' Scott writes. 'Is the weather breaking up? If so God help us with the tremendous summit journey and scant food. Wilson and Bowers are my standby. I don't like the easy way in which Oates and Evans get frostbitten.'[33]

It is true, Taffy is not only badly frostbitten white on the nose and cheeks, his fingertips are badly blistered. With that, his morale is extremely low. For the humble Taffy, being one of the five first men to the Pole would have secured him the financial independence he has never known to this point. And *now* what does he have to look forward to? Not a lot.[34] And the truth of it is that his body is breaking down more quickly than those of the others. Despite being far and away the largest man among them, selected almost as a human workhorse for his tremendous capacity to haul the sledge, no allowance has been made to give him more food than the others. On top of everything else, he is starving.

As to Titus, though Scott can see that his face is just as frostbitten as Taffy's, what he cannot see yet is that the big toe of the Soldier's left foot is turning blue-black.

Even Scott's 'standbys', the men he always feels he can count on, are suffering. Due to the onset of snow-blindness, by now Wilson cannot make out the track ahead. And Bowers is suffering frostbite of the nose and cheeks.

With food and men spent, and having faced the second full blizzard since beginning the return journey from the Pole, Scott thanks God when a reluctant sun sheds a tepid light on the grim black flag of 1½ Degree Depot at 2.30 pm on 25 January.

25 January 1912, Cape Denison, Mawson and his men build their house on rock

Their living quarters are taking shape before their eyes, under their swinging hands, as they cheerily toil away. Despite the whipping winds, there is much good-natured banter as they work.

When assembling the roof, McLean loses his footing and rolls mercifully harmlessly to the ground, clinging to the chimney he has used for support. Ninnis, believing a hurricane has struck, reaches over and holds to the pipe inside the hut, receiving a head to toe covering in soot. All one can see of him are his brilliant eyes gleaming out from this ashen shroud. Ah, how they laugh – nearly as hard as when they first witnessed the 16-stone radio-operator Walter Hannam try to move around on skis. A giraffe on roller skates would have more poise!

Mertz, meanwhile, is nailing slats on the inside of the roof with his customary fervour but chooses a nail so long it lightly punctures the bottom of Bickerton, who is outside fixing the two layers of tar paper into position.[35] He yelps, and, as Laseron describes it, there is 'more universal joy'.[36] On another day, when a hammer is dropped on Walter Hannam's head, the entirely innocent Mertz apologises on the reckoning that *someone* should do so – resulting in the Swiss, to his astonishment, learning a whole new host of swear words courtesy of the outraged Hannam. Yet more laughter . . .

Through all the high hilarity, though, the work goes on, and what was merely a skeletal frame soon starts to have walls and fixtures inside. The 24 foot by 24 foot hut has become the living quarters, with the men's double-bunks placed around the walls. Only Mawson has a tiny room to himself, at the far end, while a darkroom in one corner is reserved for Hurley to develop his photographs.

The now adjoining 16 foot by 16 foot small hut has, as planned, become the workroom, complete with the carpenter's bench, dynamo and wireless outfit, lathe, stove and a workbench for the zoologists. The roof of both huts is pitched at 35 degrees, steep enough to ensure the snow will slide off it and shallow enough for the shattering wind to flow over it rather than right against it. On three sides of the main hut, the roof extends down far enough beyond the walls to build an enclosed veranda, which becomes a storehouse and shelter for the 19 dogs that will stay here. (Wild and his men have taken the other nine.) On the windward side, cases of the heaviest provisions are piled up in the manner of an extra wall, to prevent the wind exerting too much pressure on the walls of the hut or getting under the eaves to lift the roof off.

25 January 1912, *Framheim*, Amundsen and his four comrades make it back to base

It is so typical of the Chief. Instead of arriving back at *Framheim* in the middle of the day, he playfully plans to have them get there at 4 am when their companions will be fast asleep and . . .

And all quiet now.

With just 11 surviving dogs left to pull the two sledges, this is relatively easy, and the five hale, hearty, heroic adventurers gather at the front door of *Framheim*. They planted that solitary Norwegian flag at the South Pole together and now they make their entrance together, having travelled 1725 miles in the last 97 days. The return journey of 863 miles has been accomplished in just 39 days, at an average rate of 22 miles per day. But *quiet*, Roald says. Creeping through the front door, filled with joy to be back after accomplishing their glorious feat, they close the door behind them and are officially home safe.

The first of their comrades to stir is Jørgen Stubberud. He is startled to see five familiar faces grinning down at him – is this a dream? – before one by one the other occupants awaken from their deep slumber with a typical momentary start; the party were not expected back for another ten days. Amundsen has himself been surprised at how quickly they have made it there and back from the Pole, including having covered on one extraordinary day an amazing 62 miles. But here they are, all right!

'Where's the *Fram*?' asks Amundsen of the room, and he is soon relieved to learn that all is well, she has simply put to sea after her arrival on 9 January due to bad weather and is soon to return.

'And what about the *Sørpolen*?' Lindstrøm says to Amundsen. 'Have you been there?'

'Yes, of course; otherwise you would hardly have seen us again,' laughs the Chief, indulging in coffee and hot cakes, which taste like sweet perfection itself after days of privation.

'*Ja, borte bra, hjemme best.*' It was good outside, the jubilant men agree, but still better at home.[37]

Back safe in the bosom of *Framheim* and the company of their comrades, the reality sheets home. They really have done it! Amundsen takes the opportunity to weigh himself. He has put on a few pounds.

As Amundsen himself would go on to note of their general good nutrition, 'The best proof was, that we always felt well and were never raving about food, which has been so common in all longer sledge journeys and an infallible sign of deficient nourishment.'[38]

26 January 1912, Cape Evans, the first of Scott's support teams gets back

Is there a doctor in the hut? At last there is. Having travelled over 1100 miles in three months – over 400 miles more than Scott's previous farthest south mark – the First Support Party (aka the Doctor's Party) reach Hut Point on this afternoon. At a respectable average of 16 miles per day, they have covered the total distance of 573 miles in 35 days, and, as ever, it is Cherry-Garrard's words that best capture the journey:

> We had the same dreary drag, the same thick weather fears and anxieties which other parties have had. A touch of the same dysentery and sickness: the same tumbles and crevasses: the same groping for tracks: the same cairns lost and found: the same snow-blindness and weariness, nightmares, food dreams . . .[39]

They were preceded, of course, by Meares, Demetri and the dogs, who together have paved the way for the following returning parties by rebuilding the cairns razed by the blizzard that raged from 5 until 8 December 1911.

Meares and the dog teams' own return home – arriving three weeks earlier, on 4 January – was greatly hampered by soft summer snow that slowed down the dogs and then the unexpected blizzards. The other problem was that, because they were 17 days later than planned in turning back, they were perilously short of food on their own sledge and had no alternative but to significantly dip into the supplies depoted for the three parties yet to return – taking a little butter, 50 biscuits and a day's provision for two men from each bag of the three weekly units at each of the depots between Lower Glacier and One Ton.

It means that, starting with the First Support Party, all the returning parties will be forced to come back on progressively less rations than originally depoted for them up until One Ton Depot. During January, One Ton has been resupplied by a man-hauling party, but without the power of locomotion provided by Meares's dogs, that man-hauling party were unable to carry any of the dog food and fewer rations to One Ton than Scott stipulated in his original instructions to Meares.[40] The upshot is that any relief party coming out to One Ton Depot in the future would have insufficient dog food there to be able to continue further south to help Scott and his men back from the South Pole.

30 January 1912, Cape Denison, Mawson's Winter Quarters are finished

It is a significant date in the life of the expedition. It is the day when the roof is completed, the basic interior of the hut is finished and the building is ready to accommodate them. To mark the occasion, Dr Mawson gathers all the men around him as he stands by the rocks on the side of their Winter Quarters. He christens the two huts and makes a brief speech thanking his men for their fine work. And then, as they all take their helmets off, the Union Jack and the Australian flag are hoisted side by side, and their leader formally claims possession of this region of Antarctica in the name of the King – *the King!* – and the British Empire. The men give three hearty cheers and then quickly put their helmets back on, as the freezing wind has been nipping their ears, and frostbite on such delicate extremities is always a danger.

By way of further celebration, that evening the men have their first sit-down meal together, cooked by Douglas Mawson himself, on their own stove, from supplies they have brought with them, leavened by kills of penguins and seals in their own front yard. For all of them, it is wonderful to be safe and warm and well fed inside, while the bitter wind continues to howl outside. From the moment that *Aurora* left them 11 days earlier, the gale-force winds have rarely abated. Though reluctant to inform his team, Mawson is well on his way to the conclusion that, in Adélie Land, 'the average local weather must be much more windy than in any other known part of Antarctica'.[41]

Still, for the moment they are safe and warm inside. In this brief time of rest and reflection after all the frenzy of their activity,

Belgrave Ninnis sums up his view of their position on this continent in strikingly philosophical terms in his diary:

> From the creation, the silence here has been unbroken by man, and now we, a very prosaic crowd of fellows, are here for an infinitely small space of time, for a short time we shall litter the land with tins, scrap timber, refuse and impedimenta, for a short time we shall be travelling over the great plateau, trying to draw the veil from a fractional part of this unknown land; then the ship will return for us and we shall leave the place to its eternal silence and loneliness, a silence that may never again be broken by a human voice.[42]

6 February 1912, Cape Evans, after being farewelled a year before, Scott's *Terra Nova* finally returns

Laden with Indian mules, more Siberian dogs and such relief supplies that the expedition might require for the second year, on this cold morning *Terra Nova* at last draws alongside the fast ice at Cape Evans, after an exceptionally long and arduous journey. Having left Lyttelton seven weeks earlier, they first picked up the Wicked Mate, aka Captain Victor Campbell, and his men at Cape Adare before dropping them at Evans Cove, north of the Drygalski Ice Tongue, on 7 January so they might undertake a month's geologising.

Since then, *Terra Nova* has spent the best part of a month trying to force a path through the ice floes crowding McMurdo Sound to reach Cape Evans. The fact that on this day they have at last achieved their goal brings relief to both the crew of *Terra Nova* and those gathered at Cape Evans, who have anxiously been waiting for this moment.

8 February 1912 and two days thereafter, Upper Beardmore Glacier, Scott's party battle on

For the last three weeks, since starting on their return journey from the South Pole, the men have been struggling, and weakening with that struggle. All of them are suffering, none more than the huge Welshman, Taffy Evans, whose hand wound has refused to heal and is getting worse by the day. In the freezing conditions, on an increasingly poor diet and in his run-down state, the wound has begun to badly fester and his fingernails are falling out. Despite the best ministrations of Bill Wilson, this and Taffy's mess of other afflictions – suppurating blisters and frostbitten face – are bringing this great snowman down.

But does Taffy care? By now, their formerly jocular companion has turned so morose that it is hard to tell, but the evidence continues to build that he is giving up. Three days earlier, Scott and Taffy Evans took a bad tumble down a crevasse, Taffy hitting his head, and his mental state has been dubious since. 'I fear,' Scott confides to his diary, 'Evans is becoming stupid,' before deciding the last word is too harsh and changing it to 'dull'.[43]

Meanwhile, the frostbite on Oates's nose and cheeks has worsened, and he has reluctantly revealed to Wilson, though not the Owner, that his painful big toe is now completely black with the same – not that he is one to ever show pain; he carries on regardless. But Taffy and the Soldier are not the only ones suffering. Over the past week, Wilson's own leg has been so swollen that he has relinquished his skis to Bowers and is now travelling on foot. Scott has also come a 'purler' and painfully injured his shoulder. Of the five, only Bowers – good old Birdie, he is such a trooper – seems to be travelling well.

Beyond their injuries and conditions, though, the principal problem is that all of them are slowly starving, getting thinner and colder by the day as they lose their last reserves of fat. Such is the energy they are expending through the heavy work they are doing, exacerbated by the high altitude and cold – for the lower the temperature, the more energy the human body must burn to get its own temperature to normal range, in the same manner as a hut must burn more coal to make a comfortable temperature inside – not even full rations would be enough to sustain them. But making matters even worse is that they are finding it progressively more difficult to locate their food depots. And when they do finally make it to Upper Glacier Depot, it is only for Bowers to discover that the depoted biscuit box is mysteriously short one full day's allowance. The only explanation is that one of the parties preceding them to the depot has taken it, which is deeply disturbing.

Notwithstanding the extremity of their situation, however, Scott now makes a couple of extraordinary decisions. The first is that, despite the weather being conducive to travel, he deems it worthwhile to all but stop for a day and a half so that Bowers and Wilson can take geological samples from the foothills of Mt Darwin and Mt Buckley.

They are thrilled with what they find. 'Wilson,' records Scott in his diary, 'with his sharp eyes, has picked several plant impressions, the last a piece of coal with beautifully traced leaves in layers, also some excellently preserved impressions of thick stems, showing cellular structure.'[44]

It is true that the importance of these fossil finds is enormous. It is proof that Antarctica once had flora and fauna flourishing. The true measure of how important Scott personally sees the find is that, in his second extraordinary decision, he acquiesces to Wilson's wish to add 35 pounds of rock samples to their sledge, before – *altogether now men and heave extra hard* – they set off again.

Three days later, the men find themselves lost in heavily crevassed country that should be familiar but isn't. A dispute breaks out whether to head right or left. They end up heading left, only to find it even more crevassed and so icy that their perpetually slipping, sliding, skittering skis are close to unworkable. The men keep falling into crevasses every minute and are lucky not to suffer terrible injuries or worse. Seeing a smoother slope in the distance, they make their way towards it but then find themselves in a different kind of turmoil, a place where the irregular crevasses give way to huge chasms, which are closely packed together and very difficult to cross. Scott's rising desperation shows in his diary entry that night: 'There were times when it seemed almost impossible to find a way out of the awful turmoil in which we found ourselves.'[45]

But does Scott abandon the dead weight of those rock samples? He does not. Apart from everything else, such rocks provide a real point of difference to Amundsen. Yes, the Norwegian conquered the South Pole first, but he, Scott, arrived there only a short time later and has advanced the cause of science to boot, as witness, among other things, those precious rocks.

In the wake of their struggle, and their slower than anticipated rate of return, Scott feels he has no choice but to reduce rations. Not surprisingly, the huge Taffy Evans, who needs more food than them all – but gets no more, because the rations are divided evenly – is now so weakened that he can no longer help make camp for the night. He simply sits there, mumbling incoherently. Every day now, as they set off, he trails further and further behind, resulting in longer stops to allow him to catch up. 'Taffy,' Scott writes, 'is nearly broken down in brain, we think. He is absolutely changed from his normal self-reliant self. This morning and this afternoon he stopped the march on some trivial excuse.'[46]

11 February 1912, Winter Quarters, Mawson's party receive a surprise visitor

On this morning, the cheeky 22-year-old chief magnetician, Eric 'Azi' (short for his favourite word: azimuth) Webb, bursts into the hut to announce that a ruddy great elephant seal has arrived in their harbour and is making cumbersome progress over the rocks near the shore! An elephant seal venturing onto the Antarctic mainland is an uncommon spectacle, and, as one, the men excitedly spill out of the hut, Hunter pausing only to grab his trusty rifle along the way. They arrive on the scene to find that Johnson the sledge dog – living up to his namesake, world heavyweight boxing champ Jack Johnson – has the great beast bailed up and is actually snarling and baring his jaws at the massive creature from the deep, which is nearly 50 times the dog's size.

With just one snap of its mighty mouth, Johnson's head would have simply disappeared, the way a dog eats a peanut, but now, on catching sight of the men, the elephant seal instantly loses interest in the mad mutt and begins lumbering towards these insolent tall creatures who would invade his regal domain.

Now living up to his own name, biologist Jack Hunter lines the sea beast up between the sights of his rifle and, before the creature can make a slow getaway, shoots him dead at close range. The elephant seal measures a good 17.5 feet in length and 12 feet around the fattest part of its girth, and they estimate its weight at just under four tons.[47]

Before the carcass can freeze stiff and become unworkable, the men immediately employ block and tackle and set about raising and flaying their quarry, saving the impressive skin and skull for their biological collection. Dog-carers Ninnis and Mertz butcher over a ton and a half of the meat and blubber, which will be used throughout the winter – the meat to feed their 19 ever-ravenous dogs and the blubber to keep the hut fires burning. Blubber, in fact, burns so well that it can turn the stove-top red hot – though on such occasions they have to be careful that the 'oddments [constantly hung above the stove] like wolf-skin mitts, finnesko, socks, stockings and helmets, which had passed from icy rigidity through sodden limpness to a state of parchment dryness' do not get too hot and burn.[48] Oddly, blubber also proves useful as an application to frostbite.

Meantime, others of the men are also, as the occasion arises, killing penguins and Weddell seals, whose carcasses are soon snap frozen by the natural air temperature, and these are carefully put by Herbert Dyce Murphy, the short and slight storeman, in a cellar beneath the hut's front porch, which is designed to be used as a meat store.

And though that meat store proves to be an effective place to keep the 15 frozen carcasses of lambs, seals, penguins and this elephant seal, there is a problem with it. That is, it is an extremely difficult spot for the 30-year-old Murphy to get in and out of, let alone to hack one frozen carcass away from another in. The solution? Despite having been left out of Shackleton's *Nimrod* expedition, purportedly for being too effeminate – there's no doubt he has a soft and rosy complexion, high-pitched voice and beautiful blue eyes – Murphy has three Arctic expeditions to his credit and is a man of considerable initiative.

He works out the way to do it is to push a dog through the trapdoor, let it grab one of the penguin carcasses on top and then, once the dog springs back out, grab the meat from its slavering jaws. It works well, right up until the day that the dog in question manages to get a rare bit of Sunday mutton and this time refuses to release it. Instead, the dog springs out and away from the outstretched hands of the grasping and gasping Murphy, who then spends the next hour charging madly around their nascent camp in wild pursuit, while the other men howl with laughter. Thereafter, Murphy decides he must do the job himself.

Murphy's redeployment as a storeman has been quite a come down. He was to have led the second landing party, somewhere between here and wherever Wild is being dropped, yet Murphy feels honoured to simply remain part of the AAE, even in a reduced capacity.

Mid-February 1912, off the north coast of Antarctica, Davis takes a chance with *Aurora*

It is strange to gaze closely upon a coast that few eyes have ever seen before, and none from this close. In *Aurora* over the previous three weeks, Captain Davis has been keenly aware of the privilege of his position as the ship closely follows the contours of the Antarctic coastline, pushing westward – though the compasses are practically useless this close to the Magnetic Pole. The British Admiralty chart on the bridge of *Aurora* shows only odd bits and pieces of land, as reported by Dumont d'Urville and Wilkes and a couple of others, but for the most part it is absolutely blank – until Davis's officers lightly sketch in the coast as they see it. It is a great satisfaction to be able to close at least some of the gaps on that vague spiderweb of a map of Antarctica he had seen in Shackleton's office four years earlier. He later recounts:

> The unknown land seemed to rise in an almost unbroken curving slope until, at a height of approximately 3000 ft, it met the horizon to the southward. This was a very different topography to that of the Ross Sea area. One expected to find here the same awe-inspiring and dramatic spectacle of mountain peaks and glaciers that had astonished and delighted one in Victoria Land. But here, so far as one could judge by the contour of the ice-cap, the land hidden beneath it might well consist of rounded slopes and rising plains, the grazing lands, perhaps, for untold herds of prehistoric animals in days before the age of ice.[49]

As *Aurora* continues, they are confronted by ever more ice, including an enormous glacier tongue, protruding so far out into the Southern Ocean that they are nigh on a week in getting past its northern extremity to the other side. By this time, all trace of actual land has disappeared, and, as Davis puts it, they know they are 'looking at no ordinary coastline but at one that had been overwhelmed by an all-engulfing flood of ice.'[50]

But for a place to land, there is little on offer – no more beaches, inlets or safe harbours are apparent. Facing the passing men are just huge and unrelenting ice cliffs. The plan of dropping sledging-party provisions at regular intervals along the coast is clearly out of the question. There appear to be no places to drop Wild and his men, let alone provisions for their sledging parties, and the situation becomes ever more desperate as the days pass.

The second party now confronts the fact that it is losing precious time and even more precious coal. The more time that passes in these days of mid-February, the more chance there is that they themselves will be frozen in on *Aurora*. And the further they go – they are already 1500 miles to the west of where they dropped Mawson's party, which is three times more than the plan – the less coal reserves the ship will have to get back to Hobart. Already, the radio of Wild's Western Base will be useless for receiving messages from the Mawson party at Cape Denison, because it can only do so over a distance of 500 to 600 miles.

In the view of Captain Davis, it has now come down to a matter of hours before he must drop the party, not days. But where? All they can see are the high ice cliffs before them. Davis is at his most desperate when, at 8.45 on the morning of 15 February, they spy a promising high ice-shelf formation, similar to what Davis and Wild previously saw at the Great Ice Barrier but significantly lower. What is more, as they continue along it, by noon they come to a point where a few hundred yards of ice floe butts up against a part of the ice cliff that is only 80 feet high, and against this snow that has been blown over the cliff has formed a drift like a ramp in the lee of the cliff. Is it really possible? Could it be done?

Frank Wild certainly thinks so, and in no time at all the experienced Yorkshireman has led an investigative party across the ice, up the snow ramp to the top of the ice cliffs and beyond it. Upon his return, he reports to Davis that at the top they can see land less than 20 miles away, and he is certain that what he was standing on was the blue ice of a glacier, meaning it would be stable enough to establish their Winter Quarters upon.

A key decision beckons. In some ways, it is pure madness to drop men for a year upon ice in a part of the world where huge chunks breaking off into the ocean to eventually melt into nothingness is as natural and unremarkable a process as autumn leaves falling to the ground in other parts of the world. It is nothing less than the equivalent of ignoring the biblical admonition that a man must build his house on solid rock as opposed to shifting sand. In this case, they are considering putting men on ice that soundings reveal is floating on 200 fathoms of water.

And yet Wild is adamant. They have come this far. They have all their equipment and supplies. He is sure the ice is stable and they will be okay. What to do? It is difficult to imagine Davis, the expedition's second in command, returning to Hobart with the news that the Australasian Antarctic Expedition has only managed to establish one base in Antarctica, instead of the targeted three, while bringing back a third of the landing party staff. However, with Mawson's second base already consolidated into the main base on a spot already far to the west, if the Western Base is not established here, that will be exactly the situation. They simply do not have time or coal to find anywhere else on this coast – and that is if such a place even exists, which Davis is starting to doubt.

Reluctantly, Captain Davis finally agrees – though he does feel gloomy about it – that at least they may start unloading stores while he thinks about it further, and they can see in that time if there is anything to suggest it is not stable after all.

Done!

17 February 1912 and the day thereafter, six miles south of Lower Glacier Depot, for Scott's party, the situation takes a turn for the . . .

This dull, overcast day sees the party struggling through freshly fallen snow that clogs the sledge runners and creates extreme difficulty underfoot. Although Taffy has slept well and says he is feeling fine, only a half an hour after they set out his ski shoes come away and he drops far behind the sledge. He is ailing so badly that their pace has been halved.

Concerned, Scott stops to prepare lunch, yet after quite some time Taffy is still only seen far off in the distance behind them.

Now the alarm is raised, and the four party members ski back to the aid of the stricken Taffy. Reaching him first, Scott – whose affection for the Welshman has remained steadfast – is immediately shocked by the sight of this former laughing giant now dishevelled on hands and knees, highly distressed with an animal look in his eye. His hands are exposed and frostbitten, and, in a series of grunts, he manages to tell his leader he thinks himself to have fainted.

Leaving Oates by the collapsed man's side, Scott, Wilson and Bowers hurry back for the sledge, and once they have retrieved it they quickly transport the comatose Evans to the tent. An awful responsibility now falls on Scott, and there is no way around it. The brutal truth is that, with Taffy lying there insensible, their supplies depleting by the day and the dreadful winter starting to overtake them, 'the safety of the remainder seemed to demand his abandonment'.[51]

But could they really do that? Leave a living man in the polar wilderness, so as to save themselves? Has it come to this?

Mercifully, Scott is spared the decision. From midnight, Taffy becomes ever more still, his breathing more shallow, and at 12.30 he breathes no more on this earth. Finally, the old Antarctic campaigner may rest – forever, here at the foot of the Beardmore Glacier. Scott writes:

> It is a terrible thing to lose a companion in this way, but calm reflection shows that there could not have been a better ending to the terrible anxieties of the past week. Discussion of the situation at lunch yesterday shows us what a desperate pass we were in with a sick man on our hands at such a distance from home.[52]

In fact, there is another notably sick man among them at this time doing his best to hide it and to soldier on regardless. For Lawrence Oates, what has been mere frostbite of his feet has started to turn gangrenous – that is, the actual blood vessels and tissue have begun to die, to rot. A red line marks the border between the living flesh and the dead flesh, and as the days go by that red line keeps moving and more of his body dies. It makes every step an agony, but Oates does not wish to burden the others with his problems and continues on the best he can.

19 February 1912 and the day thereafter, Hut Point, another of Scott's men returns

When a near-dead Tom Crean staggers through the door at Hut Point at 3.30 am, the foundation stone of another staggering story is laid. For most of the last six weeks since separating from Scott's Southern Party, Crean, Teddy Evans and Lashly have been pushing their way back through dreadful conditions, first hit by a three-day blizzard while they were still on the plateau, and then losing their way to the top of the Beardmore Glacier.

This has so taken its toll that by the time they made it back on track and to the bottom of the Beardmore Glacier, Teddy Evans had been faltering from the effects of full-blown scurvy, with his stiffening and swollen legs turning green with bruises, his gums ulcerating and his teeth loosening. Solidly in harness since the day the last motor sledge had given up the ghost three and a half months earlier, Evans is now so totally exhausted that the scurvy has its tentacles wrapped around him and is rapidly drawing him ever down. At One Ton Depot, a little over a week earlier, that condition descended to the point where Crean was sure that Teddy Evans had died. Fortunately, that was not true, as Evans was still compos mentis enough to feel Crean's hot tears on his face, roughly coming to, with a weak kind of laugh. But he was certainly close to the point of death.

Lashly recorded that Evans was 'turning black and blue and several other colours as well'.[53] When fully roused, Evans, with what could easily be assumed to be his dying breath, had given direct orders that he was to be left in his sleeping bag with what food they could spare while Crean and Lashly pushed on without him, to save themselves.

No, sir. Not going to do that, sir. Though they had only minimal rations left and, having covered over 1500 miles, were beyond exhausted themselves, Crean and Lashly strapped Evans to their sledge and struggled on. Pausing now and then to dribble some precious drops of brandy down their leader's throat, they reached Corner Camp on 18 February.

And it is here that the likeable Irishman rose to the occasion. For, leaving Lashly with Teddy Evans, Crean 'strode out nobly and finely',[54] making the 39-mile dash for Hut Point without crampons and carrying nothing more than two biscuits and a stick of chocolate, to raise the alarm.

He has arrived 18 hours later only just ahead of a terrible blizzard that has been roaring up behind him. Now, Atkinson gives Crean a tot of brandy followed by some porridge, which the exhausted man immediately throws up. 'That's the first time in my life that ever it happened, and it was the brandy that did it,' jokes Crean.[55]

By the following day, once the blizzard has blown itself out, Atkinson is leading a relief party to go and get Lashly and Evans. Though it is a close-run thing – a thing with frostbite nipping at its extremities – they are able to get them back to Cape Evans.

Ever afterwards, Teddy Evans would say that in his entire naval career this was the only time he had given a direct order only to have it disobeyed.[56]

20 February 1912 and the day thereafter, Shackleton Ice Shelf, the Western Party's decision is made

And now they are finally finished. By virtue of all hands on deck working over the past five days at a furious pace – not only on the deck but also on the ice shelf, the flying fox and the summit of the 60-foot ice cliff – all of the material for the prefabricated hut and all of the supplies, including 12 tons of oh-so-precious coal, have indeed been put at the top of the ice shelf. (At Davis's suggestion, they have named the formation the 'Shackleton Ice Shelf', by virtue of the fact that they spotted it on the great man's birthday.)

By the time everything is finished, it is just gone midnight. In the early hours of this morning, Davis approaches final-decision time. Well, after all their effort to unload, he can hardly give an order to pack it all up again, so for Wild this decision is a foregone conclusion, but the good captain does insist on one thing before agreeing to it. Frank Wild must write him a letter, making clear that it is not Davis but Wild himself who is insisting on staying on the Shackleton Ice Shelf. Wild soon produces it:

S. Y. Aurora,
Shackleton Glacier
20.2.1912

Dear Captain Davis,

. . . There will probably be some discussion about the position of this base, and no doubt some authorities will consider we are taking unjustifiable risks, and were this a barrier I should be of the same opinion. However, I am convinced that it is a glacier and with practically no movement. It is quite possible that during the twelve months of our stay here small portions will break away from the edge, but at the distance back at which I intend to build the hut I consider we are certainly as safe as Amundsen on the Ross Barrier.

You have made a good survey of the site yourself and will be able to satisfy any of the Party's relatives that they will be as comfortable here as is possible in the Antarctic . . .

Yours ever,
Frank Wild[57]

Look, it will hardly save Davis from the most severe criticism if Wild and his men subsequently perish, but it is something.

With talk rife among the crew regarding the precariousness of the ice-cliff encampment, Wild speaks to each member of his party individually, offering them the chance to immediately return with *Aurora*. 'If it is good enough for you, it is good enough for me,' each expedition member, to a man, replies.[58]

And so they are unanimous.

As Captain Davis and his men make ready to leave, one of Wild's men, Morton Moyes, says to him pleasantly, 'Have a good trip home.'

And they don't call him Gloomy for nothing, as Captain Davis is as quick as he is pointed with his reply: 'You'd better hope I do as nobody but me knows where you are and you'll be lost forever if I don't get home.'[59]

It is a terrifyingly fair point. But the decision is taken and now they must get on with it.

At 7 am on 21 February, with blankets strapped to their backs, Wild's men scramble over the side of *Aurora* then wave and cheer from their position on the sea ice as the sturdy little workhorse of a ship sails away and . . .

And watch out! Just an instant after the ship has left the shore, a massive piece of the ice shelf breaks away and tumbles down from the cliff to hit the sea with massive force. The result is a huge wave that not only causes *Aurora* to roll heavily but also breaks up the very part of the floe where they have landed their stores. It is a narrow escape, but at least the ship is away safely.

From the party's position high above the ice shelf, it takes a long time for *Aurora* to finally disappear from view. No fewer than 2500 miles from the nearest point of serious civilisation, Hobart, there are few people on the planet more isolated than they are.

And the men on *Aurora* are thinking of them in turn, none more than the skipper, as he gazes back on the spot where he has left the men he is ultimately responsible for, no matter what the letter in his pocket says. 'A black "oasis" in a white waste of snow! Was this an ice-shelf, attached to the land, on which we were leaving them?' wonders Davis.[60] Or is it a piece of ice destined to soon be part of the Southern Ocean, leaving Wild and his men to face a certain watery death?

PART FOUR

STRUGGLES

Chapter Eleven

Settling

*Thus February came and went. Already we had slipped into this
new life as if it had always been. Day by day the outside world faded
farther from our thoughts. It was indeed hard to imagine we had
ever been puppets tied to the routine of cities. Even thoughts of home
came as memories of a remote past. We lived in a world of our own,
a primitive world, in which the only standards were efficiency and
utility, and in which, in an all-satisfying way, we made our own
news, devised our own pleasures, and were busy with our own work.*

Charles Laseron, *South with Mawson*

Misfortunes rarely come singly.

Robert Falcon Scott, *Scott's Last Expedition*

21 February 1912, Cape Denison, Mawson settles in

Ah, but in terms of isolation, Mawson and his men run Wild and
the Western Party close. A month since being left here, and three
weeks after settling into their hut, they are now preparing to do
what is necessary to get their many scientific projects under way.
And there is much to do. From the first, Mawson has noted the
likely antediluvian history of this place – just near the hut, there
is evidence that the whole area was once covered by an ice sheet
that has now receded slightly, leaving behind the telltale grooves
and highly polished rock surfaces as traces of what once has been,

just as he saw in the Flinders Ranges – but now he and his fellow scientists want to find out everything they can about current conditions.

21 February 1912, Great Ice Barrier, Scott's Southern Party suffer another terrible day

Apart from the death of Taffy, it has been their worst day since turning back from the South Pole – a brutal, debilitating, devastating day of slow, agonising, exhausting progress.

Though they hoped for less freezing temperatures after leaving the high altitude of the Polar Plateau, things have in fact only got worse. And again, it is not just the discomfort of those temperatures that hurts them, nor even that because of such freezing conditions they need to burn through more fuel to do such things as melt snow for water. Fluctuating temperatures ranging between minus two and minus 17 degrees (at times as much as ten and 20 degrees below average for that time of year) continue to make the surface ever less conducive for their skis and the runners.

After the midday sun melts the top layer of snow, the surface refreezes and sandy, granular snow (known as sugar snow) is created. Scott likens it to 'pulling over desert sand, not the least glide in the world'.[1] It means the sledge does not gliiiiiiide so much as grip and grind.

Rather than fly across the surface, thus, the runners of their sledges tend to plough down, often to the point where the crossbars themselves hit the snow. Worse, as underfed and overworked as they are under these snow conditions, the men's rate of deterioration is increasing, making the sledges even *more* exhausting to pull. On this particular night, Scott writes in his diary, 'We never won a march of 8.5 miles[2] with greater difficulty, but we can't go on like this.'[3]

21 February 1912 and the day thereafter, Southern Ocean, Davis struggles to escape Antarctica's icy clutches

Just after 11 pm on this night, on the bridge of *Aurora*, Davis is suddenly as frantic and as fearful as he has ever been in his life, as his ship tries to break free of the pack of the massive and menacing ice-soldiers that has now suddenly surrounded the trembling ship. At first, in the face of it, he tries having the ship lie doggo, bringing it to a dead halt so he can hopefully see a way forward, but it is soon apparent that the bergs are moving, actually *closing in* on them! The obvious danger is that they will soon be hemmed in, frozen in place and unable to move for the winter, so the only alternative is to go at the bergs and try to make a break for it.

Now, Davis is a man who is serious by nature, a man truly at home on the high seas – bellowing orders when required, singing from the bridge when things are travelling well. Tonight, though, there is certainly no singing.

For the cries from the lookout are coming thick and fast: 'Ice to port!', 'Ice to starboard!', or 'Ice ahead!'. And Davis responds in kind, in an endless staccato: 'Port!', 'Starboard!', 'Steady!', 'Hard-a-port!', 'Full steam ahead!' and so on, as the ship tries to dodge her attackers. Still, the ice-soldiers cede nothing and keep coming. Just before midnight, the Gods of Freeze even send in their biggest soldier of all. Davis has just given the order to steer away from a berg that looms large on their starboard bow when, as he records it:

a veritable wall of ice seemed suddenly to rise up, like some enormous and menacing ghost, out of the haze before us, right across our course. There was no room to turn and not a moment to be lost. We were embayed. 'Full speed astern' was the only thing left.[4]

445

Full speed astern it is, and once more they just manage to avoid crashing into a massive iceberg.

And so it goes until the restless dawn arrives, giving enough light that Davis can at last see clearer water to the north. Reluctantly, the waters of Antarctica release their icy grip upon *Aurora* and, for the moment, the little ship is free to go.

But Davis knows only too well that had it not been for a merciful absence of wind, their fate would have been different indeed.

Last week of February 1912, Cape Denison, Mawson's men turn to science

It is time to begin their constructions for the purposes of science beyond the hut. Though they have been taking regular meteorological observations since 1 February – and the barometer and barograph can remain inside the hut – Mertz and Ninnis build two 'Stevenson screens', box-like structures with four louvred sides to hold the other key instruments. The boxes have one side on a hinge to allow access to the instruments, while all sides allow the free circulation of air without the instruments being blasted by the wind or affected by the sunlight. One box, right next to the hut on the eastern side, contains the thermometer, thermograph and hygrograph, while close by is the nephoscope, which measures the motion of the clouds.

Because the hut is situated in a small gully, the Campbell-Stokes solarimeter (recording hours of sunlight every day) and the anemometer and anemograph (respectively recording wind speed and direction) are located at the top of a small hill 450 feet to the east and 94 feet above sea level, on Anemometer Hill. The anemograph is located in the second Stevenson screen.

All of the instruments are attached to needles with ink buds, connected to slowly revolving drums upon which reams of graph paper are folded so that the changing conditions can be clearly graphed. Every day – rain, hail, shine, snow, gale, blizzard, summer, spring, winter, autumn, with *no* exceptions – the drums have to have the springs that power them rewound, the daily charts with their valuable recordings collected and new paper put in. The nibs of the pens must be kept full of special non-freezing ink.

Down by the water, a spot is found to drill through the ice, so that a float attached to a vertical wire can be lowered upon the water. As the float rises and falls with the tides, a geared pen above the ice rises and falls with it, drawing a line on a piece of paper wrapped around the slowly revolving drum that is the tide gauge.

All is set up so that, for the next year, the party will be able to record with extraordinary precision the ever-changing conditions they are enduring, and the men set to keeping records with a will, always determined that there will be no mishaps on their watch.

Despite being busy himself with myriad other matters, including getting ready for a forthcoming sledging journey to find out more about the region in which they have landed, Mawson has, of course, been right in the thick of each installation, just as he is quick to ensure that all data is accurate and precisely recorded.

In faraway Australia, at least in less academic circles, a man with his name might be known as Doug or Dougie. But not here. These intellectual and academic young men start calling him Dux Ipse, Latin for 'the leader himself', a sobriquet that seems to nicely sum up the intellectual, slightly aloof nature of the man.

Mawson's patrician nature notwithstanding, Frank Hurley would later claim that they 'looked up to him not only as a leader but loved him as a comrade and a man'.[5] This may not be the universal view, with Laseron noting that he is 'sometimes as stern as billy oh!'. Yet from behind an exterior that eschews familiarity, Mawson also proves to be, according to Laseron, 'Far more of a comrade than any of us thought he would be . . . he is such a worker, for from the start he has done more than any two of us.'[6]

Part of his work is spending enormous amounts of time, often while the others are resting, getting things organised. This includes, particularly in these early weeks in the hut, preparing a multitude of notices setting out all manner of procedures from cleaning duties to just who is on the roster to take the magnetic and meteorological readings. Meticulous in his approach, Mawson provides written instructions, so that everything is set out clearly and all can know their role. Cooking, for example. Do you need to know just what it entails, when it must be done and what must be served? Well, here it is, posted by Mawson on the wall of the tiny but efficient kitchen, which lies at the northern end of the hut, right next to Frank Hurley's darkroom:

```
The COOK is responsible for the culinary
matters and will be assisted by the messmen.
Duties commence at 7 am and continue until
   the washing and cleaning up are completed
   in the evening.
Meals will be served respectively at 8 am,
   1 pm, and 6.30 pm.
The 'piece de resistance' of dinner shall be
   as follows:   ,
   Monday - Penguin
   Tuesday - Seal
   Wednesday - Canned meats
   Thursday - Penguin
   Friday - Seal
   Saturday - Variable
   Sunday - Mutton.
   . . . The COOK is in charge of the main hut
   stove unit and shall continue to keep the
   mean hut-temperature above freezing point
   and not exceeding 45F.⁷
```

24 February 1912, South (Lower) Barrier Depot, in Scott's Southern Party, Christopher has the last neigh

It is the way of the world . . . or at least this part of the world. Whereas they had begun this journey 116 days earlier confidently striding out, before shortening their step somewhat as the journey across the Barrier began to sap their strength, and then staggering up the Beardmore Glacier, where their steps turned into a limp, now . . . now they are reduced to a bare shuffle. For on this day, they at last make it to Southern Barrier Depot, where, 12 weeks before, they left the remains of the highly troublesome pony Christopher. Little do they know . . .

For even in death the wretched pony causes them desperate grief. All this way, they have been looking forward to eating the brute's flesh, only to find – they can barely believe it, and certainly not stomach it – that his flesh is rotten. Just one bite makes them gag, and there is nothing to do but throw it away. It seems likely that one of the returning parties has dug up Christopher and not sufficiently buried him and . . . a few bursts of bright sun have done the rest. Or perhaps, after all, Christopher was indeed bad to the bone.

All they can do is tighten their belts another notch and keep going.

28 February 1912, Germany, with Paquita

No sooner has Paquita's ship arrived in the German port of Bremen after her long voyage from Australia than she posts a letter to Douglas. True, there is no way he will be able to actually read her letter until nearly a year later, when *Aurora* would return to pick up the expedition, but the two have agreed to write anyway, to put down their news as it happens, as a way of staying spiritually close to each other. She reports that she has had a wonderful trip to Europe, where she intends to catch up with many of her relatives in Holland. She played deck quoits with a charming young Frenchman she met, loved visiting the city of 'Colombo with its exquisite colouring, dirty old Port Said . . . and now Messina with its pitiful ruins'.[8]

Mostly, though, she has missed him. It has been hard for her seeing other couples wandering hand in hand on the deck, cuddling, dancing, talking, dining together when she is not only all alone but also with her fiancé in something close to the most remote spot on the planet.

'Here I have been longing and longing for you and now I must write. You said truly when you said that a sea voyage was redolent of love and longing. It is. I lean over the side and in the water see you – oh I think I love you now even much more than when we parted. How simply glorious it will be when we are on our trip together.'[9]

Sometimes, all but unconsciously, she would see a man with a silhouette like Douglas's and her heart would leap, and then she would remember, no, she was still by herself. She couldn't think straight for missing him, couldn't even read to take her mind off him. She writes:

Oh darling, we are far apart, aren't we? Does it ever come to you with a rush . . . If only nothing is happening to you but I think I should feel it . . . It is no use wishing you success because when you get this you will be coming back and it will be nearly over. But I know you have had success.[10]

29 February 1912 and the day thereafter, Cape Denison, Mawson steps out for the first time

Not yet, he hasn't, but he is working very hard towards it. And yes, he is missing Paquita greatly, though there is some chaff in the hut on this day that, given it is 29 February, it is a very good thing that they are all safe in Antarctica and can't be besieged by women asking them to marry them.

Still, just after 5 pm, Mawson, together with the astronomer, Lieutenant Robert Bage, and the meteorologist, Cecil Madigan, make their expedition's first significant foray away from the relative warmth and safety of the hut, to get a feel for the area they are in, understand the lie of the land and discover something of the conditions they would find. The first step is getting the sledge up the steep, long slope of the rise of the polar ice sheet to the immediate south of their hut and then trekking some five miles inland, at which point they find themselves in 'a great, wan, icy wilderness',[11] before the distant white skyline of a far higher hill that rises to a good 2000 feet in altitude. And beyond that? That is what they are intent on finding out, though they decide to do it by man-hauling, rather than using the dogs, as the animals are clearly not yet in good shape for such an arduous journey.

But it is not easy for the men, either. As it turns out, the wind is so strong, blowing the snow on the ground at them like a river, that they cannot proceed. After securing the sledge up the hill at a distance from the hut of one mile and 264 yards – according to the precious sledge-meter wheel – they beat a hasty retreat, before trying it again at noon the next day, when it goes better.[12]

Retrieving their sledge, they continue south, and as they proceed they are careful to plant flags every mile or so in the frozen terrain so they can be certain to find their way back. They get as far as five and a half miles before the weather closes in, and they camp for the night, a little anxious to be so far removed from the warmth and stability of the hut but getting used to it little by little. However, the following morning the gale becomes so strong it is overwhelming, and Mawson decides to again anchor the sledge and return to the hut, following the flags they have planted. They make it, just, and are much wiser for the experience.

They have penetrated the hinterland enough to get an impression of the inland ice as 'an unbroken plateau with no natural landmarks'.[13] And they have good reason to believe that such a passable surface may go a whole lot further, to the far horizons and beyond. From that hinterland, 'a vast solid stream of ice flowed, with heavily crevassed downfalls near the coast',[14] and yet, as difficult as it was in the wind, they managed to traverse it. In warmer weather, it should be much easier. All they need do now is continue their preparations and get ready for the coming spring, when the sledging parties can hopefully head out in earnest in both directions along the coast and at angles slightly inland.

The hut they have returned to, however, is not quite the oasis it was. For by now the wind is so strong, so relentless, that it is finding its way through every tiny chink in the Winter Quarters' armour – much of the timber, which had become sodden on the deck of *Aurora*, has twisted a little in the freezing conditions – meaning a great deal of energy, time and resources must be spent sealing those chinks. When they are outside, however, they just have to learn to live with those winds . . . and, for the most part, so they do, because they have no choice.

In their first days after *Aurora* sailed away, when the wind blew at hurricane force, the men fell over and were swept away with ever greater velocity until they were hard up against the sastrugi some 30 yards or more away. This obliged them to stay mainly indoors. Over time, however, as the wind blows with ever more ferocity and frequency, this becomes problematic. To stay indoors when the wind is howling would mean staying indoors almost all the time. So they adapt.

Bit by bit, they learn how, by wearing Swiss crampons – specially designed shoes with sharp studs on the bottom to dig into the ice – it is possible to 'hurricane-walk'. That is, by keeping your body rigid and thrusting your torso forward on the wind, it is possible to gain a bizarre point of equilibrium at an angle closer to zero than 45 degrees. Then, by digging your crampons into the ground and bracing your feet against every tiny projection of rock or ice, you can, step by step, go about your business. Those unequipped or less game are reduced to crawling along on hands and knees like infants. But for those who have crampons and who practise, it is found to be possible to move fairly comfortably in a 70-mph wind and stay standing in 80 mph.

At such velocity, the rushing wind is a living, killing thing, slapping your face, pulling your hair, tearing at your entire body, billowing into your clothes, into every tiny nook and cranny where it can get a purchase, even as the breath is sucked from your lungs and your ears are filled with the roar of a thousand banshees screaming your death song. And then it gets stronger and faster still.

In 90- and 100-mph winds, not even the best of the men can hurricane-walk: there is no last man left standing, and all are brought back to the same level, wriggling about on the ground like snakes, giving the wind as little surface as possible on which to get a grip. It is best to have your ice-axe with you, in case you are bowled over and find yourself sliding straight towards the Southern Ocean.

Certainly, it is extraordinarily difficult to experience such conditions, but as scientists it is also fascinating to experience 'katabatic' winds first-hand.

For they know that what is happening is that the freezing air on the Polar Plateau is denser and heavier than the far warmer air above the water by the coast where they are situated. The warmer air rises, to be replaced by the dense frigid air pulled down by gravity from the plateau, where the temperature is usually 15 to 20 degrees colder than the coast. And the spot where they have made their home, beneath a glacial slope pointing down towards the sea, increases these katabatic wind speeds even more. They are in one of the few places in all of Antarctica where 'an open sea throughout the year lies in direct contact with a steep shore',[15] and the result is they are in fact living in the windiest place on earth at sea level, frequently suffering the onslaught of a veritable avalanche of air. While the average wind speed in Melbourne is 8 mph year on year, here it is 44 mph.

As scientists, though, they note not merely its extraordinary speed but also its particularities. By observation, they establish that no matter its strength, its direction is always coming from within a point of south-south-east, while high above them they note by the drift of the clouds that the wind there is coming from nearly the exact opposite direction.

1 March 1912 and the day thereafter, Mid-Barrier Depot, death begins to stalk Scott's party close

Disaster. Sheer disaster. Though hugely relieved to arrive at the depot that they left almost 14 weeks earlier, in an identical situation to that at the South Barrier Depot they find that the thing they most need apart from food – paraffin oil, to heat their food, melt their ice to water and heat their tent – is in devastatingly short supply. Fuel tins that were expected to be full to the brim only have a little sloshing around at the bottom. How has this happened?

A large part of it seems to have been their positioning: the red tins have been left at the top of the cairns both for accessibility and visibility. Alas, just as the warmth of the sun may have rotted the flesh of Christopher, it appears to have also vaporised the fuel, and a significant quantity has escaped – either through a flaw in the leather container seals or possibly through the tins' seams, on occasion contaminating the food supplies beneath.[16] And though it

Portrait of Ernest Henry Shackleton as he appeared in the frontispiece of his *Nimrod* expedition (BAE 1908–09) book, *The Heart of the Antarctic*, published by William Heinemann in 1909. (Bridgeman Art Library)

On 16 January 1909, Mackay, David and Mawson (L to R) raised the Union Jack in the place reckoned to be the South Magnetic Pole before beating hasty retreat back to Relief Inlet. (Mawson Centre, South Australian Museum)

The South Magnetic Pole Party relieved by *Nimrod* at Relief Inlet on 4 February 1909. (Mawson Centre, South Australian Museum)

Give that man a smoke. The Southern Party – Wild, Shackleton, Marshall and Adams (L to R) – safely back aboard *Nimrod* having come within 97 geographical miles of the South Pole. (Mawson Centre, South Australian Museum)

On his return to Adelaide in April 1909 following the *Nimrod* expedition, Mawson is borne aloft by his students and carried from the train station to the university. (Mawson Centre, South Australian Museum)

On 27 January 1911, Scott's Eastern Party were astonished to discover Amundsen's ship *Fram* already in the Bay of Whales. (Bridgeman Art Library)

Roald Amundsen in polar kit.
(Bridgeman Art Library)

Royal Navy Commander Robert Falcon Scott was just 33 when he led the *Discovery* expedition (BNAE 1901–04) to Antarctica. On his return, Scott was soon promoted to captain. (Bridgeman Art Library)

Recruited from the 6th Iniskilling Dragoons, famed horseman and Boer War soldier Captain Lawrence Edward Grace Oates took great care of the white Manchurian ponies during their month-long stabling aboard *Terra Nova* at the end of 1911. (Bridgeman Art Library)

The *Terra Nova* expedition's Winter Quarters, Cape Evans, with the magisterial Mt Erebus prominent in the background. (Bridgeman Art Library)

With pipe and pen, 'the Owner' in his den at Winter Quarters, Cape Evans. Note the fur mitts hanging from the wall above his head. (Bridgeman Art Library)

Captain Scott's birthday was celebrated with a sumptuous dinner on 6 June 1911. Scott sits at the head of the table, with Bill Wilson on his left, and Bowers second on Wilson's left. Oates is standing on the left as viewed. Note the men's traditional sledging flags, proudly hung from the ceiling. (Bridgeman Art Library)

The *Terra Nova* expedition's Winter Quarters, Cape Evans, after the winter of 1911. Scott can be seen standing in the centre holding a ski pole, with Oates second on his right. Bill Wilson is sitting in front of Scott, clasping his wrist in his hand, with Bowers on his far right and Edgar Evans second on his left next to Crean on the end. (Bridgeman Art Library)

Three men work as one to man-haul their sledge over sastrugi during a blizzard. Scene painted by *Terra Nova*'s chief scientific officer and expedition artist Dr 'Bill' Wilson. (Bridgeman Art Library)

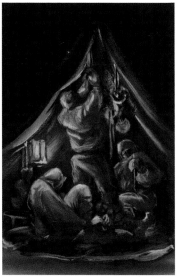

Dr 'Bill' Wilson's painting shows how cramped the conditions are with three men in a pyramid tent, let alone four, let alone five. (Bridgeman Art Library)

Cold reality. Forestalled by over a month, on 18 January 1912, Scott, Bowers, Wilson and Evans (L to R) discovered Amundsen's tent *Poleheim*, 'The Home of the Pole', at the South Pole. (Bridgeman Art Library)

In a rough polar equivalent of committing bodies to the depths, Scott's men entombed the tent containing the bodies of their leader, Wilson and Bowers in snow, and a cross fashioned from a bound pair of skis was placed on top. (Bridgeman Art Library)

Dux Ipse of the Australasian Antarctic Expedition, 1911–14, signed four months before the AAE departed Hobart bound for Antarctica. (Mawson Centre, South Australian Museum)

Rrrravishing! Mawson was instantly attracted to Paquita Delprat when they met over dinner at her father's home in Broken Hill in 1909. (Courtesy of Emma McEwin and Gareth Thomas)

In the stillness of a late afternoon, there remains no question: Douglas and Paquita are deeply in love. (Courtesy of Emma McEwin and Gareth Thomas)

Mawson and Shackleton in the latter's Regent Street, London, offices in 1910, planning the expedition that, following Shackleton's withdrawal, was to become the Australasian Antarctic Expedition. (Mawson Centre, South Australian Museum)

Mid-February 1912, *Aurora*, drawn up against the fast ice at the AAE's western base atop the Shackleton Ice Shelf, 1500 miles west of Mawson's main base, attracts local interest. (Mitchell Library, State Library of New South Wales)

Captain John King Davis, master of *Aurora* and second in command of the Australasian Antarctic Expedition. (Mawson Centre, South Australian Museum)

Ever the geologist, Mawson is seen here examining an outcrop of exposed gneiss rock in the vicinity of his Winter Quarters at Commonwealth Bay. (Mawson Centre, South Australian Museum)

The AAE's youngest member, 19-year-old Percy Correll, kneels at the edge of an ice cliff in the vicinity of Commonwealth Bay. (Mawson Centre, South Australian Museum)

Roped to an outcrop, Percy Correll takes in a view over Commonwealth Bay. The Barrier can be seen stretching off in the background. (Mawson Centre, South Australian Museum)

View over Commonwealth Bay from the AAE's Winter Quarters. (Mawson Centre, South Australian Museum)

By wearing Swiss crampons – specially designed shoes with sharp studs on the bottom to dig into the ice – Mawson's men find it possible to 'hurricane-walk' around Winter Quarters at Cape Denison. (Mitchell Library, State Library of New South Wales)

You know things are slow during the winter months when Frank Hurley's trimming of Jack Hunter's beard attracts such an interested crowd. (Mawson Centre, South Australian Museum)

The AAE celebrates midwinter's day at Commonwealth Bay, 21 June 1912. Mawson is in the dark coat, Ninnis is second on his right and Mertz is front centre with moustache. (Mawson Centre, South Australian Museum)

At the end of the long winter, the inseparable Mertz 'n' Ninnis (L to R) attend to their charges in preparation for their Far Eastern journey with Mawson. (Mawson Centre, South Australian Museum)

Robert Bage cooking hoosh, and Frank Hurley in his sleeping bag, in Aladdin's Cave, the AAE sledging parties' home away from home, excavated during August 1912. (Mawson Centre, South Australian Museum)

During the spring sledging journeys, the temperature dropped so low that the men's helmets froze to their faces and 'ice masks' formed. Premature removal could result in loss of beard and skin! (Mawson Centre, South Australian Museum)

Mertz leads his willing team up the ice slope behind Cape Denison. Note the dogs in fan formation. (Mitchell Library, State Library of New South Wales)

Mush, you dawgies, mush! (Mawson Centre, South Australian Museum)

10 November 1912, day one of Mawson's Far Eastern journey. The leader rests against one of the Party's sledges on the short march to Aladdin's Cave. (Mawson Centre, South Australian Museum)

Solid ice covered with snow is often no more than a snow bridge across a bottomless crevasse. (Mawson Centre, South Australian Museum)

The cut-down half-sledge with cooking box and mast man-hauled by Mawson for a month during his return from the Far Eastern journey. (Mitchell Library, State Library of New South Wales)

Memorial cross and plaque created during the AAE's second winter to honour Ninnis and Mertz. (Mawson Centre, South Australian Museum)

is a devastating error on the part of individuals unknown, as with everything else, Scott must bear the ultimate responsibility.

Men in the Antarctic without fuel are almost inevitably destined to be frozen men, and as on this day the temperature drops as far as minus 40 degrees, that freezing will not take long if they run out. Yes, they still have a little fuel left from their last depot, but that cannot last long. To add to their many woes, the temperature has plummeted still *further*, and day by day they must face temperatures ten to 20 degrees below average, and 40 to 50 degrees lower than Teddy Evans and his men experienced just a month before.

The most pressing problem, though, is the fuel and the fact that they simply don't have enough of it. Again using the calculus of catastrophe, a desperate Scott records their perilous position in his diary on the following day after lunch: 'With most rigid economy it can scarce carry us to the next depot . . . 71 miles[17] away.'[18]

All of their thoughts now focus fiercely on the salvation in the form of paraffin and biscuits that should await them at the Mt Hooper Depot – the spot that Teddy Evans's abandoned motor-sledge party established three and a half months earlier – if they can just get there.

After all, prior to departure 19 weeks previously, on 20 October 1911, Scott formally instructed Meares to bring the dogs out to meet the Southern Party:

about March 1 in latitude 82 or 82.30. If you are then in a position to advance a few short marches or 'mark time' for five or six days on food brought, or ponies killed, you should have a good chance of effecting your object.[19]

True, those orders to Meares had been complicated by the fact that the dog-handler and his dogs stayed with them two weeks longer than planned, meaning he had been four weeks late back to Cape Evans, but hopefully something would have been sorted out.

They press on the best they can. But it is hideously difficult. In terms of pulling, the men soon realise they have lost a quarter of their power after the now seriously struggling Oates reveals his frostbitten, gangrenous feet, all the toes turned black as . . . death.

'Misfortunes rarely come singly,' records Scott.[20]

And sometimes they really do announce themselves with a darkening sky, a further sharp drop in the temperature and an ill wind growing in strength. For just when they are most in need of benign weather, the cloudy columns of snowdrift they can see advancing from the south soon hit them, and this wretched wind blowing in dark and stormy weather makes it seem as if the full-blown winter coming from the Pole they have left has finally overtaken them. The following morning, it takes them an hour and a half to get into their foot gear.

May God help them, indeed, because it is starting to look like Providence will not.

Early March 1911, Cape Denison's Winter Quarters, Mawson's men build up

And now the focus of Mawson's party switches to mounting the rest of their scientific program. One of Mawson's principal aims in this field is to continue his research on the magnetic fields, which he first began during his expedition with Shackleton four years earlier, particularly focusing on how the position of the South Magnetic Pole changes over time.

To do this properly – and that is the only way that Dux Ipse accepts *anything* being done – the men now busy themselves finishing off another two small structures, known as the Magnetograph House and the Absolute Magnetic Hut. They are 50 yards apart around 400 yards north-east of the main hut, far enough that there will be no magnetic influence on the sensitive recording equipment that those huts will contain. It is for the same reason that the huts are constructed with copper, rather than iron, nails.[21]

Once the Magnetograph House is finished, the chief magnetician, Azi Webb, will oversee the efficient installation of the instruments, including the magnetograph. All up, the equipment will precisely record the variations in horizontal and vertical components, as well as the absolute value, of the total magnetic force, minute by minute, hour by hour, around the clock and allow them to monitor sudden large, irregular variations referred to as 'magnetic storms'.[22]

Ensuring they are not carrying anything magnetic – such as knives, belt buckles and even boot fittings – Webb and his assistant magneticians will take turns manning the nearby Absolute Magnetic Hut to calculate standard values as a check against the automatically recorded information.

Because Mawson's party is soon due to take part in synchronised magnetic readings with the German Antarctic expedition led by Lieutenant Wilhelm Filchner and other observatories at low latitudes, the erection of these huts is a priority.

4 March 1912 and six days thereafter, One Ton Depot, Cherry-Garrard's Dog Party look for Scott and his men

The checklist is sobering:
- The dog expert Meares is in fact going home, 'recalled by family affairs'.[23]
- The still seriously scurvy-stricken Teddy Evans is shortly to be sent back to England on *Terra Nova.*
- Dr Atkinson is busy nursing Teddy.

That leaves . . . the young and enthusiastic Oxford graduate Apsley

Cherry-Garrard, along with Demetri and two teams of dogs, to head out into the wilderness to One Ton Depot, 140 miles south of Hut Point, and possibly further, to meet up with Scott's returning party and help them get home. No matter that in his whole life Cherry-Garrard has 'never driven one dog, let alone a team of them'[24] and is no expert on navigation. It has to be him as, effectively, he is the last man left standing.

Just where this meeting point with Scott may lie is nigh on impossible to predict, dependent as it is on the Southern Party's rate of progress, unknown since the return of Evans's final support party. Matters have been further confused by Scott's lack of clear instructions to the respective returning parties regarding where he is expecting the Dog Party to get to. He has not even been totally clear as to just whose responsibility it is to get a new supply of dog food to One Ton Depot, so that this Dog Party, when it gets there, can easily keep going further south to the Mt Hooper Depot and even beyond. All is confused.

Still, it is hoped that Scott and his men will be somewhere in the area around One Ton Depot, and before leaving Cape Evans Atkinson told Cherry-Garrard, 'If Scott [has] not arrived at One Ton Depot before you, you must judge what to do.'[25]

So be it. Making his calculations based on the final support party's rate of return, Cherry-Garrard has been straining his eyes the whole way on the reckoning that Scott and his men may already be *north* of One Ton Depot, and his fervent hope is to either see their ethereal figures emerge from the snowy sleet or, on a clear day, spot them as tiny specks in the distance.

Scanning . . . scanning . . . scanning. Nothing. Nothing. Nothing.

After eight days' sledging in deteriorating conditions, Cherry-Garrard, Demetri and the dogs do indeed reach One Ton Depot on this day – in full-blown blizzard conditions – to find not only that Scott is not there but also that he and his men have not yet been there. That can only mean they remain somewhere to their south, between here and the South Pole.

What to do? The situation is now delicate. Cherry-Garrard and Demetri have hauled a maximum sledging load for that time of the year: food for the men themselves for 21 days; food for the dogs for 24 days; and a further two weeks of supplies for the Scott party, including fuel and requested delicacies. It is this amount of dog food, though, that is the most telling factor in the decision Cherry-Garrard must make, as, amid all of Scott's confused instructions, the bottom line is that One Ton Depot holds not one *crumb* of a dog biscuit.

The mathematics of it get even more grim as the blizzard closes in for four of the next six days, as they deplete the supplies they do have. It is still possible to keep going a bit further south for a day or so, even if, in the conditions, it would be difficult and they would risk missing the Southern Party coming the other way. Still, unaware of Scott's abominable situation some 65 miles south of Mt Hooper Depot at this very time, it certainly does not appear to be a matter of extreme urgency that he do so. In fact, Cherry-Garrard recalls Scott mentioning on the outward journey that his party held sufficient supplies to be able to return to Hut Point on full rations as late as 27 March or even early April. And didn't Scott also say – reiterated in Atkinson's instructions before they left – that the purpose of the Dog Party is only to speed the Southern Party home, rather than 'succour' them?

Following Scott's instructions to protect the worn-out dogs for the following season, Cherry-Garrard even increases their daily rations as a way of combatting the unseasonal and extreme cold that sees the temperature plummet to minus 40 degrees. He still has nine days of dog food in hand, and so Cherry-Garrard must finally give an answer to the question to which Atkinson has instructed him to apply his judgement: go on or hold on one more day at One Ton Depot and return on the remaining eight days of food?[26] Kill one of the dogs for food, to give them the capacity to go even further south? After wrestling with the dilemma for some time, Cherry-Garrard finally takes decisive action . . .

6 March 1912, 65 miles south of Mt Hooper Depot, Scott's Southern Party struggle on

'God help us, we can't keep up this pulling, that is certain,' Scott has written in his journal. 'Amongst ourselves we are unendingly cheerful, but what each man feels in his heart I can only guess. Pulling on foot gear in the morning is getter slower and slower, therefore every day more dangerous.'[27]

Now, three days later, Scott recognises that their situation has moved beyond desperate – it is critical. Even as they manage to struggle just over six miles forward, the witches' tempest shrieks with no sign of abatement.

No one is more affected than Lawrence Oates, who by now has such a swollen, frostbitten and blackened left foot that he has to slit his finnesko up the front to allow it on. Oates's greatest hero, of course, is Napoleon Bonaparte, and just as the French emperor had so famously lost all but 40,000 of the 450,000 soldiers who invaded Russia in the summer of 1812 only to still be caught there in that cruel winter, Oates is now experiencing what so many of those soldiers experienced: trying to get back to safety, clumping forward through a frozen wasteland, undernourished, over-frozen and forever teetering on total collapse.

And though there is little Uncle Bill can do for him, the good doctor doesn't stop trying, so much so that Scott grows concerned over dear Bill's self-sacrifice. Oates's parlous condition means he is now unable to pull the sledge, yet the Soldier marches on, only stopping to sit on the sledge while the others search for the track. His condition is coming to resemble that of the tragic Taffy shortly before he died, and they all know it.

Scott writes, 'If we were all fit I should have hopes of getting through, but the poor Soldier has become a terrible hindrance, though he does his utmost and suffers much I fear.'[28]

Scott realises that, truly, their only hope is that the dogs have been to Mt Hooper to replenish supplies there, most particularly oil, because without that they are extremely unlikely to pull through.

Whatever happens, though, 'I should like to keep the track to the end.'[29]

6 March 1912, London, Kathleen Scott hears the news . . .

Wonderful! Kathleen Scott can barely believe it is true, but an unending series of phone calls from reporters are the cause of her joy. A rumour has started circulating that Captain Scott has become the first man to conquer the South Pole and has arrived back at base safely! Does Mrs Scott know anything? No, she does not, but surely such a rumour must be based on something, mustn't it? *Surely* confirmation will arrive shortly? When no confirmation does come, she decides to rein in her joy until such times as it does. But still nothing.

The day passes and the phone calls slow . . .[30]

7 March 1912, Cape Evans, *Terra Nova* gets ready to leave without Scott and his men

It is time to go. The acting commander in Scott's absence, the still seriously scurvy-stricken Teddy Evans, is brought aboard *Terra Nova*. In the exact path of Shackleton before him back in 1903, Evans is to be invalided home. In his absence, Atch Atkinson – who has closely attended Teddy since his dire return from the south – officially assumes command.

With the pack ice starting to close in, *Terra Nova* reluctantly turns north for Lyttelton without Scott's polar party, while also abandoning Campbell's Northern Party to their fate at Evans Cove, north of the Drygalski Ice Tongue. (Twice over the last month, *Terra Nova* tried to break through the pack ice and twice she failed. The crew simply have to hope that the Wicked Mate and his men will be able to get through the winter on their own and perhaps make their own way back to Cape Evans in the next spring.[31])

It is a pity that *Terra Nova* is not able to take either party back, but on the other hand there is, really, concern only for the Wicked Mate's party and not for Scott's. For while the Wicked Mate and his men are going to have adapt to the unforeseen circumstance of not being relieved, as far as anyone knows Scott's party is still on track and on time.

7 March 1912, Hobart, Amundsen arrives aboard *Fram*

Early this morning, a little the worse for wear, an unidentified barquentine enters the Derwent River under power. In due course, she responds to the Mt Nelson signal station: she be *Fram*, come back from deep within the Antarctic Circle, from out of the Bay of Whales in the Ross Sea. News out, the crowd gathering by the docks are soon disappointed, as *Fram* drops anchor in splendid isolation some distance off Battery Point.

Once Amundsen arrives on shore by launch, the members of the press gang, who gather like baby chicks around a mother hen, are also let down. In the manner of so many explorers who have a contract for exclusive rights with a major newspaper – in this case, it is with London's *Daily Chronicle* for £2000 – Amundsen refuses to answer any questions regarding his farthest south and whether or not his party have claimed the coveted crown.

'Please do not bring in the Pole, but say rather when I got so near to the Antarctic regions, which I had already visited, I felt I must make another voyage there before turning to the northwards,' dictates the 'dour Norse sea king', appearing to believe his own press.[32]

Faithful to his contract he may be, 'but the "Silence is Golden" puts a very sordid aspect upon the heroism of exploration,' writes a nonplussed Hobart *Mercury* reporter.[33]

What Amundsen does say is that he is keenly interested in Mawson's expedition and that, from what he has heard, the Australian would make a 'clever leader and that the expedition should have valuable and interesting results'.[34]

Like Shackleton, Amundsen has also sworn his crew to silence, and soon the Chief is whisked away to the Norwegian consul's residence, from where he sends the scoop, in a typically coded, brief cable to his brother Leon at home in Norway. Feverishly decoded by Leon, it proves to read: '*Ja!* – Pole attained fourteenth–seventeenth December 1911. All well.'[35]

As Leon knows, the most important thing now is to first inform the King, before letting the press and the rest of the world know.

Alas, alas, initially in London there is confusion, and the first of the newspaper banners shrieks, 'SCOTT AT SOUTH POLE – BRILLIANT VICTORY'.[36] Then come the first of the garbled corrections, the cables saying: Amundsen arrived South Pole, states Scott has reached the pole. In her home, Kathleen Scott is besieged by newspaper reporters, all with their own versions of those cables, but this time she refuses to let herself go. Such cables are worthless, she says, as they are unsigned, and they would only make themselves and their papers ridiculous by publishing them.

'But they heeded me not and published far and wide,' she confides to the detailed diary she has been keeping so her husband, when he returns, can know all of her and young Peter's life without him.[37] The day becomes a pandemonium of telegrams, phone calls, visitors and insistent reporters trying to get a comment out of her. Wary, and worried, she refuses to respond, simply sending a short note to *The Times* and *The Morning Post*, saying she has no reason to believe such reports. The best she can, she tries to concentrate on completing a bust of her friend, Aubrey Waterfield.

And then, the denouement. A worldwide exclusive, simultaneously shared by *The Daily Chronicle* in London and *The New York Times*, flashes the true news of Amundsen's historic success:

AMUNDSEN REACHES THE SOUTH POLE; STAYS FOUR DAYS, DEC. 14 TO 17, PARTY ALL WELL HE TELLS THE NEW YORK TIMES.[38]

'Captain Amundsen has attained the geographical South Pole, the long sought for spot, and that finishes record breaking as far as the ends of the earth are concerned,' writes Shackleton in an exclusive article for the same paper.

'The whole world has been discovered,' enthuses the paper itself.

The news is like a flaming comet, and as one the planet gravitates towards it with eyes ablaze. Nowhere in the heavens nor on earth is the news more passionately celebrated than in Norway, where one paper joyously proclaims, 'NORWAY'S FLAG AT THE SOUTH POLE. Today, town and country put out all flags. We are all Roald Amundsen's fellow countrymen,' and the rhyme in an Oslo variety theatre runs:

Roald Amundsen ran,
Faster than Scott can.
Miles ahead of Scott,
Roald to the Pole has got![39]

With regard to Scott, the English-language press's initial stoical optimism – maybe he has actually beaten Amundsen to the Pole or arrived simultaneously? – soon gives way to the realisation that the glorious crown of being the first to reach the Pole (either north or south, for that matter) will never be worn by an Englishman. At least they could focus on the considerable contribution Scott's party will have made to the advancement of science.

'England will wait most anxiously for news of the Scott expedition,' opines the *Chicago Daily Tribune*.[40]

When news of Amundsen's success reaches Kathleen Scott's ears, the explorer's wife is immediately thrown into a state of shock and despair. Mrs Scott has long harboured a distinct dislike of Amundsen, and Shackleton's public recognition of the Norwegian's success provokes her to privately exclaim of the disloyal Anglo-Irishman that she would 'willingly assist at that man's annihilation'.[41]

Where, oh where, is her husband now?

9 March 1912, Mt Hooper Depot, Scott's Southern Party discover the wrong kind of broken seal

After the most bitter pulling of their lives, pushing their exhausted and starving bodies far beyond the limits they were previously aware of, Scott, Bowers, Wilson and Oates make it to the Mt Hooper Depot. Their most earnest hope is to see a support party waiting for them with dogs, or even that the depot has been resupplied, but . . . there is . . . nothing.

The depot is there, just as they left it in mid-November, but that is all. *That is all!* The only thing leavening their grievous desperation at finding their dreams dashed is that it is at least something to have made it to this repository of food and fuel, and eagerly they scrabble the snow away to find that . . . much of the fuel has evaporated.

Again, the problem is possibly some kind of inadequate lid seal or defect in the tin seams. It is now more unlikely than ever that they can make it to One Ton Depot, 77 miles away, and if Scott is not mistaken, this is a death warrant, perhaps for them all, but certainly for Oates.

He writes in his journal that evening, 'Things steadily downhill, Oates's foot worse. He has rare pluck and must know that he can never get through.'[42]

That, Titus does – almost.

The Soldier nevertheless has just enough of the spark of life left in him to ask Bill Wilson on this night in the gasping, whispery wisp of a voice of one who is likely not long for this world whether Uncle Bill thinks he has any chance of living.

Wilson looks at him, considers it and decides to lie.

'I do not know,' he says simply, but with great compassion.[43]

But Scott does, for he has overheard the conversation and now writes in his journal, baldly:

In point of fact he has none. Apart from him, if he went under now, I doubt whether we could get through. With great care we might have a dog's chance, but no more. The weather conditions are awful, and our gear gets steadily more icy and difficult to manage. At the same time of course poor Titus is the greatest handicap. He keeps us waiting in the morning until we have partly lost the warming effect of our good breakfast, when the only wise policy is to be up and away at once . . . Poor chap! It is too pathetic to watch him; one cannot but try to cheer him up.[44]

They now, really, have only two chances left of survival. The first is that they make it to One Ton Depot. This is an unlikely prospect, such terrible condition are they in, but one they must try for. And the second is that a relief party is on its way to them, with dogs and food and fuel . . .

11 March 1912 and several weeks thereafter, Cape Denison, Mawson and his men send signals

In terms of major infrastructure to install at Cape Denison, what remains are the two tall wireless masts at a far enough distance away from the huts that if they are blown over they will not come crashing down upon it.

It requires some serious grunt and engineering. Each mast has four segments, and each of those segments needs to be secured with ten stout 'strops' of rope anchored into hard rock to hold it against a wind that always wants to flatten it, like everything else above ice level. The problem is that the work to raise those segments can only be done in comparatively calm weather, which is rare, and . . .

And what is that?

What is what?

That . . . *silence*. Every now and then, there is a lull in the all-but-ceaseless roar of the wind, and it always stuns the men. Charles Laseron records:

> Our ear-drums commence to throb as with a great noise. Somebody speaks and his voice cracks like a whip on the stillness. For the wind has stopped, and, accustomed as we are to its howl, the silence can literally be felt. For a while we speak almost in whispers, our heads are ringing and we feel very uncomfortable.[45]

But hasten!

For with every rare lull in the roar, there is a mad dash in the hut as everyone rushes to put on their Burberrys, gloves, balaclavas and beanies, and shortly thereafter the hut disgorges through the veranda exit 'a crowd of muffled figures . . . dragging ropes, blocks, picks, and shovels'.[46] Within minutes, all hands are employed, 'collecting rocks as weights, boring holes in the hard rock, or digging foundations for the masts themselves'.[47]

In a radius of 80 yards around where the two masts will stand, ice holes are dug. Cairns of heavy boulders are gathered as the men use dynamite to blast deep holes to hold each lowest section of mast – a ten-inch-square, 30-foot-long piece of Oregon timber.[48] The three higher sections than this are also 30 feet long, though progressively thinner, and if all goes well the masts will get to 120 feet high – but there remains a lot of work to do, and freezing work it is, frequently causing the nip of frostbite.

Always, the men return to the hut with great relief. It is *unimaginable*, horrifying to even think of, what it would be like to be caught out in such temperatures without a warm shelter to retreat to.

11 March 1912, Great Ice Barrier, Scott's Southern Party face the toughest choice

Finally, Scott wheedles out of Wilson the easiest way to solve all their problems. It turns out that in his old friend's medical kit there are sufficient opium tablets to put them all to sleep, painlessly, forever.

At Scott's insistence, the extremely reluctant and deeply religious Wilson – for whom taking one's own life is a sin – gives Scott, Bowers and Oates 30 tablets each.

Should they find themselves near the point of death, unable to stand it any more, with no further point in suffering needlessly, then these tablets will make it easy for them. For himself, Wilson keeps a vial of morphine handy. This will not kill him, but at least it will ease the pain.

If the blizzard stops, and *if* the party can quickly get going again, they still have an outside chance of getting to One Ton Depot, which Scott calculates as now being 63 miles away. At best, he estimates, they can make seven miles a day . . . but they have food and fuel for only seven days – bringing them up 14 miles short. They need a miracle. They really *do* need to see men with dogs coming their way, bearing supplies and help.

12 March 1912, Hobart, Captain Davis has a homecoming of sorts

Shortly after noon, *Aurora*, under the tight control of Davis, steams up the Derwent River, passing *Fram* still lying at her anchorage in Sandy Bay. Having been informed by the pilot of Amundsen's success, as *Aurora* passes *Fram*, 16 years her junior, the ship from the Mawson expedition dips her flags in a show of respect, as a proud mother might honour the success of her child. Still not content, Davis and his crew crowd the deck and offer three mighty cheers for *Fram*, Amundsen and his brave crew, who have won the honour of being first to the Pole.

Aurora makes fast to the pier (with only nine tons of coal left in her hold – the equivalent of the smell of an oily rag for the ship's engine) and, once ashore, Captain Davis continues to honour Amundsen's victory. He tells the *Mercury*:

> I was surprised to hear that the *Fram* was in Hobart but was very pleased to hear that Captain Amundsen had returned safely, having reached the South Pole. Those who have followed his previous work will probably not have been at all surprised at his success. We are anxiously waiting news of Captain Scott, and we hope that he also will return with a full measure of success.[49]

Meanwhile, cables have continued to pour in from all parts of the globe congratulating Amundsen and his men on their achievement, including ones from the Royal Geographical Society and the former president of the United States Theodore Roosevelt. Now, for the first time in the history of Hobart, two mighty and pugnacious polar vessels belonging to separate Antarctic expeditions are in the port. Time to celebrate!

13 March 1912, Western Base, Frank Wild and his men break the ice

Since having been dropped off by *Aurora* three weeks earlier, Wild and his men have devoted all their energy to getting themselves established, and that is precisely what they are doing on this early morning. After having breakfast at 6 am, they get to work putting up the masts to hold their antenna and by 8.30 am are just getting them into position when . . .

When before their eyes another huge chunk of the ice shelf on which they have made their home, on which their entire existence depends, calves off, and, with a resounding roar, many thousands of tons of it fall into the ocean. 'The tremendous waves raised by the fall of this mass smash into fragments all the floe left in the bay'[50] and take away the snow hill they have been using to get up and down the cliffs from their hut to the shore and back, meaning they will have no further chance to hunt seals and penguins. All that remains between them and the water is 'a perpendicular cliff, sixty to one hundred feet above the water',[51] and their old landing place has been completely obliterated. It is, notes Wild in his diary, 'a rather serious matter'.[52] Quite.

The only good thing? The ice on which they have built their home is still there. But it is a worry all right.

Somewhere, surely, Captain Davis is stirring restlessly, his worst nightmare barely averted, this time . . .

13 March 1912, Hobart, Captain Grumpy meets a happy man

The following day, Captain Davis boards *Fram* to pay his personal respects to Amundsen and is mightily impressed. 'After seeing the *Fram*, and her equipment,' he shortly afterwards tells the *Examiner*, 'it was easy to understand why Captain Amundsen returned successful. Every little detail had been thought out with the greatest care.'[53]

Returning the honour, Amundsen goes to lunch aboard *Aurora*, where Captain Davis, following the flavour of the day, toasts Amundsen's victory. Amundsen responds by saying that he has a keen interest in the success of Mawson's expedition and is glad that things have got off to a good start.

He has nothing but high praise for Davis's 'splendid' seamanship in successfully completing all he has had to do and for *Aurora*'s seaworthiness in accomplishing this.

To back up his words, responding to Mawson's request, Amundsen arranges to transfer 21 of his fine-looking Greenland dogs, including one that accompanied Amundsen to the Pole, to the quarantine station to be picked up by *Aurora* on her relief journey to Antarctica.

15 March 1912, Great Ice Barrier, Cherry-Garrard and Demetri . . . head back to base

For Cherry-Garrard, five days earlier it had begun with a simple cry of 'Hut, hut', a sharp flick of the whip and a nod to Demetri. And with that they had started their trip . . . back to Cape Evans.

After long consideration, Cherry-Garrard has decided to return to Winter Quarters and trust that Scott's party – which includes his leader, Scott, his mentor, Bill Wilson, and good friend Birdie Bowers – will be all right.

It had been a particularly brutal last few days. The dogs, as wild as the weather, had started fighting among each other, the weather turned blank with blizzard and night temperatures continued to languish at around minus 30 degrees. Demetri's health further deteriorated, and they lost their way in the thick fog and began to 'turn circles'.

Still they had kept going, however, and – after recovering from the fright of being lost – now that Cherry-Garrard is just approaching those Winter Quarters he is relieved. He hoped to be returning with the Scott party, of course, but he is not worried over the decision he has made not to go in further search of them.

There was no particular reason to have concerns about Captain Scott's Southern Party, and his primary duty has been to ensure the safety of Demetri and himself. Had the two gone on further to the south in search of the others, they would have cut into their precious few supplies, in any case, and it was Cherry-Garrard's view that it would be better to leave the entire two weeks of provisions, including treats, at One Ton Depot for Scott and his men, and head back to the sanctuary of Hut Point.

Now, with one final drive, they force the spent dogs through the white wall towards the refuge, and once inside the safety of Winter Quarters at last they recount their journey and go to bed. None of the other men in the hut is concerned about the Scott party either.

15 March 1912 and the day thereafter, 32 miles south of One Ton Depot, beware the ides of March

For two weeks now, Oates has been bravely marching on feet in such terrible condition that every step causes crippling pain. His time of pulling the sledges is long gone. With one foot badly swollen, black and gangrenous, he limps and staggers rather than marches and is all but done in, trailing behind like a broken-down Frankenstein's monster, a spectre of their worst nightmare at their heels. For he is what they fear they will become.

And though the rest of them are in a much better condition than Oates, all intuitively understand that if he can no longer walk, it is out of the question for them to put him on the sledge and drag him, for even if he were the lightest of the party – and not the heaviest, as he is – they are simply not strong enough. Yes, he is at the end of his tether, but to have him at the end of *their* tether would be a certain death warrant for them all.

What then?

When asked while at Cape Evans before setting out what should a man do if he has become a burden to his mates, Oates unequivocally replied that the party should carry a pistol for just such an occasion, and 'if anyone breaks down he should have the privilege of using it'.[54]

But, of course, now Oates has no pistol, and at lunch on 15 March, after they have marched all morning into an unrelenting northerly wind at a temperature of minus 37 degrees, Oates tells Scott he can go no further and that he wishes to be left behind in his sleeping bag.

Scott is, surely, sorely tempted to accede to the request. Without Oates, they will not have anyone holding them back, and all of their own food intake can increase by a third. As it is, however, Scott, Bowers and Wilson unanimously urge Oates to soldier on the best he can.

That night in the tent, at much the same spot on the Barrier where Oates so strongly argued with Scott that One Ton Depot should be situated, at 80 degrees south, the Soldier withdraws into himself, barely able to utter a word. Nevertheless, he does briefly rouse himself to give Wilson his diary, asking him to take it to his mother and to tell her that she is the only woman he has ever loved.

And also tell her that he is sorry he couldn't write her a last note, but his frostbitten fingers prevent it. Oates furthermore speaks briefly but fondly of his regiment, hoping that they will remember him well.

Scott knows that this brave soul has not got long:

> Titus Oates is very near the end, one feels. What we or he will do, God only knows. We discussed the matter after breakfast; he is a brave fine fellow and understands the situation, but he practically asked for advice. Nothing could be said but to urge him to march as long as he could.[55]

That night, his condition so deteriorates that Oates hopes he will expire in his sleep. Alas, the brave Soldier awakens the next morning to the same tragedy, the same entirely hopeless situation.

In the tent, it is minus 40 degrees. Outside, in the howling blizzard, it is surely another 20 degrees colder. No one speaks, as that would require energy they do not have, and, besides that, there is nothing really to say. The others do note, however, some feeble movement from the direction of Oates's sleeping bag, as the Soldier struggles first to extract himself and then to get himself into a crawling position, without bothering to put his boots on over his grotesquely swollen sock-clad feet.

Clambering over their outstretched legs, he painfully moves towards the tent flap, manages to wobble to his feet and then looks back to the others before speaking his first words of the morning: 'I am just going outside and may be some time.'[56]

. . .

With that, Captain Lawrence Edward Grace Oates lets himself out from the tent[57] and goes forth . . . and within minutes he is no more. This brave soldier is just one day shy of both his 32nd birthday and the second anniversary of the day he received the cable from Scott telling him he has been successful in his application to join the expedition.[58]

The men who remain behind are overwhelmed with a mixture of emotions.

Scott honours him with warm words:

We knew that poor Oates was walking to his death, but though we tried to dissuade him, we knew it was the act of a brave man and an English gentleman. We all hope to meet the end with a similar spirit, and assuredly the end is not far.[59]

For his part, Wilson would subsequently take the time to write a heartfelt letter to Oates's beloved mother, Caroline:

Dear Mrs Oates,

This is a sad ending to our undertaking. Your son died a very noble death, God knows. I have never seen or heard of such courage as he showed from first to last with his feet both badly frostbitten – never a word or sign of complaint or of the pain. He was a great example.

. . . if ever a man died like a noble soul and in a Christian spirit your son did – Our whole journey's record is clean and though disastrous – has no shadow over it. He died like a man and a soldier without a word of regret or complaint except that he hadn't written to you at the last, but the cold has been intense and I fear we have all of us left writing alone until it is almost too late to attempt anything but the most scrappy notes.

God comfort you in your loss.

Yours sincerely,

E A Wilson[60]

Once the blizzard lifts later that day, though the wind blows at force four and the temperature remains at minus 35 degrees, it is time for them to move on once more. When they emerge from the tent, of course they look for some sign of Oates – he cannot have got far – but there is no clue. No doubt his body will have been covered by snowdrift. In any case, finding him is beside the point. He is dead, and they must try to live. They must move as quickly as they can.

Carefully, they offload Oates's sleeping bag, a camera and their theodolite, so as to reduce weight. At Wilson's special request, they are sure, however, not to leave behind the 35 pounds of rock specimens containing the fossilised remains, as he judges them to be of great scientific significance.

18 March 1912, Cape Denison, with Mawson and his men, as the heavens play opening night

While the coming winter brings terrible travails, some compensation is provided by the fact that it also brings scenes of unimagined beauty. Even during blizzards and fierce winds, for the most part the sky remains clear, and many is the night they are able to see, in all its glory, aurora australis, the stunning light-show in the northern skies.

'These were the nights,' Mawson records, 'when "curtains" hung festooned in the heavens, alive, rippling, dancing to the lilt of lightning music.'[61]

As wonderful as these spectacles are, however, the gasps of awe coming from onlookers in polar climes is not their only effect on earth. When the show is at its height, such disparate things as the edges of helmets, the corners of boxes and the ends of mitts begin to glow with a pale blue light, which sometimes works itself all the way up into a small electric shock.

Nowhere is this phenomenon more marked than down in the Magnetograph Hut, where at the height of the aurora event the nightwatchman finds the edges and wire stays of the screen outlined in a fashion reminiscent of a pyrotechnic display. The exact cause of it all is not obvious, only that it is connected to the aurora, and that when that phenomenon is occurring, there are 'magnetic storms' here on earth.

In normal circumstances, the dip on the vertical compass attached to the magnetograph points down at an angle of about 87 degrees, though that varies day by day and even minute by minute by as much as a degree – all of it recorded on the revolving drum. And yet, as the veils of the aurora rise and fall to the horizons, so too does the magnetograph suddenly flicker wildly, like the metronome on a piano keeping time to this visual melody from the heavens.

19 March 1912 and a week thereafter, Great Ice Barrier, the final days of Scott's Southern Party

Despite extreme exhaustion and the woeful weather, over the two days since losing Oates, Scott's party make one last-ditch effort and travel a little over 20 miles until they arrive at a point where they simply cannot go on, as a blizzard closes in and they must stop or die in their tracks. Now, they are just 11 geographical miles[62] away from the supplies stored at One Ton Depot the previous February and replenished several times since. But when they wake the following morning, the blizzard has not abated even a jot. If anything, it has become fiercer. Scott's attitude at this point is a curious mixture of refusal to give in and fatalism as to the inevitable result. 'We have decided to die naturally in the track,' writes Scott.[63]

Scott's feet, his pride just two days ago, are gone – with his right foot so horrifying that, even if he does make it back, it will have to be amputated. By this day, 20 March, they have just two days of food left, and the day after just enough fuel to make two cups of tea apiece. In short, lying in their tiny tent in the middle of the white desert, as the very heavens rage at their existence, it is becoming ever more obvious: they have shot their bolt. On 22 and 23 March, the blizzard is as bad as ever, the fuel is gone and the food might as well be.

Around this time, Bill Wilson writes to the woman whose memory has warmed his soul for months – if not his freezing body now – his beloved wife, Oriana: 'Birdie and I are going to try and reach the Depot 11 miles north of us and return to this tent where Captain Scott is lying with a frozen foot.' Wilson continues, saying that if he does not make it:

I shall simply fall and go to sleep in the snow, and I have your little books with me in my breast pocket . . . Don't be unhappy – all is for the best. We are playing a good part in the great scheme arranged by God Himself, and all is well . . . I am only sorry I couldn't have seen your loving letters, and Mother's and Dad's and the Smiths', and all the happy news I had hoped to see – but all these things are easily seen later, I expect . . . God be with you – my love is as living for you as ever . . . We

will all meet after death, and death has no terrors . . .
We have done what we thought was best. My own dear
wife, good-bye for the present . . . I do not cease to pray
for you — to the very last . . .[64]

Still the blizzard rages, though, and Wilson finally does write to his parents:

Dear old Dad and Mother,

The end has come and with it an earnest looking forward
to the day when we shall all meet together in the
hereafter. Death has no terrors for me. I am only sorry for
my beloved Ory and for all of you dear people, but it is
God's will and all is for the best. Our record is clear and
we have struggled against very heavy odds to the bitter
end — two of the 5 of us are already dead and we three
are nearly done up. Scott's foot is badly frostbitten so
that he can scarcely walk. Dear old home folks how I love
you all and how I have loved to think of you all — bless
you. I have had a very happy life and I look forward to
a very happy life hereafter when we shall all be together
again. God knows I have no fear in meeting Him — for
He will be merciful to all of us. My poor Ory may or may

not have long to wait – I am so sorry for her. However we have done all for the best believing in His guidance and we have both believed that whatever is, is His will, and in that faith I am prepared to meet Him and leave all you loved ones in His care till His own time is fulfilled.

Now God be with you all,

Your own loving Ted.[65]

Despite Wilson's ongoing hope that the blizzard will abate long enough to allow them to make a push on One Ton, such are the conditions, and so overwhelming is their weakness that another attempt to sally forth is simply not possible. The good man, Wilson, thus summons his last ounces of strength to write a final note to his beloved Oriana:

I leave this life in absolute faith and happy belief that if God wishes you to wait long without me it will be to some good purpose. All is for the best to those that love God and oh, my Ory, we have both loved Him all our lives. All is well . . . All the things I had hoped to do with you after the expedition are as nothing now, but there are greater things for us to do in the world to come . . . One of my notes will surely reach you.

All is well.[66]

26 March 1912 and four days thereafter, Corner Camp, Atch nearly gets it right

In the continued absence of the Scott party, it is decided that a search party needs to be sent. Taking 18 days' worth of provisions on their man-hauling sledge, Atch Atkinson and Patrick Keohane set off, into a howling gale and temperatures of minus 40 degrees. By the time they reach Corner Camp, both men are stunned by how difficult the going is. The terrible weather, bitter cold and approaching winter make further progress south impossible. Besides which, there is no point.

Though he doesn't say anything to Keohane, in his own mind Atkinson is 'morally certain that the [Scott] party had perished'.[67]

29 March 1912, 12.5 miles from One Ton Depot, Scott writes in his diary for the final time . . .

In that tiny tent, in that raging blizzard, the last flicker of life is at last . . . finally and forevermore . . . extinguished.

Scott's last diary entry, 29 March 1912, ends with these words:

Every day we have been ready to start for our depot, but outside the door of the tent it remains a scene of whirling drift. I do not think we can hope for any better things now. We shall stick it out to the end, but we are getting weaker, of course, and the end cannot be far. It seems a pity but I do not think I can write more. R. Scott.

For God's sake look after our people.[68]

Chapter Twelve

The Winter Months

During the winter months we had all been drawn together, but
between Mertz and Ninnis there existed a very deep bond. Mertz, in
his warm-hearted, impulsive way, had practically adopted Ninnis,
and his affection was almost maternal. Ninnis, less demonstrative,
reciprocated this to the full, and indeed it was hard to dissociate
them in our thoughts. It was always 'Mertz and Ninnis' or 'Ninnis
and Mertz', a composite entity, each the complement of the other.
Charles Laseron, *South with Mawson*

[Winter descended] with the shriek of a thousand angry witches.
Captain John King Davis, *High Latitude*

5 May 1912, Cape Denison, the cold takes hold at Mawson's Winter Quarters

Curious. Just as a tame cat or dog can engender a great sense of companionship, so too in this wilderness had the teeming seals and penguins been able to give Mawson's men some feeling that they were *not* all alone here, on the edge of this frozen continent. But then, first by the hundreds, then by the dozens, then by the handful, and then one by one, those seals and penguins started to disappear back into the warmer ocean to see out the coming winter, until, as the last penguin flopped into the water and away, they really had found themselves all alone . . . and have now been all alone for *weeks.*

Getting darker now. Getting colder. Getting windier.

Best to keep busy, and though performing their scientific duties can be rather humdrum, that only serves to make festive occasions all the more festive when they do occur. Things such as celebrating birthdays. On this day, it is Mawson's and Hannam's turn, and the occasion is celebrated with a sumptuous dinner cooked by Hurley and Hunter. Hurley, obviously with some time on his hands – as the only part of the dark that photography loves is the darkroom – produces the cover image for an impressive birthday menu, designed by expedition cartographer Alfred Hodgeman. The result befits such celebratory fare as 'Penguins on horsebacks with beans', which will be accompanied by wine, port, Russian stout, café noir and, of course, cigars.

Mawson is a firm believer in having such fare on occasional call:

Luxuries, then, are good in moderation, and mainly for their psychological effect. After a spell of routine, a celebration is the natural sequel, and if there are delicacies which in civilization are more palatable than usual, why not take them to where they will receive a still fuller and heartier appreciation . . .? So we did not forget our asparagus and jugged hare.[1]

5 May 1912, Holland, Paquita gives Mawson a cake

Down in The Hague, where the Delprats have rented a house for the duration of their European stay, Paquita is celebrating her fiancé's birthday in her own fashion, in the company of family and friends who have gathered to celebrate the special day of a man, over 10,000 miles away, whom most have never met.

Missing him particularly desperately by now – it is over six months since she last saw him and she is still not halfway through the time they must spend apart before they can marry – she and her mother have baked a cake, atop which is piled whipped cream in the manner of a mountain, with nothing less than a dollop of nougat, representing a tent, upon it. And it goes on. Beside it, there is a tiny 'marzipan sledge and dogs and the flag of the Southern Cross flying on a pole of angelica'.[2]

And there is Douglas! Well, at least a tiny model of him, made out of chocolate and pink fondant, standing by the flag and tent. They toast him. They sing 'Happy Birthday'. Paquita blows out the candles on his behalf and makes her wishes.

Not long afterwards, she writes him a letter:

9 Wagenaarweg

Haag

My Douglas, mine,

I'm feeling so absolutely healthy and happy tonight despite the distance between us that I want to write to you. I wrote you a letter on your birthday but it wasn't a success. I know you thought of us thinking of you then.

And we did. It was you all day long. Lots of aunts and things sent flowers. There was one huge bouquet just like a wedding one! Then one aunt gave 'Us' a silver old Dutch spoon. They make a lot of fuss over a birthday here more than English do.

I hope you don't mind but I'm quite Dutch. I've never

been so patriotic as now. I'm so awfully proud of my country and next year when we are together we must find time to come here, so that you can meet all our relations (and there are a heap) and see my Holland.

I got your letters safely and just when I was wanting something from you. How different our lives are at present! My man, I wish I had been there to help you when you were so worried before you landed. What a lot we shall have to tell each other when we meet again . . .

I hope everything goes well with you now. We aren't worrying about not hearing per wireless yet. But I hope we do soon hear. Scott will return about the same time as you. I hope you come first. He will be disappointed at Amundsen's getting [to the Pole] first. How thankful we are that you aren't bound for there. Don't you go and stay away another year!

You're under contract to return next year less than a year from now . . .

And as for Mother I don't know how I shall ever leave her even for you. Yes I do though. There is only one you. I'm sure you don't love me as I do you. Women always love the most and miss the most. Well I wouldn't like you to *miss me as much as I do you.*

With my whole heart and my lips

Your

Paquita[3]

Mid-May 1912, Cape Denison, Mawson and his men gather at 'Hyde Park Corner'

In his tiny room, at the end of each day, Mawson is likely to be at his desk, writing his journal, compiling his lists, writing formal instructions for his men and collating the scientific data gathered thus far . . . Occasionally, he glances up at the risqué painting given to him by Paquita, which he now has pinned above the desk, upon the wall of his small partition – *The Swing*, by Jean-Honoré Fragonard – showing a Frenchman looking up a lady's skirt as she rises high on a swing.

Being in such an environment and working so hard, it is important for the others that they be able to relax and keep themselves entertained as well. Beyond the books they have brought with them, and the records they could play, much of that entertainment comes from . . . themselves. While in the 'outside world', the ability to be able to play a musical instrument, recite a poem or tell a story might be valuable, here it is highly prized, and the men quickly become aware where each other's skill lies.

The young geologist from Melbourne, Frank Stillwell, for example, can play the piano, and though they don't happen to have one handy, they *do* have a small accordion, which on many a night Frank is prevailed upon to play while they all sing along, often finishing up with the grand finale of 'Auld Lang Syne', bellowing out the well-loved words they know so well.

Other times, Charles Laseron thrills them all with his composition of a comic opera he has entitled *The Washerwoman's Secret*, and while Hurley proves to be a great organiser of gambling games he is also a great practical joker with an amazingly theatrical bent, to the wonderment of them all. At one point, when all are gathered around the table for dinner and he is sure he has their complete attention, he stands at one end and begins to sing a riotous song he has written about Dux Ipse's abilities at shooting birds. Right at the climactic moment, he brings to his shoulder a small wooden gun he has fashioned for the occasion and, as he makes to fire it at a wooden duck that he has placed at the other end of the table, a bell loudly rings, just as if he were in a carnival shooting gallery!

It gets better still. As recounted by Charles Laseron:

There were also numerous loud bangs from beneath the table, where a little carbide had been brought into contact with water by pulling a string and inverting a number of small tins. The lids blew off with quite convincing reports. Moreover, from various points in the roof Antarctic penguins and skua gulls dropped in every direction on those sitting beneath, while the gramophone funnel descended as an extinguisher on Alfie Hodgeman's head.[4]

Oh, how they roar!

A favourite activity of them all in quieter, more regular times is to smoke their pipes as they listen to the gramophone, which must be regularly rewound. With only a limited number of records, of course each one becomes exceptionally well known, and this one, with its stirring climax of a loud clash of cymbals, is surely Mertz's favourite, because it is so similar to his personality. As a matter of fact, they refer to it as 'Mertz killing seals', being so 'suggestive of his emphatic methods'.[5]

A universal favourite is a chorus from *The Mikado*, and there are frequent animated and sometimes heated discussions as to just what the exact words to the refrain are. It goes . . . *'something, something . . . the Lord High Executioner . . .'* but what is that *something*? It sounds for all the world like 'Japara', which coincidentally is the material their tents are made from, but, of course that doesn't make sense. Again and again, they put the needle on the gramophone back a little, as they huddle close and strain their ears to get it, but it simply escapes them. At least, however, many happy hours are spent discussing it, their minds fastening upon this little bit of civilisation they have brought with them to this polar wilderness and savouring every second of it.

In the absence of any formal entertainment, or games, or listening to records, the default position is to gather night after night, after dinner, in the part of the hut known as 'Hyde Park Corner' – formed in the angle between the top bunks of Ninnis 'n' Mertz and the bottom bunks of Bickerton and Madigan – where they can debate points great and small, argue over anything and everything, recite poetry, do readings of various books or simply tell stories.

In the latter regard, the favourite of them all is Herbert Dyce Murphy, who proves to be a superb raconteur with a seemingly inexhaustible fund of yarns from his staggeringly colourful past. Now, it is not that Murphy – born the son of a very wealthy Queensland grazier and educated in Melbourne, London and Oxford, the last only until he dropped out – tells *all* of his most intimate stories, but he is one with a particular predilection for wearing women's clothing. This is a passion and talent he discovered while attending Oxford and has engaged in thereafter. It was he, after all, who had been rejected from Shackleton's *Nimrod* expedition because he had been too effeminate. Regardless, he has for a long time been comfortable with exploring the feminine side of himself and has been quite open about it.

When, in his early 20s, he had been living in London and fell out of touch with his mother for several months, she journeyed there unannounced and arrived at his church one Sunday morning. There, she found her son in his familiar pew, dressed as the most feminine woman in the establishment – with a hat, veil, long-sleeved jacket, gloves and gorgeous long skirt.

Sitting down beside him, his mother had delicately written, 'Who are you?'

'I am your daughter, Edith,' her son had written back, in his equally elegant hand.

She replied, 'I always wanted a beautiful daughter.'

Acceptance!

And well, one thing led to another, and in the early 1900s Murphy worked as a spy in France and Belgium. Dressed as a woman and presenting himself as an Australian heiress, Edith Dyce Murphy, he travelled the French railways taking notes on railway infrastructure and resources, before returning to London where, for many years, still dressed as a woman, he lived with an elderly sea captain who was very generous to Edith/Herbert in his will. He also has three Arctic voyages on his résumé.

'His stories have a curious suggestion of truth,' Laseron would later write of them. 'They are convincing and at the same time too impossible to be true. For Herbert is a genius, who from an ounce of fact can manufacture a mountain of entertainment.'[6]

And so it would go, night after night, gathered in the smoky bonhomie of Hyde Park Corner as, in his light tenor voice, Herbert tells his yarns. They laugh and carouse and carry on before, at last, it is time for bed. Now, as the blizzard continues to rage, and the howling wind makes the roof creak wearily in protest, one by one they head off to their bunks, usually leaving as the second-last man up the nocturnal Bage, who is often to be found doing some sewing or fixing up one of his gadgets.

And then Bage, too, rises, stretches, says 'Goodnight' to the nightwatchman and goes to his bunk for some precious shut-eye.

Charles Laseron's account of what usually then happens is evocative:

> The night-watchman rises from the table and puts some coal on the fire . . . It is nearly midnight, and preparations must be made to take the usual observations. It is a serious business this, though the weather screen is but a few yards from the hut on the eastern side.[7]

First of all, the watchman draws on his Burberry trousers, which he ties tightly with tapes around his ankles and waist:

> Then comes the balaclava, and over it the burberry helmet. Woollen mittens come next to protect the wrists, and over all the blouse, which is tied at the waist, neck and wrists to prevent the entrance of snow. Finally, fingerless woollen gloves complete the outfit. The barometer is read, and the result noted in the record book; then the main adventure begins. Passing into the outer room, from thence to the porch, he crawls through the snow tunnel into the veranda of the main hut . . .
>
> He now calculates his distance—one—two—three—four—five yards. Now comes the plunge into the unknown. At right angles he makes a rush, and his hand gropes blindly about him. Here it is at last – a thin strand of wire, vibrating shrilly in the wind. As his fingers make contact with the wire, blue sparks spring forth, and the metal rim of his helmet also glows with blue flame. This is St Elmo's fire, an electric discharge caused by the friction of the particles of snow. But at this moment he is not concerned with the superstitions of the old-time mariners, but instead hauls himself carefully upwards, his mind on the immediate task.[8]

Making his way out to the instruments, he hangs on for grim death against the marauding wind and manages to open the door of the screen, turn on the small electric switch attached to a battery and, in the resultant tepid light, get his eyes to within a couple of inches of the gauges to read the results, take a mental note, and then close it all up again, before retracing his steps with the same difficulty as before.

> He finds the entrance and plunges through with a feeling of relief. In the porch he takes off his burberries, shakes the snow from them, and with his hand melts the ice from his eyes. His balaclava he leaves on until he is in front of the fire, for it has become frozen fast to his beard, and it is apt to be painful to pull it off too suddenly.
>
> In the warm hut again his cheek feels rather numb, so he looks at himself in the glass and sees a round, shrivelled patch about the size of a shilling. It is a frost-bite, and he rubs it gently to restore the circulation. It tingles a bit as feeling comes back, and an hour later there is a blister in the place. He takes the record book and makes an entry, curiously similar to other entries for many pages back:
>
> 12 midnight. Temp. -18°F, wind about 80, thick drift.[9]

One other thing not to forget, and it is the great pleasure of all nightwatchmen: at midnight, they must turn over the calendar on the wall. Another day has passed, bringing them a day closer to the darkness leaving, the warmth returning, the summer's keenly anticipated sledging journeys beginning and, thereafter, going home . . .

However, that still seems a long, long way away. And in the face of it all, the bitter cold, their ongoing isolation, some men begin to struggle spiritually, their mood starting to match the growing blackness.

But Xavier Mertz is not one of them. He writes in his diary:

Although I am uncertain about the present or the future and I know that Switzerland lies far away, I have never felt such satisfaction and peace in my life . . . Raving weather whips up my nerves and blood. The stress caused by natural phenomenon is not to be compared with stress in our civilised world. A lot of people can't understand why we travelled to an unknown land. The danger, laborious work, and cold weather wouldn't tempt them. If they could see our satisfaction and enjoy the life with us, they would understand. They would realize how, in this area, hard work and life's difficulties bring delights. I love this cold area in the same way that I love my Alps, with their natural beauty and dangers.[10]

Although by this time, outside tasks are down to a bare minimum, still there remains a little building work to do, in the few precious daylight hours when the conditions are good enough to allow it.

By now, it is so cold, even on good days, that all activity outside must be extremely vigorous and for a short time only, or a case of frostbite would be the all but certain result – requiring heavy rubbing in the first instance, even as you get as close as you can to the stove, to try to restore circulation to the affected flesh.

One job that occupies the party's attention at this time is assisting Bage in building the astronomical observatory, on the eastern side of the main hut. This new building requires many tons of stones for its foundations, and many hands pitch in to carry them from the nearest pile, some 20 yards away, though the bases of many of those stones are frozen in the ice and they can only be shifted by heavy use of crowbars.

After that rock collection is exhausted, it is Ninnis and Mertz who rise to the occasion. They take the opportunity of putting their dog-teams through their paces by loading up the sledges with stones from further afield and then careering across the ice-flat towards Bage and the others, who unload the sledges before the men are cheerfully off again, with the shivering dogs yelping short and sharp and constant in their eagerness to get going.

Little by little, the men and the dogs become used to each other, the dogs growing ever more responsive to the men's commands. With the sledge laden once more, Ninnis and Mertz get the dogs started with a touch of the whip and some shouted imprecations. Then, once the sledge is properly going, they jump aboard, with Mertz habitually on the lead sledge singing, as Mawson would remember it ever afterwards, 'some quaint yodel song, [with] Ninnis, perhaps, just behind upbraiding a laggard dog'.[11]

Mawson, for one, is not surprised to see the two Europeans so heavily involved in all facets of the work. A few weeks earlier, when it was noticed that the ropes anchoring the still inoperative wireless masts were badly chafed, meaning the whole thing was in danger of falling to the ground, Mawson noted that it was Ninnis 'n' Mertz who were the first to help the wireless operator, Hannam, secure them, an action not necessarily duplicated by some of the others.

'I was sorry to see,' he noted crisply in his diary, 'that others, who were not engaged on special work, excused themselves and one even refused to go. With all due consideration for the frailty of such individuals, this is scarcely a brotherly feeling, to say the least of it.'[12]

But Ninnis and Mertz? Well, they could not be faulted, and Ninnis, particularly, has come a long way from the callow and lazy youth that, on *Aurora*, Davis doubted was up to the task.

10 May 1912, Sydney, at the Lyceum Theatre, another curtain rises

Roll up! Roll up!

And so they do. If not quite in their thousands, then at least in their hundreds, as some of the film that Frank Hurley shot on the trip to the south – from Macquarie Island right up until *Aurora* had departed Cape Denison, before sending it back on that very ship – has been made into a film called *With Mawson in the South*. In Sydney's finest theatre, the film is played after a special address by Professor David, and to the accompaniment of a 'full orchestra and effects'.[13]

The film will go on to play in Melbourne and Hobart, and if the prime hope of Mawson – that it will do such good box office that a chunk of the expedition's bills will be paid – is not realised, at least it generates some publicity and gives interested parties some clue as to what conditions are like far, far to their south, where the ice men are living.

June to August 1912, Cape Denison, the darkness deepens at Mawson's Winter Quarters

It was a dark and stormy night . . .

On the other hand, as this particular dark and stormy night now goes all but around the clock, day after day, for weeks on end, it is barely worth noting any more.

All but beaten now, the sun glows for no more than a short period each day, and even then it's not high enough to be anything more than a frozen red orb on the horizon before it quickly slinks away out of sheer embarrassment as the more powerful forces of darkness crowd close.

With that darkness has come ever more freezing temperatures and ever more powerful winds. In March, the average wind velocity was 49 mph, which was more than matched in April with an average of over 50 mph, with only three days of relative calm. On one particular day in mid-May – the 14th – the average had been no less than 90.1 mph, lifting the average for the fortnight to above 70 mph.

Beyond the scientific value of such measurements, they also

add to the entertainment: one of the most popular activities is the monthly Calcutta sweep as to what that month's average wind speed will be. All of the punters keenly anticipate the second-last day of the month, when the available numbers are put on display, just as if they are horses in the Melbourne Cup, and the auction takes place, presided over by Cecil Madigan, who, as the man who takes the monthly readings, is the one person who cannot bet himself, as he already knows the approximate result. For currency, there is nothing so gauche as money available, so instead they bet from their weekly ration of 30 squares of chocolate.

'How much am I bid for an average of 70 mph?'

'I bid twenty-one squares!'

'Twenty-three squares here.'

'I bid twenty-five squares!'

And so on. It provides endless revelry and even some oddly good-hearted sorrow when, on one occasion, Archie McLean is found to be unable to pay his chocolate debts and declared bankrupt, meaning that some of his precious personal effects, such as candles, matches and tobacco, are placed on the block for another auction, so that his honour can be restored.

Others are able to form a syndicate, and by hook and by crook, and by pooling their resources, they manage to corner the whole chocolate market for weeks ahead.

One of the strangest phenomena of all, beyond the fact that there are wind gusts approaching 200 mph – they still can't get used to it – is that even in the middle of such a tempest you can often see the stars above twinkling, with nary a cloud in the sky. By the light of these stars and the moon reflecting off the ice, it is as though one is living in an ethereal twilight world, albeit with a screaming banshee devil of a wind and a cripplingly low temperature to spoil it.

In such conditions, fulfilling even the most quotidian of chores is a trial, and, as Mawson discovered on the *Nimrod* expedition, the colder it gets the more energy men require just to survive.

Take getting water for the hut. Every drop must be melted from ice, and that ice must be chipped from outside, no matter the weather. (*Most* important is that the ice must come from a place well distant from anywhere the dogs have been – as yellow ice is a disaster.) Getting water is the primary job of Dr Leslie Whetter – a rather prickly New Zealander – and he is rarely happy about it, particularly when the weather is inclement, which is pretty much always.

With an assistant grimly hanging on to a box, Whetter holds a pick. Both must brace against any small ridge they can find to prevent themselves from being swept away by the wild wind. But it is not a matter of simply swinging the pick in the same spot of ice to break it up, because to begin with it is difficult for Whetter to grip the handle properly with his thick mitts, and, each time he lifts it, it is caught by the endlessly varying gusts of wind, making it nigh on impossible to hit the same place twice. This means that what chips are gathered for the box are small, and even such pieces as fly from the point of the pick are instantly caught by the wind and have to be gathered back in.

'The box itself,' Laseron later recounts, 'even when partially filled, is sometimes lost, wrenched from the hands and swept away to sea. No wonder Whetter sometimes growls at the cook's demands for ice, and the cook, in turn, resists requests for water for such frivolous purposes as washing.'[14]

Whetter's particular mistake is to growl at Dux Ipse during breakfast on 4 June, asking when 'winter's work' would begin, assuming that winter's work would mean that instead of having his men working all day every day seven days a week, Mawson might at last give them half a day a week of free time.

In response, Mawson is terse: 'Never, as there is too much work to do.'[15]

Whetter is aggrieved, though as this tends to describe his natural condition, it is unremarkable. Outside, the wind keeps blowing strongly all day, just as it does day after day.

Inside the hut, though, things are cosier than ever, helped by the fact that an enormous drift of snow has first built up against its southern wall and then all but covered it – to the point that the only entrance to the hut is through a tunnel into the snowdrift and then via a trapdoor in the roof of the veranda.

For those with duties outside, it is, therefore, an extraordinary thing when they are finished to go from the roar of the terrifying tempest to a sudden hush and then, only a few seconds after that, hear the strains of a gramophone playing Nellie Melba mixed with gales of laughter from another section of the hut. If they are really lucky, they are also greeted with the wonderful aroma of Mertz's speciality, which is omelette made of eggs long ago snaffled from the penguins. They have very small yolks with very large whites and, surprisingly, 'no fishy taste whatever'.[16]

One whiff of Mertz's masterpiece and they know heaven is just up ahead.

For Mertz is one of the few in the hut *not* to hold guaranteed membership of what is known laughingly within the hut as the 'Crook Cooks' Association', nor even their brother guild, 'The Society of Muddling Messmen', that group of unfortunates who at every mealtime are assigned, on a rotating basis, to help the cooks do the most menial of work. For true membership, one has to have committed a 'championship', as in some mistake such as dropping a dozen plates or burning the porridge, sufficient to attract the derisive mirth of the entire hut and a cry of 'Championship! Championship!'[17]

One notable Crook Cook is a junior member (whose name is not recorded) who forgot the crucial ingredient of baking powder in making a loaf of bread. The resultant 'championship' was *so* inedible, so hard that not even the dogs outside would eat it! (Great hilarity results, heightened when it is first found days later in the gathered rubbish that lies to the north of the hut, and then, *months* later when they are digging out a tunnel, they find it again – the loaf of bread that refuses to die.)

Another championship occurs when Ninnis, very carefully following Mrs Beeton's famous cookbook, decides upon a salmon dish for lunch. Now, let's see: 'Take one tin of salmon, 2 oz of butter, 2 oz of flour, pepper and salt to taste.' Well, as there are 18 of them to feed, it should be a simple matter of roughly multiplying those quantities by four, which means . . . 4 tins of salmon, 8 oz of flour, 8 oz of butter, and . . . yes, I suppose . . . 8 oz of pepper and 8 oz of salt! Well, it *did* seem rather a lot, but that is what the recipe seems to say and so that is what he does.

'The funny thing,' Charles Laseron recounts, 'is that the dish looked all right as it came nicely browned from the oven. I . . . was aroused by the howl of anguish that followed the first mouthful. Ninnis never heard the last of this . . .'[18]

For his part, the true 'artist' among them, Hurley is always concerned with how the food *presents* rather than whether it tastes good or not, always insisting, for example, on making pastry very hard so it would 'stand up in the form of a ship or some grotesque shape',[19] always guaranteed to cause high hilarity.

And this is the hut at its best: a place of laughter, camaraderie and care entirely removed from the oft-cataclysmic chaos and total frigidity of the world outside. Though the average temperature inside the hut is only around 45 degrees – similar to the interior of an icebox at home – compared with the frozen wastelands that lie at its door, being safe inside it feels like lazing in front of a roaring fire.

'Once passing through the vestibule and work-room,' Mawson later describes it, 'one beheld a scene in utter variance with the outer hell. Here were warm bunks, rest, food, light and companionship – for the time being, heaven!'[20]

Certainly, it is a curious kind of heaven, one where the 'air pulsates as the roof bends inwards beneath the pressure of the fiercest gusts',[21] but for the men inside the hut that only heightens the sense of privilege that they are not outside.

One thing they all look forward to, as this cruellest of all possible winters gets a true grip on their hut, is midwinter's day on 21 June, a date of legendary significance for all those who have wintered in the Antarctic. This is the day, of course, that marks the very heart of the winter, meaning that every day thereafter the summer is on its way to returning and the forces of light, thought to have been so completely routed by the forces of darkness, will begin their improbable fightback. After being pinned down for so long, restricted to appearing as a glow just above the northern horizon for only 30 minutes around noon each day, soon, they know, it will start to change. Soon, the golden orb of the sun will begin to gain confidence and start to strike out in all directions, rising higher, shining brighter, appearing earlier and lasting longer each day.

And when that shortest day finally 'dawns' – the first day since they have disembarked that Mawson frees them from duties for the entire day – they are not at all disappointed. For with that dawn, just after midday, the wind suddenly falls away, almost as if acknowledging that a crossroads has been reached, and the men are nearly all able to get outside to enjoy the precious light, coming from the moon and even the aurora. After the sun goes down, they manage to go on small ventures around and about the hut, exploring the nearby ice caves and the abandoned penguin rookeries as they glory in the sense that from this point on it can only get better, lighter and warmer.

That evening, the hut is adorned with flags, all the men are dressed in their least dirty cardigans and neckcloths, the table groans under the weight of festive fare, and they enjoy a wonderful meal followed by toasts to the King and each other, together with speeches. And then comes 'a musical and dramatic programme, punctuated by choice gramophone records and rowdy student choruses . . . Outside, the wind was not to be outdone; it surpassed itself with an unusual burst of ninety-five miles per hour.'[22]

'At midnight,' as Mertz fondly writes in his diary, 'the party came to an end, and it was the beginning of Ninnis's birthday. We gave him congratulations, presents and ovations, then we went to bed.'[23]

Over on Shackleton's Ice Shelf, Frank Wild and his men have had a similar celebration. Though on this day the temperature has plummeted to minus 38, still nothing can quell their joy that this auspicious date has been reached. So thrilled is Wild himself that he has proclaimed a general holiday throughout the land he has unofficially named Queen Mary Land. That evening, they too have a celebratory dinner followed by speeches and toasts and a gramophone concert.

With the darkest point of the winter now passed, the focus of Mawson and his men turns to preparing their sledges for their spring trips. Packing them is an art form, the masterpieces of which display a perfectly balanced lightweight load where the things that will be most often required are placed in the most easily accessible spots and nothing crucial is left behind.

At Cape Denison, Mawson supervises the practice packing of the sledges particularly closely. Let us begin with the box at the front of the sledge carefully filled with everything from surveying instruments – such as the theodolite, to measure vertical and horizontal angles, so we can record the contours of the land we see – to photographic equipment, meteorological measuring gear, tools, weapons and ammunition, and a medical kit.

Most crucial – and Dr Mawson insists on this – is that each man makes his own harness out of stout canvas. This is because, firstly, it is important that the harness – which they will attach to themselves to haul the sledge forward – is comfortable. Far more crucial, though, is that if they fall down a crevasse, their lives will likely be hanging by a thread, and it is important that all of that thread – in fact, the canvas of the harness, attached to a rope tied onto the sledge – be fashioned by the man concerned. So long as the canvas holds, and the sledge doesn't follow them in, they can likely be hauled to the surface or even, *in extremis*, pull themselves to the surface.

A lot of work is also put into the tents that they will carry, and into practising how to erect them.

These tents, to be sure, are already designed to withstand fierce winds – pyramidal in structure, with a low pitch supported by five bamboo poles so that the wind will be more inclined to flow *over* them than through them, blowing them away – but Mawson is not satisfied.

Realising how impossible it will be to mount such a tent in a full-blown blizzard, he insists that the bamboo poles be ready-sewn and secured inside the tent, so the whole thing can be mounted as one piece with three men working together. That done, Mawson's men are obliged to practise raising the tent again and again just outside the hut, most particularly when the wind is at its worse, until they get the hang of it.

First, they must cut large blocks of ice or hard snow to act as ballast and then lay the whole of the tent with its apex pointing straight into the wind and the tent entrance on the top side. Now, as one man crawls inside, the tent is slowly raised, with every foot raised giving more shelter to the men on the lee side. The job of the man on the inside is to spread the three windward legs as wide as possible so that the material is taut . . . all while not getting blown over . . . and while giving the other men the chance to heap the ballast on the specially designed long flaps at the tent's base. Then a canvas tent floor is laid and the reindeer-skin sleeping bags set out. These bags have the tiniest slit at the top, just large enough for a man's body to fit inside. Once a fellow is in the bag, that slit can be narrowed to nearly nothing, allowing the occupant to be snug as a bug in a rug, practically as if in the womb of a reindeer. Though lack of oxygen could be a minor problem, the key is to have the slit just wide enough for you to breathe easily, allowing your own hot breath to warm the entire bag.

Another thing that occupies them greatly is preparing and packing the food to be taken out on their sledging expeditions. The apportioning and packing of the foodstuffs, which include Plasmon biscuits, pemmican, butter, Glaxo, cocoa, chocolate and tea, together with preparation of sledging 'compounds', takes up weeks on end. The pemmican compound is prepared by shaving down the pemmican and mixing it with hand-ground Plasmon biscuits before being carefully weighed and placed into small calico bags. After that, those small bags will be put into larger canvas bags, or 'tanks', designed to hold rations for a week or a fortnight. Cocoa compound, made up of cocoa, Glaxo and sugar, is similarly dealt with.

As to dog food, it is Ninnis 'n' Mertz who look after it – just as they have made the dog harnesses – and they are often to be found drying seal meat over the stove. The reason the seal steaks are dried and not cooked is that this reduces their weight by fifty per cent, and that is always a prime consideration.

And so the winter proper passes. While other animals in freezing climes have the luxury of sleeping or resting through the northern winter, not so Mawson's men in the south.

Their winter must be spent actively preparing for the coming spring, and as the weeks pass the sense of expectation rises. Indeed, there is so much for all of them to do that, despite the constant protests of Whetter, Mawson insists they continue to work until dinner each and every night – that's right – seven days a week.

All of their sledges are ready and packed long before that spring arrives, and, as early as the morning of 21 July, Mertz and Ninnis are feeling sufficiently confident that as the wind temporarily drops away for the first time in weeks they may even be able to start ferrying loads of food to the top of the plateau, where they can depot it.[24]

31 July 1912, Cape Denison, Mertz has a particular reason to celebrate

At the end of this long day, Mertz writes joyously in his diary:

> The wind rages and howls above the roof. The grey clouds and the light snow drifts create a gloomy atmosphere. My thoughts linger in Switzerland where now it's the middle of summer. For the National Day, fires are lit on the mountains. The whole country celebrates 1 August. In the evening, in 'Adélie Land', we also celebrated this day. The Englishmen joined me for this holiday. The red Swiss flag with its white cross was hoisted. For the first time since the earth exists, this flag flutters in Antarctica. I am very proud. Honouring this day, Swiss courses were dished up. 'Lenzburger' vegetables and fruits and 'Decksens' coffee and Swiss Leckerli biscuits. During the cup of coffee, I made a speech about Switzerland, pointing on a map to the mountains, valleys, and lakes. After that Mawson pronounced some very sensitive words. We had a toast to Switzerland.
>
> As a second toast was to me, I had to sit out, and kept my mouth shut. Nin, my oldest friend here, gave Switzerland three cheers, and wished me all the best. These signs of sympathy from my comrades were so warm that I never lived such a 1st August until now. A Swiss has never moved so far away from his homeland, as I did, and no Swiss can feel more intensely than me, how the homeland is beloved.[25]

9 August 1912 and five days thereafter, Cape Denison, Mawson tests the wind . . .

On this morning, after the worst of the winter has passed and sufficient daylight has returned, Dux Ipse judges the time is right to make another foray to see what they can see. He sets out in the company of Madigan and Ninnis, this time with dog teams, only to find, alas, that the lull of wind at their hut does not exist higher up. The steep grade softens a little as they rise, and though the hard glacier ice is beset by light sastrugi and small crevasses, by the time they have struggled up to an altitude of 1000 feet – by which point they can no longer see their tiny hut, nor even the islands offshore – that wind is blowing at them so strongly that it is impossible to proceed.

After making camp a little over three and a quarter miles inland, the next day they get their bearings once more. To their far north, they can see the darkness of the blue sea, lightly peppered with the white of the icebergs. But all around them in every other direction it is white, pure white, without any discernible landmarks, apart from the fact that as they look to the south that white clearly moves higher. It is lifeless, utterly lifeless, bar themselves and their dogs.

As they set off further to the south and the sight of the sea disappears, they become more aware than ever of the importance of their compass in heading in the right direction, for there is no other thing with which to get their bearings – except the fact that the wind itself usually blows from the frozen heart of the continent, to their south.

Though with the strength of that wind it is difficult to keep going, they are able to get to the sledge that was abandoned five months before, five and a half miles from the hut. It is with some satisfaction that Mawson notes it is where they left it and still intact, if showing the wear and tear of having been in such a wind for so long. So, too, an aluminium cooker, the windward side of which has been burnished to sparkling by the irrepressible winds. A bonus is that they also find the remains of one of Madigan's puddings, which is carefully thawed out over their Primus cooker and consumed in double-quick time – tasting as fresh as if it were baked just an hour before. Due to the wind still blowing as strongly as ever, Mawson decides to make camp once more.

As this area is at the point where the ascent ends and the plateau truly begins – just under six miles from the hut, in a clearly distinguishable part of the great whiteness all around – it is decided that it is an excellent place to locate a depot. Given, however, the intensity of what appears to be year-round continuous howling winds, Mawson deems they should excavate a cavern at the site, beneath the icy surface, which would provide far more shelter than anything constructed above ground.

Using ice-axes and some small shovels they have carried with them, they immediately start chopping and digging upon a small fissure in the ice, and by the end of the next day the men are snugly ensconced in their new home, which is a roughly cuboid chamber with six-foot-long sides and a roof about five feet high. Entrance is afforded via an almost vertical shaft with a tent cover for a door, before opening into what is effectively an underground igloo, with an ice roof thin enough that the light from the outside world comes as something of a translucent glow, making the ice walls within sparkle.

Once inside this subterranean refuge, the blizzard is banished and the eerie silence, together with the sparkling of ice crystals, creates an atmosphere of sitting among jewels and treasures, reminding Mawson of the fairy grotto in *Lady Betty Across the Water*. As he records, they call it Aladdin's Cave, as it has 'walls sparkling like diamonds'[26] and is 'a truly magical world of glassy facets and scintillating crystals'.[27]

Compared to a tent with its furiously flapping canvas, Aladdin's Cave is a luxury hotel. If water is required, ice is simply hacked from the walls to be melted over a Primus. Shelves are also cut into the walls for Sir's convenient placement of everything from eating implements and diaries to boots. A place is provided so clothes can be hung to dry, by wetting the corner of each garment and freezing it to the wall. As to the call of nature, a convenient crevasse connected to the cave provides commodious egress for all unwanted matter.[28]

After carefully marking the site of Aladdin's Cave with a huge black flag attached to a bamboo pole that pokes out from the top of a large snow cairn, on 13 August Mawson, Ninnis and Madigan begin a foray further south but are beaten back by the weather and return to their icy oasis that night. In thick weather, with a hurricane at their backs, yet without the trailing dogs that have fallen behind somewhere in the drift, they arrive once more at Winter Quarters on 15 August.

The dogs, knowing there is just one source of food and warmth in the whole area, should not be far behind.

1 September to mid-September 1912, Cape Denison, spring springs forth

It is truly wonderful to have made it through the winter, as characterised with typical eloquence by Charles Laseron:

> As the first rounding of the Horn is to the sailor, so a winter in the ice is to the polar explorer. It puts the hallmark on his experience. Having successfully emerged from the embryonic stage, he is now fully fledged, and can take his place in the select fraternity.[29]

Helping the upbeat mood of Mawson and his men after surviving the trials of the winter is the return of more normal conditions.

In recent weeks, the wind has lessened a little and the daylight hours have increased. With the greater capacity to do work outside, on this very day the men complete the first section of the three-section masts for the antenna to be suspended from. In fact, they have long since decided it will be impossible to get all four sections up, but they will try to get the third sections, the top-gallant masts, attached. For the moment, it is enough to suspend the antenna 65 feet above the ground, and Hannam begins to send messages. True, there is no response from Macquarie Island, but there has to be a small chance that the messages are being received, and so he continues to send them.

In these early days of September, the weather continues to improve, and they are treated to a fabulous five days straight of an almost surreal calm. The seals are the first to answer nature's clarion call of warmer times ahead, as they flop ashore and, at least initially, sleepily bask in the frigid sunshine for all the world as if they are bathers on Bondi Beach at the height of summer – a new craze that was just taking off at home when they left. Mawson's men are delighted to see them, and they waste little time in killing the first of the seals for their meat and blubber.

Such perfect weather offers Mawson the opportunity to send out three trial sledging parties, so they may reconnoitre at least the beginnings of the routes they will be on in a couple of months' time, get some crucial experience and test the equipment. All of the men are under strict instruction, however, to go no further than 50 miles from the hut and be back within 14 days.

Webb, McLean and Stillwell's party get away on 7 September in a 56-mph wind that soon builds to 80 mph, even as day temperatures drop as low as minus 20 degrees. As they soon learn, it is impossible to proceed in such conditions, and they are obliged to lay up for three days, digging out – against the possibility that their tent might be whisked away by the tremendous winds – a cave that becomes known as The Cathedral Grotto. After nine days out, they return, having covered a distance of less than 12 miles south of the hut.

As to the South-Eastern Party of Ninnis 'n' Mertz and Murphy, after departing on 11 September, they, too, are quickly thrown into the deep end of harsh experience when they quickly find themselves ascending the glacier behind the hut in 50-mph winds as they encounter frequent crevasses – making less than six miles for the day. The following day, the glacier surface is even worse, and they travel less than three miles, finally being obliged to beat a hasty retreat after having made it just 18 miles from the hut.

And finally, the Western Party of Madigan, Close and Whetter set out on 12 September in the same fierce winds . . . only to disappear for 14 days. Given the experience of the other parties, it was expected they would quickly return, but it is not until 26 September that they finally, mercifully, arrive to tell their tale to the relieved throng.

Madigan recounts to his rapt audience that, despite the conditions, they actually made it to 50 miles out and managed to establish a depot with a black flag flapping on a wide, featureless plain. But they suffered terrible hardship, too, as they stumbled their way back through strong snowdrift while constantly capsizing their sledge in steep country. In winds of up to 75 mph, it had taken them over *an hour* to pitch a tent, and it had only got worse. They had had to haul their sledge over three-foot-high sastrugi in blizzard conditions.

Not surprisingly, all of them are the worse for wear and have varying stages of frostbite on various parts of their extremities, from eyelid to nose to chin to fingertip to toe. Madigan ends his story with a riveting description of how the temperatures became so low that his helmet froze solid to his face. He is greeted with a silence so profound that you could hear an icicle drop, and probably do. Either that, or it was his nose.

30 September 1912 and a week thereafter, Cape Denison, a signal is sent . . . and received

Today is the day. Finally, after much work over many months, the men feel the aerial stands at a sufficient height that they may at last be able to contact Macquarie Island. That evening after dinner, they crowd around Hannam as he sits at his wireless, all of them with the fervent hope that the first real long-distance messages from their base to Macquarie Island, and hopefully from there on to Australia, are about to be sent and received. Perhaps, soon, they will be able to communicate back and forth with their families!

Mawson writes, 'The sharp note of the spark rose in accompanying crescendo and, when it had reached its highest pitch, Hannam struck off a message to the world at large.'[30]

They all eagerly wait, but there is no response. Yes, the men can hear 'atmospherics' – radio reception noise caused by electromagnetic disturbances in the atmosphere – which indicates that something is working, but Hannam cannot hear any messages from the outside world.

Nor are there any responses the following night, or on subsequent nights. The one thing they all do note, however, is that because the wireless works off the effects of electrical induction – sending a strong current across a conductor moving through a magnetic field – it means that the air in the hut is effectively alive with it, and there is great joy evinced when everyone conceives 'a mania for "'drawing" sparks'.[31] Merely by moving any part of your body to within a short distance of a metallic object, it is possible to have a delightful spark leap the distance. A particular favourite is 'to brush one's head against one of the numerous coils of flexible metal gas-piping festooned about the place. Sparks immediately jump the interval with startling effect'.[32]

That amusement aside, Hannam keeps going in the hope that

even though he can't hear Macquarie Island, they might possibly be hearing him . . .

And, sure enough, in faraway Macquarie Island and Australia, they actually can hear something. It sounds like 'the voice of a deaf man crying out in the darkness', and like 'the outermost ripples caused by a stone thrown into the middle of a pond'.[33] In short, next to hopeless, but still it is something, an indication that something is happening down at Cape Denison where Mawson and his men were left.

Not all of what is happening at Mawson's hut, however, is happy.

How to get to the bottom of Mawson's most recent flare-up with Whetter? Perhaps by starting with Whetter's inflamed piles as a reason for his grim mood. From Mawson's side, however, the fact that Whetter seems to have spent the better part of the last six months sitting on that backside for so many hours a day reading is a significant pointer as to the likely cause.

One way or t'other, the bottom line is that Dux Ipse has had a gutful of both the assistant doctor's indolence *and* insolence. The two had their first confrontation over Whetter's laziness as far back as June, and Mawson has ever after been rueing the day he took this laggard on.

Whetter has not backed off an inch in his constant campaign to have the leader relent on the seven-days-a-week work routine. Despite several stern talks, the fact that Whetter continues to work all of two hours a day has hardly supported his case that the men be allowed to finish work by 4 pm and be granted Sundays off.

Mawson, who by now has taken to recording detailed notes regarding Whetter's recalcitrance, at one stage overhears the medico suggesting Ninnis follow his lead and turn in for an afternoon nap around 4 pm as preventative to feeling tired the following day. Ninnis, a tireless worker who typically hits the hay no earlier than 11 pm, fails to quite 'cotton on' to the good doctor's advice.[34]

Matters come to a head on 3 October, when once again the assistant doctor fails to obey Mawson's order to cut ice, preferring to read in bed. Whetter believes he has done enough work for the day, and when confronted by Mawson he declares that cutting ice is not the reason he came on the expedition.

'[You're a] bloody fool to come on the expedition if that was the case,' Mawson uncharacteristically snarls.

'Bloody fool yourself, I won't be caught on another one,' responds Whetter insolently.[35] The workload has been so onerous, Whetter continues, that some of the men have been drawing out their work so as not to be immediately assigned a new duty.

Well aware that this is the practice of at least three of the expedition members, at dinner that night Mawson relents. General duties and scientific work aside, from here on the men may knock off at 4 pm and Sundays will be free. Fittingly, the first to fully benefit from the new regime is the hard-working Swiss. Mertz celebrates in his diary:

6 October. My birthday. The first free Sunday . . . Percy gave me a nice book about photography, Hannam a book by Shackleton, Dad McLean a volume by Chateaubriand, and Mawson an English collection of poems. From Whetter, Hodgy and Nin I received cigarettes, so now I have 150 altogether. All of us appreciate Madi's cooking. From time to time we were treated to tasty delicacies. The plum pudding was cooked by Mawson's fiancée. The lady seems to have talent for cooking. In the pudding, Hodgy found a ring (will marry), and Murphy a thimble (remains single). Of course this pudding was served in my honour. In his speech Mawson complimented me, and then 'cheers!' rang out with 'Many happy returns of the day!'[36]

12 October 1912 and the day thereafter, Cape Denison, the sound of a falling body is heard

As the forces of darkness recede, so too, encouraged, do the forces of life begin to surge forward. On this day, late in the afternoon, from the freezing waters of the Southern Ocean the first penguin of the season, with extraordinary athleticism, suddenly springs out and comes 'waddling up the ice-foot against a seventy-mile wind'.[37]

For its trouble, the penguin is quickly captured by Archie McLean, who puts it under his coat, takes it back to the hut and unveils it to the gathering, where the tiny animal receives a welcome almost as rapturous as the one he receives later on when he is on their dinner plates.

Alas, winter is not done with them yet. For the next day is one that the men on this expedition would ever after refer to as 'Black Sunday'. That evening, Mawson and his men are all seated for dinner while a hurricane rages outside. It is so powerful that the whole hut is quivering under the assault of the freezing air that is tearing down the slopes at them, with speeds that Dux Ipse reckons to be as high as 220 mph. The wind is not continuous but comes in savage gusts, the freezing exhalations of an angry continent intent on blowing them away.

After one particularly ferocious gust, as all the timbers quiver once more, a sudden loud crack is heard, followed by the 'sound of a heavy falling body'.[38] For an instant, they all fear that the roof of the hut itself has caved in, but that does not seem to be the case, for it is soon apparent that there is no sudden rush of freezing wind pouring in upon them. It is the messman who finds the answer. He has no sooner poked his head out of the trapdoor than he sees that the northern wireless mast has crashed to the ground, as three wire-stays have broken. All that work, all that energy, all of their combined expertise – the first top-gallant section on one mast was completed just a fortnight before – now lies in a shattered mess of ropes and broken sections.

Right on the point of opening full communications, they are suddenly totally isolated again. It could have been worse – it could have crashed down on the roof of the hut, threatening their very existence –

But it couldn't have been much worse.

14 October 1912, The Hague, Paquita writes of good news and bad news

Mawson's fiancée has had a busy time of it over the European summer, visiting the delights of such places as Milan, Lucerne and Vienna. Oddly enough, one of the chief delights of the Austrian capital was its cold weather, which made her feel closer than ever to her man by giving her some sense that she was experiencing just the barest little bit of what he was experiencing.

Most importantly, though, she knows that the time of their separation is drawing to a close and that now, in a matter of mere months, they will be both returned to Adelaide, to be together again and to marry! She writes to him on this day:

First of all I love you even more than when you left and there has not been a day – an hour almost – that you have not been in my thoughts. You will have a warm welcome on your return – my arms are open for you already as I think of it . . .

We shall be very happy when you return with the separation behind us. Dear, I know you have done good work down there in the cold — you and your little hutfull of men.[39]

As to his comment to her in a letter brought back by Davis in March that he has been finding this expedition less cold than his last expedition with Shackleton, she is in no doubt as to the reason:

Of course, it is my love that does it. I warm you every night. You are safer there in a way than many here . . . I can almost feel your arms round me and involuntarily as I write lift my face to yours. Seventeen months without one caress! One embrace. We shall have something to make up for.

With my heart's whole love to you my lover

from your
Paquita

PS. You will have later news than I can give from Campbelltown. Am afraid Mrs Mawson is not so well. But hope for the best darling.[40]

Mid- to late October 1912, Cape Denison, let the winds of hell do their worst

Though the wind remains extremely strong over the next

fortnight, with an average velocity of 56.9 mph, the calms are becoming more frequent – no longer do one's ears throb with silence when it arrives.

Despite that wind, however, more and more penguins start to appear, making their way back to their rookeries, where they start to build their simple nests from pebbles. Soon, the skua gulls, snow petrels and storm petrels reappear too. Weddell seals, soon to pup, heave themselves from the water and flop upon the shore.

Cape Denison is waking from its frozen hibernation and returning to beautiful and bountiful life before their very eyes.

Nearing the end of the month, though, Dux Ipse starts to become notably tense and restless – and *not* just whenever he happens to gaze upon the enduringly recalcitrant Whetter. Despite his expectation that the wind would have markedly fallen away by now, allowing them to get away on their sledging expeditions, still it blows on and on, day after day, delaying their departure – a real problem, for the sledging season is a limited one at the best of times. They simply *must* get away soon if they are all to complete their trips and return to the hut by 15 January, when *Aurora* will have returned to take them home.

Finally, Mawson decides they can wait no more.

On the still blustery morning of 27 October, after the weekly Sunday service, Dux Ipse gathers the men around him and grimly tells the assembly about the sledging program: 'No matter what the weather, the main parties start . . . and let the winds of hell do their worst.'[41]

The program that awaits, he says, is one that, 'if carried out successfully, is all that remains to make the Expedition a huge success'.[42]

Six parties of three will set off into the Antarctic wilderness, each assigned to explore a different section of uncharted territory, all to depart, ideally, within ten days.

List of Parties

1 A Southern Party composed of Bage (leader), Webb and Hurley. The special feature of their work is to be magnetic observations in the vicinity of the South Magnetic Pole.

2 A Southern Supporting Party, including Murphy (leader), Hunter and Laseron, who are to accompany the Southern Party as far as possible, returning to Winter Quarters by the end of November.

3 A Western Party of three men – Bickerton (leader), Hodgeman and Whetter – who are to traverse the coastal highlands west of the hut. Their intention is to make use of the air-tractor sledge, and the departure of the party is fixed for early December.

4 Stillwell, in charge of a Near-Eastern Party, is to map the coastline between Cape Denison and the Glacier Tongue, dividing the work into two stages. In the first instance, Close and Hodgeman are to assist him; all three acting partly as supports to the other eastern parties working further afield. After returning to the hut at the end of November for a further supply of stores, he is to set out again with Close and Laseron in order to complete the work.

5 An Eastern Coastal Party composed of Madigan (leader), McLean and Correll are to start in early November with the object of investigating the coastline beyond the glacier immediately to the east.

6 Finally, a Far-Eastern Party, composed of Mawson with Ninnis 'n' Mertz, assisted by the dogs, are to push out rapidly overland to the southward of Madigan's party, mapping more distant sections of the coastline, beyond the limit to which the latter party would be likely to reach.[43]

Mawson hopes his own Far-Eastern Party will push far enough east to link the eastern limit of the Australasian Antarctic Expedition's charting with the western limit of sledging expeditions launched by the men Scott – *more quiet gnashing of teeth* – left at Cape Adare.

6 November 1912 and four days thereafter, Cape Denison, once more unto the breach dear friends, once more . . .

The landscape, obliterated by raging blizzards and snowdrifts, dashes Mawson's hopes of getting any of the parties under way on this day, as he hoped. And yet, as the weather sufficiently abates the following afternoon, the Southern Supporting Party make a dash for it – only to find themselves 1000 feet up the glacier when the wind returns, forcing them to put down their sledge and head back to the hut for the night.

By 8 November, however, the winds have moderated enough so that it is once again manageable for the men to move around outside. After the false start the day before, the Southern Supporting Party will be able to get away today, together with the Near-Eastern and Eastern Coastal Parties. Cheered off by the others, in the late morning Murphy, Hunter and Laseron are the first to leave, to be followed later in the day by the other two groups.

The next morning, while a particularly heavy drift sweeps through Cape Denison, delaying Mawson's and Bage's parties from setting out, Ninnis 'n' Mertz seize their opportunity.

Since the penguins returned to lay their first eggs, there have been constant expeditions to the rookeries to grab fresh batches of the greenish beauties far larger than a duck's egg and about twice the size of a chicken's.

And now it is time for a fresh raid. Fighting off the penguins, the two brothers in arms return from the fray with an impressive count of 22 eggs and with Mertz sporting one pair of ripped Burberry trousers courtesy of a particularly annoyed penguin who wants a piece of him to take home to show his mother.

While Mertz composes three omelettes for his comrades, Mawson takes time to write to Paquita:

This is the first occasion since landing in Antarctica that I have addressed myself to you in writing, though daily a warm glow of life feels to have crept in to me coming from the far distant civilised world and of course it can be from none other but you. I have concluded once again that it is nice to be in love, even here in Antarctica with the focus of the heart strings far away.[44]

The next morning, however, on the rescheduled day of departure for his own group, Mawson is a tad troubled after a vivid dream the night before about his father, whom he has been worrying about anyway because he knows that, right then and there, Mawson Snr is on his own expedition to the farthest reaches of New Guinea, charting his own new territory.[45] What to do to soothe his soul? He dashes off a few more lines of his letter to Paquita:

10 November, 1912: The weather is fine . . . though the wind still blows. We shall get away in an hour's time. I have two good companions, Dr Mertz and Lieut. Ninnis. It is unlikely that any harm will happen to us but should I not return to you in Australia please know that I truly loved you. I must be closing now as the others are waiting.[46]

Ninnis has already closed off the final lines in his own diary, which he will leave behind him with his other personal effects: 'I must close my writing now, maybe for two months, maybe for good and all, for who knows what might happen during the next two months . . .'[47]

Before Mawson's Far-Eastern Party and Bage's Southern Party depart, there is something they all want – indeed, after last night, *need* – to do . . .

How the soon to be departed clamour around Chef Mertz at the stove, hoping to savour the final omelette for the road – the final omelette 'fore they go – knowing it will likely be many weeks of straight pemmican and hoosh before they once again have the pleasure.

Together in harness, the Southern Party bid their fond farewells and start man-hauling, only to be immediately shocked by just how difficult it is to exert serious physical force after months of relative inactivity in the hut.

'Our way lay up a steep slope,' Hurley noted in his diary. 'Going was very hard, and not being in good sledging "NICK" our muscles felt the strain of the heavy hauling and overburdened sledge.'[48]

And so it is that, at 12.30 pm on this splendid afternoon in spring, Mawson finally sets out to play his own part in the realisation of his long-held dream. His fervent hope is that the AAE sledging journeys will firmly stamp Australia's crampon-clad footprint on the part of the Antarctic landscape that lies directly below Mawson's homeland.

With the help of Ninnis 'n' Mertz and the full complement of the expedition's remaining 17 dogs (even though many of the bitches are rather inconveniently in pup) pulling three sledges, he will chart the coastline and geologise a possible 500 miles east, where no man has ever gone before. With *Aurora* due to return on 15 January, Mawson has just 65 days to complete his self-assigned, groundbreaking, ground-*charting* mission.

Everything has been worked out to the tiniest detail. Here, starting off on the irregular coastal slopes, the third sledge is carried atop another. For now, the one man who is not driving a team of dogs walks alongside one of the sledges. However, in time the party will fall into a regular procession typically comprising a front-runner (usually Mertz on skis), followed by the other two driving the sledges initially laden with 1723 pounds of equipment and supplies.

Waving them off now are the yet to depart Western Party members Bickerton and Whetter, and Hannam, whose job it will be to keep the home blubber fires burning.

As Mawson and his men head up the slopes, wisps of their shouts are carried back to the remaining men by the wind – 'Hike, hike, hike!' – and they soon disappear into the whiteness.

The final sledging frontier awaits . . .

Chapter Thirteen

Into the Wide White Yonder

There can be no question as to the value of dogs as a means of traction in the Polar regions, except when travelling continuously over very rugged country, over heavily crevassed areas, or during unusually bad weather. It is in such special circumstances that the superiority of man-hauling has been proved. Further, in an enterprise where human life is always at stake, it is only fair to put forward the consideration that the dogs represent a reserve of food in case of extreme emergency.

Douglas Mawson, *The Home of the Blizzard*

12 November 1912 and three days thereafter, 11 miles south of One Ton Depot, with the Scott search party

In the bleak, flat, white landscape that lies before them, a sudden bump is always noticeable, and this is just such a case. As the search party sent to look for Captain Scott treks across the seemingly endless white terrain, Silas Wright suddenly notices that, a half mile out to the west, an odd-looking large white mound is throwing a small shadow on the whiteness all around.

In fact, so odd is it that while Wright tells the men on his mule train to keep going, he heads over to investigate, and the nearer he gets to it, the more he is stupefied.

Could it be?

Yes . . . yes . . . indeed, it probably is. For, poking about six inches or so out of the snow in front of the mound, he can see the tips of what appear to be two crossed skis. Suddenly feeling that he is in a sacred place, Wright furiously starts to signal for the others to come hither. He does not wish to shout out to them to come quickly, as it would be 'a sort of sacrilege to make a noise. I felt as if I were in a cathedral and found myself with my hat on.'[1]

Eventually, the whole party, including their leader, Atch Atkinson, cautiously approach where Wright is standing. There is no danger, per se, but they are fearful of what they are about to find. Absurdly, at this point, despite the passage of a year without contact from Scott or his people, they are still clinging to the hope of finding some signs of life in the wilderness.

Finally, they stand before the large lump.

And yes, this looks like . . . *Silas scratches back the snow covering, revealing light, unbleached drill canvas* . . . a tent.

There is a collective intake of breath at the discovery. Slowly now, as the rest of the party watch, mesmerised, Silas gently, cautiously, and illogically hopefully, pulls the flap of the tent aside as they all peer inside. And there they are, perfectly preserved, just as if they closed their eyes for the last time only a minute earlier. Bill Wilson and Birdie Bowers are in their separate sleeping bags, their faces upturned. Their skin is yellow and glassy from the cold, with many blotches of frostbite.

It is obvious by the way that Wilson's and Bowers's bodies are wrapped up that they died first and that Scott carefully and even lovingly laid them out. Uncle Bill, at least, looks peaceful enough, with his hands crossed on his chest, though he is in a half-sitting position, the prayer book his wife gave him before departure lying open by his side. (Ten months earlier, Scott told Oates of his decision not to put One Ton further south that, 'Regret it or not, I have taken my decision as a Christian gentleman.' Clearly, now, they have all died as Christian gentlemen.)

Oddly, Bill has an expression on his face that almost seems the faint smile of one who knows that he is about to meet his maker and looks forward to it.

As Tryggve Gran later describes it:

I had often seen the same look on his face in the morning as he awakened, as he was of the most cheerful disposition. The look struck us to the heart, and we all stood silent in the presence of this death.[2]

Birdie is much the same, resting in peace, though his arms are not crossed and he is lying on his side as if asleep.

The truly shocking vision, though, is that of Robert Falcon Scott, their leader, who is also half-sitting, with his back to the tent pole, one arm stretched out towards Wilson, and, 'between his head and the pole . . . his diary, apparently in order that its broader surface might provide an easier support than the pole'.[3]

One of the party, Petty Officer Thomas Williamson, would never forget the vision: 'His face was very pinched and his hands, I should say, had been terribly frostbitten . . . Never again in my life do I want to behold the sight we have just seen.'[4]

Nor did Tryggve Gran: 'It was a horrid sight . . . It was clear he had had a very hard last minutes. His skin was yellow, frostbite all over.'[5] When the others go inside, Gran stays very firmly outside, never feeling more Norwegian than now. It was simply not his place to be inside that sepulchre of British mourning.

And yet, though the men have all too obviously been dead for many months, there is a protocol that must be observed, and as both doctor and leader of the party, Atkinson asks the others to withdraw so he can make a medical examination of each man, as well as perform the last rites, and this is done.

That completed, carefully, in the manner of a man moving

around a tomb, for that is exactly what he is doing, Atkinson now gathers the diaries, documents and journals the men carried with them, together with the letters they wrote in their final days. Ever afterwards, Gran would remember hearing what sounds like a pistol shot ring out but is in fact the sound of Scott's frozen, withered arm breaking, as Atkinson lifts it to retrieve his diary.

On the first page of diary number three, Scott has written, 'Send this diary to my wife,' but then has crossed out the last word and replaced it with 'widow'.[6]

Among the other diaries, documents and letters is, of course, the note and the letter that Amundsen has penned, asking Scott to pass them on to the Norwegian King, the first confirmation that the rest of the Scott party have of the Norwegians' success.

Upon Atkinson telling the others of this, Crean, in tears, strides across to Tryggve Gran and offers his hand in personal congratulations that his country has been the first to the Pole.

'Sir,' he says, 'permit me to congratulate you. Dr Atkinson has just found Scott's diary, where it is written that our people found the Norwegian flag when they came to the South Pole.'[7]

Gran, also in tears, grasps the Irishman's hand and thanks him.

Gran is so moved by the manner of the Englishmen's death that, 'I just felt that I envied them. They died having done something great. How hard death must be for those who meet it having done nothing.'[8]

Outside, Atkinson continues to carefully go through Scott's diary and the letter to the public, so they can all know just what happened to the party.

The diaries of the other men, however, which contain letters they have written to their own loved ones, remain unopened under the protocol that their families have a right to read them before anyone else.

The news of the manner of Oates's death, when Atkinson tells them, makes a deep impression on them all. As Wright records in his diary that night, 'knowing that he had no hope and realizing he was a drag on the Party, he walked out into a blizzard about 19 m south of here. A damn fine finish.'[9]

What now, though? Well, they died here together, and here together they would remain. This will be their tomb, and in place of an epitaph on a tombstone Atkinson writes some words on a piece of paper and places it in an envelope beside Captain Scott. It reads:

Captain R. F. Scott, C.V.O. R.N.
Dr E. A. Wilson, and
Lieutenant H. R. Bowers, R.I.M.

As a slight token to perpetuate their gallant and successful attempt to reach the goal. This they did on 17 January 1912, after the Norwegians had already done so on 14 December 1911.

Also to commemorate their two gallant comrades:
Captain L. E. G. Oates, of the Iniskilling Dragoons, who walked to his death in a blizzard willingly about 20 miles[10] south of this place to try and save his comrades beset by hardship;

Also of Petty Officer Evans, who died at the foot of Beardmore Glacier.

The Lord gave and the Lord taketh away. Blessed be the name of the Lord.[11]

And now, carefully, just as if the men inside were sleeping and were not to be woken, the living men remove the poles supporting the tent so that the canvas collapses down upon the bodies. They then spend the rest of this day and some of the next heaping snow upon it, turning the burial site into a large mound, in a rough polar equivalent of committing the bodies to the depths. Upon the mound, they place a pair of skis, bound together to form a Christian cross.

At this point, as the wind whistles around, and the nearly midnight sun dips low above the Pole, reflecting from the iridescent clouds an ethereal light over the whole scene, the service proper gets under way. To begin, Atkinson reads out Scott's 'Message to the Public', which includes an account of the noble death of Oates. So moving are the words, so emotional the occasion, so haunting it is to make the words of the dead man lying before them live again, Atch must pause every now and then to gather himself but then finishes with the strong words that are effectively the epitaph on the snowy tomb before them:

> The causes of the disaster are not due to faulty organisation but to misfortune in all risks which had to be undertaken . . . The loss of the pony transport . . . The weather . . . The soft snow in lower reaches of glacier. Every detail of our food supplies, clothing and depots . . . worked out to perfection . . . I do not think human beings ever came through such a month as we have come through . . . We should have got through . . . but for the sickening of . . . Captain Oates, and a shortage of fuel in our depots for which I cannot account.
>
> We took risks, we knew we took them; things have come out against us, and therefore we have no cause for complaint, but bow to the will of Providence, determined still to do our best to the last . . . Had we lived, I should have had a tale to tell of the hardihood, endurance, and courage of my companions

which would have stirred the heart of every Englishman. These rough notes and our dead bodies must tell the tale, but surely, surely, a great rich country like ours will see that those who are dependent on us are properly provided for.[12]

As the graveyard group around the mound press together tightly, Atkinson again composes himself to read the Christian Burial Service, together with a chapter from Corinthians, and then, all together, they sing Scott's favourite hymn, 'Onward Christian Soldiers', particularly appropriate for the occasion. No matter that the sung words are instantly whipped away by the wind, they sing it with gusto to, if not wake the dead, at least stir them a little:

Onward, Christian soldiers, marching as to war,
With the cross of Jesus going on before.
Christ, the royal Master, leads against the foe;
Forward into battle see His banners go!

As they finish, there is a full ten seconds of complete silence, bar the wailing wind, and then, more or less together, they snap to. It is time to get on with it, come what may. In Antarctica, it is always time to get on with it, for to falter is to freeze, to dally is to die.

The most urgent task now is to find the noble Oates to give him, too, the Christian burial he deserves. An emotional Atkinson is particularly insistent on this, as Oates was his closest friend on the expedition. Carefully, scanning the landscape as they proceed slowly south, they look for him, but wherever his body lies he is clearly completely covered by snow and ice. The only sign of the Soldier that they can find is his sleeping bag, located 15 miles to the south of Scott's final camp. Inside the bag is the discarded theodolite, his finneskos and socks. One of the finneskos is slit down the front, evidently to get his gangrenous foot into it.

Despite their failure to locate Oates's body in the early morning of this 15th day of November, they erect a cross, on the base of which they write the inscription:

Hereabouts died a very gallant gentleman,
Captain L. E. G. Oates of the Iniskilling Dragoons.
In March 1912, returning from the Pole, he walked
willingly to his death in a blizzard to try to save his
comrades, beset by hardship.

And then they head back to Cape Evans, with Atkinson keenly aware that some months hence he will have to break to the waiting world the terrible news of Scott's tragedy.

15 November 1912, Queen's Hall, London, Amundsen is not cheered by three cheers

Gentlemen, gentlemen, gentlemen . . .

Dignitaries and notables, members of the Royal Geographical Society and their friends have turned out to the Queen's Hall in a fair number to hear the Norwegian chap, Amundsen, deliver his paper giving details of his Antarctic venture. (True, when Peary had been similarly received two years earlier by the Royal Geographical Society to talk of his North Pole conquest, they had to book the much bigger Royal Albert Hall, but Peary had not been competing with an Englishman. This tidy little Queen's Hall will just have to do for the Norwegian.)

Introducing the guest speaker, the president of the society, Lord Curzon, declares:

In the field of exploration we know no jealousy. Even while we are honouring Capt. Amundsen, I am sure his thoughts no less than ours are turned to our brave countryman, Capt. Scott, who is still shrouded in the glimmering half light of the Antarctic and whose footsteps reached the same pole doubtless only a few weeks after Amundsen. The names of these two men will perpetually be linked, along with Shackleton's, in the history of Antarctic exploration.[13]

Hear, hear. Hear, hear. A rough rumble of approval rolls through the room, amid the thick pall of British protocol. Not joining in any such positive rumble in the presence of *that man* is Kathleen Scott, who has knocked back a front-row seat at the top table in preference to sitting relatively anonymously in the top gallery.

Similarly, while Amundsen's own speech, in which he details what they did and how they did it, seems to be reasonably well received, in Kathleen's view, as she would describe it to her husband in her diary later that night, it was 'plucky, but dull and of a dullness!'.[14]

And then it is none other than Sir Ernest Shackleton (whose brother Frank just happens to be currently under arrest for an alleged part in the theft of the Irish Crown jewels) who proposes a generous vote of thanks to the Norwegian.

Hear, hear. Hear, hear.

And then it happens . . .

At the end of the actual speech of thanks for Amundsen's address, Lord Curzon – the Norwegian explorer would ever after maintain – makes a remark that wounds Amundsen to his core. After noting the manner in which Amundsen and his men have managed to be the first to get to the Pole, Lord Curzon turns to Amundsen and says, 'I therefore propose three cheers for the dogs.'[15]

Three cheers for the dogs . . . three cheers for the dogs . . . three cheers for the dogs . . .

Amundsen, at least the way he recounted it ever afterwards

(though there would be bitter dispute as to whether Lord Curzon ever did say those five words[16]), could barely think straight for the sting of the insult he had just suffered.

17 November to 1 December 1912, 63 miles to the east of Cape Denison, Mawson, Ninnis 'n' Mertz experience pride before several falls

A week into their trek, Mawson is well satisfied, even proud, with the progress they are making and the work being done. With regular stops so he can set up his theodolite to chart the landscape they are covering – while Mertz boils the hypsometer to measure altitude and, between them all, several times a day, they record magnetic variation and meteorological conditions – they continue to push east over sometimes difficult but never impassable terrain. As they trek, Mawson is getting to know his two companions a lot better. While it is one thing to have been merely *around* them along with dozens of other men on a ship or with 18 of them in the hut, it is quite another to be with them day after day, every day, in extreme conditions, facing obstacle after obstacle, all of them putting their lives in each other's hands.

Mawson is extremely impressed with both of them. On the odd occasion that Belgrave Ninnis is not known as one half of Ninnis 'n' Mertz, he has been nicknamed 'Cherub' by the others, due to his rather beatific baby face and the fact that he has a complexion as pink and white as that of any girl. However, he is strong, generous in spirit and resilient.

Though both Mawson and Mertz already have a lot of experience in covering severe frozen terrain like this, now Ninnis, too, becomes expert in such things as being able to spot the telltale wavy lines on the surface that can indicate the presence of the edge of a crevasse, where extreme care must be taken. He learns how it is best to cross such snow bridges square on, to get across them as quickly as possible, and becomes ever more proficient at running his dogs so they exert maximum pulling power, which is no small art.

As to Mertz, notwithstanding that it seems he has a predisposition to suffering snow-blindness, Mawson is more confident than ever that he has made the right choice in picking him. With that curious combination of toughness and cheeriness, 'X', as they sometimes refer to him, is close to the ideal sledging companion.

Together, the men push on, taking their bearings principally from 'shooting the sun' and examining the distance travelled on their sledge-meters.

In the bigger picture, highly prized for all of them in this unending white terrain is when they spy new landmarks. Such a thrill occurs at 5 pm on this afternoon of 17 November when they crest a ridge at an altitude of 2600 feet to see before them the splendid vision of 'a fine panorama of coastal scenery'.[17] On the far-eastern horizon, they spy the very glacier tongue projecting into the Southern Ocean that *Aurora* first followed to make her way into Commonwealth Bay and delight to see, as Mawson puts it, 'its long wall touched in luminous bands by the south-western sun'.[18] Directly in front of them, they see a wide valley, and beyond that again there is a deep indentation in the coastline, which means they will have to soon steer a more southerly course to be able to get around it.

They make camp that evening at 7.30 pm, well advanced into the wide valley. With the next day dawning bright and beautiful, they make good progress before that evening something even more exciting appears on the distant horizon to their south-east, so exciting that they alter course to get a better look.

To their amazement, bit by bit, a rather imposing mountain starts to rise from the ice before them . . . and by the following evening again they are close enough to be standing at the lip of a large glacial valley, where they can see the glacier they must cross sweeping by the eastern side of this 1750-foot-high mountain.

Of the many pleasures of travelling where no man has gone before, the privilege of marking fresh geographical features in one's journal and naming them is one of the foremost. And so, just as Mawson named the feature discovered the previous day Madigan Nunatak, in honour of his valued expedition member Cecil Madigan, on this occasion Mawson decides to call the completely snow-clad mountain ahead of them Aurora Peak, in honour of the worthy ship that has not only brought them to these parts but in six weeks' time will, hopefully, be taking them away again.

The next day, a long journey crossing that glacier commences, with the icy slopes of the other side so far away they can only just discern them. Though the dogs perform well, the day after that there is something more than a mere hiccup with their finest hauler, Ginger. This particular 'hiccup', from her nether regions, on this day produces no fewer than 14 puppies, which is some explanation for why she uncharacteristically cut loose after lunch the day before. Of course, there is no question of the puppies being nurtured, and there is really only one choice, which is carried out. They have no sooner come into the world than they are killed and given to the other dogs to feed on.

It is yet another example of where, as was elucidated by Captain Cook 140 years earlier, things that would have revolted a civilised spirit while in Europe simply have to be accepted in this part of the world.

In this glorious new world, every day seems to bring a fresh vision, previously unseen by the eyes of man – though sometimes the fresh vision also indicates problems to come.

On 21 November, after a difficult morning's sledging through a strong wind and heavy drift, things calm and visibility improves enough that they can see what they must face: 'a glittering line of broken ice, stretching at right angles to our path'.[19]

A more immediate problem is that they now find themselves in a part of the glacier filled with crevasses, through which the dogs are regularly falling before being hauled back.

The party stop for lunch in a place surrounded by many such terrifying abysses, and while Mertz prepares a meal – on today's menu is, let's see, *hoosh* – Ninnis and Mawson go to take a photo of a nearby open crevasse. Returning, they pass on either side of the tent, and the next thing Mawson knows he hears a strange sound and rushes around to find Ninnis rather as he found Edgeworth David four years earlier, hanging onto the lip of the crevasse for his very life as his legs dangle over a gaping maw of nothingness. Mawson soon drags him to safety, and, lying on their bellies looking down into the black depths, they both realise with a shudder just how close Ninnis has come to disappearing forever.[20]

Pushing on, by the afternoon of 24 November they have risen to the far side of the glacial valley enough to see the glacier they have just crossed in all its magnificence, 'extending out to sea as a floating tongue beyond the horizon. Inland, some 20 miles to the south, it mounted up in seamed and riven "cataracts" to a smooth, broad and shallow groove which wound into the ice-cap.'[21]

They continue to use Aurora Peak to get their bearings and are sad to see it finally sink back into the whiteness as they continue to the east, where the western wall of a second major glacier is now becoming apparent, lying around 145 miles east of their Winter Quarters. Mawson has been expecting to see this glacier, as it is clearly noted on the map left by Charles Wilkes some 70 years earlier, of which he has a copy now.

Crossing this glacier, beginning on 27 November, proves problematic, as the steep slope to get down it is covered with sastrugi and continues for 1000 feet. The only way to get through this is to let most of the dogs loose – in the confidence that they will return to the only source of food, which is what they have for them on the sledges – and let gravity plus two dogs a sledge do the work. Even then, it is chaotic, as the sledges prove uncontrollable and turn over many times before the bottom is reached.

Once the dogs come back to them and are put back in harness, one bitch, Betli, is missing and is never to be seen again, presumably fallen into a crevasse. She joins the roll call of the dog-dead. (Jappy and Fusilier have previously been shot for, literally, not pulling their weight.) The next day, the bitch Blizzard is also shot for her trouble, as with all the work she has weakened so much she is more valuable as a food source to the other dogs than as a puller. Still, even without her the conditions have improved so much that they make 16 miles on the day.

Over the next couple of days, the three men continue crossing the glacier – only narrowly escaping on one occasion losing an entire sledge and dog team down a crevasse – until, at last, on the evening of 30 November, with the 12 dogs remaining, they are able to get to the higher reaches of the eastern side of this second major glacier, where they camp.

The following morning, as they move a little further, get a smidgen higher and can get their bearings, Mawson suffers a keen disappointment. Based on the Wilkes map, he was expecting to now come over this lip of the glacier's edges and see a vista of land before them to the north-east. But there is nothing but . . . sea!

'It is obvious we have been deluded by Wilkes's reports,' he writes in his diary, 'for it appears that no land exists in that [north-east] direction, and if Wilkes saw anything it can hardly have been more than a barrier edge.'[22]

After carefully checking angles and calculating approximate distances with his trusty theodolite, Mawson carefully redraws the map to reflect the now proven reality. He then changes their course so as to move further inland and hopefully traverse less crevassed terrain than that typically found where the glaciers begin to enter the sea. As they proceed, the only notable complication is that the weather has acknowledged the first official day of summer by warming up to the point where it makes the snow sticky and difficult to move across, meaning Mawson again must adapt their plan. To try to minimise this problem, he changes their schedule so that they travel at night, when it is colder and the snow firmer.

9 December 1912 and four days thereafter, 287 miles east of Winter Quarters, Mawson's Far-Eastern Party meet a 'wasp's nest'

How very, very odd. On this day, from out of nowhere, and even though they are well inland, suddenly a snow petrel appears and briefly circles over Ninnis's sledge before quickly disappearing. Where has it come from? Where has it gone to?

They press on.

While it has been initially exciting to be in a place where one's every step is where no man has trodden before, by this time, well by this time . . . *plod* . . . *plod* . . . *plod* . . . most of that thrill is gone.

Five weeks and 287 miles into their icy odyssey away from the hut, all three of the party are looking forward to soon putting their feet exactly where they *have* trodden before – to getting to the point where they can turn back and head for the safety of Winter Quarters. Hopefully, of course, they will arrive before *Aurora*, which should be chugging back towards Antarctica within a fortnight to take them back to Hobart. (Oh, Hobart! From their current position in the wilds of Antarctica, that tiny Tasmanian town seems like London or Paris, the height of civilisation.)

The going has not been easy, and the distance they have traversed is a lot less than Mawson hoped for. In an effort to increase the number of miles they can cover before turning back, on 12 December he comes up with a new plan.

They will abandon the recently damaged sledge of Ninnis at this campsite and very carefully redistribute the load from the discarded sledge across the remaining two.

For Mawson has thought it through. He reasons that if one of the sledges is to tumble into a crevasse atop a crumbling snow bridge, it will most likely be the first sledge – so it will be the wisest thing to have the most important supplies on the second sledge, pulled by the best dogs. And though that second sledge is admittedly 50 pounds heavier than the first sledge, that weight will rapidly diminish in coming days as they and the dogs eat their way through much of the supplies it bears.

Mawson also decides that in a couple of days' time, they will establish another depot where they can leave most of their gear and make a quick dash as far east as they could safely get, before returning to the depot, collecting their supplies and beginning the long haul back to Winter Quarters.

All happy, all good, all . . .?

No, Ninnis is not happy. It has nothing to do with Mawson's announced plans and everything to do with the whitlow – a very painful and pus-filled infection – atop one of his fingers. It has been troubling him for a week, to the point where he has lost sleep over it. After a terrible and nearly sleepless night, on the morning of 13 December, before setting off, he asks Mawson to lance it, which the expedition leader does, the pus suddenly bursting forth. While Ninnis recovers, Mawson and Mertz get on with re-arranging the sleds, and they are soon under way.

At 4 pm, they encounter what Mertz describes as 'a wasp's nest' of crevasses.[23] However, they negotiate a course circumventing the crevasses with 'pretty well clear luck' and, having reached safer ground, camp after an eight-and-a-quarter-mile day.

14 December 1912 and the day thereafter, 311 miles east of Winter Quarters, Mawson has to say farewell

And some days are just like this. After all the blizzards, all the problems, all the falls down crevasses and the terribly hard yards gained, suddenly it all comes together and they are able to positively *zoom* along. Mertz is in his customary position, in front on skis, loudly singing his Swiss student songs. Mawson is 30 yards behind on the lightly packed first sledge, pulled by the weakest six dogs. And the cheerful Ninnis – who, since his finger was lanced, has slept well for the first time in a week – brings up the rear, another 40 yards back again, with the heavily packed sledge pulled by the strongest dogs.

All is right with the world, everything is as good as it could possibly be, they are not far from the point where they will turn around to be homeward bound and . . .

And suddenly, Mawson looks up to see that Mertz has lifted a ski pole of warning, of something unusual up ahead. It is not cause for huge alarm, for Mertz has done this many times in his role as the veritable scout of their expedition – it just means be careful.

After Mawson reaches the point where Mertz has given the warning, he stops his sledge to look around for what might have warranted it, but, seeing no immediate indication of anything untoward, he hops aboard the sledge to set about calculating the latitudinal observations they have taken at noon. But wait . . .

Briefly casting his eyes to the ground, he now does see, after all, the signs of a snow bridge: the small depression in the terrain where the overlying snow takes on a slightly different appearance, and the tiny telltale wavy line that marks the edges of a crevasse. Danger.

Quickly turning behind him, Mawson shouts a warning to Ninnis, who is now walking by the side of his own sledge. At Mawson's call, the young Englishman immediately swings the leading dogs around to cross any hidden crevasse front on – to minimise his time on the dangerous part – rather than cross it as Mawson has done, diagonally. Satisfied that Ninnis is safe, Mawson returns to his calculations and continues forward.

The near silence of that beautifully benign day, peppered only by the panting of his dogs and the creak of the runners, is suddenly if lightly broken by a weak and plaintive whine from one of Ninnis's dogs. Assuming it is because the dog has just had a touch from the Englishman's whip on its lazy behind, Mawson playfully says to young George, the laziest dog of his own team, 'You will be getting a little of that, too, George, if you are not careful.'[24]

But there is no time to continue even this imaginary conversation. For now, Mawson becomes aware that Mertz has stopped and is looking back, open-mouthed, to a point behind him. Mawson turns around to see what is up with Ninnis and . . .

. . .

And Ninnis is not there.

Mawson continues to stare for a few moments, *willing* Ninnis to suddenly reappear, nearly sure that the head of the young army officer will bob up in a second as he comes up over a dip in the terrain. But Mawson cannot remember any such dip in the last 30 seconds, and Ninnis does *not* suddenly emerge. There is just Mawson himself, Mertz, the panting dogs, the sorrowful, whistling wind and nothing else . . . until they both suddenly hear it.

Again, it is the whimper of a dog coming from the direction where Ninnis was last seen. Mawson begins to run back, still hoping that he will suddenly see Ninnis at the bottom of a dip, or at the very least his sledge, with the rope trailing downwards to the suspended Englishman.

But upon this vast vista of whiteness, there is nothing, stone-cold motherless *nothing*, until he comes upon a crevasse that has broken in, 'a gaping hole in the surface about 11 ft wide'.[25] Leading up to the far side of it, he can see the ski tracks of Mertz and the sledge tracks of himself and Ninnis. But coming from the hole there are only the tracks of himself and Mertz.

Mawson looks over the edge, not knowing what he will see, but fearing it greatly. It is worse, much worse than he can have possibly imagined.

He gasps. There is seemingly no bottom to this crevasse. Just as he said 'let the winds of hell do their worst' before they all departed, this is surely the place where those winds have come from. All he can see is a dark abyss, going down, down, down, with just one ledge visible about 150 feet below, on which he can see only a food bag and a moaning, writhing dog, whose back appears to be broken as only its front paws are moving. Beside it is a dead dog and what looks to be the tent and a crucial bag of food supplies.

Appalled and shocked by the horror of it all, Mawson calls down into the depths for 'Ninnis . . .! *Ninnis . . .!* NINNISSSSS . . .!' But wherever he is, he is so far down that there is not even an echo . . . and certainly no reply from him.

And now, Mertz, equally stunned, has arrived, and he too is calling for his best friend, in his thickly accented English – 'Ninnähs! Nin-näähs!' – but there is no response. Both men are in shock, not believing that this terrible thing has really happened and yet being confronted with the evidence before them.

For the next three hours, they continue to call forlornly, all while the dog with the broken back dies before their eyes. In response to the call, there is only the silence of the tomb. But still they cannot bring themselves to stop calling. That would be giving up. That would be accepting that Ninnis is dead and that the vast majority of their food supplies is gone – two things that neither of them is prepared to acknowledge.

In pauses between their shouting, however, they discuss how it is that they got across the snow bridge while Ninnis didn't. Whereas Mertz was on skis and Mawson was sitting on his sledge, Ninnis was walking beside the more heavily laden sledge. Was all the sledge weight together with his own weight – coming directly down through his feet – enough extra pressure per square-inch to punch a hole in the snow and take the rest of it with him? Had their own weight so weakened the snow bridge that it had become nothing more than a lethal trapdoor, waiting for him?

They look for options, for something constructive they can do. What about climbing down into the crevasse to look for him? No. By putting all their alpine ropes together, they still can't even reach the supplies on the ledge below, let alone go any deeper than that to look for Ninnis. Besides, the crevasse is far too wide to lay the remaining sledge across as a support.

Bit by bit, the enormity of what has happened really does hit them.

'We could do nothing, really nothing,' writes Mertz. 'We were standing, helplessly, next to a friend's grave, my best friend of the entire expedition.'[26] Not only is their dear friend Ninnis dead, but they have also lost their best six dogs, all of their dog food, four-fifths of their own food supplies, their tent and one sledge, together with such crucial things as their spade and ice-axe, and, not least, Mertz's windproof Burberry trousers, which Ninnis was carrying with him on this surprisingly warm day. All at a point when they are 311 miles east of the nearest succour, on the wrong side of some of the most treacherous and unforgiving country on the planet. For a short time, they both feel completely lost and helpless, until their survival instinct kicks in and they are moved to action.

The most urgent thing, of course, is to get out of this field, which may well be strewn with lethal crevasses all over. To get their bearings, both men leave the remaining sledge and carefully, oh so *carefully*, trek a further five miles in a south-easterly direction to reach a vantage point so they can look down upon the terrain they must cross.

There is no question they must turn back – immediately! Without adequate food, clothing and camping equipment, they will be lucky to survive the march home. Having encountered such dangerous crevasse-filled country towards the coast, they have long planned to return to Cape Denison via an inland route. This means they have laid no depots to resupply from, as they would have done had they intended to get home along a retraced route.

As the two men stand there, gazing to the north, suddenly, from out of nowhere, a snow petrel appears, which flits about for a short time before flying away.[27] It looks like the petrel that appeared above Ninnis, from out of nowhere, just a few days earlier. Strange.

It is time to get to grips with trying, however vainly, to close the gap between them and safety. Carefully, they negotiate their way back to the remaining sledge and get themselves organised. It is time to discard whatever is not absolutely necessary to their survival, bar the records they have taken, as it is unthinkable to discard their whole *raison d'être* for this journey.

As to food, there is just enough on this surviving sledge to keep them alive for maybe 11 or 12 days, and judging from the duration of the journey to this point it will take at least 35 days to get back to Winter Quarters.

Right now, so conscious are they of the grimness of their food situation that they decide the only meal they can allow themselves is to boil up some old and empty food-bags they are about to discard in order to make some exceedingly thin soup.

For food for the dogs, they have next to nothing . . . other than the dogs themselves. Clearly, as those dogs weaken, they will have to be shot and fed to the other dogs . . . and themselves, to help make up the rations they are missing. (Somewhere, the spirit of Captain Cook, if not Mr Forster's dog, stirs.) In the meantime, the dogs will have to make do with whatever can be found for them. Mawson throws them some mitts and rawhide straps that are no longer needed, and the dogs begin fighting for the few precious morsels.

Watching the dogs snapping and snarling at each other, right beside the crevasse where Ninnis has died, both men feel as miserable and as vulnerable as kittens caught in a terrible snowstorm. They will fight to survive, but they are up against forces so much more powerful than themselves that the odds against their coming out of this alive are overwhelming. But – and this is no small thing – at least they have each other, and that really is something to cling on to.

As Mawson later reflects upon it:

> When comrades tramp the road to anywhere through a lonely blizzard-ridden land in hunger, want and weariness the interests, ties and fates of each are interwoven in a fabric of friendship and affection. The shock of Ninnis's death struck home and deeply stirred us.[28]

By 9 pm, they are finally ready to go, bar one thing. They need to formally acknowledge that Ninnis is dead. They have been putting off doing any kind of a service for him to this point, because any such service was a denial of even the slimmest of hopes. But now it is time. The Australian and Swiss stand by the edge of the crevasse, their uncovered heads bowed, as Mawson slowly and solemnly intones the burial service, his words carried away on the growling wind: 'We therefore commit his body to the ground, earth to earth . . .'

At its conclusion, there is a brief silence, leavened only by the wind whipping across the maw of Ninnis's open grave, until Mertz, still deeply shaken by what has occurred, shakes Mawson by the hand and offers a sincere, broken, 'Thank you.'[29]

All Mawson can say is, 'May God help us.'[30]

In the wake of the unspeakable tragedy, Mawson and Mertz, two tiny dwarves on a vista of snow-white nothingness, take stock.

What they are left with are six dogs, barely one and a half weeks' supplies for what at best will be a four-week journey, two sleds and . . . very little hope. The only saving grace is they still have some kerosene, a Primus cooker and a spare tent cover.

The men's thoughts now turn to the importance of immediately retracing their steps to the 12 December campsite of two days before, where they know they can salvage some abandoned gear from the damaged sledge, including a broken shovel, which may now prove invaluable.

The question is, will they be able to get to it before dropping from exhaustion, for resting without a tent for protection is out of the question.

The spot where Ninnis disappeared is a terrain of low hills, and they now return through it, with Mertz again going ahead on skis, while the dogs slowly and painfully pull the sledge up the slopes, as Mawson walks beside. At the peak of each hill, Mawson climbs on board, and all together they charge like mad things down the other side, the dogs hot on the heels of the seemingly crazed Mertz.

Yes, there is the constant danger of falling into another crevasse, but such is the extremity of their situation now that dying from falling into a crevasse is only a possibility, whereas not getting back to the abandoned sledge and its tent in time would make death a certainty. They *have* to race, and race they do, with their sledge lurching fearfully from side to side as, in Mawson's mind, 'Death and the great Providence' fight a bitter duel to decide their fate. In such a race, knowing that speed is of the essence for Providence to have a chance of winning the duel, there is little time to grieve for the dear, departed Ninnis.

'We strove to forget it in the necessity of work, but we knew that the truth would assuredly enter our souls in the lonely days to come.'[31]

Not only is there little grief, there is also not much fear. Mawson's mood is one of almost numb resignation. If Death wins in this fight against Providence, then so be it. And yet, for the moment, Providence holds her own and they pass over far more dangerous-looking crevasses than the one that has claimed Ninnis, without any damage whatsoever.

Finally, after only five and a half hours of this downhill madness, following their outward tracks, they have covered the entire 24 miles, and at 2.30 am on 15 December they spy their discarded sledge up ahead.[32]

It is a valuable resource, and no sooner have they arrived than Mertz is at it, taking one of the runners of the sledge and breaking it in two. In conjunction with his skis, this will give them the four stanchions they need, lashed tightly at the top in the manner of an Indian tepee, four feet above, around which they can put the spare tent cover that has mercifully survived on Mawson's sledge. By piling plenty of snow-blocks around its base, they prove to have a serviceable shelter, even if there is absolutely no room inside for one of them to change even his mind.

As they lie there, exhausted, their dire plight hits them anew and they discuss just which direction they should head in from here.

There are two choices. One is to return as quickly as possible to the coast, which, though it is the longer route, would give them a greater chance of shooting some seals for sustenance. The other is to stay with their original plan and return inland, via the shorter route, using the ten days' ration they have, supplemented by the meat from their six dogs.

In the end, they decide on the second option, the one with less distance and fewer crevasses. Give them anything but a route with a lot of crevasses. Beyond everything else, they must get back to the Winter Quarters at Cape Denison before *Aurora* would have to leave without them.

14 December 1912, *Terra Nova* leaves Lyttelton, New Zealand, as *Aurora* arrives again in Hobart

At the first glint of the Lyttelton dawn, all is shipshape and ready to go on *Terra Nova*. It is so early when she casts off, at 5 am, that there is only a light sprinkling of friends and spectators on the wharf to farewell them. Commander Teddy Evans is eager to get under way and leave New Zealand so they can 'sail south to lift the veil', as one Antipodean paper expresses it.[33]

Yes, it was a bitter blow to him to have been turned back from the assault on the Pole by Scott, not to mention having nearly died shortly thereafter, but after returning to England to rest and recuperate he has now recovered both his health and his good humour and is keen to return to pick up all the expedition members, most particularly the Scott party returned from the Pole. At the request of Professor Edgeworth David, they will be taking a different route to the south this time, to take fresh soundings and do some dredging work on a previously unexplored part of the sea bed. If all goes to plan, Evans expects to get to the Antarctic edge late in the second week of January.

Just a few hours later, *Aurora*, under the command of Captain Davis, arrives once more in Hobart, after a long excursion of over a month taking soundings between Hobart and Macquarie Island, and Macquarie Island and Auckland Island, south of New Zealand. The most interesting thing discovered is an underwater ridge south of Tasmania and extending towards Antarctica. The top of the ridge is just 500 fathoms deep, while either side it is 2400 fathoms. The existence of this very ridge was previously posited by Professor David as the remains of a land bridge once connecting Australia to Antarctica, before the seas rose, and Davis has been extremely excited to establish its existence.

For now, *Aurora* must replenish her stocks and get ready to depart in just under a fortnight's time to head back to Cape Denison to pick up Mawson's men, as well as Wild and his men at the Western Base.

15 December to 26 December 1912, heading towards Cape Denison, Mawson and Mertz's dogs grow nervous

Although all the dogs started out well enough, all of them bar Ginger have weakened terribly.

A single shot rings out in the polar morning, its crack rolling across the stark bleakness with nary a single obstacle to raise an echo, and the weakest of the dogs, George, is dispatched. Shortly thereafter, large pieces of George are being fed to the other dogs, while small pieces are being lightly sizzled on the lid of the aluminium cooker being held over the Primus stove, the makeshift tent filling with the sound of the hissing stove and the fragrant aroma of cooking meat.

Still some 287 miles from the hut, Mawson and Mertz sit there, gnawing on the stringy meat for their breakfast, in rough if companionable silence. Sometimes, there is really nothing you can say, is there, George? . . . George? For that is the way they are thinking of him, rather than as an anonymous piece of meat. And, by George, he has a strong, musty taste.

Mertz loved George with a passion, the same way that Mawson still loves Pavlova, now gnawing on George at Mawson's feet, and for the Swiss man the meal is particularly ghastly. For Mawson, the only part of George that is remotely pleasurable to eat is his soft and mushy liver, which slips down fairly easily. On the other end of the scale are his paws, which can only be digested after being stewed for a very long time. (The recipe could well have been to put George into the water with a stone, and when the stone is soft, George will be ready to eat.)

The other dogs, however, are ravenous, and their far more powerful jaws and lower levels of sensitivity make notably short work of the rest of George, wolfing down his meat, his skin and even his fur, before crunching through his very *bones*. In short order, apart from the scraps of meat that Mawson and Mertz have put aside for their next meal, there is nothing of George that remains, with even his eyes, ears, genitals and anus consumed by the dogs.

Mawson suddenly realises that in the madness and misery of the loss of Ninnis, they have forgotten something important. They have overlooked raising the Union Jack at the farthest point east that they have trekked, effectively claiming this part of the planet for Australia and the British Empire.

This is soon put to rights on this early evening of 15 December 1912 as they plant the flag and formally name this newly discovered territory King George V Land, with Mawson perhaps wondering quietly at the futility of a ceremony no one is likely to ever learn of, but at least it is done.

Finally breaking camp at 6 pm, they start off strongly and in this land of the midnight sun are able to keep on walking in the low glow of the early morning hours. Not that finding the right direction is easy. It is not simply a matter of getting out their compass and following it, for, this close to the South Magnetic Pole, their compass is not too much to the north of useless. Or maybe to the south of useless . . . it is always very hard to say.

The only way they can now be sure they are heading in their direction of due west is by orientating their march at right angles to the sastrugi, whipped up by winds that run almost directly north–south. When freshly fallen snow covers the sastrugi, they need to halt from time to time, dig down and examine the underlying formations to ensure they are on course.

All of it is exhausting, and not just for them, as the remaining dogs, too, are suffering terribly. On the early morning of 17 December, after completing another 16 miles, Johnson – once strong enough to try to take on an elephant seal – has become too weak to carry on. Mertz has no recourse but to shoot him and cut him up.

And so it goes: night after night of sheer exhaustion, stumbling, pressing on, resting briefly, shooting a dog, eating it and moving on again, with the loss of each dog of course meaning that they must take progressively more of the weight of hauling the sledge themselves, all while their remaining dogs get increasingly exhausted and thin. On 21 December, one dog, Haldane, falls down a crevasse, and though he is saved soon afterwards drops in his tracks and also has to be shot. His carcass, like poor Johnson's, is added to their food supplies.

Through it all, they have kept moving, and on the upside they have covered an approximate 115 miles since Ninnis's death, meaning they are now under 200 miles from the safety of Winter Quarters.

Against that, they are rapidly deteriorating physically, as, on reduced rations and doing more work than ever, their bodies have no choice but to effectively eat themselves. First their fat, then their muscle mass reduces accordingly. Though immediately after the loss of Ninnis they have been able to travel as much as 20 miles in a day, that daily tally is now dropping in line with their strength and their number of dogs. On a bad day, it goes as low as just ten miles, and it has become progressively more difficult to erect their tent as they weaken. When the temperature drops, it is a particular problem for Mertz, as his Burberry over-trousers were lost with Ninnis's sledge, leaving him only with his thinner Jaeger woollen under-trousers – though, oddly, he finds that when he sweats, that sweat instantly freezes into a thin crust, which gives him at least a little protection from the wind, in the same manner as an igloo.[34] This is one positive thing, in a litany of woes.

It is not simply that the terrain, which is littered with a riot of high sastrugi, soft snow and crevasses, is difficult to traverse; it is that the often overcast weather and heavy drift obscures the sun, which prevents them seeing a clear way forward.

And finally, there is this. Over the last week, Mawson's dog Pavlova has just about given up the ghost. Mawson now carries the waning, whining canine upon his sledge, prolonging, for as long as possible . . . the moment that has now come. Having hauled the heavy sledge uphill, Mawson acknowledges to himself that Pavlova's final curtain has arrived.

Always conscious of lightening the load, they have recently discarded their rifle, meaning that Mawson must take to this sweet-natured animal with his knife. God help him.

A small whimper, a shattered gurgle, and soon enough it is over, as he begins to harvest Pavlova's body for nutrition, right down to the very marrow of her bones for soup. Through it all, Mawson is able to at least gain some moral strength by repeating to himself some of his favourite lines from the stoical philosophy of Marcus Aurelius: 'If thou art pained by any external thing, it is not this thing that disturbs thee but your own judgement about it. And it is in thy power to wipe out that judgement now.'[35]

By Christmas Eve, the two exhausted men reach the middle of the second of the glaciers that they crossed after leaving Winter Quarters, leaving them still with 160 miles to get back to safety.

On this night, Mawson's imagination works overtime as he has a bizarre dream involving rows of giant confectioner's cakes four feet in diameter with inbuilt fuses that, once lit, set in train a chemical process that completes their cooking.

Look at the size of them! Their colour! Their smell! The ingenious scientific way in which they could be cooked, even . . . well, even when in a tent in Antarctica! Albeit disappointed, he has room for but one cake; he makes his selection and hurries off to the counter to make payment. But now, when skipping off down the street, he suddenly realises he has forgotten the cake. Alas, upon returning, a closed door bears the sign 'Early Closing'.

Early Closing . . . Early Closing . . . Early Closing . . .

He wakes with a start. The wind is howling.

Oh. There is no cake shop. He is in a tent in Antarctica, with Mertz, who is snoring. He is hungry. He is always hungry. He is *starving*. At least there will be a reasonably good meal on the morrow, even if it is less traditional Christmas fare – an altogether different kind of Pavlova. For, ever the pragmatist, Mawson soon sets about turning the remains of his favourite dog, once held in the arms of and cuddled by the greatest ballerina of her day, into a stew, all while he does his calculations.

Given they are 160 miles as the crow flies from Cape Denison, and are travelling at an average of 15 miles per day, he works out that every day they can have just six ounces of dried food, down from the original allocation of 34, augmented with around eight ounces of dog meat, which will hopefully be sufficient to survive on. It all helps distract him somewhat for a short time, but Mawson cannot help but think of Paquita on this Christmas morning, wondering precisely where she is and what she will be doing, apart from, he hopes, missing him as terribly as he misses her. No doubt, wherever she is, she will be having a real Christmas meal, with all the trimmings.

Suddenly, he remembers the two half-biscuits secreted in a pocket for this very day. He proffers one to Mertz, who has now woken up and is sitting close by, and the two men wish each other 'happier Christmases in the future'.[36] Mertz, forcing down some of Pavlova with a little 'festive' butter, hopes 'to live to share many merry Christmases with my friend Mawson, but if possible, as a real festive occasion in the civilized world'.[37]

A future that starts now. For, at 2.30 am in this land of the midnight sun, they are up and away and depart into a 15- to 20-mph wind in a west-north-west direction.

While Mertz leads the way on skis, Mawson is hunkered down in his harness, hauling the sledge on his own through the snowdrift up a gradual incline.

After ten miles, up on a ridge, Mawson pauses to assess the situation. They are on the plain of that second major glacier they crossed after leaving Winter Quarters. Its ridges rise to the land on the far side, and he calculates they are now roughly 150 miles away from the hut, 68 degrees 41 minutes south, roughly halfway home. At 9.30 am, they pitch camp, heat the dreaded dog dish for dinner and fall yet again exhausted into deep sleep. Then, upon rising at 10 pm, they consume yet more of the dog stew, washed down by cocoa, and set off. A real Christmas to forget . . .

15 December to 26 December 1912, Adélie Land, Christmas comes to the other parties

Meanwhile, the other groups set in train from the hut to all parts of Adélie Land are struggling on in their own fashions, the best they can. As Christmas comes a'jingle-jangling along, Robert Bage's Southern Party – comprising himself, Frank Hurley and Eric Webb – are on their return march from their thwarted attempt to get to the South Magnetic Pole, after constant gale-force winds had prevented them. (At least, however, their data has allowed for an update of its position to be calculated, proving it has moved from the time that Mawson, Mackay and David claimed its conquering on the Shackleton expedition four years earlier.) Now, though, after turning back 'half glad, half regretful'[38] that the wind is going their way, they are under full sail over occasionally high and hard sastrugi – with Webb, nevertheless, still stopping the party at regular intervals to record his magnetic readings, while Hurley takes his opportunity to document the passing scenery in timeless images. (This has not been easy, with Hurley noting in his diary at one point, 'My camera is a bugbear and using it a nightmare. Every time I have to set the shutter I have to take a number of tiny screws from the front and bend the mechanism into shape . . . with frostbitten fingers!'[39])

Because food stocks have run so low, the men have decided to hold over any festive meal and celebrations until they reach their

200 Mile Depot, a further two days' march from their current location, meaning Christmas Day itself is spent negotiating sastrugi, trying to stop the sledges from overturning and fighting the 30-mph winds.

Meanwhile, the Eastern Coastal Party, led by Cecil Madigan, is making good progress, and Christmas finds the men already on the comeback trail from their farthest point travelled along the eastern coast, across the same two great glacier tongues that Mawson and his men crossed higher up.

As they make their Christmas camp on a broad glacier tongue that protrudes into the sea on the George V Land coast, little do they realise that their colleagues Mawson and Mertz are atop that same glacier further inland at around 1500 feet.

Chief Chef Madigan prepares a penguin dish equal to the occasion, and all men retire with their sheets of frost to their ice beds that night sated and content.

The Western Party of Frank Bickerton, Alfie Hodgeman and Dr Leslie Whetter, who, as planned, did not leave Winter Quarters until 3 December, laboured long and hard as they made their way around the western coast of Commonwealth Bay. Just a day after setting out, their air-tractor – which had been towing four sledges – had been rendered useless after its propeller had been smashed, and they had man-hauled one heavily loaded sledge thereafter in rough hurricane winds up to 80 mph. Though that had been a disappointment, the next day they made an important discovery: the first meteorite found in Antarctica, a large lump of over two pounds, which they carried with them thereafter. From there, it was just heavy hauling with little break in the supremely difficult conditions . . .

The melt from the snowdrift having almost totally destroyed their sleeping bags and ground sheet, a very unpleasant Christmas is spent in a cramped, snow-encrusted tent at high altitude and roughly 158 miles from Cape Denison.

Meanwhile, Frank Wild and his men at their base on the ice floe

1500 miles to the west of the hut have been going well. They have built their own habitation, 'The Grottoes', on the ice, and though in the first blizzard they lost their radio mast, and despite the fact that at one point their hut was nearly completely buried in snow, the main thing is that they have never woken up to find themselves atop a massive but diminishing iceberg in the Southern Ocean, as some of them have feared.

And they have gone on sledging trips to explore their territory. While Harrisson and Moyes have remained at the base, the rest of the men have split into two parties, with Wild taking his three-man sledging party to the east, as the leader of the other party, Doc Jones, takes his two men to the west – each party exploring and mapping much of the surrounding coast as they go.

Alas, Wild's own push to the east was stopped only 147 miles from their base due to an impassable field of crevasses in a glacier.

At a spot 120 miles east of their Western Base, on this day Wild's party celebrates Christmas with a surprise plum pudding – put there by Moyes – chased down with a snifter of spirits from the medical store. Following dinner, the Union Jack and Australian Ensign having been hoisted, Wild takes it upon himself to take possession of the land 'for King George V and the Australian Commonwealth'.[40]

As to Doc Jones, his three-man expedition, which includes George Dovers and Arch Hoadley, left the Western Base on 7 November, headed west, and after a long and difficult journey manage on this very day to scale the loose-rubbled slopes of their destination, the volcanic plug of Gaussberg! Their every step sends whole square yards of the volcanic fragments sliding down, and – after a pause for Christmas lunch, which includes the plum pudding they have brought all this way – they soon arrive at the cone at the summit, where they find two cairns that had been left by the Germans of the ship *Gauss*, when they discovered this volcanic plug a decade earlier.

After leaving their own record, in their own cairn, the three men begin the descent. They decide that, on the following day, they will begin their journey back to the Western Base, some 234 miles to the east as the petrel flies, or 300 miles for them, due to relay work. And yet, they must push hard. It has taken seven weeks to reach this point, and they know they must return to their base before 30 January, when the men of *Aurora* are due to return upon their fine ship to pick them up.

Speaking of whom . . . there could be little greater contrast provided on this day than the position of Captain John King Davis and his crew on *Aurora*. Now fully provisioned and ready to go, the ship is securely docked once more in the port of Hobart, and the crew are dining the day away in that finest of establishments, Hadleys Hotel. The food is excellent, the beer is plentiful and the toasts to absent friends – on Macquarie Island and Antarctica – are many. So hilarious and high-hearted is the gathering that Davis has some fear, as he weaves his way back to the ship, that some of the crew may continue too long into the night and struggle to make their 10 am departure the next day, when they will be at last heading south to pick up, hopefully, *all* of those absent friends. Time and again throughout the year, Davis has worried most particularly about where he has left Wild and his men, and he is getting more anxious as the time now approaches to see whether they are all right, or whether he has made the worst decision of his life.

Boxing Day 1912, Hobart, *Aurora* leaves with a fair sea, a following wind and a Norwegian gift

Fortunately, all the sailors are there on time, and at 10 am sharp under a clear blue sky *Aurora* draws away from Hobart dock, cheered on by the crowds of well-wishers. Loaded on board – ready for the contingency of some expedition members staying for another year – are 35 sheep, 521 tons of coal and a fair amount of mail, plus, having stopped by Macquarie Quarantine Station, the 21 dogs presented to the expedition by Captain Amundsen. By noon, they are steaming towards Storm Bay – Antarctica bound!

28 December 1912, on the western side of the farthest east glacier, Mawson and Mertz play a game of shut-eye

And so they plod on, still over 135 miles away from the hut. Mawson notes:

> Tramping over the plateau, where reigns the desolation of the outer worlds, in solitude at once ominous and weird, one is free to roam in imagination through the wide realm of human experience to the bounds of the great Beyond. One is in the midst of infinities – the infinity of the dazzling white plateau, the infinity of the dome above, the infinity of the time past since these things had birth, and the infinity of the time to come before they shall have fulfilled the Purpose for which they were created. We, in the midst of the illimitable, could feel with Marcus Aurelius that 'Of life, the time is a point'.[41]

If only they didn't feel so ill! Neither Mawson nor Mertz is quite sure of what exactly they are suffering from, only that it is getting worse. It is a day when they almost envy their last dog, Ginger, whose suffering is ended by one sudden slash of the knife across the neck. After some brief twitching, she is instantly at peace. Certainly, lying dead there in the snow, her eyes glassy, the blood from her neck slashing the whiteness, fate has not been kind to her, but has it, possibly, been kinder to her than to them? After all, Ginger feels no more exhaustion, no more pain, while they are suffering practically across the gamut of human ills.

Their next meal consists of the precious contents of Ginger's skull, which Mawson throws into a pot and boils until it is ready. To decide who gets which side of the difficult to divide head, they use the tried and true 'shut-eye' method. Mertz closes his eyes and Mawson points to one side of the skull, before saying, 'Whose?' Mertz then says 'mine' or 'yours', and they eat from their respective sides.

Using wooden spoons they have made from one of the discarded sledge runners, they scoop out her brain, which, a little like the liver, is mercifully soft.

New Year's Eve 1912 to 6 January 1913, further west of the farthest east glacier, Mertz gets a lift

It strikes Mawson at the time as a slightly curious request. Mertz asks whether it would be all right if he doesn't have the dog meat on this day but instead eats exclusively from their normal rations. Maybe it is the dog meat itself that is making him feel so ill?

Mawson agrees, and that evening they dine like kings – *kings!* – eschewing the stringy remains of Ginger and instead having a couple of biscuits, covered with a thin layer of butter, together with some hot tea. (The only downside being that it makes them feel hungrier.) Alas, the following day, New Year's Day 1913, if anything Mertz feels worse, and instead of trying to 'blunder along in bad light',[42] Mawson decides it best they remain in the tent so Mertz can rest.

The problem, as Mertz notes in his diary on this first day of the New Year, is even clearer to him now than it was the day before: '*Das Hundefleisch scheint mir irgendwie nicht zu bekommen.*' ('The dog meat doesn't seem quite to agree with me.')[43]

It is at least a day when they can talk – there is little opportunity when they are pushing forward through the sludge or lying exhausted in their tent at the end of the day. After close questioning from Mawson, Mertz admits for the first time that he has been getting terrible abdominal pain. As Mawson has a constant gnawing sensation in his own stomach – otherwise known as hunger – this does not worry him unduly, as he presumes Mertz just has it worse. Still, as Mertz prefers on this day not to eat biscuit or dog meat, Mawson allows him some Glaxo from their precious stores, while he helps himself to a generous slice of Pavlova.

If there had been a choice at this point, then of course Mawson would have moved them both off dog meat, but, of course, there is no real choice. The only way they can make their normal rations last the distance is to return to the dog meat.

Two days later, Mertz's strength appears to be all but gone, and it is all the Swiss man can do to get up and out and into his harness. And even when they do get under way, it is obvious to Mawson that Mertz – now with the added woe of frostbitten fingers, as the weather has turned even colder – is simply incapable of pulling his weight. Most of the hauling falls to Mawson, and despite making good time they are again forced to stop and camp.

To some extent, the cause is obvious. Both are slowly starving, their stomachs and joints ache, their nails are detaching, their hair is falling out and their skin is sloughing off in sheets. They are red raw in many sensitive places, most particularly around their thighs and groin. The cast-off skin inevitably works its way down into their socks, requiring them to regularly clean them out as best they can.

With such gnawing hunger and constant cold, sustained sleep is closer to an abstract notion than a reality. And yet, while Mawson is conscious of his own ills, he has become aware that his companion, Mertz, is suffering even more than him.

By the morning of 6 January, the situation has become so grim that the Australian has to help Mertz get out of his sleeping bag, and when it becomes obvious that the Swiss has no strength left to haul the sledge, the leader has no choice but to offer him a lift upon it.

Mertz, his face grey, his eyes flat, sways in the fiercely buffeting wind. He appears unsure whether or not to accept the offer. After all, this is what they have been doing to dogs. When they can no longer pull, they have been placed on the sleds to keep them alive just a little longer, so their meat will be fresher when they are shot or knifed at the next camp.

But yes, he knows he has no choice and clambers onto the sledge, but after only a short way he becomes so freezing through inaction that they are forced once again to prematurely pitch camp. Food is now *obsessing* them. Mawson attempts to cheer up a significantly depressed and feverish Mertz by suggesting that when they are aboard *Aurora*, which will be waiting for them once they get back, Mertz will once again serve up his trademark penguin-egg omelettes par excellence. It does not seem to help.

7 January 1913 and two days thereafter, 97 miles south-east of Cape Denison, Mawson prays to God

Mertz's appalling condition has delayed their travel to the point where Mawson has long realised any further days spent resting will inevitably mean their scant supplies will be exhausted even sooner. While only 97 miles from Winter Quarters – a relatively short distance for healthy men – it's 'a lengthy journey for the weak and famished!'.[44] Desperate to keep moving, the previous evening Mawson convinced Mertz that on this morning he would be placed on the sledge, where, cocooned in his sleeping bag, he would be transported under sail.

Now that the time has arrived to dress Mertz for departure, however, Mawson soon realises that despite the reasonable weather, once again this day will be without travel. His companion appears all but incapable of movement, and the only possible course is inaction. But inaction means certain death. Mawson records in his diary:

> This is terrible. I don't mind for myself but it is for Paquita and for all the others connected with the expedition that I feel so deeply and sinfully. I pray to God to help us. I cook some thick cocoa for Xavier and give him some beef-tea – he is better after noon, but very low. I have to lift him up to drink.[45]

During the afternoon, Mertz's only real movement is that he soils his trousers, which requires Mawson to clean him up, before attempting to sit him up to take a little food. However, Mertz refuses any sustenance and now grows ever more delirious.

Nearing midnight, he appears to have some kind of fit, his whole body shaking as his eyes roll back in their cadaverous sockets, and it is some time before this internal bodily storm – with a source of energy that has completely escaped Mertz in previous days but is now strong enough that Mawson must hold him down – subsides around midnight.

Mertz is peaceful now, his ravaged, skinless body finally able to find blessed calm.

Mawson is decidedly less so. There is no way of getting around it – if he is to have any chance at all of getting back to base, Mertz must either rapidly improve or die quickly. They simply cannot stay where they are. It is with those desperate thoughts that Mawson finally drifts into an extremely restless sleep.

He awakens at 2 am and notes that Mertz is notably still. He reaches out and tentatively touches his face. It is not just cold but frozen. Mertz has breathed his last. His duty is done, and he has passed into 'the peace that passeth all understanding', as Mawson puts it.[46] His verdict is straightforward: 'Death due to exposure finally bringing on a fever, result of weather exposure and want of food.'[47]

For hours after the death, Mawson lies in his bag, turning

everything that has happened over and over in his mind – strangely, the body of Mertz lying beside him offers a curious kind of companionship – as he tries to work out just what his own chances of survival are, beyond the obvious, which is next to none.[48]

His own physical condition is such that he is not far off collapsing himself, too weak even to hold himself up in certain positions, and his body is rotting from lack of nutrition before his very eyes, as frequently snow-blinded as they are. His every waking moment is one of constant pain clutching at him from within and without – hunger eats at his innards, frostbite at his every extremity, while his red-raw scrotum is little more than an agony factory. Though it cannot be denied that the sole upside of Mertz's death is that his own food supply has suddenly doubled, it is still very doubtful whether the meagre rations of dried food and remaining dog meat will be enough to get him back to the hut, even if something else doesn't kill him first. After all, he is not even sure if he will be able to break and pitch camp single-handedly.

The question has to be asked: should he just give up? It is so snug in his bag, it is such a bowl of total chaos outside it, he is still 97 miles from the hut and . . . he feels so tired . . . so *tired* . . . he is so alone and his situation so entirely hopeless . . .

Still, just as he has gained inspiration in the past from the words of Aurelius, he now gains some strength by reciting to himself some favourite lines from the Canadian Kipling, Robert Service, the same man whose poetry had inspired him long ago when he was sitting in the Refectory at the University of Sydney:

Buck up, do your damndest and fight,
It's the plugging away that will win you the day.[49]

But always, of course, he comes back to the main thing: Paquita. He must at least *try* for her. Just weeks away from beginning her journey home from Europe, so she can meet him upon his return, she is waiting for his news, *willing* him on to safety. To honour her love, he cannot simply curl up and not go forward.

He resolves to make an attempt to survive against all the odds, formally recording in his notebook:

> For many days now Xavier's condition has prevented us going on and now I am afraid it has cooked my chances altogether . . . However I shall spend today remodelling the gear to make an attempt. I shall do my utmost to the last for Paquita's and supporters' and members of expedition's sakes . . .[50]

He hopes to at least get close enough to the hut that he can build a cairn in a sufficiently prominent spot to catch the eye of a search party, so his story could be told and Paquita would know what happened to him, and of his enduring love for her.

One thing is obvious. He need no longer haul any of Mertz's gear. And, with nearly half the load abandoned, why doesn't he proceed with just half the sled as well? For the rest of the day, Mawson uses a pocket tool to laboriously saw the wooden sled in half. He then makes a mast out of one of the discarded halves of the sledge and uses the other rail to make a spar. For a new sail, he takes Mertz's Burberry jacket and whatever other material he can find and sews them together.

It all takes a great deal of time. Together with the blizzard that confines him to the tent for most of the day of Mertz's death, it is not until the evening of 8 January that Mawson is able to gently drag the body of Mertz in his sleeping bag outside. Then, after delicately putting his friend's face beneath the hood, he carefully piles snow blocks around his body – ashes to ashes, dust to dust, snow block upon snow block upon body upon snow block – before raising 'a rough cross made of the two half-runners of the sledge' at his head.[51]

Exhausted, Mawson moves back into his suddenly empty tent. It is the next day before he can get out again to read the same burial service that he conducted over the gaping grave of Ninnis, but even with that accomplished the weather is still too bad for him to recommence trekking.

Chapter Fourteen

A Close-Run Thing...

[Antarctica is] a land where loneliness weighs like a giant pall,
[where] there is an ever-present feeling of a hostile presence,
hovering and waiting for a chance to strike ... One had the
impression of fighting, always fighting, a terrible unseen force.
Charles Laseron, *South with Mawson*

8 January 1913 and three days thereafter, Adélie Land, Robert Bage's Southern Party receive a royal reception

Things are getting desperate. For the last two days, they have been wandering, lonely as a cloud, looking for a depot that simply refuses to be found. A 'lucky peep' of the sun at noon on 6 January allowed them to align themselves with the exact latitude of that depot, but despite their resolute marches back and forth along it, east and west, it seems to have disappeared! And they are all but out of food.

Bage has thus decided, and Hurley and Webb have agreed, to make a dash to where they think Winter Quarters lies, 67 miles to the north.

Desperate to make the sledge as light and fast as possible, they ditch just about everything non-essential, including 'dip-circle, thermometers, hypsometer, camera, spare clothing and most of the medical and repair kits',[1] leaving only what little food they have, plus the tent to sleep in and the precious records they have so painstakingly gathered from the journey. So desperate are they to lighten their load that Hurley even abandons his precious camera, while being careful, of course, to keep the exposed negatives. With one of his eyes bandaged because of snow-blindness, and all of his comrades near collapse, the photographer records his worst fears in his diary on that evening of 8 January, that 'another two days of this will about make statues of us'.[2]

Things become even more desperate the following day as they battle through a 60-mph wind with dense drift. At least they are not going directly into it, but as it is coming from their south-east, the tendency is for it to keep blowing them off course.

Nevertheless, after camping that night on all-but-empty stomachs they press on throughout the following day the best they can, and just before midnight on 10 January they spot the most blessed thing: Aladdin's Cave! With some of the pemmican and biscuits that have been there now in their bellies – and a wonderful night's sleep within the shelter of its walls – they make it back to Winter Quarters the following day, just after dinner, completing a journey of 600 miles. There, they are welcomed with 'a Royal reception and were carried into the Hut where Good Old Close had a banquet prepared for us'.[3]

'We three,' Bage noted, 'had never thought the Hut quite such a fine place.'[4]

11 January 1913 and the day thereafter, approaching the nearest glacier to Cape Denison, Mawson is close to leaving more than his mere footprints behind

At last, a beautiful, calm day, with bright sunshine and a good surface heading off down a gentle slope. It is just made for cutting down the distance between him and the hut, and Mawson sets off with as much of a spring in his step as his total exhaustion and his overall physical decrepitude will allow.

Alas, after only two miles his feet feel so lumpy and painful that he is obliged to stop and examine them. Using his sledge for a chair, and sitting in the bright sunshine, he slowly takes off his boots . . . and very nearly peels away the bottom of his feet with them. To his horror, what he sees is that 'the thickened skin of the soles had separated in each case as a complete layer, and abundant watery fluid had escaped into the socks. The new skin underneath was very much abraded and raw.'[5]

First, Ninnis had gone. Then the dogs had gone, one by one. Then, Mertz had gone. Now, his *feet are in danger of going*, as his soles are actually separating from the rest of him. All he can do is to try to care for them the best way he can, which in this case is to smear the new skin with lashings of lanoline and then take bandages and wrap them around his flapping soles to try to hold them in place . . . before painfully putting over the whole lot 'six pairs of thick woollen socks, fur boots and a crampon over-shoe of soft leather'.[6]

Time to move off? Not yet. So bright is the sun, so calm the wind that he decides to take advantage of it. Taking off most of his clothing, getting back to nature right in the middle of nature at its most awesome, he lies back and lets mother sun warm him, renew him, allow the life force within him to begin to glow again. His reward is that a pleasant 'tingling sensation seemed to spread throughout my whole body, and I felt stronger and better'.[7]

This day, he does indeed cover a fair distance – six and a quarter miles – which is greatly to the good, though his new-found strength does not endure long, and he stops at 5.30 pm, unable to go further. The rest of the evening is spent applying much of the contents of his medical kit to himself, trying to look after those parts of his body, not just his feet, where the skin is festering or inflamed, or rubbed red raw.

The following day, the wind is too strong and the snowdrift too fierce to allow him to move out of his tent, which is frustrating, but at least it allows him precious time to rest his even more precious feet.

13 January 1913, Cape Denison, Australia has won the First Ashes Test

One moment, all of those at the hut are just as they ever were – alone, under a clear sky, a bright sun and a howling wind – and the next moment radio operator Walter Hannam steps outside from their lunch to see the launch from *Aurora* just ten yards off coming to a mooring in Boat Harbour.

In an instant, he starts waving his arms and shouting, 'The ship! The ship!'[8] before rushing inside to alert the others. As soon as Captain Davis and his companions step ashore, they are awash in the welcome of hairy, wild creatures in the very place where, the year before, they left relatively well-groomed young students from the finest universities of Australia and New Zealand.

Those boys of a year ago had short hair and neatly trimmed beards, clothing without patches and were fleshy in a well-fed sort of way. These men, however, and they really are now all *men*, are little more than blazing sets of eyes staring through all the hair – 'their full-grown whiskers bleached almost white by the frost',[9] their faces matured through having known many hardships and their bodies lean and strong. A wild tribe indeed, they joyously dance around the new arrivals and yell with excitement and delight. Davis and the others look closely but cannot see the particular man they are looking for.

'Where is the Doctor?' asks Davis.[10]

Not back yet, Cap'n. Still out there with Belgrave Ninnis and Xavier Mertz. Like all the others, they are expected back in the next two days.

Come to the hut!

Aurora has arrived complete with provisions of fresh fruit, lamb, newspapers and . . . most importantly, mail. The men fall upon the scores of letters come to them from loved ones, with some men having as many as a hundred missives, even as they devour apples, oranges and the like. And then to the newspapers. Strangely, these do not quite hold the allure they are expecting.

After a wonderful win in the First Test against England at the Sydney Cricket Ground, Australia had, against the natural order of things, gone on to lose the next four Tests, and the Ashes; a massive ship called *Titanic* had run into an iceberg on her maiden voyage across the Atlantic, with many lives lost; there had been a war in the Balkans; and, most interestingly, Scott was spending another year in the Antarctic.[11]

But there isn't a lot more that is really gripping. It seems to Charles Laseron, for one, that while reading things from day to day is interesting because you know what's happened on preceding days, so you can read it in context, without that context they are dull. As a matter of fact, the thing that *Aurora* has brought for them that most interests them is the libretto of the song that has been driving them crazy all these months, so they can at last establish what the missing words of *The Mikado* are.

A furious scrabbling through the pages and they have the answer.

It is . . . 'defer to . . .'. Of course! Why couldn't they work that out? The refrain goes:

Defer, defer,
To the noble Lord, to the noble Lord,
To the Lord High Executioner!

Of *course*!

In the meantime, Captain Davis, who now resumes his position as Mawson's second in command – and in the Doctor's continued absence, expedition leader – is getting up to date on where things are with the expedition. Of the six groups that have gone out, just two, the Southern Party of Bage, Webb and Hurley, and the Near-Eastern Party of Stillwell, Close and Hodgeman have returned, while the others are still out.

According to Dr Mawson's instructions, all parties are due to be back at the hut by 15 January 1913, and the men in the hut are expecting all the others to come in over the next two days. For now, the men content themselves with reading their letters and beginning to pack up, ferrying much of their luggage and all of the specimens they have gathered over the last year out to *Aurora*, at least when the weather allows. They want to be all ready to go once the last of the sledging parties is in.

13 January 1913, 93 miles from Cape Denison, Mawson hears artillery fire

First, it is a little black dot on his far horizon, all but imperceptible . . . then it becomes a knob . . . and then a boulder . . . and then it starts growing before his very eyes. Can it be . . .? Yes . . .? Yes . . .?

Yes! The further he walks on this suddenly glorious afternoon, dragging the sledge behind him, the better he sees it and recognises it. Way off to his west, about 20 miles, on the other side of the first glacier that they crossed eight or so weeks earlier, the same Aurora Peak that mournfully sank beneath the whiteness two months earlier is now slowly, ever so slowly, rising up to greet him like a courtly old lady of the Antarctic. Most importantly, this enables him to roughly fix his position, and he knows that next to that peak is the plateau leading onwards to Winter Quarters.

It is so thrilling for Mawson that he would have kept going towards it, but with the difficult surface playing havoc with his feet he camps at eight o'clock that evening, having made just on five and three-quarter miles after a late start to the day.

When he removes his boots to examine his feet, they are worse than ever: red raw, oozing pus and beginning to smell . . . rotten. Despite the joy of now fixing his position, it is debatable just how long he will be able to go on for, something he is contemplating when . . . it happens.

Mawson is lying exhausted in his tent when suddenly a shot rings out. And then another. They have come from outside and are quite distant, but they are shots all right! And then there is still another . . .

Four years before, when Mawson was at the Drygalski Depot with the Professor and Mackay and they heard shots, which proved to be *Nimrod* looking for them, he had the energy to charge out to investigate. Now, however, it is all he can do to gather himself and get up and out of the tent to see what is happening. By the time he has done so, yet more shots ring out. It sounds less like rifle fire than distant artillery. How this can possibly be, up here in the polar wilderness, so far from anyone, let alone anyone with big guns, he has no idea . . . and in fact it takes a little while to work out.

But he more or less does. It is the glacier. As he steps outside the tent, the noises continue, and, though roughly random, if there is a pattern it is that it seems to start higher up the glacier and move down it in the direction of the sea. There is no disturbance to the glacier itself, but he theorises that it is something to do with the re-freezing and splitting of the ice, owing to the evening chill releasing 'great jets of imprisoned air'.[12] This thing he is on is not just dead ice lying there but is rather like a living thing. It is a massive and even monstrous river of ice moving slowly down a mountain, gouging and cracking as it does so. It lives, it breathes, it swallows, it crackles, it fires off like artillery and does so for the next 90 minutes before it stops and Mawson is able to drift off into a fitful frozen sleep of gnawing hunger and painful joints every time he moves, not to mention his ever more red-raw scrotum and agonised feet.

16 January 1913, Cape Denison, Madigan comes back ag'in

After the excitement of *Aurora*'s arrival, tension has risen over the last couple of days as first 14 January and then the due date of 15 January pass with no further sign of any of the missing sledging parties. But then, on this afternoon of the 16th, Cecil Madigan's party appears high on the slope at the back of the hut, and just minutes later they, too, are being warmly welcomed, having been away for 71 days. They have done well and have made a journey of 259 miles to the east as far as longitude 150 degrees 27 minutes east, surveying the entire coast as they went.

17 January 1913, 70 miles from Cape Denison, Mawson puts a foot wrong

In the land of the midnight sun, there is no 'rise and shine' to start the day, there is simply 'rise and get busy'. Another day, another desperate, clawing and painfully slow struggle. And that is just to get up and out of his frozen sleeping bag . . .

After that, the familiar, dull routine must be followed. He must gather in his frozen mitts that hang from the tent pole, brush away the crystals of ice that have formed on them overnight, put them on to his aching hands and then gather in snow that he can melt to drink, cook a bit of Ginger for his breakfast, squeeze his frostbitten and grotesquely swollen feet into his frozen finneskos, roll up his dank sleeping bag, strike his makeshift tent and its pathetic poles, load up his sad half-sledge with his Nansen cooker and poor excuse for food together with his pitiful personal belongings – all of it now under that wet powder of snow that covers everything – and prepare to get under way. All that remains now is to fight the agony of his frostbitten fingers to rig up the stand-in sledge sail, pull on his gut-wrenching harness and begin to hike, hike, hike, just like the beast of burden he feels.

On this day, the weather is no more vicious than usual – which is not to say it is not appalling – and yet the clouds are so thick overhead and the snow falling so heavily that the light is terrible, limiting his ability to spot danger ahead. But he has little choice. If he does not continue, he must face cutting down his already pitifully meagre rations not just to the bone but right to the marrow of those dog bones to compensate for more lost time. He decides to push on. But it is dangerous all right. Time and again, he becomes aware that he is standing right over a crevasse, and all he can do is thank Providence that he is . . . *suddenlyfallingfallingfalling* . . . 'So – this is the end!'[13] STOP.

From walking gingerly over the snow, just two miles on from his starting point that morning, Mawson only has the barest instant to realise that a snow bridge over a crevasse has given way beneath him, before he really is falling into the abyss, tumbling down, down, down. Strangely, despite how fast it all happens, he still has time for two conscious thoughts. The first, surprisingly calm thought is that his life is about to end, with the sledge likely to fall down right upon him and that he is to go the way of Ninnis. The second thought is that it will be a *terrible* waste of the uneaten food that he could have enjoyed if only he had known he was going to die anyway . . . when suddenly his harness pulls tight and he finds himself hanging some 14 feet below the surface.

Up above, remarkably, his half-sledge has stuck fast between the two lips of the narrow crevasse opening. All that separates him from eternity is his severely strained harness swinging him back and forth and, more problematically, his own will to live. For does he still have it?

Mawson has removed his outer clothes due to the warmth of the day, and now his gaping blouse is completely filled with snow cascading from above. Weakened by days of constant hunger, he quickly chills in the significantly lower temperature within the crevasse.

Yet who is he not to accept Providence's chance, though that chance is slimmer than the rope now chafing at the lip of the crevasse? Slowly reaching up, in the near darkness, he manages to get his bare hands, deformed by frostbite, around a knot in the rope and laboriously pull himself a foot or so upwards. Every muscle is screaming as he does so, calling on energy reserves that by rights should simply not be there. A brief pause, with his legs wrapped around the rope to help maintain the height he has won, and then he goes again and gets another foot higher. And again, and again and again.

After a desperate and seemingly endless struggle, he is right to the top and manages to pull himself onto the overhanging ledge that the rope has cut into when . . . the whole thing collapses. He tumbles down, in full expectation that the sledge will fall in after him, but again it holds, and again he finds himself agonisingly suspended above the abyss. It is exactly as it was before, except that he is even weaker.

This time, the temptation is nigh on overwhelming to simply surrender the fight. All he has to do is slip out of his harness – the work of a second – and it will be all over.

'A chance to quit small things for great – to pass from the petty exploration of a planet to the contemplation of vaster worlds beyond,' is how he thinks of it.[14] Yet, recalling that cruel fate of Ninnis's dog, he balances eternal liberty against the thought of 'a fall on some ledge below me and [to] linger in misery with broken bones'.[15]

And yet, and yet, again his will to live proves to be at least the equal of those hopeless thoughts. For one thing, there would be 'all eternity' to contemplate those vaster worlds beyond, while 'at its longest, the present would be but short'.[16] He feels better and marginally stronger for the thought.

Plus, there is this. Twice now, Providence has given him another chance by stopping the sledge falling upon him, and somewhere in the world Paquita is awaiting him, expecting him to return to her. While that may not be possible, he is determined that his death will only come after he has fought it to his very last ounce of strength.

Far from 'shuffling off this mortal coil', as Shakespeare would have it, he must once more get his hands around this mortal coil and try to heave himself to safety. His hand moves of its own accord towards the rope . . .

And so, the long haul upwards begins again. Hand over hand, legs wrapped around the rope like a monkey, pausing with each gain until sufficient strength returns to go again, he inches higher. This time, it takes even longer, but at last, at *last*, with indeed the last ounce of energy he has in him, he emerges feet first and, still gripping tight to the rope, vaults his fully extended body out onto the solid ice. And then he 'swoons'.[17] His soul and his will to live have written a cheque for energy that his body simply cannot pay, and, broken, he lies on the snowy ground for a solid hour without moving, practically comatose, right beside what was meant to be his open grave.

Finally, however, he stirs, stands, and bit by bit retrieves his sledge, unpacks his tent, and cooks and consumes 'a regular orgy' of dog meat.[18] He climbs into his sleeping bag and thinks things over. For some reason, the words of the Persian philosopher Omar Khayyam appeal to him:

Unborn To-morrow and dead Yesterday,
Why fret about them if To-day be sweet?[19]

And today *is* sweet. He is still alive, despite everything! And it is good, so good, to be out of the wind and with some food and tea in his belly. He can't help but contemplate how glorious it would be to stay here . . . well, *forever* . . . sleep, eat his fill and stay warm in his sleeping bag until the end. As far as he knows, he is in a field of crevasses and what has just occurred to him will happen again as soon as he sets off once more. He knows, without a skerrick of doubt, that if he falls into another crevasse, just as he has done today, he will not have sufficient strength to climb out again. The horror of what has occurred, and of what might occur in the morning, keeps him awake that night as he tries to *think* his way out of his terrible predicament.

And, sure enough, somewhere in the early hours an idea comes to him. If he is destined to go down into a crevasse once more, why not make it easier next time? Why not fashion a rope ladder out of the cords he has, so that, so long as the sledge doesn't tumble in with him, he can just climb up and out? One end of it would be secured to the bow of the sledge, while the other could be carried over his left shoulder, loosely attached to the sledge harness. He resolves that as soon as he is up and about the following day, he will begin fashioning exactly that . . .

18 January 1913 and the day thereafter, Cape Denison, a false alarm, and an alarm . . .

At 1 am, just outside the hut, a cry goes up and echoes back from the nearby penguin rookeries. Another troupe has been spotted, heading their way, coming from the west, and it looks like they have dogs with them. It is probably the Dux Ipse and his men!

But no, when the distant dots form up into real men, they prove to be Bickerton, Whetter and Hodgeman, who have no dogs and report that they reached a point 149 miles west before coming back. Welcome, welcome!

The hut is briefly abuzz and then settles down for the night, waking to the cold reality. All the sledging parties are safe and accounted for, bar the one that had been on the longest and most dangerous journey of all. Mawson, Mertz and Ninnis are still missing, and they are now three days overdue. With every passing day that they continue to be absent, a growing sense of anxiety grips the hut, as bit by bit the feeling builds that something terrible must have happened to them out there. Captain Davis writes in his diary:

> I cannot help feeling a bit anxious, as it is so difficult to know what to do for the best. We shall have to do something soon, as we cannot remain here waiting for one party and sacrifice Wild's. If they turn up in a day or two, all well. If they do not, I shall have to start making preparations for leaving a party here for a second winter.[20]

Shortly thereafter, Captain Davis tells radio operator Walter Hannam that he wants the men on the ship and those on the shore to combine to resurrect, more solidly this time, the topmast of the radio antenna that had blown down in October, so that whatever happens thereafter there could at least be contact between Cape Denison and the outside world. And this is important, for he further advises that if the Doctor's party fail to turn up soon, then six men will have to be left here for another year, on the chance that the Mawson party turn up after *Aurora* has left. That party would also be able to record key scientific data for another 12 months, which would be an important contribution to the overall success of the expedition, so it is important that the final group selected has a wide array of skills.

The first volunteer to stay is the new radio man, Sidney Jeffryes, whom Davis has brought from Australia, which thus allows Hannam to go back on *Aurora* to Hobart. Though Captain Davis still can't quite believe that the Mawson party won't turn up at any minute, he also starts taking soundings from the others as to who else might volunteer to stay.

Preparations begin. Supplies, including more coal, start being offloaded from *Aurora* so the remaining men will have what is necessary to get them through, while dozens of penguins and seals are slaughtered and their meat put into storage. Though everyone is busy, the mood remains one of quiet grimness, keen eyes constantly scanning the far horizons for the hoped-for black dots coming over the lip of the hill and always finding the same thing.

Nothing.

18 January 1913, Cape Evans, Captain Scott's ship arrives to pick them all up

With all her flags flying and cabins prepared to celebrate the return of their long-lost companions on the Scott expedition, *Terra Nova* enters McMurdo Sound. Soon, every telescope and binocular aboard that has been trained on Cape Evans picks out two men standing outside their old familiar hut.

As the ship approaches the fast ice, Captain Teddy Evans seeks out the familiar figure of Captain Scott among the group of 19 men gathered as one by the shore to receive them.

'Are all well?' he hails to them through a megaphone as the ship cuts her engines.

. . .

Finally, it falls to Victor Campbell, whose party eventually walked back to Cape Evans from Evans Cove, to reply. 'The Southern Party reached the Pole on 18 January last year, but were all lost on the return journey – we have their records.'[21]

Evans quietly orders the flags be hauled down and the anchor dropped as Atkinson and Campbell mournfully come aboard.

18 January 1913 and the day thereafter, 69 miles from Cape Denison, Mawson presses on

Though at the end of this day he has not moved far, the main thing is that he is at least a little closer to Winter Quarters, and he is still alive.

Yet sleep does not come easy this night, as the gaping maws of the surrounding crevasses emit yet more 'loud booming noises, sharp cracks and muffled growls'.[22] It is now as though the crevasse field is not only alive but also angry at him for not being dead yet. With each growl, boom and crack, he can feel the vibration, and Mawson concludes that the ice on which he is travelling is 'in rapid motion'.[23]

The anxiety is debilitating. A few days previously, he felt that his physical condition was actually improving. Now, he knows, with the strain of it all, that his health is going backwards fast.

The following morning, Mawson resolves 'to go ahead and leave the rest to Providence', and mercifully, kindly, Providence once again proves to be on duty.[24] In the middle of this crevasse field, time and again as he wallows through the deep snow, his feet and legs break through the snow bridge into space, and twice he falls all the way through into the abyss. But in the former cases he is able to haul himself out with his arms, and in the two latter cases the rope ladder works perfectly.

19 January 1913, Cape Evans, Scott's men and the cross they bear

In the wake of the dreadful news, the men decide among themselves that they must build for Scott and his final party a fitting memorial: a massive cross made of West Australian jarrah hardwood, to be erected upon Observation Hill. Once completed by *Terra Nova*'s carpenter, it is over 12 feet high and weighs nearly 300 pounds. It is a long process to get the two beams up the hill and into position facing the spot where the dead men lie, around 170 miles away. In the two days necessary to do the work, there are many willing hands and backs available.

To complete it, they inscribe upon its horizontal limb the sacred names of the dead, while, at the suggestion of Apsley Cherry-Garrard – and overriding the views of those who think there should be a biblical quotation because 'the women think a lot of these things'[25] – they carve into the wood the appropriate words from Tennyson's poem 'Ulysses': 'To strive, to seek, to find, and not to yield.'[26]

The final inscription reads:

IN MEMORIAM
CAPT R.F SCOTT R.N
DR E.A WILSON CAPT L.E.G OATES INS. DRGS
LT H.R BOWERS R.I.M
PETTY OFFICER E. EVANS R.N
WHO DIED ON THEIR
RETURN FROM THE
POLE MARCH
1912
TO STRIVE, TO SEEK
TO FIND
AND NOT TO
YIELD[27]

Before it, in the shrieking wind, the small grieving group manages to give three sad cheers and snap off a few photographs, before heading back to the welcome warmth of their ship.

20 January 1913 and the day thereafter, approaching Commonwealth Bay, Mawson sees a sign

So wretched are the conditions on this day, so exhausted and weak is he, that it is 2 pm before he can resume his march, though at least by this time the wind is coming from behind him, which proves to be of considerable assistance. Still, the drift is so strong that he can see nowt of his surroundings and the only thing he can be sure of is that the ascent of the rising hills on the west side of the glacier has commenced, and every step takes him a little higher. By the time he makes camp that evening, he has made just two and a half miles.

The first true breakthrough comes just after noon the next day, when after the wind and drift falls away and the sun starts to shine benignly, far away to his north he suddenly can see the sea.

'It looked so beautiful and friendly that I longed to be down near it.'[28] At the end of this day, he has covered a good six miles but is exhausted by the heavy pulling.

22 January 1913, Cape Denison, Captain Davis calls for volunteers

In the lustrous light of the evening, Captain Davis has come ashore to make an inspection of the work on the wireless masts, which he notes with satisfaction has been done solidly and is nearly complete. Already, Hannam, Bickerton and the heavily bearded new radio fellow, Jeffryes, for whom Antarctica is still a place of wide-eyed wonder, are busily hauling the rest of the radio equipment into position. It shouldn't be long before they will be able to begin transmissions.

It is a pleasant thing to be ashore in relatively calm weather, away from the cloistered confines of *Aurora*. In an all too rare opportunity to be alone with space around him, Davis decides to take advantage of the moment to walk a mile up the slope. He rises to a point where, gazing back down, the Winter Quarters looks like little more than a heap of stones. Beyond that, he can see *Aurora*, of course, and beyond that again the dark water of the ocean to the north, leavened by the occasional white of a berg or an ice-covered island. On this fine evening, it all looks so beautiful, but . . .

'. . . but what a terrible, vast solitude, constantly swept by icy winds and drift, stretches away to the south!'.[29]

On this seventh day that Mawson and his men are overdue, it is hard not to be constantly thinking of them. Again and again, he looks up the icy slopes stretching away to the far southern horizons, hoping against hope to see three black specks starting to descend, but there is nothing but the all too empty whiteness. It is a good thing that his plans for a group to stay behind for another year are well advanced.

Davis has already decided that Cecil Madigan will be the best man to command the party that will remain in Winter Quarters. Madigan excelled in his leadership of the Eastern Coastal Party and is well liked by all in the hut. Most importantly, when Davis approached him about the possibility of staying, Madigan pronounced himself willing, even though it meant deferring his scholarship for another year.

With him and Sidney Jeffryes, Captain Davis has chosen Robert Bage, Frank Bickerton, Alfred Hodgeman and Archie McLean to stay on. Archie's account in his diary seems typical of their collective attitude: 'I have consented to stay as one of the relief party. Capt. Davis asked me and I accepted, considering it was my duty to the Expedition and to Dr. Mawson.'[30] In McLean's mind, a duty to a dead man – or at least an almost certainly dead man – is a duty nevertheless, and the others feel broadly the same.

It is on this evening that Davis has the formal announcement of the new plans posted upon the hut wall. In the announcement, he notes that in so doing he is following Mawson's stated wishes of what to do if they did not return, and that his own instructions to them in this matter:

> are for the present intended as a precaution. I know that I can
> rely on everyone doing his best to assist the work of the search
> parties, the establishment of the winter station for another year,
> the rigging up of the wireless installation and the furthering of
> all work in connection with this proposed relief party.
> J. K. Davis[31]

23 January 1913, approximately 55 miles from Cape Denison, Mawson struggles

Another very difficult day. Though the sun is visible in the early hours, by 8 am the clouds have come down and the winds gone up and Mawson is engulfed in 'a swirl of driving snow'.[32] He presses on, the best he can, though the swirling wind becomes so strong that the sledge frequently capsizes by the sheer force it. Under such circumstances, it is impossible to walk straight, so all he can do is meander along in what he hopes is the right direction. At least the snow underfoot is soft, which helps with his sore feet, even if it does make the sledge harder to pull. By 4 pm, however, he is so cripplingly exhausted, so eyeballs-rolling gone that he knows he must stop, after having covered no more than three and a half miles in a straight line. With his last ounce of strength, he spends the next two hours getting the tent up in the high wind and then collapses, entirely spent, inside.

24 January 1913, Cape Denison, Captain Gloomy comes to a gloomy decision

In the wardroom of *Aurora*, Captain John King Davis is holding a crisis meeting. Dr Mawson, Ninnis 'n' Mertz are now nine days overdue, and the rest of the party are all running out of time.

Davis simply cannot keep *Aurora* here indefinitely in the hope that the lost ones will turn up, for he risks being trapped by the pack ice, in which case the men would all have to spend another year here, and Frank Wild and his men, 1500 miles to their west, would likely perish. Davis is only too aware that, vis-à-vis those faraway men, time is of the essence to be able to safely pluck them out and get away again. Not only will their stock of food and coal be all but gone, the issue is the sea around them freezing over. As Davis is keenly aware, at the same time of the year, 11 years earlier, the German Antarctic Expedition under Drygalski in the *Gauss* were hopelessly frozen in, being forced to remain there for a year before getting away again. Last time, it took him just over a month to leave here and be able to drop Wild. This time, although they will be quicker, as they now know precisely where they are going, even leaving their departure as late as 30 January will be cutting it fine. They *have* to get away.

After discussion, Captain Davis announces his plans. They will begin to unload all the stores they have that can be spared from the ship's own supplies to sustain the half-dozen men who will remain here for another year. A relief party, composed of Frank Hurley, Alfred Hodgeman and Archie McLean, will set out the next day to push into the south-eastern hinterland, where it is expected the lost men will be coming from. They will take with them a supply of food and, if no trace of the men is found, set up a depot marked by black flags at the farthest point they reach, being absolutely sure to return to base by 30 January, when *Aurora* must sail.

And, as per Mawson's instructions, Davis will simultaneously take *Aurora* down the coast to their east to look for signs of them, just as they did four years earlier in *Nimrod* when they found Mawson, Mackay and Professor David at the Drygalski Depot.

25 January 1913, Cape Denison, the relief expedition for Mawson departs

And so they move. At 8.30 am on this morning, Alfie Hodgeman, Frank Hurley and Archie McLean head off into the teeth of a 50-mph blizzard. Under normal circumstances, they would have waited until the blizzard had passed, but this is an emergency. They are just five days away from *Aurora* having to set sail, and it is urgent that the Mawson party be located if at all possible. As it turns out, even finding Aladdin's Cave is not easy, as the snowdrift is so strong that it obscures the icy oasis the first time they pass it. But they cannot simply stay there.

The searchers intend to get as far into the Mawson party's presumed route of return as possible in the time remaining, in the certainty that Mawson, Ninnis 'n' Mertz will have all but entirely run out of food, so getting supplies out to them might make all the difference between life and death. If they are still alive, that is.

Five days is all they have to find out.

29 January 1913, 27 miles from Cape Denison, Mawson gives thanks to Paquita

Had Dickens written it, it might have gone like this: 'It was the best of times, it was the worst of times, it was the *very* best of times.' The best of times came the day before, when at 1 pm he finally reached the 3000-foot crest of the plateau he was plodding up for the previous three days and at last saw signs that he was in the vicinity of

Commonwealth Bay. For there, sure enough, on his north-western horizon, was the darker patch on the clouds he was looking for, the 'water sky' that indicated a vast patch of water was ahead.[33] This was no longer a nameless wilderness. He knew where he was, where he was going and that evening, for the first time, really felt as if Winter Quarters was getting closer. And yet, he was still so exhausted, so near collapse, that his salvation remained far from assured: 'For the last two days my hair has been falling out in handfuls and rivals the reindeer hair from the moulting bag for nuisance in all food preparations. My beard on one side has come out in patches.'[34]

And now, at two o'clock the following afternoon, Mawson is staggering along, wondering if his fate is, after having come all this way, to simply collapse and never get up again. He has been strong. He has fought the good fight. He has survived to this point against extraordinary odds. But there is only so much his body can bear. He has just two pounds of food remaining, which will not go far, his feet and face are frostbitten, possibly gangrenous, and his spirits are as ever caught between a general desperation about all things and a specific desperation to survive come what may.

But in the end, it is exactly as they say: the darkest hour is right before the dawn. For right there in the gloom caused by his mood, the deep cloud cover and the strong 50-mph wind, he spies through the drifting snow something dark up ahead a short distance away to the right, something out of the ordinary, something that is not of nature but is of . . . man! It is not a man – for it is about twice the height – but it is the next best thing. It is a snow cairn! Stumbling towards it, Mawson sees that wound around the snow blocks is some black cloth, on top of which is, can it be . . .? Yes, it is . . .! The distinctive red of . . . a 'Paquita bag'!

Fifteen months earlier, Paquita made lots of brightly coloured bags so he and his men could have something cheerful to look at amid all the whiteness, and now here is one of them, *indeed* cheering him up no end.

With suddenly feverish hands, he opens the bag to find food and a couple of notes. The first of the notes reads:

Aurora arrived Jan 13. Wireless message received. All parties safe. Amundsen reached Pole December 1911 – remained three days. Supporting party left Scott 150m from Pole in the same month. Bage reached 300m SE 1,7' from magnetic pole, Bickerton 160m west. Aeroplane broke down 10m out. Madigan went 270m west.

Good luck from Hodgeman, Hurley, McLean.[35]

Another, smaller note tells him his exact bearings at this point, the direction in which he would find Aladdin's Cave, just 21 miles away and the fact that the search party left the cairn at 8 am that very day, which was just six hours earlier! They had camped the night before only five miles from his own camp, and had it not been for the blizzard-like conditions, in all likelihood he and they would have been able to see each other.

These are but tiny regrets, however. The most amazing thing is that he has stumbled upon the cairn in the first place. In that vast white horizon, in drifting snow, the odds of it are later likened by Charles Laseron to 'one chance in a thousand . . . [like] finding a buoy in a fog at sea, when even its existence was unsuspected'.[36]

As it is, Mawson is just so relieved to have contact, his first contact with what is effectively the outside world in three months, and to have some real food to put in his belly. Redoubling his efforts, his spirits soaring – maybe he really *will* live to see Paquita again – he reorients himself and begins the long trek towards Aladdin's Cave. And from there, of course, it would only be a short trek to Winter Quarters itself, the small hut that had once seemed little more than a primitive shack but that now appears to him as nothing less than El Dorado.

The problem he has now is that ten days earlier, upon reaching the western side of the first glacier east of Winter Quarters, he had thrown away his battered and tattered crampons to lighten his load. But now he has reached the coastal slopes with their blue ice, he is unable to walk even a few yards without falling over, putting him in a dangerous situation. But at least the wind is strong and coming from behind, so by setting full sail and sitting on the sledge he is able to continue, even having the comfort as he does so of nibbling on the precious food they have left him and feeling some strength start to return to his limbs.

At the end of the day, he has made a fair distance, about 14 miles, but by his estimation he has headed too far to the east of Aladdin's Cave. Alas, when he changes direction to move further to the west, the wind hits the sledge amidships, making further progress impossible. The only thing he can do is make camp for the night.

29 January 1913, Cape Denison, *Aurora* ships out

In the continuing absence of Dr Mawson and his party, one thing is now obvious to Captain Davis. If they are still alive, they will have no food left. They had taken provisions for 63 days, and that was 80 days ago. Thus, if they are still alive, the only sensible thing for them to do would be to hug the coast in the hope of killing penguins and seals. So that is why on this day he has *Aurora* and her crew cruising along the coast to the east of Cape Denison as he goes looking for them.

And the other thing for sure is that Captain Davis is not going to have it happen twice to him. Four years earlier, as chief officer of *Nimrod*, he learnt a valuable lesson when he omitted to properly scan the one part of the coast that counted – where Mawson and the South Magnetic Pole Party were found – and was only able to miraculously correct his error when his captain insisted they do it again and get it right.

This time, Davis is barely willing to trust anyone else and relentlessly scans the coast himself, looking for a flag, a sledge pole, a cairn, *anything* out of the ordinary to indicate that the Doctor might be there, but there is nothing, absolutely nothing. They fire rockets at regular intervals and fly a kite at 500 feet to announce their presence to anyone a little back from the shore, but the Antarctic coast stares blankly back at them.

30 January 1913, 13½ miles from Cape Denison, Mawson makes a case for survival

Still the blizzard blows, and Mawson, so close to safety, and acutely aware that *Aurora* will have to leave within a day or two for fear of being iced in, is desperate to finish the last 13½ miles he estimates it will take to get there. What he most needs are crampons and a break in the weather, and while there is nothing he can do about the latter, he spends most of this day trying to fashion himself the former out of the things he has with him. Taking the box that held the theodolite, he breaks it into two big pieces of wood and then, using whatever screws and tacks he can get from the sledge-meter, together with some ice-nails he still has in his repair bag, he turns the underside of the wood into two pincushions. By then strapping these pieces of now-studded wood to the bottom of his boots, he is ready to go again.

At least for a little way. He is able to push west again for a short spell before the wind picks up once more and he must make camp.

31 January 1913, off Cape Denison, with Davis aboard *Aurora*

No luck. For over two days, those aboard *Aurora* have searched the coast, but they have seen not the slightest sign. Reluctantly, when they reach the tip of the first glacier tongue east of Commonwealth Bay, Davis comes to the conclusion that he must call off the search.

It is time to get back into Commonwealth Bay, anchor off Cape Denison, pick up those members of the expedition who are coming with them, load the last of their gear and their samples, and get away as quickly as possible.

Alas, just as they are on their approaches to Cape Denison, a strong gale from the south-east blows up, making it way too dangerous to start a boat ferrying from ship to shore and back again. Before too long, the gale has picked up to hurricane force. Davis, increasingly frantic about the passage of time, has no choice but to drop anchor and wait for the hurricane to blow itself out. But it does not, and nor do the anchors hold.

With squalls exceeding 80 mph, Davis is powerless to keep the ship in position within the shelter of the cliffs, for even with the engine roaring on full, it is not strong enough and *Aurora* is blown out to sea again and again. Each squall announces itself with a great 'booming roar, with a sound almost like that of heavy calibre gun-fire',[37] at which point the ship is tossed around like a toy in a bathtub, and only when the wind has decreased to 'a mere fiendish howl' can they manage to crawl back, until the next burst of frozen fury hurls her seaward again.

1 February 1913, on the approaches to Cape Denison, Mawson breaks through

For two days, Douglas Mawson has been effectively trapped in his tent, using his time to eat, to get some of his strength back and to work on the crampons to make them more effective. And now, late in the afternoon, the wind at last subsides enough for him to once more get under way when . . . he sees it!

For, as the wind diminishes, the infernal snowdrift starts to dissipate, and away to his west he now clearly sees the beacon, complete with the black flag waving, that marks the entrance to Aladdin's Cave.

His spirits soar, his staggering step quickens and at seven o'clock that night at last, at last, at *last* he is able to make his way to the cave entrance, undo himself from the wretched sledge harness and tumble inside.

There, he finds the most extraordinary things: three oranges and a pineapple! They have been brought to Antarctica all the way from distant climes, and the search party has left them there for him on the one-in-a-hundred chance he is still alive.

And he is, by his own indomitable will. By God, by Providence, which he believes in more firmly than ever, he is alive!

Still, he cannot quite believe it as he sucks on the delicious fruit – of course frozen as hard as a cricket ball – and as the trickle of the orange juice slips down his throat like the nectar of the gods, he has the wonderful realisation that he need never again set up a tent in these wretched climes.

The cave offers perfect protection from the screaming blizzard, which is to the good. What is to the very bad is that this particular blizzard would appear to have staggering staying power, making it unimaginable to venture out into. Only five and a half miles from the Winter Quarters, albeit down a steep, icy slope, Mawson has no choice but to sit there, wondering what is happening back there. Has *Aurora* left? Have some men been left behind at the hut?

Is he now the sole human for hundreds and even thousands of miles in any direction? It feels as if he is the last man left standing on a frozen continent . . .

First week of February 1913, Cape Denison, time to go

It is time. Time to face reality. In all likelihood, Dr Mawson, Ninnis and Mertz are dead. Nearly two and a half weeks since they were due, there has been no sign of them. Their food would have long ago run out, and the howling blizzard outside is as sure a sign as any that the brief Antarctic summer is nearly at an end and the demons of winter will soon be screaming for their very souls. Even if the lost men are still alive, they cannot last long in these conditions. For some time, the men at the hut had clung to the slender hope that their fellows had merely suffered some minor accident to delay them, but now even that hope is gone.

In the hut, the expedition members who are due to return to Australia with Captain Davis have packed and are ready to go – waiting only for the weather to break, so the ship can send in a launch to pick them up – while the six members who are to stay here for another year on the extremely slender chance that the missing men turn up are settling in. Those who are going are torn between joy at the thought of returning home and guilt that they are not one of the six unlucky ones staying behind.

Outside, on Commonwealth Bay, every now and then those brave enough to venture outside can see *Aurora* in the blizzard. She is fighting with every ounce of power she has to hold position just off the coast. In those winds, the anchors are useless, and all she can do is go full steam ahead straight into the wind and have a contest with nature. Sometimes, nature gets the upper hand and carries her out of sight. Sometimes, *Aurora* gains brief superiority and momentarily appears again, like a phantom ship beating into the wind from out of the swirling spray, into the lee of the jutting ice cliffs . . . but then she is gone again.

Aboard *Aurora*, gazing to the shore, they can sometimes see a burst of the blizzard hurtling down the slope, picking up surface snow as it goes and then blasting it across the waters straight at them, until the shore disappears in the cloud that engulfs their ship. Sometimes, the cloud is so thick they cannot see the aft of the ship from for'ard. Men *lived* in such conditions for a year? It is shocking. The only upside the sailors can see, as recorded by one of the *Aurora* crewmen, Stanley Taylor, is that 'we do not need to shave. We just take off our happy hooley and let a spray wet our whiskers and when they freeze we just break them off.'[38]

For those in the hut, as the days pass with still no break in the weather and no sign of the missing party, it becomes more obvious than ever that there will be no miraculous reappearance of the missing trio, and a pall of abject grief hangs over them. Charles Laseron feels it particularly strongly, writing in his diary:

> This is 2.30 am, and perhaps the last night I shall spend in Adélie Land. For the last week every night was to have been the last, but we are still here. The same old stove in front, the same old corner where the nightwatchman sits and reads – or thinks maybe – for the last time I feel . . . homesick – home and the green trees and sunshine [await]. The same old bunks are occupied by the same old chaps, that is nearly all – but there are three vacant. The poor old chief – we loved him with all his faults, Ninnis, Cherub as we called him, and [Xavier] whose Swiss heart was one of gold, are up on the plateau somewhere. Oh that awful plateau . . . blizzard ridden, treacherous, the most desolate, cruellest region in the world. January has entirely gone, and winter is . . . on the land again. Last month was a month of [terrible] emotions.[39]

8 February 1913, Aladdin's Cave, Mawson makes his move

It is time. Time to get going. For the last week, Mawson has been a prisoner in the oasis of his dreams. It was wonderful to get to Aladdin's Cave, but he has become so increasingly desperate for the wind to drop that he has been sitting outside the cave for hours at a time, waiting for a lull that never comes.

In extremis, this very morning he reaches his decision, similar to the admonition he gave to his men five months previously: let the winds of hell do their worst, he is going to go. He simply cannot wait any longer. He *has* to get back to Winter Quarters on the forlorn chance that *Aurora* will still be there. He will sit on the sledge as long as possible and have it blow him along and . . .

And what is that? The wind . . . it is . . . lessening. It really is!

He must go, *now*.

He wants . . . no, *needs* . . . to make that ship before she departs so he can all the sooner be reunited with Paquita. Doubling the rope beneath the sledge – putting several turns around the runners, so as to give it more friction and act as a brake – and again putting himself in his hated harness for the times when he can't allow the gravity and wind to take the sledge downwards on its own, he sets off.

This time, the going is easier, and after a couple of miles the wretched wind abates even further and the day soon turns glorious, calm and clear, almost as if after Antarctica throwing everything it has at him it is prepared to bathe him in its best for the last leg . . . No hard feelings, and all that.

Coming now over the lip of a large hill, a month after the death of Mertz and nearly two months after the death of Ninnis, a sudden, stunning vista appears before him. A bay! Is it . . .? It is! The exact shape! Commonwealth Bay! The Mackellar Islets! And down there are the familiar rocks around Winter Quarters! His spirits soar, his heart sings . . .

And then . . . he sees it.

As he gazes from his elevated position atop the hill, something catches his attention. On the far horizon, way out to the north-west, he can see a tiny speck, with what looks to be a thin stream of smoke coming from it. In an instant, he recognises it for what it is. It is *Aurora*. He has missed her by just a few hours. He has made it all this way only to be condemned to arriving at an empty, abandoned hut . . .

. . .

Or has he? Again, looking closer, right down by the hut he can see first the familiar contours of the basin of the boat harbour and then movement around it! There, he sees three men working at something on one side of the harbour, three tiny dots of indeterminate shape that really do look just like this:

. . .

Feeling almost as if he is in a dream, he cries out.

Down by the hut on this day, Frank Bickerton and two others are working away when Bickerton looks up to see the most extra-ordinary thing. High up on the hill, he suddenly notes something black against white and looks closer. Under the circumstances, he can be forgiven for taking a second or two to realise what he is seeing, as seemingly unlikely as seeing an oak tree in the desert, a baby swimming in the middle of the ocean, *life* where all is thought to be arid. For it is a man! And he is walking, or at least staggering, towards them out of the polar wilderness.

Bickerton shouts, at which point the other two men look up and see the figure too.

For his part, through his fog of exhaustion, Mawson sees the distant stick figures wave at him, and then the men start running, first towards the hut. (As it happens, McLean is in there preparing dinner when the new radio man Jeffryes bursts in upon him and yells excitedly, 'There's someone coming down the hill!'[40])

After the dots emerge from the hut, Mawson quickly loses them as they disappear behind the steep rise of the hill that lies between him and them. As absurd as it sounds, it almost seems as if they have run away to hide from him.

Minutes pass, and all Mawson can do is to keep going, his heavy breathing and the crunching of the snow the loudest noises as he hauls his sledge forward, down the hill . . .

And then there it is! The brow of a head is bobbing above the brow of the hill, the full head now of a man approaching at pace, soon joined by other bobbing heads all around. In short order, the first head proves to have a torso and legs attached, and a complete, breathless man appears before him. It is Bickerton!

Bickerton now stands there, gazing in stunned amazement upon this scarecrow of a man hauling a half-sledge behind him. Rake thin, with a splotchy, frostbitten face, he has a beard grown down to his chest and is clearly only just managing to stay standing.

It couldn't be . . . could it? It must be!

Dr Mawson, he presumes?

A few croaked words from the man, and he confirms it. Dr Mawson is alive, and this is he!

In an instant, there is great rejoicing from Bickerton and the others who have now arrived. Archie McLean has left a shoulder of mutton ready for the oven where it stands and rushed up to join them. However, their rejoicing does not last long.

After only a few more croaked words, Mawson hears that the ship indeed left just a few hours earlier, and they come to understand that Ninnis 'n' Mertz, those two fabulous men, are dead. And though this is only confirmation of what they have already strongly assumed, still the tragedy of it hits them. Together with the joy of Mawson's own survival.

The mood of the whole group is now a curious mix of elation, devastation and sheer exhaustion, with Mawson himself encompassing most of the last, as he heads with the group down the hill, now mercifully relieved for the first time in three months of the weight of the sledge.

Some 15 minutes later, it happens. Like the spirit of Oates, who has been outside for some time . . . Douglas Mawson once again steps inside the warmth of a civilised construction, the very Winter Quarters he feared he would never see again.

Upon entering the hut, Mawson's primary feeling is of course relief, and profound gratitude to Providence for having ensured his deliverance against all odds. For the last several weeks, he has barely allowed himself the hope of survival and has instead concentrated on 'reaching a point where my remains would be likely to be found by a relief expedition'.[41] But now he finds himself alive and safe. He feels entirely overcome with 'a soft and smooth feeling of thanksgiving'.[42]

Out on *Aurora* this evening, Captain Davis is on the bridge, gloomily navigating the ship north-west through the pressing ice pack, considering the terrible fate of his great friend Mawson with his tragic companions, when he looks up to see his radio operator Hannam hovering with a stunned look on his face. It is 8.30 pm on the evening of 8 February. The young man begs to inform the good captain that he has just received a wireless message that is most urgent. Captain Davis takes the proffered piece of paper, quickly scans it and gasps, as he receives 'the biggest shock of my life'.[43]

It reads:

```
To Capt Davis.
Aurora.
Arrived safely at hut. Mertz and Ninnis dead.
   Return and pick up all hands.
Signed Dr Mawson.[44]
```

Stunned, delighted and devastated all in one – to Hannam, Davis appears to 'age all at once'[45] – the captain immediately gives orders to the helmsman of *Aurora* to put the wheel hard a'port, and they are racing back to the hut the best they can, through the heavy pack ice that is pressing them close. The mood aboard the vessel is black, as the news of the certain deaths of Ninnis 'n' Mertz hits them hard.

Their last shred of hope concerning their possible survival is now crushed, and from the moment the word spreads, crew members 'walked around the ship on tiptoe and spoke in whispers',[46] even though the grief is leavened somewhat by the news of the survival of Dr Mawson.

The exception to this mood is Captain Davis. He is, in fact, mightily annoyed, bordering on outright angry, at having been recalled. Yes, it is good that Mawson has survived, but as captain he has a responsibility to all of the men on board, plus Wild and his men, who await them, and heading back to pick up those at the hut means that he is putting at risk *all* three groups. The days spent searching for the Mawson group have depleted their coal reserves severely, and they simply don't have *time* to do this – a problem compounded by the fact that the harsh coastal wind has now started blowing hard enough that he can hear the first shrill notes of it hitting the rigging.

'Why did they recall us?' he writes in his diary. 'It simply means that we are going to lose Wild for the sake of taking off a party who are in perfect safety.'[47]

A part of his frustration is that it is not possible to communicate with Mawson directly about the situation, as on the ship they have a receiver but not a transmitter. At Macquarie Island, however, they have a receiver and a transmitter, and at this very time wireless operator Arthur Sawyer takes off his headphones, stunned, and reviews the message he has just overheard by pure happenstance from those at Adélie Land to those on the good ship *Aurora* – it has been months since they have had contact. Dr Mawson is alive! But Mertz and Ninnis are dead. Sawyer is personally saddened in the extreme, as he liked Ninnis, particularly, a great deal and recalls how he used to say how lucky he was to be on this expedition as it meant he was missing out on a whole year of duty in ghastly India. And now he is *dead*.

Gathering himself regardless, Sawyer hurries off to inform the base leader George Ainsworth, before returning to his post and trying to reach Adélie Land to get more details. He has no luck but is at least able to pass on the news to Hobart, where it is greeted with similar exhilaration and sadness. Mawson is *alive*! The news is out.

All quiet, back at Winter Quarters. In the next room, an emaciated man who is safe, warm, fed and in a comfortable bed for the first time in over three months is sleeping the sleep of the dead, the near-dead and the dead-exhausted. Douglas Mawson plumbs new depths of unconsciousness as every now and then one of his men takes the liberty of coming into his partitioned room and gazing down upon him, to ensure that he is breathing. His reappearance that afternoon has stunned them, as have even the barest rudiments of his story. But his survival is still far from assured. So devastating is his physical condition – his body riven by starvation, most of his extremities frostbitten, the soles of his feet a mess of puss, his skin flaking, his internal organs suffering – that there is a real fear they may lose him still. Lifting the mood of the men regardless, however, is that *Aurora* should now be on her way back to them, and they won't have to spend another year in this godforsaken land after all! They begin to quickly pack, ready to leave, likely the following morning.

9 February 1913, aboard *Aurora*, Captain Davis has never been gloomier

At eight o'clock the following morning, *Aurora* again enters Commonwealth Bay, pounding straight into a very strong southerly wind that carries with it enough snow that the combined force hits the ship like God's fist. Nevertheless, they have steamed close enough to their original anchorage to be able to see the Pilot Jack – the white-bordered Union Jack used by the merchant fleet, and in this case an arranged signal that Mawson has returned – flying from the wireless mast. However, so powerful is the wind, so strong the waves, so dangerous the conditions that it is simply not possible either to get closer or to send the motor launch to go and pick up the men from the shore. There are volunteers to try to take the whaleboat in, but Captain Davis flat out refuses to let them go, as the wind is so strong, the waves so high that it would certainly be swamped.

In the meantime, though inside the hut Jeffryes is furiously sending messages saying they hope *Aurora* can wait a few days more, those messages are not getting through. On the ship, Hannam is listening closely to his radio but receives nothing. The gods, and the atmospheric conditions, are simply against them. From the bridge of the ship, Davis's chief officer is using semaphore flags to signal the message 'Send Instructions',[48] but still there is no reaction, let alone instructions.

From *Aurora*, it looks as if the hut is filled with dead men – though in fact, since the ship has been spotted entering Commonwealth Bay, inside they are joyously packing all their records, instruments and personal effects so they can be quickly taken down to Boat Harbour, once the weather calms and *Aurora* can get the motor launch in.

The one bit of contact between ship and shore comes mid-morning when the men on the ship see a figure appear on the hill, wave briefly, then quickly disappear. The seamen continue to gaze at the hut, the snow positively stinging their eyes, but there is no further sign of any movement. But the wind remains so strong that there is simply no chance to get closer in.

Frustrated beyond all measure, and acutely aware that they are chewing up both precious coal and even more precious time, all the supremely exasperated Davis can do is keep steaming back and forth across the bay – through vast fields of highly dangerous pack ice – hoping for a break in the weather. A sure indication of the kind of danger they are in comes every ten minutes or so, when it simply isn't possible to completely avoid a berg, and instead of sliding by it they glance against it, so everyone is hurled forward and sideways, and the ship shudders from stem to stern. Yes, the ice-soldiers that they so narrowly escaped a year earlier are now clearly massing for another attack.

By 5 pm, the weather is worse, the wind higher, the barometer lower and the haggard Davis's worry deeper. Desperate, he calls a quick meeting in the wardroom for all those of the land party he has just taken on board. Speaking in spare, low tones, he explains the situation to the gathered men and says he feels that he has no choice but to proceed to pick up the Western Party as they are in grave danger, while those at the Winter Quarters are relatively safe, with full supplies for another year. He cannot see the sense in risking the lives of those on *Aurora* and the men in the west by waiting for the gale they are now in to blow itself out – it could last anything from a day to a week – when to take the alternative course is to maximise the chances for everyone to survive. He feels, he says, that they must go.

That is . . . unless anyone else has any ideas?

In response, there is silence, bar the sound of the wind howling through the rigging above, which seems to some of them to be confirming the rightness of the captain's view. And then one of the land party speaks: they have confidence in Captain Davis. Whatever he decides, they will stand by him in accepting responsibility for those actions.

Hear, hear. Hear, hear. Hear, hear . . .

With this view unanimously endorsed, Davis uncharacteristically brightens somewhat and announces his decision. 'Well, gentlemen, I think we should go at once to the relief of Wild's party.'[49]

And so they do, with Davis quickly telling Gray, the second officer, to hoist the ensign and dip it as a signal of farewell. At 6.50 pm, Captain Davis gives the key command of this expedition: full steam ahead to the north-west.

In celebration of its victory, the wind whips up anew, sending the ship scudding across the storming sea.

Chapter Fifteen

Now Is the Winter of Our Discontent

Situated as we were, Time became quite an object of study to us and its imperceptible drift was almost a reality, considering that each day was another step towards liberty – freedom from the tyranny of the wind. In a sense, the endless surge of the blizzard was a slow form of torture, and the subtle effect it had on the mind was measurable . . .

Douglas Mawson, *The Home of the Blizzard*

The long Antarctic winter was fast approaching and we turned to meet it with resolution . . .

Douglas Mawson, *The Home of the Blizzard*

'Polar madness' can erupt without warning. You can get it when someone sits in your chair. You can get it while they are combing their hair. It can come at any time . . . dishing up chow or telling them how! As a matter of fact, some have it right now. It might be as trivial as the way you dress. It might be as provocative as being served a glass of chilled urine at dinner. It might just be the sound of your voice . . .

Tom Griffiths, *Slicing the Silence*

10 February 1913 and several days thereafter, Winter Quarters, the six men remaining awake to news

The following day, when the marooned men come out of the hut, there is no sign of *Aurora*! Nor that afternoon, nor that evening. Reality starts to set in. They actually are going to have to spend another *year* here. It is a bitter blow so soon after they thought that they would shortly all be on their way back to their families, but there is simply no way around it. True, they do have the faint hope that after picking up the Western Party Captain Davis might be able to bring *Aurora* back to retrieve them, but that is regarded as highly unlikely.

For his part, Mawson is so stunned to have survived the 629-mile round trip, and so weak, he has neither energy nor emotion to express frustration, while the others realise that their position is at least a lot more joyous than it had been at the same time the previous day – Dr Mawson is alive!

And following them around . . .

Time and again over the next few days, they look up, or turn around, to find their leader hovering close. Somehow, after everything that he has been through, his long journey solo across the ice, he now feels a spiritual need to be close to other humans. It is not quite that he is a lost puppy seeking solace, but he is certainly unrecognisable from the slightly aloof, patrician figure with whom they arrived in these parts.

As Mawson himself describes his first few weeks back in the hut, he does 'little else than potter about, eat and doze, with frequent interruptions from internal disorders'.[1]

10 February 1913 and four days thereafter, news from New Zealand stuns the world

It is just after half-past two in the morning of 10 February 1913, the most silent watch of the night, when . . .

What's that? For a few restless souls sleeping near the water, the unmistakable muffled sound of an engine is heard, coming from just beyond the heads of Oamaru Harbour, midway down the east coast of New Zealand's South Island. *But who would be moving in or out of my harbour at this ungodly hour?* Straining his eyes in the gloom, the lighthouse keeper can see what is either a small phantom come from the aquatic netherworld where all lost ships go, or a real ship, a small one, with three masts. No lights ablaze, no flags a'flying, she appears indistinctly abject and forlorn.

A signal from the nightwatchman at the harbour entrance is quickly flashed out to her in Morse code: 'What ship is that? What ship is that?'[2]

No reply.

Again, he signals, impatiently opening and shutting the shutters in a slightly faster manner, insisting on a reply. 'What ship is that? Please identify. What ship *is* that?'

And now a signal comes back, still not identifying itself but informing the nightwatchman that they are sending a dinghy ashore. Other night owls aroused around the harbour watch closely, if silently, as – can it be? – yes, in the dim light of the wan moon, a dinghy is seen to be ghosting towards the shore.

As it pulls into Sumpter Wharf, it is met by the stunned nightwatchman, who asks its crew what ship they are from. The four men reply that they 'don't know', before two men alight, while the other two in the dinghy immediately head back to the ship.

The nightwatchman, in a surprisingly familiar accent – for Neil MacKinnon is a Scotsman – tells the two who have alighted that they had better start cooperating or he'll call customs and the police. The men, in British accents, reply that he is quite welcome to call anyone he pleases. Meanwhile, by this time other people are aware that something is up, have been drawn to the lights on the shore and want to know just what is going on, but the Englishmen have no interest in telling them.

At last, however, the men soften a little and explain to the night-watchman what they need and why they need it. After hearing their urgent request, the nightwatchman quickly wakes the harbour-master, Captain James Ramsay, who is instantly cooperation and hospitality itself, inviting the two men to stay the rest of the night on the floor of his modest cottage – an offer they happily accept.

As soon as the post office opens the next morning, the telegraphist's finger works the Morse key, as directed by one of the men from the dinghy. For the first time, heavily coded word of Scott's unsuccessful attempt on the Pole is sent out, intended for the bereaved relatives and friends so they shouldn't learn first-hand of their losses through the press.

Under agreement with Central News, who are Scott's sole agents for worldwide distribution of his cabled story (and who have paid £2500 for the rights), the first instalment of the story of the death of Captain Scott and his four companions – penned by Teddy Evans and including Scott's 'Message to the Public' – then heads out first to Christchurch, and from there to the wider world, with the story first breaking in London's *Daily Mail*.[3]

Another cable goes to the War Office in London to formally inform the British authorities what has happened to some of their finest officers.[4] For the ship just outside Oamaru Harbour is none other than *Terra Nova*, and the men in the dinghy are Dr Edward Atkinson and Lieutenant Harry Pennell, rowed ashore by Tom Crean, with one other.

Tom Crean, meanwhile, with his companion, has returned on the dinghy to *Terra Nova*, reporting to Evans, in a thick Irish brogue, 'We was chased, sorr, but they got nothing out of us.'[5] Yet despite the crew's best intentions, the next day the regional papers announce that *Terra Nova* is back and has landed two men at Oamaru, 'supposed to be Scott and one of his officers'.[6]

The real news, however, is out.

When *Terra Nova*, with her ensign at half-mast, pulls into Lyttelton at dawn the following morning, it is to find that the world has changed. As recorded by Cherry-Garrard:

> How different it was from the day we left and yet how much the same: as though we had dreamed some horrible nightmare and could scarcely believe we were not dreaming still . . .
>
> Indeed we had been too long away and the whole thing was so personal to us and our perceptions had been blunted: we never realised. We landed to find the Empire – almost the civilised world – in mourning.[7]

And so it is.

The harbourmaster, arriving in the tug with Pennell and Atkinson, on learning the news first-hand, soon breaks down and weeps. And now, as the men of *Terra Nova* come ashore, the locals of Lyttelton form a grieving guard of honour for them. So affected is Atkinson by once again being in the middle of the mourning, awakening his own grief to a new pitch, that, as is soon reported by the papers, 'he is gone into the country to rest'.[8]

On this same day, Oriana Wilson is on a train coming into Christchurch when she becomes aware that a newspaper hawker at a station she has stopped at is shouting excitedly some news to do with the 'South Pole', and 'Scott expedition' . . .

What is it?

'All found dead!'

For the news has indeed burst on the stunned world, first via the pages of the *Daily Mail*, beneath the headline:

DEATH OF CAPTAIN SCOTT
LOST WITH FOUR COMRADES
THE POLE REACHED
DISASTER OF THE RETURN
STARVATION IN A BLIZZARD
FINDING OF THE BODIES
FATE OF THE LAST THREE

We regret to announce that disaster has overtaken the British Antarctic Expedition. The news is brought by the expeditionary ship *Terra Nova*, which arrived in Oamaru, in the south of New Zealand, yesterday from the Antarctic.

Captain Robert Falcon Scott reached the South Pole on January 18 last year. He died ten weeks later on 29 March, and with him perished his four comrades in his dash to the Pole. Their names are:

Captain Scott, R.N. Expedition leader, ultimately responsible for all aspects of the expedition.

Dr E. A. Wilson, chief of scientific staff, zoologist and artist.

Lieut. H. Bowers, of the Royal Indian marine, in charge of the commissariat.

Capt. L. E. G. Oates, of the Iniskilling Dragoons, in charge of the ponies.

Petty-Officer Evans, of the Royal Navy, in charge of the sledges and equipment.

Thus the British Antarctic Expedition which set forth with such bright hopes has ended in the deepest tragedy – in a tragedy unmatched in Polar annals since the disaster which befell Sir John Franklin and 129 officers and men in the Arctic in 1847–8.[9]

The editorial of the *Daily Mail* is nothing less than the overture for the full symphony of violins, trumpets and cymbal clashes that is to follow in that same paper:

A great blow has fallen upon the nation. Captain Scott has attained the goal of his life's endeavour, but the price he has paid is his life . . . they have died for the honour and greatness of their country as truly as any seaman or soldier who falls in battle. And by her they will be ever lamented and their memory cherished as a sacred inheritance.[10]

The words of the former Poet Laureate, Alfred, Lord Tennyson, from many years before, on the death of the explorer Sir John Franklin, are quoted prominently:

Not here! The white South[11] has thy bones; and thou
Heroic sailor soul
Art passing on thine happier voyages now
Towards no earthly Pole.[12]

From the pages of the British press, news of the deaths of Scott and his men reaches into the far corners of the British Empire, spreading out across the western world and then beyond. The outpouring of global grief it generates – as both the grandeur and tragedy of what has occurred seem to have combined to form a patriotic tidal wave of emotion – is unprecedented.

Nowhere, of course, is the grief so great as among the dead explorers' families.

Scott's mother, Hannah Scott, is hosting a tea party in her quiet home at Henley-on-Thames – all ivy, picket fences and smoke from the chimneys – when a knock on the door reveals a uniformed boy with a peaked cap proffering a telegram from London, a telegram that is opened by Captain Scott's sister. That good woman tries the best she can to break the news to her mother gently, to save her 'the pangs of such a sudden and painful shock', but, of course, there is simply no stopping the outpouring of grief that results.

Scott's three-year-old son, Peter, is playing with his blocks, in the care of his maternal grandmother – Kathleen Scott left for New Zealand several weeks earlier, telling her son 'I am going to fetch him home'[13] – when the news comes to that very home. By way of explanation for the black, pressing pall of grief that hangs over the house, young Peter is told by his grandmother that 'Daddy is ill', until she can muster the strength to tell him the truth.[14]

He had been just ten months old when his father had departed on *Terra Nova*. The veil of babydom had no sooner been lifted than, with the help of his mother, Peter had started tracking Daddy's progress by helping his mother place tiny flags on the map of Antarctica, and the place names were among the first words he had ever learnt.

'Mother has gone to fetch *him* back,' he has constantly been declaring to household servants, in his mother's absence, 'and then she is going to bring *him* home and I am going to meet *him* at the station.'

Alas, as the grandmother and those house servants now know, that will never happen.

Elsewhere, all across the nation, other children are badly affected. In the preceding two years, many of them have saved their sweet money and collected pennies to raise funds so that their schools might sponsor aspects of Scott's expedition. They know full well, and have even studied, which party would be using the specific tent their school's money has purchased, which pony they have nicknamed, which school's sledge they have dragged . . . and now they know which of their travellers lies frozen, dead and buried in the sleeping bag they have worked so hard to contribute to the cause.

The *Daily Mail*, meanwhile, appeals for the public to make donations so that the debts of the expedition can be cleared, 'as well as for provision for the dependents of the dead, and a temple of fame worthy of those British heroes'.[15]

Amid it all, however, there is some muted criticism, even from members of Scott's original expedition. Herbert Ponting is to the point in his own quoted remarks:

> It is my genuine personal opinion that had Scott had dogs with him on the last journey, this disaster would not have happened. But Scott did not like the idea of employing dogs and then having to kill them. It is an interesting point whether such an act is justifiable where human lives are being affected.[16]

For the most part, though, such words are lost in the tide of national grief that is at its height in Great Britain and high enough to simply swamp the rest of the British Empire and the English-speaking world from there, before making its way to all other parts of the globe.

On the late morning of 14 February, three days after the news breaks, a requiem service is held at St Paul's Cathedral, where it is standing room only inside, with no fewer than 10,000 people outside. Inside, the sovereign King George V himself sits near the centre of the front aisle, almost like any other member of the congregation, which includes members of other polar expeditions, foreign ambassadors, leading members of the government and opposition and representatives 'of all the great nation's activities'. As the service begins, King George is seen to 'bow his head a little and then straighten his back, as if to brace himself against the onset of great emotion . . .' as the muffled drum of the dead march from *Saul*, played by the Coldstream Guards, begins. And now the king kneels along with the rest of the congregation as a special prayer is offered and all of them repeat in full the names of the five men who died among the snows. 'We humbly leave in Thy Fatherly keeping the souls of our brothers Robert Falcon Scott, Lawrence Edward Grace Oates, Edward Adrian Wilson, Henry Robertson Bowers, Edgar Evans.'[17]

There is something about the manner of their deaths, the heroism of it, while on a patriotic calling for the Empire – the *Empire!* – that strikes not just a chord but also a hymn, and the nation weeps as it sings with patriotic passion. At St Paul's, that hymn is most appropriate to Scott and his men:

> While I draw this fleeting breath
> When my eyelids close in death
> When I soar through tracts unknown,
> See thee on thy judgement throne,
> Rock of Ages, cleft for me,
> Let me hide myself in thee.

Simultaneous to this service, to try to help the children understand and appreciate the glory of their men's deaths, a special account has been written in language they can comprehend and is read out in every elementary school in London, as well as in another 50 towns around Great Britain:

> Children, you are going to hear the story of five of the bravest and best men who have ever lived on the earth since the world began . . . they feared no danger, never complained and did their very best, each one willing to give up his life for the others, and when they knew that there was no hope for them, they laid down their lives bravely and calmly like true Christian gentlemen . . .[18]

And so it goes. A *Daily Mail* journalist happens to overhear a group of boys discussing the death of Captain Oates as they linger after school at the gates.

'He was a brave man,' says one.

Another replies proudly, 'He was a British officer!'[19]

Indeed, the adulation for the manner of Oates's death is universal.

When the telegram from the War Office arrived at the home

of Lawrence Oates's mother, Caroline, at Gestingthorpe in Essex, to inform her of her son's death, she was mercifully not there to receive it, as she was down in her London flat at the time. It is her eldest daughter, Lawrence's older sister, Lillian, who hears the news first, when she sees a newspaper poster on a London street, blaring the dreadful tidings. Buying a paper with shaking hands, she soon takes in that the worst has happened and with heavy heart and heavier tread goes off to find her mother and break the news.

That good woman would at least be heartened by the adulation for the heroic act of her son that is reflected across the nation. For just as there is the service at St Paul's, so too are many other services held around the country as the nation mourns with an intensity usually reserved for the death of monarchs alone. Shackleton's words to his wife Emily three years earlier – 'I thought, dear, that you would rather have a live ass than a dead lion' – have particular resonance now. For Scott, though dead, is now being lionised as never before, and far more than had he lived, even if he *had* beaten Amundsen and his men to the Pole.

As to the Norwegian expedition leader, he is on a lecture tour in New York, capitalising on his own stunning feat, when the news hits and he is asked for his reaction. 'I am unwilling to believe the report is true,' he states flatly. 'I was reported to have died and so was Shackleton.' Shortly thereafter, however, his tone changes, as if he has accepted it as fact after all. 'Scott was a brave man,' Amundsen says, 'whose first thought was for the safety of his men. He took no thought of his own danger or comforts. I am grieved beyond measure at the report.'[20]

He reserves special words, though, for Lawrence Oates:

Oates went bravely, you know, out into the blizzard that his sickly condition might not hinder the others. He knew the others wouldn't desert him so he deserted them. That was an epic deed

– wonderful, wonderful! A great sacrifice – but it did no good.[21]

For his part, Shackleton, first up, also simply refuses to believe it. He tells the *Daily Mail*:

> I only hope there has been some mistake. Everyone knows that a polar exploration is largely a game of chance . . . If the reports are true and Captain Scott has been lost it will be a tremendous blow to explorers the world over. To me it is a fearful shock to think the man I served under may be gone.[22]

It is Rear Admiral Robert Peary, however, the self-proclaimed conqueror of the North Pole, who is the most eloquent:

> Mingled with their feelings of sorrow, there must be a swelling sense of pride to the countrymen and relatives of Captain Scott and the other heroes with him that they made 'good' and by their courage and dogged persistence carried the British ensign to that far and frozen goal that they had set out for. It is a splendid tragedy – a splendid epic, written like many another British epic dotted over the globe in a language which every creed and race and tongue of man can understand. Captain Scott's name and work are imperishable, and as eternal as the icy heights on which he died.[23]

Mid-February 1913, Cape Denison, the ether strikes back

Success! After seemingly endless difficulties with all of the radio equipment and antenna, on the night of 15 February, Sidney Jeffryes is doing what he has been doing every night – firing up the petrol engine that runs the dynamo that sends the electrical current he needs to send the radio signal up the mast and out on the antenna, even as he secures his headphones – when suddenly something happens. He hears something! He clearly hears the base at Macquarie Island sending the Morse code weather report to Hobart.

Once told, the others immediately crowd around the 27-year-old as he tries to join in their conversation, and though it doesn't work on this occasion, all are excited. Five nights later, it gets better still. Jeffryes has no sooner sent out a message to Macquarie Island – where all the men in Ainsworth's team have agreed to remain at their post for another year so that the radio link between Cape Denison and Hobart can be maintained – than he hears their distinct reply: 'Dah-dah-dit, dah-dah-dah, dah-dah-dah, dah-di-dit, dit, di-di-di-dah, dit, dah-dit, di-dit, dah-dit, dah-dah-dit.' ('Good evening.')[24]

True, something then breaks, but they know they are close.

In the meantime, bit by bit, Douglas Mawson is coming back to himself, getting physically, mentally and emotionally stronger, less dependent on the others to look after him and more capable of looking after himself. It is a slow process, grounding himself back in the real world, such as it is, but one thing that helps is reading, over and over and over again, the four letters that his Paquita had written between February and October of 1912 and which, courtesy of *Aurora*, had been waiting for him at the hut when he got there. After all the coldness he has known, all the fear, all the sense of total isolation, here, *here* is love, warmth and companionship, as she assures him:

You will have a warm welcome on your return. My arms are open for you already as I think of it . . . Don't I long for the first quiet hours together. I make no promises to meet you as I can only answer for myself and not for my family on whom it depends. But my heart will be there if not in flesh in spirit.[25]

He *aches* to be with her in turn. What, he frequently wonders, is she doing right now?

Mid-February 1913, Gulf of Aden, aboard *Roon* on the Indian Ocean, as Paquita gets news

Oh dear. Oh dear, oh dear. On this fine day, out in the middle of the Indian Ocean, Henrietta Delprat, Paquita's mother, answers a knock on her door to find a cabin boy standing there. Begging your pardon, Madam, but the captain has asked me to pass this cable on to you. She opens it and gasps. Her future son-in-law, Douglas Mawson, has met with disaster in the Antarctic, and though he has narrowly survived, his two companions, Xavier Mertz and Belgrave Ninnis, are dead!

On the bunk before her, Paquita lies sleeping. How will her daughter react when she hears the news? Not quite sure what to do, but needing some moral support, Henrietta drops the cable on her bed and goes next door to the cabin of her other daughter to talk to her and get some advice.

Awaking to the sound of the door opening and closing twice within the space of a minute, Paquita opens her eyes to see the cable on her mother's bed, and her mother gone, just as the door opens once more as her mother returns, with a devastated expression on her face. Wordlessly, Henrietta Delprat hands Paquita the cable and says to her, 'You must be thankful . . .'[26]

And, ultimately, Paquita is: devastated that two of Douglas's companions have died, but thankful at least that he is still among the living. She also feels an overwhelming sense of gratitude to those men in the hut who have sacrificed another year away from their own families so they can look after him. Bless them.

18 February 1913 and three days thereafter, Pacific Ocean, between Tahiti and Raratonga, aboard RMS *Aorangi*

Though not classically beautiful, Kathleen Scott is an alluring woman. She is something of the toast of the ship, frequently invited to dine at the captain's table. After all, she is married, don't you know, to the dashing Captain Robert Falcon Scott, the polar explorer who is due back in Dunedin very soon. She is on her way to meet him, coming via a cross-continental trip through the United States before embarking from San Francisco.

Kathleen spends her days chatting to all and sundry, playing whist with those lucky enough to make up her four, but on this day she is taking some sea air in her deckchair, not feeling very well, when she looks up to see the troubled-looking captain looming above her . . .

Might he have a word with her in his cabin?

Of course.

Strangely, the nautical gentleman seems to be almost ill when they arrive at the Master's cabin and is distinctly grey of complexion. What on *earth* can be the matter with the good man? She is not long in finding out.

'I've got some news for you, but I don't see how I can tell you,' he says.

'The expedition?'

'Yes.'

'Well, let's have it.'

With his hands shaking, the captain passes her a piece of paper on which is written a message that the ship's wireless operator has received from the Marconi station in San Francisco just a few minutes earlier:

```
Captain Scott and six others perished in a
blizzard after reaching the South Pole January
18th.27
```

She staggers momentarily and then quickly straightens.

'Oh, well, never mind!' she says to the kindly old captain. 'I expected that. Thanks very much. I will go and think about it.'

Kathleen then goes about her business, in the first instance to receive an hour and a half of Spanish tuition. She then returns to her cabin, where she records in her diary:

I acquitted myself well . . . I was sure I could control myself . . . My god is godly. I need not touch him to know that. Let me maintain a high, adoring exaltation, and not let the contamination of sorrow touch me.[28]

Nevertheless, as she emerges once more from her cabin to play five games of deck-golf, she can't help but notice a young third officer who, 'like a big dog sits by me and is sorry'. Only later does she find out that his job, assigned by the captain, is to ensure she does not throw herself overboard.[29]

'It is good that I do not firmly believe in life after death,' Kathleen records in her diary, 'or surely I would have gone overboard today.'[30]

Stoically, she goes on. Two evenings later, as the ship approaches Raratonga on the Cook Islands, she is alone with the wireless operator as more details emerge, including the fact that, instead of dying of exposure as she thought, they had suffered the even more ghastly death of starvation. Now, her control wavers.

'The operator is an Irishman,' she records in her diary. 'We have never had any conversation. He just hands me the papers as he has finished writing them. I took my papers and went to bed; I didn't want to hear any more.'[31]

23 February 1913, Shackleton Ice Shelf, Frank Wild sees a 'penguin'

In these waning days of February, the situation of Frank Wild and his companions is beyond desperate. For the past year, they have survived, and even prospered on occasion, fulfilling all their scientific tasks – meteorology, geology, biology, magnetic observations – and completing all their sledging expeditions, reaching out to the east and west of their base, but for the last three weeks their anxiety day by day has risen with the ongoing failure of *Aurora* to pick them up. The ship had been scheduled to appear on 30 January, but they had continued to search the horizon in vain.

With winter already starting to close in, and few supplies beyond penguin and seal meat and next to no coal to get them through the long, dark, freezing night, their survival will be a close-run thing if the ship does not arrive. All the men can do to heighten their chances is to lay in more of that meat, by killing more seals and penguins, and that is their task on this morning – quietly, desperately, ever conscious that any day now these aquatic wonders will be returning to the ocean for the winter.

Out on *Aurora* this morning, Captain Davis is feeling almost equally desperate. He is the one, after all, who had taken the responsibility the year before of leaving the men camped on the ice. If they are now dead, or disappeared – perhaps the cliff where he left them has by now floated out to sea? – then it will be on his conscience and his record for the rest of his life. It has in fact been an extraordinary journey just to get back here, bashing westward, ever westward, through blizzards and bergs alike. Vast fields of pack ice have constantly thwarted progress, and though he is navigating 'by guess and by God'[32] and danger has attended their every torturous mile, Davis has decided that even in darkness, even with bergs everywhere – and despite what happened to *Titanic* a year earlier – he wants his ship for the most part at full speed. This is so he can be certain she will answer the helm quickly, with the bonus that, if they survive, they will get to Wild and his men all the sooner. And it has more or less worked, because Davis now knows he is roughly in the area, even though there is no sign of the Wild party.

All of his crew are out on deck as they steam past cape after cape, bay after bay, looking for the tiniest sign of human life, but there is still nothing. Presently, Davis can stand it no more, and even though he knows that the third mate, De La Motte, who is up in the crow's nest, would have called him the instant he has seen anything, still he calls out, 'Can you see the hut, Mr De La Motte?'

'No, sir,' the third mate replies gloomily, before softening a little and trying to offer the cap'n *something*. 'But I can nearly see it.'[33]

The resultant roar from Davis would have done Roaring Tom himself proud and gives those on *Aurora* the first real laugh for some time.

What's that?

At 11.20 on this freezing morning, Frank Wild and Dr Evan Jones have descended from the ice cliff to retrieve a sledge when their attention is drawn by some tiny movement out on the pack ice. At first, they think it is a penguin, but then the stunned realisation hits. It is a crow's nest, followed by the mainmast of a ship. It is *Aurora*! Their ship has come in! Shouts of joy abound as the men on shore realise they are saved after all, curtailed only by Wild giving orders to Jones to head back to the others and tell them to instantly start getting their gear, records and specimens down to the water's edge.

There they are! Distant figures waving on the lip of the high ice confirms to Davis that there is a God after all, and he instantly alters course. They're *alive*! In an instant, his worries of the last year are swept away with the wave of sheer relief that now washes over him. Even then, however, it is the Devil's own work to get close, as the little ship bashes and breaks its way through the broken floe to get to the solid ice at the bottom of the cliffs where *Aurora* dropped the land party the year before.

By the time the ship is getting close, Wild and his men are waiting patiently for her at that spot, and now a new fear hits Davis and his men. How many of the 'castaways' are there? Are they about to find out about another calamity, just as happened at main base when they arrived there? Anxiously, Davis begins to count the distant figures to see if any of the eight are missing.

One, two, three . . . they keep counting . . . until they get to . . . *20*?

Have these blokes somehow been *breeding*? And then they realise: the shorter group to the side of the main group is in fact an interested gathering of Emperor penguins, just come along to check that everything is shipshape.

From the shore comes the sound of a resounding three cheers as Wild and his men offer thanks for their salvation to the captain and crew of *Aurora*. The captain and crew return the three cheers in kind.

As before, once the ship is moored alongside the floe, it takes some time, amid all the warm handshakes, to work out just who is who, and Wild's men have similar problems with Mawson's men who are onboard – even though the latter by this time are looking more human than they were a few days earlier.

And, as before, these wild men are not only overjoyed to see the arrivals but also pleased to quickly take them back to their quarters for the last year, to show them around. Davis and his men are stunned to climb the hill, to visit the hut, which is half-covered by the winter snows, and see how these men have been living 'the lives of troglodytes. Tunnels extended into the drifts on every side – tunnels that had been used to store the food cases in order to save the ceaseless exertion of digging them out of the snow above.'[34]

By the time the men return to the ship, with their two surviving dogs, more Emperor penguins have gathered to farewell them, solemnly bowing their salutations. 'They were very stately and dignified,' commented Charles Laseron admiringly, 'and lacked the bustling self-importance of the Adélie penguin.'[35]

After the men pile on board with all of their gear, it is only a short time before they are under way. For all the joy of everyone being safe and well, there is still no time to lose.

24 February 1913 and into March, Winter Quarters, there is another breakthrough

At last, some 15 months after Mawson planned, their whole radio system is now working, which is an enormous step forward. A slew of excited messages about how they are getting on at Winter Quarters is traded for what is happening in the rest of the world. Mawson is, of course, deeply saddened to hear of the death of Scott and his companions, as their first bit of news from beyond their shores. There but for the grace of God . . .

Then Mawson sends another message, this one to Lord Denman, the Australian governor general, to apprise him of their situation and the death of his loyal comrades, while also requesting of the King his 'royal permission to name a tract of newly discovered country to the east, "King George V Land"'.[36]

Of course, the person with whom Mawson is most keen to make contact is Paquita, but for the moment that is not possible, as she is still on the high seas heading back to Australia. At least he is able to get confirmation from her father via a brief exchange of messages that she is fine, which is something. Against that, he also receives news of his father's death three months earlier, while on his own trip to New Guinea – curiously, at the time he had the disturbing dream about his father – which saddens him.

And there are terribly difficult cables to send, too. Several days after the radio has begun to work, after gathering the spiritual strength necessary, Mawson reluctantly hands to Jeffryes two cables destined for distant shores that he has been working on with heavy heart – messages that simply now must be sent via Macquarie Island and Hobart, to England and Switzerland:

> Deeply regret to advise you by wireless Lieut. Ninnis killed instantly December fourteenth by falling into crevasse whilst sledging. Dr Mawson.[37]

And:

> Deeply regret to advise by wireless telegraph the death of Dr Mertz on January seventh whilst sledging from causes arising from malnutrition. Dr Mawson.[38]

The news of the deaths also provides more headlines for the English press soon afterwards:

NEW TRAGEDY OF THE ANTARCTIC
DEATH OF TWO EXPLORERS
MESSAGE FROM DR MAWSON
FATE OF BRITISH OFFICER
LEADER AND SIX MEN LEFT BEHIND
Two more explorers have lost their lives in the Antarctic. One is Lieutenant B. E. S. Ninnis, of the Royal Fusiliers, and the other Dr Mertz, a Swiss champion ski-runner.

Lieutenant Ninnis fell in a crevasse (fissure in snow or ice) on 14 January, and was instantly killed . . .[39]

In response to the news, Sir Ernest Shackleton is quick to the point:

A portion of the press is speaking of the Mawson Antarctic Expedition as a tragedy. Undoubtedly the deaths of Lieutenant Ninnis and Dr Mertz are sad, but they are the outcomes of accidents which come in the ordinary course in all Polar expeditions. Apart from these two accidents the expedition seems to me to have been a brilliant one.

When the story comes to be written of Mawson's journey it will, to my mind, be a fascinating one, for I can imagine the lonely struggle he made, his two companions dead, moving northwards[40] through blizzard, snow, and fog over crevasses for three weeks on his lonely way. Knowing Mawson as I do, I am not surprised at his achievement. To a man of less equable temperament or less determination the result would have been fatal.[41]

Back at Cape Denison, many further communications follow, including a full report to Professor David of exactly what the last year has consisted of, and there is a flood of messages back, of both sympathy and congratulations. Lord Denman sends a message expressing his sorrow at the death of Ninnis and Mertz, a sentiment royally echoed by the King himself, who also graciously allows that Dr Mawson may 'affix the name, "King George V" Land, to that part of the Antarctic continent lying between Adélie Land and Oates Land.'[42]

Other cables, of course, of far less momentous content are also flowing back and forth, and it is quite a frequent occurrence that those who have gone to bed before midnight awake to find a pile of messages awaiting them, which is the highlight of their day – taking the place, in many ways, of a morning paper.

Whatever news is general and of common interest – more details on the death of the Scott party, for example – is discussed over breakfast 'from every possible point of view'.[43] (Being careful, of course, to talk quietly, so the nightwatchman can at last get some sleep.)

While this is a wonderful thing for most in the hut, the actual process of receiving the distant messages places a great strain on the radio operator, Jeffryes, for whom it involves long hours of tedium interspersed with signals through such difficult things as atmospheric static, the sometime howling of the dogs, noises within the hut and interference from the aurora australis and St Elmo's fire. On a bad night, he spends hours on end trying to send or receive a single message, all for no result, and when it is particularly bad he can try for a whole week – enough to send any man spare. Fortunately, though, he seems mostly to cope. One of his key duties is sending through to Hobart the daily weather reports from Cape Denison, and though it frequently takes a long time to do this, they usually do get through by evening's end.

14 March 1913, Port Esperance, *Aurora* returns

For all the still half-frozen wild men who spent the previous year on Antarctica, this is a magic time. They have survived. They have done well. They are on their way home. And the sea is now calm, after battering the ship as she headed north through the Southern Ocean. And there, up ahead, on the far-northern horizon, they can see land! Tasmania, ho!

Sure enough, as they steam into Port Esperance – on Tassie's far south-western coast – they can spy, for the first time since two Decembers earlier, green hills! And they can even sniff the scent of trees on the wind – a scent that they had not previously known existed but do now, after a year without. But it gets better still. For there, do you see? There are the shapes of houses emerging from between those trees. Civilisation!

But now a greater wave of excitement quickly spreads through the men eagerly lining the rail near the bow of the ship. For the more eagle-eyed among them have just spotted something that tops all the rest put together, something that makes them jostle each other in their eagerness to get their hands on the field-glasses so they can get a better look. There is a figure standing in a garden at the front of a cottage.

Is it . . .? Can it be . . .?

Yes, it is. It is a girl.[44]

March to May 1913, Cape Denison, autumn in the Winter Quarters

Shortly after *Aurora* arrives in Hobart, back at Cape Denison Mawson and his men learn over the radio that Davis has succeeded in picking up Wild and *all* of his men, and the whole lot of them have returned safely. Mawson is not long in sending Davis instructions to proceed with all pace to England, where he believes his friend will have the best chance of raising the funds necessary to meet the bills attendant on them staying in Antarctica for another year.

In the here and now, though, there is great rejoicing to hear the news from Hobart, and an all too rare evening of exuberance follows, in what is otherwise a dour time.

For . . . the ambience in the hut is now entirely different to what it was just a few months earlier, when, just before they headed out for their summer sledging expeditions, the whole place crackled with optimism, laughter, excitement, *life*. Then, there were 18 of them crowded around the dinner table, in Hyde Park Corner, smoking their pipes, playing instruments, listening to records, telling stories and laughing into the night. Then, there were the effervescent Ninnis 'n' Mertz, the riotous Hurley, the spellbinding Herbert Dyce Murphy, with his endless supply of stories. Then, the delicious waft of Mertz's penguin omelettes had filled the entire hut.

Now, now there are just seven of them quietly rattling around in the suddenly cavernous shelter, of whom one, Mawson, still has a long way to go before resuming his full place in the life of the hut, such as it is.

While the bunks of 11 men now lie empty, there are none emptier than those of Mertz and Ninnis, their absence a constant reminder to all of their dreadful fate. They're still out there, of course, both of them, their bodies perfectly preserved in their frozen resting places, and it is impossible not to think of that too. Their deaths hang like a black shroud over the entire hut, a pall that does not dissipate as the days and then weeks pass. Some nights, Cecil Madigan can hear Frank Bickerton 'sobbing under his blanket'[45] as he grieves for his dear friends.

As time hangs heavy on all of their hands, it is impossible, too, not to reflect on how close they came to being safe aboard *Aurora*, to now being home with their families, only to be here, in this frozen wasteland, once so invigorating and fresh but now, as Mawson himself puts it, 'decidedly duller'. For that which once was new no longer is, and, in Mawson's words, 'the field of work which once stretched to the west, east and south had no longer the mystery of the unknown'.[46]

The one thing that helps is that they are relatively busy. For Dux Ipse is determined that this year will be more gainfully than painfully spent, gathering data for a total of two years and not just the one previously planned, and this means that the seven men must do what nearly three times that number have previously accomplished.

Now, for example, McLean, as well as keeping the biological log and making general observations, does all the ice-cutting and coal-carrying. (And he also, apart from pursuing his personal passions of collecting and preserving parasites from birds and fish, throws many sealed bottles with messages in them into the ocean, in the hope that information can be gained, if they are picked up, about the direction of the currents.)

For his part, Bage takes over Webb's role as magnetician, while also being astronomer and storeman. Bickerton, beyond his regular role as general mechanic, also, as radio engineer, has his hands full most nights, ensuring the link to Macquarie Island is up. Hodgeman, as assistant meteorologist, is responsible for continuing to collect a lot of the scientific data on a daily basis, as well as, in his role as cartographer, spending 'much time drafting, engaged upon the maps and plans of the Expedition'.[47]

And then there is the final member of the troupe, the new man, Sidney Jeffryes. Mawson first met him over two years earlier when he applied to join the AAE, and though he rejected his application then, this time he has been employed by the expedition secretary, Conrad Eitel. Jeffryes has continued to be kept more than busy, night after night, into the wee hours – when the transmissions work best – trying to send and receive messages, not always with success, but still going hard all the same. Of them all, Jeffryes, being relatively new to it, still gazes with wonder upon the environment, and, for the most part, he seems to fit in.

Mawson himself is kept busy collating much of the data and information recorded in the previous summer's sledging, while also drafting the book he has agreed to write for William Heinemann, detailing the entire expedition. In the latter task, he has the great help of McLean, a highly literate man who, with the exception of Mawson's epic sledging trip, has of course lived through much of what Mawson is wanting to describe. As well as writing some chapters from scratch, McLean works hard on compressing and refining Mawson's drafts and greatly contributing to the book's overall style.

Beyond such professional duties, however, the fact that there are seven of them in the hut makes the division of chores relatively easy, with each man obliged to spend one day a week being the cook and one night a week being nightwatchman.

And so the hut settles down to wait the year out, with mixed degrees of ease. It is perhaps most difficult for Mawson himself in these early weeks, as he is not yet recovered from his physical and emotional ordeal and frequently pushes himself too hard. To try to relax, he often reads – including *The History of War and Peace* by G. H. Perris – but even reading can be fraught. Though he finds fascinating the book by Frederick A. Cook, *Through the First Antarctic Night* – concerning the ill-fated expedition of Adrien de Gerlache in 1897 – parts of it deeply shock him. For, as Cook so evocatively details, not long after the darkness of the polar winter night descended, it brought with it a terrible melancholia, and, from there, madness was not far behind.[48]

Speaking of which . . . even though they have not begun their own second polar winter in this hut, Mawson himself sometimes fears for his own sanity. Though flesh is slowly returning to his bones and he has stopped shedding skin, he still cannot sleep well, is frequently anxious far beyond an immediate cause, is irritable and sometimes irrational, has terrible headaches and keeps thinking of his own near-death experience and of the all too real deaths of Ninnis 'n' Mertz, now reunited in death.[49]

The spectre of their bodies out there in the frozen wastelands is something that continues to haunt Mawson in the darkness, a darkness that is now starting to rapidly lengthen as winter approaches. 'I find my nerves are in a very serious state,' he quietly confides to his diary in late March, 'and from the feeling I have in the base of my head I [have the] suspicion that I may go off my rocker very soon.' The cause, he feels, is obvious. 'Too much writing today brought this on.'

The way forward, in his own opinion?

'Take more exercise and less study, hoping for a beneficial turn.'[50]

In the meantime, in an effort to keep everyone else's spirits up, at the beginning of April Mawson asks McLean to resuscitate an idea he had the previous winter of producing a monthly magazine, called the *Adélie Blizzard*, in the tradition of the *South Polar Times*, which Shackleton and Bernacchi edited during the *Discovery* expedition and which was continued by Cherry-Garrard during the *Terra Nova* expedition, along with *Aurora Australis*, which had been produced during the *Nimrod* expedition.

McLean could be the editor and all of them could make contributions in the form of poems, articles, stories or anything that took their fancy 'on every subject but the wind', as Mawson put it.[51] It included anything and everything from 'light doggerel to heavy blank verse . . . original articles, letters to the Editor, plays, reviews on books and serial stories . . . within the limits of our supply of foolscap paper and typewriter ribbons'.[52] It is McLean's idea to have a column exclusively devoted to news of the day, incorporating the more interesting of the cables that have come to them from the outside world over the wireless.

The plan got nowhere the previous year because Mawson himself had carriage of it and neither he, nor anyone else, had time to produce anything, absorbed as they were with getting themselves established and then in making preparations for their summer sledging journeys. This time, it should be easier.

True, in the absence of a printing press, each edition has to be laboriously typed up and pasted onto the pages, but McLean is nothing if not energetic and proves to be up to the task – so much so that he is himself admitted as a member 'by wireless to the Journalists' Association (Sydney)'.[53]

The first edition is a particular success, with McLean reading some of the best of it to the others over dinner one evening, to their great amusement. After that, the one and only copy of the newspaper, running to 40 pages, is passed from hand to hand. Extra, extra, read all about it!

'An "Ode to Tobacco" was very popular and seemed to voice the enthusiasm of our small community,' Mawson later recalls, 'while "The Evolution of Women" introduced us to a once-familiar subject.'[54]

There also continues to be some wonderful correspondence coming and going, courtesy of Jeffryes straining at the radio night after night. To Mawson, none is more important than the cable he sends to Paquita on the first day of April, by which time he knows, from his previous correspondence with her father, that she should be just returned to Adelaide from her long sojourn in Europe. After long thought, he composes and sends a telegram that makes clear that while he still loves her, he realises that her own feelings may have wavered during their long absence from each other:

```
Deeply regret delay stop only just managed
to reach hut stop effects now gone but lost
most my hair stop you are free to consider but
trust you will not abandon your second hand
Douglas stop[55]
```

Oh, the relief, the indescribable relief when all but instantly Paquita replies with her own cable, not long after her ship has reached Port Adelaide:

```
Deeply thankful you are safe stop warmest
welcome awaiting your hairless return stop
regarding contract same as ever only more so
stop thoughts always with you stop all well
here stop months soon pass stop take things
easier this winter stop speak as often as
possible stop[56]
```

So she will indeed be waiting for him upon his return, which is the best news imaginable. From that initial exchange of cables, the two begin to write infrequent letters to each other – alas, letters that will have to wait many months to be read by the other, as Mawson is reluctant to tie up the precious radio link on purely personal matters – but even in such few letters as there are, the warmth of their love for each other is affirmed again and again.

In his first letter to her, Mawson confides just how poor his physical, mental and emotional states were when he returned, which was also the reason he was inclined to liberate her from her commitment to marry him. 'Though this demonstrated my physical ability at the time,' he explains, 'it was a great shock to my entire system and the effects of it left me more than ever convinced that I did not merit your appropriation.'[57]

Her letter, written only a short time afterwards, seeks to record the warmth of her feelings for him, and all the more so for what he has been through:

My Douglas,

Oh my dear, dear man. If only I could come with this letter. Oh that terrible journey all by yourself if I could have had it instead of you – did my love help you then? It is worth less than nothing if it didn't . . . Miraculously spared to do great things – a life is not spared like that for nothing and I shall help you do them. Poor, poor Ninnis and Mertz. Correll tells me they were so much liked. Mertz was not so wiry as you. They both knew the risks they took. Thank heavens their deaths were not due to anything that could have been prevented . . .[58]

Still, he must understand that while her love for him has not changed, it is quite possible that *she* has changed:

> Douglas I have grown so much older in these months and I came back from Europe with my head full of things to discuss with you. And now everything has to wait. I feel the need of you now — am at a sort of turning point . . . I do want you so badly.[59]

It is precisely the love he needs to help keep him warm during the long, dark night to come, and already there are signs that it is not far away.

When a lone penguin stands on a rocky ledge overhanging the freezing ocean, steels himself, dives in and is not seen again, 16 April 1913 is marked down as the last sign of summer disappearing this year.

Happier communications come from Australia, where Mawson and his men are being lionised *in absentia*:

```
24.5.1913
Via Rfc. Sydney
We boys and girls and teachers of Fort Street
Public high school assembled on Empire Day
and send greetings to old Fort Street Boys,
Douglas Mawson, Archie Maclean . . . and all
their comrades who are doing their duties by
our Empire in Antarctica -
Professor David University
```

```
24.5.1913
To Professor David University
```

```
Sydney University via Rfc
Dr Mawson and colleagues heartily thank the
girls and boys of Fort Street Public High school
for their kind and sympathetic message.[60]
```

That afternoon, to celebrate Empire Day, the isolated seven raise the Union Jack and give three resounding cheers for the King.

It is good to have something to celebrate in a hut that used to crackle with so many of them . . . though for the most part they are all getting on well. Mawson does, however, have some worry about the strain that is starting to show on their new chum, Jeffryes.

A couple of nights after Empire Day, Mawson awakes near midnight and comes out to find the notably scruffy and hirsute 27-year-old asleep at his post. What's more, to judge from the lack of messages sent or received, he has clearly been that way for most of the evening. This, despite the fact that the conditions for transmitting are very good. And even when Mawson, highly irritated, wakes him, the Queenslander can only get a very little done before, on Macquarie Island, Sawyer goes to bed.

Part of the problem, Mawson confides to his diary, is that 'Jeffryes stops up all day – goes for tiring walks, etc, and then is not fit to keep an alert watch during the 8 to 12 hours. This is bad management.'[61] All this, and the fact that Jeffryes 'appears to have no conception of scientific analysis', makes Mawson wonder more than ever if they have the man they need for the job at hand. He suspects not. The one thing Jeffryes does appear to have passion for is constantly checking the stays on the antenna – he is always tightening them – and while that is admirable, it is not enough.

However tight the stays, it is Jeffryes himself who becomes increasingly slack and loosened as the days go by, and he is ever less frequently at his radio post at his designated time of 8 pm. Usually, in Mawson's experience, when he reprimands any of his men for breaches of discipline or this very kind of slack behaviour, the problem is solved, because they get the message and amend their ways. But this proves not to be the case with Jeffryes. For there is more, much more. Mawson discovers that not only has Jeffryes not been sending the nightly weather reports from Antarctica, which is a key part of his duties, he has also not been sending other cables given to him.

Something has to give, and alas, in the first instance at least – despite Jeffryes' sterling efforts in the matter of keeping the stays for the antenna tight – true winter is no sooner upon them than the wind becomes so strong on the morning of 7 June that several vicious gusts take out the top and part of the middle section of the main wireless mast. From that moment on, their 'morning newspaper' of fresh messages to wake up to has ceased, along with their capacity to get messages through to Australia.

On first inspection, there seems to be no chance of ever repairing it. However, as is the way of such things in Antarctica, where 'needs must' always takes precedence over 'can't be done', it is not long before the men begin discussing the ways it just might be repaired. In the meantime, the already slack Jeffryes becomes slacker still, as it is no longer possible for him to engage in the one activity that he has been brought there for, and his mind becomes ever more idle and troubled.

Mid-June 1913 and the rest of the month thereafter, Penarth Harbour, the people quietly gather

And so . . . the end.

In the early hours of 14 June, *Terra Nova* comes to anchor off the island of Flat Holm, the Welsh Dragon fluttering from her mainmast just as it did that day she departed. For *Terra Nova* is now returned to Cardiff, whence she had set out with such hope, three long years ago. With this return, the pledge that Scott made in response to the warmth and generosity of their Cardiff farewell is honoured.

At 11 am, Kathleen Scott and her son, Peter, Oriana Wilson and other family members of those on the expedition are transported out by tug to *Terra Nova*, while a vast crowd of loyal well-wishers line the docks and lock bridges to welcome the men home.

Little Peter Scott, with a burly officer in tow, wanders the ship in the very footsteps of that great man, his father, Captain Scott, stopping on the upper deck to pat the dogs. Here, Commander Teddy Evans presents him with his own white cap and lifts him up to the rail, from where the boy playfully acknowledges the cheers of the crowd.

Together with Mrs Scott and Mrs Wilson, however, *Terra Nova*'s crew do not respond to the cheers, choosing to remain respectfully silent. Commander Evans is bravest of all in the face of tragedy. Returning home to London back in April on *Otranto*, his wife, the 'wildly beautiful' Hilda, suffering from peritonitis, tragically died while the ship was off the coast of Naples. Evans rejoined *Terra Nova* in the Scilly Isles, off the south-west coast of England.

As *Terra Nova* now slowly steams to her berthing place, the guns are fired and the huge crowd cheer and press forward to catch a glimpse of her passing by.

By the end of June, *Terra Nova* has been sold to Bowring Brothers, a well-known Newfoundland sealing operation, and the days of her Antarctic exploration draw to an end. By that time, however, at least all of the letters that Scott's party wrote in the tent before their deaths have found their way to their loved ones.

For all of those recipients, it is extraordinary to be reading the words of men who have been dead for more than a year, speaking to them, effectively, from the grave. Perhaps the most moving part of the letter from Scott to his wife, Kathleen – which she in fact received earlier, when handed to her by her brother, Wilfrid Bruce – begins where he writes of his greatest regret:

You must know that quite the worst aspect of this situation is the thought that I shall not see you again . . . How much better has it been than lounging in too great comfort at home — but oh, what a price to pay — to forfeit the sight of your dear, dear face . . . Oh, but you'll put a strong bold face to the world.[62]

He also writes of their son, Peter:

I had looked forward to helping you to bring him up, but it is a satisfaction to know that he will be safe with you . . . Make the boy interested in natural history if you can. It is better than games. They encourage it in some schools. I know you will keep him in the open air. Try to make him believe in a God, it is comforting . . . and guard him against indolence. Make him a strenuous man. I had to force myself into being strenuous, as you know — had always an inclination to be idle. I want you to take the whole thing very sensibly, as I am sure you will . . . You know I cherish no sentimental rubbish about remarriage. When the right man comes to help you in life you ought to be your happy self again — I wasn't a very good husband but I hope I shall be a good memory . . .[63]

The indefatigable Bowers has written to his mother, in pencil, on leaves torn from his diary:

22 March 1912

My own Dearest Mother,

As this very possibly will be my last letter to you I am sorry it is such a short scribble. I have written little since we left the Pole but it has not been for want of thinking of you and the dear girls. We have had a terrible journey back. Seaman Evans died on the glacier and Captain Oates left us the other day. We have had terribly low temperatures on the barrier and . . . our sick companions have delayed us till too late in the season which has made us very short of fuel and we are now out of food as well. Each depot has been a harder struggle to reach, but I am still strong and hope to reach this one with Dr Wilson and get the food and fuel necessary for our lives.

God knows what will be the outcome of the 23 miles[64] *march we have to make, but my trust is still in Him and the abounding grace of my Lord and Saviour whom you brought me up to trust in . . .*

When man's extremity is reached God's help may make

things light and thus the end will be painless enough for myself. I should so like to come through for your dear sake. It is splendid however to pass with such companions as I have and as all of us have mothers and 3 wives you will not be alone . . . no shame however and you will know that I struggled to the end . . .

But take comfort that I died at peace with the world and myself – not afraid . . .

Your ever loving son to the end of this life and the next when we will meet and where God shall wipe away the tears from our eyes.[65]

22 June 1913, Cape Denison, Bage and Bickerton dress up

Under the circumstances, it is hard not to compare this midwinter's day celebration with the one the previous year. Then, it had been a riotous affair involving 18 men untroubled by tragedy, extending into the next day as they had gone past midnight to encompass birthday celebrations for Belgrave Ninnis, who was officially in his 25th year on the stroke of twelve o'clock that night.

Now, it is a rather more subdued gathering, of just seven men, six of whom have been here the previous year and remember all too well the whole night and its aftermath. Yes, this night's cook, McLean, does make an extra effort and the menu does bear the foreword: 'Now is the winter of our discontent, made glorious summer . . .'[66]

And, as Mawson notes in his diary, 'Bage and Bickerton dress up in coloured togs.'[67]

But it is just not the same . . .

July 1913, Cape Denison, the strain begins to show

And then, as is always the way in the middle of the penetrating darkness of polar winter, madness begins to stalk wherever it finds mental weakness of any kind. In this instance, it descends upon . . . Sidney Jeffryes, their radio operator.

Though in the early days of arriving at the camp, he had been agreeable and hard-working, over time he has changed, slipping into an odd, nervy kind of moroseness where it is clear that he is struggling more than the old hands are to get through the winter months.

After that first time of Mawson discovering him asleep at his post, it has become worse, as his behaviour has grown progressively more slovenly: caring less and less how he dresses and behaves; no longer participating in conversations; and appearing quite ambivalent about whether he will or won't attend to his cooking and cleaning duties.

Though Mawson tries to relieve the workload on the radio man by allowing him to cook only one meal every six days, even then the results are those of a man who simply doesn't care any more, to the point that it becomes dangerous. The reason the oven explodes on one occasion is directly due to Jeffryes' carelessness. Even making tea is beyond him, as he is known to serve it up when the water has not fully boiled! The fact that the antenna has gone down, sparing him his nightly duties, does not help, as Jeffryes seems to get only worse.

One night at dinner in early July, Madigan is talking about something he has been reading in *The Hound of the Baskervilles* when

Jeffryes, thinking he is being referred to, suddenly asks Madigan into the next room so they can have a fight about it. Mawson is able to assert his authority and quell what may well have been a violent fight. After pondering it overnight, however, Jeffryes is even more outraged than before, and while Madigan is in the gangway filling his lamp with kerosene the radio man pushes him, 'asked him to fight again, and danced around in a towering rage'.[68]

'McLean,' Mawson records soberly on 7 July, 'thinks [Jeffryes] is a bit off his head. I think that his touchy temperament is being very hard tested with bad weather and indoor life. A case of polar depression. I trust it will go now.'[69]

It doesn't. A few days later, Jeffryes comes to Mawson to advise him that if he has been a bit out of sorts lately, it is because, as a younger man, he ran a little wild with women and it has left him with venereal trouble, causing nightly emissions. He thinks the solution is for McLean to give him some poison. Mawson is not sure that is the answer and is more convinced than ever that Jeffryes is 'off his base'.[70]

And he is not getting back to it any time soon. He sleeps badly during the day, arises for dinner looking terrible and goes to bed again, muttering darkly in the dark. The whole hut is on edge, not knowing what is going to happen.

Well, Jeffryes is going to tell them what is going to happen. He is going to get *answers*, that is what is going to happen. He comes to see Mawson again and wishes him to state clearly 'all the accusations imputed against me'.[71]

He is not impressed with Mawson's response that there are no accusations against him and that everyone wishes him well. If that is true, Jeffryes asks, why are the others always 'referring to the *Aurora*'s Log?' And, for the life of him, he 'cannot see what Captain Davis has to do with the wireless'.[72]

Such nonsense questions demonstrate to Mawson that it is all now more than getting out of hand, and he is certain they are sharing the hut in the long, dark night with a lunatic. So is McLean, writing in his diary on 11 July:

> I'm sorry to record that Jeffryes has shown undoubted signs of delusive insanity, but I'm hoping that his delusional state will pass off as we may be able to remove the cause. It has come as a bit of a shock to us, but for some time (a few weeks) suspicious symptoms have been apparent.[73]

Mawson is concerned enough that he writes a formal report about Jeffryes' behaviour, for possible use later should there be an issue: 'I don't judge him on wireless results at all – I judge him on his general behaviour and appearances. Absolute selfishness in every way – no *esprit de corps*.'[74]

Well, Jeffryes is on to their game all right. He knows what all six of them are about, not just Mawson. Obviously – jealous of the success he has had in keeping the wireless mast in order as long as he did before it broke – they all want to *murder* him. Well, maybe not Mawson himself, but certainly the others. And while they are planning their murder, they are deliberately trying to both *hypnotise* him and keep him awake at night to unsettle him![75] And *none* of this would have happened if McLean had not started analysing his urine to deduce things from his past.[76]

Jeffryes is both stunned and saddened by what has occurred. 'Having no experience in these matters,' he would later record of his feelings, 'I never for a moment dreamt that it would lead to insanity and although I noticed it, I never stopped my efforts. Evidence of something wrong first appeared in Madigan and McLean who continually gave vent to cowardly insinuations.'[77]

But when Jeffryes warns Mawson about this, the leader does *nothing*! Worse still, Mawson tries to put him under a 'magnetic spell', which puts him in a 'permanent state of mental thought transference'.[78]

Desperate, he writes a letter to his sister, Norma, in Queensland, that he hopes will record what has happened to him:

Antarctic Winter Qtrs

July 13th 1913

To Miss N Jeffryes

Bougunda

The Range Toowoomba

My Dear Norm.

I am to be done to death by a jury of six murderers who are trying to prove me insane originating possibly from the jealousy of six of them . . . my services to this expedition have found their reward in death. I commend you to God's care and if they will only give me the chance I can show them that I am quite prepared to die like a man . . . Farewell to all. I am unable to prevent their folly and so must die a martyr to their bloody mindedness.

Affectionately yours,
Sid[79]

On the same day, another letter from Jeffryes is written to a friend, Mrs Fox, in Sydney:

Little did I dream when the Dr and yourself saw me

off at Sydney that I should ever have to write you. You remember how eager I was to make good well it has brought against me the charge of insanity and I am being hounded to death by Dr Mclean and other members of the expedition.[80]

Still not content with that, he also decides to write to Dr Mawson, to formally set down his fears:

Antarctic Winter Qtrs
July 13th 1913

Dr Mawson
Leader Australasian Antarctic Expedition
You have been previously warned that you were almost on the eve of a dastardly murder. I have found it impossible to make you believe that I am in a perfectly normal state of mind owing to McLean's endeavouring to weave a chain of evidence around myself, which evidence you are determined to act upon . . .
Sidney A. Jeffryes[81]

In anguished harangues at other members of the hut, Jeffryes lets them all know that once he gets back to Australia, he will report their actions to the authorities. And yet, fiends that they are, *still* they won't stop plotting against him!

In the face of it all, Mawson feels like his own brain is 'on the point of bursting'.[82] Having only recently worried about his personal grip on sanity, he has some sympathy for Jeffryes but must do everything he can to ensure the madness doesn't spread.

One thing that helps Mawson calm himself is to continue to write letters to Paquita, as it reminds him of the life beyond this tight little hut enshrouded in the darkness:

Winter Quarters

15 July 1913, 3 am

My Darling Paquita,

I simply love these hours that are devoted to writing to you. You are divinely sent to me to make life happy, and your influence is a power even here: Can you guess how much more potent when I am at your side? When I feel your breath? When lip touches lip? How great a thing love is.

Your fresh and healthy girlhood – your trust – your love – your tenderness. All these things are ever before me, and in this frozen, austere solitude loom up as giant angels . . .

Dearie my mind has been hurt again this last week. Shall I tell you what happened? Well, it is said in a few words but so sad and has had its depressing influence upon us. It is this – Jeffryes the wireless operator left here by Capt. Davis has lost his reason – I trust it will not be permanent, but it looks bad for he is not strong brained and should never have come down here. Capt. Davis should not have brought him but only good was meant. He has had very much less strain on his mind than anyone else and so we conclude must have had a weak brain originally. He has to be watched the whole time.

Do you know where I would like to be just now? In your arms, my head on your breast, all care forgotten. Oh, Dearie, is it too much to ask that Providence will some day grant this? At times it looks so far away.

Think how gloriously near each other we might be had Capt. Davis waited another 10 hours before leaving, as it was then calm and we could have gone off . . .

I am just feeling a little bit serious tonight you see. However the time is passing and in 5 months we should be away from here – and then!

Darling kiss me as I you in token of our deep wove bond.

Douglas[83]

Alas, alas, despite the warmth of such communications, Mawson's refusal to use the wireless – when it was working – for little else other than matters of science and business means that Paquita is not privy to them, something that inspires her own writing to him a few weeks later:

Are you frozen? In heart I mean. Am I pouring out a little of what was in my heart to an iceberg? Oh, for a few private dear words. Why haven't you sent me a few coded words and trusted to my finding it out! Can a person remain in such cold and lonely regions however beautiful and still love warmly? You were not in love when with Shackleton.

How I long to hear about all this. That you love me just as much. Lean over the Aurora's side and say it to the breeze – perhaps I shall hear it. Don't laugh it isn't a laughing matter. I love you to distraction and if when you return you find I am too warm! Well I can't help it. I own now I was rather cold before you left through ignorance of everything. Oh dear let's get to business! [84]

Finally, on 27 July, back at Winter Quarters, matters come to a head when Jeffryes formally tenders his 'resignation'. He is no longer one of them, no longer a part of the expedition, and will not cooperate from this point on. Mawson is confronted, not just with a madman in the hut but also with the danger of the madness spreading. In an effort to excise it, he gathers all of his men around the table, including Jeffryes, and places Jeffryes in a kind of public isolation.

Reading his words carefully from the notes he has taken, he points out that for those who would resign from the expedition, 'the accommodation houses are few and far between in the Antarctic'.[85]

However, all are to remember that it is not Jeffryes' fault that he is mentally ill, and he must understand that none of them bear him any ill will because of it. At this point, the wireless man stands up and, in a remarkably lucid speech, apologises for his actions and only wishes that everything he has done and said could be forgotten, so that he can get back to work. Mawson thanks him and assures him that it is all forgotten . . . but the following day Jeffryes is just as he was and refuses to work.[86]

For the moment, the situation remains in an extremely uncomfortable stalemate. After all, Jeffryes could hardly be confined to quarters. All of them are effectively *already* confined to quarters. Even with the odd quick forays outside, they all have to beat a quick retreat back inside the hut or be frozen to death. And Jeffryes can hardly be tied up, no matter what kind of a danger they think he might represent to either themselves or himself. In the confined space of the hut, it is simply unimaginable to hold a man prisoner for months on end until Davis is due to relieve them in December.

Fortunately, Jeffryes really does settle down a little, seeming to concentrate on not letting the others try to hypnotise him or letting Dr Mawson put him under one of his 'magnetic spells'. Which is fine with the others. All they can do is to monitor him closely and hope that the coming of the spring will remedy things. It is, in fact, the advice of McLean that when spring returns, so too will the better part of Jeffryes' mind, and his 'nervous exhaustion' might pass.[87] That would be wonderful, because, apart from everything else, Jeffryes is now refusing to wash and has started to smell terribly.

In the meantime, the worthy Bickerton, a very capable can-do kind of man, has been prevailed upon to learn how to understand and send messages in Morse code, against the time when the men hope to have the wireless back up and running. All they need, they hope, is for some calm weather to return, so they can do the work necessary.

August and September 1913, Cape Denison, spring comes around

Mercifully, spring comes early this year, with the first of the Weddell seals appearing from out of the ocean to flop upon the icy shore in late August, some six weeks earlier than they appeared the year before.[88] Flocks of petrels also soon appear, and shortly thereafter the penguins.

By then, they do indeed have the mast for the antenna repaired, which is a blessing. As it turns out, though, the aurora australis throughout September is so brilliant and constant that it proves difficult to send or receive messages, no matter who has the headphones on. Bickerton does his best, but the process remains slow. Alas, when they give Jeffryes another go, thinking he has come around, he is caught 'transmitting a false message in Mawson's name'.[89] And, as before, that is just the start of it. For the madness soon returns. Personally, though, Jeffryes is firmly convinced, as he gravely informs Mawson, that the only two who are *not* mad are himself and Dux Ipse. (And, just quietly, he is not so sure about Dux Ipse.) Worse still, he is constantly transmitting these views to the outside world.

The best Mawson can, he tries to hide his extreme frustration, but no such restraint is required in his diary. He writes on 9 September, 'It is madness to let a lunatic humbug us like this. He is not rational in ordinary talking, how can he be with the wireless?'[90]

Three days later, Mawson can bear it no more and writes Jeffryes an official warning:

Winter Quarters
Commonwealth Bay
Sept. 12, 1913
To Sidney Jeffryes,

Sir,

On account of your eccentric behaviour in the past, and the supreme importance of the duties involving trust and confidence placed in you in connection with the sending of the wireless messages, I wish to remind you that, should any further breach of faith on your part be discovered you will be held responsible on arrival in Australia . . .
D. Mawson
Leader A.A.E.[91]

Nothing changes. The Jeffryes problem goes on and on and on, and it is with some feeling that Mawson would later record for Paquita his thoughts that, 'Most of my time during this winter was occupied in keeping myself and others sane . . .'[92]

21 September 1913, Toorak, Paquita gets it off her chest

The traffic outside has fallen away to nothing, the family have all gone to bed in their new home here in Melbourne and all is as silent as the creeping frost as Paquita, in her dressing gown, takes up her pen at midnight and begins to write a very important letter to her absent fiancé. The window is open, and it is so cold her teeth are chattering, but it helps in a strange sort of way to relate to Douglas and to crystallise her thoughts. She feels sad but determined.

To this point, all such letters have been more an exercise in talking to herself than anything else, but not this one. This one will get to him in a matter of mere weeks as *Aurora* – which she has seen just this afternoon in a Port Melbourne dry dock – will soon be on her way to pick them up and she will be carrying this letter with her. It gives Paquita's writing more of an immediacy, an urgency to tell him how she is truly feeling and what he may expect when they soon meet. After beginning sweetly, 'My very dear Douglas,' she is not long in getting to the nub of it:

Douglas, do you want to go again? You don't know what it is meaning to me not to be able to hear anything from you. My pen has not its usual fluency in writing to you. It seems like writing to a wall. I want to know the trend of your thoughts and whether – oh I suppose you do though. There is no reason why you shouldn't like me as much as before. But this everlasting silence is almost unbearable. I don't want to doubt you dear but I'm afraid of the fascination of the South . . . Will a calm life ever satisfy you? I have seen unhappiness where I thought all was well. Calm homes also have skeletons in a cupboard it seems. I want you to reassure me that all will go well with us and our love.

I long for our meeting but in a faint way dread it . . .

There is more, much more, but one thing in particular she feels he should know before returning: 'I am not a child any longer as before you left.'

And she finishes:

It's time I went to bed. It looks so cold and uninviting. My knees and arms are frozen. But I'm too cold to shut the window.

Oh Douglas don't don't let Antarctica freeze you. If I only had some words to go on with. Just another caress to think of. I need it so much. It would be selfish if I wished you missed me as I do you. But men don't love as women.

Not as this one, anyway.

Your Paquita[93]

22 September 1913, Cape Denison, Jeffryes takes action

Wonderful. Things seem to be going a little better for Jeffryes. After dinner on this night, he is even lucid enough to put a record on the gramophone. Alas, when McLean ventures a tepid remark to the effect that he never could understand that particular piece of music, Jeffryes is appalled. He not only announces he is moving out but also follows through, to the point of beginning to pack his bags. After two hours of standing at the veranda door, he returns inside. Dux Ipse has been proved right: accommodation houses really are few and far between in the Antarctic.

Mid-November 1913, Cape Denison, in everlasting memory of . . .

As their time at Cape Denison draws to a close, there remains one particularly important task for the men, and now Mawson pushes it through. It is the construction of a wooden memorial cross to the perpetual memory of their lost comrades, Ninnis 'n' Mertz.

On a wonderfully calm evening, that cross is erected on the highest point of Azimuth Hill, overlooking the sea, just a few hundred yards to the west of the hut. With the time for leaving Antarctica rapidly approaching, Mawson takes pause at this poignant moment – when, as if to mark the occasion, the harsh conditions have given way to a scene of unparalleled beauty – to take it all in.

It is just two hours before midnight, a time when in most parts of the world all is dark. But not here. Here, the most exquisite natural colours are lit upon:

> the canvas of sea and sky. The northern dome is a blush of rose deepening to a warm terra-cotta along the horizon, and the water reflects it upward to the gaze. Tiny Wilson petrels flit by like swallows; from their nests in the crannies of the grey rock hills come the love carols of the snow petrels; seals raise their dark forms above the placid surface; the shore is lined with penguins squatting in grotesque repose. The south is pallid with light – the circling sun. Adélie Land is at peace![94]

13 December 1913, Cape Denison, there is a reunion

And now is the hour. For the third time in the last three years, Captain Davis guides *Aurora* into the now familiar embrace of Commonwealth Bay. This has been the easiest passage so far, not simply because he knows precisely where he is going but also because the weather for once – for once! – has been, if not quite benign, at least not vicious.[95]

And, as the perfect punctuation point for the trip thus far, instead of Cape Denison being beset by a coastal blizzard, it is relatively calm. Captain Davis, Frank Hurley, Jack Hunter and two of the Macquarie Islanders that they have picked up on the way through climb down a rope ladder from *Aurora* into the small whaleboat that has been put over the side, and they set off together.

'Give way together!'[96] Davis gives the order, and from that moment all are as unaccustomedly quiet as the whispering wind, heightening the sense that they are right at the point of a momentous occasion. As they approach the shore, everything seems just as it was, bar a large memorial cross they can see at the top of Azimuth Hill, which they know from their previous communications was erected several weeks earlier, as a memorial to their lost comrades. And still the whispering wind urges them forward, and still the sense of momentousness heightens.

And, sure enough . . .

Just as they enter the tiny harbour, they hear a familiar voice ring out. 'Turn out, you chaps! The BOAT is here!'[97] It is Mawson's voice, and here he is, coming down to the water to greet them as they spring ashore.

As Davis warmly pumps his hand, the sea captain is overwhelmed with a sudden feeling of intense relief: 'Relief that [Mawson] was manifestly alive and well, relief that I had been able to do my duty. My life has given me few moments that have been more rewarding.'[98]

In short order, Davis invites Mawson and his men back on *Aurora*, where a hearty breakfast has been prepared for them, and – amid the eggs, bacon, toast, orange juice and coffee – Mawson tells the story of his expedition, in a low, quiet voice, to his rapt audience.

For the first time, many of the crew get a close look at this now legendary figure, and one of them, Herbert Goddard, records his impression in his diary:

> Noticing Dr. Mawson closely one can read leader on his face. He looks in general very tall, fairly broad shoulders for a young man. Speaks firm but nice. A substantial man, eats what given him, not a little bit of this etc. One cannot help but like him. He's very active, always up and doing.[99]

Quickly packed up, they are soon aboard *Aurora* and on their way, with great mirth arising from the fact that practically the last thing they see as they leave the hut is the petrifaction of that same loaf of bread cooked nearly two years earlier, now 'an icy pedestal near the Boat Harbour.'[100] *Still,* it goes on!

And yet, in the end, Mawson's next actions bespeak the man he is. For surely any other expedition leader, away from home for over two years, miraculously saved and at last on a ship that could take him back to be with his fiancée and a hero's welcome, would have given the orders for full steam ahead for home! But not Douglas Mawson. He is, first, last and always, a scientist eager to expand the field of human knowledge. His strong view, and he will countenance no other, is that they owe a duty to those many people who 'had subscribed money to send the ship to the Antarctic for the third time and he is determined that it should not all be spent for the sole purpose of his own and his companions' rescue'.[101]

True, he still makes some time for Paquita, as his thoughts turn increasingly towards their forthcoming reunion, and he writes some very warm catch-up letters to her: 'My love for you and duty to you was the real insentive [*sic*] which finally availed in my reaching the hut [and] I shall never regret the struggle through which it dragged me.'[102]

Not enough? Still probably not enough. Now in receipt for the first time of the letters she has written to him, where she has poured out her anguish at his seeming distant coldness, his letters get warmer as they go on, meaning he will have a tidy pile to hand her when they meet. 'Believe me Paquita, I have never at any time loved anybody as I love you. Never had it entered my head before I met you to wed anybody. This is perhaps one reason why I love you so much.'[103]

And yet, there is no question of that love getting in the way of their very important research. For the next six *weeks*, thus, *Aurora* conducts scientific investigations all around the Mackellar Islets and the glacier tongue nearest the hut before exploring the coast of Queen Mary Land and the current contours of the Shackleton Ice Shelf. Then, and only then, do they turn for home.

26 February 1914, Gulf St Vincent, *Aurora* takes the men back to Adelaide

It is not so much that the men arrive at the Australian coast as the Australian coast comes out to them, the folds of land reaching forward to embrace them in its loving grasp as the ship blow-bobs her way forward. As one, those of the ship's company allowed to be on the upper decks gaze with longing at the land they are approaching, eager to be back upon it.

It is the most perfect late summer's day imaginable, with nary a cloud in the sky, nor a wavelet that doesn't sparkle in the bright sunshine or a bird that doesn't sing. As *Aurora* arrives at the entrance to the River Torrens, the sailors are soon joined by Professors Edgeworth David, Orme Masson and George Cockburn Henderson, alighting from the Harbour Authority's launch, all to be hail-fellow-well-met by Mawson and the other members of the expedition. From the bridge, Captain Davis gazes down upon the scene with a great deal of pleasure: 'When one thought of what this small group of explorers had endured, the loneliness of more than two years of exile, one understood a little of what this moment must have meant to them.'[104]

And what a scene awaits them as *Aurora* draws close to her berth off the semaphore signal station. The foreshores of the Torrens are simply white with people, all in a festive, welcoming mood. The women – ah, the *women!* – are in lovely light skirts and blouses, with broad-brimmed hats, holding 'gaily-coloured parasols',[105] while the menfolk stand in their shirt-sleeves.

And how they clap! How they cheer! Louder and louder and louder. So loud that Davis can only just hear the river pilot say to him, 'Tell the mate to make her well fast. That'll do the engines.'

Davis does exactly that, though he is obliged to use a megaphone to make his order to the mate heard: 'Vast heaving! And make fast!'[106]

As Douglas Mawson makes his way down the gangplank, he is instantly swamped by people. There, right in the middle of the throng, the man whom everyone wants to get to, to shake hands with, to clap on the back, to offer words of congratulation to, is the man who used to be merely a well-known university lecturer in these parts. He is now nothing less than a national hero.

'The welcome home, the voices of innumerable strangers – the hand-grips of many friends – it chokes me – it cannot be uttered!'[107]

Mawson is finally home.

Earlier that day, another ship has sailed down the River Torrens, one coming from Melbourne, where the Delprat family have so recently moved. On board are Paquita and her mother, and no sooner has Paquita come ashore than she has seen in the 'Stop Press' column of the Adelaide *Advertiser* that the ship bearing Douglas is then and there on the approaches to Port Adelaide.

Quickly now, Mother!

The two ladies race to disembark, and they catch a train to their hotel, where they find a message that they are to 'wait for Douglas there'.[108]

And so they have . . . and now . . . here he is!

As he enters the room, Paquita has a momentary start as she compares the image of him she has carried in her head for the past two years with the man who now stands before her. She just has time to think, 'Yes, of course, that's what he is like!' before Douglas says, 'You have had a long time to wait . . .'[109]

That she has. And there have been times when she has wavered, wondering if it could work after their being so long apart, but, as soon as they embrace, she knows everything is going to be all right. So does he.

It has all been worth it. It was the thought of this moment that helped him find the strength to pull himself out of the crevasse over a year earlier; it is the reality of it now that gives him confidence that he has the prospect of a full life ahead with his beloved Paquita.

And he looks forward to it more than ever.

Epilogue

*Have you ever seen the midnight sun? Have you ever flirted with
the penguins and beguiled them into parting with their eggs when
you were hungry? Have you ever seen the snow, nothing but snow,
miles upon miles, and then more miles, all around and underneath?
If you ever had experienced these, and a few more attractions the
Antarctic has to offer, you would not ask me why I am going back.*

Douglas Mawson, before speaking to the Canadian Club of Montreal in 1915

Just a month after being reunited with Paquita, on 31 March
1914, Mawson and she were married in Melbourne's Holy
Trinity Church, with none other than Captain John Davis as
the best man.

In her biography of her husband, Paquita recounted the scene of
Davis arriving at Mawson's hotel on the morning of the wedding.
Davis was holding a bottle of champagne that Paquita's father had
given him the night before, only to find the groom in an entirely
mismatched suit, with frock coat, waistcoat and trousers originating
from different outfits.

'You can't possibly get married like that!' Davis expostulated.

'Nonsense,' replied Mawson, 'I haven't got my dress trousers
here, they must be in my luggage at the Delprats'.'

'We must go and get them.'

'Oh no, Paquita won't mind,' Mawson replied airily.

It is here, by the bride's account, that Davis tried to take matters
in hand by suggesting they quickly jump in a car to get his proper
trousers, adding, gloomily, 'We'll probably be late.'

'Paquita won't mind that either,' Mawson replied, entirely

unruffled. 'People often have to wait at weddings.'

'Not the bride,' Davis shot back, now starting to panic. 'It's only the bridegroom who can be kept waiting, never the bride.'

By any measure, it was a fair point, and finally Mawson reluctantly agreed, and they ordered the car to be brought to the hotel driveway for them, at which point Mawson noticed for the first time the champagne that Davis was carrying.

'What is this bottle for?' he asked.

Davis explained that it was a gift for him from Paquita's father, should he need either calming or strengthening.

'Have it yourself,' said Douglas, 'I'm all right.'[1]

So Davis did.

For all that, the wedding went off well, being nothing less than the society wedding of the year.

And yet there was little time to tarry in a traditional honeymoon. For Mawson had work to do, most particularly to try to pay off the many debts that the expedition had incurred. This meant that, as soon as the morning after the wedding, the newly-weds headed up the gangway of the SS *Orama*, bound for England via Adelaide (in which city they couldn't help but notice the locals reading reports of their wedding while admiring the many photos). Aboard the ship with them was none other than Captain Davis and Dr Archie McLean, the latter of whom Mawson would continue to work with through the remainder of the voyage to produce his book on the expedition: *The Home of the Blizzard*.

It was as good an introduction as any to Paquita as to what married life would be like, for, though her new husband would indeed prove to be a good and faithful man, he would always be a hard-worker, perpetually pushing back the frontiers of science with much the same energy as with his every dogged step he had pushed back the frontiers of the unknown in Antarctica. For the moment, though, his primary professional focus remained on paying off his considerable debts.

Certainly, he was now a national and even an international hero, but in the tradition of polar explorers before him, that heroism had not allowed him to easily skip across the gap between his expedition's costs and its net amount of sponsorship and earnings. In Mawson's case, that gap was some £8000, which, while minor compared to the *Nimrod* and *Terra Nova* expeditions, was nevertheless an enormous amount when it was the responsibility of just one man.

The solution Mawson had proposed was for the Australian Government to purchase *Aurora* and all her scientific equipment for use as an oceanographic and coastal survey ship for the price of, shall we say . . . £15,000? If the Government accepted, it would have allowed him not only to pay his creditors but also to pay for the subsequent publication of the Australasian Antarctic Expedition scientific reports, which he would have to begin writing when he returned to Adelaide. Alas, the Government did not accept his offer.

A lesser price then?

No.

Mawson was obliged to sell *Aurora* to Sir Ernest Shackleton for his forthcoming Imperial Trans-Antarctic Expedition at the bargain-basement price of £3200. Yes, it was only a little over a fifth of what Mawson wanted and needed, but against that it was, after all, Shackleton who, three years earlier, had put his weight and name behind raising finances for the AAE, including purchasing *Aurora* – so there was a certain sympathetic symmetry in the ship going back to him for his own expedition.

The bottom line – the key one at the foot of Mawson's personal balance sheet, the one that kept glaring at him – was that he still remained in debt to the tune of £5000. This was one reason to be heading to London now. For, apart from his honeymoon, Mawson hoped that old England could provide the publishing and financial opportunities that Australia simply could not.

After disembarking at Plymouth, Mawson's party headed up

to London by train and on 3 May 1914 were greeted at Victoria Station like the long-lost friends they were by Sir Ernest and Lady Shackleton, Frank Wild and others. Hail fellow, well met, and very, very good to see you, old bean! And here is your bride!

For all that, Mawson was not widely feted in London in the same way that Shackleton himself had been after the return of *Nimrod*. For one thing, Mawson was only an Australian, and for another the epic of Scott's tragic but heroic death still had such a grip on the popular imagination that all new polar adventures were judged against it, and none could measure up. Mawson's story was a good one, true, but he had not been engaged in something so popularly magnificent as trying to beat a deceitful foreigner to the South Pole and . . . well . . . no one on his return journey had gone *outside* . . . they had just died.

Nevertheless, Mawson remained a man in demand in certain elite circles. From the moment of arriving in London, he, with Paquita and Davis in his magnificent trail, was swept up in an unending series of scientific meetings, interviews, lectures, appointments with his publisher, audiences with royalty and engaging in whatever fund-raising activities came his way.

So over-committed was Mawson that Paquita and he were often obliged to attend separate events, with Gloomy Davis acting as her escort and his fill-in. 'I've often told Captain Davis that I could never have got through my honeymoon without him,' Paquita wrote. 'As long as I wore a hat when everyone else did, and was there on time, everything was fine for Douglas.'[2]

Any gaps in Mawson's schedule were automatically filled by his continuing to work with McLean on *The Home of the Blizzard*. And then, while McLean kept working, Mawson would go on to his next commitment, including some devastatingly difficult ones.

The first was to visit the parents of Belgrave Ninnis in their London home, so that Mawson could give a personal account of what had happened as well as express his deepest condolences.[3]

The second was to 174 Buckingham Palace Road, the home of Captain Scott's wife . . . *widow* . . . Kathleen Scott. Over dinner on 21 May 1914, Kathleen generously proposed that Mawson accept £1000 from the profits of *Scott's Last Expedition* – the two-volume book comprising Scott's *Terra Nova* journals, which had been published the previous November – to be put towards meeting the AAE's debts. It was Kathleen's feeling that Mawson was due this money, perhaps in partial recompense for the as yet unrewarded role that the Australian had had in her late husband's plans to land his men at Cape Adare. The only condition she placed upon it was that her contribution remain anonymous in the public domain.[4] Agreed? *Agreed!*

Kathleen was now a woman of some means, as Scott's final wish – 'For God's sake, look after our people' – had been handsomely realised. The president of the Royal Geographical Society, Lord Curzon, had led the appeal for the public to donate at least £30,000 so that the debts of the expedition could be cleared, 'as well as for provision for the dependents of the dead, and a temple of fame worthy of those British heroes'.[5]

The response, led by the King and Queen, who donated £100 apiece, had been magnificent, and the requested money was raised in just three days. That amount kept building until it got to £75,000. After £30,000 was put towards the outstanding debts, another £12,000 had been donated to Cambridge University to help establish the Scott Polar Research Institute as a memorial to Captain Robert Falcon Scott and his four companions – a place where polar travellers and explorers could meet and where material of polar interest might be collected and made accessible for research. When it opened its doors, it would have none other than Scott's former expedition member, Australian Frank Debenham, as its first director.

The rest of the money was divided between the widows and families of the survivors, though not equally. While Kathleen received £8500, the widow of Taffy Evans was given just £1250.

Scott's mother and sisters were given £6000 between them, while £3500, administered by the Public Trustee, was put aside to provide for Scott's son, Peter, until he was 25 years old, at which point he would be given the full amount.

That was not the end of the money for the Scott family. The government of the day also decreed that Kathleen, his mother and sisters share an annuity of £300, of which Kathleen received £100, while Peter was awarded £25 a year until he was 18. The King decided that, seeing that if Scott had lived, he would have been made a Knight Commander of the Order of the Bath, Kathleen should be granted the 'same rank, style and precedence' of a knight's widow and was now to be known as 'Kathleen, Lady Scott'.[6]

The two volumes of *Scott's Last Expedition* had been an immediate success, and when Kathleen sent the first copies to the First Lord of the Admiralty, he dropped her a note in reply:

Dear Mrs Scott,
. . . It is most kind of you to send me the two volumes, which I shall read with the deepest interest at my first moment of leisure. I have already had great pleasure in looking at the admirable illustrations. This book is a worthy memorial of one of the greatest achievements of our time.

Yours sincerely,
Winston Churchill[7]

Of Kathleen Scott's many passions, beyond championing the reputation of her late husband, a key one was continuing to shape statues, and only a few weeks after the visit by Mawson and Paquita the one she had done of Bill Wilson was unveiled with great pomp and ceremony, on the promenade of his home town of Cheltenham, where it remains to this day.

In attendance, of course, was Wilson's widow, Oriana, who in fact would remain a widow for the rest of her days, treasuring to the end the last letter her beloved had penned to her, 'stained by the icy film of his dying breath', as one of his key biographers, Isobel Williams, so eloquently expressed it.[8]

To the last, many of the men who had been on that fateful expedition to the South Pole with Scott kept in touch with Oriana and were frequent visitors to her home in Cheltenham, most particularly Frank Debenham and Apsley Cherry-Garrard. The latter never overcame the guilt he felt for being unable to do more to save Scott's party when with Demetri and the dogs at One Ton Depot.

For his part, Mawson would – with Paquita's full blessing – keep in close touch with Kathleen Scott, and the two remained dear friends and correspondents for the rest of their lives.

Kathleen would remain faithful to her husband's dying wishes that she feel no compunction about remarrying. After seeing off many suitors – including none other than the great Norwegian explorer Nansen – she married the politician Edward Hilton Young, who later became Lord Kennet of the Dene, making her Baroness Kennet.

On 9 June 1914, Lord Curzon rose to introduce Douglas Mawson to the assembled gathering at Queen's Hall in London:

> We are here tonight to welcome the return to this country of the members of one of the most remarkable expeditions that has ever sailed into the Polar regions, an expedition remarkable for the scientific results which it has brought back . . . still more remarkable for the extraordinary fortitude under the most difficult circumstances that man can conceive which was displayed by its members . . .
>
> All men of science will confirm what I say, that there has been no Antarctic expedition the results of which, geological, glaciological, or in the way of throwing light on the past history of our planet, have been richer than that of which we are going to hear an account.[9]

In a room that included Ninnis's father, together with the likes of Shackleton, Davis, Wild, McLean, Hodgeman, Bickerton and Madigan, Mawson rose to acknowledge the applause on behalf of them all, before giving his own comprehensive address, aided by lantern slides of Hurley's splendid images.

It was of course, once more, Sir Ernest Shackleton who rose to his feet to move a motion of thanks. 'It was of great interest to me,' he stated, 'that Mawson and Davis, who for the first time went south on our last expedition, should have made one of the best expeditions ever carried out in the Antarctic.'[10]

The motion was passed unanimously by this august gathering of the British exploring and scientific community, and, to finish formal proceedings, Lord Curzon conveyed congratulations not only to Mawson and his men, 'but also to the Australian Commonwealth, the young nation which has sent forward an expedition which has been so successful and done so much for the progress of geography and of our knowledge of these remote and inhospitable regions'.[11]

Yes, a great honour for Mawson, but there would be more to come. On Monday, 29 June 1914 – the day after, by the by, the assassination of a relatively obscure heir presumptive to the Austrian–Hungarian throne, Archduke Franz Ferdinand, in faraway Sarajevo – Mawson was received by the King himself, and in the Throne Room at St James's Palace was knighted by one and the same. Arise, Sir Douglas.

Over the years, many more honours followed in recognition of his work in Antarctica, including the Royal Geographical Society's Founder's Medal, the King's Polar Medals (silver, with two bars, for the *Nimrod* expedition and the AAE, and bronze for the British, Australian and New Zealand Antarctic Research Expedition), the gold medals of the American, Chicago and Paris Geographical Societies and the Bigsby Medal of the Geological Society of London.

Thereafter, while the redoubtable and indefatigable McLean was left behind in London to keep going on the manuscript for *The*

Home of the Blizzard, with the former Royal Geographical Society librarian and polar historian Hugh Robert Mill, Sir Douglas and Lady Mawson set off for Australia, with only one detour. That was a quick trip to Basel in Switzerland, where they arrived on 22 July, allowing them to spend time with Xavier Mertz's still deeply grieving family.

It was while on the way home to Australia, when their ship was near Aden, that they heard the news. War had broken out, and at that moment all matters polar fell a long way back when it came to capturing the public imagination.

Against that, war had occurred at a time when Sir Ernest Shackleton was again the focus of wider attention as he was about to leave England in command of the Imperial Trans-Antarctic Expedition, with the stated intent of making the first crossing of the continent via the South Pole, a journey of 1800 miles. The irony of what had happened to Captain Robert Scott and Dr Bill Wilson did not escape Sir Ernest, who once observed to a colleague that within a mile of the spot where Scott and Wilson had discussed Shackleton's own imminent death, ten years later 'Wilson and Scott were both dead and I was still alive'.[12]

No matter that he had been lucky to survive, that did not stop him wanting to go south again. This expedition involved two ships, *Endurance* and *Aurora*. *Endurance* was to drop a team of six at Vahsel Bay in the Weddell Sea and begin the trek, while *Aurora* – commanded by none other than Captain John Davis – would go to McMurdo Sound, where a supporting party would venture out onto the Barrier and establish supply depots all the way to the Beardmore Glacier.

When the hostilities with Germany broke out, the new Shackleton expedition was just days from departure. What to do? Shackleton was in no doubt and immediately offered his expedition to the war effort. It was not accepted. No less than the First Lord of the Admiralty, Winston Churchill, instructed them to proceed with their original plans, and they did so, leaving on 8 August 1915.

Alas, before Shackleton's shore party could even be landed in Antarctica, his ship *Endurance* became trapped in pack ice off the Luitpold Coast, on the eastern shore of the Weddell Sea, on 19 January 1915, and began to be slowly crushed between its freezing jaws. She finally sank on 21 November 1915. Shackleton's finest hour had arrived . . .

After abandoning hope that the piece of floating ice on which they had made camp would eventually drift towards the safety of an island, Shackleton ordered the crew into the lifeboats. After five terrible days, the three lifeboats made it to Elephant Island on 15 April 1916 – the first time that any of the men had stood on solid land in just under 500 days.

In the most revered episode of his career, on 24 April Shackleton then left the bulk of his men safely behind on Elephant Island, under the command of Frank Wild, while he took five men in one boat – including the very same Tom Crean who had saved Teddy Evans's life by walking 35 miles on his own during the final stages of the Scott expedition – and headed across the ocean, through the towering seas, to the faraway South Georgia Island in search of help.

It was only through extraordinary seamanship and navigation – sailing their tiny boat through waves so big that, as Shackleton recorded, 'often our sail flapped idly in the calm between the crests of two waves'[13] – that they made it to the uninhabited southern side of South Georgia on 9 May that year. In a feat never accomplished before, and only rarely since, after leaving two men behind on the island, Shackleton then led Crean and Frank Worsley up the cliffs and over mountainous terrain for the next 36 hours to get to the whaling station at Stromness, where they were at last able to get help. Oh so typically, despite disaster after disaster, Shackleton's courage and leadership were able to get all his men home safely from the whole calamitous *Endurance* expedition.

In 1917, Davis in *Aurora* captained the relief expedition to McMurdo Sound to rescue Shackleton's other party, which had remained on Ross Island throughout the whole *Endurance* drama still entirely unaware of what had happened. Sadly, three of the ten men previously landed from *Aurora* had perished.

After such a narrow escape from complete catastrophe, a different man than Shackleton would have been content to put on his slippers, take up his pipe, tell his stories of extraordinary derring-do over the years and do very little for some time. But, having been re-acquainted with the drug of adventure and fame once again, it was hard to get used to quiet times. Though too old to formally enlist, he served briefly as a major in the army during the Great War and was part of a mission to north Russia, but it was just not the same as it had been, and as he forlornly wrote to his wife, the ever-faithful Emily, 'I feel I am no use to anyone unless I am out facing the storm in wild lands.'[14]

Sir Douglas Mawson, meantime, had returned to Adelaide with Paquita in the last half of 1914 to take up his position, after three years away, at the University of Adelaide – while still remaining devoted to continuing fund-raising lectures to pay the ongoing debts of his expedition. Satisfying his creditors was far from easy at a time when the nation's attention was entirely elsewhere with the coming of the Great War, but he continued. He had to.

There were many disappointments. One of his great hopes was that the full-length version of Frank Hurley's cinefilm of the AAE expedition would grip the nation's imagination and that the healthy flow of box-office receipts would pay down the debt. But it did not. With a war on, such a film seemed rather beside the point, and for the same reason his mooted speaking tour of Great Britain in the New Year was cancelled, even as his publisher Heinemann delayed the release of *The Home of the Blizzard* in the UK – and therefore Australia, as there was no Australian publisher – on the grounds that the public would only be interested in 'war and its combatants'.[15]

So, after just one term of lecturing at the University of Adelaide in late 1914, Mawson and a pregnant Paquita travelled to London, and while Paquita almost immediately headed home to Australia, on 2 January 1915 Mawson continued on to the USA and Canada, where *The Home of the Blizzard* was due to be published by Lippincott in January.

After four months away from his wife, during which he had missed the birth of his baby girl, Patricia, and met with only limited success in America, it was time to head home. Mawson arrived back in Adelaide in May 1915. Even then, he would not have the luxury of staying with his family for long. For duty called . . .

Having offered his considerable skills to the Australian Department of Defence, with no satisfactory position arising, he headed to England on the reckoning they may make better use of his talents. With Paquita and Patricia installed with the Delprats in Melbourne, Mawson returned to England via America in March 1916.

The famed explorer had no sooner landed than he was seconded as an executive member on the Admiralty Committee for the relief of Shackleton's Imperial Trans-Antarctic Expedition – something he was, of course, uniquely qualified for and very happy to give his advice on.

In the meantime, he was also appointed as a captain – later rising to major – by the British Ministry of Munitions. Based in Liverpool, he devoted his energies to overseeing the shipment of high explosives and poison gas from Britain to Russia.

For a man of his capacity and creativity, contributing to the war effort in this manner was not remotely rewarding work, but Mawson felt it to be his duty, and at least his loneliness was alleviated when Paquita came to join him in Liverpool, after having to leave two-year-old Patricia with her mother. Of course, it was a difficult separation from their child, but both felt it was unfair to bring a baby into the middle of a war. Their second daughter, Jessica, was born in London during an air raid in late October 1917.

After Armistice was declared on 11 November 1918, the Mawsons returned to Australia the following March aboard *Euripides*, accompanied by Professor Edgeworth David. The Prof, too, had had a busy war, serving as a consultant geologist to the Australian Tunnelling Battalion in France, during which time he had plummeted down a 70-foot shaft and had to go to hospital to recover.

On arrival in Melbourne, a journalist from *The Argus* interviewed Mawson, who expressed his hopes that at the forthcoming peace conference in Versailles, Australia might be formally allocated that quadrant of Antarctica with the coastline that he and his men had explored and already planted the flag on for their country, saying, 'I think that we may fairly claim that section of Antarctica between 90 degrees and 180 degrees should be under the control of Australia . . . There are immense areas of coal bearing country in the Antarctic.'[16]

Only a short time thereafter, Mawson arrived back in Adelaide and picked up the strands of the life he had left behind. The good thing was that, within a year of their return, the Mawson family was living in Jerbii, the dream house Mawson had conceived during his second winter in Antarctica, which was built on the Brighton one and a quarter acre given to him by his father-in-law.

More difficult, however, was that while he had been away, his old friend Walter Howchin – the ordained Methodist minister, who took a biblical view of geology – had been made honorary Professor of Geology at Adelaide University, something that miffed the younger man more than somewhat. It was only after Howchin retired in 1921 that Mawson became a Professor and Head of the Department of Geology and Mineralogy.

Though the celebrated polar explorer and professor settled down to a far more suburban life, some of his former polar contemporaries just couldn't manage it. For it was also in 1921 that Shackleton headed off on his *Quest* expedition, the objectives of which included the exploration of the coast west of Enderby Land and some of the little-known sub-Antarctic islands.

Like a Greek tragedy, disaster struck. While stopped off in Rio de Janeiro on the way south, Shackleton fell so ill that his doctor recommended he return to Britain. Shackleton, however, still a British bulldog to his core, would have none of it – *none* of it, do you hear? – and was on *Quest* as she headed for her next port of call, South Georgia.

It was there, in the early hours of 5 January 1922, that the expedition doctor and veteran of the *Endurance* Alexander Macklin, passing Shackleton's cabin, heard a whistle from within. He entered to find the leader looking gravely ill. Shackleton, covered with a single blanket, did not have the energy or the will to get another one from the bottom drawer.

Finding him in an unusually quiet mood, Macklin judged the time was right to again suggest that Shackleton take things more easily.

The Boss responded, 'You are always wanting me to give up something, what do you want me to give up now?'[17] At which point, Shackleton's own heart gave up, and he died. He was just 47, a genuine lion of a man who more or less died in action. At the request of his wife, Emily, he was buried there at South Georgia.

As to Amundsen, the surprising thing is that despite his prodigious feat in beating Scott to the Pole, his renown never remotely approached that of his main rival. So gripping were the details of Scott's journey, so powerfully eloquent the Englishman's writing of their venture, so poignantly tragic the whole saga . . . that, at least in the English-speaking world, Amundsen was chiefly referred to only as the necessary villain to better establish Scott's sainthood.

And, such was the way that story was generally told, it was inevitable that instead of Amundsen's expedition being celebrated for what it was – a brilliantly executed mission with a stunning result – it was portrayed in the light of being 'ungentlemanly'. There was the *foreigner*, Amundsen, sneaking up on Scott in a jolly unsporting fashion and embarking on a coarse 'race to the Pole', with little dressing of science around it and nothing to show for it in terms of expanding knowledge of the planet.

Such accusations troubled Amundsen deeply, and in his autobiography he made reply, asserting strongly that English schoolchildren were taught that Scott was the discoverer of the South Pole. On the off-chance that any of the Brits remained un-offended, he went on to assert that the British were 'by and large . . . a race of very bad losers'.[18]

During the Great War, Norway remained neutral, allowing Amundsen to make more than enough money for his next expedition by supplying 'neutral' shipping to the Allied powers. Most of his profits went into building and supplying his new ship, *Maud* – named for the Queen of Norway – which he subsequently used to fulfil another life-long ambition, becoming just the fourth man to forge the North-West Passage around Siberia, though he was subsequently unable to make his way to the North Pole.

That frustration was at least partially remedied in 1926, when, pouring his energies into air adventures, he, with one Lincoln Ellsworth, managed to fly the airship *Norge* from Spitsbergen in northern Norway to Alaska *over* the North Pole. Oscar Wisting travelled with Amundsen and thus these two became the first men to have seen both poles.

All up, Amundsen continued to live an exciting but highly dangerous life, filled with risks that he did not just accept but embraced. Like Shackleton, not for him retirement from adventure and the comfortable life, and, just like Shackleton . . .

On 18 June 1928, Amundsen was flying on a rescue mission with a French pilot searching for a party of Italians whose airship had come to ground while returning from the North Pole . . . when they disappeared. Later, parts of the flying boat they were in were washed up on the Tromsø coast in the far north of Norway, but of the men themselves or the main body of wreckage there was never any sign. It is thought they crashed in the Barents Sea.[19]

(As to Amundsen's famous ship, *Fram*, she is magnificently displayed in The Fram Museum by the harbourside on the edge of Oslo. As Australians continue to revere Gallipoli, in part because it was the first widely celebrated and united act of a newly formed nation, so too do the Norwegians continue to celebrate Amundsen and his men being first to the South Pole as the first great act of their own nation, which established itself as separate from Sweden in 1905.)

With the death of Amundsen, Mawson became the last man left standing of the principal four explorers of the Heroic Age. One reason was that the other three had died 'with their boots on', after continuing to live risky lives well after the achievements that had first gained them international attention. Mawson, on the other hand, had for the most part eschewed anything that looked like an expedition and, apart from geological field trips with his students, lived a far more suburban life – with the principal axis of his existence extending no further than between the University of Adelaide and his home.

Once installed in his professorship, Sir Douglas had felt a renewed urgency to finish publishing 'the scientific fruit of his labour', the scientific reports from the AAE. Therein lay a saga. Because of the war, neither the Fisher nor the Massey governments of Australia and New Zealand respectively had found any money to put towards the publishing of the reports. Only the South Australian Government had dug deeply enough to enable 17 reports on zoology and biology to be published by 1919.

Even once the war was over, funding to continue publishing remained hard to come by, the more so because the South Australian Government peremptorily announced it had no more money to give to the project. Desperate to keep going regardless,

Mawson managed to secure funding from the New South Wales Government, which agreed to publish the reports until 1925, to the value of £5000, on one crucial condition. In return for the money, Mawson was to deliver to the New South Wales Government everything that had come back from Winter Quarters on the AAE – all the photos, diaries, logbooks, sledges and gear, samples, collections and all documents and papers scientific, financial and otherwise.[20]

For Mawson, this went against the grain. Though he took the money, he held out for many years on handing the material over, claiming he needed much of it to write the reports, before reluctantly handing over a substantial amount, but not all, of it. Still, during the course of the next three decades, no fewer than a staggering 96 AAE reports were published in 22 volumes, the final report being published in 1947.

In the meantime, Mawson had continued to establish his academic credentials as a geologist and teacher. His university department, boosted by the addition in 1922 of his old comrade from Cape Denison, Cecil Madigan, prospered under his leadership.

Even all these years later, Mawson remained passionate about establishing the ancient history of the Flinders Ranges, and he was able to uncover evidence of 1000-mile-long glacial beds. He was well regarded by his students as a man and highly respected as a teacher.

It was not, however, that his academic career was without its frustrations. Although his great dream had been to succeed Professor Edgeworth David as the chair of Geology at the University of Sydney, when the time for the decision came, the retiring David himself did not support him! Instead, the Prof placed the considerable weight of his own support behind another man, none other than Leo Cotton, who in 1907 had been – with Mawson, David and Armytage – the fourth Australian who travelled down to Antarctica on *Nimrod*, though Cotton had come straight back.

In the final vote in December 1924, Cotton prevailed over Mawson by ten votes to eight – a surprise to all, and a rather crushing blow to the man who came second, given Mawson's stature, academic qualifications and achievements in the field.

In somewhat of a turnabout, in 1926 Mawson was offered the inside running on the most prestigious academic post in the land, the University of Sydney vice-chancellorship, which among other things would have made him Cotton's superior had he secured it. However, by this time the focus of Mawson had switched to returning once more to Antarctica – albeit in a far less risky manner than during his first two ventures – and he withdrew his name from contention before any formal offer could be made.

By now, Antarctica was no longer the totally remote area it had once been, and there was in fact a growing amount of commercial activity on its shores, particularly in the realms of whaling, where, from the mid-1920s on, the Norwegians (*sniff*) were becoming ever more active – right to the point of attempting to annex areas of Enderby Land. And this was all in spite of the fact that at the 1926 Imperial Conference, the British had listed Enderby Land as one of seven areas, including Wilkes Land, over which the British had asserted a claim of sovereignty.

But the Norwegians didn't seem to care!

Mawson's particular concern was that unregulated Norwegian whaling would see the Scandinavian country encroaching on, and even making territorial claims within, the very area that his own expedition had worked so hard to secure: the shore lying south of Australia. Equally concerned, the French – simply on the basis that their man Dumont d'Urville had sighted Adélie Land in 1840 – had quickly declared sovereignty over that whole area on the Ross Sea side of the 'Australian Quadrant'.

The solution? Mawson strongly and persistently urged the Australian Government to carry out a fresh expedition to Wilkes Land to reassert sovereignty, for reasons that were 'firstly, political;

secondly, economic and commercial; thirdly scientific,'[21] with Mawson instructed by the Australian prime minister to 'plant the British flag wherever you find it practicable to do so'.[22]

Only after two years of politicking, with the Norwegians up to their old tricks and again preparing to make fresh land claims, did the British agree to throw their support in with an Australian and New Zealand expedition. In early January 1929, Mawson, as the driving force behind this expedition, was declared leader of the British, Australian and New Zealand Antarctic Research Expedition (BANZARE).

The British flag would be raised along the coast, charted with the aid of an airplane, between Enderby Land and Oates Land, and British sovereignty would be claimed on the understanding that it would be Australia that retained control of the entire territory. At the same time, the expedition would undertake scientific work, including hydrographic surveys and meteorological observations.

And so, Sir Douglas Mawson returned to Antarctica with – who else but? – Captain John Davis. By this time, Davis had settled in Australia, and in 1920 he became the Commonwealth director of navigation – a position he had to take leave from to go on this very important journey.

The symmetry with the past was completed by the fact that not only was Davis Mawson's first choice as captain and second in command, they would be sailing in none other than *Discovery*, the ship that had been used for the first Scott expedition, in 1901–04. (The first choice of vessel would have been *Aurora*. However, she had vanished without a trace in 1917 while transporting coals *from* Newcastle to Chile.) *Discovery* left Cardiff for Cape Town on a program to be carried out over two voyages: 1929–30 and 1930–31.

Alas, this expedition was destined to cause conflict between the two old friends. Under the structure they both agreed to, Davis assumed command of the vessel only when Mawson was not aboard, but . . .

But just as had been the case between Captain Rupert England and Shackleton two decades earlier, Captain Davis retained the ultimate power to overrule the expedition leader's orders should it be his assessment that the ship was in danger. Conflict between the two men became very serious, to the point where Davis left after the first expedition was over.

Though the whole venture was entirely different from previous ones in that it was ship-based – while also fulfilling Mawson's long-held dream of using a light plane to help to survey the coast – the men did take the opportunity to visit the hut at Cape Denison once more, with Mawson stepping ashore on 4 January 1931. Unfortunately, he left no record of his feelings on this occasion, so one can only imagine his thoughts, but it was surely deeply emotional to see the cross commemorating Ninnis and Mertz, to begin with. The hut remained standing, though inside it resembled a 'fairy cavern', with delicate ice formations abounding.[23]

But to business. For it was while on this shore trip that Mawson engaged in what had long been planned as the definitive claim for these lands, to keep the pesky Norwegians at bay. With flag in hand, they climbed to a small hill just to the east of the hut, where a flagpole had been erected. One expedition member, Stuart Campbell, recorded the event in his diary:

> We formed a mass around the foot of the mast and [Mawson] slightly embarrassed read the Proclamation. Hurley filmed it. There was some difficulty at first because the instructions said to form a hollow Square but owing to the nature of the ground this was impossible. Still one can only hope and pray that our omission of this very important rite does not arouse any international complications. Then after a lot of argument as to which wire should be pulled the captain hoisted the flag . . . Then sang *God Save the King*. Another photo. We then cheered again for the cinematograph and sang *God Save the King* for

the cinematograph again. Then sang *God Save the King* for the cinematograph again. And thus were thousands of square miles of virgin ice clad land claimed for His Majesty King George V by his dearly beloved servant Douglas Mawson (what a bloody farce).[24]

It was complicated, and Mawson himself was not comfortable with the process.

Nevertheless, there were many other activities to bolster this claim. During the course of the two voyages, with the aid of the aircraft, a large part of the coast from Ross Sea to Enderby Land and beyond was mapped for the first time and shown to be continuous. Beyond all the flag-waving and planting, the significant geographic BANZARE data that was produced also supported the *Australian Antarctic Territory Acceptance Act* of 1933, which formally claimed the 'King's sovereignty' over all Antarctic territory lying south of latitude 60 degrees south and between longitudes 160 degrees east and 45 degrees east.

In 1936, the Act came into force and, by arrangement with the British Government, the 'Australian Antarctic Territory' was formally established.

Looking at the body of Mawson's work, the renowned Australian geographer Sir Archibald Grenfell Price paid Mawson the following tribute:

Although future generations may continue to afford a high place to the gallant men of several nations who reached the South Pole, or who died in the attempt or achievement, they will, I think, pay increasing honour to the man who, of all southern explorers, gave the world the greatest contributions in south polar science and his own people the greatest territorial possessions in the Antarctic.[25]

Put together, the work of the four explorers of the Heroic Age really was enormously helpful in increasing understanding of the past, present and future of the planet. Even while Scott was at last closing in on the South Pole and Amundsen was returning from it, a German geologist by the name of Alfred Lothar Wegener was putting forward the theory to a conference in Germany on 6 January 1912 that the continents had *not* remained unmoved since time immemorial. His address, which crystallised previous speculations, ran directly contrary to other theories in vogue at the time.

Instead, he postulated that there was once a 'supercontinent', which broke up into individual pieces that then migrated.[26] The fragments drifting south ultimately formed Australasia, Antarctica, South America, India and parts of Africa. The frigid period of Antarctica developed as its fragment migrated to its current region at the South Pole. Another supercontinent, Laurasia, remained predominantly in the northern hemisphere. The union that once existed between a habitable Antarctica and Australia when part of Gondwana was thought to have lain between the north coast of Antarctica and the south coast of Australia, including Tasmania. The east coast of South America was once connected to the west coast of Africa.

Wegener hypothesised that continents (together with the seabeds) sat on large underlying plates that drifted on the earth's magma, causing the continents to move at much the same pace as fingernails grow. Relative to the size of the earth, the crust was thin, and thus the theory of plate tectonics rapidly developed from Wegener's theory.

One thing was certain in ensuing discussions. The 30 pounds of rocks with their fossilised remains that Scott and his men had brought back from their expedition to the South Pole – and in some ways gave their lives for – established beyond all doubt that Antarctica had once been a part of a much warmer region, and that it had been joined in some fashion to the other continents. Once taken to Britain and examined, they were found to contain the ancient remains of a seed plant in the genus *Glossopteris*, dating back a quarter of a billion years and also found in India, Australia and America. So all theories of the history of the planet generally, and Antarctica's history specifically, had to encompass that fact.

Nevertheless, Mawson was not a believer in Wegener's theory and instead was an adherent of the 'land bridge' theory. While this allowed that there was once a connection between Antarctica and the other continents, it maintained that this connection was by 'land rays' – narrow bridges of land at sea level, exactly like the Central American isthmus – stretching between Australia, New Zealand and South America, rather than the continents themselves ever being joined. Perhaps, it was proposed, as the sea levels had risen, those land bridges had disappeared beneath the waves and so the continents had become truly separate.

And yet, with knowledge gained from the AAE, which allowed for the comparison of the geological structures and rock types on that stretch of coast from Cape Adare to Gaussberg with those from the southern shores of Australia, the evidence for some connection between the two continents was steadily strengthened, and support for Wegener's theory grew in turn.

As to the frozen remains of Captain Scott, Birdie Bowers, Bill Wilson, Lawrence Oates, Taffy Evans, Xavier Mertz and Belgrave Ninnis, they are, of course, perfectly preserved and entombed in ice in Antarctica . . . though not in the same place they all died. All of them have, as part of the Antarctic ice, been slowly, inexorably, moving towards the sea ever since, as the ice in Antarctica has done for tens of millions of years. (The glacial movement includes what are now known as the Ninnis Glacier and the Mertz Glacier. While other men, when they die, usually have a small piece of tombstone with their name on it, in the case of Ninnis and Mertz, Mawson had decided to name the two major glaciers they had traversed in their expedition after them.)

Just when the bodies will emerge again to drop into the ocean is, of course, a moot point, but in his excellent book on the life and death of Lawrence Oates, *I Am Just Going Outside*, the author Michael Smith recounts consulting in 1991 with Professor Charles R. Bentley, of the University of Wisconsin, who, at Smith's behest, had done his own calculations. The reckoning of the Professor was that in the time since his death, Oates's body would have been subsumed to a depth of about 75 feet, and he would be moving slowly northwards at a rate of about 2000 feet a year, which would accelerate to around 3000 feet a year as he got close to the Ross Sea. At that rate, Oates's body will be encased in a giant chunk of ice that should calve off the Barrier and into the Southern Ocean around the year 2275, and when that berg melts, his body – ashes to ashes, dust to dust, ice to water – will be released from its frozen sarcophagus.[27]

Upon the same calculations, that will be around 25 years after the bodies of Scott, Bowers and Wilson are similarly liberated, as they were that bit closer to the Southern Ocean when they died.

While Mawson's passion for Antarctica enriched and in many ways defined his life, it certainly did not come without cost. In her excellent book *An Antarctic Affair*, his great-granddaughter Emma McEwin says it is likely that:

> the experience shortened his life. It very probably explains his recurring boils, as well as the acute arthritis he suffered in old age, the latter of which he endured with the same courage and stoicism he had shown on the Far-Eastern Sledging Journey. In the last years of his life, he would fly to Melbourne for Antarctic meetings and fly back on the same day to avoid having to dress himself the following morning because he could rarely manage without Paquita's help.[28]

After retiring from Adelaide University in 1952, at the age of 70, Sir

Douglas Mawson lived for another six years, enjoying his time with his wife, his daughter and his grandchildren. Alas, while at home on 14 October 1958 he suffered a fatal stroke and died at the age of 76 – about 45 years later than he thought he was going to die, when he fell into the crevasse. He had outlived Ninnis 'n' Mertz and Scott by 46 years, Shackleton by 36 years and Amundsen by 30 years.

Such was the regard in which Mawson was held, he was accorded a state funeral, and, following Anglican tradition, the bells of St Jude's Church at Brighton, where his funeral was held, tolled 76 times – once for every year of his life. He was buried there, just a short distance from where he and Paquita had lived for nearly all of their married lives.

Vale, Sir Douglas. You were a great scientist, a great explorer and a great Australian.

Notes and References

Abbreviations used

AAE   Australasian Antarctic Expedition (1911–14)

MC   Mawson Centre, Adelaide

ML   The Mitchell Library, Sydney

NE   *Nimrod* expedition (British Antarctic Expedition 1907–09)

SPRI   The Scott Polar Research Institute, Cambridge

SUA   Sydney University Archives, Sydney

TNE   *Terra Nova* expedition (British Antarctic Expedition 1910–13)

Prologue (pp. 1–8)

1. Paquita Mawson, p. 15.
2. Ibid.
3. Ibid., p. 23.
4. Eitel, 'The Spell of the South', press article, p. 1, MC, 144AE.
5. Douglas Mawson, interview with/letter to James Fisher, 18 August 1956, SPRI, MS1456.
6. Shackleton, 'A New British Antarctic Expedition', p. 331.

Introduction: Discovering Antarctica (pp. 9–47)

1. Colon, p. 63.
2. James Cook, *Voyage Towards the South Pole*, p. 6.
3. See the website of the Museum of Australian Democracy, 'Secret Instructions to Lieutenant Cook, 30 July 1768', www.foundingdocs.gov.au/item.asp?dID=34.
4. Cherry-Garrard, Vol. I, p. xx.
5. James Cook, *Voyage Towards the South Pole*, p. 170.
6. Ibid., p. 445.
7. James Cook, *Three Voyages Around the World*, p. 222.
8. Weddell, pp. 53–4.
9. There were later claims that one American sealer, John Davis, actually set foot on Antarctica in 1821.
10. D'Urville, p. 470.
11. Ibid., p. 471.
12. Wilkes, p. 299.
13. Ibid.

14. Wilkes's non-existent 'Termination Land', mapped in February 1840, is close to the western limit of the Shackleton Ice Shelf but to its north. At his closest approach to the actual coast, Wilkes was near Commonwealth Bay.
15. Larson, p. 27.
16. Ibid., p. 31.
17. In 1841, the South Magnetic Pole was located inland, west of McMurdo Sound in Victoria Land.
18. Larson, p. 36.
19. Cherry-Garrard, Vol. I, p. xxiii.
20. Ross, p. 219.
21. *Birmingham Daily Post*, 27 December 1872.
22. Mill, 'The *Challenger* Publications', pp. 360–1.
23. Nansen, p. 29.
24. Ibid., p. 316.
25. Bull, p. 218.
26. 'The International Congress of 1895', p. 292.
27. Frederick Cook, p. 208.
28. Ibid.
29. Flaherty, p. 40.
30. Cameron, p. 135.
31. Borchgrevink, 'The *Southern Cross* Expedition to the Antarctic', p. 383.
32. Bernacchi, pp. 69, 78–9.
33. Ibid., p. 132.
34. Borchgrevink, *First on the Antarctic Continent*, p. 135.
35. Bernacchi, p. 233.
36. Ibid., p. 261.
37. Markham, *Lands of Silence*, p. 447.
38. Larson, p. 43.
39. Robert Falcon Scott, *Voyage of the Discovery*, Vol. I, p. 24.
40. From the maps of Ross and then Borchgrevink, Scott knew enough of the Ross Island vicinity to investigate McMurdo Sound in the hope it would allow a ship to winter without suffering severe ice pressure.
41. Today known as the Transantarctic Mountains.
42. Armitage on Shackleton, memo to Mill, 24 May 1922, SPRI, MS367/1.
43. Begbie, p. 26.
44. Robert Falcon Scott, *Voyage of the Discovery*, Vol. II, p. 91.
45. Armitage on Shackleton, memo to Mill, 24 May 1922, SPRI, MS367/1.
46. Huntford, *Shackleton*, p. 116.
47. Ferrar Glacier was later named by Scott in honour of the party's geologist, who had partially ascended it the previous season.
48. Robert Falcon Scott, *Voyage of the Discovery*, Vol. II, p. 186.
49. Ibid., p. 308.

50. Ibid., p. 188.
51. Ibid., pp. 195–6.
52. Ibid., p. 196.
53. *The Times*, 12 February 1907, p. 12.
54. Robert Falcon Scott, 'Miscellaneous notes and plans for Antarctic exploration made before and during the British Antarctic Expedition 1910–1913', SPRI, MS1453/29.
55. Ibid.
56. Robert Falcon Scott, letter to Shackleton, 18 February 1907, SPRI, MS1456/23.
57. Ibid., undated but shortly after 18 February 1907, SPRI, MS1456/23.
58. Robert Falcon Scott, letter to Scott Keltie, 20 February 1907, quoted by Roland Huntford in *Scott and Amundsen*, p. 216.
59. Robert Falcon Scott, *Voyage of the Discovery*, Vol. II, p. 83.
60. Ibid., Vol. II, pp. 89, 90.
61. Robert Falcon Scott, letter to Shackleton, undated but shortly after 18 February 1907, SPRI, MS1456/23.
62. Edward Wilson, letter to Kathleen Scott, 17 January 1911, SPRI, MS1488/2.
63. Ibid., letter to Shackleton, 28 February 1907, SPRI, MS1537/2/14/15.
64. Shackleton, telegram to Robert Falcon Scott, 4 March 1907, SPRI, MS1456/24.
65. Ibid., letter to Robert Falcon Scott, 17 May 1907, SPRI, MS1464/25.

Part One: With Shackleton

Chapter One: Go South, Young Man, Go South (pp. 51–92)

1. Douglas Mawson, letter to Edgeworth David, 28 September 1907, ML, MSS 3022/1.
2. Jacka and Jacka, p. xxvii.
3. Riffenburgh, *Nimrod*, pp. 36–7.
4. Shackleton, *Heart of the Antarctic*, Vol. I, p. 27.
5. Jacka and Jacka, p. xxvii.
6. Burke, p. 48.
7. Hansard, Friday 13 December 1907, pp. 7491–3.
8. Ibid.
9. Marshall, NE diary, 7 January 1908, SPRI, MS1456/8.
10. Priestley, extract from NE diary, undated, SPRI, MS1456/9.
11. Davis, *High Latitude*, p. 71.
12. Ibid., p. 59.
13. Ibid., p. 60.

14. Ibid., p. 83.
15. Marshall, NE diary, 9 January 1908, SPRI, MS1456/8.
16. Huntford, *Shackleton*, p. 198.
17. Marshall, NE diary, 9 January 1908, SPRI, MS1456/8.
18. Ibid., 12 January 1908, SPRI, MS1456/8.
19. *The Sydney Morning Herald*, 5 February 1908, p. 9.
20. One thousand four hundred nautical miles equals 1610 statute miles.
21. Davis, *High Latitude*, p. 78.
22. Ibid.
23. Robert Falcon Scott, *Voyage of the Discovery*, Vol. I, p. 147.
24. Davis, *High Latitude*, p. 79.
25. Burke, p. 65.
26. Daly, p. 135. According to Armitage, if Shackleton had followed his plan and established his base on the Ross Ice Shelf he would have reached the Pole. Also, Shackleton was hampered by finances and could not afford to take the number of dogs Atkinson had advised. (Armitage on Shackleton, memo to Mill, 24 May 1922, SPRI, MS367/1.)
27. Priestley, 'Prelude to Antarctica', SPRI, MS1097/20/1.
28. Marshall, NE diary, 22 January 1908, SPRI, MS1456/8.
29. Davis, *High Latitude*, p. 78.
30. Ibid., pp. 81–2.
31. Shackleton, *Heart of the Antarctic*, Vol. I, p. 120.
32. In actuality, the ponies were found to optimally pull around 650 pounds due to surface conditions.
33. Shackleton, *Heart of the Antarctic*, Vol. I, p. 238.
34. Jacka and Jacka, p. xxviii.
35. Douglas Mawson, letter to Mill, 18 July 1922, SPRI, MS100/75/6.
36. Marshall, NE diary, 26 February and 16 March 1908, SPRI, MS1456/8.
37. Ibid., 16 March 1908, SPRI, MS1456/8.
38. *The Sydney Morning Herald*, 13 April 1908, p. 7.
39. Shackleton, *Heart of the Antarctic*, Vol. I, p. 99.
40. Burke, p. 69.
41. Davis, *High Latitude*, p. 87.
42. Ernest Shackleton, letter to Emily Shackleton, 22 February 1908, SPRI, MS1456/25.
43. Burke, p. 80.
44. Wild, memoirs, p. 35, ML, MSS 2198/2.
45. Shackleton, *Heart of the Antarctic*, Vol. I, p. 219.
46. Wild, memoirs, p. 34, ML, MSS 2198/2.
47. Burke, p. 77.
48. Shackleton, *Heart of the Antarctic*, Vol. II, p. 308.
49. Edgeworth David, 'The Ascent of Mt Erebus', in Shackleton, *Aurora*

Australis, the first book ever written, printed, illustrated and bound in the Antarctic, published during the 1908 winter.

50. Shackleton, *Heart of the Antarctic*, Vol. I, pp. 187–8.
51. Larson, p. 128.
52. Shackleton, *Heart of the Antarctic*, Vol. I, p. 192.
53. Huntford, *Scott and Amundsen*, p. 227.

Chapter Two: Into the Night and Out into the Wilderness (pp. 93–129)

1. Priestley, NE diary, 23 March 1908, SPRI, MS1097/1.
2. Larson, p. 123.
3. Douglas Mawson, *Home of the Blizzard*, Vol. I, Heinemann, p. 188.
4. Ibid.
5. Griffiths, p. 317.
6. Burke, p. 83.
7. Priestley, NE diary, 3 August 1908, SPRI, MS1097/1.
8. Shackleton, *Heart of the Antarctic*, Vol. I, pp. 147–8.
9. Burke, p. 86.
10. The return distance from Cape Royds and Cape Evans to the South Pole is generally quoted by both Shackleton and Scott as 1760 miles. However, for ease of reading I have rounded this figure up to 1800 miles.
11. In actuality, the Party sledged up to a ton of supplies and equipment a total of 1260 miles (including 740 miles of relaying in 122 days). It remains one of the greatest unsupported man-hauling journeys in the history of Antarctic exploration.
12. Shackleton, *Heart of the Antarctic*, Vol. II, pp. 73–4.
13. Ibid., Vol. I, p. 23.
14. Ibid., Vol. II, p. 127.
15. Ibid., Vol. I, p. 259.
16. Ibid., p. 261.
17. Ibid.
18. Ibid.
19. Shackleton, letter of instruction to Douglas Mawson, 28 October 1908, SPRI, MS1456/24.
20. Jacka and Jacka, p. 16.
21. Ibid.
22. This large glacier is today known as the David Glacier. The Drygalski Ice Tongue is one of the few formations where its name and that of its major glacier are not the same. When Scott named it in 1902, he was unaware of its glacial source lying in the hinterland. Hence the use of the term 'ice tongue' rather than 'glacier tongue'. The Drygalski Ice Tongue may be up to 30 miles in length, although as sections break off this is quite variable.

23. Four geographical miles equals 4.5 statute miles.
24. In actual fact, this location is 12 miles north of Granite Harbour.
25. Shackleton, *Heart of the Antarctic*, Vol. II, p. 110. Note Shackleton has paraphrased Edgeworth David's letter, though the sign-off is from the original letter. Cf. the original, Edgeworth David, 'Miscellaneous notes', SPRI, MS1408/2.
26. Ibid., Vol. I, p. 267.
27. Ibid., p. 268.
28. Ibid., p. 269.
29. *West Coast Times*, 7 January 1908, p. 2.
30. Jacka and Jacka, p. 19.
31. Shackleton, *Heart of the Antarctic*, Vol. II, p. 133.
32. Jacka and Jacka, pp. 24–5.
33. Shackleton, *Heart of the Antarctic*, Vol. I, p. 289.
34. Wild, NE diary, 21 November 1908, SPRI, MS660/5.
35. Shackleton, *Heart of the Antarctic*, Vol. I, pp. 296–7.
36. Wild, NE diary, 27 November 1908, SPRI, MS660/5.
37. Shackleton, *Heart of the Antarctic*, Vol. I, p. 308.
38. Marshall, NE diary, 3 December 1908, SPRI, MS1456/8.
39. Wild, NE diary, 3 December 1908, SPRI, MS660/5.
40. Shackleton, *Heart of the Antractic*, Vol. I, p. 310.
41. Wild, NE diary, 7 December 1908, SPRI, MS660/5.
42. *The Sydney Morning Herald*, 17 April 1909, p. 13.
43. Marshall, NE diary, 14 December 1908, SPRI, MS1456/8.
44. Wild, NE diary, 24 December 1908, SPRI, MS660/5.
45. Ibid., 28 December 1908, SPRI, MS660/5.
46. Ibid., 31 December 1908, SPRI, MS660/5.
47. Adams interview with James Fisher, 5 October 1955, SPRI, MS1456/63.
48. Ibid.
49. There remains debate as to the accuracy of his distance calculations and whether he ever made it this far south.
50. Shackleton, *Heart of the Antarctic*, Vol. I, p. 347.
51. Wild, memoirs, p. 48, ML, MSS 2198/2.
52. Ibid.

Chapter Three: Getting Home (pp. 130–67)

1. Later analysis came to the conclusion that while they were not exactly at the South Magnetic Pole, they had indeed reached its vicinity with good precision. The exact South Magnetic Pole was not reached until 2005.
2. Shackleton, *Heart of the Antarctic*, Vol. II, p. 181.
3. Ibid.

4. Ibid., p. 182.
5. Ibid., p. 257.
6. Jacka and Jacka, p. 45.
7. Shackleton, *Heart of the Antarctic*, Vol. I, p. 352.
8. Burke, p. 99.
9. Ibid., p. 101.
10. Frederick Evans, 'Narrative of Proceedings of the British Antarctic Expedition 1907–1909', p. 4, SPRI, MS369.
11. Shackleton, *Heart of the Antarctic*, Vol. I, p. 355.
12. Ibid., p. 354.
13. Wild, NE diary, 31 January 1908, SPRI, MS660/5.
14. Shackleton, *Heart of the Antarctic*, p. 358.
15. Jacka and Jacka, p. 44.
16. Ibid., p. 45.
17. Ibid.
18. Ibid., p. 46.
19. Ibid., p. 45.
20. Ibid., p. 46.
21. Ibid.
22. Mackay, 'Diary of A. Forbes Mackay', 3 February 1909, p. 63.
23. Ibid., 6 February 1909, p. 64.
24. Shackleton, *Heart of the Antarctic*, Vol. II, p. 211.
25. Davis, *High Latitude*, p. 106.
26. Mackay, 'Diary of A. Forbes Mackay', 6 February 1909, p. 65.
27. The land-based location for the South Magnetic Pole – an inaccurate science – was last measured by Barton in 2000. The Northern Party's South Magnetic Pole journey was not exceeded until the long traverses exploring the Antarctic Peninsula during the late 1940s; that is, their record was to stand for about four decades. The Commonwealth Trans-Antarctic Expedition (CTAE) 1955–58 sledged 2160 miles in 99 days.
28. Triangulation was the method they used, which involves establishing a baseline (i.e. the base of a triangle) on which the observer stands. To work out the distance from the baseline to the feature one is plotting, an angle is taken from either end of the baseline to the feature. With each angle known and a triangle created, simple trigonometry will give you the distance to the feature.
29. Brocklehurst, NE diary, 5 February 1909, SPRI, MS1635.
30. Davis, *High Latitude*, p. 104.
31. Shackleton, *Heart of the Antarctic*, Vol. II, p. 217.
32. Huntford, *Shackleton*, p. 234.
33. Shackleton, *Heart of the Antarctic*, Vol. II, p. 57.
34. Wild, NE diary, 4, 6 February 1909, SPRI, MS660/5.

35. Ibid., 19 February 1909, SPRI, MS660/5.
36. Ibid., 23 February 1909, SPRI, MS660/5.
37. Wild, memoirs, p. 52, ML, MSS 2198/2.
38. Shackleton, *Heart of the Antarctic*, Vol. I, p. 369.
39. The Glacier Tongue is fairly dynamic, and sections calve often. It nevertheless can provide protection for a ship from strong wind, especially when this comes from the south.
40. Shackleton, *Heart of the Antarctic*, Vol. II, p. 223.
41. Brocklehurst, NE diary, 25–28 February 1909, SPRI, MS1635.
42. Wild, memoirs, p. 54, ML, MSS 2198/2.
43. Vince's Cross was erected in honour of R. N. Seaman George Vince, who lost his life on Scott's *Discovery* expedition.
44. Mackay, NE diary, 5 March 1909, SPRI, MS1537/3/1.
45. Davis, *High Latitude*, p. 109.
46. Ibid.
47. Ibid.
48. Wild, memoirs, p. 54, ML, MSS 2198/2.
49. Ibid.
50. Marshall, NE diary, 22 January 1908, SPRI, MS1456/8.
51. Ibid., 9 January 1908, SPRI, MS1456/8.
52. Ibid., 5 March 1909, SPRI, MS1537/3/1.
53. Ibid., 22 January 1908, SPRI, MS1456/8.
54. Shackleton, *Heart of the Antarctic*, Vol. II, p. 227.
55. Wild, memoirs, p. 57, ML, MSS 2198/2.
56. Ibid.
57. Branagan, p. 171.
58. *The Sydney Morning Herald*, 25 March 1909, p. 9.
59. *Evening Post*, 29 March 1909, p. 2.
60. *The Sydney Morning Herald*, 24 March 1909, p. 9.
61. Larson, p. 165.
62. *Daily Mail*, 25 March 1909, p. 5.
63. Ibid., p. 4.
64. Ibid., p. 5.
65. Ibid.
66. Ibid.
67. Ibid.

Part Two: Three Men Get Organised

Chapter Four: Australian Heroes (pp. 171–208)

1. Reconstructed from two different sources: Branagan, p. 204;

The Sydney Morning Herald, 31 March 1909, p. 8.

2. *The Sydney Morning Herald*, 31 March 1909, p. 8.
3. Ibid.
4. Ibid., 2 April 1909, p. 6.
5. Ibid.
6. *The Advertiser*, 21 April 1909, p. 7.
7. Ibid., 22 April 1909, p. 8.
8. Daly, p. 152.
9. Robert Falcon Scott, letter to Darwin, 23 March 1909, SPRI, MS1456/23.
10. *The Times*, 16 June 1909, p. 10.
11. *The Observer*, 20 June 1909, p. 9.
12. Ibid.
13. Huxley, p. 218.
14. Shackleton, letter to Robert Falcon Scott, 6 July 1909, SPRI, MS367/17/1.
15. Edward Wilson, letter to Shackleton, undated, 1909, SPRI, MS1537/2/14/15.
16. Larson, p. 164.
17. *The Survivor: Douglas Mawson*, ABC TV, 1982.
18. *Chicago Daily Tribune*, 2 September 1909, p. 1.
19. Ibid., 7 September 1909, p. 1.
20. *The New York Times*, 8 September 1909, p. 3.
21. *Chicago Daily Tribune*, 10 September 1909, p. 6.
22. *Los Angeles Times*, 3 September 1909, p. 14.
23. *The New York Times*, 16 September 1909, p. 1.
24. Preston, p. 101.
25. 'Luncheon to British Antarctic Expedition', p. 22.
26. *The Observer*, 20 June 1909, p. 9.
27. Douglas Mawson, *Home of the Blizzard*, Vol. I, Heinemann, p. xiii.
28. Ibid.
29. Davis, *High Latitude*, p. 134.
30. By way of contrast, Shackleton's *Nimrod* expedition garnered only 400 applicants.
31. Cherry-Garrard, Vol. I, p. 2.
32. Robert Falcon Scott, *Voyage of the Discovery*, pp. 191–2.
33. Evans was planning a Welsh expedition, for which he had already successfully obtained support in Wales. In consequence, the *Terra Nova* expedition sailed from, and returned to, Cardiff.
34. His full name was Thomas Griffith Taylor.
35. Shackleton, *Heart of the Antarctic*, Vol. I, p. 86.
36. Mason, p. 94.
37. Robert Falcon Scott, *Voyage of the Discovery*, Vol. I, p. 340.

38. Ibid., pp. 342–3.
39. Markham, 'The Antarctic Expeditions', p. 476.
40. Ibid., p. 475.
41. Ayres, p. 33.
42. Ibid.
43. This was referred to as Cape North at this time.
44. Jacka and Jacka, p. 53.
45. Edward Wilson, letter to Edgeworth David, 24 February 1910, ML, MSS 3022/2.
46. Jacka and Jacka, p. 53.
47. Douglas Mawson, letter to Geikie, dated only 'Monday' (probably in late January, early February 1910), SPRI, MS1517/1.
48. Ayres, p. 32.
49. Ibid., p. 34.
50. Jacka and Jacka, p. 53.
51. Davis, *High Latitude*, p. 145.
52. Ibid.
53. Huxley, p. 225.
54. Shackleton, letter to Robert Falcon Scott, 21 February 1910, SPRI, MS367/17/2.
55. Oates forever after wore a built-up inner sole in his left shoe to try to hide his limp.
56. Fiennes, *Captain Scott*, p. 172.
57. Gran, p. 10.
58. Mill, *Life of Sir Ernest Shackleton*, p. 166.
59. Gran, pp. 10–11.
60. Ibid., p. 12.

Chapter Five: Departures (pp. 209–41)

1. Draft agreement, Douglas Mawson–Shackleton, 16 May 1910, MC, 8DM.
2. Jacka and Jacka, p. 54.
3. *Daily Mail*, 2 June 1910, p. 5.
4. Pound, *Scott of the Antarctic*, pp. 189–90.
5. Edward Evans, *South with Scott*, p. 13.
6. Preston, p. 123.
7. Paquita Mawson, pp. 42–3.
8. Smith, p. 101.
9. Preston, p. 124.
10. Debenham, *In the Antarctic*, p. 1.
11. Ibid.
12. Oates, letter to his mother, Caroline, 14 August 1910, SPRI, MS1016/335/1.

13. *The Observer,* 17 July 1910, p. 6.

14. *The Times,* 18 July 1910, p. 7.

15. Filchner, p. 108. Filchner's *Deutschland* expedition entered the Weddell Sea in December 1911 and discovered Luitpold Coast and the Filchner-Ronne Ice Shelf (originally named after the German Emperor Wilhelm II). Disaster struck, however, when the ice shelf that Filchner attempted to establish a base on calved off, soon followed by the *Deutschland* becoming trapped in an ice floe, drifting until September 1912 before breaking free in December 1912. During this time, the captain of the ship died, and a *Lord of the Flies* scenario was played out between the men, who resorted to sleeping with their guns to protect themselves from each other.

16. Paquita Mawson, p. 47.

17. When the ponies were lined up at the dockside for transportation, one of the ponies, suspected of suffering from the contagious disease glanders, was rejected and only 19 ponies were shipped.

18. Huxley, p. 227.

19. In addition to these 30, Scott also takes to Antarctica two Eskimo dogs given to him by Commander Robert Peary, plus a New Zealand collie, making 33 in total.

20. Scott refers to the ponies as 'Siberian'. However, excepting the two largest, they were Manchurian.

21. Meares, letter to his father, 22 August 1910, p. 1, MS-0455 (courtesy of Royal BC Museum, BC Archive).

22. The North Pole controversy is far from settled. It is generally thought that neither Cook (1908) nor Peary (1909) made it, although Peary came within a couple of degrees.

23. Edward Wilson, *Diary of the Terra Nova Expedition*, p. 45.

24. Huntford, *Scott and Amundsen*, p. 287.

25. Ibid.

26. Amundsen, *South Pole*, Vol. I, p. 45.

27. Ibid., p. 130.

28. Wheeler, p. 158.

29. Edward Wilson, *Diary of the Terra Nova Expedition*, p. 51.

30. Huxley, p. 240.

31. Gran, p. 14.

32. Huntford, *Scott and Amundsen*, p. 303.

33. Gran, p. 14.

34. Paquita Mawson, p. 43.

35. *The Sydney Morning Herald*, 14 October 1910, p. 8.

36. Oates, letter to his mother, Caroline, 24–31 October 1911, SPRI, MS1317/1/3.

37. Smith, p. 115.

38. Oates, letter to his mother, Caroline, 23 November 1910, SPRI, MS1016/337/1.
39. Seaver, notes on Oates, SPRI, MS1012.
40. Ibid.
41. Oates, letter to his mother, Caroline, 17 November 1910, SPRI, MS1016/336.
42. Ibid.
43. Williams, p. 103.
44. Paquita Mawson, pp. 43–4.
45. *Evening Post*, 24 November 1910, p. 3.
46. *Poverty Bay Herald*, 24 November 1910, p. 2.
47. *Evening Post* (NZ), Volume LXXX, issue 126, 24 November 1910, p. 3.
48. Gran, p. 14.
49. *The Advertiser*, 29 November 1910, p. 6; *The Register*, 24 November 1910, p. 8.
50. Oates, letter to his mother, Caroline, 23 November 1910, SPRI, MS1016/337/1.
51. Edward Wilson, *Diary of the Terra Nova Expedition*, p. 62.
52. Oates, letter to his mother, Caroline, 28 November 1910, SPRI, MS1016/338.

Chapter Six: Journey to the Bottom of the Earth (pp. 242–78)

1. Douglas Mawson, *Home of the Blizzard*, Vol. I, Heinemann, p. xiv.
2. *The Sydney Morning Herald*, 8 September 1911, p. 9.
3. Edward Wilson, *Diary of the Terra Nova Expedition*, p. 65.
4. Cherry-Garrard, Vol. I, p. 51.
5. Ibid., p. 49.
6. Robert Falcon Scott, *Scott's Last Expedition*, Vol. I, p. 8.
7. Edward Wilson, *Diary of the Terra Nova Expedition*, pp. 67–8.
8. Ibid., p. 68.
9. Though there is no record that this is the particular song they sang, this was a popular sailor's song at the time.
10. Edward Wilson, *Diary of the Terra Nova Expedition*, p. 68.
11. Paquita Mawson, pp. 47–8.
12. Flannery, p. 7.
13. Ibid., p. 9.
14. Ibid., pp. 10–11.
15. *The Bulletin*, 29 December 1910, p. 22.
16. Paquita Mawson, p. 51.
17. Robert Falcon Scott, *Scott's Last Expedition*, Vol. I, pp. 50–1.
18. Ibid., p. 61.
19. Ibid., p. 78.
20. Ibid., pp. 68–9.

21. Ponting, p. 64.
22. Robert Falcon Scott, *Scott's Last Expedition*, Vol. I, pp. 65–6.
23. Cherry-Garrard, Vol. I, p. 64.
24. Bruce, letter to Kathleen Scott, 27 December 1911, SPRI, MS1488/2.
25. *The Advertiser,* 12 January 1911, p. 8.
26. *The Argus,* 16 January 1911, p. 6.
27. Hansard, Friday 13 December 1907, pp. 7491–3.
28. Amundsen's actual date of arrival in the Bay of Whales was 13 January 1911, but he believed it to be 14 January because he did not correct for crossing the International Date Line (which lies between Ross Island and the Bay of Whales), as reflected in the early documents used in the research of this book. Later versions of these documents were somewhat erratically amended, so for consistency I have adhered to the dates given in the original sources throughout the book.
29. Amundsen, *South Pole*, Vol. I, pp. 49–50.
30. Robert Falcon Scott, *Scott's Last Expedition*, Vol. I, p. 71.
31. Cherry-Garrard, Vol. I, p. 218.
32. Smith, p. 163.
33. Oates, letter to his mother, Caroline, 22 January 1911, SPRI, MS1317/1/1.
34. Huxley, p. 255.
35. Bruce, letter to Kathleen Scott, 27 February 1911, SPRI, MS1488/2.
36. Campbell, p. 11.
37. Huntford, *Scott and Amundsen*, p. 330.
38. Priestley, TNE diary, 4 February 1911, SPRI, MS1097/2.
39. Bruce, letter to Kathleen Scott, 27 February 1911, SPRI, MS1488/2.
40. Amundsen, *South Pole*, Vol. I, p. 205.
41. Oates, letter to his mother, Caroline, 22 January 1911, SPRI, MS1317/1/1.
42. Gran, p. 59.
43. Robert Falcon Scott, *Scott's Last Expedition*, Vol. I, p. 120.
44. Oates, letter to his mother, Caroline, 24 October 1911, SPRI, MS1317/1/3.
45. Ibid., 28 October 1911, SPRI, MS1317/1/3.
46. Robert Falcon Scott, *Scott's Last Expedition*, Vol. I, p. 119.
47. Ibid., p. 129.
48. Cherry-Garrard, Vol. I, pp. 126–7.
49. Ibid., p. 139.
50. Gran, p. 64.
51. Oates, letter to his mother, Caroline, 23 November 1910, SPRI, MS1016/337/1.
52. Robert Falcon Scott, *Scott's Last Expedition*, Vol. I, p. 130.

Chapter Seven: Trials and Errors (pp. 279–306)

1. Ayres, p. 45.
2. Davis, *High Latitude*, p. 144.
3. Seaver, notes on Oates, SPRI, MS1012.
4. *Daily Mail*, 28 March 1911, p. 9.
5. Douglas Mawson, letter to Kathleen Scott, 5 April 1911, SPRI, MS1453/138.
6. *Daily Mail*, 28 March 1911, p. 9.
7. Jacka and Jacka, p. 55.
8. Paquita Mawson, p. 48.
9. Masson, letter to Professor Edgeworth David, 16 May 1911, SUA, Edgeworth David, Reference P011, Series 7, Correspondence 1911.
10. 'Sydney Girl', letter to Professor Edgeworth David, 14 July 1911, SUA, Edgeworth David, Reference P011, Series 7, Correspondence 1911.
11. Kathleen Scott, letter to Douglas Mawson, 25 April 1911, MC, 13AAE.
12. There is no documentary proof of this meeting, but that is the way the deal would have been struck, and when Mawson got back from his own expedition, one of his first cables was to the *Daily Mail*.
13. Herbert Ponting included the event in his film of the expedition.
14. *Daily Mail*, 8 May 1911, p. 9.
15. Ibid.
16. *Daily Mail*, 9 May 1911, p. 7.
17. *The Times*, 9 May 1911, p. 10.
18. Ibid.
19. *Daily Mail*, 11 May 1911, p. 5.
20. Ibid., 13 May 1911, p. 6.
21. Robert Falcon Scott, *Scott's Last Expedition*, Vol. I, pp. 210–11.
22. Ibid., p. 211.
23. Ibid.
24. *The Sydney Morning Herald*, 8 September 1911, p. 8.
25. Griffiths, p. 23.
26. That silk doll remained in Sir Douglas Mawson's proud possession for the rest of his long life. His granddaughter Paquita Boston remembers it sitting in the glass cabinet in Sir Douglas and his wife Paquita's drawing room. It is now proudly displayed as part of the Mawson Collection in the South Australian Museum.
27. Davis, *High Latitude*, p. 154.
28. Ibid., p. 155.

Part Three: Antarctica Under Siege

Chapter Eight: Under Way (pp. 309–53)

1. Davis, *High Latitude*, p. 157.
2. Ibid., p. 158.
3. Ibid.
4. Mertz, AAE diary, 30 July 1911, p. 2, MC.
5. Davis, *High Latitude*, pp. 158–9.
6. Ibid., p. 159.
7. Amundsen, *South Pole*, Vol. I, p. 388.
8. Huntford, *Scott and Amundsen*, p. 393.
9. In actuality, the distance marched from the top of the Beardmore Glacier to the South Pole was closer to 350 miles.
10. Robert Falcon Scott, 'Miscellaneous notes and plans for Antarctic exploration made before and during the British Antarctic Expedition', 1910–13, SPRI, MS1453/29
11. Debenham, *Quiet Land*, p. 104.
12. Oates, letter to his mother, Caroline, 22 January 1911, SPRI, MS1317/1/1.
13. Robert Falcon Scott, *Scott's Last Expedition*, Vol. I, p. 309.
14. Young, p. 134.
15. Douglas Mawson, *Home of the Blizzard*, Vol. I, Heinemann, pp. 21–2.
16. Ayres, pp. 56–7.
17. Wild, memoirs, p. 61, ML, MSS 2198/2.
18. Griffiths, p. 24.
19. Mertz, AAE diary, 8 August 1911, p. 5, MC.
20. As detailed by Alasdair McGregor in his book *Frank Hurley: A Photographer's Life*, there are a couple of versions of this story, both put out by Hurley himself. One story, in the *Lone Hand*, Vol. 2, No. 2, 2 November 1914, has it that Hurley asked Mawson to ask the guard to let him go to Mittagong. The other story, in the book *Argonauts of the South*, has it that Hurley effectively ambushed Mawson, having bought his ticket beforehand, by simply turning up in his compartment. I have plumped for the first story as the earliest version and therefore the one most likely.
21. Frank Hurley, letter to Douglas Mawson, 29 September 1911, AAE Records, 1 December 1910–1 December 1915, ML, MSS 171/14.
22. Frank Hurley, *Argonauts of the South*, p. 13.
23. Ibid.
24. Douglas Mawson, letter to Frank Hurley, 20 October 1911, ML, MSS 171/14.
25. Margaret Hurley, letter to Douglas Mawson, 6 October 1911, ML, MSS 171/14.

26. Douglas Mawson, letter to Frank Hurley, 12 October 1911, ML, MSS 171/14.
27. Frank Hurley, letter to Douglas Mawson, 12–13 October 1911, ML, MSS 171/14.
28. Douglas Mawson, letter to Frank Hurley, 20 October 1911, ML, MSS 171/14.
29. Laseron, *South with Mawson*, p. 8.
30. Hall, p. 65.
31. Douglas Mawson, *Home of the Blizzard*, Wakefield Press, p. 7.
32. *Kalgoorlie Western Argus*, 10 October 1911, p. 30.
33. Wild, memoirs, pp. 63–4, ML, MSS 2198/2.
34. Amundsen, *My Life as an Explorer*, p. 44.
35. Oates, notes on ponies, 31 October 1911, SPRI, MS1317/2.
36. Seaver, *Birdie Bowers of the Antarctic*, p. 152.
37. Williams, p. 210.
38. Oates, letter to his mother, Caroline, 28 October 1911, SPRI, MS1317/1/3.
39. Bowers, letter to Kathleen Scott, 29 October 1911, SPRI, MS1488/2.
40. Robert Falcon Scott, *Scott's Last Expedition*, Vol. I, p. 297.
41. Paquita Mawson, p. 68.
42. Ibid., p. 51.
43. Robert Falcon Scott, letter to Kinsey, 28 October 1911, SPRI, MS761/8/33.
44. Robert Falcon Scott, *Scott's Last Expedition*, Vol. I, p. 307.
45. Edward Wilson, letter to Kathleen Scott, 31 October 1911, SPRI, MS1488/2.
46. Robert Falcon Scott, *Scott's Last Expedition*, Vol. I, p. 314.
47. Ibid., p. 320.
48. Smith, p. 176.
49. Bowers, extracts from TNE diary, 29 November 1911, SPRI, MS782/5.
50. Originally named Mt Haakonshallen, after a Norwegian castle of the same name. Amundsen later changes the name to Don Pedro Christophersen, after his then current patron.
51. Amundsen, *South Pole*, Vol. II, p. 45.
52. Ibid., p. 47.
53. Nineteen and a quarter geographical miles equals 23 statute miles.
54. Amundsen, *South Pole*, Vol. II, p. 62.
55. Ibid., p. 60.
56. Ibid., p. 63.
57. Ibid., p. 65.
58. Hannam, AAE diary, 21 November 1911, ML, MSS 384.
59. Smith, p. 177.
60. Edward Evans, *South with Scott*, p. 178.

61. McLean, 'Through the Roaring Forties', p. 2, ML, MSS 382.
62. Chester, p. 20.
63. Douglas Mawson, *Home of the Blizzard*, Vol. I, Heinemann, p. 22.
64. McLean, AAE diary, undated, ML, MSS 382/2.
65. Laseron, AAE diary, 26 November–2 December 1911, ML, MSS 385.
66. Smith, p. 180.
67. Cherry-Garrard, Vol. II, p. 335.
68. Seaver, *Edward Wilson of the Antarctic*, p. 271.
69. Ibid., p. 272.
70. Wright, TNE diary, 28 November 1911, SPRI, MS1437/6.
71. Ninnis, letter to Zip, 1 December 1911, SPRI, MS1564/4.
72. The *South Polar Times*, produced by Shackleton during the *Discovery* expedition, was resurrected on the *Terra Nova* expedition under Cherry-Garrard's editorship.
73. Edward Wilson, *Diary of the Terra Nova Expedition*, p. 177.

Chapter Nine: To the South! (pp. 354–93)

1. *Northern Territory Times and Gazette*, 1 December 1911.
2. *The West Australian*, 4 December 1911, p. 6.
3. Frank Hurley, *Argonauts of the South*, pp. 16–17.
4. Ibid.
5. Davis, *With the Aurora*, p. 17.
6. Huntford, *Scott and Amundsen*, p. 467. This occurred on 11 December 1911.
7. Griffiths, p. 36.
8. Harrisson, AAE diary, 7 December 1911, ML, MSS 386, CY1188.
9. Douglas Mawson, *Home of the Blizzard*, Vol. I, Heinemann, p. 28.
10. Paquita Mawson, pp. 58–9.
11. Edward Wilson, *Diary of the Terra Nova Expedition*, p. 212.
12. Robert Falcon Scott, *Scott's Last Expedition*, Vol. I, pp. 338–9.
13. Cherry-Garrard, Vol. II, p. 349.
14. Edward Wilson, *Diary of the Terra Nova Expedition*, p. 213.
15. Davis, *High Latitude*, p. 121.
16. Douglas Mawson, *Home of the Blizzard*, Vol. I, Heinemann, p. 32.
17. This windfall subsequently paid the costs of hiring the *Toroa*.
18. Robert Falcon Scott, *Scott's Last Expedition*, Vol. I, p. 341.
19. Edward Evans, *South with Scott*, p. 162.
20. Paquita Mawson, p. 57.
21. Author interview with Paquita's great-granddaughter Emma McEwin.
22. Robert Falcon Scott, *Scott's Last Expedition*, Vol. I, p. 343.
23. Bowers, TNE diary, 14 December 1911, SPRI, MS559/20.
24. Robert Falcon Scott, *Scott's Last Expedition*, Vol. I, p. 345.
25. Amundsen, *South Pole*, Vol. II, p. 122.

26. Ibid., p. 121.
27. Gran, p. 153.
28. Flannery, p. 24.
29. Amundsen, *South Pole*, Vol. II, pp. 125–6.
30. Ibid., p. 132.
31. Kløver, p. 352.
32. A kamik (also known as a mukluk) is a soft reindeer- or sealskin boot, originally worn by Arctic aboriginal people, including the Inuit and Yupik.
33. Amundsen, *South Pole*, Vol. II, p. 133.
34. Cherry-Garrard, Vol. II, p. 363.
35. Wright, TNE diary, 19 December 1911, SPRI, MS1437/6.
36. Ibid., 20 December 1911, SPRI, MS1437/6.
37. Cherry-Garrard, Vol. II, p. 364.
38. Ibid., p. 381.
39. Ibid.
40. A kedge anchor is a light anchor used for moving or turning a ship. This technique is termed 'kedging'.
41. Robert Falcon Scott, *Scott's Last Expedition*, Vol. I, p. 357.
42. Bowers, TNE diary, 25 December 1911, SPRI, MS782/5.
43. Ibid.
44. Amundsen, *My Life as an Explorer*, p. 145.
45. Laseron, AAE diary, 29 December 1911, ML, MSS 385.
46. Douglas Mawson, *Home of the Blizzard*, Vol. I, Heinemann, p. 52.
47. Frank Hurley, *Argonauts of the South*, p. 42.
48. Oates, letter to his brother Bryan, 3 January 1912, SPRI, MS1495.
49. Bowers, letter to his mother, Emily, 3 January 1912 (misdated 1911), SPRI, MS1505/3/5/9.
50. Seaver, *Edward Wilson of the Antarctic*, p. 277.
51. Edward Evans, *South with Scott*, p. 207.

Chapter Ten: Cape Denison (pp. 394–439)

1. Paquita Mawson, p. 61.
2. Ninnis, letter to Zip, 6–8 January 1912, SPRI, MS1564/4.
3. Douglas Mawson, *Home of the Blizzard*, Vol. I, Heinemann, p. 62.
4. Davis, *High Latitude*, p. 168.
5. Mill, *Life of Sir Ernest Shackleton*, p. 159.
6. Young, p. 157.
7. Douglas Mawson, *Home of the Blizzard*, Vol. I, Heinemann, p. 4.
8. Six geographical miles equals seven statute miles.
9. Five geographical miles equals six statute miles.
10. Seventy-four geographical miles equals 85 statute miles.
11. Robert Falcon Scott, *Scott's Last Expedition*, Vol. I, p. 370.

12. Twenty-seven geographical miles equals 31 statute miles.

13. Robert Falcon Scott, *Scott's Last Expedition*, Vol. I, p. 373.

14. Edward Wilson, *Diary of the Terra Nova Expedition*, p. 231.

15. Robert Falcon Scott, *Scott's Last Expedition*, Vol. I, pp. 374–5.

16. Bowers, letter to his mother, Emily, 17 January 1912, SPRI, MS1505/3/9.

17. Smith, p. 206.

18. Edward Evans, *South with Scott*, p. 232.

19. In fact, it is one of the sledge runners used to mark Amundsen's second, five-mile locus to be sure he has included the Pole and is not the Pole itself. Hinks writes, 'They had passed the Pole on their right hand half a mile away, and gone a little too far' (p. 167).

20. Eight hundred geographical miles equals 920 statute miles.

21. Robert Falcon Scott, *Scott's Last Expedition*, Vol. I, p. 376.

22. One hundred geographical miles equals 115 statute miles.

23. Robert Falcon Scott, *Scott's Last Expedition*, Vol. I, p. 377.

24. Flannery, p. 29.

25. Douglas Mawson, *Home of the Blizzard*, Vol. I, Heinemann, p. 69.

26. Davis, *High Latitude*, p. 169.

27. Davis, *With the Aurora*, p. 32.

28. McEwin, p. 54.

29. McGregor, p. 51.

30. Douglas Mawson, *Home of the Blizzard*, Vol. I, Heinemann, p. 88.

31. McGregor, p. 52.

32. Flannery, p. 27.

33. Robert Falcon Scott, *Scott's Last Expedition*, Vol. I, p. 380.

34. This estimation of Taffy's dependence on being first to the Pole to achieve financial independence comes from Trygvve Gran in his diary, *The Norwegian with Scott*, p. 216, presumably based on previous conversations with him.

35. Despite Laseron's claim that the roof layers were of felt ruberoid, it is the observation of those repairing Mawson's huts that it was in fact two layers of tar paper.

36. Laseron, *South with Mawson*, p. 45.

37. Amundsen, *South Pole*, Vol. II, p. 174.

38. Amundsen, 'The Norwegian South Polar Expedition', p. 13.

39. Cherry-Garrard, Vol. II, p. 381.

40. It was originally planned that Meares's party would return north to be back at Hut Point by 10 December, allowing sufficient time for the dogs to recover before resupplying One Ton Depot in late December/ early January.

41. Douglas Mawson, *Home of the Blizzard*, Vol. I, Heinemann, p. 95.

42. McGregor, p. 39.

43. Robert Falcon Scott, *Scott's Last Journey*, p. 8.
44. Robert Falcon Scott, *Scott's Last Expedition*, Vol. I, p. 389.
45. Ibid., pp. 390–1.
46. Ibid., p. 393.
47. Douglas Mawson, *Home of the Blizzard*, Vol. I, Heinemann, p. 33.
48. Ibid., p. 137.
49. Davis, *High Latitude*, p. 171.
50. Ibid., p. 180.
51. Robert Falcon Scott, *Scott's Last Expedition*, Vol. I, p. 394.
52. Ibid.
53. Cherry-Garrard, Vol. II, p. 395.
54. Edward Evans, *South with Scott*, pp. 224–5.
55. Cherry-Garrard, Vol. II, p. 407.
56. After the expedition was over, the King awarded Lashly and Crean the Albert Medal for their bravery in saving Evans.
57. Davis, *High Latitude*, p. 182.
58. Wild, memoirs, p. 112, ML, MSS 2198/2.
59. Author interview with the niece of Morton Moyes, Monica Moyes, August 2011.
60. Davis, *With the Aurora*, p. 53.

Part Four: Struggles

Chapter Eleven: Settling (pp. 443–81)

1. Robert Falcon Scott, *Scott's Last Expedition*, Vol. I, p. 396.
2. Eight and a half geographical miles equals ten statute miles.
3. Robert Falcon Scott, *Scott's Last Expedition*, Vol. I, p. 397.
4. Davis, *High Latitude*, p. 184.
5. Frank Hurley, *Argonauts of the South*, p. 121.
6. Laseron, AAE diary, 18 February 1912, ML, MSS 385.
7. Douglas Mawson, 'Operational Instructions and Hut Notices', MC, 43AAE.
8. Flannery, p. 31.
9. Ibid., pp. 30–1.
10. Ibid., p. 32.
11. Douglas Mawson, *Home of the Blizzard*, Vol. I, Heinemann, p. 100.
12. Jacka and Jacka, p. 59.
13. Douglas Mawson, *Home of the Blizzard*, Vol. I, Heinemann, p. 99.
14. Ibid.
15. Laseron, *South with Mawson*, p. 67.
16. This last, known as 'tin disease', may be the reason why such vast

amounts of oil were lost. Amundsen's tins were composed of silver solder and remained unaffected. Tin disease is said to have caused the buttons on the uniforms of Napoleon's troops to disintegrate in the 1812 winter.

17. Seventy-one geographical miles equals 82 statute miles.

18. Robert Falcon Scott, *Scott's Last Expedition*, Vol. I, p. 402.

19. Edward Evans, *South with Scott*, p. 162.

20. Robert Falcon Scott, *Scott's Last Expedition*, Vol. I, p. 402.

21. The important thing was to avoid anything magnetic – no iron, steel, etc. – in the construction of or anywhere near the huts. Thus, their buildings were brilliant examples of a joiner/carpenter's work, held together by wooden dowels. Where metal was used – nails, brackets, etc. – this was either copper (soft) or brass (harder). Wind- and waterproofing were with tar-felt or similar.

22. Douglas Mawson, *Home of the Blizzard*, Vol. I, Heinemann, p. 154.

23. Cherry-Garrard, Vol. II, p. 429.

24. Ibid., p. 417.

25. Ibid., p. 416.

26. At an average of 18 miles a day, and allowing eight days to return, the Dog Party may have only proceeded another nine miles south.

27. Robert Falcon Scott, *Scott's Last Expedition*, Vol. I, pp. 402–3.

28. Ibid., p. 405.

29. Ibid.

30. Kathleen Scott, *Self-Portrait of an Artist*, p. 107.

31. The Northern Party's plight during that winter is well described in Raymond Priestley's *Antarctic Adventure*, including such details as the excavated cave they lived in, which they named Inexpressible Island, with sailors' and officers' quarters demarcated down a drawn line in the compacted snow, and their survival on what local food they could catch.

32. *Mercury*, 8 March 1912, p. 5.

33. Ibid., 9 March 1912, p. 4.

34. Ibid., 8 March 1912, p. 5.

35. *The New York Times*, 8 March 1912, p. 1.

36. Kathleen Scott, *Self-Portrait of an Artist*, p. 107.

37. Ibid., p. 108.

38. *The New York Times*, 8 March 1912, pp 1, 12.

39. Huntford, *Scott and Amundsen*, p. 529.

40. *Chicago Daily Tribune*, 8 March 1912, p. 1.

41. Huntford, *Scott and Amundsen*, p. 531.

42. Robert Falcon Scott, *Scott's Last Expedition*, Vol. I, p. 405.

43. Williams, p. 210.

44. Robert Falcon Scott, *Scott's Last Expedition*, Vol. I, p. 406.

45. Laseron, *South with Mawson*, p. 78.
46. Douglas Mawson, *Home of the Blizzard*, Vol. I, Heinemann, p. 149.
47. Laseron, *South with Mawson*, pp. 63–4.
48. Douglas Mawson, *Home of the Blizzard*, Vol. I, Heinemann, p. 151.
49. *Mercury,* 13 March 1912, p. 6.
50. Douglas Mawson, *Home of the Blizzard*, Vol. II, Heinemann, p. 55.
51. Ibid.
52. Wild, memoirs, pp. 75–6, ML, MSS 2198/2.
53. *Examiner,* 14 March 1912, p. 6.
54. Ponting, p. 288.
55. Robert Falcon Scott, *Scott's Last Expedition*, Vol. I, p. 406.
56. Ibid., p. 408.
57. There has been a great deal of debate as to whether Oates was assisted in undoing the flaps to the tent to make his exit, as the strings were complicated and by this point his hands and fingers were little more than frostbitten bits of blackened and gangrenous flesh.
58. There is some doubt as to the date of Oates's death, as Scott himself lost track of the date, with the relevant entry reading: '16 or 17 March. Lost track of dates, but think the last correct.'
59. Robert Falcon Scott, *Scott's Last Expedition*, Vol. I, p. 408.
60. Edward Wilson, letter to Caroline Oates, undated, SPRI, MS482.
61. Douglas Mawson, *Home of the Blizzard*, Vol. I, Heinemann, p. 157.
62. Eleven geographical miles equals 13 statute miles.
63. Robert Falcon Scott, *Scott's Last Expedition,* Vol. I, p. 412.
64. Seaver, *Edward Wilson of the Antarctic*, pp. 293–4.
65. Edward Wilson, letter to his parents, undated, SPRI, MS1344.
66. Seaver, *Edward Wilson of the Antarctic*, p. 294.
67. Robert Falcon Scott, *Scott's Last Expedition*, Vol. II, p. 211.
68. Ibid., Vol. I, p. 410.

Chapter Twelve: The Winter Months (pp. 482–520)

1. Douglas Mawson, *Home of the Blizzard*, Vol. I, Heinemann, p. 184.
2. McEwin, p. 61.
3. Flannery, pp. 36–8.
4. Laseron, *South with Mawson*, pp. 62–3.
5. Ibid., p. 71.
6. Laseron, *South with Mawson*, p. 81.
7. Ibid., p. 72.
8. Ibid., p. 73.
9. Ibid., p. 74.
10. Mertz, AAE diary, 26 May 1912, p. 67, MC.
11. Douglas Mawson, *Home of the Blizzard*, Vol. I, Heinemann, p. 173.
12. Jacka and Jacka, p. 78.

13. *The Sydney Morning Herald*, 11 May 1912, p. 9.
14. Laseron, *South with Mawson*, pp. 72–3.
15. McLean, AAE diary, undated, ML, MSS 382/2.
16. Laseron, *South with Mawson*, p. 113.
17. Douglas Mawson, *Home of the Blizzard*, Vol. I, Heinemann, p 139.
18. Laseron, *South with Mawson*, p. 51.
19. Riffenburgh, *Racing with Death*, p. 82.
20. Douglas Mawson, *Home of the Blizzard*, Vol. I, Heinemann, p. 130.
21. Laseron, *South with Mawson*, p. 71.
22. Douglas Mawson, *Home of the Blizzard*, Vol. I, Heinemann, p. 175.
23. Mertz, AAE diary, 21 June 1912, p. 74, MC.
24. Douglas Mawson, *Home of the Blizzard*, Vol. I, Heinemann, p. 192.
25. Mertz, AAE diary, 31 July 1912, p. 83, MC.
26. Jacka and Jacka, p. 106.
27. Douglas Mawson, *Home of the Blizzard*, Vol. I, Heinemann, p. 195.
28. Laseron, *South with Mawson*, p. 101.
29. Ibid., p. 95.
30. Douglas Mawson, *Home of the Blizzard*, Vol. I, Heinemann, p. 153.
31. Ibid.
32. Ibid.
33. *The Register*, Adelaide, 9 December 1912.
34. Jacka and Jacka, p. 104.
35. Ibid., p. 115.
36. Mertz, AAE diary, 6 October 1912, p. 102, MC.
37. Douglas Mawson, *Home of the Blizzard*, Vol. I, Heinemann, p. 209.
38. Ibid., p. 211.
39. Flannery, pp. 39–42.
40. Ibid.
41. Riffenburgh, *Racing with Death*, p. 97.
42. Frank Hurley, AAE sledging diary, 10 November 1912, ML, MSS 389/1.
43. I have paraphrased Mawson's words in *Home of the Blizzard*, Vol. I, Heinemann, p. 215 to retain the air of immediacy.
44. Paquita Mawson, p. 76.
45. Mawson later took this as a premonition of his father's death, which occurred around this time.
46. Paquita Mawson, p. 77.
47. Riffenburgh, *Racing with Death*, pp. 101–2.
48. Frank Hurley, AAE sledging diary, 10 November 1912, ML, MSS 389/1, CY 1423.

Chapter Thirteen: Into the Wide White Yonder (pp. 521–62)

1. Wright, *Silas*, p. 346.
2. *Daily Mail*, 8 May 1913, p. 6.
3. Ibid., 14 February 1913, p. 5.
4. Huxley, pp. 305–6.
5. Ibid., p. 306.
6. Robert Falcon Scott, *Scott's Last Expedition*, Vol. I, p. 439.
7. Gran, p. 216.
8. Edward Evans, *South with Scott*, p. 252.
9. Wright, TNE diary, 12 November 1912, SPRI, MS1437/6.
10. Twenty geographical miles equals 23 statute miles.
11. *Daily Mail*, 14 February 1913, p. 5.
12. Robert Falcon Scott, *Scott's Last Expedition*, Vol. I, p. 417.
13. *The New York Times*, 16 November 1912, p. 2.
14. Larson, p. 24.
15. Amundsen, *My Life as an Explorer*, p. 45.
16. The controversy broke in 1927, after an article appeared in the American magazine *World's Work* in July, followed by the release of Amundsen's autobiography, *My Life as an Explorer*, that same year. The secretary of the Royal Geographical Society, at the request of Lord Curzon, immediately wrote to Amundsen asking if he accepted responsibility for his words and drawing his attention to the January 1913 edition of the journal, where Lord Curzon is recorded as saying at the conclusion of Amundsen's speech, 'I almost wish that in our tribute of admiration we could include those wonderful, good tempered, fascinating dogs, the true friends of man, without whom Captain Amundsen would never have got to the Pole. I ask you to signify your assent by your applause.' Amundsen, however, did not accept this rendition and despite the request of the Royal Geographical Society refused to apologise. In November 1927, he tendered a hastily accepted resignation. The Geographical Society report on the series of events that ultimately led to the resignation of one of their most highly honoured members (in 1907, Amundsen had been awarded the Gold Medal 'for splendid work in the north polar region') appears in 'Captain Roald Amundsen and the Society', pp. 572–5.
17. Douglas Mawson, *Home of the Blizzard*, Vol. I, Heinemann, p. 222.
18. Ibid.
19. Ibid., p. 227.
20. Ibid.
21. Ibid., p. 230.
22. Jacka and Jacka, p. 140.
23. Mertz, AAE diary, 13 December 1912, p. 119, MC.
24. Douglas Mawson, *Home of the Blizzard*, Vol. I, Heinemann, p. 239.

25. Ibid.
26. Mertz, AAE diary, 14 December 1912, p. 120, MC.
27. Douglas Mawson, *Home of the Blizzard*, Vol. I, Heinemann, p. 241.
28. Ibid.
29. Ibid.
30. Jacka and Jacka, p. 148.
31. Douglas Mawson, *Home of the Blizzard*, Vol. I, Heinemann, p. 243.
32. Ibid., p. 244.
33. *The Advertiser,* 18 December 1912, p. 18.
34. Douglas Mawson, *Home of the Blizzard*, Vol. I, Heinemann, p. 241.
35. Aurelius, p. 134.
36. Douglas Mawson, *Home of the Blizzard*, Vol. I, Heinemann, p. 252.
37. Mertz, AAE diary, 25 December 1912, p. 124, MC.
38. Frank Hurley, AAE sledging diary, 21 December 1912, ML, MSS 389/1–2.
39. Ibid., 15 December 1912, ML, MSS 389/1–2.
40. Douglas Mawson, *Home of the Blizzard*, Vol. II, Heinemann, p. 104. Frank Wild was acting without royal consent, and the name 'King George V Land' was subsequently given to the land that Mawson's Far-Eastern Party discovered east of Commonwealth Bay. Wild's area was ultimately included as part of Queen Mary Land.
41. Ibid., Vol. I, Heinemann, p. 255.
42. Douglas Mawson, *Home of the Blizzard*, Vol. I, Heinemann, p. 256.
43. Mertz, AAE diary, 1 January 1913, p. 126, MC.
44. Douglas Mawson, *Home of the Blizzard*, Vol. I, Heinemann, p. 258.
45. Jacka and Jacka, p. 158.
46. Douglas Mawson, *Home of the Blizzard*, Vol. I, Heinemann, p. 259.
47. Jacka and Jacka, p. 158.
48. Fifty years after the death of Mertz, when medical science had advanced exponentially from where it was in 1913, the theory was proposed, and broadly accepted, that what had most likely killed the Swiss man was an excess of vitamin A from eating dog liver – now understood to be poisonous.
49. Douglas Mawson, *Home of the Blizzard*, Vol. I, Heinemann, p. 260.
50. Jacka and Jacka, p. 158.
51. Douglas Mawson, *Home of the Blizzard*, Vol. I, Heinemann, p. 260.

Chapter Fourteen: A Close-Run Thing . . . (pp. 563–600)

1. Douglas Mawson, *Home of the Blizzard*, Vol. I, Heinemann, p. 305.
2. Frank Hurley, AAE sledging diary, 8 January 1913, ML, MSS 389/1-2.
3. Ibid., 11 January 1913, ML, MSS 389/1-2.
4. Douglas Mawson, *Home of the Blizzard*, Vol. I, Heinemann, p. 308.
5. Ibid., p. 261.

6. Ibid.
7. Ibid.
8. Eitel, 'Bound for the Ice', press article, pp. 11–13, MC, 144AAE.
9. Davis, *High Latitude*, p. 197.
10. Eitel, 'Bound for the Ice', press article, pp. 11–13, MC, 144AAE.
11. Laseron, *South with Mawson*, p. 163.
12. Jacka and Jacka, p. 160.
13. Ibid., p. 161.
14. Douglas Mawson, *Home of the Blizzard*, Vol. I, Heinemann, p. 265.
15. *Chicago Sunday Tribune*, 14 February 1915, p. 12.
16. Douglas Mawson, *Home of the Blizzard*, Vol. I, Heinemann, p. 265.
17. *Chicago Sunday Tribune*, 14 February 1915, p. 12.
18. Ibid.
19. Douglas Mawson, *Home of the Blizzard*, Vol. I, Heinemann, p. 265.
20. Davis, *Trial By Ice*, p. 52.
21. Robert Falcon Scott, *Scott's Last Expedition*, Vol. II, p. 270.
22. Douglas Mawson, *Home of the Blizzard*, Vol. I, Heinemann, p. 266.
23. Ibid.
24. Ibid.
25. Cherry-Garrard, Vol. II, p. 566.
26. *Daily Mail*, 14 February 1913, p. 5.
27. Robert Falcon Scott, *Scott's Last Expedition*, Vol. II, pp. 270–1.
28. Douglas Mawson, *Home of the Blizzard*, Vol. I, Heinemann, p. 267.
29. Davis, *With the Aurora*, p. 91.
30. McLean, AAE diary, 22–25 January 1913, ML, MSS 382/2.
31. Davis, *High Latitude*, p. 206.
32. Douglas Mawson, *Home of the Blizzard*, Vol. I, Heinemann, p. 268.
33. Ibid., p. 269.
34. Jacka and Jacka, p. 165.
35. 'Notes Left in Aladdin's Cave and Out in the Field', MC, 48EE, 290113. By way of interest, the chairman of the Mawson's Hut Foundation, David Jensen, actually found this note lying in a pile of papers at the South Australian Museum in 1997. He told me, 'This historic little note just fluttered to the floor as if demanding to be seen.'
36. Laseron, *South with Mawson*, p. 192.
37. Davis, *High Latitude*, p. 212.
38. Stanley Taylor, Diary, 2 February 1913.
39. Laseron, AAE diary, 4 February 1913, ML, MSS 385.
40. McLean, AAE diary, 8 February 1913, ML, MSS 382/2.
41. Jacka and Jacka, p. 172.
42. Ibid.
43. *Aurora* Log Book, 8 February 1913, ML, MSS 171/25.
44. Douglas Mawson, telegram to Davis, 8 February 1913, MC, 28AAE.

45. Hannam, AAE diary, 8 February 1913, ML, MSS 384.
46. Stanley Taylor, Diary, 8 February 1913.
47. Davis, *Trial By Ice*, p. 61.
48. McLean, AAE diary, 13 February 1913, MSS 382/1.
49. Laseron, *South with Mawson*, p. 176.

Chapter Fifteen: Now Is the Winter of Our Discontent (pp. 601–56)

1. McEwin, p. 167.
2. Cherry-Garrard, Vol. II, p. 572.
3. Gennings to Kinsey, correspondence with Central News Ltd, 14 February 1913, SPRI, MS559/164.
4. Smith, p. 241.
5. Cherry-Garrard, Vol. II, p. 573.
6. *Poverty Bay Herald*, 10 February 1913, p. 5.
7. Cherry-Garrard, Vol. II, pp. 572–3.
8. *Daily Mail*, 13 February 1913, p. 5.
9. Ibid., 11 February 1913, p. 5.
10. Ibid.
11. In the original, Tennyson uses the word 'North', but the *Daily Mail* changed it to fit with Scott.
12. *Daily Mail*, 11 February 1913, p. 4.
13. Ibid., p. 5.
14. Ibid.
15. Ibid., 15 February 1913, p. 5.
16. Smith, p. 247.
17. *Daily Mail*, 15 February 1913, p. 5.
18. Ibid., p. 3.
19. Ibid.
20. Ibid., 11 February 1913, p. 5.
21. Smith, p. 249.
22. *Daily Mail*, 11 February 1913, p. 5.
23. Ibid., 13 February 1913, p. 5.
24. Douglas Mawson, *Home of the Blizzard*, Vol. II, Heinemann, p. 134.
25. Flannery, pp. 39–40.
26. Paquita Mawson, p. 102.
27. Kathleen Scott, *Self-Portrait of an Artist*, p. 120. It was of course Captain Scott and *four* others, but, according to Lady Scott's account, that is the text of the cable.
28. Ibid., pp. 120–1.
29. Huxley, p. 309.
30. Young, p. 155.
31. Kathleen Scott, *Self-Portrait of an Artist*, p. 123.

32. Davis, *High Latitude*, p. 222.
33. Laseron, *South with Mawson*, p. 177.
34. Ibid.
35. Ibid., p. 178.
36. Douglas Mawson, telegram to Lord Denman, 24 May 1913, ML, MSS 171/40.
37. Douglas Mawson, telegram to Inspector General Ninnis, 24 February 1913, ML, MSS 171/40.
38. Douglas Mawson, telegram to Mertz family, 24 February 1913, ML, MSS 171/40.
39. *Daily Mail*, 26 February 1913, p. 5. The date is a mistake in the press. Ninnis actually died a month earlier.
40. This is an error on Shackleton's part. While Shackleton's expeditions were along the north–south axis, Mawson's was far more on the east–west axis.
41. *Daily Mail*, 7 March 1913, p. 7.
42. Lord Denman, telegram to Douglas Mawson, 29 March 1913, ML, MSS 171/40.
43. Douglas Mawson, *Home of the Blizzard*, Vol. II, Heinemann, p. 136.
44. This line appears in Laseron, *South with Mawson*, p. 183.
45. McEwin, p. 238.
46. Douglas Mawson, *Home of the Blizzard*, Wakefield Press, p. 315.
47. Ibid., p. 317.
48. Frederick Cook, pp. 208, 308–9.
49. Though Mawson does not cite these symptoms specifically, Dr Michael Cooper of Sydney, a student of Antarctic medical history, tells me these are the classic symptoms of those having trouble with their 'nerves'.
50. Jacka and Jacka, p. 185.
51. Douglas Mawson, *Home of the Blizzard*, Wakefield Press, p. 319.
52. Ibid.
53. Ibid.
54. Ibid.
55. McEwin, p. 157.
56. Paquita Delprat, telegram to Douglas Mawson, 2 April 1913, ML, MSS 171/40.
57. Flannery, pp. 56–7.
58. Paquita Delprat, letter to Douglas Mawson, 21 April 1913, MC, 52DM.
59. Flannery, p. 58.
60. Fort Street High School students, telegram to Fort Street old boys in Antarctica, 24 May 1913, ML, MSS 171/40.
61. Jacka and Jacka, p. 191.
62. Pound, *Scott of the Antarctic*, p. 302.

63. Robert Falcon Scott, *Scott's Last Expedition*, Vol. I, p. 415.

64. Twenty-three geographical miles equals 26 statute miles.

65. Bowers, letter to his mother, Emily, 22 March 1912, SPRI, MS1505/1/1/3/115.

66. Douglas Mawson, *Home of the Blizzard*, Vol. II, Heinemann, p. 148.

67. Jacka and Jacka, p. 194.

68. Ibid., p. 196.

69. Ibid.

70. Ibid.

71. Ibid., p. 197.

72. Ibid.

73. McLean, AAE diary, 11 July 1913, ML, MSS 382/2.

74. Douglas Mawson, report on Jeffryes, MC, 177AAE.

75. Jeffryes, letter to Eckford, *c.*July 1914, ML, MSS 7064.

76. Jacka and Jacka, p. 197.

77. Jeffryes, letter to Eckford, *c.*July 1914, ML, MSS 7064.

78. Ibid.

79. Sidney Jeffryes, letter to his sister Norma Jeffryes, 13 July 1913, MC, 177AAE.

80. 'Cape Denison: The People – Sidney Jeffryes', website of the Department of Sustainability, Environment, Water, Population and Communities, Australian Antarctic Division, Australian Government, www.mawsonshuts.aq/cape-denison/people/sidney-jeffryes.html.

81. Jeffryes, letter to Douglas Mawson, 13 July 1913, MC, 177AAE.

82. Jacka and Jacka, p. 198.

83. Flannery, pp. 91–2.

84. Ibid., p. 97.

85. Griffiths, p. 174.

86. Flannery, p. 91.

87. Douglas Mawson, *Home of the Blizzard*, Vol. II, Heinemann, p. 151.

88. Ibid., p. 152.

89. Griffiths, p. 173.

90. Jacka and Jacka, p. 205.

91. Douglas Mawson, letter to Jeffryes, 12 September 1913, MC, 177AAE.

92. Flannery, p. 125.

93. Ibid., pp. 101–3.

94. Douglas Mawson, *Home of the Blizzard*, Wakefield Press, pp. 330–1.

95. Davis, *High Latitude*, pp. 228–9.

96. Ibid., p. 229.

97. Ibid. Hurley's account of this – on p. 111 of *Argonauts of the South* – is quite different. According to him, there was no one there to greet them, and when they entered the hut, Mawson simply looked up and said, "'Halloa . . . back again" – as casually as if we had merely returned

from an excursion between breakfast and dinner.'

98. Davis, *High Latitude*, p. 229.
99. Quilty and Goddard, p. 198.
100. Douglas Mawson, *Home of the Blizzard*, Vol. I, Heinemann, p. 140.
101. Davis, *High Latitude*, p. 230.
102. Flannery, p. 122.
103. Ibid., p. 124.
104. Davis, *High Latitude*, p. 233.
105. Ibid.
106. Ibid., p. 234.
107. Douglas Mawson, *Home of the Blizzard*, Vol. II, Heinemann, p. 277.
108. Paquita Mawson, p. 102.
109. Ibid.

Epilogue (pp. 657–81)

1. Paquita Mawson, pp. 104–5.
2. Ibid., p. 107.
3. In the Great War to come, Ninnis's regiment, The Royal Fusiliers, were cut to pieces on the bloody fields of Flanders, and the likelihood is that had he not lost his life in Antarctica, Ninnis would have lost his life there, which was something that at least allowed Ninnis's mother to accept his death. 'Somehow death in an icy crevasse seemed more fitting to his youth than slaughter in the mud of Flanders, however sacred the latter became to us all,' wrote Paquita (*Mawson of the Antarctic*, p. 170).
4. Riffenburgh, *Racing with Death*, pp. 180–1.
5. *Daily Mail*, 15 February 1913, p. 5.
6. Ibid., 25 February 1913, p. 5. She became 'Kathleen, Lady Scott' (not 'Lady Kathleen Scott'). The former is her title derived from that of her husband (while the latter would have been a courtesy title in her own right, which was not given).
7. Churchill, letter to Kathleen Scott, 12 November 1913, SPRI, MS1488/2;BJ.
8. Williams, p. 276.
9. Shackleton, 'Discussion: Australasian Antarctic Expedition, 1911–1914', p. 285.
10. Ibid., p. 286.
11. Ibid.
12. Fisher, p. 68.
13. Griffiths, p. 34.
14. Fisher, p. 435.
15. Ayres, p. 105.
16. *The Argus*, 30 April 1919, p. 9.

17. Wild and Macklin, p. 64.
18. Amundsen, *My Life as an Explorer*, p. 44.
19. 'Obituary: Captain Roald Amundsen', p. 397.
20. This is why today the New South Wales Mitchell Library holds much valuable AAE material and not the Mawson Centre in Adelaide, as one might expect.
21. Griffiths, p. 113.
22. Ibid.
23. Ibid., p. 118.
24. Ibid., pp. 119–120.
25. Fred Jacka, 'Mawson, Sir Douglas (1882–1958)', pp. 454–7.
26. Today, the supercontinent theory is generally accepted among the scientific community.
27. Smith, p. 261.
28. McEwin, p. 145.

Bibliography

Published Sources

Books

Amundsen, Roald, *My Life as an Explorer*, Doubleday, Page & Company, New York, 1927

    The South Pole: An Account of the Norwegian Antarctic Expedition in the Fram, 1910–1912, Vol. I, II, John Murray, London, 1912

Aurelius, Marcus, *The Meditations of Marcus Aurelius Antonius*, George Long (trans.), The F. M. Lupton Publishing Company, New York, undated

Ayres, Philip, *Mawson: A Life*, Melbourne University Press, Melbourne, 2003

Begbie, Harold, *Shackleton: A Memory*, Mills & Boon Ltd, London, 1922

Bernacchi, Louis, *To the South Polar Regions*, Hurst and Blackett Ltd, London, 1901

Bomann Larsen, Thor, *Roald Amundsen*, Sutton Publishing, Stroud, 2006

Borchgrevink, Carsten Egeberg, *First on the Antarctic Continent*, C. Hurst & Co., London, 1980

Boston, Paquita, *Home and Away with Douglas Mawson*, Jessica McEwin (ed.), Paquita Boston, Carnarvon, Western Australia, 2000

Branagan, David, *T. W. Edgeworth David: A Life – Geologist, Adventurer, Soldier and Knight in the Old Brown Hat*, Paul Cliff (ed.), National Library of Australia, Canberra, 2005

Bull, Henryk Johan, *The Cruise of the Antarctic to the South Polar Regions*, Edward Arnold, London, 1896

Burke, David, *Body at the Melbourne Club*, Wakefield Press, Kent Town, South Australia, 2009

Cameron, Ian, *To the Farthest Ends of the Earth*, MacDonald Futura Publishers, London, 1981

Campbell, Victor, *The Wicked Mate*, Bluntisham Books, Eskine Press, Alburgh, Norfolk, 1988

Cherry-Garrard, Apsley, *The Worst Journey in the World*, Vol. I, II, Doran, Constable & Company Ltd, New York, 1922

Chester, Jonathan, *Going to Extremes*, Doubleday, Sydney, 1986

Colon, Cristobal, *The Log of Christopher Columbus*, Robert H. Fuson (trans.), Ashford Press Publishing, Southampton, 1987

Cook, Dr Frederick, *Through the First Antarctic Night*, Doubleday, Page & Company, New York, 1909

Cook, James, *Three Voyages Around the World*, Longman, London, 1821

Voyage Towards the South Pole, and Round the World, Echo Library, Teddington, 2007

Crane, David, *Scott of the Antarctic*, HarperCollins Publishers, London, 2006

Daly, Regina W., *The Shackleton Letters: Behind the Scenes of the* Nimrod *Expedition*, The Erskine Press, Norwich, 2009

Davis, John King, *High Latitude*, Melbourne University Press, Melbourne, 1962

Trial By Ice: The Antarctic Journals of John King Davis, Louise Crossley (ed.), Bluntisham Books, Erskine Press, Alburgh, Norfolk, 1997

With the Aurora in the Antarctic 1911–1914, Andrew Melrose Ltd, London, 1919

De Gerlache de Gomery, Adrien, *Summary Report of the Voyage of the Belgica, The Belgian Antarctic Expedition, 1897–1898–1899*, Hayez, Brussels, 1904

Debenham, Frank, *In the Antarctic*, Murray, London, 1952

The Quiet Land: The Diaries of Frank Debenham, Bluntisham Books, Erskine Press, Alburgh, Norfolk, 1992

Dickens, Charles, *A Tale of Two Cities*, Macmillan/Tor Classics, London, 1989

Doorly, George S., *In the Wake*, Sampson Low, London, 1937

D'Urville, Jules Sébastien César Dumont, *An Account in Two Volumes of Two Voyages to the South Seas*, Vol. II, Melbourne University Press, Melbourne, 1987

Evans, Edward, *South with Scott*, Collins Sons and Co. Ltd, London, 1921

Fiennes, Ranulph, *Captain Scott*, Hodder & Stoughton, London, 2004

Mind Over Matter: The Epic Crossing of the Antarctic Continent, Sinclair-Stevenson, London, 1993

Filchner, Wilhelm, *Ein Forscherleben*, Eberhard Brockhaus, Wiesbaden, 1950

Fisher, Margery Turner and James, *Shackleton and the Antarctic*, Houghton Mifflin, Boston, 1958

Flaherty, Leo, *Roald Amundsen and the Quest for the South Pole*, Chelsea House Publishers, New York, 1992

Flannery, Nancy Robinson (ed.), *This Everlasting Silence: The Love Letters of Paquita Delprat and Douglas Mawson 1911–1914*, Melbourne University Press, Melbourne, 2000

Fletcher, Harold, *Antarctic Days with Mawson: A Personal Account of the British, Australian, and New Zealand Antarctic Research Expedition of 1929–31*, Angus & Robertson, Sydney, 1984

Franklin, John, *Narrative of a Journey to the Shores of the Polar Sea*, Vol. 2, Ed. 3, John Murray, London, 1824

Gran, Tryggve, *The Norwegian with Scott: Tryggve Gran's Antarctic Diary 1910–1913*, Geoffrey Hattersley-Smith (ed.), Her Majesty's Stationery Office, Oslo, 1984

Gregor, G., *Swansea's Antarctic Explorer: Edgar Evans, 1876–1912*, 'Studies in Swansea's History' series, No. 4, Swansea City Council, Swansea, Wales, 1995

Griffiths, Tom, *Slicing the Silence: Voyaging to Antarctica*, Harvard University Press, Cambridge, 2007

Hall, Lincoln, *Douglas Mawson: The Life of an Explorer*, New Holland, Sydney, 2000

Hannam, Walter, 'Antarctic Exploration', in *The Port Hacking Cough*, L. G. Taylor (ed.), Pt III, IV, Simmons Ltd, Sydney, 1919

Bibliography

Hayes, J. Gordon, *Antarctica: A Treatise on the Southern Continent*, The Richards Press Limited, London, 1928

Headland, Robert, *A Chronology of Antarctic Exploration: A Synopsis of Events and Activities from the Earliest Times Until the International Polar Years, 2007–09*, Bernard Quaritch, London, 2009

Huntford, Roland, *Scott and Amundsen: Their Race to the South Pole*, Abacus, London, 2005

Shackleton, Abacus, London, 2009

Hurley, Frank, *Argonauts of the South*, G. P. Putnam's Sons, New York, 1925

Huxley, Elspeth, *Scott of the Antarctic*, Pan Books Ltd, London, 1979

Jacka, Fred, 'Mawson, Sir Douglas (1882–1958)', *Australian Dictionary of Biography*, National Centre of Biography, Australian National University, Canberra, 2011, http://adb.anu.edu.au

Jacka, Fred and Eleanor Jacka, *Mawson's Antarctic Diaries*, Allen & Unwin, Sydney, 2008

Kløver, G. O. (ed.), *The Roald Amundsen Diaries: The South Pole Expedition*, Fram Museum, Oslo, 2010

Larson, Edward J., *Empire of Ice*, Yale University Press, London, 2011

Laseron, Charles Francis, *South with Mawson: Reminiscences of the Australasian Antarctic Expedition, 1911–14*, Angus and Robertson, Sydney, 1957

Mallery, Richard, *Masterworks of Travel and Exploration*, Ayer Publishing, New Hampshire, 1970

Markham, Clements R., *The Lands of Silence: A History of Arctic and Antarctic Exploration*, Cambridge University Press, Cambridge, 1921

Mason, Theodore K., *The South Pole Ponies*, Dodd, Mead, New York, 1979

Mawson, Douglas, *The Home of the Blizzard*, Vol. I, II, William Heinemann, London, 1918

The Home of the Blizzard, Wakefield Press, Kent Town, South Australia, 1996

Mawson, Paquita, *Mawson of the Antarctic*, Longmans, London, 1964

McEwin, Emma, *An Antarctic Affair: A Story of Love and Survival by the Great-Granddaughter of Douglas and Paquita Mawson*, East Street Publications, Bowden, 2008

McGonigal, David, *Antarctica: Secrets of the Southern Continent*, Global Book Publishing, Sydney, 2008

McGregor, Alasdair, *Frank Hurley: A Photographer's Life*, Viking, London, 2004

Mill, Hugh Robert, *The Life of Sir Ernest Shackleton*, William Heinemann, London, 1933

Mills, Leif, *Frank Wild*, Caedmon of Whitby, Whitby, North Yorkshire, 1999

Murphy, David Thomas, *German Exploration of the Polar World: A History, 1870–1940*, University of Nebraska Press, Nebraska, 2002

Nansen, Dr Fridtjof, *Farthest North: Being the Record of a Voyage of Exploration of the Ship Fram 1893–96, and of a Fifteen Months' Sleigh Journey by Dr Nansen and Lieut. Johansen with an Appendix by Otto Sverdrup*, Vol. I, George Newnes, London, 1898

Pemberton, Max, *Lord Northcliffe*, Hodder and Stoughton, London, 1920

Bibliography

Ponting, Herbert G., *The Great White South: Or With Scott in the Antarctic*, Gerald Duckworth & Co. Ltd, London, 1950

Pound, Reginald, *Evans of the Broke: A Biography of Admiral Lord Mountevans*, Oxford University Press, London, 1963

Scott of the Antarctic, World Books, London, 1966

Preston, Diana, *A First Rate Tragedy: Robert Falcon Scott and the Race to the South Pole*, Houghton Mifflin Company, Boston, 1998

Priestley, Raymond Edward, *Antarctic Adventure: Scott's Northern Party*, E. P. Dutton & Co., New York, 1915

Quartermain, Leslie Bowden, *South to the Pole*, Oxford University Press, London, 1967

Riffenburgh, Beau, *Nimrod: Ernest Shackleton and the Extraordinary Story of the 1907–09 British Antarctic Expedition*, Bloomsbury, London, 2005

Racing with Death: Douglas Mawson – Antarctic Explorer, Bloomsbury, London, 2009

Ross, James Clark, *A Voyage of Discovery and Research in the Southern and Antarctic Regions: During the Years 1839–43*, Vol. I, John London, Newton Abbot, Devon, 1847

Scott, Kathleen, *Self-Portrait of an Artist: From the Diaries and Memoirs of Lady Kennett, Kathleen, Lady Scott*, John Murray, London, 1949

Scott, Robert Falcon, *Scott's Last Expedition*, Vol. I, II, Leonard Huxley (ed.), Dodd, Mead & Co., New York, 1913

Scott's Last Journey, Peter King (ed.), Duckworth, London, 1999

The Voyage of the Discovery, Vol. I, II, The Copp, Clark Co. Ltd, Toronto, 1905

Seaver, George, *Birdie Bowers of the Antarctic*, John Murray, London, 1947

Edward Wilson of the Antarctic, Naturalist and Friend, Butler & Tanner Ltd, London, 1951

Shackleton, Ernest Henry (ed.), *Aurora Australis: The British Antarctic Expedition 1907–1909*, Bluntisham and Paradigm, Alburgh, Norfolk, 1986

The Heart of the Antarctic, Vol. I, II, William Heinemann, London, 1909

Smith, Michael, *I Am Just Going Outside: Captain Oates – Antarctic Tragedy*, Spellmount Ltd, Staplehurst, Kent, 2008

Taylor, Griffith, *With Scott: The Silver Lining*, Smith, Elder & Co., London, 1916

Watson, Moira, *The Spy Who Loved Children: The Enigma of Herbert Dyce Murphy 1879–1971*, Melbourne University Press, Melbourne, 1997

Weddell, James, *A Voyage Towards the South Pole Performed in the Years 1822–1824*, Longman, Rees, Orme, Brown & Green, David & Charles, London, 1827

Wheeler, Sara, *Cherry: A Life of Apsley Cherry-Garrard*, Vintage, London, 2002

Wild, Frank and Alexander Macklin, *Shackleton's Last Voyage*, Frederick A. Stokes Company, New York, 1923

Wilkes, Charles, *Narrative of the United States Exploring Expedition*, Vol. II, Puttnam & Co., New York, 1856

Williams, Isobel, *With Scott in the Antarctic: Edward Wilson – Explorer, Naturalist, Artist*, The History Press, Stroud, 2008

Wilson, D. M. and D. B. Elder, *Cheltenham in Antarctica: The Life of Edward Wilson*, Reardon Publishing, Cheltenham, 2000

Wilson, Edward, *Diary of the Terra Nova Expedition*, Blandford Press Ltd, London, 1972

Wright, Charles S., *Silas: The Antarctic Diaries and Memoir of Charles S. Wright*, Colin Bull, Pat F. Wright (eds), Ohio State University Press, Columbus, 1993

Young, Louisa, *A Great Task of Happiness: The Life of Kathleen Scott*, Papermac, London, 1996

Journal articles

Amundsen, Roald, 'The Norwegian South Polar Expedition', *The Geographical Journal*, Vol. 41, No. 1, January 1913

Arçtowski, Henryk, 'The Antarctic Voyage of the *Belgica* During the Years 1897, 1898, and 1899', *The Geographical Journal*, Vol. 18, No. 4, October 1901

Borchgrevink, Carsten Egeberg, 'The *Antarctic*'s Voyage to the Antarctic', *The Geographical Journal*, Vol. 5, No. 6, June 1895

'The *Southern Cross* Expedition to the Antarctic, 1899–1900', *The Geographical Journal*, Vol. 16, No. 4, October 1900

'Captain Roald Amundsen and the Society', *The Geographical Journal*, Vol. 70, No. 6, December 1927

von Drygalski, Erich, 'The German Antarctic Expedition', *The Geographical Journal*, Vol. 24, No. 2, August 1904

Evans, Edward, 'My Recollections of a Gallant Comrade', *The Strand Magazine*, December 1913

Hattersley-Smith, Geoffrey Francis, 'The History of the Place Names in the British Antarctic Territory', *British Antarctic Survey Scientific Report*, Cambridge, 1991

Hinks, Arthur Robert, 'The Observations of Amundsen and Scott at the South Pole', *The Geographical Journal*, Vol. 103, No. 4, April 1944

'The International Congress of 1895', *The Geographical Journal*, Vol. 8, No. 3, September 1896

'Luncheon to British Antarctic Expedition, 1910', *The Geographical Journal*, Vol. 36, No. 1, July 1910

Markham, Clements, 'The Antarctic Expeditions', *The Geographical Journal*, Vol. 14, No. 5, November 1899

Mawson, Douglas, 'The Australasian Antarctic Expedition', *The Geographical Journal*, Vol. 37, No. 6, June 1911

'The Australasian Antarctic Expedition, 1911–1914', *The Geographical Journal*, Vol. 44, No. 3, September 1914

Mill, Hugh Robert, 'Captain England and the *Nimrod*', *The Geographical Journal*, Vol. 61, No. 6, June 1923

'The *Challenger* Publications', *The Geographical Journal*, Vol. 5, No. 4, April 1895

'Obituary: Captain Roald Amundsen', *The Geographical Journal*, Vol. 72, No. 4, October 1928

'Obituary: Frank Wild', *The Geographical Journal*, Vol. 95, No. 3, March 1940

'Obituary: Sir Ernest Henry Shackleton, CVO, OBE', *The Geographical Journal*, Vol. 59, No. 3, March 1922

Priestley, Raymond Edward, 'Scott's Northern Party: The Scott Memorial Lecture', *The Geographical Journal*, Vol. 128, No. 2, June 1962

Quilty, Patrick G. and Peter H. Goddard, 'The Lower Deck on *Aurora*: H. V. Goddard's Diary, 1913–14', *Polar Record*, Vol. 40, July 2004

Quilty, Patrick G. and Gillian Winter, 'Robert Falcon Scott: A Tasmanian Connection', *Polar Record* (available on CJO 2011 doi:10.1017/S0032247411000283)

Reader's Digest, 'Antarctica: Great Stories from the Frozen Continent', originally from the University of California, 1985, digitised, 2009

Shackleton, Ernest, 'A New British Antarctic Expedition', *The Geographical Journal*, Vol. 29, No. 3, March 1907

'Discussion: Australasian Antarctic Expedition, 1911–1914', *The Geographical Journal*, Vol. 44, No. 3, September 1914

Newspapers and periodicals

The Advertiser (Adelaide)
The Argus (Melbourne)
Birmingham Daily Post
The Bulletin (Sydney)
Chicago Daily Tribune
Chicago Sunday Tribune
Daily Mail (London)
The Evening Post (Wellington)
Examiner (Launceston)
Geelong Advertiser
Kalgoorlie Western Argus
Los Angeles Times
The Manchester Guardian
Mercury (Hobart)
Montreal Herald
The Morning Bulletin (Rockhampton)
The New York Times
The Northern Territory Times and Gazette (Darwin)
Oamaru Mail
The Observer (London)
The Observer Magazine (London)
Otago Witness
Poverty Bay Herald (Gisborne, New Zealand)
The Register (Adelaide)
The Spectator (London)
Star (Canterbury)
The Sydney Morning Herald

The Times (London)
The West Australian (Perth)
West Coast Times (New Zealand)

Unpublished Sources

Abbreviations used

AAE Australasian Antarctic Expedition (1911–14)
MC Mawson Centre, Adelaide
ML The Mitchell Library, Sydney
NE *Nimrod* expedition (British Antarctic Expedition 1907–09)
SPRI The Scott Polar Research Institute, Cambridge
SUA Sydney University Archives, Sydney
TNE *Terra Nova* expedition (British Antarctic Expedition 1910–13)

Diaries and journals

Blake, Leslie, R., AAE diary, MC
Bowers, Henry Robertson, TNE diary, SPRI
Brocklehurst, Philip, NE diary, SPRI
Bruce, Wilfrid, TNE journals, SPRI
Evans, Frederick P., NE narrative, SPRI
Hannam, Walter, AAE diary, ML
Harrisson, Charles, AAE diary, ML
Hurley, Frank, AAE sledging diary, ML
Laseron, Charles, AAE diary, ML
Mackay, Dr Alister, NE diary, SPRI
Marshall, Eric, NE diary, SPRI
McLean, Archie, AAE diary, ML
Mertz, Xavier, AAE diary, MC
Priestley, Raymond Edward, NE diary and TNE diary, SPRI
Sawyer, Arthur, AAE diary, ML
Shackleton, Ernest, NE diary, SPRI
Taylor, Stanley, Diary (self-published online at http://antarcticdiary.wordpress.com/
 tag/stanley-taylor)
Wild, Frank, NE diary, SPRI; memoirs, ML
Wilson, Edward, TNE journal, SPRI
Wright, Charles, TNE diary, SPRI

Correspondence and papers

AAE administrative correspondence, notes and records, MC, ML
Amundsen, Roald, telegram to Robert Falcon Scott, 5 October 1910, The Fram
 Museum, Oslo

Armitage, Albert, memos, SPRI

Aurora Log Book, ML

Bostock, Mrs A. C., correspondence, SPRI

Bowers, Henry Robertson, correspondence, SPRI

Bruce, Wilfrid, correspondence, SPRI

Delprat, Paquita, correspondence, MC

Edgeworth David, Professor, correspondence, SUA

Eitel, Conrad, articles, administrative papers, MC, ML

Evans, Edward, correspondence and speech notes, SPRI

Ferris, Graeme, 'February 10th 1913: A Morning to Remember', North Otago Museum, acc. no. 76034

Fisher, James and Margery, interviews, correspondence, notes and facsimiles of key period documents, SPRI

Hurley, Frank, correspondence, ML

Hurley, Margaret, correspondence, ML

Jeffryes, Norma, correspondence, MC

Jeffryes, Sidney, correspondence, MC

Mackay, Alister Forbes, 'William S. Bruce Papers and Diary of A. Forbes Mackay', 31 November 1908–6 February 1909, J. Pitman (ed.), manuscript held at the Royal Scottish Museum, Part 2, Natural History 8, The Royal Scottish Museum, Edinburgh, 1982

Mawson, Douglas, correspondence, MC, ML, SPRI

McLean, Archie, correspondence, MC

Meares, Cecil, correspondence, Royal BC Museum, BC Archive

Messages transmitted by wireless to and from Cape Denison via Macquarie Island, ML, MC

Mill, Hugh Robert, 'Life Interests of a Geographer, 1861–1944: An Experiment in Autobiography', privately issued, Sussex, 1945, ML, 7753805

NE administrative correspondence, notes and records, SPRI

Ninnis, Belgrave, correspondence, SPRI

Oates, Lawrence Edward Grace, correspondence and notes, SPRI

Scott, Kathleen, correspondence, MC, SPRI

Scott, Robert Falcon, correspondence, miscellaneous notes and papers, SPRI

Seaver, George, notes on Oates, SPRI, MS1012

Shackleton, Ernest, correspondence and papers, SPRI

TNE administrative correspondence, notes and records, SPRI

Watkins, Hugh, correspondence, MC

Wilson, Edward, correspondence, ML, SPRI

Index

Index